JAGUAR
SALOON CARS

JAGUAR
SALOON CARS

Paul Skilleter
with competition chapters by Andrew Whyte

Foulis

Haynes

This book is a companion volume to

Jaguar Sports Cars 2nd Edition by Paul Skilleter (F453), in preparation

Together with the following Foulis titles, they form a comprehensive history of Jaguar:

Jaguar Sports Racing & Works Competition Cars to 1953 (F277) by Andrew Whyte
Jaguar Sports Racing & Works Competition Cars from 1954 (F319) by Andrew Whyte

ISBN 0 85429 596 8

A FOULIS Motoring Book

First published April 1980
This second edition published 1988
Reprinted 1989

© Paul O. Skilleter & Andrew J.A. Whyte 1980 & 1988

Published by:
Haynes Publishing Group
Sparkford, Nr. Yeovil, Somerset BA22 7JJ

Haynes Publications Inc.
861 Lawrence Drive, Newbury Park, California
91320, USA

British Library Cataloguing in Publication Data
Skilleter, Paul
  Jaguar saloon cars.
  1. Jaguar automobile—History
  I. Title
  629.2'222   TL215.J3

  ISBN 0-85429-596-8

Library of Congress catalog card number
87-82840

Editor: Rod Grainger
Layout design: Rowland Smith & Joe Fitzgerald
Artwork production: Graffiti
Printed in England by: J.H. Haynes & Co. Ltd

Contents

MARK

Introduction

This book was literally on the presses when the shocking news came through of Andrew Whyte's sudden death, at the age of 51, from a heart attack. I was at Jaguar's Browns Lane factory at the time and I was waiting for him in the limousine shop: we were collaborating on an article for the new *Jaguar Quarterly* magazine which editorially we were producing together. But all thoughts of such ventures were banished on hearing the news – I had just lost one of my best friends, someone who had been an inspiration and who by example and by gentle suggestion had had an enormous impact on my own approach to writing about Jaguar.

This was my own first, selfish, reaction but the real loss is born by his family: Wendy, cruelly widowed for the second time, and her daughters (Andrew's step-daughters) Louise and Sarah. One can only hope they will take some small comfort in the fact that Andrew's own writings will be a lasting memorial to him: he will never be matched in his field, and the whole Jaguar movement owes him a huge debt. Read this magnificent contribution on Jaguar saloons in competition in this volume: in detail, accuracy and breadth it will never be equalled. Enjoy it, and pay your own respects to one of the greatest figures in the Jaguar world.

P.S., May 1988

Introduction to the Second Edition

The first edition of this book went to press two months before John Egan arrived at Jaguar. Since that time much has changed at Browns Lane, and in early 1980 it would have been beyond imagining that within four years Jaguar would not only be making an annual profit of approaching £100m, but would also be an independent company again. How wonderful that Sir William Lyons should have lived to see that happen; it was very noticeable how, as Jaguar pulled itself out of the mire, Sir William himself was brighter and more cheerful during his last months.

Sir William died on 8 February 1983 at the age of 83; the founder of Jaguar Cars had gone – but not before he had handed the torch to a worthy successor in John Egan. The two men had spent much time talking and it is to Sir John's eternal credit that he did not, as so many new leaders have done in various fields, reject all the old thinking but instead listened, and learnt, from what had gone before. He even read books like this one! Sir John's management techniques may be up-to-the-minute, but he has also contrived to retain the true Jaguar culture, so that 'his' Jaguars have remained 'real' Jaguars.

In my view it is this blending of modern methods with traditional Jaguar virtues that is Sir John's greatest achievement. It mirrors the achievements of his engineers in continuing to reconcile other aspects – technical ones, like combining superlative handling with an outstanding ride – which might have been considered by others as incompatible. James Randle, Jaguar's engineering director, is similarly conscious of Jaguar's heritage and considers the thinking of his predecessors extraordinarily good. He will mention Bob Knight, Walter Hassan and Claude Baily, but it is obviously Bill Heynes who commands his greatest respect.

I have been privileged to get to know William Heynes, CBE, a little, and while there is universal acknowledgement of his work for Jaguar, as I learn more about his career it becomes increasingly apparent to me that the full contribution he made to the success of the Jaguar car is not yet fully appreciated. For Bill Heynes was far more than the company's chief engineer. His contribution, especially, perhaps in the critical post-war years, was enormous and it was Heynes who co-ordinated and progressed for Lyons the whole difficult business of getting Jaguar operational again after 1945 and turning the new post-war range of cars into reality. This was all over and above his crucial part in designing the XK engine and in the design programmes that resulted in the Le Mans winning C- and D-types, and in the engineering systems which carried Jaguar through more than three decades, right up until the launch of XJ40.

The arrival of XJ40 was, of course, the most significant event at Jaguar since the original XJ6 of 1968. Naturally a full description of the new car is included in this edition, together with other new models which have come along since 1980, including the 'High Efficiency' V12 engined models, the 3.6 XJ-S, and the convertible XJ-S which reached the marketplace at the same time as this book.

These new models, and the successful launch of XJ40, paint an optimistic picture of the future for the newly independent Jaguar Cars plc. The path ahead may not *always* be smooth, but at least it is now clearly visible; and that certainly wasn't the case when I concluded my 1980 introduction ... Meanwhile, further exciting developments are underway at Browns Lane and, who knows, when in five or eight years' time a third edition of *Jaguar Saloons* arrives, maybe we'll be discussing four wheel drive and possibly even a true successor to the Mk 2 saloon at last. We shall see!

Paul Skilleter
Hornchurch, Essex
January 1988

Introduction to the First Edition

Those who have read *Jaguar Sports Cars* will know what to expect in this volume, as I have followed much the same pattern. Each chapter therefore deals with one particular model or family of models, more or less chronologically – and if because of this some background history is occasionally repeated, then I've allowed it to do so in order to 'set the scene' in each case.

The Jaguar saloon (or *sedan* to my American friends) has always been the major preoccupation at Browns Lane, and Sir William Lyons has always concentrated his main efforts and ambitions on the company's successively more impressive and refined *closed* models – the sports cars have really been subsidiary products, manufactured in smaller numbers and indeed only made possible through the use of components developed for the saloon car range. Thus to the factory, and to the historian, this book is probably a more important work than my preceeding one on the open two-seaters, even if at first sight the subject appears to be less glamorous.

Personally, I am an enthusiast for every type of Jaguar, open or closed, and I've certainly not found the research involved in this book to be any less fascinating than that undertaken for *Jaguar Sports Cars*. But it has certainly proved to be more complex, largely due to the greater number of models, which themselves have grown in complexity as the motor car has become ever more sophisticated.

As with *Jaguar Sports Cars,* I have tried to describe each car not only in terms of its design and specification, but also from the point of view of what it is like to drive and own – both in its contemporary surroundings when new, and today. The reader will also find that in most cases the cars have been compared with their rivals of the day, and that where they have been found lacking, I've recorded this too – for only in this way can their true characters emerge.

I've been enormously fortunate in persuading Andrew Whyte to contribute the competition chapters of this book, which he has done despite heavy commitments which include several long-awaited Jaguar titles of his own. So for the first time, the competition career of the Jaguar saloon has been laid out clearly and in great detail, and I for one have found it fascinating reading. Andrew is, of course, uniquely qualified to write about Jaguar, having worked at Browns Lane for many years (though he is currently freelancing in the motoring field); also, he has himself covered a number of the national and international events he describes, including some while on the staff of *Motoring News*.

Both Andrew and I have been greatly helped in our task of recording the history of the Jaguar saloon by the car's own excellence – again and again, the Jaguar's superiority over most other cars in its class (if indeed there were any) shows through clearly, whether in performance, refinement, competition prowess or sheer style. Thus this book must emerge as another tribute to the man who began it all, Sir William Lyons, and to the team of designers, engineers and shopfloor workers who over the years have turned his unique concepts into successful realities.

Paul Skilleter

Paul Skilleter
Martley, Worcestershire
February 1980

Acknowledgements

With a book the size of this one, written over a number of years, it is an almost impossible task to acknowledge and adequately thank all those who have willingly contributed material and time. Inevitably there must be some names which memory fails to recall, but I hope these will feel included in my general thanks to everyone who has made this book possible.

To begin at the factory, I must record my gratitude to those who cheerfully put up with my numerous visits to Browns Lane – particularly Alan Hodge who took the brunt of them, and who with his small enthusiastic staff in the Special Facilities Department never failed to meet even my most obscure requests.

Of the engineering staff at Browns Lane, my thanks must go to Tom Jones whose responsibilities lie in chassis development, and who devoted valuable time answering questions on all the post-War range. I would also like to put on record the part which the late Peter Craig, Plant Director, played in my researches; one of the busiest, and most loyal executives at Jaguar, his contribution was vital in recording the company's post-War history. As a person too he made a deep impression on me, and his premature death in 1977 was a tragedy.

Of those no longer working at the factory, I must thank Claude Baily for spending hours answering my questions on the evolution of the XK and V12 engines, in which he played a vital part – as did Walter Hassan, who also endured a layman's questions on engineering subjects.

These were some of the men who produced the car, but it is largely through the comments of the contemporary motoring press that we evaluate the status and success of a vehicle in its own time. Thus we motoring historians owe an enormous debt to journals such as *Autocar, Motor, Autosport* and *Road & Track*. Having been privileged in the past to work for *Motor* for some nine-years, I know at first-hand the meticulous hard work which goes into the compiling of road-tests published by these magazines, and the effort expended to ensure the accuracy of performance figures and all the other data contained in them.

I would therefore like to extend my thanks to the editors of *Motor* and *Autocar* – Tony Curtis and Ray Hutton – for allowing me to use the archives of both journals. In particular I have spent many hours at the London office of *Autocar* researching obscure details right back to 1922, and am very grateful to Anne Palmer and Warren Alport for their patience and help.

The pictorial content of this book has also relied to an important extent on *Motor* and *Autocar* photographs, and indeed it is not overstating the case to say that the negative archives of these IPC magazines amount to nothing less than part of our national heritage, such is their unique record of Britain's motoring past. As a photographer myself, I would like to pay tribute to the skills of the Temple Press and Iliffe Press (as they were) cameramen past and present who created these pictures – often inspite of appalling conditions, and in the face of

11

technical limitations unknown by many in the field today. I would therefore like to record the names of the late George Moore of *Motor,* Maurice Rowe and Peter Burn of the same journal, and Ron Easton and Peter Cramer of *Autocar;* not forgetting the photographic department staff at *Autocar,* including Len Roffey, Bill Banks, Bill Heasman and Mary Smith.

A large proportion of the pictures in this book came from Jaguar's own archives though, and I'm very grateful to Roger Clinkscales, head of the photographic department at Browns Lane, for allowing me to spend many days sorting through old negatives – without the extension of this unique privilege, *Jaguar Saloons Cars* would only have been half the book that it is.

Leaving the motoring press and Jaguar, I would like to thank Mr MacVitie of Rothwall and Milbourne (one of Jaguar's oldest-established dealers) for the loan of vital service records going back to 1946, which helped enormously in chronicling production changes to post-War Jaguars. Then Mr and Mrs Christopher Jennings once more spent some hours recalling early S.S. days, while Alan Gibbons of the S.S. Register, and S.S. restorer David Barber, both contributed a vast amount of detail to the story of the pre-War Jaguar and S.S. David Middleton also assisted on the subject of the rare Jaguar tourer, while Geoff Shimmin gave me the benefit of his intimate knowledge of 'Mk IV' and Mk V cars. Jack Rabell, 'Mk IV' Registrar of the Classic Jaguar Association, contributed much of interest on these cars too.

Also from the States, I am indebted to Paul Borel and Tom Hendricks for large quantities of rare Jaguar literature which played an important part in piecing together the story over there. Ed and Karen Miller from the same continent, and Ron Beaty of Forward Engineering here at home, helped with XJ material, while Ron also regailed me with many illuminating stories of his years as an experimental engineer at Browns Lane.

Amongst the many others I would like to thank are: John Bolster, Tom March, Roland Urban, Philippe Renault, John Harper, Graig Hinton, Raymond Legate, Alan Townsin, Les Hughes (himself author of a book on Jaguar's Australian history) and Heinz Schendzielorz (of Victoria, Australia).

Then I must single out Andrew Whyte for not only contributing the entire section on Jaguar's competition history (see Introduction), but also for guiding me through Jaguar lore generally, and helping me differentiate between fact and fiction. Andrew also gave generously of his own painstaking research into S.S. and Jaguar production figures to help complete Appendix Two.

To my publishers, especially John Haynes himself, I would like to extend my thanks for patiently awaiting a long-overdue manuscript, and for assimilating almost twice the number of words originally agreed upon... I'm grateful to Tim Parker for originally offering me the con-tract, and to his successor Rod Grainger who has had to cope with me thereafter.

Finally, this book has not been completed without much sacrifice by my wife June who has been supplanted by my typewriter for the past three-years. If this book is a success, it will be largely due to her support and understanding – quite apart from her own contributions in the form of the Index, and in weeks of copy-reading.

P.O.S.
February 1980

Acknowledgments to Second Edition

The bulk of the research which makes up this new edition was compiled with the aid of the people mentioned in the original Introduction but, of course, many others have been involved since in the preparation of new material, especially concerning XJ40 and the new XJ-S variants.

I would like to begin again at the factory and thank Sir John Egan not only for his assistance in the past but for ensuring that we Jaguar historians will have lots to write about in the future! I'm grateful to the current engineering staff at Jaguar for spending time explaining to a non-engineer the intricacies of XJ40 design and development, especially Jim Randle, Trevor Crisp, Rex Marvin, and Richard Cresswell. Paul Walker provided information on 3.6 XJ-S development, and Colin Cook of the public affairs department was of great help in obtaining factory data, as was the ever-willing Ian Luckett of the Special Facilities department at Browns Lane.

I would like again to acknowledge my debt to Bill Heynes, who has consistently spent much time patiently recalling how earlier Jaguars were evolved. 'Lofty' England has also once more contributed information and 'de-bugged' parts of the manuscript in his usual masterly style, and, of course, Andrew Whyte has updated his suberb review of the Jaguar saloon in competition despite heavy commitments to further new titles of his own (which include the second part of his overall history of 'works' involvement in competition, and a book entirely on the XJ40). Gilbert Mond of the Austin Swallow Register 'overhauled' Chapter One and made a number of welcome suggestions on the early years.

At Haynes Publishing, it is now Mansur Darlington who has to suffer my chronic inability to keep to deadlines, but to whom I'm very grateful for his polite and consistent pressure, without which there might not have been a second edition of this book! And finally, it is my family and in particular my wife, June, who have had to endure long hours on the typewriter when house, garden and even cars have desperately required my attention. Again, without such a back-up at home, this revision might not have been completed.

P.O.S.
January 1988

Part One

The design and evolution of the S.S. and Jaguar saloon

Chapter One

Swallow

... there is no wonder that so many youthful belles find a Swallow just the very thing to make life complete and well worth living.

The Autocar

If Mr. Thomas Walmsley had not decided to close his coal merchant's business in Stockport, Cheshire, and move to one of the better districts of Blackpool, that popular seaside resort on the Lancashire coast, it is just possible that the Jaguar story would never have happened. But he did, and unwittingly brought about the meeting between two young motorcycle enthusiasts that was ultimately to effect the whole British motor industry.

* * *

The true beginnings of Jaguar can still be traced back to the busy town of Stockport, just seven miles from the great city of Manchester in the smoke-laden air of the still coal-burning industrial midlands. There, Tom Walmsley would leave his main depot at Reddish station and travel back to his house a little way out from the town centre at Woodmoor; "Fairhaven" it was called, with the pastural address of Flowery Fields, and on his return he might well have been greeted by the spluttering bark of a motorcycle being started up – son William had had an early tea and was off to visit his girlfriend on his noisy Triumph again ....

The Walmsley's were a well-to-do family, and William had plenty of spare time and pocket money to indulge his love of tinkering with things mechanical. The Great War was only a couple of years over, and swords were still being beaten into ploughshares: for William Walmsley, in

1920, this meant purchasing crates of War-surplus Triumph motorcycles, pulling them apart, and selling the reconditioned models to a public which had an ever-increasing appetite for almost any form of mechanical transport.

Then, innovation! Dissatisfied with merely turning out the same old bikes as everybody else with a spare shed and a set of spanners, Walmsley took his first step into the realms of coachbuilding – his machines began to appear, in very small numbers, with a sidecar attached; and very attractive the *ensemble* looked too.

His cousin, Mr W.H. Axon, then a young apprentice at Talbot Garage, Stockport, well remembers watching the first sidecar come together in the summerhouse of the big detached house at Woodsmoor, with Walmsley being assisted by his future brother-in-law Fred Gibson. The finished result was impressive, and not at all like the pram-shaped encumbrances usually foisted on the two-wheeled brigade by the dozen-odd sidecar manufacturers of the period, who had only just grown out of the wickerwork bath-chair approach to the subject.

Walmsley's sidecar was finished in gleaming, polished aluminium, with eight separate aluminium panels mounted on an ash frame to form an octagonal, bullet-shaped carriage which has often been likened to the Zeppelin – an all too recent memory in the 1920s. The tubular chassis was 'bought-out' from the Birmingham firm of Haydens, the wire wheel usually being covered by a polished aluminium wheel disc which heightened the modern, streamlined effect.

Mr Axon recalls that the very first 'Swallow' sidecar built was registered with its motorcycle at Stockport Town Hall on January 28th 1921, the bike carrying the number DB 1238. Several more appeared to have been made at Stockport, still very much on a home-made basis with the trimming being done by Walmsley's sister, and then his wife after he married. Befitting its limited production and high quality, the Swallow sidecar was expensive; a basic price of £28 being quoted, with £4 extra for the rather claustrophobic hood, a lamp and wheel disc. It was sold locally, by word of mouth it seems, with the claim that it was "Made to sit in, not on!". At the most, one a week was completed, and there didn't appear to be much chance of this modest rate of production increasing drastically.

Then came the move to Blackpool, and a change of scene. King Edward Avenue, almost within sight of the sea front, is made up of large, solid, brick-built houses with grey slate gabled roofs and bay windows. Number 23 must look now very much as it did in 1921 when the Walmsley family moved into its new home – a typically respectable, middle-class Englishman's semi-detached residence set in the better side of town. At the end of the garden adjacent to a lane, there was – and still is – a small

Behind number 23 was this little alleyway, and in these outbuildings Walmsley constructed his sidecars. The young William Lyons became a frequent and keenly interested visitor. *Photo: P. Skilleter*

Walmsley's Blackpool home at number 23 King Edward Avenue, photographed as it is now but little changed from the early 1920s. Outside this staid, middle-class residence would often be parked a gleaming new sidecar combination, a centre of attraction for every boy in the district. *Photo: P. Skilleter*

brick outhouse, barely large enough to accomodate more than a couple of cars, and it was here that William Walmsley recommenced his sidecar activities.

Almost in the next road was another motorcycle enthusiast who didn't fail to notice that dashing silver sidecar which was often parked outside the new arrivals' house; his name was, of course, William Lyons, the only son of a Blackpool piano and music shop owner. Before long, he too, joined the small group of Swallow sidecar owners. However, his interest did not stop with ownership; the twenty-year-old Lyons was keen to enter 'the trade', for besides his motorcycle racing activities – with such machines as Nortons and Brough Superiors at the nearby Southport Sands – he had also tried car salesmanship. So it wasn't long before he realised that the Swallow sidecar might well represent the business opportunity he was looking for, as he was certain that the product deserved a much larger market than the one Walmsley was catering for. Walmsley agreed with Lyons' ideas for expansion, and obviously thought that it would be very useful to have the go-ahead youngster around to look after the paperwork and see to the business side of his activities. Certainly it can be said that William Walmsley always remained far more interested in designing and tinkering with things than he was in becoming embroiled in the organisation and structuring of the company that was being formed.

The Swallow Sidecar Company came into being on September 4, 1922 – it might have been a little earlier except that it was found that Lyons hadn't reached the legally required age of 21 (Walmsley was then 30). Finance for the project was in the form of a £1000 overdraft facility guaranteed jointly by Tom Walmsley and William Lyons senior, both parents thus expressing much confidence in the scheme (this sum would have purchased a four-bedroom house in those days).

The first step was to find better premises, and soon the business was in full swing at 7–9 Bloomfield Road, a tall, narrow building of drab brick, old even then but which stands to this day. Swallow had the two upper stories, and with a workforce of six or seven men, production of sidecars increased rapidly. So rapidly in fact, that within a year part of a warehouse in Woodfield Road was acquired for the despatch department, and soon afterwards a two-storey corner building in John Street, almost opposite the main factory, also had to be leased.

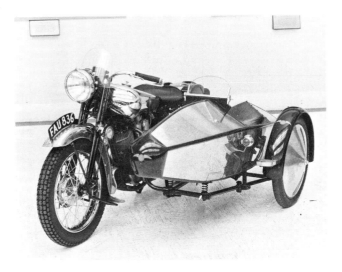

While this picture shows a later model, it illustrates well the impressive mirror-finish aluminium 'zeppelin' styling of the Swallow sidecars, and it is easy to see why they attracted purchasers.

Within a year of starting business, Swallow were exhibiting at the Motorcycle Show, and as time went by could display a wide range of 'chairs'; Swallow sidecars were also adopted by such leading motorcycle firms as Brough Superior, Dot and Matador.

Swallow's first factory was at Bloomfield Road *(top)*, but soon had to be supplemented by premises at Woodfield Road *(left)* and John Street; all were leased not bought, of course. *Photos: P. Skilleter*

Much more space was created by a move in autumn 1926 to Cocker Street; sidecar production was expanded and coach painting and trimming taken on as a prelude to proper coachbuilding. This is the building as it is today. *Photo: P. Skilleter*

Sidecar construction at the Coventry works. Considering the amount of handwork employed it was a very streamlined operation, with a capacity of 100 or more units a week. Note the small jig in right foreground used for slotting together the sidecar frames. *Photo: Jaguar Cars*

Not everyone would have predicted this success – cars such as the Bullnose Morris and the new Austin Seven threatened to bring cheap motoring to all, and it was being said that this competition would be too much for the spartan sidecar. Ultimately this would be a correct prognostication, but not for another 40 years; in the early 1920s, the Swallow Sidecar Company flourished with production of an expanded range of sidecars creeping up towards 100 units a week and, with yet another project around the corner, it was soon time to search for even larger premises.

These were found in a considerably more modern building than the one in Bloomfield Road, situated in a quiet, semi-residential area of Blackpool and formerly occupied by Messrs Jackson Bros and previously J. Street, "Motor Body Builders, Est. 1896". It was on the corner of Cocker Street and Exchange Street (both names were usually included in advertisements, making it sound more impressive), and the centralising of operations certainly helped production – which, incidentally, was somewhat seasonal in that demand for the sidecars reached its peak on three separate occasions in the year, Easter, Whitsun, and August Bank Holiday. This meant that while manufacture continued at a fairly even pace, during those three periods every spare hand was set-to in the despatch department, packing and crating the completed sidecars.

Meanwhile, the motor industry itself had been suffering a number of setbacks as the depression took hold in Great Britain, finally manifesting itself in the General Strike of 1926. One large well-established company which suffered was the Austin Motor Co Ltd at Longbridge, Birmingham, but was pulling through helped to a large extent by Herbert Austin's new 'baby car', the Seven, which had been launched in 1922 – the same year as the Swallow Sidecar Company.

The Austin Seven is one of Britain's greatest small cars, and one of the major reasons for its success was that it renounced the 'cycle-car' approach to cheap motoring – with all its attendant horrors of chain drive, noisy air-cooled engine and bent-wire-and-canvas coachwork – and instead was, in effect, a large car scaled down. It had a 'real' engine, a water-cooled four-cylinder, two-bearing unit of 696 cc (later 748 cc), four wheel brakes (though until 1930 only the fronts were worked by the footpedal, the rears by the handbrake!), a good three-speed gearbox, and efficient if basic coachwork capable of holding four people. It was indeed, "the motor for the millions", and helped to bring motoring to all, remaining in production (with various changes) up until World War Two.

Lyons and Walmsley were more than aware of the Austin Seven's success – after all, while their sidecar order books showed otherwise, the new generation of light cars which the Seven looked like inspiring might ultimately ring the death knell of the sidecarriage. In any case, their sights were set on expansion and the Seven appeared (literally) to be the vehicle.

As with virtually every production car of those days, the Seven was based on a separate chassis frame, with the coachwork being dropped onto it as a complete (and usually prefabricated) unit. In the case of expensive, luxury motor cars, the manufacturer might only supply the running chassis, which would then be fitted with coachwork to the customer's requirements at an independent coachbuilders. Swallow decided to combine the two approaches – acquire the running chassis of a *cheap* motor car, and fit it themselves with a completely new, high quality body of fashionable design. The end result was a car that was still cheap to buy and maintain, but was at the same time individual.

This snapshot of a rather modified Swallow from Jaguar's archives is captioned 'the very first Swallow Seven', but while it has the cycle wings (which turned with the wheels) of the prototype, it carries a 1928 production model radiator cowling; so it remains rather a mystery!

The Austin Swallow was soon refined into this rather more substantial vehicle, with a continuous wing line and running boards; a detachable hardtop with vent was a novel 'extra'.

Swallow was not the first company to employ this formula, but they were undoubtedly the most successful. The Austin Swallow Seven made its appearance in May 1927, and an extremely pretty car it was too; it had been given a neat two-seater body, with a distinctive 'bowl' tail and a rounded nose, built of aluminium panels on a wood frame. The Seven's 'A' frame and mechanics were untouched, although to support the new body it was necessary to fit some angle iron at the sides; likewise, the car's transverse leaf front spring, and cantilevered quarter-elliptic rear springs, remained as they were. Outside, you certainly couldn't tell it was an Austin, and of course the interior was completely new too; the plain Austin dashboard was supplanted by Swallow's own mahogany version and new, comparatively luxurious, seats were installed. There was a detachable hardtop if required, which added £10 to the modest price of £175. This low initial cost, coupled with perky good looks and a touch of exclusivity, ensured that the Swallow Seven became an instant commercial success.

The extension of Swallow's skills into the motor car market required yet more staff, and it was necessary for labour to be recruited from the industrial complexes of Birmingham and Coventry, especially men with car assembly skills. To them, building the Swallow bodies presented little difficulty, although one or two short-cuts had to be resorted to. For instance, the Austin's radiator filler neck was half an inch too high for the special Swallow cowl, and this problem was solved by placing a piece of wood on the neck and striking it sharply with a hammer, thereby depressing it neatly into the header tank by the required amount! "I am sure Sir Herbert Austin, as he then was, would not have approved, although it was a perfectly sound job!", wrote Sir William years later.*

That stylish radiator cowl which was so much a feature of the early Swallows brought another minor problem – the Austin starting handle which tinkled about at the front was not long enough to clear it, and an old Blackpool hand recalls having to hacksaw through the one-inch steel and re-weld it with an extension let in! All by hand at first, although it is also remembered that Lyons was constantly searching for more efficient ways to do things, and would introduce a machine to do a job wherever he could.

* This little anecdote may relate to Austin's introduction of a taller radiator in May 1929; earlier original cars show no signs of this 'dinging' today.

By mid-summer 1927, there was a brief excursion into another make - Morris. Instead of the 1.8-litre Oxford with which Cecil Kimber had embarked on his MG programme a couple of years earlier, Swallow elected to use the 1550cc Cowley but, perhaps because of the success achieved by Kimber's factory-backed project, the two-seater design evolved by Swallow for this chassis wasn't proceeded with, and it seems that few Morris Cowley Swallows were completed. Unfortunately, none appear to have survived and even photographs of this V-windscreened Swallow are a rarity.

So, it was the Swallow Seven which gave the chance of greatly increased sales, and it was essential for Swallow to establish proper retail outlets. Accordingly Lyons drove a two-seater Swallow to London in order to visit a new and "forward thinking" business that had recently sprung up.

"My visit to Henlys was the occasion of my first meeting with Frank Hough and Bertie Henly, the two partners. Hough was a dynamic man with a determination to do things quickly; Henly was the steadying influence and he was also the finest salesman I have ever met", wrote Sir William.

The deal concluded that day, at 91 Great Portland Street, far exceeded William Lyons' best hopes, as in return for exclusive distribution rights "... south of a line drawn from and including Bristol to the Wash", Henlys gave him an immediate order for 500 cars! A somewhat amazed Lyons made the return journey to Blackpool, wondering just how he was going to produce that sort of quantity, which was to include a saloon version, which Henlys thought essential.

Early and late Austin Seven Swallow saloons are shown here, the 1930 car nearest the camera having a wider radiator shell compared with the later 1931 or 1932 model just down the line.

The spindly 'A' frame of the Seven undergoing body-mounting at Foleshill; it was used more or less as it arrived from the Austin Motor Company, with no attempt at tuning or modification.

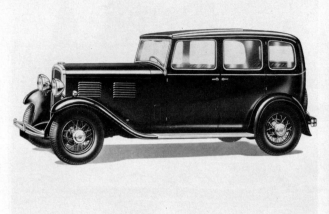

Before the 'Lyons' treatment, the basic off-the-shelf motorcar looked like this – a 1932 Standard Big Nine in this instance, all very straight-laced and angular.

Body construction in Coventry, with panelling commencing as each frame is finished off; the aluminium tail of the two-seater (on right of picture) was made up of some six individually-shaped pieces of metal welded together, the welds being ground down and hand-finished to produce invisible seams.

The pressure was now really on, but although production rose to nearly 12 cars a week (plus well over 100 sidecars) it became obvious that for reasons of space and the right sort of manpower, another move would have to be made. There were also subsidiary problems, such as Longbridge despatching chassis orders in bulk and causing much consternation at Blackpool Talbot Road Station, as it was impossible for Cocker Street to accomodate the full consignment, which to the great displeasure of the stationmaster meant that rolling stock and sidings were tied up for weeks!

There was only one place to go, and that was the midlands car manufacturing area of Birmingham/Coventry with its pool of skilled labour and every type of industrial facility. Thus Lyons set out to reconnoitre the Coventry district, driving from Blackpool in his own Swallow Seven (flat out all the way, "including the corners", by his own recent admission!) to investigate likely sites.

The most promising turned out to be what had been a shell-filling factory at Foleshill, on the Nuneaton side of Coventry; these Holbrook Lane premises comprised four separate buildings, two of which were being used by a firm supplying fabric bodies to Hillman, but the other two were empty. The owners were keen to sell outright, but Lyons managed to obtain a lease instead. "It was five times larger than the premises we occupied in Blackpool and I felt it was a tremendous step forward".

A lot of work was needed on the building itself though, which was in "terrible condition" – the contractor's quote for repairing it was five times greater than

Swallow's total assets (!), so a gang of labourers was engaged and the place was made shipshape by the company itself – which had been retitled in 1927 as the 'Swallow Sidecar & Coachbuilding Co.', this more accurately reflecting its activities.

The move to Foleshill was completed by early November 1928, but all did not go smoothly at first – almost unbelievably it was discovered that the main electric feed cable had been stolen, and even worse, it cost £1200 to replace. Then very inconsistent results were obtained from the new steam-bending equipment used for the body frames, and it was only through the arrival of Cyril Holland – the coachbuilder who had originally sketched out the Swallow Seven but had sought to stay in Blackpool – that total disaster was averted. However, with these difficulties resolved Sir William recalled that:

"It was a most exciting time. We worked from 8 o'clock in the morning until 11 or 12 o'clock at night, for we aimed to raise production from 12 a week to 50 a week within three months. We knew we could only do this by adopting a new method of coachbuilt construction .... Whereas in Blackpool each body-maker had been responsible for the complete framing-up of the body, the latest method used for volume production was the machining of the wooden parts in specially constructed jigs, so that they could be assembled rather like a jigsaw puzzle.

"This saved a tremendous amount of labour, but the introduction of the method caused us many headaches. In fact, we were in such trouble at one time that the body-makers approached me en bloc and told me that the whole thing was too complicated and doomed to failure, and that we should resort to the old method. We perservered, knowing that the economies could be very considerable, and before Christmas we had achieved our 50 bodies a week. We were really in business!''

Lyons also transferred his search for efficiency into Swallow's wages structure. In a manner somewhat ahead of his time, he made a time-study of all the major operations on the assembly line, priced them according to the time allowed for each, then printed books of vouchers. There was one book for each car, every voucher covering one or more of the operations and valued according to the price that job had been costed at. When the operation had been completed, the man wrote his name on the voucher which, after it had been countersigned by the foreman, would be handed in at the end of each day. Then all that the single wages clerk had to do was add up the value of each operative's vouchers and make up his wage packet accordingly. Not everyone liked these various schemes, particularly those amongst the newly recruited Coventry people, but they found that it worked and most stayed.

In 1929, Swallow felt able to extend their range of coachbuilt bodies, and employed their tested formula on a number of other 'plebian' chassis. These were the Fiat 509A (quite an advanced car mechanically with a 990cc overhead-cam engine, and a best-seller in standard form in Italy), the 1287cc sidevalve Standard Big Nine, and the Swift 10. The small Coventry firm of Swift possessed a sound reputation for reliability if not for excitement, although the 1190cc 'P' model used by Swallow had the optional 'sporty' wire wheels; while Swallow remained faithful until the end, Swift could not withstand the competition from giants such as Austin and Morris, and ceased production in 1931.

All were given the same basic 'Swallow' look, with a low roofline projecting over the windscreen (which was often in 'V' form), two doors, curved rear-quarters and a stylish wingline. Plus, most importantly, an imaginative choice of duo-tone colour schemes, nine in all for the 1930 season, including Cherry Red/Maroon, Sky Blue/Danish Blue, and Cream/Violet – a contrast to the normal choice of dark blues, bottle-greens, browns and (mainly) black offered by most manufacturers. No wonder that the Swallow stand at the 1929 Motor Show – their first visit to Olympia – was usually crowded.

The only car with sporting pretensions that Swallow 'repackaged' was the Wolseley Hornet. A victim of the slump, Wolseley had been taken over by Morris in 1927 while in the middle of developing a 'small six' engine of only 1271cc with the novelty of an overhead-camshaft; the idea was to bring true six-cylinder smoothness to the mass market. Morris Motors Ltd took advantage of the work done and produced a four-cylinder version of the engine which, complete with ohc, was fitted into both the Minor and the MG Midget for 1929. Wolseley were

allowed to continue with the six-cylinder design and in April 1930, the Wolseley Hornet was announced.

Rather in contradiction of its quite advanced mechanical specification, no sporting versions were offered, just the rather uninspiring saloon. No wonder then, that it attracted coachbuilders in droves - by the end of 1930, these included the Hoyal Body Corporation, Gordon England with beetle-backed offering, Hill & Boll, Coventry Motor & Sundries Ltd, Avon, and Whittingham & Mitchell who were under contract to London Wolseley distributors Eustace Watkins. All this enthusiasm notwithstanding the fact that prior to October 1930, one had to purchase the entire car rather than just a rolling chassis!

Swallow, who entered the fray in January 1931, thus faced considerable competition, but their tasteful treatment of the subject, incorporating a rather beautiful pointed tail, has stood the test of time and the Swallow Hornet can probably be adjudged the prettiest of the bunch. Wolseley production improvements were included in the Swallow's specification, so that from September 1931 the car was given a 4-speed helical tooth gearbox and three inches more track, which helped offset its rather high, narrow look. Two and four seater styles were by then catalogued by Swallow.

Foleshill also adopted the Hornet Special chassis announced in April 1932, with its new pistons giving a 6:1 compression ratio and duplex valve springs to accomodate its maximum rpm of 5000 - which equated to a respectable 80mph odd in top gear . Bigger (9-inch to 12-inch) brakes, an oil cooler and a remote control gearlever were also added to its specification, and the tail section of the bodywork revised. The Swallow Hornet Special cost £255 in two or four-seater guise, though in 1933 the foursome went up by £5. By now, Maltby, Corsica, Hardy and Patrick had added their own designs to those already available.

The Special chassis was always supplied without bodywork, incidentally, and Wolseley's own apparent lack of interest in producing a finished sporting version themselves can almost certainly be traced back to pressure from Morris Motors, who did not want in-house competition to MG. The Swallow Hornets, produced up until the end of 1933, were to be the last proprietory chassis rebodied by Lyons and Walmsley.

Rather less sporting but much more significant in Swallow's development was the Standard Ensign 16, also of six-cylinders, which was announced from Foleshill in May 1931. The Standard Swallow 16 was given similar coachwork to that of the smaller 9, including a radiator grille which clearly foreshadowed that of the S.S.1; but most importantly, it was the big, smooth 2054cc sidevalve engine with its robust 7-bearing crankshaft that made the greatest impression on Lyons and Walmsley, and by the time the Swallow 16 was on sale, Lyons had already laid his plans for a very much more ambitious project.

Precursor of the S.S.I. was in many ways the Standard 16 which Swallow happily re-bodied; above all it introduced the company to the large, strong and smooth Standard 6-cylinder power unit. Introduced in May 1931, it cost £275, plus £7.10s extra if you wanted a sunshine roof. This car was photographed recently by Stuart Sadd.

Sportiest of the Swallows was undoubtedly the Hornet version; it was also about the most attractive of the open Swallows as this photograph of this 1932 model two-seater demonstrates. *Photo: Autocar*

Meanwhile, the mainstay of Swallow's production, the Seven, had not been left alone. Fixed front wings with half valance had replaced the original cycle-type in September 1927, while for 1929 the front wings were given a full valance and a 'dummy' dumb iron cowling fitted beneath an altered radiator cowl which now incorporated the starting-handle aperture in the surround instead of the grille. The radiator cowls on these Swallows were, incidentally, polished aluminium.

The Austin was given further attention for 1931, in the shape of a new radiator grille, the bulbous nose being replaced by a new design of shallower depth, wider at the bottom than the top, and with a centre bar. The assembly, apart from the honeycombe mesh, was chromium plated, that type of finish having replaced nickel on Swallows in 1930. Cellulose paint was now being used too, instead of coach enamel and varnish. Scuttle ventilators of the picturesque ship-type became fixtures on the scuttle, these also being used on the Standard and Swift models. The Swallow Seven saloon had its split bench front seat replaced by individual bucket seats.

It was in 1930 that Maurice Sampson and F. Gordon-Crosby of *The Autocar* visited Holbrook Lane, passing Dunlop, White and Poppe, and Riley to reach the Swallow factory. Obviously intrigued and impressed by the company's progress in the few short years it had been at Coventry, they had come to see for themselves the "Swallow's Nest", where, as Maurice Sampson put it, "a well-known strain is hatched, matched and despatched".

Immediately noted by the visitors were the efficient methods of production described earlier, beginning with the saw mill. "The saw mill in the Swallow's nest is an extremely important part of the structure. In this mill every single piece of wood used in the frame of the body must be cut and shaped with such accuracy that all the pieces can be put together on a jig without the slightest hand fitting. On emerging from the mill the pieces are brought to the erecting shop, where, with two lads at each of the four erecting jigs, the pieces are put together, glued and screwed, and are off the jig in a very few minutes above one hour per body... The precision with which each piece went into place was quite fascinating to watch..."

This rate of frame production – potentially 30 a day – could, Sampson observed, easily swamp the panelling

The Swallow stand at the 1930 Olympia Motor Show, featuring an example of the revised 1931-model Austin Swallow with its less bulbous nose and a central rib to the radiator. Next to it is a Standard Nine, and behind a Swift.

department next door, where progress was slowed by the necessity to produce a perfect finish on the aluminium panels, "a tedious and expensive operation...but properly flatted and rubbed down a finished aluminium panel is highly attractive and a thing of grace and beauty, as befits a swallow."

Next came the paint. "There is no false modesty about the colour schemes here. They are out to provide bright colours, and to do their bit to make our roads as gay as possible. You hardly ever see a one-colour Swallow on the roads, just as you never see a one-colour swallow in the air. Just at present a combination of greens, or green and black, or green and white seem to be the most popular schemes." Trimming followed, the body then being taken out of the trim shop on a little hand-drawn cart to be mounted on its chassis. "There are rows of Austin Sevens, Swifts, and Standard Big Nines waiting for their pretty burdens, and it seems to take very little time

to fit the body to the chassis. Then more polishing and a final look over, and the elegant ensemble goes into the big store-room to await the owner or his agent... I hope the weather is fine when the Swallows fly away from their nest. I should hate to think of their plumage being splashed as they pass over that dreadful bit of road between Dunlop and White and 'Pops' ere they reach Holbrook Lane."

Refinements to the Seven continued, and it was announced towards the end of 1931 that safety glass was to be fitted all round, and sports silencers and fishtail exhaust became standard fitments. At the same time eight new colour schemes were made available. Perhaps because it would soon become obsolete, prices of the Swallow Seven were dramatically reduced too, the saloon coming down from £187.10s to £165, and the two-seater from £165 to £150. For Swallow, the days of mere coachbuilding were nearly over ....

Chapter Two

The S.S. I and II

Let it be pointed out that these S.S. cars are not just built round a certain popular chassis. The design is original and distinctive.

The Motor, January 31, 1933

Swallow had been hinting about a new car in the motoring press ever since July 1931, when *The Autocar* of the 31st of that month carried a very full description of "a marvellously low-built two-seater coupe of most modern line" in a nicely controlled 'leak', describing accurately the salient features of its coachwork and mechanical specification. Lyons was certainly intent on wetting the appetite of his potential customers well before the actual goods were on sale, and backed-up such editorial mentions with mysterious advertisements urging the reader to "Wait! The S.S. is Coming ...".

So when the S.S.1 emerged into the public eye on the occasion of the 1931 Motor Show at Olympia in October, it was with a confident air and without embarrassment, despite an appearance that was truly *avant-garde.* Perhaps the only unfortunate aspect of that otherwise triumphant launch was that the organisers of the Show, showing a distinct lack of appreciation and foresight, insisted that the new car be relegated to Swallow's old position in the coachwork section of the Show, instead of enjoying a stand in the Manufacturer's Hall as was its right as truly a new make.

In a show where originality of design and execution was notably absent from the offerings of the 'big names', the S.S.1 stood out. It wasn't simply a case of instant success and acclaim, though on the whole the car received very enthusiastic reviews, and there were certainly no novelties in its mechanical specification or method of construction. No, the overriding impression one gains from distilling eye-witness accounts and written opinion both was that the S.S.1 was *different* - it "struck a new note" as an experienced journalist on *The Motor* recalled some years after it had caused that initial furore. There was nothing quite like it, anywhere, and the motoring pundits of the early 1930s found themselves unable to catagorise it, or bracket it alongside anything else.

The initials by which the car was known were not quite so new, however, and were quite familiar to the keener members of the motorcycling fraternity as George Brough had used S.S. (suffixed by such as "80," "90" and "100") as a model name for his superb two-wheeled machines. Brough Superior owner William Lyons obviously decided that "S.S." would suit his purposes too, especially as the name met the approval of Maudslay and Black of the Standard Motor Company. Although this approval was not gained without "long argument", recalled Sir William, "which resulted from my determination to establish a marque of our own". The meaning of the letters was conveniently left open. "There was much speculation as to whether S.S. stood for Standard Swallow or Swallow Special – it was never resolved", said Sir William.

The S.S.1 was a medium-sized coupe with a major part of its proportions given over to an extremely long bonnet, which began behind a stylish radiator grille set well back between the front wheels and ended in a small, low, passenger compartment with two doors. The multi-louvred side panels of the bonnet emphasised its length, and so did the absence of running-boards between the helmet-type wings. The coupe top had been given a 'leather-grained' finish, this material extending to the separate luggage compartment which sat behind the bodyshell proper. Dummy chromium hood-irons decorated the rear side-quarters behind the doors, but as if to make up for the lack of a true folding head, a sliding-roof was fitted as standard - this was specially made for Swallow by Pytchleys to present an unbroken roof-line when closed, the normal sliding-roofs of the period moving back above the roofline.

One cannot say that Swallow – or Lyons – was the very first with this type of approach to bonnet/passenger-space apportionment; a long bonnet combined with low build had been showing signs of becoming a trend amongst more sporting vehicles for the previous couple of years, with examples of the style being mounted on proprietory chassis by a few continental coachbuilders, and even by established British concerns as Gurney Nutting and Mulliner on such as 6.5-litre Bentleys (complete with fabric roofs). But these were generally expensive 'one-offs', and in any case, Lyons took the theme much further - and brought it to the semi-mass production market at a price many could afford. In a critical review of the 1931 Show, the S.S.1 was about the only vehicle in the bodywork section at Olympia which that most analytical of journals, *Automobile Engineer*, felt able to single out for comment on its appearance - "a very attractive car that is, if anything, in advance of the times ..."

It was a brave step to break new ground when large sections of the motor industry, particularly coachbuilding concerns, were feeling the economic pinch and pulling in their horns - "It is not to be wondered at, that in difficult times such as these, body builders have hesitated to make alterations that might have a doubtful effect on sales" quoth *Automobile Engineer* in understanding tones. Indeed, time would tell that the coachbuilders' trade was a dying one, which maybe is one reason why Lyons and Walmsley staked so much on a single, innovatory move in October 1931.

However, it would be wrong to suppose that this was a major reason for the appearance of the S.S.1, which was born chiefly of William Lyons' increasing frustration through having to design his bodies to fit other people's idea of a chassis. In particular, it was very difficult to achieve the fashionable long, low look using chassis produced by most car makers of the period. Through the position of their engines and the mounting of their suspension, these proprietory chassis really only lent themselves to the 'sit-up-and-beg' style of bodywork which, despite Lyons' flair for curves and colour, were all too similar to the contemporary staid family saloons.

The only answer was a specially designed chassis frame, and during 1930 this was put in hand at the Rubery Owen

works. As for power plant, transmission and suspension, the Standard Motor Company became the natural choice as supplier - not only had Lyons already built up a good relationship with Standard's chairman and managing director R.W. Maudslay and general manager John Black (who had come from Hillman in 1929, after marrying one of the many Hillman daughters), but also the notably smooth and reliable Standard 16 engine had all the characteristics which would suit the intended new car very well. It was soon arranged that Standard would accept the new chassis frame from Rubery Owen, fit it with engine, transmission and axles, and deliver it to Holbrook Lane as a running unit all ready to take its new bodyshell. Thus Swallow were relieved of having to put in any new machinery, and could merely continue their existing bodybuilding activities - but with the big difference that now, they could boast of using a chassis designed and assembled exclusively for them.

The new chassis frame was 'U' shaped in section, and all its main features were directed towards achieving the lowest body-line possible. From the front dumb-irons backwards, the side members ran parallel until they reached a cross-member under the radiator, where they tapered outwards for about a foot, then ran parallel again right to the rear of the car. Where the scuttle was mounted, the frame dropped, to continue at this level under the passenger compartment, before running up and over the rear axle.

Cross-members helped to provide torsional rigidity, assisted at the front by a transverse steel plate on which the front of the engine was mounted on two rubber buffers, but no 'X' bracing was incorporated. The long, flat nine-leaf road springs were anchored onto the outside of the frame both front and rear, rather than beneath it, again to achieve the low look. Damping was by Luvax hydraulic lever-arm shock absorbers, and the Standard axles were fitted with Rudge Whitworth splined hubs and 18-inch diameter wire wheels. Steering used the Marles-Weller cam and lever type box with Standard components linking the wheels, and the steering column was given a substantial rake which resulted in an almost vertical position for the steering wheel.

Statistically, Lyons had certainly achieved what he had set out to do - compared with the original Standard 16 saloon, the S.S.1 coupe was 13-inches lower top to bottom, the floor 5-inches lower, the track 1-inch wider, and the wheelbase 3-inches longer at 9-feet 4-inches. The heart of the car was Standard's 2054cc six-cylinder engine, which was positioned no less than 7-inches back in the chassis frame compared to the Standard Ensign from which it came; this was more for looks than for weight distribution, as it allowed the (lower) radiator to be set well back behind the wheels yet still result in an exceptional length of bonnet.

The Standard six-cylinder engine had already accrued a good reputation for reliability, and in some respects was

William Lyons' first car – the original S.S.I Coupe; long and low despite the rather high cockpit. Hood-irons were dummy of course, and the side windows had a draught-preventer included at the top. Radiator shell carried a plated cast "S.S." motif on top. This rare survivor was totally rebuilt by its Australian owner Ivan Stevens.

Head and trunk were finished in leather-grain material, and the lid of the trunk (secured by three catches) hinged rearwards to reveal luggage space and the tools carried in the lid itself. Aware of the limited rear-seat room, Henlys' later offered a dicky-seat conversion which utilised the trunk; it also seems that they helped Lyons to arrive at the S.S.I concept itself, through their market knowledge.
Photo: Autocar

quite sophisticated in its specification - the crankshaft with its seven-main bearings of 2-inches diameter was both stiff and robust, and left the factory balanced dynamically and statically; pistons were of course aluminium, and the rods were of duralumin whose light reciprocating weight gave scope for quite high revs for a unit of this size.

Unfortunately though, the engine's breathing arrangements let it down sadly; mixture was initially supplied by a single Solex carburettor on the offside of the engine block, with an abbreviated manifold feeding a tract which passed between cylinders three and four inside the block, leading to a gallery on the nearside of the engine and thence to the (side) valves .... hardly an efficient method of distributing the mixture.

Continuing Swallow policy, no changes were made to the engine in the cause of more power; in order to cope with the lower bonnet line, however, it was necessary for the fan to be removed from its usual position on an extension of the water-impellor spindle and be mounted lower down on a bracket set below the impellor, with the fan belt now extended to drive it via a new pulley. The fan blades were also decreased in size, and may have contributed to the original S.S.1's tendency towards overheating.

Power output was around 45bhp, and this could be increased to about 55bhp if the 20hp version was specified, of 2552cc and with the rather better bore and stroke ratio of 73 x 101.6mm (compared with the 16's 65.5 x 101.6mm); though this larger engine doesn't seem to have been available - or at least not publicised - until January 1932. In either case, the engine drove the rear wheels through Standard's four-speed gearbox, a single dry-plate clutch and a spiral-bevel rear axle. The gearbox had reasonably close ratios, and in conformity with current sporting practice had been fitted with a cast-aluminium extension in place of the pressed-steel gearbox lid, which carried the selector rods to a short gearlever close to the driver's hand. Final drive ratio was the higher 4.66:1 offered by Standard, more suitable for

Standard's trusty six-cylinder engine with its 'silent third' gearbox as used in the Standard 16. Only minor alterations were needed for its very successful installation in the S.S.1.

the S.S. than the usual 5.11 ratio fitted to most Standard 16s.

Brakes too were from the Standard, of Bendix-Perrot manufacture with encased cables and a mechanical 'duo-servo' action, so that mechanically, the car was easily serviced by any Standard agent.

Onto this orthodox but carefully thought out mechanical and structural basis was fitted Lyons' unique bodywork which set the car completely apart from all else. The separate, helmet-type wings were made of steel, and incorporated a centre rib; at the front, they were partially included in the main bodywork by a tastefully curved extension of the panel which ran under the bonnet sides, and at the rear, they were set into the cockpit rear-quarters. The chrome-plated radiator shell attracted much admiration with its vertical slats surrounded by a moulding which ran up over the crown to end in a motif at the top, and it was flanked by plated Lucas P.170 headlights mounted on a curved tie-bar running between the wings. Sidelights were carried on the wings.

Today, we would term the S.S.1 a '2-plus-2' - while there were rear seats, no-one pretended that they were meant for anything more than carrying children or maybe one adult sitting crosswise. In front, however, the pleated leather bench seat was quite roomy and theoretically could accommodate three abreast, the gear lever being the biggest deterrent to this arrangement.

For two people, the S.S.1 was really quite roomy, the cockpit being wider than, for instance, the S.S. Jaguar saloon which was to come four or five years later; this was due to the fact that owing to the absence of running boards, the floor could be extended outwards to a point almost in line with the outer face of the rear wheel. It was possibly the low height of the car, at 4 ft 8 ins, which gave it a slightly constricting feel.

In this context it is interesting to note that William Lyons' original design for the S.S.1 featured an even lower roofline. This, although it would certainly have given the car an even sleeker appearance, might have effected the habitability of the car, and it has been said that when Lyons went into hospital prior to the announcement date, the roofline was quickly raised without his knowledge. Thus the S.S.1 appeared with its rather upright passenger compartment, which Lyons disliked and used to refer to as a "conning tower"; almost certainly, William Walmsley was responsible for this alteration - no-one else would have dared to meddle!

Throughout the car, Swallow had maintained its usual high standard of trim and equipment. Wood facia and cappings set the pattern which was to be used in virtually all subsequent S.S. and Jaguar cars, although the finish in the S.S.1 was not the walnut which was to become so typical in later years. On the S.S.1 these were not true veneers, but special cabinet makers' finishes applied to plain boxwood, very common from around 1920 to 1940; "fiddle-back" sycamore was one, "birds eye" maple

A.G. Douglas Clease holds open the door of a very early S.S.I for the benefit of the *The Autocar* cameraman. Seats were mounted virtually flat on the floor so you sat very low in the S.S.I; seat back hinged forward to allow access to the dark confines of the rear. Note well-fitting bonnet and body sections — S.S. worked to coachbuilders' standards even if durability wasn't all that it might have been with these 'first series' S.S.Is.

another. Various patterns were to be offered on the Swallow range. The door panels were trimmed in a sun-ray pattern, the Auster safety glass windscreen could be opened, and of course fresh-air motoring was provided by the Pytchley sliding roof, the moving section disappearing underneath the rear part of the roof when opened. Lucas electric windscreen wipers, rear window blind, and roof light switch were all at the control of the driver, who faced a comprehensive dash panel carrying an 80mph Watford speedometer, electric fuel gauge, a large Empire clock, and water temperature gauge - but as yet, no tachometer.

Home comforts such as strategically placed ashtrays and a mirror and powder compact for the ladies (in the hinged lid of the glove compartment) were provided, and carpets and headlining were carefully chosen to match the exterior paintwork. *The Motor* of January 26, 1932, went into considerable detail in describing the latter:

"There is a particularly wide range of artistic colour schemes. For instance, the body and wheels may be painted Nile-blue, apple-green, carnation-red, buff, birch-grey or primrose with the head, trunk and wings in black. For those who desire a coloured head, the following schemes are available: apple-green body and wheels, olive-green head, trunk and wings; carnation-red body and wheels, black head, trunk and wings; buff body and wheels, chocolate-brown head, front and wings."

Swallow's press-release and advertising illustration of the original S.S.I — this is probably the car as Lyons really wished it to be, with a much lower cockpit (compare it with the photographs of the real thing).

Quite a mouth-watering selection! These colours were further set off by the plated Wilmot-Breeden bumpers (full length at the front), the imitation landau-arms, and the bright fittings on the luggage trunk. The spare wheel was, not unattractively, fixed to the rear of the trunk, with the rear number-plate mounted on an extension underneath together with the single rear lamp.

The success or otherwise of the overall effect was a matter of taste, but there was unanimity of opinion on one point – the amazing value for money the S.S.1 gave, at a mere £310 (or £320 with the larger engine). Yet the car bore comparison in many respects with vehicles costing twice or three times that amount.

The S.S.1 on the road

The Motor was first in print with a road test of the 16hp S.S.1 in its issue of January 26, 1932, and was rather lavish in its praise for the car's behaviour on the road, perhaps mindful of Swallow's not inconsiderable advertising budget:

> "At the wheel one is reminded very much of a racing car, for the very long and shapely bonnet suggests immense power and the lowness of build of the complete car gives an instinctive feeling of security ....
> "The writer has an enclosed car equally as fast as the S.S.1 in so far as maximum speed and even acceleration are concerned, but on a winding course of about 40 miles the S.S.1 maintained an average several mph greater than the normal saloon".

But while comparisons with a racing car might have been overdoing things a little (the correlation was much more convincing after the war when it was applied to a descendant of the S.S.1, the XK 120), nevertheless the car did manage to muster an above-average turn of speed for the early 1930s. The 16hp could reach 50mph through the gears in 20 seconds, and *The Motor* achieved 65mph in top with a car that was far from run-in.

No refinement had been sacrificed for this extra performance, however, which came from light weight (21cwt. 1qr.) and a lower frontal area, not engine tuning – although the large tailpipe used gave a low-pitched note, considered to be pleasing to "sporting-car enthusiasts". Very little mechanical noise came from the engine or transmission, "which enables one to cover long distances without fatigue".

This aspect was also helped by a well-chosen combination of springing medium and dampers, where it was noted that the usual temptation of sporting car manufacturers to obtain good handling by screwing everything up tight had been avoided by Swallow, so that a good ride was obtained without pitching or rolling. The steering more than passed muster too: " ... the wheel is rock steady, is light to the touch, and what is even more important, the car goes where it is put." Turning circle

was a reasonable 39ft. 6ins.

The Bendix cable brakes were up to par, and "the pedal action is progressive and does not demand much effort on the part of the driver to obtain an emergency pull up". This statement should be qualified however, by stating that the Duo-servo action gave the brakes a 'piling-up' action, which meant that on a heavy application it was necessary to feather the pedal in order to prevent the wheels grabbing or locking up altogether, especially in the wet.

Whether or not *The Motor* was over-enthusiastic when describing the S.S.1's performance characteristics, the magazine was correct in summing-up exactly what it was that Lyons was offering the motorist:

> "... the S.S.1 is a new type of automobile in the sense that it is a car built for the connoisseur but is relatively low priced. All the attributes of sports models are incorporated in a refined manner, and this, coupled with a striking appearance, is bound to attract enthusiastic motorists of modest means".

In other words, Lyons had introduced the affordable 'personal car', and had succeeded in getting the formula very nearly right at his first attempt.

The Autocar ran its first test of the S.S.1 a few days after *The Motor's* had appeared. It was equally enthusiastic and reinforced the points that its rival had made, commenting on the smooth and flexible nature of the 2054cc six (which would accelerate from 5mph in top without fuss), light and positive steering, stability in cornering, easy gearchange and smooth clutch. The only criticisms were a certain lack of thigh clearance below the wheel rim, and a handbrake lever that was a little too far away from the driver.

An easy cruising speed was reckoned to be 55mph, and *The Autocar* claimed a maximum of 70mph, with a fuel consumption of 22mpg - this must have been a touring figure as *The Motor* reported 18.5mpg "driven hard". *The Autocar's* summary of the S.S.1's qualities was rather briefer than its rival's but it could have been no less satisfying for Lyons to read. "The S.S.1", the writer opined, "is a very attractive car".

The S.S.II

On the Swallow stand at the 1931 Olympia Show there were three other cars besides the belle-of-the-ball S.S.1 - the two-seater Wolseley Hornet Swallow, the still-attractive Austin Seven Swallow saloon, and a diminutive four-cylinder coupe which looked like a compressed version of the S.S.1.

At first, the S.S.11 was rather overshadowed by its larger and more expensive sister, but though less ambitious under the skin, it could be said to be a more balanced and better looking car than the S.S.1. *The Motor* gave it just

The Autocar was very taken with the S.S.I and appreciated its good points at a time when many sought only to highlight its bad. The late A.G. Douglas Clease drove the car for many thousands of miles on road-tests and in rallies, and is seen here during the first national RAC Rally of Great Britain in 1932. Note that the spare wheel of this S.S.I boasts a spare wheel cover, lacking on earlier examples.

four lines in its original five-page review of the new marque, while *The Autocar* chose to ignore it altogether.

There was some excuse for this, in that the S.S.11 was - when first announced - just another Swallow rebodying exercise on a more or less unaltered chassis, despite carrying a new name. Its basis was the Standard Little Nine, complete with its 1006cc, 60.25 x 88m side-valve engine giving 28bhp at 4000rpm, and a three-speed gearbox. Surprisingly, it was a lot cheaper than the previous Standard 9 Swallow saloon, at only £210 as opposed to £250, but no doubt allowance had been made for a much higher rate of production.

In looks, it was definitely a scaled-down version of the S.S.1, having the same coupe bodywork, helmet-type wings, leather-finish top, and built-on luggage container

at the rear. Described as an occasional four-seater, the interior appointments matched those of the S.S.1 in quality, with leather seats, wind-up windows, and opening roof. The bonnet was made as long as possible under the circumstances, with the footwells being taken right into the engine compartment - where the power unit itself took up barely one-third of the space. An unusual feature were the louvres set into the scuttle sides under the bonnet, which gave extra ventilation on a warm day.

Few contemporary road tests of the S.S.11 are available for study, but *The Motor's* sister journal, *The Light Car & Cyclecar*, conducted a full test early in 1933, publishing their results in May. Sixteen hundredweight and 28bhp doesn't exactly spell performance, but *the Light Car and Cyclecar's* writer seemed very satisfied when he borrowed a

The 'first series' S.S.II with its cycle-type wings; all the major features of the S.S.I were mirrored in its styling, and it was perhaps a better-balanced design than the larger car. Original photographs of the early S.S.II are virtually non-existent, and this illustration is taken from the printed page of a contemporary journal.

The S.S.II at the Olympia Show, with Hornet-Swallow in background. This is a rare unretouched view of the car from *The Autocar* archives.

rather new example from Henlys. Despite a mileometer reading of only 100, the little S.S. appeared happy to give 40mph in third (by this time, a four-speed box was fitted, S.S. taking advantage of a Standard Motor Company update), and 60mph in top, while at 50mph "the car tours easily and with plenty of reserve for that extra bit of gradient just around the corner".

This performance was certainly better than the stock Standard 9 (an increase of some 6mph in top speed) and *The Light Car and Cyclecar* went some way to explaining the difference by mentioning that the "odd spot of engine tuning" had been carried out; perhaps the S.S.11 was an exception to Swallow's usual policy of leaving the mechanics strictly alone. A Stromberg carburettor was fitted too, instead of what would seem to be the more usual Solex or, from 1933 onwards, RAG.

The S.S.11 seemed to be a very habitable car, and it was reported that 100 miles could be covered non-stop without fatigue, with "no fumes inside the body and only a minor degree of drumming, which vanishes entirely

when the roof is slid back". No mention was made of petrol consumption over such a journey, but it would probably have been around 38mpg, judging from what the Standard Little 9 was known to return.

The car was also untemperamental and simple to drive: "It started easily from cold, but the gearlever was 'sticky' until the box had warmed up. The controls and seating position were just right. The gearlever thrust its 'nose' into our hand like an affectionate dog, the steering wheel sat nicely in our lap, the screen was close enough to give a wide range of vision, the pedal pressure light, the accelerator spring exactly as we like it." The brakes were also liked, although their tendency to 'pile-up' during a heavy application was noted – a Bendix Duo-servo system similar to that fitted to the S.S.1 was employed.

The steering was thought to be one of the S.S.11's best features, "as light as a feather, yet positive and with hardly a trace of kick" - Burman worm and nut was used on the S.S.II for 1932 and 1933, after which the Marles-Weller cam and lever system as for the S.S.1 was fitted. The car also appeared to cope well with fast cornering, thanks to the "underslung chassis, low build and 4.75 Dunlops". Interior decorations were thought to be "harmonious and pleasing", and in summing up their feelings about the car, the journal stated that:

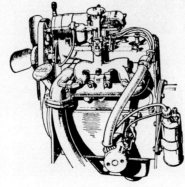

The S.S.II 1-litre sidevalve engine – hardly powerful, but smooth running and virtually unburstable, it gave the car a top speed of just on 60mph.

"... it definitely leaves behind it very pleasant recollections of effortless speed, of sweeping easily round bends, of flexibility, of something being accomplished and of something being done."

Allowing for a little over-enthusiasm, it does come

through that the S.S.11 was no freak or 'nasty special' and that Swallow had succeeded in building a spritely small car of unique looks, entirely suitable for regular use, day in, day out.

This impression is again borne out from reading *The Motor's* somewhat briefer appraisal of the S.S.11, published in January 1933. A similar top speed of 60mph was recorded, with 53mph coming up in third, and "the engine settles down to a pleasant hum at any speed between 35mph and 50mph. It will run 'flat out' all day long if desired, without sign of overheating or distress in any shape or form".

The full-width front seat was approved of, and thought comfortable for two six footers; the rear accommodation was considered suitable for children or "small adults". All in all, *The Motor's* S.S.11 "performed with great credit", and the price had been held at £210 unlike the new S.S.1 models which had, by then, undergone an increase.

The 1933 S.S.1

Swallow took full advantage of the September new-model announcements which were traditional in the 1930s to reveal a completely revised version of the S.S.1 for 1933. While sales of the original car had been far from disappointing - something in the region of 700 by that time – Lyons had from the outset been dissatisfied by some aspects of the car's styling, and knew that many improvements could be made in other directions too - and there had been a few complaints of rattling wings and dropping doors, despite Swallow's striving for quality. Those at Holbrook Lane must have worked extremely hard during the last few months of summer 1932, because in September a very much changed S.S.1 came onto the scene.

In fact, the 1933 S.S.1 was really a new car altogether, as chassis, bodywork and even the interior were all entirely different. Just the main styling theme of the original S.S.1 remained, plus the Standard engine and running gear. The result of these alterations was, without doubt, an overwhelmingly better motor car.

Immediately obvious were the car's better proportions, made possible by a longer wheelbase; the "conning tower" look had gone, thanks to an elongated passenger compartment, while a continuity of line was now provided by elegant, flowing wings incorporating running boards. The car still looked ultra-modern, but with its new, harmonised lines, it appeared handsome even to those who had remained undecided when the new *marque* had first come on the scene twelve months before.

The new chassis frame, built by Thompson Motor Pressings Ltd., gave a wheelbase of 9ft. 11ins. instead of 9ft. 4ins., and was entirely different in its construction too. It was now underslung at the rear - that is, the rear axle was positioned above the frame members, which

then ran forwards to gently rise under the dash and to curve over the front axle. Just as importantly, Swallow

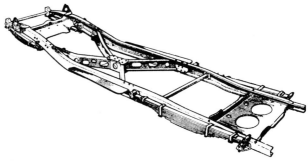

The 1933 S.S.I was almost a new car with a chassis frame of longer wheelbase and with a centre 'X' bracing to increase rigidity. Rear axle was overslung.

had adopted latest practice in chassis design by giving the frame a centre cruciform bracing, which greatly contributed to rigidity. The propellor shaft passed over this bracing, and was covered by a tunnel built into the bodywork. Long half-elliptic springs were still used, now with large Andre Hartford friction dampers; the Bendix braking system was retained with the handbrake operating on all four wheels.

Both the 16 and 20hp engines had come in for attention, although actual capacity remained the same. The major change was the substitution of an aluminium head for the cast-iron one, along with a higher compression ratio. Either a RAG type 'M' or a Solex carburettor was fitted, and the bhp was brought up from 45 to around 48, and from 55 to 62 at 3,600rpm with a 6:1 compression ratio in the case of the 16 and 20hp units respectively. An engine-driven pump brought the fuel from the rear-mounted tank, which was now of 12 gallons capacity instead of 9. It had not gone without notice at Foleshill that the 1932 cars were occasionally prone to overheating, so for 1933 a new Marston radiator block had been designed and installed.

The coachwork of the S.S.1 was, as we have seen, almost completely new, but still built to the high standards which Lyons and Walmsley had set in their early days as mere packagers. Needless to say, the main techniques developed for the speedy and efficient assembly of coachbuilt bodies on proprietary chassis during the late 'twenties were applied to S.S.1. This streamlining of operations is one reason why Swallow were able to enter the realms of semi-mass-production using what were basically still traditional coachbuilding methods, thus avoiding the need for heavy machinery with the accompanying large capital expenditure. In effect, they 'jumped two squares' in the serious game of becoming a motor manufacturer.

Not that this entailed cutting corners on quality - far from it, as can be deduced both from contemporary reports and from examination of the cars themselves

The beauty that is Swallow

Was beauty in car design ever before expressed in such striking fashion as it is in the 1933 S.S.? Olympia will again emphasize that its individuality and distinction are beyond comparison.

A full four-seater Saloon with sliding roof, comprehensive and tasteful equipment, the S.S.I is a car to be desired by the motorist of discrimination. Luxurious interior, with quickly adjustable driver's and front passenger's seats, and wonderfully comfortable "arm-chair" rear seats. Hand-buffed Hide upholstery tones with the extensive range of colour schemes. Price: 16 h.p. Model £325; 20 h.p. Model £10 extra. The S.S.II, embodying all those refinements usually associated with the most expensive models, now possesses four-speed gearbox. Price £210. Both models are exhibited on Stand 147, Olympia.

STAND 147      OLYMPIA

Manufacturers:
THE SWALLOW COACHBUILDING CO., LTD.
FOLESHILL, COVENTRY.   Coventry 8027

Southern England Distributors:
HENLYS, DEVONSHIRE HOUSE,
PICCADILLY, W.I.   Museum 7734 (20 lines).

The new-model S.S.I was announced in advertisements like this towards the end of 1932.

38

today. Said *The Motor* when describing the 1933 range, "One reason for the success of Swallow coachwork in the past has been the attention paid to detail and one finds plenty of evidence here. For example, let it be mentioned that while four coats are usually considered sufficient for a cellulose-painted job no fewer than eight coats are used in finishing the S.S. bodywork" - no doubt much to the delight of the Zofelac Paint Company who supplied the materials! The writer went on to say:

> "Every part of the coachwork is jigged to standards of fine limits, so that it is absolutely interchangeable, a point of importance not only to the future owner, but also in avoiding wasted time and therefore unnecessary cost.
> "The attention to detail is amazing, as a close examination of the cars reveals. The beautiful finish of the doors, which shut fast almost silently with a slight push, of the seating and upholstery, command admiration".

The revision of the bodywork for 1933 went right back to basics. The smell of hot Castrol not being unfamiliar to owners of the original S.S.1, much more attention was paid to bulkhead sealing, and the firewall was now mounted on thick felt all round the flywheel housing; wherever cables or other controls passed through the wall, they were carefully grommeted to exclude fumes. The pedals were boxed in, and even the engine oil-filler cap, which also acted as a breather, was given a fume

discharge pipe which ducted hot smelly air safely away under the car.

Externally, the bonnet was given extra louvres to assist the exit of warm air from the engine compartment, which helped to cut down fumes again, and promote better cooling. But most noticeable of all were of course the new wings, still with a central ridge at the front, but now sweeping back to include running boards and meet with the rear mudguards. While its height remained the same, the length of the passenger compartment had been increased thanks to the longer wheelbase, and the car now had a less severe look due to a curved, instead of straight, top rail above the windscreen. Frontal aspect was also improved by a new radiator shell, which was more slender and now tapered downwards. The rear window had been given both a plated frame and an opening facility for additional ventilation.

Occupants of the new S.S.1 enjoyed a much higher degree of comfort than before. Not only was there much more room (adults could now seriously consider a long journey seated in the rear), but also many detail features had been upgraded, of which the most obvious were the separate bucket-type front seats instead of the bench style used before. Connolly's "Vaumol" hide (the name indicating leather of the highest quality) covered the seats as before, in colours to match Swallow's usual extensive range of trim and exterior colour schemes.

The revised S.S.I Coupe did not look radically different from the front, although the curved headlamp bar had gone and the radiator shell now tapered at the bottom. The top rail of the windscreen was also given a slight curve. *Photo: Autocar*

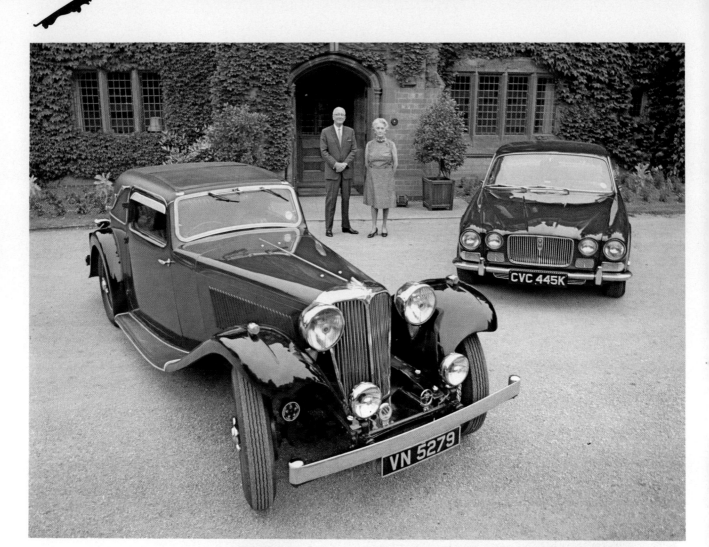

Above: **Sir William and Lady Lyons pose outside their Warwickshire home with an SS I Coupe and a Series I XJ12. The revised SS I Coupe, as illustrated by this picture, was an altogether more balanced shape, with full-length wings and running-boards, than its predecessor.** *Photo: P. Skilleter*

Right: **Interior of the revised S.S.I Coupe, showing the separate front seats; the dash layout was new too although instrumentation remained similar, including the Empire electric clock and British Jaeger speedometer. The water temperature gauge was the revolving drum-type. Note the Philco radio under the dash.**

Photo: Autocar

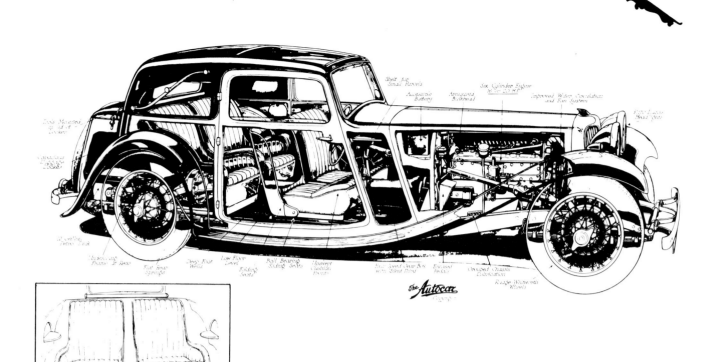

The fully-revised 'second-series' S.S.I Coupe produced for 1933, shown in cutaway form by *The Autocar*. The engine was about the only item left substantially unaltered.

Jaegar instruments now faced the driver, again mounted in a central instrument panel. The driver's ashtray had been transferred to a central position on the wide, polished wood rail which ran under the windscreen - now in figured walnut, and setting a pattern for S.S. and Jaguar dashboards which would remain up until the Mk VII. Still centered around the steering wheel boss were the hand throttle, advance and retard lever, and lighting and dipping switch, with the horn button in the middle; the choke had been transferred from the dash panel to the steering column.

A small parcel shelf ran the full width of the scuttle under the facia; the transmission tunnel below was now higher because of the underslung chassis, and therefore a straight instead of a cranked gearlever was fitted. The handbrake was still mounted on the offside of the gearbox cover. Footwell ventilation was provided by a circular vent in the side of the bulkhead, which was covered by the bonnet side panel but supplied with air by the bonnet louvres.

The rear seat passengers were equally well looked after. Making the best of the now slightly intrusive transmission tunnel, a high, well-upholstered central armrest and divide had been installed, matched by similarly contoured armrests at each side over the wheelarches. Above the latter, let-in to the rear quarters, were small cubby-holes with lids which hinged down to form small tables.

The two doors were wide enough to allow quite easy access to the rear seats as well, and they were carried on three hinges (each with a grease nipple) in order to avoid

door-dropping problems during use. They were still trimmed inside with the sun-ray pattern which *The Motor* thought was "futuristic". Without doubt, the S.S.1 was a quality motor car, and well worth the small price increase which came with all the improvements - the 16hp model was now £325, and the 20hp £335.

The 1933 S.S.1 on the road

The earliest news of how the new S.S.1 was likely to perform came from A.G. Douglas Clease, B.Sc., when on

An S.S.I in Scotland – the 1933-model coupe on test by Douglas Clease north of the border; 1000-miles were put up, over the course of a few days, without problems. *Photo: Autocar*

behalf of *The Autocar* he borrowed a pre-production car and set off to cover 1000 miles in one long weekend. Having waited while the mechanics fitted new-pattern door-locks, windscreen, dual-blade wiper and a jet control for the SU carburettor (rarely seen), Douglas Clease then set forth for Scotland, averaging 40mph in the first hour, and gained Carnforth for lunch: "So far, so good; 139 miles covered, the S.S. running as smoothly, quietly and comfortably as a dream car, the radiator temperature just below 80 deg. C., the oil pressure 30lb".

This was followed by a fast climb up Shap Fell, "and an amusing sprint alongside the huge engine of an L.M.S. Scots express, driver and stoker waving their appreciation of our greater speed, for in response to my right foot hard down the speedometer needle swung steadily up to the 80mph mark". In contrast, less smooth roads were no deterrent to the S.S. which averaged 26mph over the western road along Loch Ness - under reconstruction, it was "a mass of pot-holes, ruts, and boulders, and resembles a cart track on a new building estate".

At the end of the fourth day, Birmingham was regained after a day's run of 323 miles, which included averaging a highly respectable 46 miles in one hour. Summing up, Douglas Clease proclaimed:

"And right well had the S.S. performed. Speed it has in plenty, rapid acceleration, powerful braking, but, above all, roadholding which is uncanny in its steadiness when cornering at high speed. This is undoubtedly due to its underslung rigid frame and long flat springs, giving a low centre of gravity, but, what is important, this steadiness is not gained by any sacrifice of comfort. The steering, too, is light and precise, with sufficient self-centering action. The body is roomy and comfortable, and the seating and upholstery are such that no fatigue was felt at any time during or after this quite strenuous 1,000 miles test, a fact which vouches for the excellent driving position, easy-working and well-placed controls, and good vision".

This appraisal of the S.S.1, with its new chassis, rings rather more true than did the only marginally less enthusiastic pronouncements in the motoring press on the original 1931/32 car. It certainly did seem as if the S.S.1 was turning into an extremely competent sporting car, worthy of consideration by even a discerning motorist.

As *The Autocar* had been given this 'preview run', Swallow allowed *The Motor* to conduct the first formal road test of the new 1933 models, the magazine covering some 300 miles on each type. The 16hp and 20hp cars were thought to be of comparable performance during ordinary motoring up to 50mph, though "the larger model, however, shows to advantage when tackling hilly country, and provides a power reserve which is attractive." The 20hp S.S.1 also reached 70 mph quicker.

Top speeds were found to be 71mph and 75mph 'mean', and the 16hp could accelerate to 50mph in 23 seconds − although the latter figure does not seem representative of the new 2054cc car, as it was three seconds slower than the original S.S.1 tried by the same magazine in 1932; almost certainly, this was accounted for by the fact that the car was not sufficiently run-in to give of its best.

The general road behaviour of the car was highly praised:

"The suspension is very good. At ordinary speeds pot-holed roads are smoothed out quite satisfactorily, and at the top end of the scale there is a notable absence of rolling and pitching, the car maintaining its accurate steering characteristics. As we have already indicated, this is one of the most attractive features of the models under review. One can, for instance, go all out down a steep decline with the speedometer hovering around the 80mph mark and be sure of negotiating bends quite safely. Even a slightly built woman would experience no difficulty in parking the car in a confined space."

The Bendix brakes were found to be light and consistent, stopping the car in 27ft. from 30mph, the clutch and gearchange easy to handle and not calling "for any great finesse', two miles of third gear work did not bring the water to boiling point, and a start was easily made on a 1-in-5 hill.

The Autocar published its test in February 1933, restricting itself to the 16hp car. Apparently having the benefit of a test car with a reasonable mileage behind it, rather better performance figures were obtained − *The Autocar's* 16hp S.S.1 equalled *The Motor's* 20hp example in top speed at 75mph, and it reached 60mph from a standstill in 28.4 seconds. This same speed was readily available in third gear, so that "it can readily be understood that the car can maintain a high average speed, especially as on top gear a comfortable cruising speed of 55mph or 60mph may be kept up on suitable roads without any apparent effort".

The magazine was also pleased to note that this performance did not bring with it any temperament: "... the engine remains smooth-running and silent at any speed, either on top or on the indirect ratios, and the use of a higher compression ratio than last year has not noticeably affected the smoothness of the engine, although giving an enhanced performance".

Once more, the S.S.1's ride and roadholding were singled out for praise : "Even on a bad surface there is no feeling of unsteadiness about either front or rear axle ... it may be taken fast round bends and corners without a vestige of rolling or swaying. Altogether the S.S.1 is a well-equipped sports saloon which it is a pleasure to handle".

Just over a month later, *The Autocar* was again waxing lyrical on the subject of S.S., this time after sampling the 20hp machine. It was really quite a fast car. Just on 82mph was recorded, and this at a time when many family cars of a similar size to the S.S.1 found maintaining a true 60mph rather a wearing struggle. Fifty miles an

Wire-wheels eventually became a sporting feature of 'snob' value, but in the mid-thirties it was fashionable to cover them up; here is the S.S.1 Coupe fitted with wheel discs, which contribute to an even smoother line. Another advantage of wheel discs was, of course, that it relieved the owner of the tedium of cleaning spokes! *Photo: Autocar*

hour was gained in a brisk 15 seconds, and 60mph in 21.4 seconds, an extremely useful reduction of 7 seconds over the 16hp car.

It wasn't just flat-out speed which impressed, but the capability of the car to maintain a high cruising speed, "for when the road allows the car will glide along with practically no noise but the rush of air at an effortless mile a minute. Even 70mph can be considered a cruising speed, for the engine is then still working within its capabilities". Good brakes and steady cornering made this straight-line potential extremely usable, which doesn't always follow in fast cars. Fuel consumption was 18mpg, which was 2mpg higher than the 16hp S.S.1.

The S.S. Open Four-Seaters

Up until early in 1933, Swallow had pursued a one-model policy within the S.S.1 and S.S.II ranges, perhaps wisely concentrating on getting one car right and despatched in adequate numbers before diversifying. But now, with the S.S.1 coupe in great demand, variations on the theme could be considered in order to reach a yet wider portion of the market.

The S.S.1 having proved itself to be a commercial proposition, it was also time to run-down the coachbuilding activities in order to devote all of Foleshill's resources to making the required number of S.S.s. The last new Swallow body to be announced was on the Wolseley Hornet Special chassis as described in chapter one, but it was discontinued the same year it was introduced - 1932. That same year saw the faithful Austin Seven Swallow, in both two-seater and saloon forms, fade from production, along with the Swallow Standard 16. In any case, so far as the Austin Seven was con-

cerned, the continuity of chassis supply was by no means assured as Sir Herbert Austin had begun to get a little annoyed at the numbers Swallow were taking, all of which could otherwise have left Longbridge as proper Austin Sevens! Sidecar production was allowed to continue though, Lyons and Walmsley seeing no point in winding-up a profitable sideline that was little trouble to run.

The 'variation' was the S.S.1 tourer, announced in March 1933. It was indeed a very smart car, and was probably even better looking than the 1933 S.S.1 coupe. Said *The Autocar*:

"The graceful swept wings and running boards, the long bonnet and upswept scuttle, the low body line, the neatly folding hood, and the pleasing treatment of the rear trunk, on the lid of which the spare wheel is carried, all combine to give a sleek, low-built appearance to the car as a whole, which is the very epitome of speed."

In fact the arrangement of wings, bonnet and radiator grille were much as for the saloon, and the interior dimensions and seating - with the 'armchair' rear seats - all remained the same. The scuttle, however, was upswept in front of the driver and passenger in the manner of the times, this being intended to deflect the wind should the windscreen be folded forwards. The doors were given low cutaways to allow elbows to be rested, and "weather protection has been carefully studied" so that the rigid side screens fitted well (held in position by strong but simple locking devices) and the top, when erected, gave the car a pleasant, saloon-car feel to it. A large diameter 5-inch speedometer incorporating engine revolution markings for third and top gears was standardised.

Mechanically, the S.S.1 tourer was exactly as the sister coupe, and this applied to the price too. Captain John Black of Standard, on whom Swallow were so dependent

Above: The S.S.I open four-seater tourer, photographed next to an A.C. Doors of the tourer still have three hinges, and the folded hood is covered by an envelope. Screen could be hinged down. The A.C. had the same chassis frame, used by William and Charles Hurlock from 1932 to 1938. *Photo: Autocar*

Right: With hood and sidescreens erected the S.S.I Tourer didn't look quite so handsome; this is the 20hp car which *The Autocar* tested in used condition in 1936. Spotlamp was not a factory fitment. *Photo: Autocar*

for all the chassis hardware, was supplied with the first S.S.1 tourer to be completed, and was reported as being delighted with it. No-one appears to have formally tested the early tourers with the 2054cc and 2552cc engines, though fortunately W.H. Charnock later wrote of his experiences with a 20hp model bought new in 1933, after 12 years ownership of the car.

The biggest point in the car's favour was, thought Charnock, its smooth seven-bearing engine which gave "that undefinable untiring feel after many hours of hard driving", while its coachwork was soundly built and did not 'date' in appearance (this being written in August 1945). Top speed was thought to be about 75mph - that was with the screen down, but even so the car probably created more 'drag' than the equivalent saloon, which would explain the 5mph loss of speed compared to earlier road tests of the latter.

But further improvements were on the way, thanks partly to Standard themselves updating their range, although the S.S.1's new chassis frame, even though it had only been in production a year, was altered too. As for the S.S.II, that underwent little less than a transformation.

The 1934 S.S. Range

First, the engines; Standard had increased the size of their power units for 1934 and of course Swallow followed suit. In the case of the 16hp and 20hp engines, the stroke was taken from 101.6mm to106mm (a measurement to become very much associated with S.S. and later Jaguar) with the bore sizes remaining at 65.5mm and 73mm respectively. Just as importantly, the breathing arrangements were revised; the single RAG carburetter was removed to the nearside of the engine where a new alloy inlet manifold with centre hot-spot fed four ports in the block, two siamesed and two single. A new exhaust manifold, on the nearside as before, ended in a downpipe which swept forwards away from the bulkhead so that the passenger compartment remained cooler.

There were internal changes too: the oil pump was now of the submerged type, disclosed on removing the sump - previously it was mounted externally on the side of the block. A spring-steel timing chain tensioner blade was fitted, and the dynamo was now driven by the fanbelt instead of by the timing chain (previously, adjustment of the latter had been carried out by moving the dynamo). Cooling was improved by a new water pump which replaced the rather primitive impellor/thermo-syphon arrangement. The basic design and construction of the 1934 block and timing chain case was to be used throughout S.S. and Jaguar production right up until the 2.5 litre Mk V of 1951.

Attached to the S.S.1's engine was an improved version of Standard's gearbox, which now had synchromesh on second, third and top gears - Standard and S.S. were the only makes to offer this advantage; most Standards had a freewheel device attached to the gearbox, but Swallow elected not to offer this (incidentally the company apparently experimented with both the Wilson pre-selector and the Cotal electric gearboxes but none were offered in an S.S. or Swallow). The engine was mounted on rubber pads at the front, and held in two Silentbloc bushes on the rear engine mounting plate.

Then, conscious that the S.S.1 was still not particularly roomy inside, Swallow increased the car's track by two inches, and widened the chassis frame accordingly. This additional inch either side made a useful difference, and rear seat passengers were also given more footroom, as the centre cruciform bracing had been moved forward slightly as well, which meant that the rear footwells could be enlarged. The half-elliptic springs were now wider, and had Silentbloc bushes fitted to their rear mountings though the fronts still had shackle pins incorporating grease nipples. Even the brakes were improved, drum diameter increasing to 12.5 inches.

Outward changes to the S.S.1 for 1934 were subtle but well executed and generally useful – but first and foremost, a further body style became available. This was a true four-light (i.e. four side window) saloon, virtually identical to the coupe but with the space occupied by the dummy landau arms replaced by a full side window. It was to become very popular.

All models had discreetly re-worked wings, particularly at the front where the wing valances were continued to form half of the apron hiding the dumb irons. At the other end, the spare wheel on the closed cars was given a metal cover, complete with decorative chrome trim round its circumference. A new quick-action hinged petrol filler cap with distinctive eared release arms replaced the former, more primitive, item.

Dipping headlights now featured as standard, and plated Lucas horns decorated the front bumper; semaphore direction indicators were standardised too. The radiator shell had been updated to include an outside filler cap, in place of the winged 'SS' decoration used on the 1932/33 cars; the maker's name was now displayed as a motif under it made up of the letters "SS" within a hexagon. The hexagon had appeared earlier in 1933 on the rear bumper bar of the S.S.1, incidentally.

Inside the S.S.1, the appointments were similar to before, although apart from the increase in room, such details as the instrument panel were changed - the hexagon theme had been carried over to the facia, with the instruments being set in bright chrome hexagonal bezels on a satin-chrome background. The figured-

The first S.S. Saloon, with four-light coachwork on the S.S.1 chassis; the extra windows must have made travelling in the back somewhat more enjoyable. This car displays the now-rare S.S. Car Club badge – the S.S. Car Club was formed in mid-1934 with Ernest Rankin as secretary. *Photo: Autocar*

Right: The 1934 S.S.I range came with a modified radiator shell incorporating a separate filler cap, the "SS" insignia being transferred to a badge carried on the nose of the shell.

Below: Instruments on the 1934 dashboard had plated hexagonal surrounds.

walnut veneer remained, and the floor was "thickly carpeted".

But it was the S.S.II which received a lot of the attention on Swallow's announcement of the 1934 range in October 1933, for it had been given the benefit of much more than a mere facelift. As had happened to the S.S.1 at the end of 1932, the S.S.II now caught up and was similarly given a new chassis frame, roughly based on that of its larger brother being underslung at the rear and fitted with a cross-bracing at the centre to increase torsional rigidity. The opportunity was also taken to lengthen the wheelbase by the considerable amount of 13 ins., which brought it up to 8ft. 8ins., while the track went up from 3ft. 8.25ins. to 3ft. 10.5ins.. This made the car 20ins. longer, 2ins. wider and 1in. higher, contributing greatly to the occupants' comfort. In fact, it was probably then as roomy inside as the first S.S.1 of three years before.

Almost as importantly, the S.S.II was provided with more power through a larger, 1343cc, engine with a bore

and stroke of 63.5 x 106mm rated at 32bhp – an increase of around 5 or 6bhp which more than made up for an extra 3cwt. or so in weight. The four-speed box had synchromesh on second, third and top gears, with a final drive ratio of 5.43:1. Engine and transmission were carried on new, three-point rubber mountings, a 'U' shaped cradle on the gearbox and two at the front of the engine. This eliminated any metal-to-metal contact, and was termed "Boyuant Power" by Standard.

Furthermore, S.S.11 customers were given a choice of power unit, as a 1608cc engine was offered too; another sidevalver, this gave about 38bhp at 4000rpm from the larger bore of 69.5mm - stroke remained at 106mm, which coincidentally was the same as the larger six-cylinder Standard engines. Coupe, saloon and tourer bodies were available on the 10hp or 12hp chassis, although the open car wasn't announced until the spring of 1934.

A chance to judge the new S.S.11's performance came when *The Light Car* published its test of a 10hp model in August 1934. In fact, not a great deal of the text was devoted to the car's behaviour in this respect, other than to say that the S.S. was "probably faster than most 10hp models", its slightly modified cylinder head and RAG carburettor serving to keep it ahead of more ordinary opposition. Just over 61mph was achieved, with the standing quarter-mile being covered in 27.4 seconds.

However, the magazine was able to say that the S.S.11's general appointments were considerably above average, and to emphasise that the car was "a full four seater" with ample room. "The two doors are wide, so that, in conjunction with the folding front seats, access to the rear seats is not difficult. The interior of the car, like the

The new S.S.II was a substantially larger and better car; the saloon version is shown here, with (above) the Foleshill works in the background (plus an S.S.I Tourer with the hood up). The rear view demonstrates the low height of the car, plus rear-end details such as the 'fly's eye' lamp and covered spare wheel; roadwheels have chromium plated rims, an S.S. feature. *Photos: Motor*

An excellent photograph of the S.S. II's interior showing its high quality trim; note plentiful use of leather and wood. This saloon also has as standard an opening rear window, rear blind (controlled by the driver) and a full complement of ashtrays. Most of these interior fittings were in chromium plate. Note also the opening roof, and the deep footwells for the rear seat passengers. *Photo: The Light Car*

exterior, is exceptionally well finished. Polished walnut is used for the door fillets and cappings, as well as for the instrument panel. Vaumol hide, one of the highest grades of leather, is used for all the upholstery, Swallow patent spring-case cushions forming the seats, while the armrests are padded with cushion rubber". The Bendix brakes and Marles-Weller steering (instead of the previous Burman) were all approved of too.

A contemporary owner's opinion of the S.S.11 is provided by this letter to *The Autocar*, written about a 1935 model which possessed a similar specification:

"After a mileage of 12,000 my S.S.II saloon is running rather better than it has ever done. In fact, this engine seems definitely to improve with use, and I do not think that it can be said to be run-in under 2,000 miles. The gear change has also become well run-in and properly free.

"Little trouble has been experienced with carburation or starting, but for the best results it is desirable to clean out the carburetters and petrol filters frequently and regularly. Starting from cold is never difficult if the battery is attended to regularly and kept well charged, and if the priming lever on the mechanical fuel pump is first used to make sure that the carburetters are properly supplied. This is important, as evaporation takes place when the car is left after a run, owing to the heat of the engine making the carburetters hot. Actually, I have had an electric fuel pump fitted as well, so that the carburetters are primed as soon as one switches on the ignition.

"Brakes are good if kept properly adjusted; they seldom need taking up. If neglected, and out of adjustment, they may be a little erratic. That, however, is one's own fault. Steering is quite light and directional, but any tendency to wander probably means that the joints and box require lubricating, also that tyre pressures may need checking.

"In brief, I am very pleased with the car, which maintains its lively performance well with only reasonable attention. – H.W."

The improved S.S.1 came up for road test during 1934, *The Motor* trying out the 20hp saloon in July. It acknowledged that the S.S.1 was one of the new breed of sports car that instead of depending on raucous power alone, was "refined... quite docile and easily handled". This docility was certainly emphasised by the car's ability to accelerate readily from 5mph in top, but the 2663cc car gave an excellent account of itself when opened up too:

"It is, however, on the open road where one really begins to appreciate the charm of the car. To sit behind the long bonnet and scuttle and feel the car literally devour a long ribbon of road has to be experienced to be appreciated. On ordinary level going the speedometer... can be run up to 77mph with little fuss, whilst under slightly favourable circumstances such as on a downgrade or with a following wind, 80mph can readily be exceeded - good going for a relatively large car with a more or less orthodox engine".

The suspension design was praised – "an ideal combination of spring strength and damping" – and the car always remained under control without steering shimmy or wobble no matter what the road surface. The wide spring base was thought to account for the "steadiness on corners which is so essential to good road characteristics". Interior appointments and appearance both received the usual approval, and the car was summed up by saying that "the S.S.1 is a car for the connoisseur who requires an automobile of outstanding appearance with a good all-round performance".

The 'Airline' Saloon and the 1935 S.S. range

Towards the end of 1934, news of developments for 1935 began to filter through; at Foleshill, revolutionary plans were already under discussion for an entirely new range of cars, but meanwhile the basic S.S.1 and II ranges

The S.S.II four-seater Tourer (above) photographed outside the Swallow works; door trim pattern seems different to that of the car interior *(right)* which has horizontal pleats. Instrumentation was very complete though, as yet, no separate tachometer was fitted – an indication of engine revs in third and top was given by additional markings on the Smiths speedometer, in the manner of the times. The clock at far left also has dual markings (giving 24-hour time), and even the fuel gauge is marked in litres and gallons.

For a while, the coupe versions were continued; this S.S.I Coupe is seen on the JCC Caravan Rally of September 1933, having won the *Concours de Confort* towing its Car Cruiser 'van. *Photo: Autocar*

INTRODUCTION

FOR 1935, the SS is again presented as a car for the motorist of discernment—a car for the discriminating—the keenly critical.

In a stereotyped age, the SS stands alone—boldly individualistic—daring to be different. At a time when mere cheapness is frequently of greater account than worth, the SS note of quality is insistent. While affinity between appearance and performance tends to become less, the SS proffers both—in full measure.

It is for the experienced motorist that the SS holds the most obvious appeal—the motorist who can appreciate the fine surge of power that answers his demand for acceleration . . . the effortless control at speeds in the seventies and eighties . . . the total lack of fatigue after long journeys at high speeds.

Notwithstanding the exacting standard set by SS in previous years, ceaseless striving for improvement has resulted in the production of even finer models for 1935. New mechanical features include the introduction of an improved induction system with two special high speed carburetters, increased compression ratio, new gearbox ratios and improved method of shock absorber mounting.

No matter in which direction personal taste inclines—closed car or open car—SS offers to the discriminating motorist something out of the ordinary . . . true individuality in performance and appearance.

SS CARS LTD., HOLBROOK LANE, COVENTRY

Pages from an S.S. catalogue proclaiming the merits of the 1935 range. The 'Specification' is for the S.S.I; the illustration at bottom left shows the interior of the saloon (the centre armrest could be omitted to special order, incidentally, but the tunnel prevented a one-piece cushion being used). *Courtesy Robert Danny Collection*

SPECIFICATION

ENGINE. Specially manufactured Standard Six cylinder. 16 h.p. : 65·5 m m. bore : 106 m m. stroke : 2143 c.c. 20 h.p. : 73 m m. bore : 106 m m. stroke : 2663·7 c.c. Side by side valves. Exceptionally stiff 7-bearing crankshaft, 2½" diameter main bearings. 1¾" diameter big ends. Aluminium pistons. Chromium iron cylinder blocks. Light alloy connecting rods. Machined combustion chambers and ports. Two special high-speed R.A.G. carburetters. High efficiency induction and exhaust manifold. Detachable high compression aluminium cylinder head. Cooling by centrifugal pump and fan with adjustable thermostat. High pressure submerged oil pump. C. ignition. Single dry plate light action clutch.

FRAME. Low underslung frame designed for extreme rigidity. The main members are triangulated in the centre by cross bracing from the dumb irons to the rear spring brackets.

TRANSMISSION. Synchro-mesh gears on second, third and top. Hardy Spicer all-metal propeller shaft and universal joints. Spiral bevel final drive. Easy to hand change speed lever.

GEAR RATIOS. 16 h.p.: Top, 4·50 ; Third, 6·18 ; Second, 9·51 ; First, 16·20. 20 h.p.: Top, 4·25 ; Third, 5·83 ; Second, 8·98 ; First, 15·30.

SUSPENSION. Ensuring smooth and steady road-holding with maximum comfort at all speeds. Long flat road springs of low periodicity, mounted on "Silentbloc" bushes. The easily accessible jacking pads ensure quick erection. Hartford friction type shock absorbers front and rear.

BRAKES. Highly efficient Bendix Duo-Servo. Hand and foot operate on all four wheels. Quick-action spring release hand brake lever of racing type.

STEERING. Marles Weller cam and lever type.

AXLES. Semi-floating rear axle with one-piece steel casing. Four pinion differential. Front axle : "H" section with reversed Elliott stub axles.

PETROL SUPPLY. By A.C. pump with auxiliary priming lever for hand operation, from 12 gallon tank at the rear of the chassis. The tank filler is of 2½" diameter with quickly detachable bayonet fixing cap.

WHEELS AND TYRES. Rudge-Whitworth centre-lock splined hub type racing wheels. 18" rims with chromium plated rim edges fitted with Dunlop 5·50 – 18 tyres.

ELECTRICAL EQUIPMENT. 12-volt set. Large type QBD 166S GC head lamps with motif to match radiator cap, and dip and switch control above steering wheel. Finger-tip operated ignition control. Stop light. Reversing light. Sports type wing lamps. Special Lucas type blended note horns, domed to match head lamps, chromium plated with grille fronts to match the radiator, are fitted to each dumb iron. Lamps and horns all chromium plated finish.

COACHWORK. The body, constructed on the soundest lines, is of extreme strength. The frame is of prime quality selected ash throughout, reinforced by aluminium and steel brackets.

DOORS. Flush fitting and exceptionally wide, ensuring ease of access. The doors are hinged on double-strength standing pillars from bottom side to control by means of special self-aligning chromium plated hinges, incorporating Enots grease nipples. Spring-loaded all-steel door checks are fitted to the bottom of the doors, secured to the chassis frame. Positive action slam locks are fitted, and each door is equipped with adjustable Bedford buffers.

HEAD. Leather grained, with chromium plated weather moulds protecting the doors, and chromium bead down hinge pillar and waistline.

TRUNK. Leather grained, with heavily chromium plated hinged security catches and key lock. The accommodation is ample, and large suit cases, also golf clubs, may be carried quite easily.

SLIDING ROOF. Quick action, self-lifting, single control operation. Perfectly flush fitting, with very large opening.

WINDOW LIGHTS. Safety glass winding type.

WINDSCREEN. Patent type of simplified design, with swept top rail, and radiused corners. Opens from the bottom and is quickly operated. Concealed hinges, obviating any obstruction of vision. Lucas duo-blade windscreen wiper. Back light, mounted in chromium channel, opens to give additional ventilation.

WINGS. One-piece pressings, with deep valances, ensuring adequate protection.

UPHOLSTERY. Finest quality Vaumol hide throughout, in a range of colours to tone with the exterior colour scheme.

CABINET WORK. Instrument panel, door cappings and fillets of polished figured walnut.

CARPETING. The floor is thickly carpeted in colours to harmonise with the exterior finish.

SEATS. Four adult passengers are accommodated in the highest degree of comfort. The rear seats are constructed as two small arm chairs, deeply sprung with Swallow patent spring case cushions and back rests. The arm rest is heavily padded with a special cushion rubber. (The arm rest may be omitted if desired, but the axle shaft tunnel renders a one-piece cushion impracticable.) Deep foot wells provide ample leg room. The front seats are constructed on similar lines to those at the rear, but there is, of course, no arm rest. The front seats are quickly adjustable by means of special slide rails, whilst the back rests hinge forward.

HEAD ROOM sufficient for the tallest passenger is made possible by the special dropped chassis frame.

INSTRUMENTS. Illuminated panel with hexagon mountings for electric clock, 85 m.p.h. trip speedometer ammeter, oil pressure gauge and radiator thermometer combined, and electric petrol gauge.

ACCESSORIES. Complete suite of interior fittings in polished chromium, incorporating interior mirror, roof lamp and switch, rear blind with driver's hand control, and ash tray. Trafficators with concealed direction arms are also fitted (self-cancelling).

DIMENSIONS. Wheelbase, 9' 11" ; Track, 4' 5½". Overall length, 15' 6". Overall width, 5' 5½". Overall height, 4' 7". Width of body inside, 4' 0". Width of doors, 3' 6". Centre of backrest to pedals (adjustable), 3' 8" maximum ; 3' 2" minimum. Height of backrest (front and rear), 2' 1". Depth of body inside, 3' 5". Back of front seat to centre of rear seat backrest, 3' 6" maximum ; 3' 1" minimum.

PRICES : £340 (16 h.p.) ; £345 (20 h.p.). With D.W.S. Permanent Jacks : 16 h.p., £345 ; 20 h.p., £350.

were kept, and added to, thanks to general acclaim and a 20% increase in sales over 1933.

In view of the distinct identity of the S.S. as a marque in its own right by this time, it is surprising to note that 1934 was the first year in which the cars were able to be displayed in the Manufacturer's section of the Motor Show, as opposed to the Coachbuilders' area. Perhaps this change of heart by the Society of Motor Manufacturers and Traders was assisted by Swallow's own change of name, to S.S. Cars Ltd. Floated as a public company, the move brought in £85,000, most of which was earmarked for the successor to the S.S. which was little more than a year away from announcement.

This change of name rightly underlined the fact that Lyons had achieved the status of a manufacturer, and that the coachbuilder role was now truly in the background – although sidecar production continued under the auspices of the reconstituted Swallow Coachbuilding Co. (1935) Ltd. Production of cars was by then running at well over 1700 per annum and increasing all the time, with no less than thirteen acres now occupied by the Foleshill factory – in fact, more land nearby had also been acquired in readiness for further expansion.

While detail improvements to the S.S. range as a whole were in evidence, star of the 1934 Show so far as S.S. were concerned was yet another new model, the Airline saloon.

This was to be one of the best-looking (though opinions varied), if not the most practical, of all the closed S.S.s. 'Fastback' styling had certainly become something of a craze in the 'thirties, with most car makers feeling obliged to take notice of its popularity by offering at least one model with the new type of curved rearquarters, and Lyons followed suite in a quite rare instance of him adopting a trend rather than initiating one, though it was apparently the idea of *The Autocar's* managing editor that such an S.S. should be made and drew up the body design for it. The S.S.1 Airline appeared on the normal 16hp and 20hp chassis.

Thus the Airline shared the mechanical updating of the S.S.1 range in general. Possibly the biggest change to the engines was the adoption of twin RAG carburettors as an option instead of the single instrument employed up until then; this duplication didn't raise the total bhp by very much – about 2bhp – but it did assist in giving the car more pulling power in the middle and upper speed ranges, with consequently better acceleration and hill climbing abilities. The 16hp was now rated at 62bhp and the 20hp at 70bhp at 4000rpm. A reduction of 3-seconds in the 0-60mph time was talked of, with a rise in compression ratio from 6.1:1 to 7:1 and a new camshaft also contributing. The capacity of both the oil pump and the aluminium sump was increased, to overcome a tendency

A rare contemporary picture of the Standard six-cylinder engine used by S.S. Cars; this is the installation in an Airline, and it includes the pump take-off from the dynamo for the optional DWS hydraulic jacking system. Note also the complicated rod linkage for the advance/retard control, running from the end of the steering column to the distributor. Column also carries the lighting switchgear. *Photo: Autocar*

towards low oil pressure. The chart below plots the changes to the cylinder head which took place from 1932 to 1935.

1932/33 Early heads (usually cast iron):	Head depth		Compression Ratio (16 & 20hp)
	16hp	20hp	
16hp part no. 36920 (1 7/8in. width)	.496in.	.590in.	5.5:1
20hp part no. 36888 (1 7/8in. width)	.481in.	.570in.	5.7:1
1934 Aluminium heads (1 7/8in. width)	.450in.	.555in.	6.1:1
1935 Aluminium heads (1 7/8in. width)	.353in.	.443in.	7.0:1
1935 Aluminium heads (2in. width)	.374in.	.464in.	7.0:1
Part no. 1934/5: 16hp equals 38211; 20hp 38943			

A further change in damping was made, with larger double Andre Hartford shock absorbers mounted transversely on the chassis and operating at the extremities of the axles, where of course the leverage was greatest. Due consideration was given to their adjustment, a special tool being included in the toolkit. The chassis itself was stiffened, by the simple procedure of reversing the 'U' section cross-members so that where they met the main chassis frame, a box-section was formed. The combination of a more rigid frame and better damping did improve roadholding further.

Other detail attentions included modified cones in the gearbox to improve synchronisation, better thermostatic control of engine water temperature (the previous revision of the cooling system had been a little overdone), and the incorporation of a filter in the drain plug of the petrol tank to prevent the pipeline to the AC pump becoming blocked; pipe diameter was also increased for the same reason.

Coachwork changes all round were minimal, although the coupe version with its leather-finish top had been discontinued – the S.S.1 range now consisted of just the four-light saloon, tourer, and the new Airline. S.S. advertisements for this last addition to the range were ecstatic:

"Here is no freakish striving for effect, but an expression of the modern trend in lines of studied simplicity. Yet, in true S.S. tradition, beauty of appearance has not been sought at the expense of comfort and roadworthiness, for in the 'Airline' there exists an almost unbelievable degree of comfort allied to a road performance which surpasses all previous S.S. achievements. With every attribute demanded by a critical age, this newcomer places S.S. still further ahead in its leadership of modern design".

Aparently the "modern trend" might have been taken even further with the Airline, for The Autocar noted that S.S. actually held back in some respects: "Believing that the British motoring public is not yet ready to accept the rounded frontal aspect which is a feature of a few streamline designs, the manufacturers have retained the

Engine compartment of 1935 Saloon, showing the twin RAG carburettors and the alloy head. Later RAG carburettors sometimes had "S.S." cast into the bodies.

Above: Unusual view of an S.S. Airline *(top),* on its fully-extended DWS jacks, during a demonstration outside the DWS works. Besides its sloping tail, the Airline treatment included twin side-mounted spare wheels and horizontal bonnet louvres.

Left: Airline interior, *(below)* showing the jacking control in use. Note the polished figured-walnut finish on dash and door cappings, and rev. counter markings on the speedometer.
Photos: Autocar

normal frontal aspect of the other models in the range''. This conservative design policy was adhered to for many years after that was written in September 1934, certainly up to the Mk V of 1948-51 which still carried a large, traditional radiator shell proudly at the front.

So the Airline was chiefly distinguished from its saloon counterpart by the roofline sweeping in a continuous length from windscreen to the base of its tail, where the curvature swept under the car. This entailed a slightly higher roofline and as the new body was longer as well (supported at the rear by extra brackets in the chassis frame), the Airline was certainly more roomy inside than the saloon, and with better side visibility thanks to the larger side windows and the pillarless construction. The fixed rear window, of half-moon shape, was also larger. The windscreen pillars at the front were carried forward 3ins. at their base to give the screen an increased rake which emphasised the streamline effect.

There were mixed reactions to the success of the body design, and Lyons himself was not very pleased with the result. In a 1972 interview with Philip Turner of *Motor*, Sir William expressed this view of the car: "I was a bit disappointed with it really. We were in a bit of trouble with headroom, so we put a bit of a bump in the roof and it therefore didn't have as clean a line as it should have had".

Inside, the Airline showed at least one major departure from normal S.S. trim, in that the seats were trimmed in plain, unpleated leather – and looked very modern because of it. This was a feature unique to the Airline, and is only to be seen in a couple of other cars from the same stable since. The trim on the door panels did not have the usual S.S. 'trademark' of the sunray pattern either, but included a map pocket in each. Also, compared to the S.S.1 saloon and tourer, the Airline's front seats had been brought forward a little which gave greater accommodation in the rear, this being made possible by the repositioned screen pillars; the backs also held full picnic trays for the use of rear seat passengers. The 'armchair' divide in the rear was kept, and the sloping tail provided extra luggage accommodation.

The wide doors of the Airline, combined with the lack of a door pillar extending to the roof, were really the car's Achilles heel - the structure wasn't properly capable of supporting the weight of the door and, together with the effects of age and vibration, the wooden frame members would begin to deteriorate. But these were longer term shortcomings: when new the Airline was greeted with the usual enthusiasm by the motoring press.

The Motor tried an Airline during 1935, and in appearance considered it "unquestionably a fine intepretation of the art of streamlining, yet the car cannot in any circumstances be considered as being markedly unorthodox... the swept tail of the passenger compartment gives an impression of correctness".

It scored quite well on the road, too. The Brooklands motor course near Weybridge, Surrey, was used extensively by the motoring weeklies for testing before the war, and that's where the Airline was extended by *The Motor's* drivers. Despite bad weather, a genuine 80mph was recorded for the flying quarter-mile, and the car covered the same distance from a standstill in 22.4 seconds. Top gear performance was good, while "the acceleration in third gear is outstanding – 40mph can be reached from a datum of 10mph in but 10 seconds''; a maximum of 65mph was recorded in that gear. Petrol consumption was a reasonable 18mpg after all this.

Ride and handling brought forth praise too, the springing "providing a suspension quite free from the bumps and jerks often associated with sporting cars of a decade ago". Cornering fast apparently brought no misgivings:

"Furthermore, rolling and pitching proved to be almost non- existent. It is possible to hurl the car round corners at the maximum speed permitted by tyre adhesion without evoking the slightest qualm, and there is just sufficient castor action in the layout of the steering to cause the car to pull out of a bend and continue a straight course again."

This quite late-model Airline, tested in April 1935, differed from earlier versions on a few cosmetic points; the twin spare wheels mounted in the front wings now had metal covers, and the bonnet louvres now ran horizontally with bright strips of trim attached.

Similar performance figures to the Airline were recorded later that year when *The Autocar* conducted one of the last road tests of the S.S.1 20hp saloon. Tested under better conditions, it exceeded 80mph easily, and achieved a best one-way speed of 83.3mph; it took 24 seconds to reach 60mph, and 15.8 seconds to gain 50mph. As a measure of comparison, a small family car of the period such as the new Morris 8 could only manage the latter figure in around 26 seconds, while such 'establishment' sporting machinery as the 2969cc Talbot 105 could only better the S.S.'s time to 50mph by 1.8 seconds – and the Aston Martin four-seater tourer was actually slower!

Meanwhile, the S.S.1 Tourer had been undergoing long term assessment by both *The Motor* and *The Autocar*. The former's example clocked up no less than 10,000 miles in four months, with only a broken fan belt intruding on its reliability record. The tourer was obviously liked by *The Motor's* staff, who considered it a real driver's car with the controls in the right place, a "delightful synchromesh gearbox", and "outstandingly good" roadholding – though with the qualification that shock absorber adjustment had to be maintained, with the best settings found to be "very tight on the front and very nearly as tight on the back".

Pains were taken to scotch rumours of poor visibility,

The Airline Saloon

A cclaimed from the moment of its introduction as "the most beautiful interpretation of stream-lining," this model is characterised by a modernity of outline dignified in its restraint. That its distinguished appearance has not been secured at the expense of practical considerations is demon-strated by the roominess of the interior, the ample head room and the extraordinarily capacious luggage compartment. The same spirited road performance typical of all **SS** products is manifest in the Airline, and is exemplified in high speed, superb road-holding and a degree of comfort without parallel.

Price, £345 (16 h.p.) ex works
£350 (20 h.p.)

Self-congratulatory prose in a contemporary brochure for the S.S.I Airline Saloon.

as it was reported that even a driver of medium height could see a long section of the front wing below the sidelight, while the ground clearance was also greater than might be expected. Long journeys were "satisfying" with a cruising speed of 70mph that could be "held indefinitely". The usual compliments were paid to the quality of fixtures and fittings, and the oft-repeated comment was made on the comfort afforded to rear seat passengers, who (unusually in an open car) sat at least as low down as the front seat occupants and were therefore largely kept out of the wind with the hood down.

The 20hp Tourer was certainly the fastest of the S.S.s, *The Motor's* example reaching 84.5mph with the screen folded flat (axle ratios had gone up to 4.25 by now, incidentally) and getting to 60mph in 23 seconds, or a second less than *The Autocar's* 20hp saloon. Petrol consumption was 18mpg "driven hard".

Not that the car was perfect - one could discern the odd piece of cautious criticism in the text, with the writer indicating that the steering could be higher geared and more direct "when the car is going fast on a gusty day or for winding roads", while the clutch and brake pedals were thought "not quite so light in operation as a woman might wish."

A.G. Douglas Clease ran *The Autocar's* S.S.1 tourer, of which delivery was taken in February 1934. This car had the single RAG carburetter, but after running-in "it was necessary to prepare the car for the RAC Rally, and as the makers were experimenting with two carburetters it was decided so to equip my car for the Rally". At the same time, an SU petrol pump giving an independent supply from the rear tank was fitted, which if desired could also supplement the existing AC pump driven from the camshaft. From new, the tourer carried two spare wheels in wells formed in the front wings either side of the scuttle, instead of a single spare wheel at the rear of the luggage trunk; also to special order were the louvres in the upper panels of the bonnet, which "alone made a difference of 5-degrees in running temperature, a fact which was taken advantage of in preparing the other cars of the Alpine team, although for this country the engine is undoubtedly over-cooled."

To save weight, the front and rear bumpers were discarded and the dumb-iron brackets at the front neatly altered to take a badge and lamp bar; this extra illumination took the form of a Desmo Safebeam fitted with a Nebulite front glass and carrying a stoneguard to match those on the headlamps. "Incidentally", wrote Douglas Clease, "stoneguards are well worth fitting on any car used for competitions, as without them I have several times had lamp glasses broken, the reflectors then suffering damage."

As rough road surfaces "had the effect of making shock absrober adjustment necessary fairly frequently", larger dampers with the Andre Telecontrol system were fitted, with the control cylinders accomodated under the dashboard in easy reach of the driver. "These shock absorbers have materially improved the already good suspension and roadholding ... so sensitive is the adjustment that half a turn will draw the comment 'That is much more comfortable' from the rear seat passengers". An experimental Delco-Remy high speed ignition system was added, this featuring a six-volt coil apparantly to boost the spark, with an interrupter wired in series with it to prevent the coil from receiving too much current from the car's twelve-volt system at low engine speeds. Most of this extra equipment had to be removed when the car was taken on the Alipne Trial in deference to the rule book, but was replaced afterwards apart from the badge/lamp bar, as the 'harmonic stabiliser front bumper' which replaced it "undoubtedly enhances the front end stability". The temporary spell with the single carburetter resulted in a "distinctly noticeable" loss of power, though, and 5mph off the top speed of 80mph.

"To sum up,", concluded Douglas Clease, "the car has proved extremely reliable throughout its 20,000 miles, much of which has been over indifferent, and sometimes very bad, road surfaces. Its only fall from grace has been for a broken fan belt, and as the spindle also drives the water impellor it was necessary to replace the belt on the road".

A further indication of the S.S.1 tourer's performance was given when *The Autocar* borrowed a used example in March 1936 from a Richmond motor dealer, a useful exercise because such a random selection ensured a completely standard (i.e. untuned) car. On acceleration, this 20hp model was actually 1.6 seconds faster to 60mph than *The Motor's* road test car, and with screen up managed a top speed of 77.5 mph, as opposed to the official road test car's 84.5 mph with screen down.

Despite having covered 14 346 miles in less than 15 months, *The Autocar* found little wrong with the car so far as its general condition was concerned: "There were no suspicious mechanical noises, and the engine possessed a great deal of power which, in conjunction with a useful gearbox, good roadholding and very powerful brakes, made up a car that was very satisfying to drive... There were no major rattles, one or two lesser examples and slight creaks coming from the region of the doors". Fuel consumption over 180 miles was around 18mpg, and the oil consumption of 1500 mpg was reckoned to be very moderate, including as it did "some hard driving at Brooklands with at least one lap of the track all out." Just over a year old, the tourer was offered at £225, compared with its new price of £340.

Interest in the S.S. range had not been entirely restricted to Great Britain, and a few cars were finding their way abroad, even if this did not amount to an average of more than around 100 a year up to 1935. Nevertheless, S.S. did manage to set up agencies in most European countries, plus others including the United States – although the days of North America becoming the company's greatest export market were far off indeed, with S.S. representation in the States appearing inconsistent and a little haphazard in those early years. It seems that the East Coast had at least three concessionaires in as many years – British Motors of New York in 1934, then Richard G. Taylor for 1935, and Hilton Motors during 1936.

Richard G. Taylor was based at the Waldorf Astoria, Park Avenue with the service facilities in 134 W. 54th St, New York, and their brochure fanfared the 1935 range of S.S. cars as follows: "To drive the 1935 model is to experience a new ideal of performance – in the smooth responsiveness of a powerful high compression engine, with sparkling acceleration ... the ultimate in smartness, grace, comfort and performance". Only 20hp models were catalogued, with the saloon retailing at $2350, the tourer at $2250, and the new Airline ("a brilliant newcomer to the SS range ... consummate style, grace and dignity ... flashing speed and acceleration, and unique roadholding") was the most expensive at $2500. It was claimed that "all spares are stocked" but it is unlikely that these early S.S. customers found it easy to maintain their purchases.

It is difficult to find contemporary overseas written opinion of S.S. models, but thanks to Fritz Fruth of Vienna we have a translated description of the 1934 S.S.1 by the *Osterreichische Touring-Zeitung,* which was impressed and enthusiastic about the revised 1934 range:

"S.S. cars have not only become so well known in a very short time because of their beautiful design, but also because of their remarkable performance which enables them to pass even the most difficult tests ... Even at high speeds we were surprised by the high standard of roadholding, and the very precise Marles-Weller steering gear is accurate and enables easy handling under difficult conditions ... In brief ... the standard equipment of S.S. cars in 1934 is very complete, very distinctive, and genuine ... generally one would say that the amount of comfort and solidity on S.S. cars would be expected in cars of a much higher class and at a much higher price".

The S.S.11 ("a diminished version of the S.S.1") was given a passing mention, but as was usual abroad, the larger engined variants attracted the most interest. Austrian distributor was Georg Hans Koch of Vienna, and he practiced what he preached by successfully driving his S.S.1 in various trials as recounted elsewhere.

In March 1935, S.S. Cars Ltd made a slight departure from tradition by announcing two new models, instead of waiting for the more usual September date. This helped underline the most significant of the two offerings, which were both based on the existing S.S.1 chassis. This was the company's first sportscar, and it was called the S.S.90.

The S.S.90 used a short wheelbase (8ft. 8in.) version of the S.S.1's frame, and was powered by the 20hp 2663cc sidevalve engine. It had all-new, two-seater bodywork with a beautiful flowing wing line developed from that of the later S.S.1s; the original car had a neat rounded tail into which was set the spare wheel, but production versions were altered to include an exposed 'Le Mans' type petrol tank and an upright spare wheel mounting.

The S.S.90 (the "90" hinting at the car's maximum speed, an mph figure which in fact it could nearly reach) aroused a great deal of interest, so much so that the

About the rarest and most sophisticated of the S.S.Is – the Drophead Coupe. As is demonstrated here, the head could be lowered and concealed in the rear trunk, with the side cantrails being stowed in the doors.

I|N the SSI Drophead Coupe will be found, not only every requirement sought by those requiring a dual purpose car, but a number of additional advantages unobtainable in any other make of car fitted with a body of the convertible type. With the head erected, this SS is, in every respect, a town coupe with that elegance of appearance inseparable from the SS marque. With the head lowered, it is completely transformed into an open touring car possessing a clean, unbroken line from bonnet to tail—an effect achieved by means of an exclusive arrangement of the head linkwork, which enables the head to be lowered into the specially designed trunk where it is invisible and, furthermore, protected from dust.

Part of the S.S.I Drophead Coupe catalogue from 1935

S.S.I interior: this picture of an unrestored saloon conveys the opulent atmosphere created by the use of high-quality materials. This cosseting was what the customer wanted, and Lyons provided it; it sold cars ...

further S.S.1 variant released at the same time was rather overshadowed. It was also doomed to a very short production run because of S.S.'s plans for 1936. The new model, termed the S.S.1 Drop Head Coupe, was if you like an 'operational' edition of the original S.S.1 Coupe, as this time the head really did drop, and the plated exterior hood irons were actually functional.

The mechanical specification and even the interior dimensions of the Drop Head were virtually identical to that of the existing saloon, but the occupants had the advantage of being able to enjoy convertible motoring when the weather was favourable, but more of the comforts of closed car motoring than the normal tourer model could give when it was not. The folding top itself was something of a work of art, as it disappeared completely into the rear 'trunk'; also, the windows wound right down into the doors, and the window frames themselves were detachable for storage in the rear locker. Thus with the hood down, a completely clean profile was in evidence, save for the slim-pillared windscreen.

Some 105 S.S.1 dropheads were made for the year that it was in production, and at £380 for the 16hp model and £385 for the 20hp, it was the most expensive S.S.1 built; as much to buy, in fact, as the competely new line of cars which were at that time taking shape at Foleshill.

The S.S.1 and 11 in retrospect

Looking back at Sir William Lyons' first car over a span of 50-odd years, it is much more difficult to assess the merits and demerits of the S.S.1 than perhaps any other car which subsequently came from that source of genious. The S.S.1 was, and is, 'different'; no-one knew quite what to make of the car when it first appeared in 1931, and perhaps we still don't now.

Notwithstanding its specially made frame, it was based on very ordinary mechanics, unexciting even in 1931 and by today's standards, crude. It performed only marginally better than a normal 2-litre of the day, and for this small privilege, the occupants paid quite dearly in terms of reduced visibility and barely adequate accommodation. Yet the looks of this (to us) cycle-winged oddity tickled the imagination of the early 'thirties, and it sold. And by virtue of sticking to well-proven, known mechanics, instead of succumbing to the temptations of tuning or of installing some more powerful but less robust power unit, the S.S.1 was tough and reliable too. So those who bought it weren't plagued by *prima donna* faults in engine or transmission, and they could get parts at their local garage. It was also extremely cheap, yet with no discernible shortcuts on quality or equipment. The packaging was right, almost at first go, even if true performance had yet to come.

Very few of the 500 or so helmet-winged S.S.1s survive, either in metal or in memory. There are recollections of the much-improved versions of 1933 onwards however, when Lyons' "designers'-eye" had played itself in, and it had been acknowledged that the car must not only look good, but be comfortable to travel in too.

19

COLOUR SCHEMES

SSI AND SSII SALOON

BODY	UPHOLSTERY	WHEELS	WINGS	HEAD and TRUNK
Black.	Brown, Silver-Black, Red or Green.	Black.	Black.	Black.
Apple Green.	Green.	Apple Green.	Olive Green or Black.	Olive Green or Black.
Carnation Red.	Red.	Black or Carnation.	Lake, Black or Carnation.	Lake or Black.
Birch Grey.	Blue or Red.	Birch Grey or Red.	Birch Grey.	Birch Grey.
Lavender Grey.	Blue or Red.	Lavender Grey or Red.	Lavender Grey.	Lavender Grey.
Dark Blue.	Blue.	Dark Blue or Grey.	Dark Blue.	Birch Grey.
Ivory.	Green, Red, Brown or Beige.	Ivory.	Ivory.	Ivory.
Cream.	Green, Red, Brown or Beige.	Cream.	Cream.	Cream.
Nile Blue.	Blue.	Nile Blue.	Black.	Black.
Crimson Lake.	Crimson Lake.	Crimson Lake.	Crimson Lake.	Crimson Lake.
Beige.	Beige or Red.	Beige or Red.	Beige.	Beige.
Olive Green.	Green.	Olive Green.	Olive Green.	Olive Green.
*Silver.	*Light Blue.	*Silver.	*Light Blue.	

SSI AND SSII OPEN FOUR SEATER

BODY	UPHOLSTERY	WHEELS	WINGS and TRUNK
Black.	Green, Red or Brown.	Black.	Black.
Apple Green.	Green.	Apple Green.	Apple Green.
Carnation Red.	Red.	Carnation Red.	Carnation Red.
Birch Grey.	Blue or Red.	Birch Grey or Red.	Birch Grey.
Lavender Grey.	Blue or Red.	Lavender Grey or Red.	Lavender Grey.
Ivory.	Green or Red.	Ivory or Red.	Ivory.
Cream.	Green or Red.	Cream or Red.	Cream.
Nile Blue.	Blue.	Nile Blue.	Nile Blue.
Crimson Lake.	Crimson Lake.	Crimson Lake.	Crimson Lake.
Beige.	Brown or Red.	Beige.	Beige.
Olive Green.	Green.	Olive Green.	Olive Green.

SSI AIRLINE SALOON

BODY	UPHOLSTERY	WHEELS	WINGS
Black.	Green, Red, Brown or Silver-Black.	Black.	Black.
Apple Green.	Green.	Apple Green.	Apple Green.
Carnation Red.	Red.	Carnation Red.	Carnation Red.
Birch Grey.	Blue or Red.	Birch Grey or Red.	Birch Grey.
Lavender Grey.	Blue or Red.	Lavender Grey or Red.	Lavender Grey.
Dark Blue.	Blue.	Dark Blue.	Dark Blue.
Ivory.	Green, Red, Blue or Brown.	Ivory.	Ivory.
Cream.	Green, Red, Blue or Brown.	Cream.	Cream.
Nile Blue.	Blue.	Nile Blue.	Nile Blue.
Crimson Lake.	Crimson Lake.	Crimson Lake.	Crimson Lake.
Beige.	Beige or Red.	Beige.	Beige.
Olive Green.	Green.	Olive Green.	Olive Green.
*Silver.	*Light Blue.	*Silver.	

Wheels on all Models have Chromium Plated edges.

*This colour scheme is £5 - 0 - 0 extra.

The above standard colour schemes offer an extremely wide field of choice only made possible by a system of production which, though highly organised, is of necessity complicated when so many variations are possible. For this reason, any deviation from the standard order of finish entails dislocation of routine involving extra production cost for which a nominal charge of £2. 10. 0. has to be made.

This page from the 1935 S.S. catalogue for touring and saloon models indicates the wide range of colour schemes that a customer could choose from.

In September 1934, *The Autocar* published this little cameo of the S.S.1 sent in by a reader. Interestingly, the writer (a Mr John A. Fletcher) owned the 16 and 20hp models consecutively:

"I have had experience of both these in 1934 form. I first ran the 16hp model, but changed after about 2,000 miles to the 20hp in order to obtain the increased performance which the latter engine naturally gives. In each case I had the coupe body.

"As regards economy of running, the difference between the two engines is hardly worth remarking upon. They both appear to do 19mpg on a long run. In just over 6,000 miles with the 20hp. I have noticed no increase in oil consumption, and it is only necessary to drain the sump – of very large capacity, no less than two gallons – every 1,500-2,000 miles. There have been practically no expenses other than the normal maintenance, the engine being superbly reliable despite consistently hard driving. It 'holds its tune' like a Rolls-Royce.

"From the performance standpoint I would strongly favour the larger engine. Corresponding figures I have estimated are as follows: – 16hp model: maximum on top, 74mph; third, 52mph; second, 32mph. 20hp model: top, 78mph; third, 57mph; second, 36mph. But this is not the whole story. The acceleration and hill-climbing of the 20hp are greatly superior, as is flexibility in traffic; the only point on which the 16hp scores is in smoothness and silence, for it is definitely more 'sweet' than its larger brother. I personally, do not object to the slightly noisier performance of the 20hp, which I consider by far the sounder investment, particularly now that the annual tax on cars is to be reduced.

"As to points applicable to either 16hp or 20hp, the chassis being the same for each, I find the road-holding excellent, but unusually sensitive to load and weight distribution. Stability is ideal with the driver and two passengers in the rear seats. Incidentally, to give valuable leg room for a tall man, the passenger's seat in front is easily removed if necessary. The car is rather too lively without weight at the back. I like the steering, which is high geared and may confuse at first those accustomed to the 'jellified' type so common on large American cars. For the brakes I reserve my highest praise: they are unquestionably amongst the best fitted to any contemporary car. The synchromesh gears are good, though

An S.S.1 in service – the saloon of Bob Harrison doing duty in New South Wales. Export was hardly a priority for S.S. in those days, but some cars did end up in various far-away parts of the globe.

I always change as with a normal box finding it quicker. "Altogether, a very fine car at a modest price."

Mrs Margaret Jennings, who as Miss Margaret Allan had driven the S.S.1 tourer on its Alpine debut in 1933, remembers being lent one of the early 16hp closed coupes to practice in before that Alpine – "the one with hardly any windows – you could hardly see out of it. We used it on a trial in Wales somewhere, and I can still remember the lack of visibility on a wet night!" Her husband, Christopher Jennings an ex-editor of *The Motor*, also recalls some rides in a 1933 coupé:

"I had a friend, Pelham-Burns, who bought this S.S.1. He didn't drive it in any competitions as far as I know – we generally considered they were too low in those days and unsuitable in other ways, but it was a very fine road car, and we had some remarkably fast passages with it. Oil pressure worried us a lot – I was used to Rileys where you could screw up the oil pressure on the side of the block, so the S.S. shook me a bit. It had nothing on tickover and precious little below 40mph, and we made a lot of enquiries thinking we must be heading for disaster, and were told that they were pretty well all like that".

Later of course, both sump and oil pump capacity were increased to help this problem of high oil temperature – as W.H. Charnock wrote of his early 1933 tourer, "the sump capacity of just over 1.5-gallons was hardly in keeping and an oil temperature of 95 deg C was usual after a few hours on a hot day" – not that this reading would worry most modern oils.

An Australian owner, Bob Harrison of New South Wales, recalls his experiences with a secondhand S.S.1, a 1934 saloon.

"I owned this particular car for two years, during which time it proved to be very reliable and enjoyable, if not fast. I found that it would cruise quite happily at speeds up to 65mph and that it would pull equally happily down to 5mph in top gear by using the manual spark retard on the steering wheel. Acceleration was definitely slow by 1954 standards, but I think it would have been reasonable in 1934.

"Braking was adequate in a straight line but left something to be desired if the front wheels were in anything but the straight ahead position. Despite outside appearances, visibility from the interior was quite good."

The Bendix self-servo brakes were in fact quite efficient in stopping the car within reasonable distances, but did require regular adjustment for consistent results; things improved with the larger drums adopted for 1934. Harsh braking would, though, result in front road spring 'wind-up' which could lead to severe tramping of the front axle in extreme circumstances. Steering tended to be heavy at low speeds, but seems universally to have been liked when the car was travelling at speed.

Certainly in the case of the post-1933 longer wheelbase cars, the S.S.1 did collect a fairly deserved reputation for quite good handling qualities, and these were probably better than the die-hard vintage brigade either knew or would acknowledge. With further improvements to damping and spring location, the S.S.1 really did turn into something of a driver's car, a hard-to-define quality which has stayed with the marque ever since. It responded to and made pleasurable any effort the driver put into the car on the open road, greatly helped by that smooth, seven-bearing crankshaft engine which, if not immensely powerful even by the standards of the 1930s, gave the S.S.1 an easy, loping gait and a cruising speed which on later models could extend into the seventies.

Some considered that it was the engine which 'made' the car, but it was all part of an overall formula which included such not to be neglected items as nicely finished accessories, enterprising colour schemes, a pleasingly sporting shape, reliability, and an extremely moderate price tag. Nothing could match the S.S. on every one of these counts, not even the established manufacturers of the day, so what hope could rival coachbuilders have of keeping up with Mr Lyons and his vibrantly active young company? They were left almost literally in the dust of the S.S., even though some – like Avon – could almost match the S.S.1 for sheer style.

Avon was probably Lyons' chief rival, at least during the Swallow era; but with the coming of the S.S.I, the Blackpool man clearly pulled ahead despite attempts by Avon to keep up. This Avon Standard was a contemporary of the S.S.I coupe, but lacking a special chassis, looks higher and less stylish than the Foleshill product. (Compare with photo on P.488) *Photo: Autocar*

The S.S.1 and 11 were allowed to fade from production during 1936, but in the meantime were sold alongside the new 'Jaguars'. They were not, however, fitted with that car's OHV engine but continued to use the sidevalve units; although it is interesting to note that S.S. were quite willing to install the 'Jaguar' OHV engine in an S.S.1 brought to them for that purpose by an owner desirous of more performance. Quite a number of cars were converted in this way during the late 'thirties by S.S. Cars' service department. Most sidevalve cars produced after the announcement of the 'Jaguar' saloons carried the 'Jaguar' radiator shell but never wore the 'Jaguar'

badge which was reserved exclusively for the new range.

As a concept the S.S.1 formula, in its more refined post-1932 guise, could probably have remained viable for longer than it did, for it has been argued that as a low-built, sporting coupe the S.S.1 was sufficiently different to the Jaguar saloons that were to follow, for it to have remained in production as an alternative model. Instead, it was discontinued after 1936, having served its purpose, for the S.S.1's success undoubtedly provided the springboard for Lyons to offer a new car, and one which no longer contained any hint of the 'special' about it.

After the announcements of the 'Jaguar' towards the end of 1935, the S.S.I and II cars were given their own catalogue (entitled "Sidevalve Chassis for 1936") – S.S. were keen to differentiate them from the new ohv models. They did get the new Jaguar-type grille however, albeit without the Jaguar badge, as is shown on this late Airline saloon awaiting restoration. Andrew Whyte has calculated that about 4,254 S.S.I-chassis cars were built, including 23 S.S.90 sports cars, and some 1,796 S.S.IIs of all types.

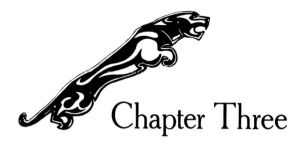

Chapter Three

The first Jaguars

The critics, when they see the new S.S. cars, will say they have grown up.

The Motor, September 24, 1935

While the S.S.1 had been systematically developed into a relatively fast, usable four seater touring car with most distinctive looks, by 1934 it was failing to satisfy William Lyons' own critical standards in various major regions such as performance, space and styling. In particular, it was becoming clear that the off-the-shelf 16hp and 20hp Standard engines were not capable of giving the exceptional performance to which Lyons aspired, and which was necessary if S.S. were to keep ahead of the opposition and remain in the public eye.

However in 1934 at Foleshill, there was no engineering or power unit departments as such, which could on the receipt of a memo commence a development programme to come up with the required new engine – everything still arrived ready-made from the Standard Motor Company, and S.S. had no real engineers, just fitters who were capable of little more than normal maintenance operations. But on the other hand, the arrangement with Standards was an excellent one, relieving S.S. Cars of the need to raise vast amounts of capital to furnish a machine shop; it would be a pity to spoil an extremely beneficial relationship if it could be avoided. But outside expertise was still badly needed.

Initially, Lyons was at something of a loss as to whom to approach for help; then, a customer (possibly driver and motoring journalist Tommy Wisdom) mentioned the name of a certain West Country engine man who for the past few years had been achieving startling results with his particular brand of cylinder head development. His name was Harry Weslake.

Exeter-born, Harry Weslake commenced his career while in the cadet airforce towards the close of the First World War, developing a new type of carburettor which after the war was sold to a number of motorcycle people – MacKenzie, Lightweight Excelsior – under the trade name of "WEX" (Weslake-Exeter). It proved suitable for racing purposes, and so Weslake was drawn into the engine tuning business.

Then he made his gasflow discoveries whereby he realised that if the amount of air going through a cylinder head could be accurately measured, then the head's efficiency could also be measured, as the more airflow obtained, the greater the horsepower produced. Thus an entirely new field of engine development was born: it was now possible to arrive at the correct porting and combustion chamber shape for any engine in a completely scientific and repeatable manner. The inspiration for this? A meter at Weslake's father's gas company ....

So a meeting was arranged between Lyons and Weslake. As told to me by Weslake a couple of years before his death in 1978, this first link with S.S. was partly on his own initiative too, for reasons totally unconnected with Lyons' company – fiercely independent and never overawed even by the mightiest captains of industry,

Harry Weslake, a key figure in the story of the original Jaguar, photographed outside his Rye, Sussex premises shortly before his death in 1978. *Photo: P. Skilleter*

Weslake had recently fallen out with Cecil Kimber of MG, and was wondering who he could work for to upset Kimber and his newly planned 2.2 litre SA saloon range.

The quietly-spoken Lyons was no doubt slightly taken aback by his new consultant when they first met at Foleshill, for Weslake walked into his office and said: "Your car reminds me of an overdressed lady with no brains - there's nothing under the bonnet!" This was hardly an orthodox method of striking up a good working relationship, especially with someone like Lyons, but that was Harry Weslake's style; and because all the parties concerned generally knew that he could deliver the goods, it worked.

Anyway, the conversation continued. "What do you want to do?" queried Lyons; "we need 90bhp". Weslake's answer was an immediate "Put the valves upstairs". Which is exactly what he proceeded to do, after signing a contract with S.S. which stipulated a pass-out performance of not less than 95bhp. Monitoring the development for S.S. also on a consultancy basis was R.F. Oates (of Penzance, Cornwall, not too far from Harry's original home), a well-known engineer who had previously been in charge of O.M.'s British-based experi-

mental department for eleven years, until that same year (1934) O.M. faded from the scene after being taken over by Fiat. Dick Oates was also known as a successful driver, with many wins at Brooklands mainly with O.M., Maserati, Alvis and Amilcar sports cars.

The 2.5-litre SS Jaguar

The basis of the new engine was to be the same six-cylinder Standard unit which the S.S.1 had used - its strong, seven bearing crankshaft and well-proven block were still adequate, so there was little point in going to the enormous extent of a complete re-design, though some improvements to the bottom end were certainly made. Weslake therefore concentrated on developing an entirely new cylinder head with overhead valves.

The arrangement of the head was quite orthodox so far as its basic layout was concerned, the Weslake expertise being mainly applied to the breathing of the engine. The valve gear on top of the head was robust, with a heavy rocker shaft being attached by studs to the top of the head by six strong brackets. The rockers were separated by spring distance pieces, and there was an oil feed to the rocker shaft for the lubrication of the rocker bearings. The hollow pushrods were sited on the nearside of the engine, and tappet adjustment was initially effected by locking nuts on a threaded section at the top of the pushrods, though this was later to be changed. The valve gear was enclosed by a handsome, polished aluminium cover with an oil filler cap set into the top.

It was the porting of the cylinder head which drew upon Weslake's knowledge, for it was not a completely orthodox design, instead having an internal gallery cast into the centre of the head from which the mixture was drawn. The two one and a quarter in. SU carburettors were bolted directly to the head and so fed this gallery direct, without an inlet manifold as such. A similar arrangement was also seen after the war on the BMC's 2.6 litre engines (as used in the Austin-Healey 100/6), as Harry worked on Austin's post-War range of power units. At the centre of this internal passageway was a venturi held in position by one of the cylinder head studs, whose function it was to form a balance between the two carburettors. Short downdraught inlet ports led from the passageway to the vertical inlet valves, with similar but slightly longer exhaust ports leading to the cast iron manifold on the offside of the engine. The combustion chamber itself was lozenge-shaped, and like the ports, was machine finished. Compression ratio was a modest 6.4:1.

On the nearside of the engine, besides the carburettors, there were the 17-amp dynamo, coil, distributor, water pipe to the radiator, drive to the rev. counter, scuttle-mounted SU electric fuel pump (AC mechanical on all

1.5-litre models), fusebox and crankcase vent. The oil level dipstick was on the opposite side together with the 14mm sparking plugs, and, possibly, the side-mounted spare wheel might also have been better placed on the offside, as it would have allowed better access to the distributor and other items needing regular maintenance – except that it was safer in this position for the person who was to remove it by the roadside in the event of a puncture.

As before, the bottom half of the engine was made up of a chrome-iron block, though now the old sidevalve chest was covered by a single plate instead of a two-section item. The pistons were a new type with Invar struts instead of skirt slots, with Duralumin connecting rods containing a steel oil-feed pipe which ran from the big end to the floating gudgeon pins - this pipe used to be of copper, but was found to be rather fragile. The crankshaft was made from manganese molybdenum steel and now incorporated balance weights, while the use of steel-backed white metal bearings allowed larger diameter main and big-end journals in the existing housings – these bearings were the latest type, and S.S. were amongst the first to specify them. Alongside it was the camshaft, driven by a roller chain from a pinion at the front of the engine. Distributor and oil pump drive followed the normal pattern in being driven by skew gears from the camshaft.

The pulley for the triangulated V-belt drive which operated the dynamo and combined fan/water pump was fixed on an extension of the crankshaft at the front of the engine; the fan itself was of built-up sheet steel sections. The oil was contained in a big, 2.5-gallon aluminium sump as used for the 1934/35 S.S.1, heavily finned to promote cooling. The water system was unpressurised but had a bypass-type thermostat to help warming-up.

The result of Weslake's attention to the engine came in May 1935 and was little short of dramatic. Witnessed by Dick Oates, the brake horsepower rose from a little over 70bhp with the sidevalve to 103.3bhp at 4400rpm with the new ohv cylinder head! This was something over 10% better than Lyons had anticipated and both he and Weslake were delighted; it was a great boost for morale at Foleshill, hard at work planning the new range of cars.

Additionally, Lyons managed to carry off an almost equally important diplomatic triumph, in that he persuaded Captain John Black, now Managing Director of Standard, to purchase the plant necessary to manufacture the new head, and to supply the complete engine to S.S. Important, because it once more relieved the company of heavy capital expenditure which it could not afford, and allowed all the existing cash resources to be channelled into the many other aspects of producing an entirely new car. In fact the whole project was funded on an amazingly small amount of money, even by the

The original 2.5-litre ohv engine as installed in the first Jaguar saloon. Note the polished rocker cover (with central take-off for the speedometer drive), the twin S.U. carburettors, and the S.U. electric fuel pump. Spare wheel mounting and well can be seen at bottom. *Photo: Motor*

William Heynes, the brilliant young engineer from Humber, pictured shortly after he joined S.S., tending the ohv engine in a test-bed in the still primitive development shop at Foleshill.

standards of the mid-1930s.

By early 1935, the power unit problem had been solved and William Lyons' dream of a 90mph car was a big step nearer to being realised. But while the new engine was being tested in an S.S.1 tourer and the design of the new car's bodyshell had been largely finalised, a great deal had still to be done to make these component parts into a motor car. S.S. Cars Ltd still had no engineering department of its own, and the right person was badly needed to form one, and to mastermind the development of this, the latest S.S. – and its successors.

It was Standard again which came to the rescue, this time unofficially – Ted Grinham and Les Dawtrey of Standard recommended to Lyons that he should interview a young, 32-year-old engineer who had joined Humber in 1922, and worked under them in the design office when they too had been at Humber. In fact, when Grinham had left to join the Standard Motor Company, Heynes had taken his place as head of the Stress Office in the design department. His obvious talent had made a big impression on the two men when involved on such Rootes projects as the successful Humber Pullman and Snipe luxury cars.

Thus it was that William Munger Heynes arrived at Holbrook Lane for an interview with Mr Lyons. In view

of the importance of the post – it was tantamount to putting the entire future of S.S. Cars in the hands of one man so far as the engineering side was concerned – it is not surprising that this was one of several interviews that Bill Heynes remembers attending, while Lyons assured himself that his trust was not misplaced.

Heynes started work at S.S. in April 1935, and his first job was to design a frame to carry the new ohv engine and the bodyshell which had already begun to take shape under Lyons' eye. The completed new car had to be ready by the Motor Show in October 1935 or even before; to achieve this in five months would be considered an impossible target today, but Heynes simply buckled down to the job and, with the assistance of only one draughtsman and a little help from his friends at Humber, worked quietly and competently to meet the deadline. Body and chassis met to form a complete car in time for the announcement at the end of September.

Due to the time factor, and to make economical use of existing tooling, the new chassis frame was little more than a widened version of the S.S.1's, slightly stiffened and with new spring mountings. The centre cruciform bracing remained, but the rigidity of the frame was increased by boxing-in the sections fore and aft of it, using 10-gauge steel drilled with elongated holes for lightness and for accessability.

The S.S.1's wheelbase of 9ft. 11ins. was retained, though the rear springs were now mounted inside the frame, allowing the chassis side members to come as close to the wheels as possible and thus allow a wider body. Long,flat half-elliptic springs were used as before, but the rear of each front spring was carried in a sliding block arrangement instead of a shackle, which was meant to eliminate sideways movement caused by wear. Luvax

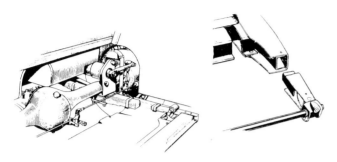

Rear springs were now mounted within the frame, and the dampers carried on the axle itself *(above)*. The front part of the chassis frame in particular was strengthened to reduce flexing and, consequently, front wheel shimmy.

hydraulic dampers were fitted, mounted on the axle at the rear (an almost unique position) and conventionally on the frame at the front. As before, the frame side members passed under the rear axle, then swept up under the scuttle to go over the front axle. "The construction in detail is praiseworthy", said *The Automobile Engineer,* "and the thoroughness of design is exemplified by the positioning of the front cross-member. The channel insert in the main member forms double stiffening

against bending with the increased width of top and bottom flange. This feature is also found in the M.G."

An entirely new braking system was installed on the chassis, and this was the very efficient Girling transverse wedge design, wherein the brake shoes were operated by a wedge, not a cam as in the Bendix system. These wedges were pulled directly by the tie-rods, and the arrangement gave a very high mechanical efficiency. The wedge actuation, together with a floating fulcrum, allowed the shoe to bear accurately on the large (13in.) diameter ribbed brake drum. Eighteen-inch wire wheels on Rudge Whitworth hubs carried Dunlop 5.50 x 18 tyres as on the S.S.1, but the plane of each front wheel rim was now brought in line with the main hub bearing and close to the steering pivots, which assisted steering accuracy.

As with the brakes, S.S. Cars had changed allegiance on the steering too; this was now manufactured by Burman Douglas, and was the worm and nut type, similar in principle to that used on the S.S.11 between 1932 and 1933. It gave a turning circle of about 38ft. from 2.5 turns lock-to-lock, compared to nearer 40ft, from the S.S.1. The steering column could be adjusted for reach, and a Bluemel spring-spoke steering wheel was fitted.

Into this chassis then was dropped the completely revised, overhead valve engine, mated up to an improved version of the existing Standard synchromesh gearbox and single plate clutch. Care was taken to mount engine and box on noise insulating rubber pads at the front, and a rectangular rubber housing at the rear, which now located on the gearbox. A one-piece large diameter open propellor shaft took the drive to the spiral-bevel 4.25:1 rear axle. Petrol for the engine was carried in a 12-gallon tank behind the axle, and pumped to the carburettors by an S.U. electric fuel pump.

The 2.5-litre S.S. Jaguar, as seen by *The Autocar's* artist. Clearly visible is the S.S.I-based chassis frame, but with the perimeter members boxed-in to increase rigidity. Steering and wheel bearings were also 'beefed-up'.

The 'Jaguar' that might have been a 'Sunbeam' – but ultimately, surely it was best that Lyons create his own legend rather than borrow another. An early 2½-litre saloon with rather strange sidelights competing in the coachwork section of the 1936 RAC Torquay Rally. *Photo: Autocar*

Enclosing this relatively orthodox but carefully designed mechanical assemblage was placed a completely new bodyshell. It was not different in the sense that it was rather too *avant garde* like the S.S.1, but it was modern and striking to 1935 eyes - "a real masterpiece of aesthetic and practical proportioning" was how *The Autocar* described it. "Today", the magazine said, "when cars tend to become more alike ... it is a pleasant duty to pay appreciative comment to a British manufacturer who has evolved a modern car appearance which follows no fashion but is more likely to create a new one... Distinction, dignity and gracefulness are evident in the new S.S. 2.5-litre Jaguar."

Jaguar? Yes, that was the name of the new model from S.S. Cars Ltd – but it was very nearly Sunbeam instead! That august manufacturer had gone into receivership in 1935 after a career which had spanned record-breaking and motor racing (including with six-cylinder, twin ohc engines). In 1920 it had combined with Talbot and Darracq to form the S.T.D. group from which many fine cars – including the remarkable Roesch Talbots of the thirties – sprang. Its last new model was the overweight, 1.6-litre ohv Dawn of 1934 which boasted a preselector gearbox and independent front suspension; it was produced alongside the Talbot 105 and the 20 and 25 Sunbeams.

Apparently a commercial failure, the constituent companies of the S.T.D. combine were put up for sale and in June 1935 the announcement came (to quote Andrew Whyte's research) that S.S. Cars Ltd was to take over the "name, goodwill, and patents of the Sunbeam Motor Company of Wolverhampton," and that S.S. would "produce a range of Sunbeam cars at their modern factory in Coventry". It was thus a surprise to William Lyons as well as to everybody else when in July the acquisitive Rootes conglomerate announced that *it* owned Sunbeam! Hence the collapse of Lyons' plan to endow his new range of cars with a name possessing built-in prestige ...

The result was a hurried search for another name, headed by E.W. 'Bill' Rankin who had joined S.S. from General Motors in 1934 to look after advertising and public relations. A short-list of animal, fish and bird names was assembled, of which 'jaguar' caught Lyons' eye – he had been enthralled as an impressionable teenager by stories from an older friend who'd served in the Royal Flying Corps during the First World War and worked on the Armstrong Siddeley 'Jaguar' engine. "Since that time, the word Jaguar has always had a particular significance to me and so S.S. Jaguar became the name by which our cars were known".

Well-balanced lines and more conventional proportions rapidly gained the new SS popularity, even amongst those who would never have purchased an S.S.I. Its power-to-weight ratio made it one of the faster British saloons, and a favourite for trial and rally work. Here a 2.5-litre saloon tackles a hill during the 1936 Scottish Rally. *Photo: Motor*

Left: The 2.5-litre Jaguar carried its tools in a bootlid tray beginning something of a tradition for Jaguar

So with a new name, new engine and new car, S.S. Cars were to take another big step forward, and, for the first time, challenge established 'prestige' makes on more or less equal terms because the new Jaguar was the virtual equal of many in its combination of performance, equipment and quality of finish.

The 2.5-litre Jaguar still bore a slight family resemblance to the S.S.1 four-light saloon in profile, as the curve on the roof and wing line were similar. But there were now four doors, a beautifully contoured integral boot following the line of the rear wings, and a completely new deep-chested radiator shell flanked by Lucas P100 headlights, although the first batch of 1936 cars may have had the smaller QK596 lamps. The sidelights were separate, and the spare wheel was set into the nearside front wing. The boot lid held a tray of tools, each in its own compartment (an arrangement first seen on the Airline), and below the number plate, the reversing light and rear lights were set into the tail panel - "two dimensional illustrations cannot give a fair idea of the artistic three-dimensional curves of the tail and wings" said *The Motor* enthusiastically.

It seems that on some early cars (perhaps just the very first), the rear doors were hung by concealed hinges from the centre pillar, with the trafficator positioned in the scuttle; but on the majority of the 1936/37 S.S. Jaguar saloons, the rear doors were hinged at the rear with the door handles adjacent to the centre pillar, and the trafficator mounted in the lower half of pillar. In both cases, a plated Mazak moulding ran along the car's waistline to emphasis the smooth lines. Matching spring-blade bumpers were fitted front and rear, and covering the front dumb-irons was a valance which continued neatly under the louvred side panels of the centre-hinging bonnet.

Under the bonnet, the engine compartment was neatly laid out and even here appearance was taken into consideration, the polished aluminium rocker cover and two two 1.25-inch S.U. carburetters contrasting pleasantly with the black-painted engine block and body-coloured scuttle. The battery was carried on the scuttle, as was the fuse box. The radiator had an external filler cap which *The Autocar* thought was "a big, honest looking affair, threaded", projecting through the chromium plated radiator shell.

Inside the new Jaguar, the general lay-out of trim had been carried over from the S.S.1 with the 'sunrise' pattern on the door panels and pleated leather seats - though the fixed rear armrest had gone, replaced by a folding one. Walnut veneer was used on the wood cappings, and the similarly finished rail above the facia contained two central ashtrays and a lever to wind open the screen. An opening roof panel was standard again.

The driver was faced by a large, thin-rimmed steering wheel which contained horn, trafficator, dip-switch and ignition controls at its centre. The instruments were grouped together in a central painted panel let into the wooden facia as in the S.S.1, but the hexagonal surrounds were gone. A large 100mph speedometer and a matching rev. counter with thin 'needle' pointers set the pattern for many suceeding Jaguars, and they were flanked by smaller dials relaying amps, fuel level, oil pressure and water temperature. The rev. counter contained an inset clock. An organ-type accelerator pedal was fitted and oval brake and clutch pedals, and a cross-stitched heel-pad of leather was set into the carpet on each side of the carpeted transmission tunnel – from which protruded the short, remote-control gearlever through a leather gauntlet, with the quick-release handbrake mounted on the nearside of the tunnel.

There was much more room inside the Jaguar compared to the S.S.1 saloon – over two-inches in height for the driver, and two-inches more across the back seat. Yet the overall length of the car was, at 14ft. 10in., actually 8-in. shorter than the S.S.1! But for those who wanted even more compact dimensions, and as the successor for the S.S.11, Lyons had also produced a 1.5-litre Jaguar.

The 1.5-Litre SS Jaguar

At a distance, and at first glance, it was hard to distinguish between the 2.5-litre and its smaller sister, so well had the scaling-down effect been carried out. Its chassis was a smaller edition of the 2.5's, the wheelbase being 11 in. less at 9ft. exactly, and the car was shorter overall by a similar amount. All the major engineering features of the larger car were retained so far as the chassis was concerned, although its Girling brakes had 12-inch not 13-inch drums, but of course the power unit was completely different.

The comparatively short-lived sidevalve 1.5-litre SS Jaguar was to be the smallest Jaguar saloon ever produced.

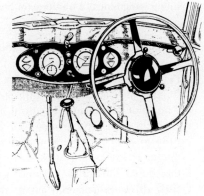

Dash and facia layout was not dissimilar to the S.S.I saloon's, but the dials lacked the hexagonal surrounds decorating those of the later S.S.Is, and a rev. counter was standard. Light switch was now dash mounted instead of on the steering wheel boss.

For the baby Jaguar – this was to be the smallest Jaguar ever produced – S.S. had retained the S.S.11's four cylinder Standard 12 engine of 1608cc, still in sidevalve form with a Salex carburetter; it was rated at 52 bhp at 4300rpm with a 6:1 combustion ratio. It drove through the Standard four-speed gearbox to a 4.75 rear axle. However, it was the appearance and luxury equipment which were to be the strong points of the 1.5-litre, these in no way being inferior to those of the larger engined car.

The final new model in the 'Jaguar' range was based on the new 2.5-litre chassis and took the form of an open tourer. This SS Jaguar Tourer is an interesting car as it provides a direct link between the S.S.1 and new Jaguars – while based on Heynes' redesigned chassis and powered by the revised 2.5-litre ohv engine, it carried what was virtually S.S.1 Tourer coachwork, and was in lieu of a true SS Jaguar drop-head version of the saloon, which was yet to come.

Possibly Lyons needed to use up, or make use of, S.S.1 tourer bodies and facilities, or maybe the resources of the small company did not stretch to making a drop-head version of the new saloon immediately (a complex type of car to make at the best of times). In any event, the SS Jaguar Tourer was something of a crossbreed and a rare one at that, with only 105 being constructed between 1935

Rarest of the SS Jaguars was the open four-seater Tourer, powered by the ohv engine but utilising S.S.1-style bodywork. This example was painstakingly restored by David Middleton of Wolverhampton. *Photo: P. Skilleter*

Interior of the Jaguar tourer was as for the S.S.I, complete with centre armrest fixed in the rear. Above the rear wheel arch can be seen the tiny picnic 'tables' which could be folded down. *Photo: P. Skilleter*

and 1937.

The instant distinguishing feature of the Jaguar tourer separating it visually from the S.S.1 tourer might have been its much bolder Jaguar radiator grille, but for the fact that very late 1935 and the few early 1936 S.S.1 tourers built also had the same radiator shell - as did the S.S. Airline saloons completed after the announcement of the Jaguar range towards the end of 1935. None of the side-valve S.S.1s ever carried the *Jaguar* badge however, the name being strictly reserved for the new overhead valve cars (except for the 1.5-litre Jaguar). And besides badging, there were other small visual differences between the S.S.1 and Jaguar tourers.

Because of the greater width of the new chassis, the Jaguar tourer's floor and sills were in fact wider than the S.S.1's, and the front wing mountings differed slightly at the front, where they folded round more towards the larger radiator. Most trim details were the same as the S.S.1's internally and externally, with the luggage compartment leather covered. The new tourer had the S.S.1's efficient hood arrangements, which took only three or four minutes to erect complete with sidescreens. Midway

through 1936 though, the Jaguar tourer was given the much larger P100 headlights which certainly did set it apart from the S.S.1 version.

While overhead valves certainly made the Jaguar tourer distinctly faster than its predecessor, for those customers with truly sporting instincts, Lyons could offer something even better. This was the SS Jaguar 100, in reality the S.S.90 with the ohv engine, and still based on what was effectively a shortened S.S.1 chassis (not on the revised SS Jaguar saloon chassis as has so often been stated). With the extra horsepower, the SS Jaguar 100 was a real flyer and amongst the fastest sports cars of the day. It was produced in very small quantities compared to the saloons (only 308 were completed between 1936 and 1940) but it added greatly to S.S. prestige.

One important aspect common to every car in the new range has not yet been touched on – price. S.S. had from the outset been known to give good value for money, but with his new Jaguar range, Lyons simply amazed everyone. He released news of the intended price structure to S.S. dealers at a brilliantly stage-managed reception at the Mayfair Hotel, London.

From the rear, the SS Jaguar Tourer was virtually indistinguishable from an open S.S.1; this car was delivered with the second number plate, incidentally. *Photo: P. Skilleter*

A contemporary photograph of the same Jaguar tourer dating from about 1937, complete with the then-owner's children. Being a 1937 model it has the larger P.100 headlamps.

A 2.5-litre Jaguar saloon was revealed to the assembled company displayed on a stage, and when the excitement had subsided a little, the seated audience was invited to write their estimate of the selling price on a card which was handed to each person. "With two scrutinisers from the gathering as supervisors", wrote Sir William years later of the event, "a comptometer operator calculated the average of all the prices handed in. This came to £632, so when I announced that the actual price was £385, it created quite a lot of excitement and, indeed, added much enthusiasm for the car".

This was truly amazing – it was actually £10 *less* than Standard's own prestige 20hp, still lumbering along with its sidevalves and a good 10mph or 15mph down on the Jaguar's expected 85/90mph maximum, while the Humber Snipe produced by Bill Heyne's erstwhile employers needed virtually an extra 1.5-litres to obtain a similar straight line performance, didn't compare when it came to looks, and cost £475. The Armstrong Siddeley 20 was listed at £550, and the cheapest (and slowest) Rolls Royce, the 20/25, was exactly £1170 *more* than the SS Jaguar's expected 85/90mph maximum, while the Lyons' disclosure.

The other new Jaguar models were just as competitively priced, with the 1.5-litre saloon perhaps even better value for money at £285 (only £7 more than the Rover 12 and £23 cheaper than the Riley 1.5-litre), the open tourer £375, and the SS Jaguar 100 £395 (here, the customer paid for low volume and speed – but there was still nothing that could approach the SS 100's performance within hundreds of pounds).

How did Lyons do it? That was a question which would be oft repeated down the years, but never was it asked more quizzically than in 1935 when the SS Jaguar was announced. Everything that the motor industry had learned appeared to dictate that to bring the price of a car down, mass production at every stage was an essential requirement to reduce the unit cost – which meant giant presses to stamp out body parts, vast, highly mechanised assembly lines to weld them together, and an annual production in the tens of thousands. Yet here was S.S. Cars, effectively in business for less than five years, with no heavy plant at all, no mechanisation to speak of, and a production potential of only a few thousand cars per annum, apparently quite confident that they could make a luxury high performance car cheaper and better than

William Lyons' dealer conventions became famous for their displays of showmanship; this is, of course, the launch of the original SS Jaguar saloon where the assembled dealers were asked to guess its price while at dinner. The average of these guesses was almost twice the actual figure of £385!

anyone else. It seemed nothing short of audacious – or if they could really do it, miraculous.

However, the 'miracle' was based on thirteen years of intensive coachbuilding, buying-in components where this was cheaper, and a cost-control system that was ahead of its time. Thus while it seemed that SS were attempting the impossible by producing in quantity a car using traditional coachbuilding practices, in fact the art had been so refined that it was hardly recognisable as such. Though an art it undoubtedly remained.

Building the SS Jaguar

The Holbrook Lane factory, as rearranged for the Jaguar, was a masterpiece of organisation. The most straightforward operation was that of building up the chassis, S.S. taking this task over from Standard who now merely sent over the engines and transmissions for S.S. to fit themselves along with brakes, suspension and other chassis components bought from other manufacturers. The new chassis assembly line was capable of supplying all the units needed and more, so that the body building department needed considerable reorganisation to cope with the scheduled output of cars.

As with all Lyons' previous cars, the basic construction of the Jaguar saloon was panelling over an ash frame. Like the S.S.1, this panelling was in steel, and to avoid the need for giant, hugely expensive presses, the entire bodyshell was made up of many small sections which could be individually made with small presses which SS did possess, or by outside contractors. In this way, the complex curves of the car's roof and tail could be built up patchwork-quilt fashion without the need for equally complex tooling. No part of the SS Jaguar's outer bodywork contained a complete panel which was more than a couple of feet long, and the average size of each 'patch' was more like a foot or so square.

When the shaped metal pieces came off the presses, they still had to be finished by hand, the edges being beaten to the right shape on a correctly contoured wooden jig with armoured corners. After this noisy business, they were stockpiled ready for the actual body building stage. The wings too were made in a similar fashion (almost certainly by H.H. Cooke & Sons of Nottingham), and the sections welded together so that complete wings would ultimately be offered up to the bodyshell.

Meanwhile, in the wood-mill the car's frame would be under construction. This sequence of operations was highly organised; timber would be drawn from a timber yard alongside, cut to approximately the right length on a pendulum cross-cut saw, then stored in the mill to be drawn upon as needed. Next, the sections of wood underwent planing for initial thickness and width, after which they would be ready for the more complex shaping operations.

It was at this stage that S.S.'s highly developed jig systems really came into their own. To shape every individual frame member, as many as thirty distinct operations might be needed (for example, to make a door post support), the wood was cut and drilled as required through the use of box jigs; despite the complex nature of the work, the accuracy obtained was such that no handwork was needed at all when these body members were later fitted together to form the car's frame. The actual milling machines were made by Guilliet in France, their worth having been well proven in the days of the Swallow Seven.

Not just the Jaguar saloon was built in this way - the procedure was much the same for the Jaguar tourer, and for the S.S.1 models which were being phased out. To avoid confusion, the various milling jigs for each car were painted in a distinctive colour and kept in a nearby store for use as required. The machined frame members themselves would also be sorted and put into a store, to be drawn on by the framework assembly shop.

Here, the work was tackled in two basic stages. First, the major sub-assemblies of the frame would be put together on jigs mounted on strong wooden tables – for example, complete roof or side sections. These were stored at one end of the shop, to wait until they could be put together to form the complete frame.

Then came the second stage, which used a larger and even more complex jig for each body, again mounted on a heavy table. Here, the operatives would glue and slot together the various sub-assemblies which had previously been built to form the complete wooden 'skeleton' of the car - all very reminiscent of a giant construction kit. The high standards of accuracy achieved in the wood shop where all the individual members had been milled will now be appreciated, as a single mistake might cause a serious hold-up as the offending member was removed before it resulted in the possible distortion of the whole frame.

While on the main assembly jig, various internal bracing battens would be fixed to key stress points, after which the body structure was removed and placed in a store to allow the glue to set. Such was the efficiency of the operation that this stage could be reached within an hour of assembly beginning!

In another part of the building, the assembled wooden door frames were meeting their steel skins, which arrived from an outside supplier already pressed to shape although needing to be flanged – this was done by sandwiching the skin between two correspondingly shaped members, and hammering up the projecting area of panel to form the flange. Then skin and frame met, to be fastened together using a pneumatic hammer.

From here on, SS's new assembly track came into play, whereby the completed body frame would be mounted on a trolley and moved from station to station for the remainder of the assembly operations. However, this

These two pictures show the main body jigs at the SS works for the original Jaguar saloon; here the prefabricated framework sections are fitted and glued together, before being panelled. The amount of work involved was considerable despite Lyons' streamlining of every operation.

procedure had been complicated by the fact that the collection of ex-shell filling factories which made up the works at Foleshill weren't necessarily on the same level, and nor was the flooring particularly even. Previously this hadn't mattered too much, because assembly had been carried out in a number of separate operations, but as soon as it was required to link everything together in the form of a modern assembly line, difficulties arose.

These were largely overcome by the construction of extremely rigid body-trucks made of angle steel and heavily braced by a large diameter steel tube welded down the centre line of the truck's frame – this was found not to put the body being carried under any sort of stress which might cause it to flex, with dire consequences later on! The frame was bolted to its truck using the same fixings which would later secure it to the chassis.

At its first stop down the assembly line, the frame received its strengthening plates and struts between the cant rails and the longitudinal roof members. The sunshine roof drainage panels followed, these being part of the lower panel in the roof recess which accommodated the sunshine roof.

The truck was then pushed on to its next stop, where all the outer panels were fitted over the wooden frame, and pinned in place. The many joins were lead-loaded and filled, contours perfected by more leading, and the whole bodyshell cleaned and washed down ready for the next stage, which was painting.

At this point, the truck was linked up with an electrically driven track, projections under the truck

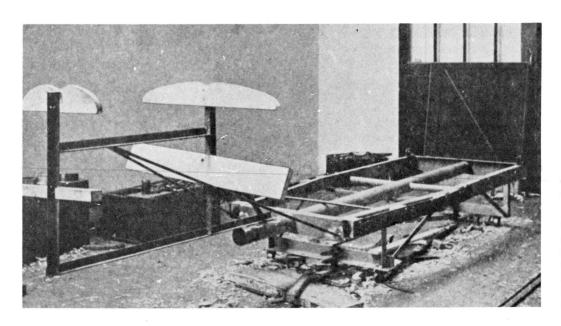

The body truck 'invented' by SS for the transporting of the Jaguar bodyshells; note the bonnet supports in front, and the tubular stiffening member incorporated in the centre of the truck.

engaging on a type of chain drive which pulled it forwards. In fact, two tracks ran through the paint shop to provide an ingenious method of ensuring a perfect colour match between bodyshell and wings, which were at this stage still separate. As a bodyshell was pulled through, so were a set of wings mounted on trestles carried on another truck. Thus both received paint from exactly the same batch, and just as importantly, the right number of wings in the right colour were automatically produced for the appropriately coloured shells.

The painting procedure itself was as follows: first came three synthetic undercoats, each followed by an hour's baking in the oven; after each baking, half an hour elapsed before the next undercoating to allow the metal to cool, while after a final three-hour session in the oven, the panels were rubbed down and given a sealing coat. After stopping, two cellulose colour coats were applied 'wet on wet' followed by an hour's baking; and finally, a 'mist coat' was sprayed on.

The body line was then taken through the trim shop, with the wings being diverted until they were required for mounting later. A high degree of organisation was evident in the trimming department too, with each body being completely trimmed in eight hours (ask a skilled craftsman to retrim a similar Jaguar today and he'll probably estimate three to four weeks at the least!). This work was divided into 16 carefully planned stages, the body taking 30 minutes to travel through each one on its track.

The roof fittings were positioned first, together with the interior lights and direction indicator wiring. Next came the fitting up of the luggage compartment lid, the direction indicators, door check straps, locks and other fittings, followed by the draught welts around the door openings and the headlining and piping. Door glasses and winding mechanisms came next, then the trimming of the quarter panels and the fitting of the screen frame (an operation which took seven men to complete!). Instrument panel and wiring, wood cappings, door panels,

carpets and seats completed the trimming work. The trim line was supplied with items made up in separate shops individually responsible for seats, headlinings, carpets and so on, these materials being deposited at 1.5-hour intervals on a bench running along one side of the trim line – enough for three bodies at a time.

Meanwhile, the chassis were being built up and made ready for accepting the body, one of the final stages being for them to pass through a spray booth for a coat of black paint. A little further on, the bodies appeared on a short length of overhead conveyor, having been unfastened and lifted from their trucks ready to be mounted on the chassis.

The method used by S.S. to mount the bodies was rather unusual; at various points the chassis frame had drilled and tapped plates rivetted to its outer side members, these matching up with vertical slots in the rocker panels under the bodyshell's doors, and in the inner wheel arch panels. With the body lowered into place, bolts were then passed through the slots and into the tapped plates in the chassis frame. Some degree of vertical adjustment between body and chassis was provided by serrated members attached to the inside of the rocker panels.

After the main body shell had been secured, on would go the wings, valances, bumpers, lights and other exterior components, then at the end of the mounting line, the cars would run down a ramp to floor level where they would receive oil, water and fuel and a greasing of the suspension and steering. Tyre pressures would be checked, the wheels tested for alignment, and then – the first test run on the road.

This first test would ensure that all major components were operating correctly, and after being washed down the car would pass to the final finishing line having had its electrical equipment tested and the headlights adjusted. Should any fault have shown up on the road, the car would be taken to another bay for rectification work, and after a further road test and wash down, would rejoin the

Painting the first Jaguars – a line of bodies, with the appropriate numbers of wings, are pulled through the paintshop on their trollies. The track running through the factory was built entirely by SS, with only the electric motors and gears being 'bought in' from outside.

main finishing line where the cars received their final polishing and touching up. Lastly, the cars were driven to the despatch area where any optional extras the customer had ordered would be installed.

We are indebted to *The Automobile Engineer* for much of the foregoing description of the building of very first Jaguars, and certainly the writer of that particular feature – who must have had an intimate knowledge of more orthodox manufacturing techniques – was much taken by what he saw. "One of the outstanding impressions of the S.S. works", he wrote, "is the ingenious manner in which systematic production methods have been applied to difficult designs, and in buildings that gave rise to a number of problems. ... a high degree of accuracy and structural strength combined with a finish that cannot fail to maintain the reputation of the S.S. Company's products".

No wonder then, that on the occasion of the 1935 Olympia Show, Harry Weslake took great delight in walking over to the MG stand where Cecil Kimber stood by his new model, the SA - which with its 2.2-litre ohv engine and pleasant styling might have stolen the show but for the new Jaguar. "How d'you like the new SS car then?" asked the mischevious Harry, and he recounted with some relish years after how the MG man "nearly had hysterics – no-one ever talked to Kimber like that!".

In fact, the SA was probably the nearest thing to a rival that Lyons had to contend with. It was similar in style to the Jaguar saloon, though with divided rear window and shallow windscreen its detail design work was probably not as neat. The SA's chassis was based on the Wolseley 18, and with a wheelbase of 10ft. 3in. and an overall length of 16ft. 1in. it was a less compact car than the Jaguar. Restricting the engine capacity to 2288cc in order to come within the 18hp taxation class meant that the SA had some 20bhp less than the S.S. to propel a similar weight, which combined with a crash gearbox having poorly chosen ratios, did not add up to a sparkling performance.

Where the SA did score was with its Lockheed hydraulic brakes and MG steering - the front axle also followed MG racing practice by having torque reaction cables, whereas the SS relied solely on the road springs for axle location. In 1937 a scaled down version appeared, the 1.5-litre VA with a four cylinder engine, but while it was appreciably quicker than any 1.5-litre Jaguar it was never on equal terms with the smaller S.S. on price, as it cost £325. All in all, the four-seater MGs had little effect on Jaguar sales, and ultimately Cecil Kimber gave best to Lyons and dropped the range just before World War Two commenced.

1935 not only brought a new car, but a fundamental rearrangement of the company too. This came about when William Walmsley "expressed a wish to retire" towards the end of the year. The exact reason for his going seems unclear; he moved to Coventry Steel

Caravans where he helped pioneer aluminium panelled caravans (notwithstanding the name of the firm!), continuing to live in Holyhead Road, Coventry until moving to Poulton-le-Fylde just a year before his death on June 4th 1961.

Technically 'the boss' perhaps, first at Swallow then S.S. (he held the titles of chairman and joint managing director), and ten years Lyons' senior, Walmsley was nevertheless a shadowy figure remaining largely in the background so far as the outside world was concerned. It was Lyons' name that usually appeared in print when the cars were mentioned, and it was Lyons who was seen on the S.S. stand at motor shows, who addressed the gentlemen of the press at the launch of a new model, and who conducted VIPs around the factory.

However it seems that this was how Walmsley liked it - indeed, he apparently made no effort to share the limelight with his partner, which would have been quite easy to achieve. Everything that one can discover about Walmsley points to the fact that, in the final analysis, he was far happier when at his drawing board, or experimenting with the cars themselves, and was quite content to allow the efficient, quietly energetic Lyons to build the company's public image. In the factory though, he is remembered as being just as industrious as Mr Lyons, always about the place and giving orders, though he was apt to take long weekends at Blackpool. Above all, it should never be forgotten that it was William Walmsley whose inspiration the original Swallow sidecar was, and that he undoubtedly played a vital part in the evolution of Swallow bodywork during the early, formative years of the company. There is some suggestion of a row when Walmsley came to leave, and possibly the relationship between the two partners had perceptibly changed from the moment that the older man had ordered the roofline of the first S.S.I to be raised while Lyons was in hospital – a move somewhat resented by Lyons. His leaving coincided with S.S. Cars Ltd being floated as a public company, so it is quite likely that Walmsley felt that he would rather not be involved in a big company regime, preferring instead to go at his own pace within a smaller business – or even to spend more time on the extensive and elaborate model railway he had installed at his home.

On his departure, Walmsley gave up all his financial interest in the company, selling his shares for cash. Initially Lyons had a 50% holding in S.S. Cars Ltd, but later acquired more shares so that he would always be in direct control of the business – and with Walmsley gone, that was the only way for him. Thereafter, S.S. – and later Jaguar – was run as an autocracy; Lyons took all the major decisions, and those he did not take himself, he knew all about. While as a limited company S.S. Cars did indeed possess a board of directors, it rarely met as such, and then only as a formality in order to satisfy legal requirements – the real business was conducted by Lyons himself on a day-to-day basis, in consultation with certain key members of his small staff.

Of these, Heynes obviously represented the engineering division, and Rankin the all-important advertising and promotion. Then there was Arthur Whittaker, who had joined when he was 19, and who became General Manager on the formation of S.S. Cars Ltd, E.F. Huckvale who looked after the routine finances as Company Secretary (a position he was to hold for 25-years), and Miss Alice Fenton. Almost uniquely in the motor-industry, there was no Sales Manager at SS, and indeed, such a position was not created until well after the War. Lyons himself, with Alice Fenton, handled this vital part of the business.

Alice Fenton deserves a separate mention at this stage; she joined the company during the Cocker Street days almost straight from school, through having worked for William Lyons' parents. Originally typist and secretary to Lyons, she soon took on much wider responsibilities and it is probably no exaggeration to say that after Lyons himself, Alice Fenton played a large a part as any individual in the company's striking climb to success.

Her role came to be sales, setting up and supplying the dealerships with new cars. A lively, cheerful person, she was also interested in music and the arts, and would be careful to discover the personal interests of the dealers she met so that they would find conversations with her easy and pleasurable. She was popular and respected amongst both those she worked with, and the dealers themselves.

Later she became Home Sales Director of Jaguar; one can discern that she put her all into the company, and perhaps it was too much, for she died prematurely while still in her early fifties in 1960.

This then was the nucleous of the small team which Lyons had gathered together, dedicated individuals all with a great loyalty to the company and Lyons himself. Talking to those who remember the pre-War days, it is clear that they did realise that they were involved in something special, a company which had flourished and grown through one of the worst recessions the motor industry had known; but they had been too busy to dwell on the matter at the time. Almost everyone worked long hours, including Saturday morning, and Mrs Connie Teather who worked in a cubby-hole office next to Bill Rankin at Foleshill recalls going in to the works every Saturday morning to do the filing from the week before, because there was certainly no time to do it during the week – not until much later was there the luxury of a filing clerk!

In monetary terms, the newly formed S.S. Cars Ltd was a success from the start, and when its first year of trading was complete, the books showed a profit of £27 960. The new Jaguar range continued to sell in numbers which were soon to prove almost an embarrassment, stretching Foleshill's capacity to the limit; and meanwhile, the motoring press had sampled and reported upon the new ohv models to a highly interested readership.

Alice Fenton, who joined Lyons as a teenage typist and who rose to become Home Sales Director in the 1950s – which is when this photograph of her at her desk was taken.

Road-testing the 2.5-Litre Jaguar

The Autocar published the first test of the 2.5-litre Jaguar, and in the second paragraph observed that "the performance is worthy of the appearance" which not everyone had thought was the case with the S.S.1. As usual in those days, great emphasis was placed on the performance available in top gear, the testers probably being old enough to remember the early days of the motor car when the gearbox was only resorted to in an emergency and a car judged almost solely by its ability to remain in top for as long as possible. By 1936, ideas had changed somewhat but low-speed pulling was investigated with at least as much enthusiasm as the car's maximum. The new Jaguar more than passed muster:

"There is a fine feeling of power in reserve on top gear – a matter of great interest to a large number of drivers. This is so much that even in traffic the car can be handled chiefly in top and third, and in hill-climbing this S.S. excels".

However, to the more sporting motorist the gearbox was there to be used, and the choice of ratios and the manner of its operation were important factors. *The Autocar* acknowledged this as follows:

"Third and second are, indeed most valuable ratios to anyone who feels disposed to use the gearbox, for they are not by any means unduly low, giving good maxima, are not noisy, and, even more important, are easily engaged since there is synchromesh for top, third and second.
"The short, rigid remote-control gear lever is in an excellent position, and the synchromesh goes through

well for all but the very fastest of lightning gear changes such as few people want to use. Occasionally in ordinary handling of the car the synchromesh is overridden and a missed gear change results".

On the whole an enthusiastic summary, but it is interesting to note that even in 1936, rather weak synchromesh was being commented on; one can then better understand why testers were to be so critical of Jaguar gearboxes right up to 1964, because up to that year the same basic design survived. Speeds on the intermediate gears were usefully high, *The Autocar* reporting 69mph in third, 46mph in second, and 27mph in first, all contributing to the car's ability to put up "remarkable averages" and quickly gain 70mph, judged a useful cruising speed "with more quickly obtainable if wanted". Maximum speed was a best of 88mph, corresponding to 4700rpm, with the rev. counter needle creeping into the red-lined sector which began at 4500rpm; mean of two-way runs was 85.7mph – all highly creditable for a very fully equipped four-door saloon.

This was usefully quicker than the lighter, lower 20hp S.S.1, but the improvement in acceleration was even more marked – the sidevalve car took 15.8 seconds to reach 50mph, and 24 seconds to achieve 60mph; the new Jaguar gained these speeds from rest in 12 seconds and 17.4 seconds respectively, times which put it amongst the sports cars of the day. "One is almost inclined to feel that the engine is larger than its actual capacity", said the journal.

However it was not just *what* it did, but *how* it did it that appealed to *The Autocar,* a point taken up in virtually every road test of a Jaguar ever since: "The smooth and quiet

Meanwhile the S.S. Car Club was flourishing, and held many events including race meetings at Donington; here some perfectly standard 2.5-litre saloons compete against an SS 100 during a 1938 meeting. *Photo: Autocar*

engine and the ease of performance, also the docile way in which the car will potter around by-ways, are facets of its behaviour which will rank equal in many people's minds to the sheer performance available". But for those who wished to motor briskly, the car's handling could keep up: "It is steady in the sports car manner on corners, can be put fast with complete confidence into an open road curve, yet is not harsh on the springing" – although the generally good ride deteriorated over what were termed "colonial" sections of road.

As was to be expected, the Girling rod brakes performed well, "acting smoothly and really powerfully with only moderate pressure on the pedal", while the handbrake could hold the car on a 1-in-4 hill. The steering achieved "an excellent balance between the firmness and accuracy desirable for a car capable of so good a performance, and lightness of control at low speeds". The gearing of 2.5-turns lock-to-lock was rated as "not specially low-geared" – what the reaction would have been to the Mk 11 saloon's 5-turns lock-to-lock some 23-years later is hard to tell!

Instrumentation and fittings all won approval as well they might, and vision was thought good although the driving mirror did not give an "entirely complete" view rearwards. The lack of door pockets were remarked upon, but the doors themselves were found to "close well without slamming". Summing-up was enthusiastic and must have delighted those who built the car:

"From experience of it over a comprehensive distance, taking in a variety of conditions with loads varying from the driver alone up to full capacity, this S.S. Jaguar does even better than one might anticipate. It is not too much to say that it is a credit to the British automobile industry, and seems almost unbelievably good at the price ..."

The Motor's test of a similar car followed about a month later, in May 1936. The journal "expected great things" and it was not disappointed. "After 400-miles on the road, backed by tests at Brooklands track, we formed the opinion that this car represents one of the biggest of the advances made by motorcar manufacturers in stepping forward from 1935 to 1936."

To us, this remark does not perhaps carry the weight that it did in 1936 – now, Jaguar is more than established as a leader in many aspects of automobile engineering, but then, 'Jaguar' was entirely new, and S.S. a name still associated with 'specials'; yet here was an authoratative technical journal of international repute saying in effect that this small company had succeeded in producing a car which was as advanced as any made by established manufacturers with decades of experience and a hundred times the resources behind them.

The car supplied to *The Motor* performed quite as well as *The Autocar's* with 60mph coming up in 16.4-seconds, and over the flying half-mile at Brooklands, a mean speed of 86.5mph was attained despite unfavourable conditions. Moreover, "given a modicum of assistance from wind or gradient, 90mph can easily be obtained, the engine showing no signs of distress', this represented almost 5000rpm, which in the mid-thirties was a very high figure for a 2.5-litre production engine to safely attain.

Even when this performance was used, the car's thirst was certainly not excessive, and a weekend of hard driving produced 19mpg over 300-miles; more restrained driving brought 21mpg "without nursing". The gearbox with its "nicely chosen ratios" was liked and the synchromesh on this car singled out for praise – "This mechanism really does synchronise the change, so that one can snap the lever through from top to third at 60mph without pause" (though the third to top and *vice versa* movement of this box was always the best). The brakes were again rated as "powerful yet smooth".

General road behaviour and the ability to put up "very high" average speeds were praised:

"The pleasure of handling the SS Jaguar is due to many contributory factors and of these the most important is the way in which the car holds the road. Combined with light high-geared steering, this characteristic makes it possible to take open main-road bends at a high speed in safety. The steering lock is good, the overall width moderate and the driver can see both sidelamps: all points that are appreciated in heavy traffic".

The Motor was more enthusiastic about the SS Jaguar's ride than its rival had been, after taking a detour to further evaluate the springing:

"After a good deal of fast main-road work we took the SS over one of the old coach roads which run across Salisbury Plain. Fairly deep ruts and grassy slopes were included in the itinerary, but the ground clearance and wing clearances proved adequate. This is not a car suitable only for billiard-table conditions .... Although very firm and stable at speed the low-hung semi-elliptics provide really comfortable riding. Pitching is practically non-existent: a fact fully appreciated by rear seat passengers".

These rather eye-catching Ace wheel discs in the optional all-chrome style were available as 'extras' – the effect must have been dazzling on a sunny day! Standing by the car is the well-known rallyist Miss J. Sleigh, photographed during the 1936 Scottish Rally.
Photo: Motor

The usual compliments were paid to the quality of the car's fittings, and *The Motor* agreed with The Autocar's summary when it concluded the test by saying: "...the new 2.5-litre SS Jaguar is a car with many excellent qualities and an outstanding road performance. To produce it at so modest a price is an engineering achievement of which the makers should feel proud". If Lyons and Heynes hadn't been so busy designing improvements for the 1937 models they probably would have been.

Road-testing the 1.5-Litre Jaguar

The 1.5-litre SS Jaguar was also tried by *The Motor,* and surprisingly the magazine's test staff concentrated on writing about the sporting nature of the car, which wasn't really its strongest point in view of the very ordinary specification of the 1608cc sidevalve engine propelling it. Possibly SS had asked if they could stress this aspect for this very reason! So the impression gained is of a medium sized, good looking car with an above average performance. To be fair, the 1.5-litre wasn't slow at 70mph, but neither was it particularly brisk on acceleration – the 0-50mph time of 19.6-seconds recorded by *The Motor* was only 0.5-second less than Standard's own Flying 12 with the same engine, while such as the Rover Speed 14, helped by ohv, could cut this down to 17-seconds.

However, it does seem that once underway, the original 1.5-litre was able to give a good account of itself, *The Motor* finding that it provided "a genuine cruising speed" of 60mph with the throttle half open, and petrol consumption even with fast driving was a reasonable 25mpg – helped by a fairly low weight of 21cwt, compared to 30cwt for the 2.5-litre car and which was only 1cwt heavier than the S.S.11.

The engine was also smooth running and quite flexible for a four-cylinder, with 8mph reckoned the lowest speed in top. The gearbox was liked, with the movement of the lever quick, and of course there was synchromesh on all the forward gears except first. The height and rake adjustment for the steering column was appreciated, and the driving position was thought "excellent", provided, it seems, the driver did not mind sitting very close to the wheel. The brakes were light in operation – "on ordinary occasions the effort required is about the same as that demanded for the clutch actuation - itself a very light operation" – with the car pulling up 'all square'; at 12in. the drum diameter was an inch less than the 2.5-litre's, but it was still ample in dispersing the heat generated.

The test concluded with the judgement that the 1.5-litre Jaguar was "a thoroughly satisfactory car with a lively performance", the price of £285 being left to speak for itself.

SS Jaguar Tourer Performance

The final new Jaguar, the tourer model, seems not to have been officially tested by anyone; all that can be referred to are comments made by the two British journals of trial runs in a "last year's experimental chassis" at the time of the SS Jaguar range's announcement, this being an S.S.1 tourer fitted with the new ohv 2.5-litre engine. It is enough to gain certain indications of the SS Jaguar tourer's performance, at least.

The Autocar found that it was possible with this car to reach a maximum speed "in the region of 90mph", and to accelerate from a standstill to 60mph in around 16-seconds, or about a second quicker than their road-test 2.5-litre saloon returned a few months later. The usual top gear flexibility was apparent too. With its folding screen facility, it does seem likely that the SS Jaguar

No SS Jaguar tourer seems to have been officially tested, but it was capable of nearly 90mph. Note 'Jaguar mascot' behind this car pictured in Singapore in 1937!

tourer was ultimately faster than its sister saloon, and a virtual 90mph maximum ties in with estimates given to the writer by owners of this rare car.

The 1937-model SS Jaguar

A year had barely passed since the introduction of the SS Jaguars when, in August 1936, it was announced that a number of detail modifications had been made to the Jaguar range, the new versions conveniently being called '1937' models. Experience and informed comment from users over the previous 11-or 12-months had shown that a number of improvements could be made, though these did not amount to anything like the wholesale alterations which the original S.S.1 had very necessarily been subjected to at the end of its first year of existence. As *The Motor* put it: "The required performance has been obtained, and it is now a matter for detailed improvement".

Although most of the changes were small in themselves, their number was quite extensive. Probably the most substantial alteration was the widening of the frame at the rear of the car to allow yet more footroom – the rear footwells had gone, and now the floor sloped gently rearwards either side of the propellor shaft tunnel. Additionally, the bottoms of the two front seats had been cut away at an angle so that legs could be stretched out more. Rear track was unaffected however.

These changes meant a wider rear cushion too, and armrests were now incorporated into the wheelarches on each side. The bucket seats were altered too, with the squabs now offering more support to the driver, who with the front seat passenger now had the use of side arm rests on the doors; Dunlopillo material was introduced for upholstering the seats.

A much revised instrument panel was now in evidence - the formerly central 5-inch rev. counter and speedometer were now separated by the minor 3-inch dual gauges and dash controls, and the oval instrument panel itself changed to a lozenge-shape. A glove compartment was now built into the facia panel in front of the passenger, which together with the map pockets in each door, served to answer *The Autocar's* comments on interior stowage space earlier in the year. Windscreen wiper operation had been revised too - having obviously been rather too audible, the motor was now situated under the bonnet instead of behind the dash, and the wiper blades could now be operated together or singly as the driver wished. Efforts had been made to improve water and draught sealing as well.

Chassis running-gear and mechanical changes were numerous, but mainly concerned details. Significantly, the suspension benefitted from larger dampers (the biggest available), and lead-coating on the spring leaves to prevent rust and noise. Steering remained as before (with its transverse instead of side steering rod, inspite of the latter being more traditional with that type of car) but accuracy was improved and 'whip' reduced by much larger mountings for the steering box, and a bigger diameter steering column with a stronger dashboard bracket.

The 2.5-litre engine appeared with a variety of refinements, although one of these effecting valve gear adjustment had actually been brought in during May 1936. The first batch of 500 2.5-litre cars (with engine nos. 249501 to 250000) had the adjustment on the pushrods, with three tappet spanners (as supplied with all side-valve models) included in the toolkit. These earlier rockers were drilled and sealed at both ends, with wicks inserted at each end. At the pushrod end, the oil went down through the 0.375-

A large number of small but sensible changes came with SS Cars' 1937-model announcement; externally, the most noticeable of these on the 2.5-litre were the P.100 headlamps, quarterlights (or 'no-draught ventilators' as the factory termed them) for the front doors, and faired-in sidelamps. Bigger shock absorbers and larger diameter brake drums improved the car on the road.

Reproduced by the courtesy of THE MOTOR.

The instruments were still set into a painted metal dash, but were now grouped so that the larger (5-inch) dials were on the outside. The choke control was missing because starting enrichment was now automatic.

carburettor. It was to be a feature on Jaguars for many years afterwards.

A new water manifold was used for 1937, replacing the two-piece one used previously – this latter incorporated a thermostat housing on top of the front section, connected to the radiator by an 'L' shaped hose. It is doubtful whether any of the old two-piece aluminium manifolds (which were connected at the centre by a rubber hose) are in use now, as most owners seemed to have replaced them with the later type – although to do so, they needed the later, slightly larger radiator block too which had the downward-pointing (instead of horizontal) top entry to mate with the new horizontally mounted, forward-facing thermostat housing.

Power output for 1937 was slightly up, from 102 to 104bhp; the compression height of the pistons was increased by approximately 0.25 inch with a corresponding increase in block height for better heat dispersal, and a shim-type gasket in place of the copper/asbestos type – all this was because early engines had shown signs of bad bore distortion and consumed large quantities of lubricating oil. Then Heynes found that when the very stiff cylinder head was bolted down, the soft copper-asbestos head gasket compressed unequally, causing distortion of the block face and bores; this was proved by bolting the head directly to the block without a gasket, after which the bores remained perfectly round. He found that the solution lay in using the Corrujoint gasket which was a 0.0015 inch thick cupro-nickel sheet with indentations around the bores and waterways; SS were one of the first to use such a gasket in production, though

inch diameter ball pin on the upper end of the pushrod, into the pushrod and out through the lower ball pin to lubricate the cam-followers. This was probably inefficient, so hence the introduction of the later rocker (with adjustable ball-pin) which had an open 0.062-inch hole at the pushrod end, through which the oil flowed out unrestricted by a wick, and thoroughly lubricated the ball pin, then travelled down the outside of the pushrod and onto the cam-followers and camshaft. The valve end of the later rocker retained its wick and was sealed, allowing a restricted oil flow to the valve stem as with the earlier type.

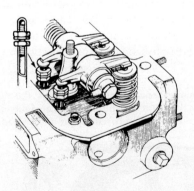

The old-type of tappet adjustment shown here, with adjustment on the pushrods, was superceeded by new rockers carrying adjustable ball pins.

Sectional drawing of the automatic enrichment device fitted to the SS Jaguar's S.U. carburettors for 1937. It was in effect an auxiliary carburettor, built into the side of the normal float chamber of one of the main carburettors; it provided various mixtures according to throttle openings, and cut out thermostatically when engine working temperature had been reached.

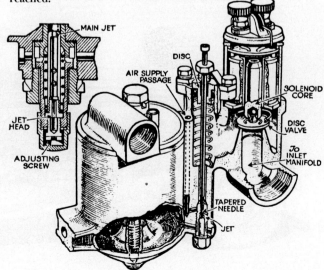

The lubrication system had not previously included an oil filter, and so the 1937 cars incorporated a Tecalemit one in the system even though it was not full-flow but of the bypass type; most engines seemed to have been modified retrospectively. The two SU carburettors were also given some protection in the form of two barrel-type air filters, these being mounted vertically alongside the engine block and leading to the carburettors via a cast aluminium air intake box. Also fitted was an automatic, thermostatically controlled, enriching device in place of a manual choke, and which was really a secondary 'starting'

the type(usually in steel) subsequently became widely used both in Britain and America. It was the rise in compression ratio stemming from the thinner head gasket which largely brought about the extra couple of horsepower.

The Standard-type gearbox came under Heynes' scrutiny too, it having suffered from being a little noisy, so the bearings were modified, and the double helical teeth were made to overlap slightly (instead of there being a gap between the rows) which made them quieter and stronger. Both the clutch and brake pedals were given curved instead of oval footplates to make them more comfortable to use. Clutch adjustment itself was improved, by making the rod from the compensator lever to the withdrawal shaft adjustable for length.

The already very adequate Girling brakes were given larger brake drums (up from 13in. x 1.5in. to 14in x 1.75in.), and were also modified to give a more progressive action by grinding the friction surfaces of the drums before fitting. Ground clearance was improved by mounting the two silencers higher, and the rear exhaust pipe was given its characteristic oval section.

From the outside, the 1937-model cars could be identified in several ways. First, the addition of quarter-lights to the front side windows was an obvious change, while on the 2.5-litre cars the sidelights were now flared into the wings (although not on every car for some reason) and larger, P100, headlights fitted - these were installed on the tourer as well, but this and the 1.5-litre saloon kept the 'torpedo' chrome-plated separate sidelights; the 1.5-litre also kept its smaller headlamps.

Prices remained unchanged though, and one indication of the value S.S. Cars Ltd were actually offering is provided by a remark in *The Autocar* – out of no less than 82 closed cars tested by that journal by the end of 1936, "the 2.5-litre Jaguar was the fifth fastest British-built closed car, and its mean speed of 85.71mph was exceeded only by others having considerably larger engine capacities, and costing from twice to nearly four times the price". Add to that a true quality finish, good roadholding and brakes, balanced styling and reliable, understressed mechanical components, and you have the Lyons formula for a successful motorcar in a nutshell. And it all evolved in less than six years.

Road-testing the 1937 models

The 1937 car came up for road test by *The Autocar* in May of that year, and the magazine was quick to sum up the major improvements: "Few cars on our roads today can be faster from point to point, for not only does the Jaguar accelerate briskly, but also – and this is every bit as important – it also handles well. It is in handling, in fact, that the latest car shows the greatest advance".

Obviously the larger dampers were playing their part, although the steering too helped improve the general handling of the car, thanks to the considerably more rigid mountings throughout:

Mr and Mrs Heynes, with the factory's (ex-Lady Lyons') 1937-model 2½-litre which displays the larger headlamps, faired-in sidelights, and quarter-lights of the later cars. *Photo: P. Skilleter*

" ... the steering has gained in accuracy, and is now really good, it has not become heavier for manoeuvring, though more effort is required for a sharp turn at low speed than at other times. The ratio is moderate, rather less than 2.75-turns being needed from lock to lock. There is good caster action, and shocks are not felt through the steering.

"The steering is accurate and firm, and requires little concentration. This car can be kept well down to the left-hand verge of the road, it can be taken fast round a corner or a series of bends on a set course exactly as the driver decides, and he can overtake at fast speeds in the knowledge of going accurately 'through the gap''.

Slight criticisms were made of the amount of wind noise (not surprising in view of the still very square shape of the car), some engine thrash when the unit was revved, and the "fairly noticeable axle movement" on poorer roads. But on the subject of sheer speed, *The Autocar* found a definite improvement – the mean maximum was now 87mph instead of 85mph, and the best timed speed was only fractionally under 90mph at 89.1mph, compared to 88.2mph formerly. Fifty miles an hour was now reached in 11.3-seconds, and 60mph in 16.5-seconds, quicker by 0.7-second and virtually 1-second respectively.

For 1937, the SS Jaguar's chassis was slightly enlarged at the rear to give greater internal width for passengers; though otherwise it still remained basically S.S.I. The company already regarded it as obsolete, however, and Heynes was busy designing an entirely new chassis. This is a tourer frame.

Fuel consumption remained uneffected, "CDU 919" returning around 20mpg over the 450 mile test. Overall, the verdict was that an outstanding car had become still better, the writer adding with some justification that "somehow one cannot help feeling that in its evolution there has been the touch of genius". Such was the extent of the impact which the first Jaguar made on its contemporaries.

Practical Motorist tried a 2.5-litre saloon in April 1937, and commenced by praising the car's general finish and equipment:

"From radiator to tool locker the car is a real precision job, every item being extremely well made and obviously of fine quality. Lift the bonnet, and you find an engine which would not disgrace a pedestal at the Motor Show – a beautiful piece of engineering, clean and polished. Open the lid of the luggage boot, and you find a second lid which, when raised, reveals the tools all neatly arranged and fitted into covered sinkings; if it is dark, they can be illuminated by a light placed inside the lid. Look at the dashboard, and you see precision instruments neatly arranged ... the controls are also well placed and of substantial design, even the switches for the indirect instrument illumination and interior lights being provided with substantial knobs .... If one were to pay twice as much, it is difficult to see how the quality could be improved".

Under way, the car was no less impressive, with the driver feeling immediately at home behind the wheel and "perfectly comfortable and safe in accelerating up to 87mph as soon as a sufficiently open road was reached". This speed appears to be a normal maximum, though in excess of 90mph was possible one-way in favourable conditions. As for acceleration: "We do not know of any other car at a similar price, and of approachable quality, which can be accelerated as quickly and easily as the 2.5-litre SS", which meant an even better 0-60mph time than *The Autocar* had achieved, less than 16 seconds being recorded on a Longines stop-watch.

The gearbox was liked and it was thought even those drivers "who prefer an automatic change device .... could not fail to be impressed with the very easy change with this silent gearbox" – although it was mentioned that obtaining bottom gear on the move (which wasn't synchronised) "is not quite so easy". On the whole, with its unique blend of performance and comfort, the car was judged to be "as much entitled to the name of 'town carriage' as 'sports saloon'.

Not that such flattering comments had the effect of introducing complacency at Foleshill; while others might have been content to rest on their laurels for a while, the young managing director of SS Cars Ltd (he was still only 36!) was already planning another major step for his company. Which, although it wasn't forseeable at the time, was to be a 'make-or-break' effort that almost ended in disaster.

Chapter Four

The `traditional´ years

It is the performance as a whole, and the style of the car, from the imposing radiator and sleek bodywork to the luxurious nature of detail appointments, that combine to produce a car of outstanding merit and appeal.

The Autocar, March 19, 1945

The success of the S.S. Jaguar car is one of the romances of the motor industry.

The Motor, May 31, 1938

Almost as soon as the new Jaguars left the factory for the dealers' showrooms early in 1936, a sales pattern developed which clearly showed that Foleshill's production capacity would be sorely stretched to keep up with an ever-increasing demand. By 1937, it was obvious to Lyons and his production manager Arthur Whittaker that their current method of building the cars, streamlined as it might have been, was far too laborious and slow. The bottleneck was the continued use of wood, with all the associated milling, shaping and assembly work which came from constructing bodies around a wooden framework.

Accordingly, the decision was made to finally say goodbye to one of the last remaining strongholds of the SS coachbuilding tradition, the elegant but outdated ash frame, and go over to an all-steel bodyshell. A corresponding programme was therefore put in hand to produce an all-steel bodyshell for the 1938 season.

There were problems from the start. As SS had no facilities for making all the new metal stampings which would replace the wooden structure of the car, it was necessary for an outside contractor to be retained for this work. The large Pressed Steel company, which already produced bodies for a number of motor manufacturers, were the obvious people to contact first. But on seeing what was required – a complete new bodyshell for a large car – Pressed Steel immediately said that they'd need twelve months to tool up and get into production.

This was no good to Lyons, who was used to making comprehensive changes to his cars in a matter of weeks, thanks to the resourceful attitude that SS applied to their problems. The only alternative if the 1938 date was to be adhered to, it seemed, was to split the work amongst several firms. But from this apparently sensible decision was to spring one of the greatest crisis the company was ever to encounter.

Oblivious of the problems ahead, Lyons instituted the design of the new bodyshell, along with a new steel sub-structure replacing the wooden frame. As before, the outer skin would be made up of a number of small panels to avoid capital outlay on expensive tooling, but instead of being pinned to an ash frame, they would now be spot welded together and also on to the new internal steel panels which replaced the frame. Few drawings were made – instead, patterns and templates were taken direct from a prototype shell, and then despatched to the various firms who were to produce the individual parts.

In due course, the panels and sub-assemblies began to arrive at Foleshill from the suppliers, amongst whom were Pressed Steel, Motor Panels, and Sankeys. Soon it was possible to begin a trial assembly of a body from all the parts, before proceeding with the work on a quantity basis using the track itself, which had meanwhile been rearranged to suit the new all-steel production methods. Imagine the horror, then, when it was discovered that the individual parts wouldn't fit together properly!

The problem was compounded because there were virtually no drawings to refer to in order to check and cross-check dimensions and arrangements - each supplier had worked to the patterns provided by SS, and now the separate components wouldn't go together to make-up a car. In fact some 25 pre-production saloons were turned out, and all were rejected by Lyons as being not up to standard; they were pushed away, with some despondency, into storage and eventually, the scrap-heap.

The cause of the trouble was tracked down to one company, which had somehow misunderstood or not followed SS's instructions properly; they were required to put the matter right (it seems that legal action may even have been taken against them by Lyons), but inevitably the delay was great and for the first three- or four-months of 1938, virtually no cars left Foleshill at all. The production line had already been geared to all-steel assembly and so no more 1937-type ash framed saloons could be made even as an emergency measure. It was, as the factory has since admitted, the nearest to bankruptcy that Jaguar was ever to come.

But thanks to William Lyon's iron nerve and a lot of work on the shop floor, SS weathered the storm. The body problem was finally sorted out, and deliveries of new cars at last began, much to the joy of many disgruntled would-be customers who had waited some months for their new Jaguar. By April 1938 some 85–100 cars were coming off the line each week, and this had been increased to more like 120 by June of the same year. Such was the recovery that on the occasion of the ordinary general meeting of SS Cars Ltd in November 1938, Lyons was able to announce that production was at full capacity, "converting what appeared to be a certain loss into a substantial profit" – which in hard figures was £29 15s. The situation had been saved.

Production traumas apart, what was the new Jaguar range like? Well, the cars looked very similar to the original 1936 Jaguars at first glance, but in reality, the changes were great. Quite apart from the virtual absence of wood they were larger and had a completely new chassis frame, plus a host of refinements besides. And, there were two new ohv engines and – for the first time – a drophead-coupe body style.

For the new Jaguars, William Heynes had designed an entirely new chassis frame, and this, while being entirely orthodox, left behind any traces of S.S.1 ancestry and embodied all the latest thoughts on frame construction. It was of all box-section manufacture with 6-inch deep side rails, and the centre drilled 'X' bracing of the earlier frame was replaced by three large box-section cross members; the first of these ran beneath the radiator over the front axle, the second across at the rear of the gearbox, and the third was placed at the front of the rear springs, carrying the latter's front shackle housings. Together with another, smaller box-section cross member at the rear of the frame which carried the rear spring rear-shackles, these members braced the two main side members which ran the full length of the car. A 'U' form cross member just behind the rear axle further strengthened the rear end of the chassis, and in conjunction with the rearmost (smaller) box section, supported the spare wheel tray and petrol tank.

Thus the frame was made up of various sections spot-welded together to form boxes, while the cross members were also welded onto the side members in order to ensure maximum rigidity. In this last respect Heynes had certainly been very successful, as the new frame was 30% stiffer in torsion than the cross-braced version it replaced, and yet was claimed to be slightly lighter at the same time, although this is difficult to believe in view of its much more substantial build.

The perimeter shape of the frame had changed too, in order to allow extra width in the body. Narrower at the front, it ran parallel towards the rear until opposite the clutch where it both dropped and diverged outwards, regaining its parallel run at the end of the gearbox; the side members then ran straight back to slope gently under the rear axle. The usual semi-elliptic springs were fitted front and (inboard) rear, lead coated as before, with Silentbloc bushes at the rear. Again, the shackle had been eliminated in the cause of greater lateral stability at the front, being replaced by a bronze bush with grease nipple. The rear of the spring was located by a sliding block arrangement, using 'Oilite' for the half-round sliding bushes, a porous (or sintered) material that was self-lubricating, being charged with oil during manufacture.

The new chassis frame for the 1938-on steel bodied cars was very rigid despite having no X-member. The new Jaguars scored over many of their contemporaries through possessing a stiff chassis and properly thought out spring and damper rates.

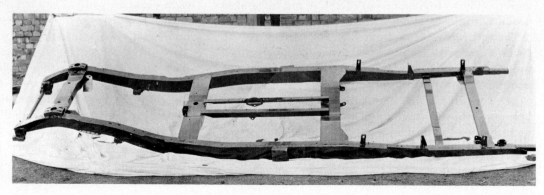

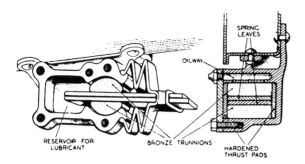

The self-lubricating sliding-roller rear spring anchorage on the front springs of the 1938-series Jaguars.

The beam-axle front suspension on the 1938-type Jaguar, showing the swivel pins, damper linkage and rod brakes; this is actually a late model 1.5-litre.

The car's front axle was the usual 'I' beam forging, with oval section arms sweeping up to carry the swivel pins on each side. These were angled to give nearly centre-point contact with wheel and road, with the swivel loading being taken on a Timken roller-thrust bearing on six-cylinder models. Each pin turned in a bush which was of course provided with a grease nipple for lubricating. Greasing was necessary every 500-miles for the swivel-pins, steering joints, front spring anchorages, fan, and water pump. Luvax dampers acted on the front axle through links which were attached to bosses forged integrally with the upswept parts of the axle beam.

Burman Douglas worm and nut steering was specified once more, the box arranged so that the steering arm described an arc across the chassis frame, the wheels being turned via a transverse rod; in this way, the side of the frame was kept clear of the steering arm drag link, an arrangement which avoided conflict in the steering and axle geometry. The steering box was situated in a forward position near the radiator, which caused the near vertical position for the steering wheel which was becoming an established Jaguar feature, and had a very rigid thrre-point mounting on the frame, which itself was locally reinforced at that point.

SS also held true to the former braking system which was by Girling, as it remained one of the most efficient mechanical designs available; possibly the company was a little conservative in not adopting hydraulic brakes, but it was probably argued that as the existing set-up was perfectly adequate for the car's weight and performance, why introduce an unknown factor by changing it? So the rod-operated system remained, the shoes being brought into contact with the big cast-iron drums by means of expander cones, which were themselves operated by direct pull-rods from the levers on the brake pedal. The leverage from the pedal operated compensator was arranged to give a 60/40 front to rear braking bias, and a safety link ensured that should any part of the system fail, braking on one axle would still be possible by both hand or foot – in normal operation, the handbrake worked on all four wheels, this car being the only Jaguar to have this feature, which was not continued after the war.

This basic chassis was to last right up until 1949, when the last cart-sprung Jaguar left the works, and indeed was to be the second-to-last chassis frame ever built by the company before progress demanded that unitary construction take over from a separate body/chassis configuration. It was a highly successful application of perfectly orthodox chassis engineering that was to serve Jaguar well for more than a decade.

For 1938, SS Cars announced that there was to be a choice of three power units – the original 2.5-litre in slightly altered form, an enlarged 1.5-litre based on the Standard 14, and a completely new 3.5-litre engine, this last creating no little excitement as it was realised that the extra power would elevate SS into the top rank of performance motor cars.

The 2.5-Litre Engine for 1938

First, the 2.5-litre. Since 1937, this was claimed to give an installed bhp of over 100, achieved largely through the rise in compression ratio as described in the last Chapter, and by improving the evacuation of exhaust gasses through the use of two 'branch' exhaust manifolds instead of the original one – later 1937 cars had this arrangement too. Each branch accepted the gasses from three cylinders, and expelled them through its separate exhaust pipe and silencer. The changes were more than enough to compensate for an extra couple of hundredweight, and add several mph to the top speed besides.

The 1.5-Litre Engine for 1938

The engine described as the '1.5-litre' was new to SS, and was based on the 73 x 106mm, 1775.8cc four-cylinder Standard 14 unit introduced in 1937; effectively though, it was two-thirds of the 2.5 Six, having the same bore,

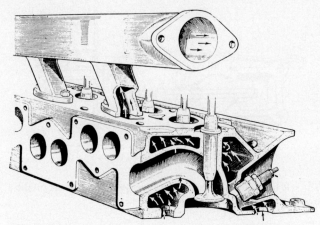

Unlike on the larger SS power units though, a crossflow arrangement of the ports was not used, and so the exhaust manifold was positioned on the same side of the head as the inlet. Attention had been paid to ensuring that the exhaust ports and combustion chamber areas in the head were adequately cooled, and water left the head via three take-off pipes to an exterior cast aluminium rail which led to the radiator – this being thought more efficient than an exit point on the head itself.

The New 3.5-Litre Engine

However it was the 3.5-litre engine from SS which aroused the most interest. Ancestry could once more be traced to Standard, but generally this 82 x 110mm six-cylinder power unit was the nearest thing to a completely new engine which had yet been produced for SS. As with the other engines in the range, it was built by the Standard Motor Company at Canley.

The bottom end of the engine followed the 2.5-litre in having seven main bearings, though steel connecting rods were used initially – there was to be some prevarication with this component however, steel or alloy rods being used in both 2.5-and 3.5-litre engines at various times as will be indicated. The 3.5-litre's block was, surprisingly, thinner than that of the 2.5, holding less coolant, and the cylinder head was fastened with two rows of 7/16-inch BSF studs instead of three half-inch BSF studs as on the 2.5 and 1.5 ohv engines (which was to make the larger engines slightly more prone to head gasket failure especially if the studs were over-enthusiastically tightened). The cast-iron head was of deep section for rigidity, and the two one and a half-inch carburetters were still bolted directly to the head as in the case of the 2.5 litre engine, via two alloy spacers, feeding an internal inlet tract.

On the opposite side of the head were two cast-iron three-branch exhaust manifolds leading to twin down

Above and below: the Standard 14hp engine and gearbox with Weslake-designed ohv head (selected as it gave more hp than a rival design submitted by Mr Grinham of Standard). A single SU was used because of mixture distribution problems with a four-cylinder engine and twin carbs.

stroke, big-end and main journals, timing gear and flywheel, though with different con-rods. As used by the Standard Motor Company, it had side valves and produced around 45bhp at 4000rpm, but for the new 1.5-litre Jaguar, an overhead valve head was used which increased this to a much more useful 65bhp at 4600rpm.

The three main bearing crankshaft and block were left much as they came from Standard, but the head of course was completely new, with vertical, pushrod operated overhead valves in lozenge-shaped combustion chambers. These had been designed in conjunction with Weslake, who say that their records show that ohv experiments for the 1.5-litre Jaguar commenced on the original 1608cc power unit. Compression ratio was 7.2:1, though later this was raised to 7.6:1. As usual, proper attention was paid to engine breathing, and an external four branch inlet manifold took the mixture from a single down-draught SU carburettor.

pipes and silencers. Conventional valve gear was used with pushrod operated rockers, although initially twin-leaf return springs were fitted between rocker and valve stem to obtain zero clearance. A large, separate aluminium water rail running the length of the cylinder head took water from the head to the radiator.

The 3.5-litre engine's displacement was 3485cc, and with a compression ratio of 7.2:1, some 120-plus bhp was claimed, which wasn't far short of the mark. It seemed that the Jaguar saloon had truly entered the 90mph class.

The new 3.5-litre engine whose 125bhp put the SS Jaguar truly into the high-performance bracket; these drawings show the rigid cast-iron block and the cylinder head with ohv valve-gear; both robust to the point of being overweight

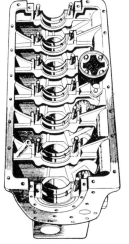
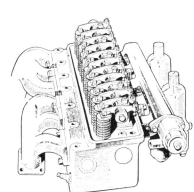

Taking the drive was a Standard gearbox similar to that used before, a double helical design with constant mesh gears contained in a cast-iron box; the gearlever was remote, and was carried together with the selector rods by the aluminium cover which extended backwards: "a simple, rigid and compact assembly" was how *The Automobile Engineer* described it, and this box was very tough and reliable too.

The drive train was continued by a Borg & Beck clutch and Hardy Spicer needle-roller universal propellor shaft to the spiral bevel rear axle of ENV manufacture. The axle casing was built from forged tubing, and the rear domed cover plate was welded in place for stiffness, the differential and drive unit being accessible via an opening at the front of the casing as previously. The Luvax (now piston instead of vane) shock absorbers were mounted on the axle casing itself, vertical links joining the chassis frame to the arms of the dampers.

Building the first all-steel Jaguars

While on first inspection the new Jaguars appeared visually much as before, in reality only the same general profile had been retained. The new chassis had increased the wheelbase an inch to 10ft. exactly on the 2.5-and 3.5-litre cars, while the track was all of 2-inches greater, which all added up to a much more roomy body. While to avoid the cost and complications of having to produce a separate chassis for the 1.5-litre car, this now used basically the same item as the larger engined cars, and the bodyshell had been standardised too. The only concession made to the 1.5-litre's reduced engine size was a

Carburettor side of the 3.5-litre Jaguar engine and gearbox; note aluminium sump, water header rail and rocker cover. This is actually a post-War unit, photographed at Foleshill.

These pictures show a post-War car, but serve to illustrate the new all-steel body very well; the rear view in particular shows how the Jaguar bodies were still made up of comparatively small panels, lead filling covering the welded seams. Note that the bodies in this production line are still carried on the original body-trucks 'invented' for the 1936 SS Jaguar. *Photos: Jaguar Cars*

smaller wheelbase of 9ft. 4.5in., accommodated by shortening the bonnet, and, of course, the frame itself. Though the wheelbase was still 4.5 in. greater than the original 1936 1.5-litre's.

The most fundamental change to the bodyshell was, of course, its new all-steel construction. This resulted in a much more efficient, if considerably noisier, assembly line; the basic layout was much as before, with virtually complete bodies eventually meeting the finished chassis at the end.

Gone was the time-consuming work in the woodmill cutting and shaping wooden frame members, and gone too was the hand-assembly and glueing of the frame ready for its panelling, except for the very small-scale production of the SS 100 (in 2.5-litre or 3.5-litre form) which was continued up until 1940. Instead, the body sub-structure was built up from pre-formed sheet steel parts as previously mentioned. Then on trolleys similar to those used for the previous range, the half-completed shell would be pulled slowly down the line as further panels and finally the outer skin were added.

It was an incredibly noisy, busy scene, well remembered by Walter Hassan who joined SS Cars shortly after the all-steel cars had commenced production. Every inch of space was used, and the gleaming naked steel of the bodies would be constantly lit up from the sparks issuing from the spot welding machines – in those days, very clumsy, caliper-like tools festooned with wires and counterbalanced by heavy weights – while all the time the nostrils would be assailed by the acrid smell of burning metal.

Once the basic sub-structure of front bulkhead, floor, rockers (or sills), rear seat pan and rear bulkhead had been assembled, the outer panels could be added. These were still in many sections, some eight or more making up the roof alone, but instead of being pinned to a wood frame, they were now flanged and spot welded together over, and onto, the steel sub-structure of the car.

This being completed, the shell moved down the track where it would be set-upon by what Hassan refers to as a "tribe called 'dingers'''; in effect panel beaters, their job was to beat out the sections where the panels didn't quite meet, getting to work with the tag-end of a file inside the car until they had succeeded in achieving a relatively good line. Then it was the turn of the lead-loaders, who would file and smooth down the joins from outside the shell, then flood the area with body solder to fill minor indentations and irregularities. The lead, which set almost immediately, would then be filed perfectly smooth so that only a minimum of stopping would be required in the paintshop. Body contours would also be perfected in the same way, so that in the building of the new shell, many pounds of lead were used.

Not that the wood mill was closed down – far from it, as it still played an important part in the business; a number of panels were made within the works, and

wooden jigs with armoured corners were required to shape the metal, or to finish items coming straight from the presses, and these were made at SS.

Viewed from the outside, the new body was seen to be sleeker and less angular than the old one, helped by the wider track and slightly longer wheelbase. Also assisting the sleek look was the fact that the front door line, bonnet sides and louvres assumed the same angle as the windscreen pillars. The same type of big, traditional radiator grille was carried at the front, but the front valance treatment was neater in that this was now formed by a casing which was in fact an extension of each front wing inwards. In the case of the larger engine cars, the impressive P100 Lucas headlights once more held sway each side of the radiator; below were twin electric horns and, mounted further out, twin pass-lights. The whole effect was dominating to say the least.

One feature of the original SS Jaguar was noticeably missing, and that was the side-mounted spare wheel in the front wing. This was now housed in the bootlid under a cover, with the tools surrounding it in rubber-filled sockets – an arrangement that was not to be permanent. One reason for this was that if the lid were to be used as an extension of the luggage boot, everything had to be unloaded to reach the spare wheel, should a puncture be suffered. So a little later, the wheel found a home underneath the boot, behind a separate hinged panel.

However the primary reason for redesigning the shell was, apart from the elimination of wood, to increase still further the amount of room inside. This aim had certainly been achieved with the 1938 car, the occupants enjoying the greater width in particular. The rear floor space was now flat, and extra leg room was provided under the front seats. In the front, the re-angled door line meant better access, and both the driver and passenger seats were wider too. The view from the driver's seat down the long bonnet was impressive, moving *The Motor* to comment in the coronation year of 1937 that "one is, in fact, reminded of the words 'might, majesty, dominion and power'''.

The 1.5-litre saloon shared most of the larger engined cars' looks, although smaller headlights were worn and no fog-or pass-lights were fitted as standard (these could, however, be ordered as 'extras' together with a chrome plated bar which was necessary for their mounting). The 1.5-litre kept its separate, plated 'torpedo' sidelights, but an identical radiator shell to the 2.5-litre. The 2.5 and 3.5-litre grilles were not identical: the 3.5-litre item was broader and had a deeper shell around the radiator cap, and had a different bonnet to accommodate it.

All three versions shared the same interior dimensions and comforts, with big, soft pleated Vaumol leather seats with Dunlopillo springing. Sound deadening had been taken very seriously, with thick underfelt on the bulkhead, under the rear seat cushions, and to a depth of half an inch under the carpets; the latter were deep pile,

The imposing frontal appearance of the all-steel Jaguar; while similar in style to the earlier car's, the front wings were brought lower, almost down to the level of the front bumper, and covered the chassis dumb-irons without a moulding outlining their shape. *Photo: Jaguar Cars*

Above: A 1938 2.5/3.5-litre all-steel saloon, this one displaying the famous leaping jaguar mascot designed by F. Gordon Crosby of *The Autocar* and sculptured by Ernest Rankin; it retailed at this time for two guineas. *Photo: Jaguar Cars*

Right: The discreetly sumptuous leather, carpet and wood interior of the 1938 Jaguar saloon; armrest could be folded up. Note rear window blind and courtesy light.

with all edges bound and piped, and with piping marking the top of the transmission tunnel where the carpet dropped away each side of the short gearlever with its pleated leather gauntlet. Heel pads were let into the driver and passenger's footwell carpets, with edge and 'X' stitching. The door trim panels contained map-pockets of pleated material in a pattern slightly reminiscent of the original SS 'sunray' design.

Attractive use was made of wood fittings inside, with wide door cappings of walnut veneer; this finish was also used on the dashboard, which had been completely redesigned. It was now all wood, and in a style which was to remain a Jaguar tradition for some 30-years, with a central instrument panel containing 5-inch rev. counter and 100mph speedometer (120mph on the 3.5-litre), combined oil pressure and water temperature gauge, ammeter, fuel gauge, cigar lighter, separate ignition switch and starter button, and 'arrowhead' light switch. The wide screen rail above contained a central handle for opening the windscreen, flanked by ashtrays, and control knobs for the individually driven windscreen wipers. Cubby holes with lids were positioned each side of the dash, smaller on the driver's side because of the steering column; manual advance and retard ignition controls were still provided around the steering wheel boss, together with a self-cancelling indicator switch. The handbrake was between the seats, and organ-type foot pedals were used.

It was all good, old-fashioned British quality, conservative even in 1938 maybe, but it was what the purchaser of a larger sports saloon expected, and so Lyons gave it to him – at an incredibly low price, for the three saloon models were, in order of ascending engine size, £298, £395 and £445.

As usual, there was nothing else on the British market to match the value for money which the new range of Jaguars offered. The 3.5-litre proved to be capable of exceeding 90mph comfortably, and you had to dig deep into your wallet to purchase something which could outrun it. Amongst the few saloons numbered in this group, the Alvis Speed 25 could touch 97mph from a similar cubic capacity, but cost almost exactly double the Jaguar at £885 for the four-light saloon (the 100mph 4.3 was £995); the Lagonda 4.5-litre needed an extra litre to return a similar figure, with £875 being asked for the chassis *alone* (the legendary V12 Rapide had a maximum of some 105mph but set you back all of £1600); while the Bentley 4.5-litre, which required an extremely spartan body to achieve much more than 95mph, was marked up at £1150 for chassis only ....

As for *direct* rivals, there really weren't any; nothing you could buy at the same price as the SS offered equal or better performance, a similar standard of equipment, and as much comfort. The "characteristic shapeliness" of the car's looks (as *The Autocar* put it) was almost a bonus. Cecil Kimber attempted to challenge it with the 2561cc WA, announced at the 1938 Motor Show; this had similar styling to that of the preceeding SA and VA models, and was to be the last big-engined MG saloon – Lyons had simply made it too hot for anyone else in the 2.5/3.5-litre sports saloon class to survive.

For the larger (16ft. 2in. as opposed to 15ft. 6in. overall length) WA was no faster than the 2.5-litre Jaguar, and distinctly slower than the 3.5, with no appreciable advantage in handling although the hydraulic brakes were a point in favour for the Abingdon car. Yet despite the backing and production expertise of the giant Morris concern, the WA cost £47 more than the 2.5-litre Jaguar, and was only £3 cheaper than the 3.5-litre car. A meagre 369 WAs left the factory, and production had been wound up before the advent of World War Two; over 1000 more 2.5-litre Jaguar saloons alone had been built in the same period by SS.

The 1.5-litre Jaguar was, pound for pound, even better value than it larger sisters, as it was sold at cost or even at a loss. In the first two-years of production, an astonishing 3754 1.5-litre saloons had been turned out by Foleshill, and in that number lies the clue to its incredibly low price tag of £298. Lyons, with considerable faith in his products, had costed for a long production run to bring down the unit price, and it was thanks to the comparatively large numbers of 1.5-litre cars sold that overhead charges were reduced and so made it possible to produce the fewer numbers of 2.5- and 3.5-litre models at the price that they were – by themselves they would have been prohibitively expensive.

Despite a performance which has always been

Well-equipped dashboard of the 1938 Jaguar, showing windscreen in the open position; note separate controls for each wiper, and telescopic steering column. Rev. counter and speedometer are for a 1.5-litre.

The 1.5-litre SS Jaguar represented amazing value for money; bonnet length was shorter but internal space and comforts were exactly as for the 2.5- and 3.5-litre cars.

overshadowed by that given by the other two engine options, the smaller Jaguar was actually amongst the quicker 1.5-litre cars of the period, and far better equipped than most. It undersold the 1.5-litre Riley by almost £15 and was no slower than this car from the old-established manufacturer just down the road from Holbrook Lane. The 1818cc Wolseley 14 might have been a contender at £285, but it was all too obviously a Morris with a different radiator grille. No, the Jaguars stood alone, in a class created entirely by Lyons.

The Drophead Coupe Jaguar

We have not yet touched upon the most opulent of the new Jaguar range, perhaps the most impressive of all the 'traditional' Jaguars. This was, of course, the drophead coupe, a body style which suited the cars well, and was offered on all three chassis.

The new variant was far from being a saloon with the top cut off and a collection of hood sticks and canvas substituted. It was a veritable work of art in its own right. The body shell itself was heavily modified, with two extremely wide doors instead of the saloon's four, and there was a certain reversion to coachbuilding techniques in that it was necessary to use wood again, particularly in the back section of the car, around the body from door pillar to door pillar. This was to replace the stiffness lost with the removal of the roof, and to provide a mounting for the soft top itself.

SS had produced one drophead before, that based on the S.S.1 in 1935, but the new SS Jaguar version was even better thought out. Termed a "wig top" in the trade because it emulated the original steel shape almost exactly, the contours of the hood were built up with layers of horsehair, and finished inside with a full headlining which folded integrally with the top – and which, unlike the S.S.1 drophead, also covered the hood mechanism. Two positions were possible – for the first, the cant rails at the front could be released and folded back by moving two spring bolts and undoing two butterfly nuts, which allowed the front peak to be removed from the top screen rail and rolled back with the material to a position just behind the driver, where it could be secured by straps; this was the *coupé de ville* position. Or, the exterior hood-irons could be 'broken' and the entire head then folded backwards to drop into a space behind the rear seat squab flush with the top of the luggage compartment, to be covered by a separate hood envelope. It was a reasonably easy operation for one person, with assistance being given by spring loading in the hood mechanism. The stylish hood-irons were, incidentally, made from bronze which ensured the durability of the plated finish.

A little interior space was lost to the drophead, rear seat passengers loosing an inch or so of the headroom because of the slightly more pronounced shelving of the roofline towards the rear, while to allow stowage room for the head, the rear seat squab was more upright and had been brought forward some three inches at the top. The contours of the front seat squabs were also slightly altered to match.

A drophead coupe body style came with the all-steel bodyshell, and was to prove extremely popular especially in countries with hot climates. When folded the hood was covered by an envelope.

This picture shows a pre-War RAC Rally competitor demonstrating the *coupe de ville* position of the Drophead's top; note straps securing hood behind driver.

Metallic-finish on a pre-War Drophead; a highly elegant car but rear vision was fairly abysmal, as witnessed by the pillar-box slit rear window. *Photo: Autocar*

The 1.5-litre SS Jaguar Drophead Coupe; this example, one of the few in existence, is owned by SS Register member Peter Pearson. *Photo: P. Skilleter*

The 2.5-litre Drophead, this one from 1938 and restored by Tom Chalmer. *Photo P. Skilleter*

The drophead Jaguars were a little heavier than their closed counterparts, but in fact lost little in the way of performance. They were imposing and eye-catching cars, the chrome plated hood-irons contrasting with the various pastel shades of hood material which were offered – French or gunmetal grey, and dark sand, though black was available if required. The chief disadvantage of the model, shared with most dropheads of the era, was a distinct lack of visibility towards the rear: with the top erected, vision was sharply cut off from the door pillar backwards. The pillar-box slit of a rear window, only 4.5in. by 22in., did little to alleviate the situation, and

wing mirrors were not even listed as extras!

Mind you, a useful range of accessories did become available to those who wanted to further adorn their cars. A popular option were the Ace wheel discs to cover the wire wheels, in three styles – black or polished aluminium at £9.17s.6d. a set, cellulosed to match the colour of the car at £11.2s.6d, or for a really dazzling effect, chrome plated all over for £13.2s.6d. These prices were slightly reduced for 1.5-litre models, which could be fitted with the same Lucas FT 58 plated fog lamps as the 2.5/3.5-litre cars for £2.12s.6d, plus £1 for the special chromium plated bar required, and 7/6d for fitting.

'Badge carriers' could also purchase a plated badge bar for 12/6d ("not suitable for fog lamps"), a translucent rear number plate (illuminated rear plates became compulsory in October 1938 anyway) with matching polished aluminium front plate at £1.7s.6d, a model K628 Philco radio set (which at 15 guineas plus £3 for fitting was still something of an expensive novelty in the late 'thirties), and a set (two) of fitted trunks for the locker at £4.4s.0d. These were fabric covered plywood, angled at the front to accommodate the slope of the boot lid as it closed; apparently not many were sold, and few survive today.

For all models, SS still provided a wide range of interesting colours – three greens, three greys, maroon, dark blue, ivory, gunmetal, honeysuckle, and black. Similar hues of trim were available for the interior, matched to the exterior paintwork, and you could specify pigskin grain leather too. If you wanted to deviate from the standard paint/trim combinations you could do so, at £2.0s.0d extra, while a non-standard exterior colour to your choice would cost £5; though this was increased to £10 if you required Pearl Essence (an attractive metallic-type finish) or white. Wheels finished in a contrasting colour incurred a charge of £5 per set of five, and a non-standard upholstery colour £2.10s.0d. So it was quite possible, using this facility of choice, to order a car which would be unique.

Testing the 3.5-Litre SS Jaguar

To *The Motor* fell the honour of first testing the new 3.5-litre Jaguar saloon; they gave it a highly enthusiastic reception. "It is a fine car with a fine performance; indeed this is so outstanding that the driver finds himself in possession of a degree of acceleration and maximum speed more in keeping with a *voiture de course* than with a full five-seater saloon". Translated into figures, this meant a 0-50mph acceleration time of nine-seconds dead, and a top speed of 91mph – the latter remarkable in view of the car's total disregard for any sort of aerodynamic efficiency. The acceleration was firmly in the top league too, the car being over a second quicker to 50mph than such revered thoroughbreds as the Speed 25 Alvis and the 4.5-litre LG6 Lagonda – at virtually *twice and three times the price* of the SS respectively!

Top gear pick-up was exceptional too, and in fact the 30-50mph time of 8.5 seconds was fractionally better than the four-speed manual XJ6 4.2 of 40 years later. But those who wanted to use the gearbox found it "very likeable" according to *The Motor*, with its close ratios and 76mph third gear. "The action of the remote control lever is so pleasant that most drivers will use the gearbox fairly constantly for the sheer driving pleasure to be obtained therefrom. The change from third to top demands simply de-clutching and pushing the lever straight through ..."

But as the journal went on to say: "Such performance

This picture has been seen before, but it is worth using simply to show the "SS" motif displayed on the Foleshill factory wall before the 2.5/3.5 saloon; plaques by door denote the registered offices of the Swallow Coachbuilding Co., and SS Cars Ltd.
Photo: Jaguar Cars

would be useless were not the roadholding, suspension, steering and brakes fully in keeping", then allayed fears by continuing, "All are just about as good as a first-class engineering and a tremendously enthusiastic executive can make them". Nor did good handling mean an uncomfortable ride for the passengers:

"Although the car holds the road as if running on rails, there is no tendency whatever towards harsh springing, and the Jaguar is one of the few cars which provides the rear seat passengers with as high a degree of comfort as that enjoyed by those seated in front. Over rough surfaces there is a gentle rise and fall, which does not increase should the road conditions deteriorate suddenly into a series of potholes.

The vertical steering wheel position was liked, and combined with a well-shaped bucket seat, was thought to "add materially to the ease with which the Jaguar is controlled". The task of affecting the right compromise between steering ratio and lightness had been successfully accomplished according to *The Motor*, "so that on the open road, while cruising at 70mph, the car is directed more by the action of the wrists than anything else". Castor action at lower speeds was quite marked, and the magazine considered that the car would be suitable for "tackling alpine passes with their numerous hairpin bends".

That other vital chassis ingredient, braking, apparently came up to scratch, though it may be an indication that increased speed was catching up with the rod-operated design when the journal merely described them, almost in passing, as "adequate", thereafter leaving the subject entirely alone. Wind noise was certainly a feature of the car's square-rigged shape, and *The Motor* did venture to say that over 70mph this blended with increased engine noise, though "the general effect is exhilarating".

Fixtures and fittings were liked as usual, including the new dash: "The instrument panel contains everything that could be required, and the design of the facia board is dignified". The spare wheel had by this time (May 1938) been transferred to a position underneath the boot floor, and below the 14-gallon fuel tank, allowing the tool tray to occupy the whole width of the boot lid, while the luggage locker itself was "large enough to enable golf clubs to be carried lengthways". So a good reception from *The Motor* on the occasion of its first road test of the 3.5-litre Jaguar.

Show time, 1938 – the SS Jaguar stand at Earls Court with Drophead and Saloon four-seaters on display, plus the one-off closed SS 100 with its foreshadowing of XK 120 lines. Few changes to the range were announced for 1939. *Photo: Motor*

Meanwhile, the same 3.5-litre engine had also been inserted in the SS 100 sports car, which gave it an electrifying performance with a quite genuine 100mph maximum. Although little more than 300 SS 100s of all types were built before production ceased in 1940, they were extremely successful in rallies and won 1st-class awards in a number of the 'classics'; they were capable of giving a good account of themselves on the race track too. At £445, the 3.5-litre SS Jaguar 100 was almost certainly the cheapest 100mph car ever to be offered to the public on a true production basis, and it did much to enhance Jaguar's reputation as a performance car manufacturer.

The 1939 SS Jaguar range

The all-steel Jaguar range had hardly been in full production four-months when the traditional mid-year 'new model announcements' of that time demanded that SS release details of its 1939 range. This was duly accomplished in July 1938, but there were few changes to report; which at least proved that the formula was right, and indeed it was not to change in essence until 1948. About the only alteration was a change of rear spring camber.

Testing the 1.5-Litre SS Jaguar

The slightly overweight 'baby' of the Jaguar range came up for test in July 1938, *The Autocar* putting the 1776cc, 26.5cwt car through its paces. But any suggestion that a reduced power to weight ratio compared to the larger engined versions had produced an uninteresting or lesser car were scorned by the journal. "Straightaway", it said, "one takes to the car, not only on account of the good acceleration it proves to possess, and its ready and quiet way of running fast, but also for its whole style ... A striking part of the running is the absence of effort or any impression of travelling specially fast at a maintained speed of 60mph or thereabouts".

True, the 0-50mph time of 17-seconds was only average for the cubic capacity, but once on the move the 1.5-litre was probably a quicker car than this figure suggests. "There is the feeling of considerable reserve existing, and ... at the more generally used rates between 30mph and 50mph this is a particularly easy running car".

And, while *The Autocar* did not consider it sufficiently important to mention the fact in the text of its road test, there was the all-important advantage of moderate thirst, 25-27mpg being listed in the data box. This compared with the 18-20mpg recorded by *The Motor* for the 3.5-litre car, and it also gave the 1.5-litre a useful touring range from the 14-gallon tank of 350 to 400-miles.

What power the engine could supply was given readily, and aided by a pleasant gearbox with a very useful close-ratio third providing almost 60mph. "The red limit area on the rev. counter starts at 4500rpm, but the needle can be taken nearly to the 5000rpm mark before the engine feels that it is being forced... The gear change is pleasing, by a short, rigid remote-control lever... The gears are satisfactorily quiet, without being silent".

One could possibly criticise the 1.5-litre for its average performance if it had been the only model made by SS; but as the same company also offered one of the quickest production saloon cars available in much the same package, it becomes unfair to do so in the circumstances. Not everyone wanted or needed a 90mph top speed, so quite rightly Lyons catered for them too, offering comfort, dignity and quality at a uniquely low price.

The Autocar's **road test 1.5-litre, willing if not exactly fast. Crossover air silencing for the downdraught SU is clearly visible, as is the sliding roof panel 'disappearing' into rear roof section.** *Photo: Autocar*

Layout of tool compartment in the 1938 1.5-litre Jaguar; note light in tool tray lid and brackets at top of boot opening to take luggage straps. *Photo: Autocar.*

Testing the 2.5-Litre SS Jaguar

The next rung up the SS ladder, the 2.5-litre saloon, was tried by *The Motor* in June 1939, just a month or so before the new – and alas necessarily short-lived – 1940 range was announced. The writer did not beat about the bush: "The 2.5-litre Jaguar is one of the best-looking cars on the road today and a prolonged road test showed conclusively that beauty, in this case, is very far from being skin deep. It is difficult to imagine a more successful blending of utility and good looks, nor is it easy to think of a car costing less than £400 which has such an inspiring road performance combined with such high-quality workmanship".

The "inspiring road performance" meant a top speed of 87mph, and acceleration to 50mph and 60mph respectively of 10.6 and 17 seconds; in other words, the 2.5-litre Jaguar could reach 60mph in the same time that the 1.5-litre took to gain 50mph. "A glance at the acceleration and maximum speed figures obtained at Brooklands show that the Jaguar is one of the fastest 2.5-litre saloon models in existence", underlined *The Motor*, which continued by saying that this performance "is accomplished without sacrifice of quietness of running or other motoring amenities".

Nor was there any suggestion of flat spots, temperament or loss of tune – this last being an especially valuable Jaguar attribute: "In point of fact", said the writer, "the model tested had been used for extensive hack work and did its thousand miles of main road motoring before the track was reached, so that one may assume sustained performance over a long period". An increasing number of Jaguar owners could vouch for that too.

However, constant use of the gearbox wasn't mandatory for the attainment of good average speeds as a 30-50mph top gear time of 9.4 seconds proves – this compares favourably with the XJ6 3.4 overdrive saloon's 9.2 seconds, though of course the older car looses out heavily in higher speed ranges. The car certainly didn't object to

fast driving: "On the road the car gives a great impression of safety, due largely to the low build and careful attention to suspension. The possibilities of high speed cornering are considerable, and during such activities the passengers do not tend to be thrown sideways... The gearbox deserves high praise because the synchromesh action is particularly effortless and rapid... The Jaguar steers accurately, and at night the head lamps throw a widespread and powerful beam. The Girling brakes have to deal with speeds approaching 90mph and do so in a downright inspiring manner".

Visibility was rated as good, and the steering wheel fell "nicely to hand". The interior design was well liked too: "... a really well proportioned exterior is so often spoilt by a flamboyant interior. The Jaguar has no tendency towards the ornate, and yet the trim leather and woodwork of the interior of the car would do credit to the finest examples of British coachwork available". Also appreciated were thoughful details like the comfortable angle of the pedals, the tools set in their individual containers, and the "general accessibility of all the working parts". So in all, another good press for SS Cars Ltd!

Testing the 1939-model 3.5-Litre SS Jaguar

Finally, a 3.5-litre saloon was tried by *The Autocar* in April 1939, the journal not having sampled the type for a full road test before that date. The performance figures were fairly consistent with *The Motor's*, 50mph being reached in 9.8 seconds through the gears, and the top gear increment of 30-50mph being covered in 8.7 seconds as opposed to 8.5 seconds for the other journal. Maximum speed was slightly down at 88.2mph mean, with a best one-way speed of just on 91mph. Fuel consumption was reckoned to be 16-18mpg, which is probably more representative of a hard-driven 3.5-litre than *The Motor's* 18-20mph figure.

The same current of enthusiasm ran through this

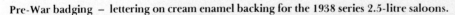

Pre-War badging – lettering on cream enamel backing for the 1938 series 2.5-litre saloons.

report as could be detected in previous Jaguar tests. It was noted that the use of a large engine did not tempt the manufacturer into burdening it with the biggest possible body, but instead retained medium sized dimensions to make a car which "can be geared reasonably high for ease of running, and at the same time afford exceptional acceleration". As for the Jaguar's character, *The Autocar* had this to say:

"It is decidedly in the category of a 'driver's car', for there is that ready response to the throttle pedal to satisfy anyone who likes to send the speedometer needle soaring on the main roads, and it handles well, too. Even on a run of the 300 mile category it is hardly possible to force it in this country, for maximum revs are 4500 to about 4800, giving rather more than 90mph, and this range of engine speed is usable comfortably on top gear.
"Somewhere around 60mph is reached almost automatically on sufficiently clear roads, and between 60 and 70 is the natural maintainable pace. On a journey the 3.5-litre Jaguar displays the highly valuable faculty of putting up nearly as good as average when no conscious effort is made to hurry as on an occasion when the driver definitely sets out to make the best use of every open stretch of road."

Some pinking was noticed on hard acceleration, but the manual retard control could be used to control it, and when picking up from below 20mph it felt better to engage third instead of top, so perhaps a little of the engine's flexibility had gone. There was also a slight noise period at 60mph in top, and "wind noise was more evident than mechanical noise at higher speeds". But under all normal conditions, the engine was "delightfully smooth ... silkily so, indeed, during leisurely driving". It was not averse to pulling and holding quite high revs for a large unit, 4800rpm being held during the maximum speed timing, which was equivalent to a full 90mph.

At these speeds the car felt "safely steady" with the well-placed steering wheel conveying only a little road movement to the driver. Some 2.75 turns lock-to-lock were required for the car's turning circle of 38ft., and one deduces that a little effort was needed at the wheel for low-speed parking manoeuvres – castor action was marked at medium to high speeds, but not lower down. The Girling brakes were quite up to standard, a light pressure on the pedal being adequate most of the time, while "a more determined pressure brings the car up sharply in an emergency".

Ride and road-holding passed muster easily, with good lateral stability in cornering and an absence of harshness over rough surfaces both being noted. The P100 headlights provided a "magnificent beam for fast night driving", and the horns were "melodious yet powerful"; all the incidental controls on the dashboard worked well and were easily reached. The luggage space was thought "decidedly useful", and the "excellent and rare" feature of a reserve petrol tank was commented on (the tap was placed beneath the filler cap on the exterior of the car).

Above: A feature of earlier Jaguars was the reserve petrol tap under the filler cap – but it did mean you had to get out and run round the back of the car to operate it, which could be a nuisance on a busy highway!

Left: The 3.5-litre SS Jaguar was an extremely fast car, capable of over 90mph and with acceleration better than that of many sports cars; *The Motor* found that cruising at, or near, maximum did not bother it either.

An interesting insight into what it was like to own and drive a 3.5-litre Jaguar in the late 1930s is provided by Rodney Walkerly, who as Sports Editor of *The Motor* drove his black 1938 saloon all over Europe, averaging some 454 miles a week and covering 20 000 miles in twelve months' motoring under all conditions. It reeled off this mileage without any attention bar routine servicing and a tappet adjustment at 10 000 miles (when only three needed altering.) To quote Rodney:

"You can buy this car from two motives: elegance of bodywork or performance on the road – for it has both in a big way... The amusing thing is that at such a small outlay you can take on anything on the road. The car goes so fast that I have been too lazy to bother about checking the speedometer, but an exactly similar car as road tested by us did 92mph on top and 76mph on third. Either my speedometer is a thought on the right side or I have a slightly better car, but, after 1000-miles of running-in at under 50mph, mine did 94mph, and once, on that bad leg of the Rheims circuit, which starts with a downhill rush and goes level for the rest, it did 96mph, and held it, three up and with luggage.

"Such a car is at its best abroad, where the roads are long and straight and high speeds become really safe. The 3.5-litre runs like a train at 70mph, with no sound from engine or back axle, and only the soft roar of the wind past the body to suggest that the speed is really quite high. ...In point of fact, the autobahn cruising speed in Germany was a steady and really comfortable 80mph for an hour or two on end, during which the thermometer never moved above 75 degrees.

"As for springing, the SS is on the sports-car side – firm and stable – but is by no means harsh at any speed. Rear-seat passengers will tell you how comfortable the back-seat ride is.

"The road-holding, of course, is famous. No need for me to talk azout how the car corners and handles generally as a sports car should, although this is a full five-seater touring saloon and by no means a racer. So far there is no appreciable wear in the springs, no rattles to the body, and no kick in the steering....

"Possibly the most noteworthy feature is the ability to reach high speeds in very short stretches of road. One touches the loud pedal a bit and the car is doing 50mph right away and 70mph a moment or two later. There is no sensation of pace at all and no difference in the handling of the car between 50mph and 80mph, except that one gets to the corners more quickly.

"Apart from the known acceleration and high speeds of the SS, there are three features which are really oustandingly good – (a) the driving position, (b) the lights, and (c) the brakes.

"The first is really well thought out. There you sit with both front wings in view, and a steering wheel which goes up or down at will, so that you can get just the right hold on it (in my case, I sit well back and keep the wheel at arm's length – I like it that way), the seat is springy, but firm, and there's plenty of elbow room plus a neat arm-rest.

"The P100 Lucas head lamps are simply terrific and the dip throws the light just where it's wanted at night when meeting other cars. In addition, the two Lucas road lights or pass lights, or whatever they call them, are 100% for fog driving and are quite powerful enough for normal night driving without head lights at all.

"Girling brakes need no introduction. I will merely say that they are right up to their job, with even so fast a car as this, wear evenly, do not get out of adjustment, and wear very slowly.

"The gearbox is the next thing which merits a word of praise. This is delightful to use. With this car you can drive in top and third all day, but if you want to go all sporty that box will play every tune you require; the change is child's play, the ratios are silent, and the effect on the car when you use the neat little handle is what they call electrifying.

"Taken all round, at £445, I can't think how they do it."

The aforegoing is a very fair word-picture of the big pre-War Jaguar saloon – tough, reliable, extremely fast and with subtle touches surprising for a car with such a relatively short pedigree. The 'simply terrific' P100 head-lamps, incidentally, were originally designed by Lucas during 1927 as a reaction to Rolls-Royce using continental lamps such as Zeiss and Marchal instead of a Lucas product. Harold Nockolds relates how "the negotiations that went on the Lucas to get them at a price Lyons could afford were long and intricate", and these also stipulated that they must carry a different medallion – that as a sop to Rolls-Royce, though the latter nevertheless remained a little peeved to see the upstart SS concern supplied with the P100!

The 1940 SS Jaguar range

As 1939 drew on the future did not look bright for the motor industry, or indeed for Europe itself, and in fact the second World War only months away; but already most of the car manufacturers had planned their 1940 range of vehicles, and so went ahead and announced them during the summer of 1939 – though probably with some doubts as to whether they would ever get into full-scale production with them. SS Cars Ltd released details of their new range in July of that year.

In a nutshell, the 1940 Jaguars were 'the same but different'; that is, no far-reaching changes had been made which effected the basic design of the cars, but on the other hand, many detail improvements were to be found.

Visually, the 1940 cars were little changed; the 'New Alto' twin-tone horns were no longer carried in full view on the front valance, and instead 'Mellowtone' horns were employed, tucked away out of sight underneath, while at the back of the car, it was apparent that the spare wheel compartment lid had been enlarged. This now extended right up to the boot lid and gave easier access to the spare wheel, which being carried higher, did not need the extra complication of a rear bumper which hinged down to allow it to be withdrawn as had been the case with the previous arrangement.

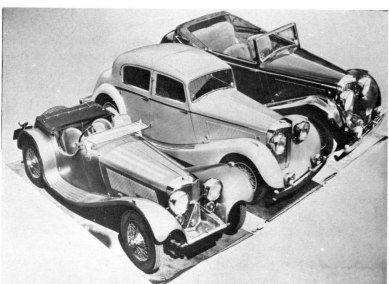

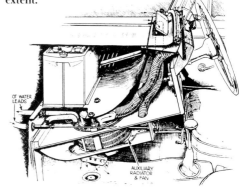

Above: **The 1939 SS Jaguar 2.5-litre, illustrated by** *The Motor* **in cutaway form.**
Left: **The 1940 SS Jaguar range of Sports car, Saloon and Drophead.**
Below: **Diagram of the 'air-conditioning' which came with the 1940 Jaguar range; flap on scuttle allowed 'fresh-air' heating and ventilation to an extent.**

But arousing most interest was what SS rather optimistically called "air conditioning". This was heralded as something of a breakthrough, though in reality it was nothing more than a fresh-air heater with a demist facility. But it should be remembered that up until then, a heater hadn't even figured as an extra for the Jaguar; and, in Great Britain indeed, it was not until the late sixties that you could be assured of this rather elementary aid to comfort being supplied as standard equipment in your average new car.

The system used by SS was simple enough by today's standards, but warranted detailed and lengthy descriptions in the motoring press to explain its workings to the reader unaccustomed to such heights of automotive refinement. To be fair, though, it was not simply a recirculatory 'fug-stirrer' but possessed a fresh-air intake which ducted clean air from a vent on top of the scuttle to the heat exchanger mounted horizontally beneath it inside

the car. This took hot water from the engine's cooling system via a valve that could be controlled by the driver or passenger. Inside the round heater element was an electric blower with a rheostat control, and this pushed the warmed air into the car interior via controllable shutters.

A secondary function of the system was to demist the windscreen, effected by ducting hot air from the heater to outlets at the bottom of the screen between glass and screen rail. It was claimed that the entire windscreen could be cleared of 30 degrees of frost "in a few seconds", but I think owners of the cars – even when new – would tend to disagree! But it was a good try, and a step in the right direction.

Widespread changes affected the trimming of the 1940 Jaguars. Completely new upholstery and door trim patterns wrought the biggest changes in this department since the SS Jaguar was first launched in 1935. The familiar – and conventional – pleated finish to the seats had been replaced by plain hides, a throw-back to the Airline pattern of 1934, and the door trim had been simplified "with the object of attaining a greater dignity in style". However, it must be pointed out that SS were not entirely consistent with their trim styles, as a picture of the 1940 range in *The Autocar* shows a saloon with pleated seats... The new style front seats offered greater lateral support through the use of side rolls, and had the further novelty of a small chromium plated handle mounted under the cushion at the front which, when turned, raised or lowered the seat. This, together with the normal fore-and-aft adjustment of the seat, and the telescopic steering wheel, certainly gave a wide range of driving positions.

Rear seat passengers were offered something new too, in the form of picnic tables of walnut veneer which folded into the backs of the front seat squabs. Smacking of gimmicry though were the ashtrays positioned above the tables which popped outwards on the pressing of a button... Luggage compartment trim had been revised, partly of course because its layout had been changed following the repositioning of the spare wheel, which also incurred a loss of space – although mitigated to some extent by a shallower lid, some two inches in height and two in depth had gone; rubber mats in the now flat-floored boot had been replaced by rubber guard strips on metal panels finished in body colour. The boot lid handle was now a vertical 'streamlined' shape, instead of the horizontal 'T' shaped item fitted from 1936.

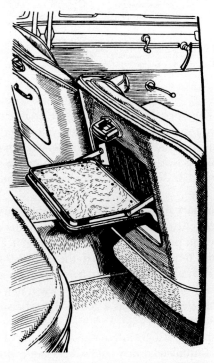

Sketch showing the picnic tables and plain leather upholstery of the short-lived 1940 range.

Rather fewer changes had taken place in the mechanical specifications of the cars; piston-type dampers replaced the previous vane-type, ground clearance was increased through revised springs, and on the 3.5-litre engine, the return springs on the valve rockers were replaced by coil springs at the lower ends of the pushrods. On the 2.5-litre steel connecting rods replaced the alloy ones (at engine no. L 1051), while the 1.5-litre now had a horizontal SU carburettor instead of the previous vertical instrument. To meet criticisms of slightly heavy steering at low speeds, the ratio had been lowered slightly on all cars, and now gave about 3 turns lock-to-lock instead of the previous 2.75.

The 'Special Equipment' 1.5-Litre SS Jaguar

There had been an interesting development in connection with the 1.5-litre Jaguar however, in that a "Special Equipment" model was introduced, the first time that SS had used the designation which after the war was to be so familiar to purchasers of the XK sports cars. As applied to the 1.5-litre, it meant that those specifying a Special Equipment car obtained not only the chassis improvements listed in the previous paragraphs, but also the 'air conditioning plant', the multi-adjustable front seats, the folding picnic tables, a better finished luggage compartment, pleated upholstery, "super beam headlights", and Lucas FT57 fog lamps.

Surprisingly, prices had not been increased although naturally the purchaser of the 1.5-litre Special Equipment models was required to find some extra cash – the SE saloon was £20 dearer at £318, and a similar increase brought the SE coupe up to £338. Still superb value for money though, by any standard.

Testing the 1940-model 2.5-Litre SS Jaguar

The Autocar managed to publish one test of a 1940 series car before such activities ceased in deference to the war effort and petrol rationing. Already, higher octane fuels were unavailable at the pump and so the 2.5-litre saloon supplied had a lowered compression ratio; this, and the loss of Brookland's outer circuit for testing, had its effect on the figures, but the car still managed to reach 80mph in less than a mile.

This was about 7mph down on the normal 2.5-litre's top speed, and at 19.5 seconds to 60mph, some 2-seconds had been lost there too. Pinking occured when accelerating from low speeds but could be minimised through the use of the ignition control still fitted, at the expense of a temporary loss of performance, but it seems that on the plus side, the lower compression ratio (affected by means of a plate between head and block) provided even greater smoothness and flexibility, the engine being quite happy

Above: **The 1.5-litre 'Special Equipment' Saloon; the car still kept its separate sidelights though.**

Left: **Wartime Jaguar: 2.5/3.5 Saloon fitted with blackout headlight attachments.**

to trickle along at 5mph in top without snatch. It still revved to 4500 or even 5000rpm if required, and cruising speeds of up to 70mph did not appear forced.

The gearbox was capable of making excellent use of this capacity for revs, and was much liked: "Third is a strikingly useful ratio, and second is admirable for the steeper kind of hill or a burst of acceleration". But more gentle techniques employing coasting and a 50mph crusing speed brought a useful 25mpg, some 20% better than normal.

The usual pleasant road manners of the Jaguar were noted: "This car is driven without need for active concentration. It goes into a corner 'on the level', is steered round by hardly more than a light finger action, and comes into the straight again 'all in one piece.' The suspension is a good compromise. It affords this stability, but is never harsh, conforming to the test that passengers and driver do not notice for any particular reason the kind of surface they are traversing". The lower geared steering had "gained in lightness...but at the same time has lost nothing in directness and accuracy of control. There is decisive but not aggresive caster action...and the driver is conscious all the time of having precise regulation over the car's position, aided by the excellence of the driving position".

Variations on the SS theme by private coachbuilders were fairly rare before the War – Maltby's Ltd of Folkestone produced this slightly Germanic Drophead for Mr & Mrs Francis Redfern, elongating the SS's tail *(right)*. Meanwhile the Saloon came in for razor-edge treatment from Mulliners of Birmingham (to the design of Capt. Black of Standards for Mrs Black) and from an unknown coachbuilder who constructed this rather more angular body *(above)*.

The new unpleated style of upholstery fitted in this saloon was considered "attractive", but of the new heater and demister, the magazine did not go into detail apart from saying that it was "of very great value". A reminder of wartime conditions was the mention of lighting – no more glorious P100 motoring, just the masked beam of a single pass-light...

With the outbreak of war in September 1939, car production had been drastically reduced at Foleshill, which was now being geared up for war work. The earliest casualty had been the coupe, a low volume car anyway for SS, and none were produced after 1939. Saloons continued to be assembled from parts in stock, 68 3.5-litre, 135 2.5-litre, and 688 1.5-litre cars leaving the factory during 1940 – the obvious popularity of the 27mpg car showing clearly in a petrol-conscious Britain!

In fact, some development work was carried out on the 1.5-litre before it too finally left the scene, the last few months of production allowing William Heynes to try out a new type of rear axle. This was the Salisbury 'hypoid' bevel drive unit, and due to its pinion being well below the centre line of the crown wheel, the propeller shaft could be lowered some two inches, which resulted in a shallower transmission tunnel and thus more room inside the car. SS Cars were pioneers in fitting this type of axle, which did not become universal until well after the war. The new axle entailed some minor changes to the chassis frame of the 1.5-litre, and a rearrangement of the brakes.

The company's accounts for the last peacetime financial year were presented to shareholders on November 22nd 1939; Lyons stating that a record trading profit

Before War work took over, Heynes introduced the hypoid rear axle on the 1.5-litre SS Jaguar which became one of the first British cars to be so equipped. *Photo: Jaguar Cars*

The Swiss coachbuilders Tuscher of Zurich remodelled one of the original 1936-type Jaguar Saloons to produce this drophead.

The closed coupe illustrated (now in the States) was also based on the original Jaguar Saloon, and bore a certain resemblance to SS's own fixed-head SS100 of 1938.

of £60,461 had been made – double that of the year before. But ever cautious, Lyons had decided to husband resources and did not recommend that a dividend be paid, due to the "financing of the reorganisation and the preliminary work prior to full (war) production, the provision of further plant and machinery, the increased taxation now in force, and the air raid protection for our employees". Also, a resolution was passed to increase the Ordinary Capital of the Company by £100 000 should the need arise, though in fact this was not to be taken up until well after the War was over.

Obviously, with its production difficulties ironed out, the new all-steel Jaguar range had been a big success. In total, 8252 cars had been built from 1938 until 1940, and when broken down, this was how the sales had gone: 1.5-litre, – 4442 saloons, 643 coupes; 2.5-litre – 1585 saloons, 273 coupes; 3.5-litre – 1071 saloons, 238 coupes. A large new extension to the factory had been completed, and the future had looked bright. But for the moment, cars would have to be forgotten, and a different sort of work undertaken....

Much important work rebuilding aircraft was taken on by SS during the War, though at first Jaguar's fitters had difficulty meeting Air Ministry standards – Sir William still thinks that in view of the desperate urgency for aircraft in those days, certain short-cuts could, and should, have been taken.

The factory at War

SS Cars took on a bewildering number of tasks as various armament contracts were entered into, effectively demonstrating the company's versatility – no less than 56 separate items were to be produced in all. The first project was the building of the flaps and other major wing components for the Stirling bomber, and so efficient were the SS fitters at the new job that Peter Craig, who was to become Jaguar's Plant Director years later, recalled that the experts from Stirling actually came down to see how on earth the output was being achieved, as it was greater than their own! Then came the repair of Whitley bombers, though this was more difficult as it entailed meeting the extremely rigid Aeronautical Inspection Directorate requirements – virtually the entire aircraft had to be dismantled and rebuilt to almost new specification. SS test-flew the finished aeroplanes from their own airfield, which had been commandeered for them at Tachbrook, near Leamington Spa.

Wellington bombers were repaired too, and thousands of small components manufactured for Spitfire, Lancaster, Mosquito, and Oxford Airspeed craft, plus gun-control parts and cartridge feed boxes in quantity. A new factory had been constructed especially for the building of the new Manchester bomber, but when this was cancelled by Beaverbrook, it was turned over to other work.

Slightly more allied to the company's peacetime work was the construction of trailers, these being made at the rate of nearly 700 a week and in a diversity of sizes and types – mule carts, 10cwt amphibious trailers, special airborne trailers, 10cwt wood trailers, and huge 6-ton fuselage trailers. The subsidiary Swallow Sidecar Company meanwhile undertook to meet the entire requirements of the Army, RAF, and Admiralty for

Just a small part of the enormous output of trailers from Foleshill. Note shelters on left. *Photo: Jaguar Cars*

Walter Hassan demonstrating the lightweight VA 'jeep'! It had an air-cooled JAP engine.

motorcycle sidecars of all types. Amongst the trailers constructed were those for Commander Wingate's famous jungle exploits – they had to be light enough to be airlifted, and capable of being pulled by mule, jeep or just manpower; they were built from rough sketches in a few days.

A number of skills which could later be applied to specialised aspects of car manufacture were learnt – particularly in connection with aluminium – and also two vehicles were built for the War Department in which could be detected future car trends. These were miniature general-purpose vehicles produced in 1944 and intended for parachute operations, replacing motorcycle combinations. Codenamed VA and VB, the prototypes were two distinctly different approaches to the same problem, although they shared quite advanced design concepts such as unitary construction and all-round independent suspension.

The VA had a passing resemblance to a dodgem-car and was powered by the well-proven but noisy 1096cc JAP vee-twin aircooled motorcycle engine, mounted at the offside rear and driving the gearbox by chain. More successful was type VB, a box-like little vehicle with large cut-outs in the side for the wheels; power unit was the sidevalve Ford 10 engine, driving the rear wheels through a three-speed Ford gearbox and an auxiliary gearbox which gave a choice of six forward ratios, the lowest being 34.38:1. The independent rear suspension was not unlike the 'E' type's and Mk 10's to come, with big hub carriers, coil springs and driveshafts contributing to wheel location. Suspension at the front was by coil springs and pressed steel (or fabricated) wishbones; brakes were hydraulic – possibly the first 'Jaguar' to have a non-mechanical system. However, by 1944 when the VA and VB projects had been completed, aircraft development had been such that full size Jeeps could now be carried, so they never went into production.

The company's final project as the War drew to a close indicates the esteem in which they were held by the Air Ministry, for SS were chosen to build the complete centre fuselage sections of the then top-secret Meteor III jet aircraft. But by that time, moves had already been made to resume production of cars, and many interesting engine and suspension experiments were in progress.

While the Holbrook Lane works had not escaped unscathed during the war years – six shops had been destroyed in a Luftwaffe raid in November 1940 – the great diversity of work had brought its advantages in that for the first time, something like a machine shop had been built up, this being at Wigston some few miles from Foleshill. But even with these occasional beneficial spin-offs, the War still proved to be a huge set-back for SS and any profits ensuing from Ministry work hardly compensated for the interruption of the company's progress and the spoiling of Lyons' plans of the late 'thirties.

Above and centre right: The ingenious VB prototype, shown during trials. Rear view displays Jaguar's first (?) attempt at independent rear suspension, which was by no means entirely dissimilar to the Mk X and E-type's of 17-years later. *Photos: Jaguar Cars*

Centre left: Many of Swallow's last sidecars looked like this – stark War Office specification 'chairs'. A marked contrast to the stylish originals with which Lyons and Walmsley began business with in 1922; the sidecar concern was sold off in 1945.

Bottom: One of the most exciting Wartime projects at SS was the construction of Meteor jet fuselages; many useful skills were picked up during this period, to be seen later exercised on such as the aircraft-rivetted D-type sports racing cars which won at Le Mans.

Petrol shortages during, and after, the War were sometimes met by devices such as this – a gas-producer plant, as seen on this pre-War 2.5/3.5 Saloon; one wonders what the effect on the rear springs was!
Photo: Motor

The most significant long-term effect of the War on SS was certainly the enforced abandonment of the intention to make bodies entirely on the premises – that is, to be independent of outside panel suppliers such as the Pressed Steel Company. It was with the object of being his own master in this respect that caused Lyons to purchase an erstwhile supplier of body parts to SS – Motor Panels. This, Lyons' first acquisition of another company, was effected shortly before the war and would have helped provide SS with the tooling and facilities to make its own body shell components.

As Sir William said in an interview with Philip Turner of *Motor* many years later: "I have often thought what might have been if the war had not broken out, for we would have gone ahead developing and would have built up a very substantial body plant. It might have altered my outlook on a lot of things and the whole history of the company might have been different". Indeed, had Jaguar achieved self-sufficiency in body tooling, it is just possible that the company might have remained independent and never fallen into the clutches of BL.

However, in the cold light of an austere post-War Britain, every possible effort and all resources had to be thrown in merely to get car production underway once more. "We just hadn't got the money, so I sold Motor Panels to Rubery Owen", said Sir William and one can detect a note of regret in this statement; Jaguar were never again to come within reach of an 'in-house' body panel facility.

SS becomes Jaguar

One of the first important post-war moves was to re-name the company "Jaguar Cars Ltd". The initials "SS" were now singularly inappropriate for an English car company, shared as they were by what had been Nazi Germany's most feared troops – the SS battalions (*Schutzstaffel*), later described by Sir William in a charmingly British understatement as "a sector of the community not highly regarded..." The decision to change

the company's name was ratified at an Extraordinary General Meeting called in March 1945, and although the major reason for the change was as already mentioned, it might well have occured anyway in order to emphasise the fact that the company's coachbuilding origins were now well in the background, and bore no relevance to the current product. This was further underlined when towards the end of the year, the Swallow Sidecar concern was at last sold, the name going to Helliwells of Walsall.

The adoption of a model name – Jaguar – for the main title of the company has at least two interesting parallels in motoring history. Mercedes was originally a model name in the Daimler range, and then the motorcycle firm P&M become known as Panther after the use of this for a model (like Jaguar, that name too was inspired by a ferocious wild animal from the cat family). Jaguar and Mercedes were of course to become great rivals both on and off the racing circuit, although Jaguar has never sought to match the output of the giant firm from West Germany.

Meanwhile, various rumours had been circulating about Lyons' intentions for the company, and as early as November 1944, SS had issued an official denial that they would enter the quantity-production market with a small car at the War's end. The go-ahead for a partial resumption of peacetime activities was received from the government some months before the end of the War, and at the same time some interesting news was received from Standard....

John Black contacted Lyons and told him that it was his intention to embark on a 'one model' policy for Standard after the war, centred around the Vanguard which was then being designed. This was to be powered by a new 2.1-litre four-cylinder, ohv, wet-liner engine, and because of this Black no longer wanted to continue making power units for Lyons. He was, however, prepared to sell the plant he had put in for the production of the Jaguar 2.5- and 3.5-litre engines, and at a very advantageous price too – its 'written down' value, which was only a fraction of its true original cost.

This was an opportunity which Lyons seized with both

hands; before the war, he had become increasingly worried about the arrangement, as Black had on several occasions considered requests by other manufacturers to supply them with the ohv engine too, and it had not been easy to dissuade him from doing so. Furthermore, Black was becoming increasingly unpredictable and imperious in his behaviour; so that any move Lyons could make towards Jaguar's independence from Standard would obviously be a wise step to take. "Therefore, within a few days I sent transport to collect the plant and sent our cheque in payment for it", recalled Lyons.

It was just as well that he did so, for shortly afterwards Captain Black proposed that they should go back to the original arrangement, and indeed put much pressure on Lyons, even suggesting that they should form a separate company together. But Lyons valued his independence highly – "I had a great admiration for John Black in many respects, but I quickly grasped the opportunity to obtain security... I saw this move as a great step towards our becoming the self-contained manufacturing unit at which I aimed."

The situation was made even more complex by the presence of the Triumph company on the market; it had been in receivership since 1939, after having sold off the motorcycle division to Jack Sangster who, with a new engine designed by Edward Turner, made a large profit during his first year of trading. The Triumph factory was only just down the road from Jaguar, and Lyons was approached by the receiver to see if he would be interested in buying. But on examining the books, it was clear that Jaguar's financial resources were not great enough to stand the risk of attempting to put the company right; so the possibility of a small or mass-production 'Jaguar' faded out of the picture for good.

It was John Black who finally bought Triumph, partly in retaliation to Lyons' refusal to join forces with him earlier, for his intention was to more or less put Jaguar out of business through competition from a rejuvenated Triumph. But inspite of producing such handsome saloons as the Triumph 1800 (which used the 1776cc ohv 'four' originally developed for the 1.5-litre Jaguar, the tooling for which alone remained at Standard) with its Mulliner razor-edge coachwork, and fast, popular sports cars like the TR2, the company never came up with even an equivalent to any Jaguar model, let alone a rival.

But having decided on an independent future, Lyons still had further hurdles to overcome. The biggest of these concerned the post-War shortage of steel, and it seemed that the only way to obtain a reasonable allocation from the government was to concentrate on building for export, as foreign currency – particularly dollars – was badly needed in a Britain left monstrously in debt after six years of war.

The export trade was one which was very little known by SS/Jaguar – to quote Sir William, "we had enjoyed only a limited export market before the war, because we had always been able to sell on the domestic market all the cars we could make. So we did not go to the expense of establishing export outlets..." It now remained to be seen if Lyons could convince the Ministry of Supply that the Jaguar was a saleable commodity overseas – and if retail outlets could quickly be established there. "We prepared a very elaborate brochure, which set out our programme for exports – the countries to which we were going to sell, the number of cars and the amount of steel we required. I delivered this personally to Sir George Turner, who was then Permanent Secretary to the Ministry of Supply, and I elaborated verbally on our plans and obtained his promise of support".

The approach was successful – within a fortnight Jaguar received a permit for all the steel which it had asked for. "This gave us a tremendous boost, because we only had to make the cars for selling which was no problem in the car-starved world. However, we did not allow this to lead us into a state of false security. We went flat out to establish selling outlets throughout the world..."

The post-War Jaguar range

By mid-1945, the job of reconverting the factory buildings to car production was well under way, and Lyons released an optimistic statement to the effect that the company was planning to meet unprecedented demand from foreign markets. The newly-arrived engine plant from Standards had been installed in one of the large bays used for the repair of the Whitley bombers, and while work was continuing, a rather nice tribute was paid to the Jaguar workforce by the Gloster Aircraft Company – they sent over a Gloster-Meteor jet, just released from the secret list, to give a thrilling flying display over the factory, demonstrating the new plane's outstanding performance and marking Gloster's appreciation of the efforts which had been put into the project by Foleshill.

The assembly track began to move in July 1945, though it was a further two or three months before cars began leaving the factory in any quantity. Like virtually every other British manufacturer, Jaguar went back into production with its basic pre-War range of cars, though a statement issued by the factory in September 1945 noted that "for the moment closed bodies only are available and the '100' series of open sports cars is temporarily out of production".

The SS 100 never reappeared, although the drophead coupes certainly did, from December 1947 onwards. Until then, just the saloons were manufactured, powered by the usual choice of 1.5-, 2.5- and 3.5-litre engines. Outwardly, there was little to distinguish the reconstituted Jaguars from their pre-War counterparts – narrower chrome waist lines were about the only instantly identifiable changes, while the P100 headlights had 2-inch instead of 4.5-inch clear centres, hinged at the bottom instead of at the top. Radiator shells looked the same as pre-War, although they were not in fact interchangeable. Naturally, with the dropping of the SS insignia, badging was different and a few words on the subject generally would not come amiss here.

The original 1936/37 SS Jaguar radiators carried a raised hexagon, enamelled blue with the letters "SS" in the centre; underneath was the word 'Jaguar' on a blue-background scroll, incorporated in a fairly heavily sculptured 'wing' emblem. The 1938/40 cars had a smoother and more simply sculptured 'wing' style, with "SS Jaguar" in the centre and engine colour-coded capacities indicated in the scroll – pale grey enamel for 1.5-litres, cream for 2.5-litres, and black for 3.5-litres; all with chrome letters and figures. The post-War radiator badging was as follows: black for 3.5-litres with chrome letters and figures, cream for 2.5-litres with chrome letters and figures; and finally pale lilac for 1.5-litres with black-infilled letters and figures. The chromed mazak 'wings' were also a slightly different shape on the post-War cars and, of course, the SS monogram was omitted. On the knock-on wheel nuts, "Jaguar" replaced "SS", and a "J" plaque replaced the hexagonal "SS" one on the rear bumper.

Body having met chassis, wiring and steering would be linked up before radiator, bonnet and wings were added.

As quickly as possible, the factory returned to car production after hostilities ceased. This shows a chassis and rear axle assembly; the frames being pulled slowly down the line on tracks. In the background, bodies are being fitted up ready to meet the completed chassis on the body mounting line. *Photo: Jaguar Cars*

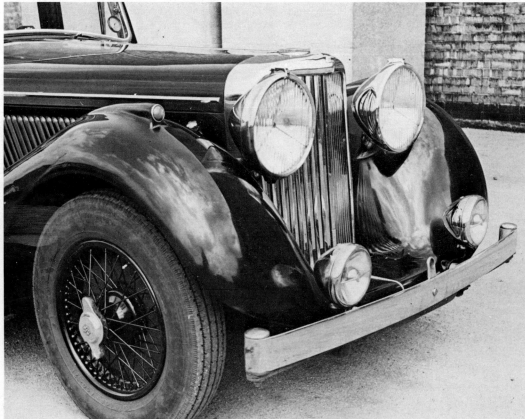

Above: The post-War Jaguar Saloon looked very much like its pre-War counterpart, but there were, in fact, numerous small changes, especially to internal panels. One of the few identifying features was the thinner body-moulding at waist level. *Photo: Motor*

Right: Front quarters of an early post-War 3.5-litre Saloon – obviously before Jaguar had organised delivery of "Jaguar" spinners to replace those with the unwanted "SS" insignia. *Photo: Motor*

Detail modifications there had been, though, making the 1946-on cars different even to the revised 1940 range. One important change was the fitting of hypoid rear axles to the 2.5- and 3.5-litre models, after the successful pioneering of that type of axle by the 1.5-litre Jaguar before the war, and after a number of successful applications by other manufacturers during the war had further proved its durability. It had the effect of lowering the propeller shaft by a useful 1.75-inches (which was in fact 0.5-inch more than on the 1.5-litre), and the hypoid also proved to be stronger than the previous ENV spiral drive unit. The change also meant a slight alteration in overall gear ratios, as no direct equivalents existed in the Salisbury range – for the 1.5-, 2.5-and 3.5-litre cars, the final drive ratios were now (ENV figures in brackets): 4.87 (4.86), 4.55 (4.50), and 4.27 (4.25). It was not enough to noticeably alter performance characteristics though.

A more minor change effecting the transmission was the adoption of needle roller bearings in the gearbox (layshaft only), while the six-cylinder engines were given an improved oil feed through a higher capacity oil pump and grooved bearings. An external Metalastic damper was fitted to the crankshaft of the 3.5-litre engine, this item being made in two parts, the outer rubber-welded to the inner. The few home market cars had compression plates installed between head and block to decrease the compression ratio in deference to the poor quality post-War fuel (some 2.5-litre cars were later fitted with special low-compression heads and so dispensed with the need for the plates). Export cars had the choice of two compression ratios – 7.6 or 6.8, 7.6 or 6.9, and 7.2 or 6.6 for the three engines in ascending capacity.

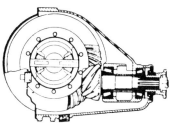

Top left: **The Production Engine Test Shop at Foleshill, with 1.5-, 2.5- and 3.5-litre units being run-up before installation. Individual power units were checked on dynometers seen right.** *Photo: Jaguar Cars*

Top right: **Diagram of the hypoid rear axle, with its low propellor shaft line, gradually adopted on all Jaguar saloons following its pioneering use on the 1.5-litre.**

Left: **The pushrod 3.5-litre engine assembly line; here the valve timing is being carried out.** *Photo: Jaguar Cars*

The 1776cc '1.5-litre' engine, alone of the three still made at Canley, was given considerably improved breathing arrangements in the form of a new inlet manifold. Pre-War, the inlet and exhaust manifolds were bolted together to form a hot-spot, and a separate three-branch water outlet rail bolted to the cylinder head had taken the coolant away; now, a new water-heated inlet manifold was used, which took the coolant from the cylinder head through three cast elbows, and ducted it afterwards to the radiator without the need for a separate rail. This produced more even inlet mixture temperatures and was claimed to raise bhp by 10%, although the same official rating of 65bhp was retained.

The braking system on all cars was updated to the Girling two-leading-shoe design, but they were still rod-operated, a feature which was to become distinctly anachronistic towards the end of the car's production run in 1949, even though they worked well and were less prone to fade than later hydraulic systems. Experiments were going on at Foleshill with hydraulic brakes of course, and *The Motor* of September 26, 1945, spent some time describing in detail a Girling hydro-mechanical system whereby the front wheels were braked by hydraulics and the rears by the usual rods; but it was never adopted for production.

Detail work carried out included some tidying-up of the Clayton 'air conditioning' unit. The heat-exchanger and electric fan were now tucked away further under the dash and were mounted centrally over the gearbox bellhousing. The battery was placed on the right in the 1.5-litre, left in the 2.5/3.5-litre cars. The scuttle panel immediately in front of the windscreen was made a couple of inches wider (which resulted in a shorter length of opening bonnet), with the curved under-bonnet section of the bulkhead being brought up to meet it; this

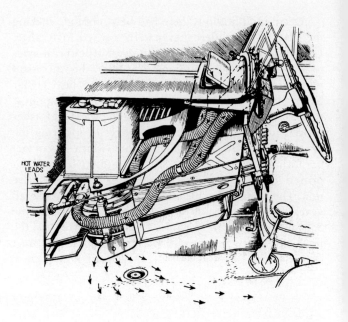

The Clayton heating and ventilation system as used for the post-War saloons – compare it with the previous layout illustrated earlier.

gave more room for a large air-intake flap and piping and allowed a "Radiomobile 100" radio receiver to be mounted under the instrument panel if desired.

The instrument panel and dash layout remained much as it had been, the instruments themselves having black-faced dials as had been the style since 1938; manual advance and retard controls had disappeared (except on the 1.5-litre which retained that facility a little longer). No more picnic tables for backseat passengers on any of the cars however, and neither were the seats upholstered in plain leather – pleats were back.

The post-war version of the 1.5-litre engine, showing the revised head-cooling arrangements – water was now ducted round a new inlet manifold, onto which bolted a horizontally mounted SU carburettor. *Photo: Jaguar Cars*

Dash panel and facia of an export
Saloon – note left-hand drive. Visible are the
new heating controls; note carpet material now
used for gearlever gauntlet on this car.

Without doubt, the most drastically altered aspect of the post-War Jaguars was their price; this was no fault of Lyons, but of an economy which had suffered large-scale inflation, and of a government which had just introduced purchase tax. Inclusive of this tax, the 1.5-litre was now £684 (or £729 for the Special Equipment saloon), the 2.5-litre £889, and £991 was asked for the 3.5-litre. But as before, by comparison to other similar cars (if there were any), this still offered astonishing value for money.

In fact by keeping the prices down as much as he could, Lyons could probably have sold the entire production at home, but he was pledged to the export trade, and export he did. Initially, Belgium represented the largest overseas market for Jaguar, having survived the war with much of her economy intact thanks to her wealth-generating colonies – and to circumnavigate the £600 limit imposed by the Belgian government for imports, a new plant was established there to assemble "completely knocked-down" cars. But the biggest potential market by far was the United States.

View of interior of a very early
post-War Saloon – but
showing new door trim panels
with rigid map pockets, and
new-style rear interior light. As
on the 1940 model cars, the
front seats display the handle
which could raise or lower
them. *Photo: Motor*

The post-War 1.5-litre Jaguar, still amazing value for money; this particular example is a 1947 Special Equipment model.

Lyons realised that with his Jaguar range he could offer the North American customer two very valuable commodities – extremely handsome looks, and exclusivity. An *Autocar* correspondent made the point that only eighteen home manufacturers served that market of four million cars annually, compared to Britain with thirty-four makes catering for an annual market of only four-hundred thousand. So if you bought a Jaguar, you bought individuality as well as style – and the privilege didn't cost too many dollars. So for the first time, there were left-hand drive Jaguars, the first such being a 1.5-litre completed in August 1947.

Jaguar in the United States

By January 1947, the first batch of new Jaguars were on their way across the Atlantic, albeit in right-hand-drive for a while. However, it soon became obvious that the complimentary back-up organisation in the States was far from satisfactory, and customers began complaining of lack of spares and poor service. Two major importers had already been established – Charles Hornburg on the West Coast, and Max Hoffman on the East – but the number and quality of the agencies who supplied the cars directly to the customer were doubtful. Lyons himself set

Jaguar found a market in the United States which exceeded their expectations – here a left-hand drive 3.5-litre Saloon awaits despatch.

sail on the *Queen Elizabeth* in March 1948 to sort the situation out, having stated that "Americans purchasing British cars must be provided with after-sales service equal to that of the American firms if goodwill is to be retained and sales are to be expanded. No sales agency agreement will, therefore, be concluded without a clause stipulating the stocking of adequate spares and the maintenance of efficient servicing facilities".

In a busy few weeks, Lyons toured the States and Canada signing up many agencies to create a complete distribution organisation for Jaguar; many of these agencies were necessarily small concerns, as no distributor of an American make was allowed to take on another franchise. However, as the name of Jaguar become more widely known and cars began to flow into the country, a big proportion grew into large and extensive organisations; on the other hand, it did take a considerable time to meet continuing criticism of inadequate parts stocking and inefficient service, which for a number of years was – to the customer – one of the biggest disadvantages of owning a Jaguar (or to be fair, most other foreign makes too).

Above: **More left-hand drive Saloons on their way abroad – note placement of number plates above bumper.** *Photo: Jaguar Cars*

Left: **A rare picture showing the optional fitted suitcases which could be ordered by the customer.** *Photo: Jaguar Cars*

No sooner had cars began to leave the production line when, on Friday January 31 1947, the works were afflicted by a bad fire. It was the biggest blaze Coventry had seen since the blitz, and it appeared to have started in rolls of felt kept on metal racks in the normal way inside one of the huge assembly shops erected during the war for the assembly of bomber fuselage assemblies. The blaze was discovered around 8.30pm, but the Coventry National Fire Service couldn't get it under control until 10pm, and a great quantity of trim material was destroyed.

Fortunately, a sheet-steel screen and the efforts of the fire brigade managed to prevent the flames reaching the paint shop next door; apart from two newly finished cars standing in the stores annex, no vehicles were damaged. The next morning, work was begun immediately to repair the damage, estimated at some £100 000, and thanks to Jaguar's suppliers who brought new materials in over the weekend, production resumed as normal on the Monday.

Accidents like that were not the only problems Jaguar had to contend with – shortages of steel and coal, power cuts, and rising prices were all part of the gloomy post-War scene with which motor manufacturers had to cope, not to mention the 'Siberian' winter of 1947 when virtually everything stopped. Many with leaders less astute than Lyons did not survive at all. But production and therefore sales began to climb, with an especially high demand developing overseas for the drop-head coupe, reintroduced at the end of 1947 on the 2.5-and 3.5-litre chassis. Very few Jaguars of any sort remained to be sold at home, and most of those were 1.5-litres, economy of running now being preferred to speed in petrol-rationed Britain.

The old pre-War range did in fact carry its age well, for all its traditional, 1930's styling – which might even have been a positive attraction to the North American customer. These Jaguars always remained very *impressive* cars, while the performance of the larger engined versions was at least average for their displacement, and they were quicker than most stock American family cars of the late 1940s. A typical Ford V8 saloon of 1947 reached 60mph in 21-seconds and had a maximum speed of 81mph for instance – figures easily bettered by the 2.5-litre Jaguar at 17-seconds and 87mph respectively. As for the 3.5-litre, a genuine 90mph was still rare on either side of the Atlantic.

Production of the Drophead Coupe was re-commenced towards the end of 1947, with the car substantially unchanged. Note overriders fitted to this American import example before despatch. *Photo: Motor*

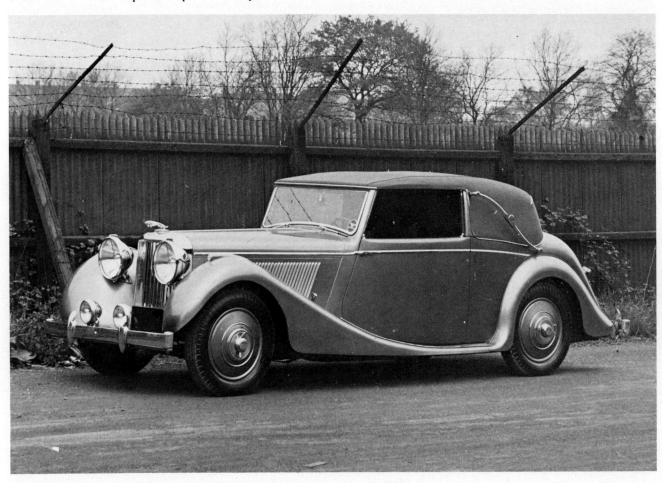

Road-testing the post-War 3.5-Litre Jaguar

The 3.5-litre figured in the newly resumed road-test activity amongst British motoring magazines, a saloon of this engine size being tried by *The Autocar* in March 1948. Despite being a ten-year-old design, it was still rated as a "front rank car" and – with the export drive firmly in mind – "a fine ambassador abroad for the high-quality British specialist car". Performance, despite inferior petrol, was impressive as ever:

"Speeds around 70mph are reached with superlative ease on any suitable clear stretch of road and are readily seen on an appreciable upward slopes. No experience in motoring can give a more vivid impression of power than this ability to climb main road gradients accelerating rapidly, and on top gear, between 60 and 70mph. Such is the smoothness and quietness of the engine that there is virtually no difference between 50 and 70mph as regards mechanical impressions conveyed to the occupants. Nor...is any real difference apparent at 80mph, though as the speed rises into these regions there is some wind noise. Because the performance is achieved in a manner which never feels 'frantic', even at the higher speeds, fast motoring in this car is not wearing to either drivers or passengers... It soon makes one feel that a 200-mile journey is something to be relished".

A top speed of 91mph was recorded, the car running on a 7.2:1 compression ratio, the higher of the two options being used on this road test car despite Pool petrol. This maximum was every bit as good as the original pre-War 3.5-litre figure, but on acceleration, the need to retard the ignition using the vernier adjustment on the distributor probably had its effect – the 30-50mph top gear time of 10.3 seconds was 1.6 seconds slower than before, and the 0-60mph time was up 2.4 seconds at 16.8.

Despite the increasing prevalence of hydraulic brakes, *The Autocar* found the mechanical system still used by Jaguar to be perfectly adequate, making the performance entirely useable and without requiring too much in the way of pedal pressures. The steering likewise had not fallen behind the times, and was found to be "quite high geared and gives firm, accurate and always safe-feeling control". Low speed parking manoeuvres revealed a certain heaviness though, a point which had been commented upon in pre-war road tests; Jaguar took note of this and, no doubt persuaded by feedback from the States too, did lower the steering box ratio before the car left production. This was effected from chassis nos. 511047 (2.5) and 612302 (3.5) and was incorporated in *all* left-hand drive cars; it gave 3.5-3.75 turns lock-to-lock. The 1.5-litre saloons ended up with a similar ratio, having had 2.5-2.75 turns in 1936/37, and 3-3.25 turns for 1938/40. The variations in turns for each was due to how the steering lock stops were set, the highest figure representing the maximum number of turns within the Burman Douglas steering box itself (hence the slight difference quoted for similar cars in road-tests and descriptions).

Surprisingly perhaps, the Jaguar's suspension and ride comfort was singled out for praise – by 1948, independent front suspension was becoming the norm, particularly on luxury cars. But there was still something to be said of a properly sorted out 'cart spring', beam axle scheme:

"The half-elliptic suspension constitutes a demonstration of the good results that can be obtained with a conventional layout. There are occasions when evidence is given of passing over bumps, or, for instance, poorly

The Autocar's road-test 3.5-litre Saloon of 1948, photographed in the Dorset House car park. Note the "J" monogram on the rear bumper, displacing the "SS" one of pre-War days.
Photo: Autocar

filled trenches across the road, but shock is not felt and an extremely comfortable ride is obtained throughout the speed range, without harshness at low speeds... For stability, too, the suspension is excellent. The knack is soon acquired of swinging this quite large car round bends at a speed with a fine feeling of balance and 'one-pieceness', and a very strong impression of safety is engendered by the riding as a whole."

Complimenting this still above-average ride and handling were the seats – "highly praiseworthy for the support they afford and the absence of tiredness experienced after appreciable spells of motoring... Soft leather upholstery of excellent quality is used, and the finish as a whole, inside and out, is of a very high order. In all respects the body is of 'specialist coachbuilder' character, one instance of which is the way in which the doors close..."

The last comment must have pleased Lyons; to retain that 'coachbuilt' feel was a fine achievement and a big sales point in a post-War era where rising costs had forced all but the extremely rich to surrender their normal practice of ordering a body from the specialist coachbuilder of their choice to have fitted onto a new chassis ordered from Rolls-Royce or Bentley (indeed, up until 1946 this had been the only way of acquiring a new example of one of these makes). Unfortunately, even the affordable Jaguar with its many expensive-car qualities would be difficult to obtain new on the home market for a number of years yet.

However, to return to the road test, the Clayton Dewandre heating system was adjudged "most efficient in keeping the occupants warm", the luggage locker was thought to be "of very considerable capacity and exceptionally well finished inside", the jacking system convenient to operate "at two points front and rear", and such engine accessories as oil filler and dipstick easy to reach. The feature of a separate petrol reserve push-pull control situated under the petrol filler cap was appreciated – "an increasingly rare and welcome fitting", although it was not to survive on a Jaguar after that model had left production.

Petrol consumption as recorded by *The Autocar* was between 16 and 18mpg, really not too bad for a 32cwt, 3485cc luxury saloon with such a blunt shape to push through the air; in the States, the figure might almost be regarded as very moderate. Despite a sliding scale according to engine capacity, petrol rationing at home did not make the bigger engined Jaguars very practical to run, but that was rather theoretical anyway as you could rarely find one. The 1.5-litre, with its easy 25mpg, was more popular and slightly more available.

Attempts were made in those fraught times to eke out the precious fluid with modifications and inventions – observant owners soon caught on to the fact that the auxiliary starting carburettor often remained in operation longer than was necessary, and took to fitting an overriding switch on the dashboard. Others experimented with the SU carburettor needles and claimed

Useful picture of the 'Mk IV' Saloon's tool kit. As owners will relate, the most-asked question is "what's missing from the oblong slot in the middle?" – that is, of course, where the tool-kit light fits when the lid is closed!

25mpg for the 3.5-litre.

As for Jaguar themselves, they were content to leave the cars alone until they reached obsolescence in the normal way, and in fact this says much for the basic design of the car, and does a great deal towards illustrating Lyons' ability to provide such superb value for money. Long manufacturing runs bring down the unit cost of virtually any article, and by keeping the 1938 range of cars in production for (effectively) at least seven years, Lyons extracted very full value from his tooling and machinary. The numbers he made were, for a specialist car, extremely impressive, the list being headed by the 1.5-litre of which no less than 12 713 left the factory.

Production changes were therefore very few; apart from those already mentioned, the 2.5-and 3.5-litre engines underwent fairly minor improvements at various times – early in 1946, after about 180 of each engine had been built, a duplex timing chain and sprockets replaced the single one, and alloy connecting rods were introduced once again (from engine nos P201 and S201), apparently for no better reason than to save on steel. At the same time, the compression plate on the 2.5-litre engine was deleted, and the cylinder head modified to give a lower compression ratio instead. The gearbox, made by Moss, was redesigned during 1946 – the double helical gears had become too difficult and expensive to machine, and could suffer from broken teeth, so the box was converted to single helical (at chassis nos 510881 and 612041 on rhd cars). With the advent of the S.H. box, the old rubber gear lever knob (C.853) disappeared, after continual use from probably the very first S.S. car. In its place was a slim plastic knob (C.1911) with raised letters that soon wore down just like the old rubber one....

The 1.5-litre Jaguar remained similarly unaffected by change, though in 1947 it too lost the manual ignition control from the steering wheel boss (from engine no. KB4252E). Some attention was paid to the front axle however, in that up to 1946 two thrust washers were used with the kingpin, and after that date a single thrust washer was employed, grooved on its upper face. The kingpin diameter itself was also increased during 1947, from 11/16-inch to 13/16-inch, and fitted with a grease nipple at the top (from chassis No. 413551 on). All cars underwent minor changes in front and rear spring camber during production, either to increase ground clearance or to further improve the car's ride.

Above: **Following the impetus given them by the War effort, Jaguar continued to build up a proper machine shop; here are a battery of Shardlow vent lathes used for crankshaft machining.** *Photo: Jaguar Cars*

Left: **This photograph shows the aluminium connecting rods used in some pushrod Jaguar engines; as with every Jaguar engine since, each rod is weighed and balanced – though the process is rather more mechanised these days and less like a grocer's shop!** *Photo: Jaguar Cars*

1948 was a year of re-investment, the profits from the new-found export trade being ploughed back into the business. Much money was spent on new machine tools, especially for the machine shop, which was being built-up by Production Manager John Silver – the intention was to make the majority of engine parts at Foleshill and expensive Archdale and Landis machines at £6-£9000 each consumed a lot of the £100 000 expanded on new tools. Obviously, this new equipment was earmarked not only for the current ohv engine range, but also for its successor already under advanced development.

The last of the 'vintage' Jaguars left the factory in early 1949, overlapping their independent front suspension replacement by several months. The twin overhead camshaft XK engine had already been announced in the XK 120 sports car, and it was quite clear that another era was approaching – one that would no longer find room for giant P100 headlights and cartsprings at each corner.

The first Jaguars in retrospect

From the very first, the Jaguar was a *driver's* car. In a retrospective analysis of its merits in practical use, this comes across very clearly right from the beginning in 1935, when the first Jaguar saloons entered service. These, the last of the wood-framed saloons, underwent a number of changes as we have seen but the initial concept was a very valid one and remained appropriate up until the MK V saloon of 1948/49.

Generally, the 1936 cars were reliable and easy to maintain, using as they did many tried and tested proprietary components – steering, brakes, gearbox, and

Flashback to 1937: Mrs. (later Lady) Lyons' 2.5-litre Saloon being tested by *The Autocar* **during the War in its 'blackout' livery; this same car now stands in Jaguar's Browns Lane entrance hall.** *Photo: Autocar*

even most of the engine. Whatever was unique to the car (like its ohv head) was well engineered and tough. *The Autocar* carried out an appraisal of a 1937 2.5-litre saloon during the war years, an example which had covered some 65 000 miles (it was actually Mrs Greta Lyons' car, and is still retained by the factory), and was able to substantiate this impression, although it was the appearance of the car which the writer commented on first:

"An interesting point from the commencement was the undated appearance. I do not think that anyone unacquainted with the details of S.S. cars which were altered seasonally between 1936 and the 1940 model that actually came into production on a limited scale could have said that this was not a 1937 or '38 car, or a '39 for that matter.

"In other words, when in 1935, as it must have been, the Jaguar design was first schemed, lines were hit upon that would look well in any company of cars five or six years later, and that cannot be said of by any means of its contemporaries. A similar remark could be made of the mechanical specification".

On the road, the Jaguar easily put 40-miles into just over an hour, returned 20mpg (with coasting), used virtually no oil – and nor did the engine "sound in the least slack or loose, and no smoke was noticeable from the exhaust". It started at the first press of the button, although "CDU 700" had been updated by the fitting of the SU auxiliary carburetter. "The steering was firm and without appreciable lost movement, the car cornered most satisfactorily, and the Girling brakes were excellent – light to operate and decisive when wanted to be so... I can call to mind many cars of various makes, showing not half the mileage of this one, that were not in nearly as good condition".

An even more convincing testimonial to the qualities of the original 2.5-litre SS Jaguar came from a 21-year-old university student in Belgium whose family had purchased one towards the end of 1936. His letter was published in *The Autocar* during May 1938, and as the enthusiastic writer was none other than future Jaguar works driver Paul Frere, it is well worth reproducing in full. Also, few early Jaguars could have been subjected to quite such a tough life as the Frere family's was!

"We bought an early 1937 Model 2.5-litre S.S. Jaguar saloon in Vienna in October, 1936 and it has now done over 30,000 miles, 26,000 miles being in one year, and it has seen every country in Europe from Hungary westward except Spain.

"First of all, regarding suitability for Continental conditions, it has proved absolutely adequate. The suspension is decidedly good for a car of this kind: two rear spring blades were broken in Calabria (Italy), where the roads are not good, otherwise it has never given any trouble, though one could wish for a little more clearance between the front springs and the chassis (I have seen that this point has been improved on the later models). Nor has the coachwork developed any serious rattle. I should not be proud to say so, but, as a matter of fact, not even a nut has been tightened on the body or the wings.

"The Jaguar is a first-class hill-climber; the gear ratios are admirably chosen for mountain as well as for fast road work. Though I tried very hard I never could get the water temperature above 80-85 deg. The brake linings are still good for at least 12,000 miles, although the car has always been driven fast on the road.

"I have done with the car everything that an ordinary saloon-owner is not expected to do with his car – demonstration runs to some fellow-enthusiasts, and private standing start acceleration competitions against their cars (a Jaguar is a somewhat rare thing over here) – in spite of all this I only succeeded in once breaking the star-pinions of the differential. This is the only breakdown and major trouble I have ever had.

"The maximum speed easily attainable, where the road permits, is about 87m.p.h by corrected speedometer reading; the maxima on the gears are about 69m.p.h on third and 43m.p.h on second at 5,000r.p.m, though, of course maximum acceleration is reached by changing up earlier. The gear box, though not truly silent, has not become obtrusive; on our car the synchromesh does not work very well, but, using double declutching, extremely fast changes can be made up and down. The car will cruise at 75m.p.h, very comfortably with a lot of power in reserve. Road-holding and steering are of a high standard and the steering has not developed appreciable lost motion.

"I never expected such a quality and resistance to wear at the price. I have no connection whatsoever with the S.S. Company, but I think it would have been an ingratitude not to record the pleasure we have had with the car."

A fine word-picture of the satisfaction given by a hard-worked 2.5-litre Jaguar; the failure of the ENV differential was unusual but not totally unknown, and the hypoid bevel Salisbury axle adopted after the war was much stronger – halfshafts have been known to break on these latter axles, but the differential itself, never (disregarding oil loss or similar catastrophe).

The differences between the 1936/37 Jaguar saloons and their all-steel replacements are better appreciated from inside the cars, for apart from the side-mounted spare wheel it is difficult to distinguish the two apart at any distance. The 1936 car feels considerably smaller and more compact from the driving seat, there being noticeably more room in the 1938 car. But like its immediate predecessor, the all-steel saloon was durable and willing, and in its element on long-distance continental hauls. The Autocar borrowed a 'hack' 2.5-litre from SS in 1938 to cover the Monte Carlo Rally, and reported that "after nearly 2000 miles over all kinds of going, and keeping up a high average such as can be sustained with ease on French roads, our already high regard for the SS rose considerably. There must be few 2.5-litre engines so willing, so responsive and with such pleasing top and third gear performance... Cruising speed on the many straights along this route was as high as 70mph, at which the engine was completely happy, but on many occasions the engine was given its head and

achieved 90mph on the speedometer (it was reading only two or three miles fast by stop-watch), a remarkable speed for a moderate sized engine averaging 20mpg and consuming oil at the rate of a gallon per 1000 miles."

Little mechanical trouble was encountered, although on one alarming occasion, every light went out – the trouble was never discovered, but Harry Teather told the writer of a similar occurance on William Lyons' personal 3.5-litre saloon; that too suffered unaccountably from total failure of the lighting system, and the Service Department spent many anxious hours trying to sort the problem out for their annoyed MD. Everything would work perfectly on test in the shop, but inevitably Lyons would bring the car back with the same complaint. An entirely new wiring loom was, in desperation, finally fitted – but it still happened. Then purely by chance the cause was discovered – when the brake pedal was depressed, it would sometimes foul on the main loom, and the resulting short-circuit would knock out the lighting system. Of course, stationary in the Service Department, this didn't show up at all... Wiring on production cars was subsequently re-routed.

The 1.5-litre cars were well liked by their owners too. Said one writing from South Africa of his 1936 sidevalve model: "I have owned this car now for two and half years, and must say I have been very pleased with its all-round performance and also the first-rate British workmanship found in every part of it. The roadholding is excellent, the Girling brakes are very good and stay so for long periods. Steering, although rather heavy, feels 'safe and positive' at all speeds."

The ohv 1.5-litre produced an equally keen response from an Autocar reader from Sao Paulo, Brazil. Said M.C. Bacellar; "From appearance to remarkable performance, one wishes for almost nothing more. The high safety factor, stability, steering and excellent four cylinder engine, as well as the rich upholstery, cannot be bettered. There is only a moderate degree of pinking owing to the inferior petrol in this country; the spring dampers require frequent recharging as they do not suit our roads. None the less, I make a monthly run between Sao Paulo and Rio de Janeiro, driving the 550 kilometres very fast and hard over a rough road, sometimes completely covered in mud; each time I take only ten hours, although with big American cars it takes me 14 hours."

The correspondent went on to say that he thought these same American cars were necessary when it came to covering really high mileages, such as the 30 000 kilometres he had achieved with a Buick over a three-month tour of North America – but perhaps he had not sampled a 3.5 litre Jaguar....

Those who did use the 3.5-litre for touring fondly recall its prowess on the open road. Nick Dyckhoff remembers his family's well: "The car was remarkably suitable for continental touring, proving reliable and comfortable over long distances. We had a detachable

This splendid picture had been reproduced before, but it is such a superb evocation of Britain's now-vanished Empire that it deserves inclusion; the 2.5-litre Saloon shown was 'on duty' in Fiji, one of many in far-flung parts of the globe where its toughness and longevity were appreciated. *Photo: Rob Wright*

luggage rack and had heavy duty springs fitted to the rear. Obviously we carried a full spares kit, but I don't recall ever having to use it. The car is remembered as thoroughly reliable. Maintenance consisted most of attention to the steering and replacement of the exhaust, but otherwise it tended to go happily from service to service.''

However, it was in the States, of course, where the big Jaguar saloons really caught on. The huge lights, the great upright radiator, and the old English, clubroom atmosphere of the interior impressed and appealed. Nearly all the cars entering North America were 2.5- or 3.5-litres, a high proportion being drop-head coupes – that model particularly captivated the average American. To quote American writer and ex-owner Rick O'Kane:

"The drop-head was classically pretty – huge Lucas

P100s, sweeping fenders and graceful Landau bars. Though I often was struck with the feeling that the designer got to the back of the car and ran out of patience; from the rear the drop-head looked like an enormous black and white beetle getting ready to scurry somewhere.

"In the final analysis, I think it was the landau bars that made the car truly pretty. They were working ones, too, part of a delightfully baroque top system. The top wasn't exactly hard to put up and down. Involved would be a better word...something you wouldn't want to do twice in the same afternoon.

"From behind the huge four-spoked wheel the aspect was pure Edwardian Glitz. Everywhere was walnut, leather and wool, and the dashboard was the fantasy of every man who likes to Operate It Himself. The dashboard was Power, Glory and Excess in All Things. There were dials to tell you the revs, miles per hour, oil pressure, amps, water temperature and time. There were knobs and switches and levers and lights and hooks and cranks to do everything from increasing the idling speed

25rpm to winding the windshield out to the horizontal if this pleased you. A man getting behind the wheel of a Mk IV for the first time is lost.

"But the visible qualities of the car were minor indeed when compared with the greatest job – the adventure of operating the thing!

"It starts easily with the push of a button and idles quite genteelly. But as you get ready to actually move, you find that no matter how you crane your neck, you can't get even a glimmering of what's happening anywhere to the rear of the car.

"The padded inside of the top looms as darkly as the universe, effectively blocking out about 180 degrees worth of fellow motorists. Why yes, there's a little slit back there, but all you can see through it are two and a half leaves on what you assume must be a tree. If you're parked on the left, the only safe way to get away from the curb is to get out, look, wait for traffic to clear completely, then quickly get back in the car and drive away before more traffic comes."

The hazards of living with a drop-head! Another shortcoming of the car highlights Jaguar's early ignorance of certain aspects of North American motoring – parking techniques. As one correspondent of my acquitance puts it: "here in the good 'ole U.S. the way you park is back till you hear the crash of metal or glass and then go forward till you hear one or the other, then repeat the process until you are somewhere near the curb." While some pre-Mk V Jaguars left the factory with overriders, almost universally the U.S. distributors fitted these to any cars arriving without them when they docked in the States.

There was a problem though – put them on the rear bumper and you couldn't get at the spare wheel, unless you managed to find some very petit ones. A number of Jaguar saloons collected two sets of overriders; it wasn't that the spring steel bumper blade of the car was particularly inadequate, just that, unfortunately, it was set lower than its opposite number on 'Detroit ironware'.

Most Jaguars entering the States seemed to have been supplied with Ace wheel discs, though equally, it appears, a good number lost them at the docks after shipment – the fitted tools often went the same way. Special vertical-

A large proportion of Jaguar Drophead 'Mk IVs' went to the United States; this example, equipped with mascot and over-riders, is being driven in a Californian speed event held early in 1949 by Roger Barlow. Second fastest time of day, after a Talbot, was set by one Phil Hill in a supercharged MGTC!

This conversion was carried out by a private coachbuilder on a pre-War Drophead, but can hardly be said to be much of an improvement with its outside boot hinges and unfaired rear number plate; it does manage to achieve a completely smooth line with the hood down, however.

dipping P100 headlights were supplied with export cars (only), both pre- and post-War, through many cars in the States have since collected sealed-beam units which have been adapted to suit.

Drive a 2.5- or 3.5-litre Jaguar today and you return to a different era of motoring. The bonnet appears to stretch a vast distance in front of you, and on the move, may gently vibrate along with the wings, the tips of which you can see. Used to the rigidity of the modern car, you have the constant impression of movement – not to the point of rattles or noticeable flexing, just a liveliness of the whole body as you travel. The steering wheel feels very large, and requires effort at low speeds, but in fast driving trembles lightly in your hands and responds quickly to input.

No longer is even the 3.5-litre a fast car in the absolute sense, though drive a healthy specimen – preferably with steel connecting rods (XK type fit!) – and you will be surprised how quickly 70mph comes up on the open road,

and how third gear will take you smartly from 40mph to 60mph to easily keep up with a normal traffic stream. The soft, leather seats are comfortable in an armchair fashion, and the ride is generally good – although poor surfaces will quickly disclose the small amount of wheel travel allowed by the semi-elliptics, resulting in a fairly harsh up-and-down movement of the car. But at the same time, roll is low and the car – with familiarisation – encourages brisk cornering, being easily balanced on throttle and steering, with the suggestion of a self-correcting tail slide as you exit from a 55mph bend in third gear.

The engine is smooth, judge it how you will, only becoming noisy above 4000 or 4500 rpm, the latter being the safe limit for the 3.5-litre, realms never needed during ordinary motoring such is the torque available from 1000rpm upwards. But even when giving the car its head, running the needle up to the red line through the gears and keeping the accelerator hard down on the straights, the engine has an unburstable feel, as if it enjoys working

After the War and with motor shows once again under way, coachbuilders had a field day with the Jaguar chassis; here are two designs by Vanden Plas (Belgium) exhibited at continental events around 1948.
Photos: Motor

Left and below: **Less flamboyant than Vanden Plas' efforts were these drophead four-seaters by Lanthenthal, the one under repair having been built for the-then Swiss distributor of Jaguars, Emil Frey.** *Photos: Motor and A.J.A. Whyte*

Reinbolt & Christie produced this quite discreet drophead coupe body on the post-War 3.5-litre Jaguar. *Photo: Motor*

131

It is thought that this rather extraordinary pseudo-American coachwork was draped over the Jaguar pushrod chassis by Swiss coachbuilder Willy Bernath; little 'Jaguar' to be seen, except characteristic wheel-discs to give the game away. Lights are set behind the lower, dummy, grille.

It was in the States that the 'Mk IV' Jaguar first attained a 'classic' status, and now the type is a regular winner in *concours d' elegance,* so it is fitting to end this chapter with a photograph of a beautifully kept example at the Jaguar Club of Southern New England's meeting of autumn 1976.
Photo: P. Skilleter

near its designed limits – happier, certainly, than the chassis at, say, 85mph.

Brakes: those new to the Girling rod system are usually surprised by the efficiency of the design – pedal pressures are a little high, but generally, one soon forgets about what is making the car slow down, which is a compliment the Girlings deserve. With the big, eighteen-inch wire wheels and the large well ventilated drums, plenty enough air circulates to eliminate fade as a cause for complaint. And provided the owner has kept the rods properly tensioned and adjusted (no great task), then unequal braking or grabbing will not be experienced. True, linkages have been known to break, but only through lack of maintenance and consequent wear – overall, the reliability factor probably exceeds that of a hydraulic system, which is undoubtedly one reason why Jaguar were slow to change in this respect.

Today, the 1.5-, 2.5-and 3.5-litre SS Jaguars and Jaguars have been firmly relegated to that category known as 'collector's cars'; despite faithful service in many parts of the world and over millions of miles, the type is rarely in use now as an everyday car. Headed by the drop-head coupe, the car first achieved its 'classic' status in the United States, where many have since been restored and bring their dignified presence to Jaguar club

meetings there. Amongst them are a number imported from Great Britain in recent years, as values rose more slowly here – although, as has been the case with other Jaguars, the differential between the two markets has narrowed, and may well end up non-existent.

Colloquially, the pre-Mk V Jaguars are often referred to as 'Mk IVs', particularly the all-steel range from 1938 onwards; this started amongst car dealers almost as soon as the Mk V was introduced, although the factory has never used the term itself. But it has become accepted parlance amongst even the most fanatic of owners or adherents, simply because it is much easier to say in conversaion than ''2.5-litre Jaguar drop-head coupe'' (for instance).

Whatever we may call them now, the sturdy old 1.5-, 2.5- and 3.5-litre saloons did much to elevate Jaguar into the 'establishment' in Britain, and made it possible to break *into* the American market, even if they did not exactly break-*through* in terms of numbers sold. However, even the 3.5-litre did not meet William Lyons' pre-War dream of a 100mph luxury saloon and, even before the War had ended its successors were being designed. It would take two stages for Lyons to achieve that ideal, but achieve it he would. No-one who really knew him doubted it.

Chapter Five

The Mk V Jaguar

... a standard of riding comfort which is outstandingly high, a standard which has not been bettered in any car of any nationality which it has been our good fortune to test.

The Motor, April 5, 1950

An honest radiator is still there, though refined in detail, by which we shall continue to recognise the breed.

The Autocar, October 1, 1948

France, April 1934, and a new saloon car had just been announced, heralded by its makers as: "a new concept in motoring". It possessed monocoque (chassis-less) construction, front wheel drive, hydraulic brakes, wet-liner engine, small wide-based wheels, and torsion bar suspension, independent at the front and featuring wishbone suspension members. Within a year, hydraulic piston-type dampers and rack and pinion steering were added to its specification too.

The "Traction Avant" Citroen was indeed a "new concept", and it was to exert a vital influence on European car design for at least two decades. Unfortunately it was too new in many respects, because it drained the resources of Andre Citroen, who bankrupted, was forced to sell out to his chief creditor, Michelin.

Technically, the car was the product of Andre Lefebvre and his talented design team at Quai de Javel, and while none of the key features embodied in its makeup were individually unique, (Lancia's famous Lambda had pioneered a production form of unitary construction, while Ferdinand Porsche was already producing a successful torsion bar suspension system), never before had they been integrated to form a single overall design. Those who tried the new car found its roadholding and stability to be quite beyond their experience, with no other vehicle able to match it on these counts – which included the best continental sports cars too!

With production difficulties overcome, the 7A Citroen

and its successors commenced a lengthy run of success which continued until 1957, over 700 000 being built (including a fair number at Citroen's Slough factory in England). Poor Andre Citroen, his heart broken by the initial collapse of his futuristic project, did not live to see the car's eventual triumph, as he died in 1935.

Naturally, the 'Traction Avant' Citroen did not fail to impress the more receptive of British automotive engineers, and one of the most admiring was the young William Heynes, particularly as he was then investigating independent front suspension for the Hillman Minx while at the Rootes' Humber factory. When in 1935 he joined SS Cars Ltd, it was equally natural that he should take this very justified regard for the French car with him; and while initially there was no time to experiment with the independence of the front wheels at Foleshill, as the new 'Jaguar' range became successfully established, Heynes did at last find time to pursue further what was obviously destined to become a trend in car design – and one which SS could not afford to ignore.

While his experiments on the Hillman Minx had been confined to coil and leaf springs, on commencing independent front suspension work for SS, torsion bars and wishbones figured from the start in Heynes' designs. At least one system was ready to be tried when Walter Hassan joined from Bentley (via Woolf Barnato) in 1938, the components machined and awaiting assembly when he arrived. While the basic inspiration for his

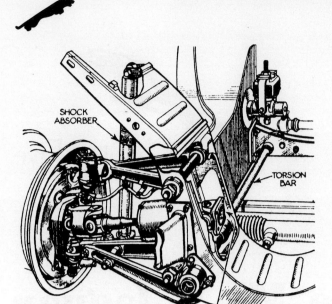

Andre Citroen's torsion bar/wishbone front suspension for the car which became known as the Light 15 in this country. It aroused much interest.

independent front suspension might have been the Citroen, William Heynes' own designs were far from being copies. Heynes was, for instance, one of the first to combine torsion bars and wishbone suspension members with ball joints carrying the stub axle – the advantage of a ball joint being its ability to accommodate movement in any direction, which on a car means the up-and-down movement of the suspension itself, and the turning of the wheels during steering.

A car was running with independent front suspension before the war, a converted 3.5-litre saloon carrying a standard body but with the necessary chassis frame modifications at the front to accommodate suspension member pick-ups. Walter Hassan remembers a great deal of work being carried out on this car over many thousands of miles; it held the road marvellously but was harshly sprung, and it was later decided that there wasn't enough wheel movement, and the springs were too stiff.

The reason why interest was centred on independent front suspension (I.F.S.) at this time was due to the defects of the beam axle/leaf spring system becoming ever more apparent as cars became more powerful and passengers less tolerant of a hard ride. Softening the springs to improve the ride made them susceptible to 'wind up' under braking, causing wheel hop or patter – which with the coupling effect of the rigid axle could also develop into a violent and self-perpetuating shimmy.

It was the research into ride and handling undertaken by ex-Rolls-Royce engineer Maurice Olley for Cadillac in 1930 that convinced General Motors (and eventually most other manufacturers) that the only way to obtain a 'soft' ride and eradicate shimmy was to separate the front wheels. Some European car makers had produced good

I.F.S. systems almost intuitively but it was GM's scientific experimentations that proved the point – although in Britain, adopting the system was often postponed by manufacturers on the grounds of cost and the generally well-surfaced British roads. Also, it was technically quite difficult to prevent roll, wallow and understeer becoming additional and less desirable characteristics of I.F.S. So Heynes and Hassan were faced with no mean task in designing a system for the Jaguar.

The I.F.S. Jaguar was run throughout the war, and was joined by one of the smaller engined front wheel drive Citroens and a "rather ugly" BMW saloon – the latter was used for an interesting experiment with 'air strut' suspension which the company was very keen on trying at the time. The strut consisted of cylinders half filled with air and half with oil with a shock absorber in between. It showed promise and was very nearly adopted, but the car tended to sink down overnight and needed pumping-up in the morning – it really required a pump like Citroen used much later on the DS19. Concurrently, the VA/VB military projects were being undertaken, but while the results of the VB's all-round coil spring independent suspension were carefully filed, they were really self-contained exercises and not related to saloon car development at the time.

Of the wishbone I.F.S. systems, two cars were run, one carrying a long wishbone arrangement with coil springs; this was a first attempt by Mr R.J. Knight who had joined

While saloon car work was progressing with the torsion bar suspension system, coil springs were used on the wartime VB project. *Photo: Jaguar Cars*

the company in 1944, and who was later to become Jaguar's Managing Director. It wasn't adopted though – "we didn't like it too much, probably because we'd done a lot more work on the other (short wishbone) one to start with", says Walter Hassan. Then three cars were tried with reversed stub-axles, but, recalls Hassan, all three failed at exactly the same mileage so that approach was abandoned too.

So by 1946/47, it was fairly clear that Jaguar's independent front suspension was to be made up of top and bottom wishbones carrying ball-jointed stub axles, with springing by longitudinal torsion bars and damping by telescopic shock absorbers. But what of the car for which it was destined?

During the War years, William Lyons had become determined that as soon as possible after the end of hostilities, he would produce the 100mph luxury saloon which for some time had been his strong ambition. To this end, a new twin overhead camshaft engine was designed and developed to provide the necessary power, and a new, streamlined body shape was already taking shape in Lyons' mind. The new independent front suspension was the third major ingredient in the outline specification for this radically different Jaguar, as yet unnamed but in fact the Mk VII saloon.

However, in relating the sequence of events at Foleshill during the mid and late 'forties, it is actually best that model names are left out of the picture for a while, because they are in this instance rather confusing and certainly irrelevant to what took place, affected as they were by outside influences. So I shall refer to the Mk VII as the 'twin-cam saloon' for present purposes.

The full story of the XK engine's development is told in the next chapter, but the unit had achieved its production form by the latter part of 1948. The chassis frame and suspension for the new twin cam saloon had been finalised even earlier, and theoretically the car could have been built, but for complications with the bodyshell. This was chiefly because for the first time, the company was to go outside for a *completed* body which would arrive more or less ready for mounting – and getting this under way in conjunction with Pressed Steel was no mean task.

So by late 1947/early 1948, Jaguar had a brand new chassis and engine virtually ready to go, but not much hope of clothing it with the totally new shell for at least a year or eighteen months, perhaps longer. While in the meantime, the beam-axle range of cars inherited from before the War was beginning to look extremely long in the tooth, and very outdated technically. The result was a good, not too old-fashioned, British compromise.

It was decided to put the new, I.F.S. chassis straight into production, and overcome the bodyshell problem by designing a more or less traditional body, which could be built up piecemeal at Foleshill as with the pre-War type cars; the shop floor was used to this sort of construction and the new steel shell could quickly and easily be made ready for production without heavy tooling costs – unlike the twin cam saloon's streamlined body, whose large panels required presses and ancilliary machinery which Jaguar did not possess.

As for a power unit, it would have taken some time to get the XK engine into full production, and it was also felt that it would be "bad policy" to place a brand-new engine in an outdated shell; so from the outset, the 'interim' car was fitted with the 2.5-or 3.5-litre pushrod engine which had been the Jaguar mainstay since 1938. Meanwhile, the small supply of XK engines which were becoming available were used in a shortened wheelbase version of the new I.F.S. chassis to produce the XK 120 sports car, launched as a mobile test-bed to see how the XK engine stood up to every-day use in the hands of the customer. Initially, a year's production of only two-hundred XK 120s were scheduled, but on announcement at the September 1948 Motor Show at Earls Court, Jaguar realised that they had vastly underestimated demand for this beautiful 120mph two-seater, and later it was put into quantity production.

Such was the birth of the Mk V Jaguar – a borrowed chassis and an inherited power unit, with a bodyshell of basically pre-War appearance but with various 'forties influences evident in such as the faired-in headlights and push-button door handles. A compromise certainly, but not as it turned out, an unsuccessful one. And above all, it allowed the factory breathing space to sort out the twin cam saloon's bodyshell tooling.

Now we can return to the question of model names. For a start, why Mk V? Well, the new model needed some sort of name, because to use the appellation "2.5" or "3.5" would confuse it with the beam axle cars. So the rather arbitrary designation "Mk V" was chosen, supposedly because it was the fifth I.F.S. prototype. True, Bentley had used the name before, but only very briefly in 1940, and only a handful of Mk V Bentleys were made – the model was redesigned and renamed in 1946 as the Mk VI Bentley.

The use of Mk V as a model name in 1948 was, perhaps, a little unimaginative of Jaguar, if only because problems were obviously going to arise when the twin-cam saloon successor to the Mk V came along – Bentley had already been using Mk VI since just after the war as mentioned above. So what did Jaguar do? Simply skip a number and call the Mk V replacement "Mk VII". This was fine, and the minor problems that resulted did not effect Jaguar at all – Bentley had to call their 1953 Mk VI successor the "R-type" (or B7) to avoid confusion with Jaguar's Mk VII which was still in production, and historians have found it consistently difficult ever since to kill persistent rumours of a 'mystery' Mk VI Jaguar that never appeared!

As we have seen, the missing model never existed. Some people have conjectured that it was the Mk V fitted with the twin cam XK engine, but while the Mk V was indeed used to test the XK engine over high mileages (and Walter Hassan remembers the XK powered Mk V as being very pleasant to drive), at no time was it a production proposition. In any case, even if the car had carried the XK engine, it would *still* have been known as Mk V, with 'Mk VI' inevitably being left out of the model sequence because of the Bentley complication. I may appear to be labouring the point, but the 'Mk VI' Jaguar ghost has wandered abroad for long enough, and deserves to be laid at rest.

While the family resemblance of the Mk V to the previous Jaguar saloons was strong, underneath the skin virtually only the engine and transmission were shared. Gone was the old underslung frame which had served Jaguar so well since the end of 1937; in its place was an entirely new one designed specifically to accommodate the independent front suspension and the re-thought rear suspension, and to provide additional stiffness.

This time, the frame ran at one level from the front to a point just before the rear axle, where it swept up sharply for about eighteen inches before tapering in thickness and dropping away slightly to take the rear spring hangers. The front of the chassis frame was also thinner in depth at its end, the 14swg side members deepening as they ran back towards the dash, where they maintained a depth of 6.5-inches until the upsweep, and a width of 3.5-inches. Both side members were of box section of course, and mainly arc-welded. Channel-section 'X' bracing was back in favour, strengthened at the centre of the 'X' by a channel-section cross-member, while at the front of the frame, a large transverse box member ran between the suspension pick-up points. A plan view of the frame showed that it tapered quite markedly towards the front end, where a narrow triangle was formed by closing plates which ran from side members to the box member which closed the forward end of the frame.

It was an extremely rigid chassis indeed, yet not too heavy: Heynes being well aware that a flexible chassis would interfere with the correct working of the suspension, besides creating rattles and creaks. The torsion bar independent front suspension for which the frame had been built was mounted neatly at the front cross member.

The new chassis, designed especially for the independent front suspension, was immensely strong and rigid with its large box-sections and cross-members; note jacking points built into the front and the 'kick-up' over the rear axle. Main side-members were in 14 s.w.g. steel. Pushrod engine is shown installed right; at least two (RHD) Mk V saloons were experimentally fitted with XK engines from new (623053 and 623173). The former was sold secondhand and survives today in North America.

Jaguar's first attempt at independent front suspension holds an aesthetic appeal which lasts to this day; with longitudinal torsion bars, there was no need for heavy and bulky suspension components to house big coil springs, so the wishbones remained slim and neat. As with the Traction Citroen, the main components were a forged top wishbone, and a single lower beam projecting at right-angles from the frame. On the Jaguar, Heynes added a further member to this I-section beam, in the form of a tubular strut running from its outer end forward to an extension of the beam's mounting under the chassis. By this triangulation, which took care of fore and aft loads, Heynes effectively made the bottom suspension component into a wishbone too.

The top wishbone was mounted on a pillar which projected above the frame, and which also took the inboard end of the Newton telescopic damper. Importantly, all inboard mountings for the suspension were via bonded rubber bushes developed by Metalastik Ltd of Leicester; no metal-to-metal contact was made at all, which significantly cut down noise, harshness and vibration. Nor was any lubrication needed, because the rubber in the bushes accommodated the turning movement of the wishbones as they rode up and down, this resistance being included in the spring-rate calculations.

The torsion bar was in effect an extension of the lower I-beam inner mounting, so that as the beam turned, so the bar twisted. As the lower wishbone mounting was some way inboard of the frame side member, being on the cross piece, the 52-inch torsion bar ran back to its rear mounting point *alongside* the frame member rather than under it as on previous Jaguar experimental designs. This rear anchorage was where a girder bisected the 'X' bracing, and it was fitted with a screw adjuster so that ride height could be altered if necessary. By taking some of the road shocks this far back in the frame, the torsion bars helped to a certain extent in reducing twisting forces on the chassis.

The balljoints which Heynes employed to carry the stub axle took the form of pins contained in cups, situated at the outer end of both top and bottom wishbones. The ball pins, hard-chromed to reduce wear, were seated in sintered bronze cups at an angle of about 70-degrees to the vertical, giving a bedding-in effect which automatically took up wear. It took much patient research to arrive at the final specification for the ball pins and cups, and the material used for the latter was to be changed at various times in the future. Both were quite easily renewed if worn, though if kept greased six-figure mileages were usually required before this became necessary.

By specifying ball joints, Heynes achieved several objectives – first, it enabled him to bring the stub axle centre line and outer wishbone pivot point closer together, which cut down the leverage applied by road forces to the joint and thus reduced stress and wear, and secondly, by accommodating both steering and suspen-

Above: Heynes' beautifully engineered torsion-bar independent front suspension – most people express surprise at its delicate simplicity, but of course it was extremely strong too. All pivots were rubber-bushed to cut down vibration; the long torsion bar anchored at the centre of the crossmember. Note the anti-roll bar in front.

Left: The independent suspension as mounted on the Mk V chassis; note air-vents in back plates to assist brake cooling – these were a mixed blessing as they also scooped-up water and grit! This particular chassis, with plated suspension parts, is for demonstration purposes – normal finish was black.

sion movement in a single joint, he avoided the use of multiple bearings or joints which might have reduced precision and certainly would have introduced more wearing surfaces. The system was completed by a rubber-mounted anti-roll-bar which was anchored under the front cross member and ran between the two lower suspension beams.

This suspension was advanced and very effective. It was used unchanged on all big Jaguars from the Mk V until the Mk 1X left production in 1960, and similarly on all XKs up to the same date. In only slightly modified form, it served on the C- and D-type sports racing cars at Le Mans, and then lived on in the 'E' type from 1961 until 1975. William Heynes and his engineering team had got their sums right from the very start.

The rear suspension on the new chassis might have looked basically similar to that of the previous cars, but important changes had been made. Above all, a much greater degree of wheel travel had been allowed for, the axle being carried on much softer springs which were six-inches longer than before; hence the kick-up of the frame as it approached the axle, to allow for the increased movement. Girling lever shock absorbers, mounted on the frame side members immediately ahead of the axle, took care of the damping. The axle was either Salisbury or ENV, although it seems that all drophead coupes – even very late ones – continued to use the ENV even after the saloon (and XK sports car) had gone over to Salisbury.

Heynes new 'independent' chassis worked so well and was so successful that it is difficult looking back to those days to remember that in the 'forties it was considered by many to be almost impossible to combine softly sprung suspension (especially if it was independent) with good road holding and controllability; roll, and that com-

Much increased wheel travel was allowed by the new chassis frame, with more flexible springs also contributing to a better ride. The lever-type damper was mounted on the inside of the frame, and the hydraulic brake pipes are also visible – plus the big handbrake cable. *Photo: Jaguar Cars*

patibility between front and rear suspensions were thought to be the most difficult problems to solve. Yet solve them Heynes certainly had, by selecting the correct spring rates fore and aft, and by effective damping.

The new suspension had been designed in conjunction with new wheels and tyres, and these added materially to the success of the chassis. At 16-inches in diameter, the steel wheels were 2-inches smaller than before, and they had wide-based rims (by the standards of the day) of 5-inches across. On these were mounted the new Dunlop Super-comfort tyres of wide 6.70 section, the Mk V Jaguar being the first car fitted with them. The combination offered much better grip than before, and the smaller diameter lowered the car's centre of gravity, which apart from being beneficial in itself, gave the car a sleek, ground-hugging look.

Steering was still Burman, using a recirculating ball steering box; the steering drop-arm moved a centre track rod with an idler arm at its other end, this assembly being isolated from suspension movement. The movement was transferred to the stub axle via short links and steering arms on the axles themselves, the whole arrangement being compatible with, and uneffected by, the up-and-down motion of the suspension. An 18-inch Bluemel telescopic steering wheel was still used, but a sign of the times was the big increase of turns lock-to-lock – 3.25 instead of 2.5 as before: North America was exerting an ever increasing influence on Jaguar....

Perhaps a little overdue, a hydraulic braking system featured for the first time on a Jaguar chassis. The brake pedal acted on a chassis-mounted single master cylinder in the normal way, with slave cylinders transmitting the effort to the brake shoes within their 12-inch cast-iron drums at each wheel. The Girling two-leading-shoe system was used, with its 'self servo' effect, the front shoes being pulled against the rubbing surface of the drums as they rotated. The handbrake operated on the rear wheels by cable in the normal way, but in a departure from their usual practice, Jaguar's engineers chose to mount the brake under the dashboard to the right of the steering column, with an awkward umbrella-handle device to operate it.

However, the reduction of wheel diameter inevitably meant a reduction in drum size, which together with increased shrouding by the solid steel wheels, meant that brake fade became a serious factor for the first time. Three generations on and the chassis would receive disc brakes, but until then, fade was to be a reoccuring problem during fast driving.

Novelty ended when it came to engine and transmission though, as the 2.5-and 3.5-litre pushrod engines from the previous range were employed as we have seen. No 1.5-litre Jaguar anymore, no doubt because Standard retained the tooling for that engine, which John Black used in the Triumph Roadster and 1800 saloon for a while, until it was finally dropped in favour of the 2088cc,

Testing the Mk V's new suspension – Walter Hassan takes the car over a rough surface and practically gets both front wheels off the ground! Place is the ex-RAF wartime airfield at Lindley, near Nuneaton, adopted as a motor vehicle proving ground by members of the Motor Industry Research Association and officially opened on October 1, 1948 – though it had been in use unofficially for some time previously.

wet-liner Vanguard engine. Nor, probably would the performance of a 1776cc Mk V have been acceptable by the quickly rising standards of the late 1940s.

These engines were used with a minimum of change, although it was thought necessary to use a slightly milder camshaft in the 3.5-litre to provide even greater flexibility and smoothness. Power output was also slightly affected by the use of a single exhaust system with one silencer instead of the former dual arrangement, though officially the power output remained at 102bhp and 125bhp for the two engines. The company had still not made up its mind about alloy connecting rods and both types were used, although steel was in fact standardised on later cars.

Likewise, the previously re-designed single helical gearbox was used, though it led to a divided propeller shaft, not seen on a Jaguar before. This was installed in order to take full advantage of the downwards offset given by the hypoid bevel rear axle, thus keeping the floor line as low as possible – the Mk V had no transmission tunnel at all in the back, the floor merely shelving almost imperceptibly from the centre down towards the doors. A rubber-mounted centre bearing supported the divided shaft just behind the centre of the chassis cross-member.

The Mk V perpetuated the traditional 'Jaguar' look when it came to appearance, maintaining a profile which was not that far removed from the original car

Above & Below: The Mk V was powered by Jaguar's existing range of pushrod engines as used in the previous 'cart sprung' saloons. These pictures show the 3.5-litre unit. *Photos: Jaguar Cars*

The Mk V's divided propeller shaft – note the rubber mountings on each side of the coupling. Large-diameter exhaust pipe passes through hole in cross-member on right. *Photo: Jaguar Cars*

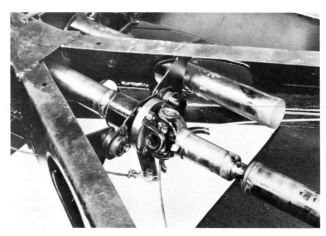

announced back in 1935. But changes there had certainly been, and not one panel was interchangeable with any of the previous model. Immediately obvious was the sloping bonnet, the faired-in headlights, the massive bumpers, and the spats covering the rear wheel openings. A closer look would reveal slimmer windscreen pillars set at more of an angle, chromium plated side window frames, and wider doors.

The styling of the Mk V Jaguar is slightly controversial today, with some people loving its squat, bulky look and others disapproving of Lyons' attempt at updating a pre-War design by incorporating what they term late-forties gimmickry. Back in October 1948 though, *The Autocar* approved of it, saying somewhat defiantly: "...it is not American or Italian styling, but British, and with dignity as well as gracefulness. An honest radiator is still there, though refined in detail, by which we shall continue to recognise the breed."

Like most Jaguars, the greater number of Mk Vs were destined for export, and Jaguar incorporated a number of lessons hard learned over the preceeding three or four years. The most visible of these were the Mk V's bumpers, the most substantial and complex seen on any Jaguar with the possible exception of the 5mph-impact defenders fitted to late XJ cars. They consisted of no less than thirteen major, chrome plated components, this total being made up of four quarter-bumpers at each end, four overriders, and a heavy bar running across the rear number plate. "It looks like a bumper salesman got to Jaguar" said one American owner plaintively. Then there were the valance plates on top, and an invisible array of spring steel brackets and supports holding the assemblies to the chassis frame.

But yes, the big radiator grille was still proudly worn, surmounted by a *real* radiator cap which screwed directly into the radiator header tank itself, and on which could

be mounted the optional leaping jaguar mascot. The grille was flanked by two pedestal-mounted fog and/or spot lamps, above which were the Lucas 'tripod' headlight units carried in pods faired into the steel wings.

The Mk V was the last Jaguar to feature a 'hinge-down' bootlid, with the inbuilt tray of fitted tools in a sea of green baize, complete with its own interior light. The luggage compartment revealed was not particularly large, although the best use was made of the space by the optional fitted suitcases, two to a set and fabric finished in a choice of two colours, black or pigskin (the drophead coupe boot was slightly different and the cases were tailored accordingly). As before, provision was made for the lid to remain open for carrying bigger loads, eyelets being fitted to accommodate straps.

Underneath, the assembly containing the rear number plate with its twin (XK 120-type) reversing lights hinged down to reveal the spare wheel compartment; clipped to the compartment wall alongside the spare wheel was the screw jack. Between boot floor and spare wheel compartment was the 15-gallon fuel tank, which had its filler cap concealed by a flap for the first time (but no longer with a reserve facility).

The new Jaguar still had a waist-line moulding, but this time it incorporated some new technology – push-button door locks. This was a departure for Jaguar, who up until then had used nothing except the old dovetail coachlock, and the new Wilmott Breedon cannistor lock was not without its problems – "we did more experimenting than Wilmott Breedon did regarding pressures, spring ratings

Almost there! Side view of the Mk V body mock-up with correct wings and side windows; though note the low-mounted spotlights, single bumpers, and wire wheel at rear! *Photo: Jaguar Cars*

Early Mk V boot and tool kit, plus spare wheel compartment underneath (disclosed by hinging-down number plate panel fixed with budget-lock). This car may be destined for a motor show as the bumper valance appears to be chromed. *Photo: Jaguar Cars*

and so on in the lock!'' recalled Peter Craig. This was one of the many minor headaches associated with the launch of any new car, and Peter remembered that while getting the Mk V ready for its introduction, he and his colleagues would often be at the factory for 37 hours at a stretch, surviving on cat-naps and eggs and bacon cooked by works manager Teddy Orr ...

The interior of the Mk V was a blend of old and new, although even the 'new' had been seen briefly before – this was the unpleated leather used on the seats, a style which had been seen in the curtailed 1940 season. The idea was not, apparently, mere fashion, as the reason given was that overseas customers had complained of dust collecting in the pleats. The use of plain leather for

Interior of very early (October 1948) Mk V saloon, showing plain-leather seats; ashtrays were later moved from the rear of the front seats to rear door cappings. Note sliding roof, with neat wood fillets surrounding it. *Photo: Jaguar Cars*

upholstering seats is always more expensive however, as any marks on the leather (scars, barbed-wire marks etc) show up at once, which means that only the most perfect hides can be used. This is probably why Jaguar returned to pleats with the Mk VII.

Deep bucket seats with a handle for height adjustment featured in the front, with a large bench seat with sharply shelving cushion in the back complete with the usual folding centre arm rest. The seat backs extended right up to the small rear window, where there was no parcel shelf. Map pockets with zips were incorporated in the door panels, and walnut veneer graced all the many wood cappings, fillets and rails. Doors were now locked from the inside by turning small plated buttons, each inscribed with an arrow and carrying the word "lock", and the door catches operated by buttons within vertical slam-handles.

The walnut finish was continued onto the dash as before, where the same basic pre-War type layout was maintained. The major revision concerned the top rail, which was now much shallower as it didn't have to accommodate a handle for opening the screen, a facility which no longer existed. Similarly, the windscreen wiper controls had been transferred from the rail to a single knob on the dash, which itself had been generally tidied up – the three minor instruments were now grouped together at the top, above the centre placed light switch and minor controls. New stylised figures graced the black-faced instruments, and the needle pointers were now much thicker.

This last was probably connected with the new type of Lucas dash lighting used, as the figures and needles alone on the dials were picked-out by a battery of four "black

violet" lights hidden up under the top screen rail to give a strange, luminous effect. Opinions differed, but many found that the low-key glow made night driving a delight. However, nobody who had practical experience with it disputed the worth of one simple innovation which came with the new dash – its ability to hinge down complete once the outer wood finisher had been removed, thereby openly displaying the mass of wiring behind it. Simplicity itself if attention was called for, compared to the dismantling and blind groping necessary with the previous models.

An 'extra' for the dashboard was a Radiomobile receiver, model RM.100 for the home market, and model 4012 for Canada and the USA. A centre roof aerial was usually specified, though the less satisfactory under-wing type could also be ordered. A small drawer filled the gap if a wireless was not fitted, supplemented at each end of the facia by the usual small cubby holes lined in green baize.

The driver sat in front of the big black 18-inch steering wheel with a good view down the traditionally long Jaguar bonnet; wing tips were still just in sight. The rear view mirror was now mounted on the lower screen rail. Organ-type foot pedals were used, with a foot operated dipswitch taking the place of the previous steering wheel boss control. The gearlever was very short and stubby, but easy to reach. Heater and demister were fitted as standard, although the main units were mounted under the bonnet, giving the engine compartment a rather cluttered look; later they were transferred back under the dash where the previous model had carried them. Finally, a sliding roof panel completed the car's equipment, disappearing backwards under the false roofpiece as before; good fresh-air ventilation could be obtained by opening the new rear quarter-lights in the back doors, their curved, heavily plated frames setting a Jaguar pattern that would continue for twenty years – even the design of the operating knob was not to change!

The Drophead Coupe MkV

Then there was the drophead coupe, rated by some as the most elegant of the old Jaguars; it certainly seemed to carry its chrome-ware a little better than the saloon, especially when finished in black cellulose with a white top. A two-door car, it differed from the saloon on a number of points, and more wood was used in its construction – the body rocker (or sill) under the doors was a single piece of timber which ran from scuttle to rear wing instead of being a hollow steel box as for the saloon, of 9-inches by 1.5-inches section; it bolted to the chassis frame extensions, and to it was fixed the running board/wings by small coachscrews. The doors were ash-framed, with a diagonal 45-degree internal bracing rod as employed in earlier Jaguars. Neither did the drophead have the pushbutton exterior door handles, but instead was given

Another early Mk V, showing the dashboard arrangements including the stylish (or stylised) instrument lettering, unique to the Mk V. Later cars had ashtrays incorporated in the top rail of the facia. Umbrella-type handbrake can be seen beneath steering column, and the trim displays the contrasting piping sometimes employed on seats and door panels.
Photo: Jaguar Cars

The Mk V Jaguar Saloon, a blend of old and new but with a certain poise of its own. The scene is London Airport, Heathrow, the plane a Lockheed Constellation.

the old type of push-down handle with a wedge-type coachlock.

The option of various different colours for the hood meant an even wider range of options in finish for the prospective purchaser, who could choose from 79 combinations of body, hood and trim colour schemes, compared with a 'mere' 25 for the saloon!

The launch of the Mk V drop-head was not without its little slice of drama, and the episode serves to illustrate Williams Lyons' strength of character when it came to the crunch. Plant Director-to-be Peter Craig was working long hours helping to finish the new coupe ready for its official presentation to the dealers. The coupe carried the same beautiful, expensive full 'wig top' of the previous model, with headlining inside and graced by plated landau bars outside – all very difficult to engineer and time-consuming to make.

"We had the coupe ready", recounted Peter, "and the deadline at the convention was 11am that Thursday morning, and we were there behind the curtains at 10am waiting for the dealer presentation. And Sir William came up and had a look, and he stood back. 'Wonderful effort, lads, but – no'. And afterwards, first thing on Friday, he wanted the body line dropping. But there was one thing about it – when the body line was dropped, the car *was*

right. He was right once again. It wasn't unusual, he was completely and utterly correct."

For most people the 1948 Motor Show was the first opportunity to examine the Mk V. This particular show was an extremely important one, as it was the first since 1938. Enough time had elapsed since the war had ended for most manufacturers to have come up with entirely new post-War designs, in which technical ingenuity and new departures in styling abounded, with independent front suspensions and excursions into streamlining and unitary construction evident on many stands.

Of the two most significant new cars at Earls Court, one was on the Jaguar stand – but it was not the Mk V. Intentionally, its limelight had been stolen by the staggering new XK 120 sports car, smuggled into the hall and revealed on the opening day. The twin cam covers on its advanced, hemispherical head, six-cylinder engine sparkled with the promise of 120mph motoring, and its graceful body lines were an object lesson in the art of merging wing and bonnet into one overall shape. The other 'milestone' car was Alex Issigonis' Morris Minor of course, and it was no coincidence that both it and the new Jaguar chassis featured torsion bar suspension – the inspiration was a common one. The Minor was to be the first British car to achieve the million mark, that produc-

144

Left: A very useful picture of the Mk V Drophead bodyshell, showing the hood frame and even the wooden members running around the top rear of the body. *Photo: Jaguar Cars*

Below: The Mk V Drophead Coupe door with, and without, its trim panel. Note steel tensioner running across the wooden door frame and the three door hinges to support the not inconsiderable weight of the assembly. *Photo: Jaguar Cars*

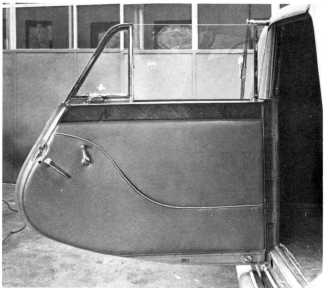

tion figure being reached in 1961, and it was outlived by only two other vehicles displayed at the 1948 London Show – the Land-Rover and the Citroen 2CV.

Not all manufacturers quite got to grips with the new fashions; quoth *The Automobile Engineer:* "far too many cars of quite good general form are spoiled by bad detail. There is far too much over fidgetiness in the way of needles, ribs and strange section bumpers, fanciful overriders and what not. Good general modelling can be quite spoiled by reckless distribution of ornamentation... Neither is appearance improved or distinction gained by providing bumpers of duplicate section, novel form, or worse still, with the important middle portion omitted."

Now the Mk V could be said to be guilty of quite a number of these transgressions which the *Automobile*

Engineer writer abhored, yet somehow the result was not the vulgar over-ornamentation that word description alone might indicate. For all its chrome and duplicated bumpers and missing centre pieces, the car carried itself well and stands as a perfectly valid design in its own right, and need not be ashamed. Or so the writer feels – others may have differing opinions! At anyrate, despite the metallic bronze XK 120 alongside, the new saloon from Jaguar drew many admiring glances, and as always, orders straight away outstripped supply.

Road-testing the 3.5-Litre Mk V

Production of the Mk V was well under way by the time

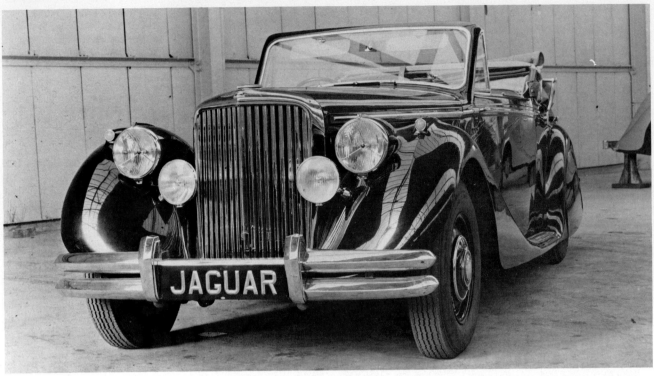

Above: Frontal aspect of the Mk V Drophead was as imposing as ever; this view also shows the hub caps, which although chromed are also partly painted.

The Mk V Drophead Coupe showing 'de ville' and closed positions of the top. This early car lacks the budget locks for the rear wheel spats which feature on later examples. *Photos: Jaguar Cars*

the model came up for test in Great Britain, the vast majority being shipped abroad of course. In view of the fact that the few which remained here were mostly 2.5-litre cars, it is possibly surprising that Jaguar chose only to loan out the 3.5-litre – but then, the 2.5-litre Mk V was by no means a brisk car, even if sweet and smooth: the performance image was probably better fostered by the larger engined car.

The Autocar liked the car's styling – "an extremely effective compromise between a car that still 'looks a car' and ultra-modern trends has been struck. After seeing the Jaguar Mk V...and the excellent and impressive line that has been achieved from whatever angle the car is viewed, one is led to wonder why it should be necessary to go further away from the sensible shapes accepted for many years past."

Perhaps, if many potential customers were as conservative as *The Autocar* (founded in 1898), it was just as well that Jaguar introduced a transitional shape, before disturbing their sensibilities with something as revolutionarily modern as the Mk VII!

However, looks apart, the performance and general behaviour of the new Jaguar needed no qualifications. "The new suspension shows great merit both in comfort of riding for all occupants and in the stability for fast cornering. The long torsion bars in front, coupled with half-elliptics in the rear, give a ride which is soft but never sloppy, and the car feels under remarkably good control. Up to the highest speeds it sits down on the road like a train, feeling completely safe". The writer also mentioned that while the new Dunlops did sometimes squeal, the suspension "does not permit roll" – which is patently untrue! However, he was honest enough to say a little later on that the brakes did fade, even if words were chosen carefully to express the thought.

As for general performance, the accent was on smooth, sustained progress rather than out-and-out speed:

"Basically, the engine has not been materially altered, but is more flexible than before, and the Mk V will trickle through slow traffic at under 10mph in top gear and pick up smoothly and swiftly when an opening offers. It is smooth and quiet right up into the eighties, though interestingly enough a slight, even subtle, exhaust burble has been permitted, a somehow attractive reminder of the 120bhp which the engine can develop, for this slight note never becomes obtrusive and is noticeable only when accelerating from low speeds.

"It is a car for long journeys, that can put 50 miles and more into the hour, one in which 200-miles leave the driver and passenger uneffected, and in which a 400-or 500-mile day would be a pleasure. Yet it is thoroughly tractable for the short pottering or shopping expedition, and very light to control. In the controls, in fact, the Mark V shows improvement parallel to that evident in the smoothness and silkiness of the latest engine and the comfort and stability of riding imparted by the new suspension."

The steering received equal praise, being light in operation and accurate. Turns lock-to-lock were quoted as 4.5 for a good turning circle for a 15ft. 7in. car of 37ft., gearing which *The Autocar* described as "fairly quick". Clutch and gearlever operation were singled out as light and pleasing, which with the "thoroughly satisfactory" driving position, made the car pleasant to drive, helped by reduced wind noise compared with the old model.

Under the stop-watch, *The Autocar* found the Mk V to be generally less accelerative than the old 3.5-litre saloon it tested in 1948. At a rather leisurely 18.9 seconds, the 0-60mph time had increased by over two whole seconds, a discrepancy which had grown to three when 70mph was reached. Apart from an improvement of a second in the

Engine installation on the 3.5-litre Mk V – centre hinged bonnet is secured by hooks visible on side panels, which are themselves detachable for better access to the carburettors and electrics. This car has the early-type heater – later on, the unit was fitted under the dash instead of in the engine compartment. *Photo Jaguar Cars*

30-50mph time, top gear acceleration was down too. Only in the top speed could the Mk V get anywhere near its predecessor, matching it exactly at 91mph.

While it may be dangerous to pick and choose one's performance figures from contemporary sources, it does seem that *The Autocar's* example was either off-song or not conducted in the timed tests with sufficient *brio*, as with no particular weight or gearing penalty, it appears to be no quicker than a good example of the earlier 2.5-litre Jaguar, which (averaging *The Autocar* and *The Motor* results) achieved 60mph in 18.3 seconds.

One would therefore like to believe that *The Motor's* set of figures for their 3.5-litre Mk V saloon are more representative of the breed, and subjective opinion suggests that they are. This car, not completely run-in, made 60mph from rest in a much more spritely 14.7 seconds, and bridged the 30-50mph gap in 8.9 seconds, an improvement respectively of 4.2 and 0.5 second over *The Autocar*. Together with an almost identical top speed of 90.7mph, the closeness of the 'passive' top gear figures and the divergence of the 'active' standing-start ones does rather point to a difference in driver technique which resulted in this discrepancy.

Compare *The Motor's* Mk V figures with its own test of the 1938 3.5-litre Jaguar, and one sees that the earlier car has a slight but not dramatic edge. At 9 seconds, it was just under a second faster to 50mph, and around 0.5 second quicker over top gear increments of 30-50 and 40-60mph. Despite its even blunter shape, the older car's maximum (at 91.8mph) was marginally higher than the Mk V's.

On the road, these differences would be too slight to notice under normal conditions, and in virtually all other respects, the independently sprung car was vastly better, and capable of putting up higher averages over mixed roads with far less strain on the driver and his passengers. It was in ride comfort that the greatest strides had been made, and perhaps for the first time Jaguar became truly a leader in this respect; the company was rarely to lose its advantage thereafter:

"The occupants of the front seats of this car enjoy a standard of riding comfort which is outstandingly high, a standard which has not been bettered in any car of any nationality which it has been our good fortune to test. There is flexibility in the suspension to give excellent shock insulation at low speeds on really rough surfaces yet there is sufficient control over the springs for the riding to remain steady when the car is travelling fast; physical comfort, resulting from the virtual absence of either direct road shocks or of undamped spring oscillations, is accompanied by mental comfort, resulting from a lack of road noise and from the car's evident stability."

So Jaguar had managed to avoid the many pitfalls lying in the path of the unwary I.F.S. designer, even though there was some work left to do, as *The Motor* suggested that the rear seat passengers were not quite so well insulated against road shocks as were the front seat occupants. But, on the other hand, the car's behaviour was not influenced by a near maximum load, a state which reduced some of its contemporaries to wallowing, understeering hulks. "It is not simply a question of the engine having ample reserves of power to handle any reasonable load without requiring noticeably more frequent use of the indirect gears", explained *The Motor*, "but also of riding comfort and steering responsiveness, which are almost equally commendable whether the

A later Mk V displaying the escutcheon on rear wheel spats covering budget-lock, and the later type quarterlight frame with a rounded, instead of pointed, front 'corner'. *Photo: Motor*

driver be alone or accompanied by a full quota of passengers and their luggage."

Despite being made technically obsolete by the XK engine, the sturdy old pushrod unit was far from being an antique. "There is a great deal of extra power on tap when the tachometer is allowed to record high rpm in the indirect gears" said *The Motor*; "there are faster cars than the Jaguar saloon...but nevertheless, the type under review, built and equipped without evident regard for weight saving, can comfortably better the speed and acceleration of American automobiles."

The willingness and power of the engine were considerable helped by the action of the clutch and gearbox, which *The Motor* also commented upon:

"A delightfully smooth clutch withstands abuse without slipping, and is coupled to a four-speed gearbox having the short central lever associated with the British sporting saloon car. Closely spaced ratios allow the keen driver to attain utmost performance at all times, or the lazy man can travel about very briskly by the technique of starting from rest in second gear and changing directly up into fourth at a convenient speed. On badly-iced road surfaces we even found it possible to start from rest uphill in top gear. The indirect ratios are quiet without being absolutely silent, and the engagement of all gears except first is facilitated by synchromesh mechanism which, without being clashproof, does eliminate the need for careful judgement of rpm".

It should be noted here that the weak action of the synchromesh is, in April 1950, already being commented on; as substantially the same gearbox was still in use up to 1964, one can again readily understand the somewhat bewildered criticisms of the box in later Jaguars ten years, or more, on.

Strangely enough, no mention was made of the car's brakes at all; perhaps they tended to fade to an extent which would have made comment ill-mannered! Or possibly, as much of the 2600 mile test was conducted in wet or snowy conditions (including an excursion into Eastern Sweden in January!), they could never be fully put to the test. Only the unfortunate pistol-grip handbrake was singled out for mention, its "awkward location" being disliked.

Of the ancilliary equipment, the heater was described but its actual performance not commented upon, the 48-watt headlights were rated as "powerful", and the horn-push (similar to the XK 120's) pleasing to look at but not sensitive enough for use on a fast car like the Mk V. The dashboard display with its full quota of knobs and switches was at first glance considered "slightly alarming" though in fact "sensibly spaced out to avoid any risk of confusion". The capacity of the luggage locker was obviously thought minimal, and Jaguar must have agreed because the deficiency was very enthusiastically remedied in the next model!

The Motor's summary of the Mk V Jaguar's character is subtle, accurate and expressive:

"What it typifies ... is not the economy vehicle such is at present forced upon a majority of European motorists by prevailing economic conditions; rather does it typify the European style of fine car, developed as an adjunct to the good life which has been evolved in the old world by centuries of civilisation.

"Like many of the products of traditional craftsmanship, the Jaguar serves a practical purpose with complete effectiveness, but it does so in a way which is emotionally pleasing rather than justifying itself in terms of the strictest economics. Thus, when assessed in terms of world markets, it is a car with no need to claim that it is the largest, fastest or the most economical car available at a given price; rather, it is a car large enough for most purposes, faster than usual without being extravagant, but above all else a car which it is a lasting pleasure to own and use".

The Mk V Overseas

So true, though comparatively few people were given the opportunity in this country to find out for themselves. A large number of Mk Vs went to the United States, and an interesting feature in *The Autocar* towards the close of 1949 allows us to gauge the American viewpoint, and compare the Mk V with its immediate predecessor.

It was the story of how Los Angeles Jaguar distributor Roger Barlow and his wife Louise delivered a brand new Mk V saloon to Spokane, Washington, a distance of more than 1 500 miles from their starting point of Hollywood. The run included the crossing of the Mojave desert where despite enormously high ambient temperatures, only a little over 80-degrees was recorded on the dashboard; running-in precluded any high speed cruising, though towards the end of the trip, some effort was made to investigate the car's higher speed potentialities briefly. Then at Spokane, the ivory Mk V with its whitewall tyres was swopped for the customer's old 1948 3.5-litre saloon for the return journey.

Louise Barlow's comments on how they found the new independently sprung car compared with its beam axle predecessor are valuable, being as it is contemporary opinion from one of Jaguar's most important markets:

"Both Jaguars performed magnificently and the trip made possible a direct comparison between the Mk V and the older 1948 3.5-litre model, as the latter was driven over the same route as the Mk V, except for the side trips to the parks. The immediate impression was that the Mk V was a larger and more luxurious car to both driver and passenger. My husband talks about the new torsion bar suspension but I'm afraid it doesn't seem very clear to me – except that I *know* that the Mk V rides beautifully at any speed over the roughest roads and never gives one the impression of being abused under such conditions. We didn't have sufficient miles on the Mk V before delivering it to the new owner to drive it flat out, but both Roger and I agreed that it felt like a faster car in the normal

Louise Barlow stops to examine desert flora on the trip to Washington; whitewall tyres were usually fitted to North American import Jaguars, and this saloon looks particularly handsome against the magnificent back-drop of the Mojave Desert. *Photo: Roger Barlow*

driving range of 70-75mph and was certainly smoother and faster in accelerating from low speeds on top gear. Steering was definitely easier at all speeds and the incredibly small turning circle was a continual source of amazement to both of us. When manoeuvering the car for pictures we found it possible to swing tight around on a normal two-way highway without having to reverse; a remarkable state of affairs.

"We both agreed that under any conditions the Mk V seemed to cruise at a 10mph higher speed than the previous model with the same effort on the part of the driver ... I almost forgot to compliment the Mk V for being such a good mountain climber ... and no matter how hard we drove coming down the mountain grades we always had plenty of braking power and never experienced what my mechanically minded husband calls 'fading'."

While the traditional aspects of the Mk V – its big impressive radiator, the wood and leather inside – appealed to the average American, it was also one of the comparatively few British cars which was also suited to

the conditions out there, in particular the long distances frequently covered as a matter of course, thanks to miles of properly engineered highway systems. While not astonishingly quick off the mark, once on the move, the Mk V Jaguar was easily able to keep up – or more likely overtake – virtually any of the home-produced automobiles, and was much more stable during cornering and braking, areas of car behaviour in which North American manufacturers remained disinterested for years.

Although drop-heads were very popular in the States, much larger numbers of saloons were in fact exported, probably because the open cars were more difficult to produce in quantity. Most Mk Vs were of 3.5-litres capacity (7831 as opposed to only 1661 2.5-litre saloons), the larger engine being preferred in overseas markets. Some 972 3.5-litre drop-heads were made, but the 2.5-litre drop-head is a very rare animal, a mere 29 being produced and only a handful apparently surviving today.

While the Mk V Jaguar was certainly a stop-gap model to an extent, demand overseas was high. Here a batch of new saloons are loaded into the *S.S. Mauretania*

The car was manufactured in left or right-hand-drive as the market demanded, with a lot of right-hand-drive Mk Vs going to Australia, where its incredible reliability and toughness were greatly appreciated in distant outposts in the bush.

On that continent, the importer was Bryson Motors of Sydney, a small but enterprising concern that after the War had offered to contract for 2 000 cars a year, having heard that Jaguar were dissatisfied with the 100 a year rate which their existing distributors felt unable to improve on. Although they then represented only Morgan and a few motorcycle companies, Lyons was impressed by Bryson's enthusiasm and gave them the concession. They only failed to reach the target set because Jaguar couldn't keep up the supply of cars! Within two years they had taken over the showrooms of the previous distributor ("the finest in Sydney") and continued to go from strength to strength.

That it was not easy to appreciate the Mk V's true worth under the restricted conditions in England was discovered by Gordon Wilkins when he borrowed a 3.5-litre to cover the 1950 Mille Miglia and visit the Turin Motor Show amongst other things. "I must confess to a slight lifting of one eyebrow when the car was delivered without any spare parts at all, other than a couple of lamp bulbs, but by the time the trip was over I realised that the manufacturers had good reason for their display of confidence". In fact the 3000 mile journey began with a late-night dash in England to pick up passengers and luggage, and a hint of the car's capabilities was given when over one deserted stretch, "63 miles were covered in just an hour without any particular effort".

Across the channel, the Mont Cenis pass was tackled despite increasingly heavy snow, "the Jaguar accelerating up to 50mph in top gear between the hairpins" despite being five-up and with a heavy load of luggage. They were the last to get across for a week. On the descent the other side, conditions were treacherous, "and what a help the old-style gear lever is in retaining control of the situation when all four wheels want to slide and a precipice yawns at the edge of the road!" commented Gordon Wilkins.

The Autocar artist Max Miller was left at Turin to draw the Lancia Aurelia, while Gordon and the Mk V went on to Brescia for the start of the Mille Miglia. It was due to commence at midnight on the Saturday, and, extending over a thousand miles of Italian roads, would not end until the dawn of the following Monday. A difficult race to cover with time for only three-or four-hours sleep a night – "in such conditions one appreciates a car which will take to the *autostrada* as its natural element and do 70-miles in the hour without stress or effort. Comfort is increased by the fact that at speeds up to 75mph the engine is virtually inaudible."

Obstructionist tactics by the local *carabinieri* at one point near Bologna meant that for a while, Gordon and the Mk V had to join the main race route itself. These roads were not officially closed to traffic during that extraordinary race, which could make life exciting for the competitors. "Efforts are made at towns and villages to divert traffic to side roads, especially with vehicles going in the opposite direction to the race, but provided a car is going fast enough in the right direction no one tries to stop it and the Jaguar rarely dropped below 80mph on the 57-miles from Bologna through Modena to Parma, where we turned north for a short cut back to Brescia.''

The race was made even more interesting that year by the entry of an XK 120 by the veteran Italian driver and local hero Clemente Biondetti. The near-standard XK put up a courageously good showing against the sports-racing Ferraris and Alfas, the amazing Biondetti forcing the car up to second place during the run from Rome to Brescia, challenging Marzotto's £5000 Ferrari, before a broken rear spring spoiled his chances.

Leslie Johnson in another XK finished 5th, and it began to be brought home to Jaguar how important these competition sorties were in promoting the Jaguar name – even Gordon Wilkins noted that he "heard people pointing out my saloon to each other in traffic blocks: 'There's a Jaguar, the British car which ran in the Mille Miglia!''. Certainly the XK120 did much to help Mk V sales, the car basking in its reflected glory, and together with the MG TC, the XK was largely responsible for truly opening up the North American market, in particular, for the European sporting car.

The homeward run was a more relaxed affair, the party taking time to eat well and take photographs; nevertheless, a running average of 47.8mph was maintained over 10-hours 33-minutes and 504-miles, which isn't slow. The total (corrected) mileage for the trip was 3376, most of it, observed Gordon Wilkins, covered at speeds of 70mph or over. Thus the fuel consumption of 16.4mpg was moderate in the circumstances, and oil consumption was nothing to be worried about at 2850mpg – it was many years before the XK engine could improve on the latter figure. Summing up, Gordon said:

"The car did not give a moment's trouble of any kind and showed an extraordinary ability to cover long distances at high speeds, without tiring driver and passengers ... Starting was instantaneous regardless of the fuel used.

"At a time when social upheavals and political divisions cause many people to have doubts about our destiny, it is a tonic to travel abroad in a Jaguar. For foreign observers its tremendous performance, delivered without fuss, seems to express the British way of doing things.''

The Mk V in production

The Mk V Jaguar changed very little during its relatively short production life. At the end of the first year, Jaguar did announce some minor changes, a number of which had already been gradually incorporated in the car's specification. The new front suspension had proved perfectly satisfactory in service, although isolated cases of premature wear had resulted in an improved upper ball joint assembly being introduced; other than that it was left alone. Mechanically, little else was done at this stage – early on, after about 100 3.5-litres and 20-30 2.5-litre cars had been built, the centre bearing of the divided propeller shaft had been given a spring

loaded mounting, and later, a stronger 'detent' arrangement had been installed in the selector rods of the gearbox to prevent accidental selection of reverse instead of first gear from rest (this was only partially successful and the reverse stop spring on any non-synchro Jaguar gearbox usually weakens with age, making for some amusing incidents at traffic lights ...).

The original method of locking the side-opening, centre-hinged bonnet, using a system of plungers and cables, hadn't proved very satisfactory so the mechanism was revised after the first batch of cars; the side panels could still be released from inside the car, but the hooks securing the panels were now worked by rods and levers, giving a very positive operation. The spats were now released using a simple T-piece kept with the tools, the budget lock on the spat being covered by a small, plated sprung cover.

Door and window sealing had received early attention too, sorbo-rubber being replaced by moulded rubber and the front quarterlight altered – the original item had a sharply pointed leading edge, the later type being rounded. These early quarterlights (or "No Draft Ventilators" as the factory termed them) differed too in that they were operated by the same captive bellcrank device that was always used for the rear quarterlights, mounted on small wooden plinths. In February 1950 front door sealing was improved through the introduction of a cast aluminium sealing fillet which fastened onto the base of the front doors – it was given a part number and could be ordered for retrospective fitting to earlier cars too.

The body-finishing line at Foleshill, where blemishes are being rectified and door gaps checked and adjusted. A visit by journalists is in progress too. *Photo: Motor*

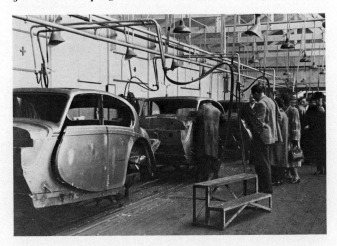

The ultra violet instrument lighting didn't last many months, the flourescent paint on the instrument figures being discontinued, although the same discreet blue panel lighting remained - it seemed to pick out the white figures on the dials quite well enough. Nor did the positioning of the interior heater in the engine compartment – that was transferred underneath the dash as in the previous model, a change accompanied by the installation of a scuttle vent in front of the windscreen (not to be confused with the existing fresh-air doors set vertically in the side panels of the scuttle, and controlled by wire handles from inside).

In January 1950, the threaded bearings at one end of the track rod were replaced by rubber bearings which did not need greasing, and in February, the front cable of the handbrake was given a pull-off spring to alleviate fraying of the inner cable. There were a few changes visible inside the car too, chiefly concerning ashtrays – these were transferred from the backs of the rear seats to the door cappings, and in the front, they became incorporated in the facia rail in front of driver and passenger.

The biggest change to the engine was the re-introduction of steel connecting rods. It was becoming increasingly clear that with age, the alloy rods could become brittle, and failures were not uncommon. Disastrous though such an occurance might appear, it seems as if damage was usually limited to the rod and piston effected, and with a new set of rods and pistons, the car would be on its way again. Another big disadvantage of the alloy rods was that due to their high coefficient of expansion, the increase in diameter of the big end eye when hot had the effect of practically doubling the clearance and loss of oil from the big end bearing, with a consequent fall-off of oil pressure.

Another January 1950 change was to the brakes; the basic hydraulic system was left unchanged, but a sliding pivot arrangement was brought in, and the rear brake assembly was no longer two-leading-shoe. All shoes, both front and rear, were now free to float on their respective anchor pivots and expander tappets, with the rear operating cylinders free to float on the back plates. Instead of operating through the hydraulic plungers on the rear brakes, the handbrake cables now worked the shoes through separate expanders and tappets located in the rear operating cylinders. Linings were also bonded to the brake shoes rather than rivetted.

The Mk V in service

One of the best remembered aspects of the Mk V was its almost total reliability, a trait which endeared the car to thousands of owners all over the world. It often remained in everyday use many years after most of its contemporaries were on the scrapheap, and certainly in Great Britain it was not that unusual to see an obviously well-used specimen going about its business as late as 1972 or 1973 – the writer purchased his late-model Mk V (625350) in 1972 just after its original owner had stopped driving. It was an enduring car, and given the most basic routine servicing would clock up enormous mileages as a matter of course. Peter Craig talked to me on this point, and recalled a letter he had received once at the factory.

"It is one of my complaint letters I've always kept – it came from a chappie in Australia who had done a quarter of a million miles in all conditions, with the temperature band being tremendous, and there could be virtually flooding conditions to the depth of 15 or 18 inches; and he requested a few spares for his car, which he reckoned would then be good enough for another quarter of a million miles! I sent him the spares free of charge."

Another endorsement of the Mk V from Australia comes from owner Bob Harrison of Cambelltown, New South Wales, who we have met before with his S.S.1. He purchased a 1951 3.5-litre saloon from his father, using it as daily transport. At 98 000-miles Bob decided to strip the engine, although he needn't have done – "the engine was in remarkable condition; the maximum bore wear was about 0.0025 inch and I could not measure any wear on the crankshaft, which was absolutely remarkable as even though the engine had regular oil and filter changes, it had done many long, fast journeys and had certainly not been spared".

"As for previous mechanical work, the gearbox required attention at about 60 000-miles after the circlip holding the front race onto the clutch shaft came adrift, and I replaced the clutch at the same time. The brakes have been relined once, the suspension ball joints renewed once, and two new tie-rod ends fitted. The rear axle has never been touched and is still perfectly silent.

"The car was always a pleasure to drive. I have often driven 500-miles in a day with no strain – it seemed happiest cruising between 70 and 80mph and would return around 20mpg on a run. It was often used to tow a caravan or a boat. Passengers always remarked on the silence and smoothness of ride. It was always hard to believe it was such a large, heavy vehicle as all the controls are light and visibility is quite good. The only criticism I have is the handbrake, which is rather ineffective and is not mounted in the ideal position under the dash."

In fact, the factory obviously became so fed-up with people complaining of the pistol-grip handbrake that after the Mk VII was announced, they marketed an official conversion kit "for installation of special handbrake" on the Mk V (part no. SD.1007); this was a centrally mounted lever based on the Mk VII design, and was much more satisfactory.

Not that tributes to the Mk V are confined to overseas users – the car did sterling service in Britain too, and was the first Jaguar to be widely used by the police, with mileages of 200 000 being quite common. A private owner, Dr Nicholas Storrs, relates his experience with the type:

"The car was put to much use, including caravan towing all over Europe and Scandinavia – a job at which

Right & Below: The Mk V Saloon was about the first Jaguar to become really popular with the police, and "JUE 114" is shown having completed more than 100 000-miles in service.

This, believe it or not, is a Mk V ... Whatever one's thoughts on the styling, this Australian hardtop coupe bodywork has a surprisingly professional air about it and is by no means worse than some excesses from European and North American coachbuilders. This particular car has been fitted with an XK engine too, a fairly easily accomplished 'swop' carried out by a number of owners at home and abroad on 'ordinary' Mk Vs. *Photo: courtesy J. Byfield*

it excelled. At about 40 000 miles a connecting rod broke while travelling quite slowly near Southampton. A new engine, with the stronger con. rods, was fitted by the local agents within 48-hours. Apart from this, it was always extremely reliable and this was the only time an enforced stop had to be made (except the occasion when the final drive ran dry, the garage having not filled it properly ...).

"Cooling and brakes were two aspects which were rather marginal. Both were accentuated by, but not confined to, towing. The cooling water would boil quite readily in traffic or when climbing hills, but this never caused damage. The brakes faded easily and I remember a number of worrying moments! The gearbox had to be used to the full when descending hills towing the caravan. Starting, on the automatic choke, was always reliable. Standard 6.70 x 16 tyres were always used and wear was fairly heavy. Eighteen mpg could be achieved with luck. I personally enjoyed using the old Moss gearbox and it certainly taught me how to double declutch properly. It seemed just as sweet and no noisier at 100 000 miles than when new. The comfort of the seats and good ride were a constant joy. It was reluctantly sold in Bedford in 1966 due to lack of space. It was bodily somewhat tatty by then but mechanically good. It always amazed me how overall good a car it was, bearing in mind that it was but a stop-gap model."

Regarding the overheating, the system was non-pressurised and a number of owners cured the problem easily and simply by ensuring that the radiator cap sealed, and then inserting a 5lb. pop-off valve in the overflow pipe – having made sure that the thermostat hadn't jammed shut.

The Autocar conducted a used-car test on an eight year old Mk V 3.5-litre saloon in 1958, and came to much the same conclusions as our private owners. It had obviously sustained a heavy mileage but in almost every way it was enjoyable to drive. Slight piston noise was audible when starting from cold, but this soon disappeared, and in fact the acceleration figures taken (0-60mph in 17.6 seconds, 30-50mph in top 8.1 seconds) were better than the magazine had recorded with their new road test car in 1949. Only the brakes were thought to be below par, as

Final polish after road-testing – unusually, this is a two-tone Mk V and it seems that although such a colour scheme was never catalogued, the factory would produce it to special order.

the pedal travel was excessive and heavy pressures were needed. Apart from that, its road behaviour was exemplary for an eight-year-old:

"This Jaguar has a remarkably good steering lock, and over the full range the control is extremely light to operate, as well as being commendably precise. This is inspite of having on the road wheels Michelin X tyres which often increase the effort of steering. First-class directional stability adds security to the car's high speed cruising ability.

"... The indirect gears are quiet but the change is not quick, as the synchromesh has become very weak; a momentary pause in neutral or full double-declutching is necessary to ensure silent gear changes. A fault is that second gear jumps out of engagement on the over-run.

"Perhaps the most impressive feature of this Jaguar – as a used car and bearing in mind its age and the low price at which it is offered for sale – is the fine mechanical order which make it so enjoyable for the driver. It is also comfortable for the passengers. The suspension ... is well damped and carries the car smoothly over bad road surfaces without pitching or jolting. Pleasant handling characteristics, and excellent behaviour without roll or vicious breakaway, are also evident when the car is driven fast on a winding road.

"Wind noise is at a surprisingly low level, and the car impresses quickly by its ability to cruise between 70mph (corresponding to 3,700rpm) and 80mph in remarkable silence. There are no rattles or squeaks. A good driving position, giving an unobstructed view of the road, and placing the driver near to the windscreen, completes the picture of enjoyment to be obtained at the wheel. The car is easy to control in traffic although rear visibility is poor."

This ability to maintain its performance was integral with the car; the big unstressed 3.5-litre engine did not produce a startling amount of brake horse-power per litre, but would continue to deliver it almost *ad infinitum*. Amongst its few failings were a slight tendency towards head gasket failure, and the oil supply to the rocker shaft was a little suspect and could result in premature wear.

The 2.5-litre Mk V has not figured very much in this chapter so far, largely because there is little contemporary literature on the type. Performance from its 2664cc, 97bhp engine was about the same as the previous 2.5-litre saloon, which meant a top speed in the region of 85-87mph (with a little more down hill!). Acceleration could just about be labelled 'brisk' by the standards of 1949, with a probable 0-60mph time of around 18 seconds – all quite enough to keep the 2.5-litre ahead of most early 1950s saloons at least, and with a close-ratio 65mph third gear combined with a willingness to rev. which exceeded even that of the 3.5-litre, it was a very pleasant car to drive even for the enthusiastic driver. The more frugally minded owner could also take delight in another of its attributes – a moderate fuel consumption. Twenty mpg was easy to obtain, and 25mpg came with a little forebearance on the throttle. In all other respects, the

The last Mk V bodyshell comes down the line, and the story of the 'traditional' Jaguar saloon closes. *Photo: Jaguar Cars*

2.5-litre shared the comforts and road behaviour of its larger engined sister.

Like their immediate predecessors, the majority of Mk Vs were put off the road eventually by body deterioration rather than by any chronic mechanical failures, particularly in climates such as Britain's with its wet roads and salted highways in winter. But even into the 'sixties it was still seen as a high-performance car, with the 3.5-litre version able to show a clean pair of heels to most 'Youngsters' over straight or twisty roads.

In its handling too, the Mk V Jaguar did not begin to feel dated until the beginning of the 'sixties, and always remained enjoyable to drive over demanding routes. For no logical reason, aspersions have been cast on the Mk V's capabilities in this respect, but in fact it was an extremely well-balanced, predictable car. After all, its chassis was deemed perfectly satisfactory by Jaguar and countless owners for almost ten years after the Mk V itself was obsolete, being used virtually unchanged on the Mk VII, VIII and Mk IX luxury saloons. It can even be argued statistically and otherwise, that the Mk V actually handled better than these cars.

Pursuing this theme, it is instructive to compare the Mk V with its twin-cam successor, and a surprising number of statistics do stack-up in favour of the earlier car. The Mk V was almost 2cwt. lighter at 33cwt. unladen, compared to virtually 35cwt. for the Mk VII; it was more wieldy, being 9-inches shorter than the Mk VII, and had higher geared steering; and its pushrod engine sat 5-inches further back in the chassis than the Mk VII's XK unit, giving a front/rear weight distribution which most chassis engineers would acknowledge as being more favourable for good handling. The ratio was 51/49 (front

to rear) for the Mk V, compared to 52.8/47.2 for the later car, the reduction in weight over the front wheels making for better steering response and less effort at the wheel.

Certainly, when the Mk V was introduced there were very few large cars in production which could match it for handling. An obvious rival might have been the Mk VI Bentley. This, the first Bentley to have standardised coachwork (formerly you purchased the chassis and had the body constructed by the coachbuilder of your choice), also had independent suspension, but it was a markedly inferior design to Heynes' torsion bar arrangement. The original Mk VI Bentley was an ill-handling car if pressed – as John Bolster remarked, it "could give the driver anxious moments, tending to go straight on if a slippery corner were entered too fast inadvertently." While the 4257cc car from Crewe was marginally faster than the 3.5-litre Mk V in the higher speed ranges, on overall performance and cornering ability the Jaguar was definitely superior, which was indeed a feat on behalf of the young Coventry company – and no need to bring in the huge price difference betwen the two cars!

Despite its traditional styling, the Mk V Jaguar was really the first *subtle* Jaguar; journey times were no longer simply a function of sheer engine power, but of a scientifically designed chassis too; and the handling and ride of the Mk V are not separated from the performance of the modern car in this respect by the same gulf which lies between today's car and the beam-axle Jaguars which came immediately before it. Lacking the brilliance of the twin-cam engine, the Mk V was not a sophisticated car, but while later Jaguars certainly instilled respect, the Mk V was equally capable of instilling affection in its owner, and that sums up the car very well.

Chapter Six

The Mk VII, VIII and IX Jaguars

There are very few cars that have a genuine maximum speed of over 100mph, give a fuel consumption of around 20 mpg, have a large saloon body, and sell at a list price of under £1,000 equipped with a radio and heater.

The Autocar, April 23, 1952

When we acquired the Mk VII, we unknowingly acquired a personality.

J.C. Robertson, *Road & Track,* July 1963

The Mk VII saloon is one of the most significant cars in the Jaguar story. For William Lyons himself, it was the attainment of a goal he had set himself many years before – the building of a true 100mph luxury saloon which would be the match of any similar car, built anywhere in the world and at any price.

And through the Mk VII came the XK engine, the power unit which for the first time made twin overhead camshafts with all their advantages practical and available to the car buying public – and which, quite coincidentally, was to power five Le Mans winners over a six-year period. It became one of the world's longest-running production engines, and continued to be Jaguar's mainstay as a power unit for almost every single type of Jaguar made from 1951 until late 1986. In overall terms of the performance and refinement breakthrough it achieved, the Mk VII is probably only matched by the equally important XJ series announced eighteen years later.

The birth of the XK engine took place during World War II; all car manufacturing activities had ceased after 1940, but that didn't mean that the subject was ignored – at Foleshill, Lyons had many plans for his company and, during the long nights of the Coventry blitz, talked over his ideas for the future with fellow-firewatchers in a small development office. Seated on the camp beds were Walter Hassan, William Heynes, and a relative newcomer, Claude Baily.

Baily had started work as a boy with Anzani, the much respected engine design and manufacturing company, and had stayed with them until their liquidation in the Depression. "I had the advantage there of doing everything," says Baily, "tracing, drawing, layout to instructions – a first class training." After working for a number of concerns (including Sunbeam and Villiers), he joined Morris Engines, where he worked on the new range of engines and gearboxes for the new Morris 8 planned for 1934/35. His biggest job was designing the new sidevalve Morris 8 engine itself, by a very simple expedient – "I was asked to draw it up from dimensions supplied by the Inspection Department, who had a Ford 8 engine, took it to pieces, and measured it all up!"

That was the extent of the SS design/development team - Heynes as Chief Engineer, assisted by Hassan and, in a slightly more junior capacity, Baily. Independent front suspension experiments had already commenced as we have seen, so it was the as yet unexplored subject of power units which was Lyons' main preoccupation. His sights were fixed on the production of a 100mph Jaguar saloon after the War, and the present range of engines were really at their limit of development.

Some 160bhp had in fact been extracted from the 3.5-litre unit before the War, using a very high compression ratio and a methyl-alcohol and benzine fuel. The engine was inserted into the SS 100 run by Tommy Wisdom, who succeeded in lapping Brooklands at over 118mph and

The 160bhp given by the works-tuned SS 100 before and just after the War provided the aiming point when the XK engine was being designed. Here the stripped '100' is shown on display next to a 'Mk IV' saloon during the 1947 Bouley Bay Hillclimb meeting.

winning a handicap race, but it was clear that the limit had been approached. "This 160bhp", reported Heynes, "had to be measured on the brake with the engine almost cold. After a few seconds the heat would build up in the head and the power fall rapidly." But the level of performance given by that engine "showed us the joy of having plenty of power", and 160bhp became the aiming point as discussions about an entirely new engine progressed at Foleshill. Only this time, it would need to be a totally reliable 160bhp, capable of being held for a hundred hours or more, non-stop ....

During these discussions, several types of engines were thought about, though in each case it was thought necessary to have two sizes of power unit, both to be produced on the same machinery. The great potential market which existed in North America for the right sort of British car just wasn't appreciated then, and it was thought that the two types would be needed in order to get the quantity up and spread the costs. At this early stage, such combinations as a V8 with a possible 4-cylinder 'sister', and a V12 with a six-cylinder variation, were "seriously considered." But whatever form it would take, the engine had "to be capable of propelling a full-size saloon at a genuine 100mph in standard form and without special tuning", and would need to be sufficiently advanced not to need drastic redesigning in order to keep up with the competition in future years.

Quite a tall order, as 100mph saloons were very few and far between in 1939, and were nearly all extremely expensive and produced in very small quantities. But at least Heynes and his team had the advantage of starting with the proverbial blank sheet of paper, a comparatively rare concession then, as now, in the industry.

Early on Heynes came down in favour of the hemispherical head, in consultation with Harry Weslake who once again was called in; this shape of combustion chamber had many advantages, including good valve throat flow, easily controlled turbulance, good exhaust valve cooling, and easy machining owing to the symmetrical form. It featured in all the company's experiments, which began in 1943 with the tacit approval of the authorities. Most of the work thereafter revolved around finding the best type of valve gear.

Bill Heynes at the drawing-board; as Jaguar's chief engineer, he lead the team which produced the XK engine.

"The whole thing was a team effort really," Claude Bailey recalls: "I worked under Heynes, who wasn't an expert on engines in those days, he was more of a chassis man, but Hassan had had some experience of course. We talked things over, and I endeavoured to put things on paper. Really it was a case of the three of us working together. I had a little office and a drawing board in one of the old wooden buildings – I was buried away a bit, it was the sort of work we didn't want everyone to see. There I did innumerable head and engine layouts on paper – many, many schemes were thought of then".

The first concrete evidence of all this paper work was a little 1360cc four-cylinder engine, 66.5mm x 98mm, built purely to prove the hemispherical head and another feature which was close to Heynes' heart – twin overhead camshafts. In fact, 20-years before, these and hemispherical combustion chambers had featured in a paper that Heynes read before the Graduates of the Institute of Automobile Engineers on the design of a four-cylinder motor cycle engine, so there was little doubt what form the new Jaguar engine would finally take right from the outset.

Code-named "XF", this engine provided much useful data before being superseded by the "XG" unit, which

The first twin-cam experimental engine built by Jaguar (or SS as they still were), featuring twin overhead camshafts and hemispherical heads.

Claude Baily, photographed in the early 'fifties; together with Walter Hassan he assisted Heynes with the design of the XK engine. Later he became head of Jaguar's power units division.

for convenience used the bottom half of the Standard-built Jaguar '1.5-litre' engine of 1776cc. It alone diverged from the twin-cam line, having an experimental opposed pushrod cylinder head based on the BMW 328 engine. The BMW 328 sports car had been the SS 100's arch-rival before the war, and was one of the few cars which could equal or better its performance, although it was about twice the price of the SS. Heynes was very friendly with one of the top 328 drivers of pre-War years, Leslie Johnson, and it was his highly developed 328 that was wheeled into the SS workshops for close examination.

However, while the "XG" ran quite well, the rather complex valve gear (which was still worked from a cam down in the cylinder block) was rather too noisy for a luxury saloon car, and furthermore the vertical inlet port arrangement was not as efficient as the horizontal design of the previous engine. So a further engine was built, and this was to be the true forerunner of the eventual production power unit.

The "XJ" was a four-cylinder, 80.5mm x 98mm 1996cc design with twin overhead camshafts in the classic mould. It was on this engine that most of the experiments involving port and head design were carried out, with Harry Weslake being closely involved. Many arrangements of valve gear and camshaft drives were tried out on the XJ (no relation whatever to the later saloon of that name, incidentally), and one version with a 12:1 compression ratio was loaned to Major Goldie Gardner, who used it in his famous EX 135 MG streamliner to record 176.7mph in August 1948. This was the first public

The 'XF' was superceeded by the 'XG' experimental engine, using the old Standard 1.5-litre block – seen here without sump.

appearance of any Jaguar twin-cam engine, and it brought the company useful publicity – 146bhp from 2-litres was very good going for 1948.

From the XJ four-cylinder came the XJ six-cylinder of 83m x 98mm and 3.2-litres capacity. It contained all the refinements which had been bred into the four-cylinder version, and the intention was to replace both the former 2.5 and 3.5 litre pushrod units with this one engine, then develop a four-cylinder version using the same tooling to replace the 1.5-litre unit. However, at 3.2 litres it was smaller in capacity than the old 3485cc pushrod engine, and tests on the road showed that it lacked low-speed torque, so the stroke was increased to 106mm. This final version was termed ''XK''.

Harry Weslake had his own version of how this increase in stroke occured, fairly late in the development programme. ''I went into Hassan's office one day and I saw 3.2-litres – I said, hey Wally, what's that. And he said, 'well, it's a hemispherical head and gives a lot more horsepower, so it can be a smaller engine'. Look, mister, I said, you can't give away 300cc without upsetting the low speed pulling, because a hemispherical head or side valve or overhead valve up to the first 2000 revs will hardly be any different – then the overhead valve will start going away from the sidevalve, and when you get up to 4000 or 5000 the hemi is miles away from everything; but down there it's no good.

''You'll find that your performance up to 60mph isn't going to be as good. You can work it out for yourself – you've got to have a bmep of 130 over 1000lbs to be equivalent to the pushrod giving 118 with 3.5-litres, instead of 3.2. Wouldn't listen to me.

''Then one day, at my office, the telephonist said, Mr Lyons to speak to you. Oh dear – 'I am a very disappointed man. The performance of the hemispherical head engine does not come up to the 3.5-pushrod in traffic or up to 60mph'. Well, I said, what do you expect. I warned your b**** up there if they reduced the capacity that's what would happen. So after a while Bill Lyons said, 'what have we got to do'. There's only one thing to do, that's increase the bore, get it back to 3.5 litres. So old Heynes said, 'we can't do that, there's not enough water between the barrels' but when you look at the 4.2-litre of today that's a lot of bilge. So they took the stroke from 98mm to 106mm. I said, we'll have that 106 stroke round our necks for the next ten-years''.

Well, that story told to me by Harry might just be as he wished to remember it, rather than what literally occured; but it serves to illustrate one point – the XK engine *has* got an unfashionably long stroke. Though thanks to the engine's incredibly robust build, this fact has never appeared to place too much of a limitation on the power which could be developed from it; which in competition form has approached 350bhp!

When announced, the XK engine produced a brake horsepower figure which was exactly on target – 160 at 5100rpm; and unlike the modified pushrod engine, it could supply this almost indefinitely. Undertaking some tests on lubricating oil, a production-built engine with no preparation except 10 hours running-in, had been held on the test bed at 5000rpm for 24 hours on full load, with 5-minutes at 5250, 5500 and 6000rpm every two hours. ''The oil temperature was maintained at 130 deg C, and the engine, when stripped, showed no ill-effects'' recorded William Heynes in his famous Paper on the Jaguar engine which he presented to the Institute of Mechanical Engineers on 14th April 1953.

The twin overhead camshaft engine had long been recognised as highly efficient, the direct action of the cams on the valves (via tappet buckets) without the need for pushrods or rocker arms reducing reciprocating weight, thus alleviating wear and allowing greater rpm in safety. But there were disadvantages – the complication and expense of driving camshafts situated in the head and not the block, extra noise, and the difficulties of having quantities of oil in the roof of the engine which tended to leak or, worse still, escape down the inlet valve guides with possibly disastrous consequences to the proper running of the engine.

This was largely why before the War, dohc engines had been confined to expensive, high performance machines often built with racing in mind, and for owners who expected to undertake fairly constant maintenance

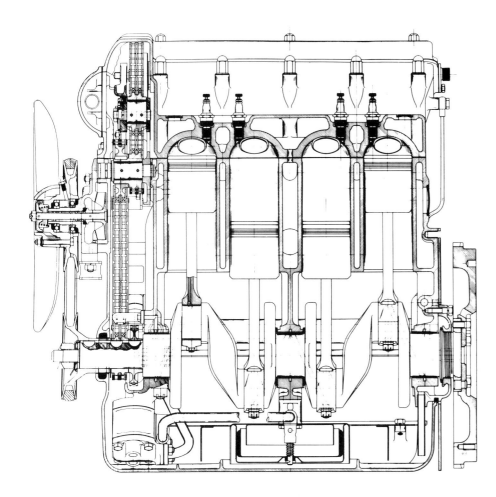

The 'XJ' four-cylinder twin-ohc engine, displaying all the major features of its larger brother. The four-cylinder Jaguar engine very nearly saw production.

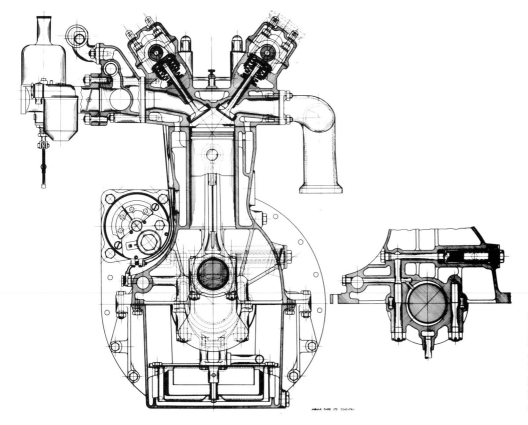

Sectional drawing showing all the salient features of the XK engine – twin overhead camshafts working on bucket tappets, crossflow inlet/exhaust, SU carburettors, and sturdy crankshaft.

and who certainly wouldn't be concerned about such things as noise. Vittorio Jano's famous dohc six-cylinder engines of the late 'twenties and 'thirties spring to mind as a primary example. This engine in supercharged form won for Alfa Romeo virtually every important European sports car race between 1928 and 1930, adding Le Mans to these achievements with the 2.3 straight-eight engine used between 1931 and 1934 at the Sarthe circuit.

Bugatti was of course another ohc adherent, and his designs in turn certainly inspired the American Duesenburg straight-eight engine, the first of its kind in the States. In production form, this gave 100bhp from 4.2-litres in 1920, then with the coming of the fabled Model J at the end of 1928, the 6.9 litre, eight-cylinder unit with chain-driven dohc and four valves per cylinder was said to give no less than 265bhp at 4250rpm.

Returning to France, the Salmson concern produced twin ohc engines from 1922, and continued to do so spasmodically after the war, finally offering a 105 bhp 2.3 twin-cam in a quite attractive coupe body which sold in very small numbers up to 1957 when the ailing company was absorbed by Renault.

In England, perhaps the most successful of pre-War twin-cam designs was the small, 1104cc high-efficiency four-cylinder unit released in mid-1934 by Lagonda, to supplement their rather more orthodox 2- and 3-litre cars. It was a model design by Tim Ashcroft incorporating many advanced features, including chain drive to the overhead cams, large (2-inch) diameter main bearings, a hemispherical cylinder head, cross-flow 90 degree valves, and twin SU carburetters. But sales did not match its advanced specification, despite it giving the small Lagonda an unburstable performance and 75mph; it was marketed as a private venture by the Rapier Company when Lagonda was reformed in 1935, but this could not save it and the type perished in 1940 after a mere 300 cars had been made.

However, all the cars powered by a twin-cam engine before the advent of the XK power unit were almost by definition expensive and difficult to maintain. The cheapest Bugatti chassis listed in 1939 was £590, and you couldn't get a closed Alfa Romeo under £1000; the little Rapier saloon cost £415, or appreciably more than the 3.5-litre Jaguar with all its space and equipment, while in the States, to purchase a Model J Duesenburg and have it bodied would leave little change out of $18,000.

Nevertheless, here was Lyons anticipating the manufacture of a twin-cam engine on a quantity basis, and using it in a soft, luxurious saloon car available to anyone with the money – and, as it turned out, for an astonishingly small amount of money, as the new car was planned to sell at a basic price before purchase tax of under £1000 – or in pre-War currency, a lot less than £500.

It was a bold move, and Lyons needed to trust implicitly his small engineering team, for it was absolutely essential that the new engine be tough and reliable, quite apart from producing the required horsepower. There was no way in which the small Coventry manufacturer could withstand a multitude of guarantee claims from incensed customers with blown engines, a fate suffered by more than one manufacturer with an unreliable product.

However, Lyons' confidence was well placed; sound initial design work and extensive development was to ensure that the XK engine would be one of the most rugged, long-lasting and efficient power units ever put into production. The basis of the unit was its massive seven-bearing EN.16 steel crankshaft with main bearing diameters of 2.75 inches – the same dimension as the almost indestructible crank of the previous range of engines. Each shaft was dynamically balanced, then balanced again statically after the pre-balanced flywheel was bolted on. Careful attention was paid to counterweighting, and torsional vibration was also controlled by a Metalastic damper.

Lubrication of the engine was by the normal type of gear pump, circulating the oil through large diameter oil passages with all holes countersunk wherever possible to prevent brittle edges breaking and allowing cast-iron debris to enter the bearings. The connecting rods were steel from the commencement of production; the lesson having been learnt from the Mk V and previous Jaguars that the expansion of the early alloy rods could lead to problems with escaping lubricant.

The block was made by Leyland, and its design was simple and strong. No liners were fitted, and the bores were found to have exceptional wearing qualities, helped by a chromium plated top ring on the alloy pistons. The oil pump and distributor were driven from the forward end of the crankshaft.

The strong seven main bearing crankshaft of the original 3442cc XK engine.

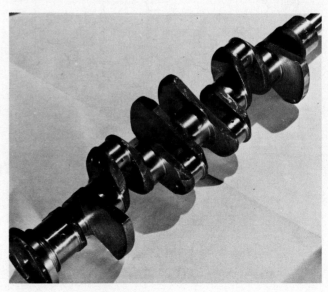

Overhead view of the XK engine's aluminium cylinder-head with cam covers removed to display the two camshafts
Photo: Jaguar Cars

The *piéce de resistance* was of course the cylinder head. It was made in aluminium, a material chosen chiefly for its light weight – 50lbs as compared with 120lbs for a similar head in cast iron. Ease of machining and handling were further reasons, and no problems were encountered with the valve seats (inserted with the head at a temperature of 232 degrees Centigrade) or the fact that the spark plugs screwed straight into the DTD 424 aluminium alloy.

As we have seen, the combustion chambers were of hemispherical shape, and a great deal of work had been carried out to discover the best way of taking the mixture to them. Much of this was done by Weslake using full-scale models of the cylinder head in wood or aluminium which then were 'flow-tested' – that is, the amount of air passing through the port would be carefully measured before and after modifications had been carried out. The better the flow, the greater the efficiency. Basically this was a very simple trial-and-error method but was, and is, very effective, and saved many hours of bench-testing with a running engine, even though it was not totally foolproof. When the final shape of the porting had been arrived at, and checked in working engines, highly accurate male cores were taken from the model, from which the pattern maker would make the core-boxes for the casting process.

Similar tests were carried out to check the behaviour of the induction pipes (or inlet manifold) which led from the carburetters. For the XK engine, 1.75 inch SU carburetters were specified, these being slightly larger than the instruments used on the 3.5-litre Mk V engine.

Having decided on twin overhead camshafts, the question next arose of how they should be turned; at first, a single, continuous chain was used, driven from the nose of the crankshaft as normal, but although this worked very well, it emitted a strange high-pitched whine which was hardly noticeable near the engine, but very clearly heard from some distance away. Walter Hassan was adamant that this just wouldn't do, and after numerous attempts to cure it with variously situated jockey wheels and dampers, a change was made to a two-stage system,

employing separate bottom and top timing chains. The two camshaft sprockets were very carefully designed, and could be adjusted to a very fine degree, while a dummy carrier could hold the sprockets still on their chain, allowing the camshafts to be removed or the head itself taken off the block without disturbing the valve timing.

As for the camshafts themselves, for the first few years of production their 'lift' was purposely kept low at 5/16-inch, so that inexperienced mechanics would not run into trouble with the valves fouling each other while the head was being overhauled. In fact, damage from careless handling was much less than expected, and later the lift was increased to a more efficient 3/8-inch.

Effective cooling of the head was important and was thoroughly investigated, with the water pump in particular undergoing a lot of development to prevent cavitation at speed. It was also ensured that the valve area received a good flow of water, although this was nevertheless possibly a little marginal around the exhaust valve. In service, early XK engines may have suffered from overheating in hot climates, but this was largely through inadequate radiator or fan performance.

Jaguar's 'two-tier' chain drive from crankshaft to cams; this early (1949) engine is of course upside-down. *Photo: Jaguar Cars*

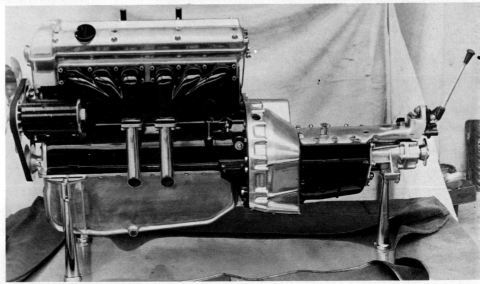

Both sides of the original XK engine as used in the first XK 120s; note attention to finish with polished cam covers and enamelled exhaust manifolds. The show engine (right) has a non-standard black oil filler cap.

Finally, even the exterior of this magnificent power unit received conscious attention, and so the handsome, polished aluminium camshaft covers, black vitreous-enamelled exhaust manifolds, and other neat external features of the engine were purposely contrived to present a graphic picture of efficiency and engineering perfection which communicated itself even to the layman.

In parallel with the new 'six' and incorporating all its main features was the four-cylinder alternative, essentially a small-bore XJ less two cylinders, having a bore and stroke of 80.5mm x 98mm and a capacity of 1995cc; it went under the name of XK however, and was rated at 95bhp at 5000rpm, which was getting on for 50bhp per litre.

Although the XK engine was designed for what was to

be called the Mk VII, a late decision was made to present it at the 1948 Motor Show in a new sports car. As related in chapter five, it was thought that this would bring the company some useful publicity and result in some equally useful 'consumer testing' under service conditions. "The engine had, of course, already been completely tooled", wrote William Heynes later, "as it was intended for the Mk VII saloon which was to be produced the following year, and it was a most welcome break for the Engineering and Production Departments that we were now going to have a reasonable quantity run off this engine plant before we came into the main production."

The XK 120 two-seater was based on a short-chassis version of the Mk V frame, with the new torsion-bar independent front suspension; this gave the car a degree

of refinement quite unknown in a sports car before, and
with 160bhp, the XK could achieve virtually 120mph
(hence its name) even in true production form, which in
1948/49 was 'racing car performance'. Scheduled for a
leisurely 200-a-year using a hand-built aluminium body,
the demand for the XK 120 immediately forced Jaguar
into commissioning Pressed Steel to make a steel body on
a proper production basis, although this programme
took nearly two years to come into effect. An 'XK 100'
powered by the 2-litre engine was catalogued but never
produced because of the huge demand for the 3.4-litre
version.

Meanwhile, the stop-gap Mk V saloon with the new
chassis but old engine was doing a brave job in carrying
Jaguar over the difficult period while the Mk VII saloon,
the most complex Jaguar yet built, was put into production. For the first time, Jaguar were going completely
'outside' for a complete bodyshell, and there were a new
set of problems to solve.

There were several interconnecting reasons why Jaguar
approached the Pressed Steel Company to make their new
body. The first was the styling of the Mk VII – the new
shape meant large, flowing panels which were not easily
made up from many small pieces as had been the case
with all previous Jaguars; indeed this was a major reason
why Lyons adopted the modern integral body/wing line,
because there was far too much expensive hand-work
involved in the building of the Mk V and previous
saloons. The use of a comparatively few, major panels cut
the time-wasting procedure of individually making and
then welding together a large number of small sections to
make up the shell.

As Lyons had been forced to sell Motor Panels to
Rubery Owen after the war, Jaguar lacked the press-tool
facilities to manufacture the large panels needed for the
Mk VII, so it was necessary to negotiate with Pressed
Steel for the supply of complete bare body shells, which arrived
at the factory on transporters 'in the white' ready for
painting and fitting to the Jaguar-built chassis. The shape
of the car was, of course, Lyons' design, but there were

many constructural details which had to be worked out
with Pressed Steel, who already possessed a vast
knowledge of this new – to Jaguar – body engineering.

The structural design and then the tooling-up for this
large and quite complex luxury car body took longer
than expected, and as already related, both engine and
chassis were ready for production two years before the
first production bodies came through from Oxford. But
when it came, the Mk VII launch was a memorable one.

With his usual flair for drama, Lyons chose to say
nothing until the Motor Show of October 1950 – and
there unveiled the new luxury Jaguar, so different from
anything which had so far emerged under that name. It
sat resplendently on a moving turntable, finished in pale
metallic blue with the chrome sparkling under the
spotlights as it slowly revolved in front of the crowds
packed against the stand's railings. No wonder *The
Autocar* aptly referred to it as the "Prima Ballerina".
Lyons himself was involved in the opening of the Show,
giving the annual message in his newly elected capacity as
the President of the Society of Motor Manufacturers and
Traders; Princess Margaret, standing in for Princess
Elizabeth who was ill, performed the opening ceremony.

The specification of the Mk VII with its twin overhead
camshaft engine, new servo-assisted brakes and
independent torsion bar suspension was quite enough to
make it the "car of the show", even if it hadn't gained the
title by virtue of its new, flowing body line alone. But
perhaps the biggest surprise and delight of all was the
price at which Jaguar were prepared to offer their new
100mph saloon – £988 basic, or the same as the XK 120
and the 3.5-litre Mk V. Keeping it under £1000 meant
escaping the top rate of purchase tax, which increased
sharply over that figure; with tax the car sold for £1,275
19s 6d; not that this was of more than theoretical interest
to British admirers – the Mk VII was firmly listed as an
"export saloon", and indeed the factory still had orders
dating back to 1946 from the home market!

This superlative value-for-money factor made it doubly
frustrating for many **would-be** Jaguar purchasers, who

not only admired the product but felt they could afford it too. The low price amazed even Jaguar employees. "I told Sir William this many times", said Peter Craig, "he could have put a two or three in front of that figure – he could have sold that car with a three in front of that figure.

"But he didn't do it – he kept it at £988. But I say that if he had put a two or three in front of it, he wouldn't have made it for the years that he did. So you get the length of run out of the tools – this is one of the secrets; he was so wise. We certainly made improvements, but we didn't change a Jaguar every other year."

In an otherwise slightly uninspiring Show, the Mk VII Jaguar stood out. The factory were so pleased with the reception the car was given that special trains were laid on from Coventry to Earls Court and all employees were invited down to see the results of their efforts. Unfortunately this did not prevent one of Jaguar's worst strikes, which broke out shortly after the Mk VII's launch and which continued for six weeks, a result of direct union confrontation. But every cloud has its silver lining – the enforced pause in production enabled the staff to thoroughly sort out a few of the remaining problems relating to the new Pressed Steel bodywork, (and in particular the front door hinges, which are recalled as being troublesome – certainly they had to support a great deal of weight).

Following its triumph at Earls Court, the show car enjoyed a similar reception at the Waldorf-Astoria Hotel in New York, whence it was shipped after the doors had closed on the last visitors to leave the London Motor Show. The American dealers were ecstatic and by the end

of November, approaching $30 000 000-worth of Mk VIIs had been reserved. So far, every expectation for the car had been realised; all Jaguar had to do now was make enough of them.

The London show car at the Waldorf-Astoria, Park Avenue, New York for the North American launch. Thousands visited the display and over 500-orders were taken in three-days.

But Foleshill, with its string of buildings of various sizes at various levels, was no longer suitable or adequate, and for some time Lyons had been searching for a better site. This was eventually located in the form of a quite modern building erected in 1939 for the Daimler company's war-work, and still used by that company after the War for the building of cars and buses. Ownership remained with the government, however, and despite it being normal policy to lease and not sell such properties, Lyons did in fact manage to secure the freehold of the building, which lay in the semi-rural village of Allesley a few miles outside Coventry city.

There was one condition attached to the sale, and this required Jaguar to take up production of the Rolls-Royce Meteor tank engine; but while the company tooled-up well ahead of schedule, the contract was finally cancelled. Later Jaguar would design a tank transporter, which was just as interesting a design as the Spitfire Merlin descendant which the original contract concerned. The move from Holbrook Lane to Allesley was accomplished in stages during 1951 and 1952, with no loss in production at all, and as well as the new buildings being far more

suitable for car manufacture, there was plenty of room for expansion in the land around the factory too.

The Foleshill works where the first XK 120s and Mk VIIs were made; the rather motley collection of buildings of which they were composed could no longer contain Jaguar's expanding production, and during 1951/52 a move was made to Browns Lane.

We have not yet examined the Mk VII saloon in detail and so discover why it appealed so much in 1950. Certainly its looks attracted, but although Lyons had very successfully adopted modern lines for his new car, he had still succeeded in retaining an instantly recognisable 'Jaguar' appearance. The shape was the result of much experimentation, carried out in Sir William's world-famous manner of working; this rarely included models or styling drawings, as Lyons liked to work directly with shape and form in full-scale mock-ups of the intended car, working with a few trusted panel men in a secret part of the body shop. There, panels would be hand-formed and arranged on a wood frame conforming to the basic engineering requirements of wheelbase, length, and engine and passenger compartment dimensions, already agreed with Heynes. It must have been a fascinating process to watch for the privileged few who were able to see 'the master' in action, and the pictures in this book show how, gradually, the final shape would emerge from a variety of themes.

Mk VII styling evolution – an early mock-up with a very untraditional front; note that two sizes of headlight are being tried, and indicators in bumper. This particular design probably dates back to the Mk V as well, which Jaguar contemplated releasing with a 'streamlined' front.

Neater, with slim XK 120-type grille – an almost 'Alfa' appearance.

Top: Roof and side windows
about right, but a dropped
front wing line is being tried.

Centre left: The Mk VII grille
is evolving, but large
headlights are still being
played with.

Centre right: Rear view of the
mock-up — boot and wing-
line not quite there yet, and
note exterior hinges.

Left: Much closer to the
finished design, with
head/spotlight heights being
experimented upon.

Front and rear wings have now been connected; note sloping centre pillar.

Below: A much more 'finished' edition of the previous design – only the wing-line now deviates from the final arrangement.

Rear view of low wing-line car, still with its Mk V bumpers.

Now a straight line between front and rear wings is being tried.

Below: Then...the happy compromise, with gentle shelving of the front wing to join the rear two-thirds of the way up. See how the wooden formers are used to make up the body shape.

The final design, with every major feature as for production, including bumpers and lights.

The prototype Mk VII next to the car it was to supplant; a marked family resemblence despite the modern treatment of wings and accessories. *Photos: Jaguar Cars.*

The last test of all, when a design was almost ready, meant that the entire shell on its wooden jig must be transported to Wappenbury Hall, Lyons' own home, where it would be viewed outside the house, in completely natural surroundings away from factory buildings – what might look right in a factory yard might not be so pleasing in the driveway of a country house. Only if successful there would it be turned over to the pattern-makers and draughtsmen to be made into a production reality.

Thus did the Mk VII emerge, blending many new features into those already seen on the Mk V and previous Jaguars. The basic curve of the roof and rear-quarters had been carried over, and so had the Mk V's curved rear side windows, while at the front, the radiator shell was still upright and recognisable, even if discreetly slim by previous Jaguar standards. Front and rear wing lines had been merged to form a sweeping line running down the side of the car, kicking up over the spatted rear wheels and then following the downward contours of the luggage compartment; in this way a continuity of line had been maintained between the new saloon and the XK 120 sports car.

It is most noticeable that inspite of the car being designed principally for the North American market, Lyons had not let his sense of good taste be influenced by the "jaws, teeth and whiskers" (as *The Automobile Engineer* put it) of the typical American sedan of the period, and the

The production Mk VII saloon, elegant despite its undoubted bulk. A drop-head version was built experimentally, in 1952, employing Wilmot Breedon power rams, but was never taken up.

Photo: Jaguar Cars

Rear-end detail of an early Mk VII; note complex ribbing on bumper blade, simplified later on, and locking flaps for the petrol tanks mounted in each wheelarch.

Mk VII was remarkably free from chrome embellishment. While this may have tended to emphasise the Mk VII's slightly bulky, slab-sided look, the restraint exercised in this direction helped prevent the car dating rapidly – even if the area of chrome was to be increased with the coming of later versions.

About the only decoration on the side of the car was the traditional chrome waist-line incorporating the push-button door handles, while substantial but more orthodox bumpers with twin over-riders were installed front and rear in place of the Mk V's chrome complexities. Sidelights were mounted integrally with the front wings, which also carried the two Lucas Y-piece

No mascot for the Mk VII, but instead this stylised jaguar head built into winged emblem and mounted on the simple radiator grille. *Photo: Jaguar Cars.*

headlights and two spot/fog lamps inset below. One slightly odd characteristic of the Mk VII was the divided windscreen, not seen on a Jaguar saloon though the XK 120 was similarly styled; Triplex had recently introduced the curved windscreen to British manufacturers, but two of the most advanced British cars of the late 'forties appeared not to notice – the Mk VII and the new Morris Minor. Both repented later, however!

Some of the Mk VII's styling features were the result of engineering changes, because while the basic chassis and wheelbase remained unchanged from the Mk V, the new XK engine, and a re-think of the interior accommodation, had brought about an engine position which was much further forward than the Mk V's. Already three-inches longer than the pushrod unit, the twin-cam engine was carried another five-inches further forward in the frame, making the radiator eight-inches nearer the front – hence the longer bonnet ending in radiator shell and wings which were well in front of the wheels.

The objective was greater interior room and it had certainly been achieved – the rear seat occupants of the new saloon had an extra three-inches of leg room thanks to the front seats being brought forward; and due to the body now extending out to where the running boards had been on the Mk V, they also enjoyed no less than five-inches of greater width. The Mk VII's front seats were each 4.5-inches wider than before, and everyone had at least an extra two-inches of headroom. Wheel arches intruded very little at the rear, the seats having been moved further ahead of the axle – this also helped provide the Mk VII's huge luggage compartment.

While nearly all Jaguars had previously been rather inadequate in this department, the Mk VII simply

More room inside than the Mk V, and plushier, heavier-looking seats too. Pleating was back, but with plain 'horseshoe' surround. This is a very early (Oct. 1950) Mk VII. *Photo: Jaguar Cars.*

excelled; the boot was almost 2ft. 6 inches deep and no less than 4ft. long, and at its widest point measured 3ft. 8in. An upright mounted spare wheel (which could be removed without disturbing the luggage) and petrol tanks hidden away in each wheel arch helped provide this enormous capacity, which challenged for size the 'trunk' of the largest American automobile. The bootlid opened

upwards, and was held by a telescopic stay; it no longer contained the toolkit however, which had been transferred to equally neat quarters concealed in the front door trim panels.

Inside the car, the main features developed in previous Jaguar saloons had been carried over, with polished walnut veneer on the dashboard, cantrails and door

Right: Where previous Jaguars had been merely average, the Mk VII excelled – its huge boot easily swallowed this quantity of luggage. *Photo: Jaguar Cars*

Below: Mounting the spare wheel upright allowed enormous depth in the boot as well as considerable length. No trim panels or smart matting here yet, though a tidy-up was to follow later.

cappings; pleating was back on the seats, which at the front were less bucket-shaped than the Mk V's although they still retained their wide range of adjustment, complete with small chromed handle to alter the height. A big 18-inch steering wheel similar to the Mk V's was used, with the dangerous-looking protruding hornpush set in the middle. Instruments and switchgear groupings were

Tools were relegated to neat compartments in each front door; spare light bulbs and spark plug are included in this one – the other held a grease gun as well.

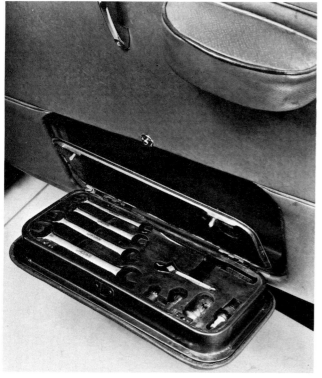

much as before, except that Jaguar had gone back to 'needle' pointers for the large speedometer and rev. counter together with more formal lettering. Instrument panel illumination was still by indirect 'ultra-violet' lighting, though without the luminescent effect of the early Mk Vs.

The heater was of course standard, with the blower unit and heat exchanger situated under the bonnet on the bulkhead and supplied with fresh air from a central ventilator in the scuttle. Additional cold air could be directed into the footwells through flap-type ventilators in the sides of the front wings, a very necessary feature in hot climates and introduced on the XK 120 at about the same time. In fine weather the sliding roof could be enjoyed.

Mechanically, the Mk VII used a similar four-speed gearbox to the Mk V, with its short remote-control lever and rather slow action. The clutch operation was hydraulic on all but the first few cars (four RHD, 51 LHD), and a divided propeller shaft led to the hypoid rear axle which was now standardised as the Salisbury 2HA unit. Wheels and tyres were as for Mk V, although later on rim width would be increased.

Important changes had taken place in the braking system, with vacuum servo-assistance now incorporated. But Jaguar hadn't simply plumbed the servo mechanism into the existing circuit, but used instead a redesigned system having two trailing shoes in the front drums, specially developed by Girling for high performance cars. The problem with the normal two leading shoe arrangement was that the inherent 'wrap-around' self-servo effect could induce fade and uneven operation. The higher pedal pressures needed by the two trailing shoe system was more than compensated for by the Clayton-

Dashboard styling took after that of the Mk V, except that the top rail was rounded; instrument figuring was more orthodox too, but the pronounced steering wheel boss remained (it was used on the XK 120 too). *Photo: Jaguar Cars*

Greater leg-room was provided in the Mk VII, helped by cut-outs in the bottom of the front seats. This is probably a prototype car as it lacks the centre ashtray on the facia. *Photo: Motor*

Dewandre servo. In the early 1950s, assisted brakes were extremely unusual, and Jaguar's bold move in fitting them to a production car prompted much discussion.

This servo had originally been developed in the 'twenties by the Belgian engineer M. Dewandre, but before the war was little used because, generally speaking, the cars of that period had large, well-ventilated brakes which were perfectly adequate for the speeds they could achieve. But with the coming of small wheels, large section tyres and the shrouding effect of modern wings, brake engineers were faced with serious cooling problems and fade became a commonplace occurance in fast, heavy cars of the early 1950s.

The Clayton-Dewandre servo used the vacuum created in the engine's inlet manifold to produce approximately double the hydraulic pressure in the braking system, in

Servo-braking was most unusual in 1950, as least in Great Britain. The vacuum booster was mounted underfloor adjacent to the centre crossmember.

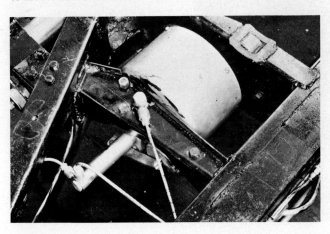

The offside front brake of the Mk VII with its two-leading-shoe arrangement. Damper has been removed in this picture. *Photo: Jaguar Cars*

relation to the effort applied to the brake pedal by the driver. Should the servo not function, direct action by the pedal on the master cylinder was still possible, though of course the driver would need to press considerably harder to obtain the same deceleration. Also, the front shoes were now self-adjusting which was an almost equally important step forward – now, when the linings wore during heavy use and the brake drum expanded as they became hot, the pedal travel would no longer increase as it did before, a friction device always keeping the shoes at the correct clearance.

While the same 12-inch drums were used, the new arrangement meant a slight reduction of 26sq. in. friction area compared to the Mk V, but overall the new brakes worked much better even taking into account the Mk VII's extra speed. The rear brakes remained the one leading and one trailing non-self adjusting system as before, and were also worked by the handbrake which had reverted to its normal position between the front seats. The servo itself was mounted on the chassis frame under the driver's floor, though for some reason no vacuum reservoir was incorporated in the system, which meant that assistance ceased if the engine stalled.

Some alterations had been required at the front of the chassis frame to accommodate the more forward position of the new engine with its four-point rubber mounting. The anti-roll bar was re-positioned behind the suspension assembly, and also, it was necessary to revise the steering arrangements to circumnavigate the extra length of engine, which resulted in extra links being introduced. Chassis engineer Tom Jones, who had joined the company in 1940 and assisted Claude Baily with the VA and VB prototypes amongst other projects, recalls that the work of designing the new layout was not without its difficulties, the additional rubber and joints promoting shimmy fed through from the central track rod. Unlike the Mk V, the column was separated from the steering box by a rubber bushed flexible coupling to reduce the transmission of road noise and vibration.

The XK engine's installation in what had been the Mk V chassis; the twin-cam unit was mounted some inches further forward than the pushrod engine had been. Note outriggers from chassis which picked-up on mountings situated on the body rockers. *Photo: Jaguar Cars*

At first, the Mk VII's steering box gave 4.25 turns lock-to-lock but this was soon increased to 4.75 turns in order to reduce driver effort. A stronger steering box mounting was also fitted. A divided steering drop-arm was another change during the first year of production, and at the same time the lower ball joint socket material was changed from the original Ferobestos material to Morganite bronze; unlike the former, the new housing required lubrication so a grease nipple was installed and the ball pin grooved.

Otherwise, the torsion bar suspension remained as for the Mk V, performing its usual excellent job; however, perhaps because of the extra weight on the front of the car, it was discovered that the suspension mounting posts on the frame were not up to the job and, after 590 RHD and 1122 LHD cars had been completed, these were

177

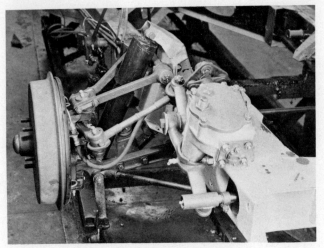

Mk VII front suspension and steering arrangements; the former incorporated ball joints, fairly common in Europe but not in the States, although Lincoln adopted them for its 1952 range.
Photo: Jaguar Cars

stiffened up. The factory considered it important enough for earlier cars to be modified retrospectively, this being accomplished with plates. Damping remained as for the Mk V, with the lever-type shock absorbers being retained at the rear, though for countries other than Great Britain and the USA, they were later uprated for better rough road control.

As the Mk VII was primarily an export car, the reaction of the North American market was of paramount importance to Jaguar, and they must have waited for the first published opinions with baited breath.

The Mk VII road-tested

Road & Track magazine's first full test appeared in October 1952, when they could report that a lot of the 'bugs' noticed in earlier examples had been successfully eradicated. "Each succeeding group of Jaguars to enter this country seems to be a little more smoothly turned out", the writer said. "After having driven four or five Mk VIIs, over a period of a year, I must say I am sold. When you look the car over carefully and compare its dollar for dollar value with anything else on the market – foreign or domestic – you are bound to admit that Jaguar gives you a lot for your money."

The car used for the actual performance testing had the later dual exhaust system but was otherwise standard; it was supplied by Peter Satori, the Pasadena distributor. For a car that weighed-in at 35cwt or so, the acceleration figures were excellent, the big saloon reaching 60mph in 12.6-seconds, and covering the standing 1/4-mile in 19.1-seconds. Top speed was equally impressive at 104mph. This could be compared with a home product such as the 5.4-litre V8 Chrysler Imperial, which wasn't too far off a

standard Mk VII in top speed (101mph) but with 41cwt to get rolling, was almost three-seconds behind the Jaguar up to 60mph.

On the road, there was really no comparison at all to be drawn between the typical American car of the period and the Jaguar; then as now, chassis design in the States lagged way behind Europe. "... I proved time and again that the American stock sedan 'just didn't have it' ... particularly when any curves were involved. The Jaguar would get through winding, hilly country without backing off from its 60/70mph cruising speed, whereas all the other traffic instinctively slowed to 45mph or less ... Without fuss the Mk VII will accelerate up to 80mph and up, without any appreciable change in roadability. The car just sits down and goes ..."

The Mk VII's brakes seemed to have stood up to enterprising driving well – "they are really wonderful" – with only a small amount of squeal intruding when they were cold. The XK engine filled the writer with admiration – "really remarkable what they get out of these engines which have about the same displacement as the Chevrolet." The luggage space impressed even a motorist used to size in everything, being described as "tremendous." The range of adjustment for the driving seat was approved of, as was the sliding roof, an unusual feature in the States.

There were niggles but they weren't fundamental ones – the long travel of the gearlever between first and second gears, and the hornpush which was too easy to brush accidentally when manoeuvering, while rear wheel patter could be provoked during a brisk take-off from rest. But that only occured when 'drag' type starts were indulged in, with the clutch being dropped at 3000rpm; hardly the sort of motoring familiar to the average luxury saloon buyer.

In Britain, it was *The Motor* which got into print first with a full road-test of the new Jaguar, in April 1952. The tone of the report was enthusiastic from the beginning. "In the opinion of the test team the Jaguar, judged upon a basis of value for money and all-round merit, is one of the best cars submitted for Road Test in the post-War years." Maximum speed was 101mph, with a best one-way figure of 103.5mph; 60mph was gained in 13.7-seconds, and the 30-50mph top gear increment covered in 7.9-seconds. So the Mk VII in its original form was 10mph faster than the previously tested Mk V, and exactly a second quicker in the acceleration ranges mentioned. Higher up the speed range the gains were much more evident, the Mk V 3.5 litre reaching 80mph in 31.4-seconds, compared with only 23.9-seconds for the twin-cam saloon.

To some extent, other aspects of the Mk VII's character showed it to be a compromise car, thought *The Motor*, due to attention being paid to American preferences in some departments. "Had it been merely a case of designing for European markets, rather quicker steering would

The Mk VII in America, looking remarkably at home on the freeway approaching Los Angeles from Hollywood; they were ideally suited to the long, sweeping roads there. *Photo: Roger Barlow*

probably have been provided, and perhaps spring strengths giving more completely roll-free cornering (at the cost of less of a 'boulevard' ride) would have been chosen." From this we deduce that *The Motor* thought the Mk VII rolled too much and could have had higher geared steering; but as the journal sensed, the car had not been built for the sports car driver, who after all could now purchase a fixed-head XK 120 if he desired that extra response and a closed roof.

That Jaguar had achieved their objective is, of course, proved by the *Road & Track* test examined earlier, where the car's handling compared to the home product was considered much superior. But even on European roads, the Mk VII was not to be scorned; helped by the optional harder shock absorbers, the car could be "power slid around a slippery corner for the fun of the thing" (as rally drivers were beginning to appreciate), and there were no vices. Even the number of turns lock-to-lock were not so noticeable on the road, as in return an exceptional turning circle of 36ft. average was given.

The independently sprung front wheels and well-sorted damping all round provided an excellent ride. "Comfort is a very strong characteristic of the Mk VII chassis ... In particular, the motion is really 'flat', so that the good riding which front seat occupants of the preceding model enjoyed has now been shared equally with the rear seat passengers. Commendably, fast driving over bad bumps does not provoke 'bottoming' ..." said *The Motor*.

The light pedal pressures needed for the new servo-assisted brakes were noted, but so was the fact that the technique of consistantly slowing a large, fast heavy car had not yet been entirely mastered:

"In ordinary driving, extremely light pedal pressures check the car's speed, but the smoothness of the Jaguar allows an occasional tendency to mild judder to be noticed – this does not, it should be emphasised, result in either snatch or loss of braking power on slippery surfaces. Use of the brakes at frequent intervals for stops from high speeds or on mountain descents did, unfortunately, produce some brake fade with the type of linings fitted to the test car, accompanied by a somewhat pungent smell; in effect, brake fade was about as easy to induce as it is on most fast and heavy saloon cars ..."

The XK engine, already sampled by the magazine in the XK 120 and memorably, the C-type, received praise although feelings were mixed about the gearbox: "The engine has a superb willingness to work hard at 500rpm or 5000rpm, and although familiarity with the Jaguar allows really 'sports car' use to be made of the gearbox, we would prefer to have a gearlever with a shorter movement, set less far below the steering wheel level, and controlling a slightly more powerful type of synchromesh mechanism. The intermediate gears are quiet rather than silent."

Of course the massive boot was commented on. "As

Underbonnet view of Mk VII; this is an early car without the front-studded cam covers. The XK engine fulfilled a Lyons ideal by propelling the luxury car at a genuine 100mph. *Photo: Motor*

regards luggage, it can only be said that the amount of space far exceeds any reasonable European expectation, the normal baggage and overcoats of five people representing considerably less than a full load." Minor grumbles concerned familiar faults with early Mk VIIs, such as imperfect door sealing and some water leaks in rainy weather. But in summing up, the journal made it quite clear that these small failings did not mar the overall concept:

> "The Jaguar is probably the best compromise yet evolved between many conflicting requirements. It provides much of the quality of finish and equipment expected on the most costly cars, at a fraction of their price. It also offers outstanding speed, with flexibility and quite a high order of silence. It provides excellent riding comfort and also a considerable degree of roadworthiness. Finally, it is extremely roomy, yet uses fuel at a rate appreciably lower than its size and speed would suggest."

In fact, the car returned an overall fuel consumption of 17.6mpg, a figure actually bettered by *The Autocar* in its test of the Mk VII published a few days afterwards. They achieved an excellent 19mpg, using the same car, LRW 173. Acceleration figures matched *The Motor's* pretty well, and a similar top speed was recorded; the car was fitted with the 8.1 c.r. domed-top pistons incidentally. General impressions of the car on the road tallied with *The Motor's* too, similar points being made about the slightly weak synchromesh and the tendency of the brakes to fade if used hard. On corners, the "general tendency of the Jaguar to understeer further inspires confidence" (technical terms such as 'understeer' and 'oversteer' were now finding their way into the increasingly scientific road test reports), and the steering "although perhaps a little transatlantic" was thought positive though not particularly light during parking.

Further opinions on the Mk VII's ability on the road had previously been furnished by *The Autocar's* Gordon Wilkins, who had driven LWK 343 in the Monte Carlo Rally of that year. While the engine remained standard, the rules allowed a change of axle ratio, so the even lower 4.55 gearing was used in place of the standard 4.27; bucket seats, extra instruments, two spare wheels, un-hitching equipment, four snow chains and an extra fuel tank helped bring the curb weight up to 36cwt – but that was nothing compared to gross weight of the previous 'recce' car, which with even more equipment, four passengers and 30 gallons of fuel totalled 47cwt. "One would not pretend that with this gross overload the car could be thrown round corners with all the abandon which is possible under normal conditions, but it travelled all the way from the Riveira to the Channel coast in that condition and happily maintained speeds up to 80mph on treacherous and slippery roads. Moreover, the suspension coped perfectly with the weight."

The car was also fitted with the early, more high geared steering which Gordon Wilkins found preferable to the later type, although he admitted the later steering would suit the average purchaser. As he pointed out, even when power assisted steering was fitted to American cars, the manufacturer still used ratios which required much wheel-twirling, simply because the customer was used to it and expected it.

With this steering, the car "handled magnificently in the worst possible conditions, sliding continously on snow and ice for hours on end... It was a hard night but it only increased our respect for the comfort and controllability of the Mk VII when driving at absurdly high speeds on snow and ice." There was a "fair degree of understeer" but less sensation of roll than with the XK 120; the brakes "inspired confidence in the worst conditions" though it was the constant barrage of snow and water which probably countered fade. It was noted that when reversing you had a two leading shoe configuration so care needed to be exercised when travelling backwards. Gordon Wilkins also recounted an interesting little story illustrating the fact that Jaguar management used the performance of their own product to full as well:

"After the Brussels Show the managing director and his wife found themselves short of time to catch the boat at Ostend, so F.R.W. England, the Jaguar service manager, held 5200rpm on top gear for most of the length of the Jabbeke highway, showing an average of well over 90mph for the distance. The opportunities for this kind of motoring may be rare, but the cars which can do it, especially in the Jaguar price bracket, are even harder to find."

The cost of a Mk VII was now £1088 basic (£1693 total, or $4170 list in the States) but how Jaguar could produce the car for this amount was still a puzzle. Gordon Wilkins again:

"A visit to the works provides a clue, and leaves one with the impression that this is an organisation which believes in putting the money into the cars. There is a fairly small and very enthusiastic staff, which seems to know how to get results quickly and economically. There is enough of oak panelling and carpeted floors to provide for the decent and civilised reception of the many distinguished visitors who find their way to the Jaguar factory, but no more. The directors' lunch room is one of the simplest and plainest in which I have ever been entertained, and W.M.Heynes, the engineering director, conducts his affairs from a small, austere office. E.W.Rankin runs public relations from a back room with bare floors in a space bounded by rough partitions, but most visitors fail to notice them because the walls are covered with a series of posters announcing world-wide sporting successes such as no other manufacturer can show."

This was an accurate description of the Foleshill offices, but within a few months the administrative section took their place too in the 'new' Browns Lane factory, with the office windows overlooking a large car park with a central flag-pole. Even there, William Lyons' own room was not large, and as Gordon Wilkins said, "I suspect that the seats and the carpets in the cars will always be softer and more luxurious than those in the offices."

Jaguar and Le Mans

As for "world-wide sporting successes", that indeed had been the case, and during 1951 a most important event occured that was to have a huge influence on the future prosperity of the company. Following the good showing of perfectly standard XK 120s in the 1950 Le Mans 24-hour race, a purpose-built sports car was pre-

pared for the 1951 event. This was the tubular-framed C-type Jaguar, powered by the 3.4 XK engine and using many production parts, including Heynes' torsion bar independent front suspension.

Driven by Peter Walker and Peter Whitehead, the C-type won the 1951 24-hour race, the first British car to do so for many years. Jaguar had chosen Le Mans as its first target because no other motor race received so much world-wide publicity, and, because of its gruelling nature, enormous prestige was attached to an outright win there. In the early 1950s, with British successes on the motor racing circuits at a low ebb, the victory was hailed rapturously at home and with great interest abroad, especially in the United States where Jaguar were striving so hard for sales.

The significance of this 1951 Le Mans win cannot be over-emphasised. As the former editor of *The Motor* Richard Jennings says, "I think it took a Le Mans win before people really fully accepted that Jaguars were a remarkable car, you know. I remember this always – there was a nagging feeling that it was too cheap for the car that it was, and that there must be some awful pay-off coming along. In fact there wasn't, but people thought there must be. But when they started winning at Le Mans, the thing changed overnight. They needed that win worse than any manufacturer I knew."

The impact which the victory had on the car buying public probably surprised even Jaguar themselves; overseas particularly it proved to be of enormous benefit. Says F.R.W. 'Lofty' England Service Manager and Competitions Manager: "I know this from personal experience. When I first started going to the States in 1948 when we were just starting to get in the market, people didn't even know what a Jaguar was. If you were in a Jaguar car people would pull up beside you and say, 'what is it?' But as soon as we won Le Mans, those who were interested in motor cars immediately knew what a Jaguar was. It had just the same effect in Europe, particularly in France where the French always go into raptures over the car that wins Le Mans. It was reflected in sales figures afterwards, spread through all the range."

Mk VII development

Meanwhile, the less heady but still essential development work had been continued and small improvements were being introduced to make the MK VII an even more satisfactory car. By the end of 1951, the original cast aluminium cooling fan on the engine had been replaced by a steel fan running at a higher speed to assist cooling especially in hot countries, while for colder climates the cylinder block was modified to accept a standard-size water heater element – this could be installed in a tapped hole above the dipstick for those wanting a quick warm-up in the morning. A two-speed wiper motor with a three-position rotary switch was fitted by 1952, followed by a Trico windscreen washer at the end of the year. To cut down oil leaks, studs were added at the front of the cam covers from engine number A7027 (engine number prefix changed to "B" at the close of 1952, recommencing with B1001).

The uprated Girling dampers already mentioned were fitted from April 1952, and could be specified as an option on British and North American cars which otherwise remained as before. The road wheels were also modified by the close of 1952 (from cars 714860 and 734987), the 5-inch rim being replaced by a stronger and wider 5.5-inch item, the extra width being offset partially outwards to give an extra 0.5-inch track. The 5.5K wheels were identified up until the end of 1955 by two depressions in the rim adjacent to the valve hole, but following that, only by a stamping in the well of the rim.

The gearbox, which had remained more or less unchanged since the Mk V days, came in for revision early in 1952; a short-shafted box, code-named SL or JL, replaced the previous long-shaft SH or JH box, together with a longer propshaft to compensate (from chassis numbers 711802 and 732209, though due to shortages some cars after this may have had the SL or JL box fitted). On the engine, modified valve and tappet guides were fitted from A6536 onwards so that the high-lift (3/8-inch) cams could be fitted if desired without any alteration to the head being necessary first. Synthetic enamel instead of cellulose was being used on the coachwork by December 1952, from body number L010744. Dust and draught sealing had also been improved by degrees, and the tendency of the scuttle to let in water eliminated too.

The Mk VII in America

An interesting and very accurate examination of the improved Mk VII appeared in the April 1953 issue of the American journal *Auto Age*, written by David Hebb. The absence of new models each year from Jaguar, almost obligatory for American manufacturers, reminded him of the Dodge Brothers slogan of the 'twenties – "no yearly models, but constant improvements." To see whether the car lived up to its promise, he tracked down eleven owners and four 'service experts'.

By North American standards, the 16ft. 4.5in. Mk VII wasn't the largest of cars, which probably explains why Hebb thought it "handled like a sports car" except for the slightly low-geared steering and softer springs; though he acknowledged that at the same time it had the capacity for touring with four or five adults and a trunk size that was "simply incredible."

In analysing the car's behaviour on the road, the eleven owners were asked what they thought about ride quality. Three found it too firm, one thought it was the car's best feature, while the other eight "found the comfort adequate, but less important than other features. The feeling of security and safety was principle among those features. One owner pointed out that comfort was closely related to speed; at low speeds the Jaguar's comparatively heavier springs and solid shocks made the ride less comfortable than the typically soft American car, but the faster one went, the less he felt the bumps." Everyone agreed that the actual performance of the car, and its useability, was "outstanding."

The Mk VII's ability to behave in traffic and on short-haul journeys was also investigated, and interestingly, in

Painting Mk VII saloons;
synthetic enamel replaced
cellulose at the end of 1952.
Photo: Jaguar Cars

view of the fact that Jaguars were generally thought not to be everyday cars in the States, two cars in the small sample were used as such. But the general opinion was that, even though the typical American car might not be ideal for shopping and school trips, "at least they could be had with a non-shift drive" – a fact which Jaguar had already become aware of.

Overheating was a normal topic of conversation amongst Jaguar owners of the period, though the majority of Mk VII owners in this instance had no complaints, "and one went as far as to say that his Mk VII was running between 180 and 185 degrees in crawling traffic on New York's Henry Hudson Parkway on a day last summer when the temperature in the sun was cracking the hundred mark. 'Coming up the George Washington Bridge,' he reported, 'there were dozens of cars lined up at the right with their hoods open. My Jaguar didn't heat up at all." One of the service men thought they all heated up, the other three reckoned that the Mk VII was no worse than any other car. It is certainly known that a number of reports of 'overheating' were due simply to the driver noticing that the temperature gauge needle had moved up a little; much later, Jaguar did away with calibrations on their gauges for this very reason.

Steering and handling were dealt with together, and Hebb was justly critical of home-bred machinery in this respect: "Our contemporary American steering, with its caramel softness, has been in vogue since 1934. In those 18-years an entire new group of drivers has come on the road, young men and women who have never experienced any other kind of steering... Some cars, when the wheel is turned, react as if there were a separate compartment under the hood that turned the wheels...

Usually the reaction to sports car steering is one of surprise, akin to the first-olive or first-martini reaction. The first ten-minutes are surprising, and after that the pleasure in the complete responsiveness of the automobile develops and increases." Set against the 36ft. turning circle, the Mk VII's 4.75 turns of the wheel still resulted, in the opinion of the writer, in this sort of "really 'sporty' steering, accurate and responsive."

Everyone concerned was unanimous on the subject of brakes – "possibly the best in the world"; while the Mk VII's brakes certainly weren't bad, the more enthusiastic approval they gained in the States was certainly due to the poor performance of the average American car in this respect, which, although often heavily servo assisted, had virtually no resistance to fade.

Looks generally aroused enthusiasm too, though two owners preferred the elegance of older Jaguars, and one criticised the "bulbous look" of the rear. All agreed that the finish was superb. One almost universal complaint was the smell of petrol after filling, apparently due to the spring loaded hinged filler cap not sealing properly (this was the subject of a factory modification on late Mk VIIs, which had stronger lids hinged at the rear instead of the front; the position of the box was also moved rearwards necessitating modified tanks). The auxiliary starting carburetter usually stayed on too long and many owners or their dealers fitted manual switches, while the "hefty dome" of the horn push was an annoyance to North American drivers too. "Ridiculous as it may seem, a little thing like this can magnify itself in importance over a period of time", commented David Hebb. Eventually Jaguar changed that too, although not until September 1954 (from chassis numbers 722083 and 738010).

The Hoffman Motor Car Company's headquarters in Park Avenue, New York, from which were handled Jaguar's East Coast sales. As can be seen, other British makes were distributed by Hoffman.

A rather attractive study of Jaguar's early-fifties products – Mk VII and XK 120 open two-seater – in North American specification. Whitewall tyres undoubtedly help the Mk VII's looks!

On servicing and reliability, the Mk VII appeared to do well with both owners and service engineers agreeing that most of the original 'bugs' had been tracked down and sorted out. David Hebb's summing-up of the Mk VII in the North American market is about as accurate as you will get:

> "All things considered, the MK VII Jaguar appears to be giving its owners what they paid for with their $4200. It is certainly no bargain counter automobile, ranking price-wise with Cadillac, Chrysler, and Lincoln. In the matter of finish and appointments it stands up with the best, and it performs and handles as well as cars costing hundreds and even thousands of dollars more. It is truly a happy compromise, slanted for the American market. Its styling is not radical, other cars are faster, Detroit automobiles are usually roomier and softer riding. But no motorcar, at this price, has achieved the combination of performance, riding quality, and handling that the Mk VII offers its owner. This combination, in turn, gives its owner an overall satisfaction in driving that is far more than transportation alone, a satisfaction that was missing in other cars costing about the same."

The Mk VII goes automatic

Just too late for mention in that feature was a new development announced in March by Jaguar which, proclaimed US sales boss Johannas Eerdmans, should double Mk VII sales in the United States. This was automatic transmission, as yet largely unfamiliar in Europe but expected by the car buyer in the States. Rolls-Royce and Bentley were amongst the few manufacturers to offer an automatic gearbox in Britain – or rather, on their export cars – and Jaguar realised that it was an essential for their cars too if they were to maintain their number-one dollar-earning position in North America.

The move had been brewing since 1952 or even earlier, and an early decision was taken to use an existing automatic box rather than attempt to develop one. So William Heynes, followed by Tom Jones, embarked upon a fact-finding mission to the home of the automatic transmission. Three rival American systems were considered, used on many Detroit cars – Borg Warner, General Motors' Hydra-matic, and the Buick Dynaflow. After a careful assessment, the Borg Warner box was selected as it had a number of features which made it appear more easily adapted for, and suited to, the Mk VII. It lent itself to a little re-engineering to suit the XK engine's torque curve, and it had a direct-drive lock-up clutch which operated on top gear; this was thought to be more efficient, as it eliminated fuel-wasting slippage through the torque converter in that gear (although it was to be discarded within the first year of production). At first the box was manufactured in the States, until a British assembly plant was established by Borg Warner near Tetchworth in Bedfordshire.

So the now-familiar "PNDLR" quadrant was to be seen in a Jaguar for the first time, located in front of the driver on the upper part of the dashboard. Normally it would have been fitted to the steering column but this would have complicated the column's telescopic adjustment. Change-up points differed to those used on the typical low-revving American V8 engines, as the six-cylinder Jaguar engine developed its maximum torque at a considerably higher rpm. A bench-type front seat was fitted when the automatic box was installed.

An early and probably experimental installation of the Borg Warner automatic gearbox on the XK engine, photographed in March 1952. It was officially offered a year later. Jaguar had investigated automatic transmissions as far back as 1946, when the Cotal electric gearbox and the Newton semi-automatic clutch had been assessed. *Photo: Jaguar Cars*

Apart from its normal function, this transmission had a kick-down switch attached to the accelerator pedal which when pressed right down would cause the intermediate gear to be selected below 60mph. At full throttle, the mechanism would change from intermediate to top at about 68mph; selecting 'Low' on the quandrant would prevent the box from changing up from first, which thus harnessed engine compression for slowing the car downhill if required. Full throttle first-gear change-up took place at about 55mph. An anti-creep device was fitted which trapped about 400lb. of hydraulic pressure in the rear brake line when the car came to a halt and the accelerator was lifted; a touch on the throttle released the brakes again. A mechanical pawl arrangement prevented the car running backwards on a hill when the lever was in the "D" (Drive) position, and another pawl came into play when "P" (Park) was selected, locking the output shaft of the gearbox and thus the rear wheels. The same 4.27 final drive ratio was retained. The system was not a sophisticated one by today's standards, but it greatly simplified driving and of course opened up a whole new market for the car in the States. It was not for the sporting driver, but in any case the automatic box was to be strictly for export only for a considerable period.

During 1953 a number of smaller refinements contributed to an even better car; the cooling arrangements were revised early in the year, with an 8-bladed fan, narrow-type fan belt, water pump with Hoffman bearing and carbon seal, an enlarged water by-pass, and a modified induction manifold being substituted for the original equipment (from engine no. B 2917). The radiator was changed too, and now had expansion chambers on top of the header tank on either side of the filler cap. A pressed steel sump took the place of the cast alloy item in June, causing the anti-roll bar to be fitted to the lower wishbone arm in order to accommodate the new sump. The brake servo was given an undershield and raised slightly. Two throttle return springs instead of one were fitted, and the engine valve springs were redesigned to prevent possible breakages.

The automatic gearbox quadrant was installed on the dash above the steering column. Also illustrated is the later type, flat, hornpush. *Photo: Jaguar Cars*

On the rear suspension, the lever type shock absorbers were replaced by telescopic dampers in August 1953 (from chassis numbers 717190 and 736872), the frame carrying an extra cross-member for the top mounting of the damper. The bodyshell was altered at the same time to provide two covered holes at the front of the luggage boot for access to the top mountings. This was definitely a step in the right direction as the telescopic damper was more efficient than the lever type, and longer lasting.

car's, though the latter was surprisingly slightly inferior at the top end, 90mph taking about 3-seconds longer to arrive.

Cruising speed was reckoned to be a very comfortable 80mph (at only 3400rpm), although really it was set only by road conditions and not through fear of overworking any of the mechanical components. Other Jaguar attributes were still present, with both roadholding and cornering "of a very high order"; steering was described

Telescopic dampers were fitted to the rear of the Mk VII from the summer of 1953. A bracket was used to bridge side and crossmembers on the chassis to provide a top mounting point. This picture also shows the two SU fuel pumps (above differential casing).

The Overdrive Mk VII

Then in January 1954, the news came that the Mk VII was to be given overdrive, in the form of the Laycock de Normanville unit which was offered as an extra on the manual gearbox cars. Unlike automatic transmission, overdrive was more familiar to European drivers, and its benefits much appreciated. The unit consisted of an epicyclic gear train attached to the output shaft of the gearbox, controlled via a cone clutch by a solenoid switch operated by the driver. It worked on top gear only, and the resulting overall ratio of 3.54:1 made for very relaxed and economical high speed cruising as it raised the mph per 1000rpm from 19.3 to 23.4. It also meant that a lower final drive ratio could be installed (4.55 instead of 4.27) which made for better top gear acceleration and flexibility. Specifying overdrive cost the prospective purchaser an extra £45 before purchase tax.

The Autocar sampled the overdrive Mk VII in September of that year and found it to return much the same performance as their original 1952 road test car, plus slightly better top gear performance and economy of running. Top speed and acceleration almost tallied with the earlier

as light and accurate and directional stability was good. The new telescopic shock absorbers must have been working well because *The Autocar* judged the Mk VII to be "very well damped." The new, high frequency horns which had been fitted from August 1953 were considered

The overdrive unit, offered from 1954, was neatly accomodated under the remote-control extension of the Mk VII's gearbox. *Photo: Jaguar Cars*

to have a "very penetrating note, a feature that is particularly useful on a fast car."

Tuning the Mk VII

Those who wanted true extra performance could always opt for the various tuning items which Jaguar offered XK 120 and Mk VII owners from early 1953. The higher lift camshafts (from 5/16-inch to 3/8-inch) have already been mentioned, and so have the 8:1 c.r. domed pistons – a 9:1 compression ratio set were available too, but the high octane petrol necessary was not readily available in Great Britain then; different distributors were required, as were carburetter needles and ignition timing.

By 1953 a number of performance options were available for the Mk VII, which could be made to go extremely fast. This December 1953 car is fitted with the big 2-inch SU H8 carburettors. *Photo: Jaguar Cars*

With 8:1 c.r. pistons, an engine thus modified was rated at about 180bhp, but by April 1953 this could be increased by at least a further 30 or 40bhp due to the availability of the C-type head. This had been developed by Jaguar following the modifications made to the XK engine for the sports racing C-type; the exhaust valves were increased from 1 7/16-inch to 1 5/8-inch with enlarged valve throats to match, the porting was revised, and it came with the 3/8 in. lift camshafts. It was available on an outright sale basis only, at £150; the original 1 3/4-inch SU carburetters could be retained, or a new inlet manifold could be purchased at £6.13s.0d which would accept 2-inch bore carburetters at £18 each. A lightened flywheel and high-speed crankshaft damper were usually fitted at the same time. Close ratio gears, uprated shock absorbers and stiffer springs all round could be obtained to improve handling, together with a high-ratio steering box giving 3.75 turns instead of 4.75.

The Mk VIIM

In September 1954 came the first and only substantial updating that the Mk VII was to receive in the course of its production. Known as the "M" model, it contained a whole array of improvements, but with no penalties at all in the way of increased cost.

Visually, considerable detail change had taken place especially at the front, where some of the accessories now displayed an affinity to those of the new XK 140 sports car. The Lucas 'tripod' headlights had been replaced by the latest J700 Lucas units, the inset fog lamps (now Lucas SFT 576) had been moved outboard to positions on the bumper valance, and L563 flashing indicators were now fitted to the front wings at the same level as the horn grilles which had replaced the fog lamps. The bumpers themselves now had a simpler profile, with the previous central 'rib' missing; higher over-riders had been fitted too.

At the rear, the bumpers now had a pronounced wrap-round effect for even greater protection, and the small circular tail lights were replaced by the larger L549 units with built-in reflectors and twin filament bulbs for indicating. These changes meant that both front and rear wings were adapted to take the new parts, and received new part numbers.

The only increase in decoration for its own sake were the Rim-embellishers now fitted to the wheels, which (for export only at first) also received tubeless tyres. Whitewall tyres, obligatory for the States, remained an option on home cars – Britain was now beginning to get an increasing number of cars, and the M version was to become the most familiar type of Mk VII on our roads. Wing mirrors were introduced as standard, but for some reason only on export cars, and oversize 7.60 x 16 tyres ("with attendant modification to the rear wheel arches") could also be specified, though the writer has never seen a car so equipped or modified.

Other extras for the Mk VII included a tow-bar (with two-ton capacity!), a choice of three radio sets (still relatively expensive, at around £50), an oil-bath air cleaner for extremely dusty conditions, and on the home market, a Continental Touring Kit in a neat case for £24.7s.0d.

However, changes on the Mk VII had gone much further than skin-deep; the 3/8-inch lift camshafts were standardised, an 8:1 c.r. engine now being rated at 190bhp at 5500rpm instead of 160bhp at 5200rpm. While the final drive wasn't changed, the gearbox ratios were made closer and worked out at 12.73 (formerly 14.4), 7.47 (8.56), 5.16 (5.84), top gear remaining direct at 4.27 for

The Mk VIIM of autumn 1954 – discreetly modified to update its appearance with wing-mounted flashing indicators, bumper-mounted fog lights, and simplified bumper section.

Below: At the rear, the Mk VIIM displayed wrap-round bumpers and new rear lights incorporating reflectors. *Photo: Jaguar Cars*

Mk VIIM engine compartment; with new camshafts the XK engine was now rated at 190bhp. Note the J.700 Lucas headlights now fitted. *Photo: Motor*

the non-overdrive car.

Interestingly, Jaguar had turned their attention to the suspension too, and had increased the diameter of the torsion bars from 15/16-inch to 1-inch, which gave a considerably higher spring rate and served to cut down roll by a noticeable extent. Formerly the front spring rate was 80lb/in at the wheel, equivalent to 128lb/in when the effect of the Metalastic bushes was taken into account; now, the 1-inch bars gave 106lb/in and 154lb/in respectively, with static deflection reduced from 7.72-inch to 6.43-inch (i.e. the suspension movement taken up merely by the weight of the car) which thus improved ground clearance.

Inside the Mk VIIM, the new flat steering wheel boss was noticeable, and although the trim and upholstery remained much the same, full depth Dunlopillo foam was now used under the leather seat covers. Incidentally, William Lyons' cost consciousness extended everywhere at the factory, even to the trim shop. Christopher Jennings remembers a mid-fifties visit to the trim shop clearly: "What I was very impressed with was the women cutting out the leather for the seats. Somebody had given them a plan which meant that they made absolutely the last ounce use of the leather – no-one went *like that* and left a big bit of leather out, they went *like this* and then miraculously there were three bits of leather for the rear

Interior of automatic Mk VIIM; note bench seat and umbrella handbrake fitted when this transmission was specified.

seats; I'm sure that was a touch of the Bill Lyons in there somewhere, and I bet you those seats cost about half as much as anybody else's and were twice as good."

Sometimes these excellent economies went wrong though; Peter Craig recalled the time when Sir William had the idea that it was unnecessary to extend the carpet underneath the front seats of the Mk VII where it couldn't be seen, and sent down orders to that effect. "But the trim shop misunderstood and just cut out the square and threw it away!", said Peter. "No-one dared tell Sir William..."

Road-testing the Mk VIIM

The Motor tried a Mk VIIM in the late summer of 1955, with the optional overdrive fitted. The acceleration figures did not show the margin over the original Mk VII tested in 1952 that was expected, the 0-60mph time of 14.1-seconds actually being 0.4-second slower. A slipping clutch was blamed for this discrepancy, but as this was said not to effect the car's top gear acceleration, which on average was no better either, an alternative view might be that the original road test was quicker than average, or that the 1955 Mk VIIM was a sub-standard example. Weight was not a factor, because – very creditably – it had remained almost exactly the same.

Economy has always been one good reason for specifying an overdrive, and *The Motor* did record an overall fuel consumption a little over 1mpg better than before, at 18.8mpg; steady-speed consumption in overdrive top at 50mph was 25.5mpg, a useful drop of 2.5mpg compared with the 160bhp car, although at other speeds the advantage was not always maintained. The worst fuel consumption recorded during the test was 15.5mpg in the Alps, and the best, 22.5mpg "for a substantial distance", all very creditable for an extremely spacious luxury car with an all-up weight of approaching 40cwt.

Top speed was up to 104.3mph mean, an increase of 3.3mph, which showed that some of the extra horsepower was getting through. Maximum speed in the 4.55 direct top gear was exactly 100mph at 5500rpm. Certainly with overdrive engaged, it was now almost impossible to overstress the engine as *The Motor* pointed out, and while in Britain high speeds could not be held for long periods, "the ability to sprint up to them for brief moments is a powerful aid towards high average speeds." These were also assisted by the improved handling, the higher front spring rates obviously doing their job: "Subtly but definitely, this latest Mk VII Jaguar feels more surefooted at speed and on corners than did its predecessors." As usual, the test staff preferred to run on the highest of the recommended tyre pressures, which improved cornering further and reduced but not eliminated tyre squeal on tight corners; only on cobbled town streets was there any sacrifice in comfort or "road rumble."

The Motor on tour with a Mk VIIM. The overdrive model in particular gave easy, untiring cruising on continental autoroutes. In England, the 'M' type became the most common Mk VII as more were released to the home market. *Photo: Motor*

The brakes behaved themselves very well, and "never showed the slightest symptoms of fade" despite extensive European motoring. Their only faults were squeal and some vibration when used hard.

Overall, *The Motor* felt that the Mk VII was carrying its years well, being "mature but in no sense obsolete", and providing outstanding value for money (with overdrive and purchase tax, the Mk VIIM cost £1679.17s.6d in Great Britain). "A small number of motorcars", the journal stated, "have so powerful a personality that they are able to impress the road tester with a key word to represent their particular quality. Such a one is the latest M type Mk VII Jaguar; the word which it conjures up is 'exceptional.'" Thanks to increased production at the new Browns Lane works, more and more people were able to sample this quality for themselves.

Of course, potential customers would soon have a choice of Jaguar four-seaters – the new 2.4-litre saloon was introduced in September 1955, its modern unitary construction marking the way ahead for the Jaguar saloon, and while it was not intended to challenge the Mk VII in terms of space and luggage capacity, it was virtually as fast. Ultimately, in Mk II guise, the new small car would outlive the Mk VII and its direct descendants, but that was years away as yet.

Refinement of the big saloon continued, with a revised automatic gearbox being fitted to the Mk VIIM by October 1954; this differed in that starts in the "D" (Drive) position were now made from rest in first gear, instead of in intermediate as before. It resulted in a considerably brisker take-off due to less power being lost in the fluid torque converter. In November 1954, the overdrive Mk VII was given the Salisbury 4HA axle in place of the 2HA unit, though the final drive ratio was not altered. Five months later, an axle modification positioned the wheels further inboard of the hub bearings, effected by repositioning the brake drum flanges on the rear hubs and 'dishing' the brake back plates to suit. The track was maintained by widening the carrier and axle tube assembly and lengthening the axle shafts.

Few alterations were made to the 190bhp power unit, though from February 1955, 3/8-inch lift camshafts were fitted to 7:1 c.r. engines too. A little later, (from engine number D.6723) a new Hobourn Eaton eccentric rotor type oil pump replaced the original gear-driven pump, and the oil pressure relief valve transferred from the oil pump to the filter head. A circular oil seal was fitted to the front of the crankshaft too. In September 1955, there was a change from the spring blade timing chain tensioner to a spring loaded Reynolds tensioner (from engine number D9869), and a nylon damper assembly fitted in place of the guide bracket.

The cooling system had undergone another change back in September 1954, when a new radiator was installed without the dual expansion chambers. About the only change visible externally was the replacement of the clear lenses of the front indicator lights with amber (February 1955), while inside, the red band on the rev. counter was moved to 5500–6000rpm instead of 5200–5500rpm, due to increased revs usefully allowed by the 3/8-inch lift cams; this took place in March 1956, from cars 724688 and 738528.

The Automatic Mk VIIM road-tested

Road & Track sampled an automatic Mk VIIM with the improved transmission, and they liked it a lot, even if "its adherence to simple styling in the face of flamboyance and sheer bad taste" was something of a novelty. The car tested (finished in strange two-tone paintwork and obviously privately owned) was the first automatic Mk VII *Road & Track* had tried, and they thought that "half the fun of driving the 1952 test car was its brilliant performance in 2nd and 3rd gears"; however, they discovered that the new transmission was certainly no "slush stirrer", with the car returning a suspiciously fast 0- 0mph time of 11.6-seconds, a second better than the 160bhp manual version tested earlier. The time to 90mph was cut by almost four seconds too, and top speed was up to a mean of 106.3mph.

What most impressed the magazine was the Mk VII's sheer road-worthiness; they could hardly have been more complimentary on this point:

"Sheer top speed, then, is at least nearly equal to any competitive domestic machine, but the ability of the Jaguar to cruise at very high speeds over rough, uneven surfaces or on winding roads is its greatest virtue. We will even say flatly that no American sedan car can keep up with the Mk VII over a crooked road. Furthermore, the Jaguar is, in our opinion, the safest high-performance sedan on the market today listed under $5000. Judged by sports car standards, its cornering powers are not phenomenal, and there is certainly very prominent tyre squeal. But this car can be cornered with a great deal of verve, and the driver knows that he is in complete control."

The writer acknowledged that the steering was no 'quicker' than the domestic product, but advised against the high-ratio steering box as the parking effort was "already a little high." As for the stiffer torsion bars, "we have yet to find anyone who can actually notice any difference under way. The Mk VII has always enjoyed the reputation of being an extremely comfortable car, and if this newest model is any different at all, it is that there is slightly less roll in a corner than before." In order to really appreciate the car's ride qualities, said *Road & Track*, the prospective buyer should take the Mk VII on "an extended test over all types of roads", not just round the block.

Like their European brethren though, *Road & Track's* testers preferred to use higher tyre pressures than normal,

Mk VIIs in church! One Dutch dealer found a distinctly non-ecclesiastical use for a disused place of worship; whether organ recitals were given to entertain customers is not known....

"as high as 38/40psi without any feeling that highway comfort was being sacrificed unduly''; as with the XK, the Mk VII responded to the helm much better in this condition, and it cut out quite a lot of the tyre squeal accompanying determined, low speed cornering. Inside the car, the writer felt that "some roominess is sacrificed" through the imposition of the bench front seat in an interior not designed for it, but otherwise "the leather and grained woodwork are...as beautiful as ever."

At the end of August, it was announced that two-pedal control was coming to the home market, so that for 1956, British buyers could specify their Mk VIIM with automatic transmission if they so desired. It cost an extra £181.6s.8d, and in May 1956 *The Autocar* reported on a car thus equipped; they found the marriage of the XK engine with the Borg Warner box worked very well.

This car was of course the M model which had superseded the earlier Mk VII, and thanks to its extra 30bhp, lost out very little on acceleration to the previous manual/overdrive saloon tried by the magazine 17-months previously. Sixty miles an hour was attained in 14.3-seconds with the automatic car as opposed to 13.6 for the manual version, and at 26.8-seconds, the 0-80mph time was only down by about a second. Top speed was 100.1mph mean, 2mph down. In fact as the journal had said earlier, in the hands of an unskilled driver, the automatic car would probably be quicker under most circumstances.

The Borg Warner box supported Jaguar's decision to employ it in the Mk VII by performing excellently; "the transmission is very quiet at all speeds, and gear changes in both directions occur without the passengers being aware of anything happening", said *The Autocar*. "The driver also finds it necessary to listen consciously for the moment when the changes take place". Full-throttle changes took place between first and intermediate at 39mph, and between intermediate and top at 68mph. Selecting Low on the quadrant would hold first gear at speeds below 40mph, useful when descending steep hills but of limited value under normal conditions. Kickdown changes from top to intermediate would take place if the accelerator pedal was sharply depressed under 60mph.

The usual limitations of automatic transmission were there of course. "One criticism of this type of transmission is that it does not allow a driver to change down in the time-honoured method for fast corners; thus for some it takes away part of the pleasure of driving, that is if one does not regard the car just as a means of getting from A to B but rather as a piece of living mechanism." Jaguar were soon to give the keen driver this extra element of control, but meanwhile, the automatic box was not obligatory in Britain so the more sporty type of driver could remain with the manual gearbox.

In keeping with the 'softer' side of the automatic Mk VII's character, the Borg Warner equipped cars arrived with bench front seats; this brought back the infamous old Mk V-type umbrella handbrake, positioned under the dash. "The brake has an indefinite, spongy feel about it" commented *The Autocar*, though with the locking action of the pawl when 'P' was selected at rest, its efficiency or ease of use was perhaps not quite so vital as with the Mk V. Another result of the bench seat installation was a reduction of a couple of inches in legroom for the rear seat passengers, though it was still ample; in exchange, they faced a handsome walnut veneer rail which ran across the back of the seat (the 'secondary collision' safety aspect was not part of automobile engineering thinking in the mid-fifties!) and which bestowed upon them a *third* ashtray. Though *The Autocar* remained unimpressed and even complained that this was "badly placed and too small – some Jaguar owners like cigars"...

The standard-equipment opening sun roof,

A late-model Mk VIIM, displaying the unpainted chrome hubcaps which came in during the mid-fifties but wearing the optional Rim-embellishers. *Photo: Jaguar Cars*

acknowledged as a feature disappearing from most production cars, was much liked, but equally, progress was beginning to show up the inadequacies of the heating and demisting arrangements – "even with the heat controls and blower fan on, a passenger in the front seat was apt to complain in wintry weather, and little or no effect could be felt at the back of the compartment."

This deficiency was inspite of the heater having been modified with larger diameter piping in 1954, and it is an unfortunate fact that by the standards of most other luxury-car manufacturers (and, let it be said, by the standards of many advanced cheap mass-production cars too), Jaguar's efforts in this direction were usually behind the times. One story, almost certainly apocryphal, quotes Sir William as saying in answer to a question on the subject, that if it was a cold day, one wore one's overcoat; but true or false, there were many owners not living in the tropics who might have believed it! The company didn't really get it anywhere near right until the XJ6 of 1968.

In most other respects, the 1956 Mk VII was up with, if not still ahead of, the crowd. "Wind and road noise is at a commendably low level, and this helps make the Mk VII Jaguar one of those deceptively fast cars. Passengers are apt suddenly to realise that they are travelling a great deal quicker than they thought. It was noticed that, on one short section of the road, the front seat passenger commented with surprise on the reading of the speedometer – which is masked to some extent by the gear selector lever – when it was recording 100mph." The lights were good enough to enable speeds like this to be reached at night, although the dipped position was thought to have a rather sharp cut-off.

Shorter drivers would have preferred a slightly higher seating position, continued the writer, but all agreed that the seats were comfortable. The car, despite its size, remained controllable:

"The car handles well. Driven fast with one up and normal tyre pressures, there was a fair amount of noise when cornering... On damp greasy surfaces slight oversteer could be provoked by use of the throttle. The big spring-spoked steering wheel is placed at an excellent angle on the adjustable-for-length column, and inspite of 4.5-turns from lock-to-lock, the car can be turned quickly in the average width road."

Finish was praised too: "The polished veneer of the facia, and door rails, the soft leather covering of the seats and door panels are worthy of a body produced by a specialist coachbuilder." Well, many of those who helped build William Lyons' special bodies in the Swallow days were still with the firm, so perhaps that's not too surprising; although in fact leather was only used on the seat facings. Other small details were liked too: "The big doors close well and firmly, and the trigger-type handles do not catch one's knees." The rear view mirror was considered inadequate, however, and the rear window small; the divided windscreen with its centre pillar was also becoming unfashionably noticeable too, but this at least was to be rectified as the Mk VII adopted a new identity.

The Mk VIII Jaguar

In October 1956, the Mk VIII arrived. It was obvious from the first glance that it didn't pretend to be an entirely new model, but there were a sufficient number of improvements to justify the new name. Visually, the car had been modernised and made more interesting by the addition of a thin chrome beading along the side of the car which followed the wing-line, this serving to break up the bulk of the car, helped by a two-tone paint finish which from then on was the normal wear, and 'cutaway' spats. A much bolder, chromium plated radiator grille surround appeared at the front, together with a Jaguar mascot, and the old-fashioned divided windscreen had gone, replaced by a full-width slightly curved screen (though interestingly, the roof pressing was never changed and continued to sport a slight 'peak' at its centre, above where the divide had been).

Mechanically the biggest change had been to the engine, which boasted what the factory termed a "B-type" head. This was a variant of the C-type head which had previously been an option on the Mk VII; its larger valves had been kept (1 3/4-in. inlet, 1 3/8-in. exhaust), with the new inlet valve angle of 45-degrees, but the standard diameter port throat of the original Mk VII head had been retained as well.

Work on the gas-flow rig had shown that increasing the valve size did indeed improve mixture entry into the combustion chamber, but that if the smaller diameter inlet throat was used, gas velocity was kept up at low and medium rpm to give improved torque in those most-used ranges. The B-type head only lost out to the C-type at very high rpm, rarely if ever used in a saloon car. Thus while the previous C-type head engine was rated at 210bhp at 5750rpm, the new B-type power unit's rating was 190bhp at 5500rpm, or the same as the Mk VIIM. The result was a much better top gear performance, with a useful increase in speed generally as well, further assisted by a dual exhaust system with twin silencers, and a new inlet manifold with a separate bolt-on water rail plus the latest SU HD6 1.75-inch carburettors.

Since the introduction of two-pedal control, an increasing number of customers were opting for automatic transmission on the big Jaguar saloons, even in Great Britain; those who wanted to combine sporting motoring with four seats were beginning to turn to Jaguar's new 2.4 saloon, and even more were won over when the 3.4 version was announced in 1957. But while most Mk VIIIs were automatics, Jaguar did not abandon driver-appeal, and built in a new, exclusive feature on all its automatic cars.

Above: **The Mk VIII Jaguar, rarest of the species, but changed externally only by the discreet chrome bodyline, duo-tone paintwork and new screen.**
Photo: Jaguar Cars

Right: **Mk VIII engine compartment; B-type cylinder head provided extra torque.**

This was the famous Jaguar "speed hold", which enabled the driver to select or retain the intermediate gear by means of a small switch conveniently positioned on the dashboard. This prevented the gearbox changing up into top gear just when the car was approaching a corner or at some other inopportune moment; it was also a less brutal method of obtaining intermediate than by using the kick-down switch, as this required full throttle, a clumsy and wasteful method of changing down in some circumstances and not helped by the strong throttle return springs usually fitted by Jaguar. The switch, which operated a solenoid fitted to the rear oil pump in the Borg Warner DG box, was the work of Tom Jones, who remembers Sir William being particularly pleased with the system, 'the boss' also giving some thought to the position and style of the dashboard switch itself; the arrangement was also the subject of a separate Jaguar patent.

Inside the Mk VIII there were lots of small changes, though the traditional leather and walnut theme still predominated; immediately obvious was the new treatment of the rear seat, which had been remodelled to suggest two individual seats, though with the armrest up, three abreast seating was just as comfortable as before. Also, the rear seat passengers now had let-down walnut veneer picnic tables facing them, and in the automatic bench seat

Jaguar's innovative "speed hold" switch introduced on automatic cars, which enabled the driver to retain or select "Intermediate" gear at the flick of a finger.
Photo: Jaguar Cars

car, a central magazine or map pocket in wood was fitted too, surmounted by an electric clock which was illuminated when the sidelights were switched on. These extra luxuries came at the expense of a small amount of lost footroom though, which became noticeable if the driver pushed his seat back to its rearmost position.

The thickness of the Dunlopillo rubber cushioning over the spring cases had been increased yet again on all the seats, and the height of the front seats had been increased in answer to complaints from shorter drivers that they couldn't see over the rather high scuttle. The

usual bench seat was fitted when automatic transmission was specified, and two separate bucket-type seats were supplied on the comparatively few cars where manual transmission (with or without overdrive) was requested. Ashtrays were now to be found let-in to the door trims, and the Mk VIII had no less than three cigar lighters – one on the dash in front of the passenger, and one in each of the centre door pillars. Above, the sliding roof remained a standard fitment.

The luxury touch was extended to the luggage compartment, which was fully lined in Hardura material – later

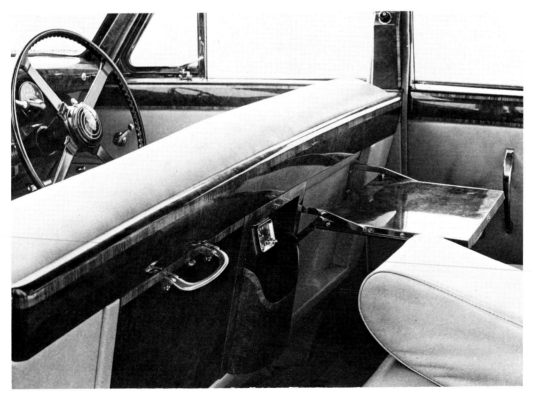

Mk VIII interior, showing the extensive use of wood, the picnic tables and magazine rack; plus the door-pillar mounted cigar-lighter and what someone described as the "boudoir" clock.
Photo: Motor

Mk VIIs had partially lined boots too, but on the Mk VIII, the spare wheel had a cover and the bootlid underside was covered by a trim panel as well. It all added up to a weight penalty over the Mk VIIM of about 1cwt, a modest increase and more than compensated for by the new B-type cylinder head.

Road-testing the Mk VIII

This was more than confirmed when *The Autocar* tried an automatic Mk VIII in January 1957, and found it much faster than their Mk VIIM tested less than a year earlier. At 11.6-seconds, it was 2.7-seconds quicker to 60mph, and no less than 11.9-seconds faster to 90mph. Maximum speed was up by a considerable amount too, the Mk VIII recording a mean of 106.5mph compared to just over 100mph for the Mk VIIM. Direct top gear increments were covered more rapidly too, with comparative 60-80mph times of 9.9 and 13.8-seconds; in fact, the overall increase in performance makes it hard to believe that it was achieved merely on an altered torque curve and not an increase in power.

The extra pace had been achieved at little expense of refinement. "The engine remains very tractable; it fires easily from cold with the assistance of the electrically operated starting carburetter, and is quiet both mechanically and in exhaust. A subdued roar at the higher rpm probably arises from the intakes." Petrol consumption was slightly up, at 17.9mpg as opposed to 18.5mpg overall for the older car, but if the driver could "curb the desire to use the car's outstanding capabilities", the journal found 20mpg a quite obtainable average – excellent for such a large car.

Surprisingly, in view of the fact that the opposition had now had over eight years to catch up, *The Autocar* thought that the car's suspension was its best point:

"The most outstanding feature of the car is perhaps the suspension system. In such a large saloon it is difficult to provide a ride which is soft enough on straight roads to give a relaxed comfort of the floating kind, yet sufficiently stiff on winding sections and bad surfaces to prevent excessive roll when the car's performance is used.

The Jaguar is a wonderful compromise – it provides an undisturbed back seat ride under all conditions, and when the car is cornered vigorously never gives the impression of getting out of hand."

The steering had remained at its normal 4.75 turns, "but only in a quick succession of tight left- and right-hand bends is this large steering wheel movement noticeable", thought *The Autocar,* particularly as it was "helped by a desirable degree and precision of self centering, for the wheel can be released to spin back through the driver's hands and come to rest in the straight ahead position.... Except at very low speeds the steering is light, which is surprising for a 35cwt car without power assistance." The compact turning circle was appreciated as always, too.

The test staff used the new intermediate speed hold extensively, preferring it to the kick-down facility, and finding that it provided "what might be described as a manually controlled three-speed box in addition to the advantages of a fully automatic transmission." Little else was said about the behaviour of the box, except for the observation that when the intermediate range was held, the car appeared to free-wheel on the over-run, this being due to the inefficiency of the torque converter under those conditions – the engine would only be turning over

Rear seat squabs of the Mk VIII were shaped individually; ashtrays were now fitted into the door panels, leaving the top rail of the facia clear.
Photo: Motor

at about half the rate compared to a fixed transmission.

The brakes, unchanged from the Mk VIIM, were "satisfactory in everyday conditions"; but pedal travel was reckoned to be considerable by normal standards, and "some fade was noticed after several successive stops from over 80mph" together with the usual vibration when they were applied at maximum speed.

The increased vision thanks to the new one-piece screen was appreciated, though the writer thought that the windscreen pillars could have been made slimmer at the same time, and the rev. counter position was beginning to annoy as it was more easily read by the passenger than by the driver. The 'ultra-violet' instrument lighting passed muster, though the new ashtray placings were not thought ideal as in the front they weren't easily reached and ash was more likely to drop into the map pockets underneath. The seats both front and rear were heartily praised: "it is impossible to imagine anyone complaining of discomfort with such luxurious appointments", while the standard of finish inside was thought to be "of a very high order, particularly so when related to its basic price."

Underbonnet details were appreciated, like the accessible fuse box and T-handle extension to the radiator drain tap, and certainly there was more room to carry out maintenance and repair than there was in the 2.4 or XK 140. The use of a mirror was advised for checking the electrolyte level in the battery.

The summing-up paragraph was almost routine in its acknowledgement of excellence:

"The Mk VIII Jaguar represents, above all, remarkable value for money. It has a high performance, but goes about its work with an equally high degree of mechanical refinement. The standard of finish and range of equipment place it firmly in the luxury class, despite a moderate cost price. These factors alone are sufficient to make the Jaguar a very desirable property, but it has in addition that elusive and indefinable feel of the thoroughbred about every part of its mechanism, which is a characteristic shared by a very limited number of the world's cars."

Prices had risen of course, and a Mk VIII with automatic transmission cost £1268 basic, or £1903 with purchase tax added. But there was still nothing available at anywhere near that price which could offer half of the Mk VIII's virtues.

Refinements for the Mk VIII

Engineering changes were few over the Mk VIII's comparatively short production run – it was the rarest of the three variants on that chassis. The engine received drilled camshafts for quieter cold starting early in 1957, and rubber interleaving on the rear springs was tried in May 1957, to be replaced by nylon interleaving by July 1958.

For cost or ease of production reasons the material for the radiator grille frame and bonnet top motif was changed from brass to die-cast alloy in July 1957 (from chassis numbers 761116 and 780870), a step regretted by enthusiasts years later who had to contend with that later metal's tendency to deteriorate badly; the same month the exhaust pipe diameters were reduced.

A more significant change occured in April 1958, when limited numbers of left-hand drive cars for certain export countries were fitted with Burman power-assisted steering. This employed a Hobourn-Eaton eccentric rotor pump driven from the rear of the dynamo shaft which provided a continuous flow of oil through the hydraulically assisted worm and recirculating ball steering box. Actual pressure was only created when the steering wheel was turned, and was proportional to the effort applied at the wheel.

This addition to Jaguar's big saloon further tailored it to the North American market, where lady drivers in particular had grumbled about the effort needed to park the car; it was becoming a universal fitment on Detroit vehicles. Sensibly, Jaguar also elected to reduce the number of turns lock-to-lock, which came down to a more manageable 3.5 and made the car considerably more responsive on twisty roads, even if some apparent 'feel' was lacking at high speeds. Cars so equipped had a "P" prefix to their chassis numbers; few, if any, stayed at home.

Then in July 1958, Jaguar offered the proprietory Reutter seats on the Mk VIII; these bulkier, more luxurious items also possessed adjustable-rake backs, a

facility which – surprisingly – was not to be offered as standard on a Jaguar until well into the 'sixties. The Reutter seats cost £42.10s. each, and could, incidentally, also be specified for the XK150. The Mk VIII was by far the rarest of the Mk VII variants, with a mere 1668 left-hand-drive examples being built, and 4644 rhd. Production continued for over a year after its successor was announced: the last Mk VIII being completed in December 1959.

The Mk IX Jaguar

Motor Show time, October 1958, and the Mk IX Jaguar made its entrance. For a car that looked exactly the same as its immediate predecessor – there's no way of telling Mk VIIIs and IXs apart if you can't see the badges – the press would seem to have hailed it with somewhat overdone enthusiasm; until, that is, one realised that some very worthwhile advances came with this latest and final variation on the Mk VII theme.

The Mk IX was, for instance, the first Jaguar saloon to have disc brakes fitted *as standard,* and the same applied to the power steering which was also original equipment. The car also became the first production Jaguar saloon to feature the 3.8-litre version of the XK engine. So in performance and refinement, the new model represented a very big step forward indeed over its twin sister.

Enthusiasts had cheerfully, but not always successfully, bored-out the XK power unit to around 3.8-litres for years, Oscar Moore probably being the first British owner to do so in 1952 with his HWM-Jaguar, though keen XK owners in the States may have beaten him to it by months or even years. Jaguar's thoughts were turned in this direction by Briggs Cunningham's experiments, and they adopted the capacity of 3781cc for their D-type Le Mans cars from 1955 onwards; further work showed that the new capacity could be used in a production engine and would give a worthwhile increase in both torque and power.

While the 3.8 engine used the same B-type cylinder head and followed the 3.4 unit's basic detail arrangements, a new block was in fact used. This incorporated liners for the first time in a Jaguar engine, because while the original block could – just – be bored straight out to 3.8-litres, a percentage would always suffer from cracking between the bores, with disastrous results as some of the lay racing fraternity had already discovered. The capacity increase was derived from taking each bore from 83mm to 87mm; dry liners were used, with the bores of the front three and the rear three cylinders being interconnected with water passages between the two 'halves'.

The new engine was rated 30bhp higher than before, at 220bhp, developed at the same speed of 5500rpm, but the increase of 11.5% in torque was even more relevant at 240ft.lb. as opposed to 203ft.lb. With the North American automobile getting a large dose of extra horses

An optional extra for the Mk VIII was the Reutter seats with their adjustable squabs.

Some not-too-serious sketches for updating the Mk VII/VIII, produced around 1958.

More trial-and-error work, this time in the metal as a Mk VII gets some experimental chrome trim. Simplicity prevailed though, for the Mk VIII itself.
Photo: Jaguar Cars

at each model announcement, this increase in both paper figures and performance on the road was very necessary to keep the big Jaguar ahead, even though the majority of owners on that continent would probably never extend the car much past half its potential on the road.

About the only other engine change was a revised cold-start system, which still used the SU auxiliary starting carburetter but instead of the rich mixture being supplied to the centre of the inlet manifold, it was ducted to four points spaced equidistantly under the manifold opposite the inlet ports. Care was taken to ensure even distribution, and the arrangement originally came through the need to provide more efficient starting in very cold countries, but was then adopted for all cars because of the improved starting and regular firing it gave generally. Lead indium bearings were standardised for the crankshaft, these also being adopted towards the end of Mk VIII production in April 1959.

The Burman power-assisted steering was as seen on some late export Mk VIIIs as already mentioned, a neat system contained almost entirely in an enlarged steering box. A large circular oil reservoir was about all that was immediately visible of the power steering on opening the bonnet. Turns lock-to-lock were 3.5 and maximum operating pressure was 650lb.sq.in.

However, the most welcome addition of all to the car's specification were the disc brakes. Conforming to Jaguar policy they were fitted to all four wheels, and were the latest Dunlop pattern with 'quick-change' pads. Big, beefy discs were fitted, 12 1/8-inch diameter by 1/2-inch thick at the front and 12-inch by 3/8-inch at the rear, each disc being gripped by square pads and twin wheel cylinders, 2 1/2-inch front and 1 7/8-inch rear. Pad area was 38.45 square inches. A new Lockheed 6 7/8-inch suspended vacuum servo supplied the power assistance, and this time a vacuum reservoir was incorporated so that an engine stall would not immediately deprive the brakes of their assistance. It was a set-up that was to prove

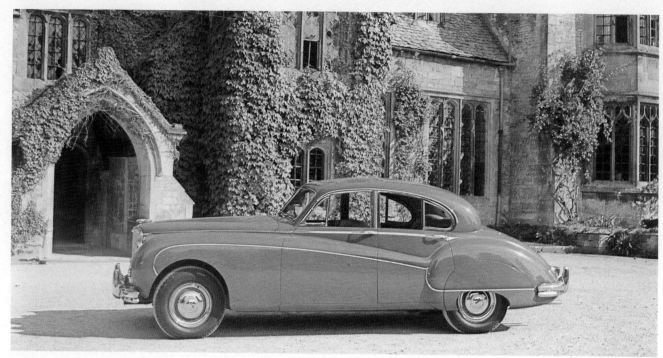

The Mk IX was externally indistinguishable from the Mk VIII from every direction except the rear, where a small "Mk IX" badge was carried on the corner of the bootlid. This is a contemporary photograph from Jaguar's archives.

entirely worthy of a 35cwt, high performance luxury car, and made the Mk IX's new-found speed completely usable.

Heating and demisting systems were becoming an ever-increasingly important part of the motor car, and by the late 1950s the customer was beginning to expect real efficiency in that department. Jaguar made an effort to comply by redesigning their heating system for the Mk IX, which now had an output rated at nearly 5-kilowatts as opposed to the Mk VIII's 3 1/2, plus an airflow up from 110cu.ft/min. to about 150cu.ft/min. To achieve this, the new heater unit was positioned much nearer the centre of the bulkhead below the external scuttle ventilator, with a vertically mounted axial-flow fan blowing air downwards to the toe-board and demisting trunking via a new heat exchanger. This meant substituting the single 12-volt battery for two 6-volt, positioned each side of the steering column.

Inside the Mk IX, it was once again the mixture as before, with detail changes – the newspaper or magazine holder in the rear compartment was now collapsible and could be locked, but other than that and the two-speed fan switch it was much as the Mk VIII. A bench seat was again fitted when automatic transmission was specified, which it usually was even in this country. Above all, the value-for-money factor had been kept too, a small across-the-range increase of £165 being the only penalty; this did bring the Jaguar saloon into the over-£2000 price bracket for the first time though, with the overdrive and automatic versions costing £2062 and £2162 respectively inclusive of tax. The manual non-overdrive car just managed to remain under £2000 at £1994.

This is an interior view of the rare manual gearbox version of the Mk IX, with separate front seats. *Photo: Jaguar Cars*

The Mk IX road-tested

Both *The Motor* and *The Autocar* tried an automatic Mk IX in 1958 and found it a significantly faster car than the Mk VIII. *The Autocar* recorded 11-seconds to 60mph, and its counterpart on the other side of the Thames 11.3-seconds . Ninety miles an hour was reached in 24.7 and 25.9-seconds respectively for the two journals, compared with the 26.7-seconds which the Mk VIII had taken a year before. Top speed was an impressive 114.3mph (113.5mph *The Autocar*), almost 8mph faster than before.

The Motor calculated that the bhp at the wheels had increased by nearly one third since the original Mk VII, and "nor did (the engine) show any roughness as the result of the enlarged cylinder bore and heavier pistons, but was on the contrary exceedingly smooth and quiet up to the rather startling crankshaft speed of nearly 6000rpm." The mid-range pulling power of the engine had usefully increased too, quite apart from its conferring out and out speed, the journal noting that the Mk IX could get from 60mph to 80mph quicker than the Mk VIII could reach 70mph from 50mph.

For *The Motor*, high speed cruising was marred by wind noise which limited sustained speeds to between 80mph and 90mph; door and window sealing must have been improved by the time *The Autocar* tried WRW 536, because "it was found that the Jaguar would cruise with extraordinary little fuss and effort at 100mph, despite the fact that this represents a crankshaft speed of just over 5000rpm, nor were there signs of distress when the car was held for several miles at its maximum speed. At 100mph, wind roar around the body is not excessive if the windows are kept closed, and the occupants can still converse in almost normal tones."

The Borg Warner box behaved well during both tests, the override switch being used to obtain maximum acceleration, intermediate being held to about 70mph (5200rpm) – although the safe maximum in this gear was nearer 80mph. First gear could be retained up to 48mph (6000rpm) by using the "Low" setting on the quadrant. The box would kick-down from top to intermediate below about 56mph, "but the change can be somewhat violent with a car of such potency, and on a wet surface its sudden, sometimes unexpected engagement on a slow corner could set the back of the car sliding" observed *The Autocar*, which preferred to use the override switch. The writer also considered that "the linkage settings of the gearbox on the car tested were not adjusted well to the car's engine characteristics, in that it would change up to top much too early on a light throttle and cause the engine to pull quite hard at low crankshaft speeds". This was a common disadvantage of these early automatic boxes, and it would need a further ten or fifteen-years' development before such problems were solved.

Needless to say, the fitting of disc brakes was welcomed by the two magazines. "The joy of disc brakes lies in their ability to continue receiving hard punishment with scarcely appreciable fade" said *The Autocar*, and the Dunlop system proved to be no exception. *The Motor* enlarged upon the topic:

"...they can be used all the time up to the limit set by human endurance, which is about 0.6g, and will remain absolutely consistent. The dominion of this latest Jaguar is thus based upon the facts that it can cruise comfortably at 100mph and can reach this figure from rest in less than 35-sec. and from, say, a brief baulk at 50mph in a mere 26-sec. Should the driver wish to pass any other road user travelling at 100mph he can do so with a margin of some 15mph and should he wish to get down from 100mph to 30mph he can do so *infallibly* within 15 car lengths on a dry road."

The brakes displayed few faults; *The Autocar* found that in damp conditions under maximum braking one or other of the rear wheels sometimes locked, while *The Motor* found that fast cornering would cause the disc to move, increasing the pad/disc clearance so that a longer pedal travel would be encountered on the first application afterwards. The poorest aspect of the system was undoubtedly the handbrake though, described by *The Autocar* as "none-too-effective."

The Mk IX's power steering, still a novel feature on British cars, was "enthusiastically endorsed after road experience" by *The Motor*. "Low physical effort is combined with an ability accurately to position the car, and a pleasing self-return action" the writer thought. *The Autocar* was not too sure:

"There were divided opinions about the Jaguar's Burman power steering. Although appreciation of this amenity is in part a matter of personal preference, judgement should not be pronounced on it after only a brief acquaintance. Jaguars have sensibly raised the ratio of the mechanism so that only 3 1/2 turns of the steering wheel (lock-to-lock) are required, compared with 4 2/3 for the Mk VIII. This results in more load and feel than is the custom with transatlantic products. The boon of power steering for low-speed manouvering is universally agreed; it is questionable, however, whether it is so sensitive as an unassisted gear at high speeds, particularly on moderately straight roads where very small deviations are necessary. Over some of the steeply cambered, undulating roads of northern France the driver was less at ease than his passenger; but on straight roads with little camber the Jaguar pursued its course with complete stability and a minimum of attention.

The Autocar was, however, slightly more enthusiastic about the Mk IX's handling than its rival, though it was considered that adjustable damper settings would be ideal. "As it is, the passengers have preference and the ride is soft – so much so that a rear seat passenger can write quite legibly while being driven at high speed over a reasonable surface. Yet this heavy six-seater, while lacking the lightening manouverability of a sports car, reacts quite well to vigorous handling. It is free from pitch, rolls

Right: Of similar wheelbase and external appearance, the limousine versions of the big Jaguar saloon were fitted out with this centre division; cocktail cabinet replaced magazine rack and extra ashtrays were provided.

Below: For an upper-crust day out – Harold Radford produced this superior picnic set, complete with tables and stove, which could be hinged-out of the Mk IX's boot!

in moderation, and springs no surprises. By driving with emphasis on its accelerative rather than cornering powers, very high journey averages can be achieved with peace of mind to all concerned.'' So the passage of eight years had not dated the car too much in this department.

The Motor was a little more cautious and thought that at the recommended tyre pressures for touring ''the car could not be given full marks for control'', it being ''immensely enhanced by using for ordinary motoring the the tyre pressures set up for the high speed attempt (37 and 34psi). No loss in passenger comfort seemed to result from this practice, and on rough roads the suspension was outstandingly comfortable and at the same time stable.''

The new heater was rated an improvement – ''now very effective as well as simple to operate'' said *The Autocar*; its opposite number agreed about the additional heat supplied but found that it was ''not unmixed with a certain smell'' and further remarked a little testily that ''there is ample cold air available from the ventilation system (plus some from the bottom edge of the front doors)...'' Other aspects of the car were beginning to date as well, such as the narrow-beam headlights ''not really equal to the exceptionally high speed of the car'' (*The Motor*), a certain lack of room in the back for longer-legged people (but ameliorated by the removal of the nylon rug), the limited arcs swept by the windscreen wipers, the remoteness of the instrument dials (with the 'ultra-violet' lighting loosing out on popularity now), and the interference of the window winder with the driver's ashtray.

Petrol consumption gave more food for thought, as *The Motor* recorded 13.5mpg and *The Autocar* less than 1mpg better; the Mk IX was the thirstiest Jaguar yet. But all agreed that considering the performance given – and the fact that the disc brakes encouraged its full use – it was

not a factor which would influence the average purchaser. *The Autocar* also recorded the quite high oil consumption of 1400mpg, indicative of the 3.8 engine's tendency towards flexing of the liners which allowed oil to escape past the piston rings.

John Bolster also tried a Mk IX, telling of his experiences in *Autosport*, February 1959. He recorded a 0-60mph time of 11 seconds, covered the standing 1/4-mile in 18 seconds exactly, and timed the car at 115mph in top. The 3.8 unit was considered even smoother than the previous 3.4, and the power steering tolerable. ''On the open road'', said Bolster, ''one tends at first to overcorrect a skid, but this can be overcome with practice. When driving on an icy road, I held the wheel only with the tips of my fingers, and in this way I soon cured myself of my clumsiness in controlling skids. This steering is sufficiently high geared to subdue the rear end when it breaks away on such surfaces.''

Quite a lot of the test was carried out in winter conditions and brought these comments on the Mk IX's handling:

''I felt at first that the tail was somewhat lively, but later discovered that this was only in the nature of a warning. If a slippery corner be entered at a fair speed, the rear of the car has some tendency to run wide, but that is all. There is no need for any sudden correction, and many drivers will be glad to be informed by this premonitary kick that an increase in speed is inadvisable... One would not advise the average owner to handle this luxury car as he would a sports model, but controlled skids may be indulged in with impunity by the more experienced conductor.''

Brakes were next on John Bolster's list for discussion, and he found that the use of discs ''has now overcome the fading problem, which greatly increases the pleasure of fast motoring...in the past the heavier Jaguars have stressed their brakes somewhat highly.'' He noticed the

By January 1960, Jaguar were experimenting with true air-conditioning; this is a Mk IX engine bay so equipped. This car also sports D-type breathing arrangements on its cam covers for some reason, possibly in view of arduous test conditions.
Photo: Jaguar Cars

slight rear wheel locking tendency commented on by *The Autocar* but the brakes were otherwise "beyond criticism". Together with the 3.8-litre engine's quoted 210bhp, they helped give the Mk IX Jaguar, in his opinion, "the highest all-round performance of any full six-seater car in the world." He was almost certainly right – the few cars which might offer the same space either couldn't match the pace, or if they could, reduced their brakes to in-effectual smoking ruin trying to maintain it over mixed roads.

Jaguar's big saloons had been inviting comparison with the 'compact' 2.4 and 3.4 cars for some time, and while they were not competing for the same sort of customer, the more advanced design of the small saloon did tend to show-up some minor deficiencies in the Mk IX; John Bolster felt that while the car's general silence and smoothness was praiseworthy, "the body is not so sensationally quiet over certain road surfaces as that of the Jaguar 3.4." The days of the separate chassis were numbered, but even as Bolster wrote, the Mk IX's successor with its unitary construction and independent rear suspension was taking shape in the more secret recesses of Browns Lane.

Mk IX production changes

The Mk IX lived out the remainder of its days quietly and without drastic changes. After about 400 cars had been made, larger diameter upper ball joints with an increased angle of movement were fitted to the front suspension, this modification being carried over at the same time (around January 1959) to the 2.4, 3.4 and XK 150. The tachometer changed from cable to electric operation six-months later (from chassis numbers 771820 and 791072), being energized by a small generator driven from the rear of the inlet camshaft.

The engine itself received a modified water pump and a screw-in adaptor instead of an elbow for the heater pipe early in 1960, and improved sump sealing. A nylon petrol line was introduced in April 1960. That rather indifferent handbrake was given an increased diameter, pre-stretched cable in June 1959, followed a few months later by stronger pad carriers with an easier method of chang-ing the pads. In January 1960, the Mk IX was given a brake fluid handbrake-on warning light in the screen rail like the new Mk II, and a plastic brake fluid reservoir in place of the glass one. The warning lights proved very popular and Jaguar later offered a kit to convert earlier cars. In the same year, larger rear lights were installed, and the heater further improved, while in February 1961 USA and Canada models received the higher-output C48 dynamo, and all cars a modified propshaft centre mount-ing assembly with larger rubbers to reduce a tendency for transmission shudder on take-off.

The Mk IX soldiered on until late 1961, when in October the Mk X assumed the mantle of top prestige model in the Jaguar range. The Mk VII series had, therefore, spanned a period of eleven years, during which time the astonishing total – for a large, specialist high performance car of this type – of more than 47 000 had been built. This figure is made up largely of Mk VIIs, approximately 31 000 having been completed, plus 10 000 Mk IXs; while the Mk VIII remains the rarest of the breed with but 6312 having left the Browns Lane works. A production run of this length goes some way towards explaining how Sir William could sell one of the fastest, largest and best equipped saloons in the world for never very much more than £2000....

The last Mk IX of all awaiting despatch. This was one of some 27 Mk IXs sold either to the Ministry of Defence or the War Office. Its official number 29DM71 is also stamped on its chassis plate, along with the designation Mk 8B. This designation was the one by which these Mk IXs were known by the military, much to the later confusion of owners and historians. This car survives and displays no specification changes from standard except in respect of the chassis plate.
Photo: Jaguar Cars

The Mk VII inherited all the ruggedness of the Mk V, and in return for a big increase in performance, its twin overhead-cam engine exacted only a small penalty in terms of more complex servicing. Indeed, it was one of the triumphs of the XK engine that it had all the advantages of a 'racing type' power unit, yet retained the capacity of the previous pushrod designs to assimilate vast mileages without major attention. Thanks to competent basic design work and a large built-in reserve of strength, the XK engine suffered remarkably few teething troubles and most of these had been sorted out in the XK 120 before it appeared in the Mk VII.

Likewise, the well-proven chassis more than matched the engine for longevity, though lack of maintenance could lead to quite rapid wear in the ball joints and the rather complex steering arrangements. The gearbox, slow as it might have been, was incredibly long-lasting and with little more than an occasional change of bearings, would happily clock up mileages of 200 000 to 300 000 miles; though inept use of the non-synchro first gear could result in chipped teeth and the need for a premature overhaul, which was another good reason for introducing the Borg Warner box to the North American market!

Even so, in that same market reliability was not a quality generally attributed to the Jaguar car, which was thought not to compare with the Detroit automobile in this respect. When analysed, the situation was that the Jaguar's major components – engine, transmission, suspension – could match the American car mile-for-mile, but it tended to be a different story when it came to ancilliary parts such as the electrics, small accessories and fittings, and to a certain extent, detail body engineering. On the rare occasions when a serious engine fault did occur, it could almost always be traced back to a lack of routine maintenance, or unnecessary and unskilled tampering by sub-standard garages.

While the Mk VII series might eventually have totalled that impressive 47 000 production figure, the rate-per-year at which the car was built was laughably small compared with that of a true mass-production car issuing from the city-sized plants of Ford or GM (or from Austin and Morris in Great Britain,for that matter). Thus it was just not possible for the small Coventry factory to put the same amount of development into every aspect of the car as the giant manufacturers were able to do; Jaguar also had to buy-out many smaller components, which inevitably meant less control over quality.

Limited resources and staff also meant limited testing – it is unlikely that before the Mk 10, any new Jaguar was taken abroad and tried under tropical conditions, for example; hence complaints such as this one from a Ceylon owner writing to *The Autocar* in 1953: "About a week after I bought the car, I was caught in a real downpour. I am afraid the car has not been made for such conditions; it leaked at the windscreen, water getting past the glass and the rubber beading. This was cured by applying Durofix along the rubber, which has to be reapplied at intervals of about three months." He also found that water entered in large quantities from the air-intake on the top of the scuttle, as the drain hole wasn't big enough. Poor draught sealing around the doors was another common fault, and only partially cured later on in production.

Building XK engines around 1953; careful assembly allied with a superb basic design resulted in a powerful yet long-lasting power unit that has been the envy of many high-performance car manufacturers. *Photo: Jaguar Cars*

Most travelled Mk IX? Alroyd Lees about to depart on another round-the-world marathon; now retired, this car is thought to have clocked-up some half-million-miles during sponsored runs for charity.

The separate-chassis construction of the Mk VII series might have attracted more specialist coachbuilders than it did; *Above:* Pininfarina produced this effort in 1956, its main body-shape hinting at the 3-litre Rover of some years later. *Right:* This two-door coupé is an adventure in 'cutting-and-shutting' by an Australian enthusiast!

This body was installed on Mk VII chassis in 1954 by Ghia Aigle of Zurich

Hardly a 'fault' as such, petrol consumption was certainly a factor in running the car which British owners often alluded to, and tried to improve, especially when encouraged by such as the Suez Crisis petrol rationing during 1956/57. This prompted Louis Giron to develop a triple-carburettor system for the Mk VII, supplementing the twin standard SU carburettors by a further smaller one mounted above, which supplied the engine with mixture until almost full throttle was given, whereupon the standard instruments would be brought in. *The Autocar* recorded between 34 and 37.7mpg during short runs at 30-35mph, and between 24.5 and 30mpg at 45-55mph crusing speeds; it was marketed at £25. Some Mk VIIs were submitted to the even greater indignity of having diesel engines fitted!

Apart from the usual Jaguar value-for-money factor, one of the Mk VII's greatest attributes was the standard of ride and handling that it set. For a large car it cornered amazingly well, and this did much to offset its undoubted bulk which would otherwise have been a hindrance when it was attempting such unlikely feats as winning in the Monte Carlo rally. On the race track, it was really only the lighter 3.4 saloon which caused the Mk VII's retirement from the scene, as it was quite capable of out-handling anything else its size. Having driven all three variants – Mk VII, VIII and IX – on the race track, the writer has proved this to his own satisfaction at least. Only the large number of turns lock-to-lock is inclined to cause

embarrassment under these circumstances!

However, by 1957, the sporting role had been firmly taken over by the 2.4 and 3.4 Jaguars both on and off the track, and the big saloon became increasingly the preserve of the older executive, or the liveried chauffeur – Mk IXs especially were favoured as official cars by a number of states and heads of governments (40 were ordered by the Nigerian Government alone!) Somehow, the Mk X which followed never quite retained the upright, British dignity of its immediate predecessor, superior though it might have been in every other department. All these variants – Mk VII, VIII and IX – were available in 'limousine' form to special order, with a fixed bench front seat and glass division. Few were produced, and these cars are a very rare sight today.

The Mk VII has definite royal connections in this country too, as Her Majesty the Queen Mother ordered a Mk VII saloon. This car became quite a permanent fixture in the royal mews, being returned to Coventry at intervals for updating. Claude Baily remembers having to rapidly surrender his personal Mk VII because Her Majesty wished to sample an automatic version – it was retained for a week, and, so the newspapers reported, the Queen Mother insisted on being driven at 100mph in it! Her own car eventually finished up equipped to Mk IX specification, with disc brakes and chrome radiator; it is now usually on display either at Browns Lane or with the BL collection of historic vehicles.

Above: Part of the 40-car order by the Nigerian government about to leave the Browns Lane forecourt in May 1960; the stately lines of the Mk IX – and its comparative cheapness – made it a favourite choice for an official car in many parts of the world.

Left: HM the Queen Mother was sufficiently fond of her Mk VII to have it regularly updated at the factory; here are the Mk VIII-type front seats being finished. *Photo: Jaguar Cars*

Variations... This hearse-bodied car was photographed at the factory in 1958, and is based on a later Mk VII or a Mk VIII. It may not have been a factory project though, in common with a number of estate-bodied Mk VIIs built privately over the years. Appleyards, the Jaguar dealers, also built two Mk IX estates to special order, one of which has survived.

While they may soon be too rare, Bill Beaman has, over the past few years, converted a number of Mk IXs to this 'roadster' specification. Full weather equipment is offered too!

While non-Californian climates took their toll of Mk VIIs, VIIIs and IXs through rust, their hardwearing mechanics and chassis saw to it that many remained in active service for years after the last Mk IX left the Despatch Bay at Browns Lane in September 1961, and they remained a relatively common sight especially in such retirement areas as Brighton and Bournemouth, right into the 'seventies. Drive one today and the sheer bulk of the car is a little intimidating at first, and a gearlever which seems miles away from one's hand doesn't make familiarisation instant. After a few miles though the high degree of comfort and silence becomes very apparent in a well-kept specimen, and – with the possible exception of parking! – the type is still perfectly suitable for every-day driving.

For no apparent reason, the Mk VII series did not acquire an appreciating 'classic' status amongst enthusiasts for many years after it became obsolete, and indeed, a 3.8 Mk II saloon in similar condition still commands an equal or higher price. But one can certainly be assured that the Mk VII, VIII and IX survivors, generous in both proportions and character, will continue to be cared for by those who appreciate their true worth and nature. It was the car which, perhaps more than any other, set Jaguar on its post-war feet.

Chapter Seven

Jaguar's first `compact´
≈ the 2.4/3.4 saloon

This is a brilliant design, breaking new ground technically in several important respects.

John Bolster, *Autosport,* December 14, 1956

It would be a false economy to specify a 3.4 Jaguar without disc brakes.

The Autocar, June 13, 1958

A "more practical XK" was how the Americans hailed the 2.4-litre saloon on its announcement in 1955, and that's not a bad description either of Jaguar's first small saloon since the original 1.5-litre. It was meant to appeal to those who didn't need or couldn't afford the majestic bulk of the Mk VII, and who found even the new two-plus-two XK 140s too restrictive for family motoring. Jaguar reckoned that the 'sporting compact' market, as yet virtually untapped by any manufacturer, might be a lucrative one; they were not far wrong.

While there might be some advantages in a 'one model' policy, the company had felt the lack of a cheaper or smaller saloon to back up the Mk VII ever since the last 2.5-litre Mk V left production in 1951. Not only would such a car bring them a whole new circle of customers, but – just as with the 'cost price' 1.5-litre – it would hoist production of any components shared with other Jaguar models, and thus bring down the unit cost for all the cars. Volume was Jaguar's aim, and volume they achieved; over 37 000 2.4s and 3.4s were built in four-years.

To Jaguar, the 2.4 saloon represented new technology. It broke fresh ground in virtually every department, and was the most ambitious and expensive project yet taken on by the company. The most complex part of the new design was the bodyshell, for it was Jaguar's first experience of unitary construction, a method chosen mainly because of its combination of lightness and rigidity. In the early 'fifties, this was fast being adopted by European manufacturers as an efficient and economical way of producing car bodies, although much work was needed on the first generation of unitary cars to solve the inherent problems with this type of design – which were to make the shell sufficiently strong in both torsional and beam stiffness, and to suppress its tendency to amplify road noise like a giant drum.

Fixed on the idea that the new car must be a true economy vehicle in every department, a smaller engine than the Mk VII's was scheduled from the very beginning; as things turned out, a lesson might have been learned from the 2-litre XK 100, and the 3.4 engine thus installed from the start – few Jaguar customers, particularly in America, truly put economy above performance.

Serious consideration was indeed given to using that four-cylinder 2-litre XK power unit, and the car very nearly appeared with this engine which had been further developed since it was first catalogued (but never used) in 1948. Fortunately the idea was dropped in favour of a new version of the XK straight-six – the four just didn't have the smoothness of the six, or its market appeal, despite the fact that it would have given little away to the eventual 2.4 in brake horsepower. But perhaps even more importantly, a smaller six could share many more components with the larger version, and thus achieve the desired increase in volume of these parts. There was also the very practical advantage of rationalizing spare parts, a very important point to consider when there are hundreds of dealerships scattered over the globe who must be kept supplied.

So the 2483cc engine made its bow, looking very much like a shorter edition of the 3.4 unit, which is exactly what it was. The same bore was retained, but the crank throw was reduced to give a shorter stroke of 76.5mm instead of 106mm; the connecting rod length was reduced at the same time, thus keeping the same 1.87:1 connecting rod/stroke ratio.

The 76.5mm stroke meant that the height of the

carburettors and the original 5/16-inch lift camshafts. In this form the engine was rated at 112bhp at 5750rpm, with a maximum bmep of 140psi. at 2000rpm, some 1400rpm lower than the 3.4 unit. A Borg & Beck single plate clutch, hydraulically operated, transmitted the power to the normal single-helical gearbox (operated by an odd, cranked gearlever in very early cars).

Before we turn to how the power unit and ancilliaries were installed, we need to examine the new body and the overall concept of the car. The decision having been made to produce a 'small' car, Heynes laid down the basic

Right: The 2-litre four-cylinder edition of the XK engine, which was in the running for use in the new compact car for some time.

Below: Jaguar decided to stay with six-cylinder smoothness for their new small car, and elected to produce a short-stroke version of the six-cylinder unit; this picture shows the difference in height between the 2.4 and 3.4 engines. *Photo: Jaguar Cars*

Bottom right: For the first time since the S.S.I, SU carburettors were exchanged for another make on a production Jaguar – this is the Solex installation on the 2.4 engine. Note also the long gearbox extension. *Photo: Jaguar Cars*

chrome iron block could be reduced too, and the almost three-inch drop from 11.5in to 8.85in represented a useful weight saving of around 50lb. over the 3.4 engine. The same big 2.75-inch diameter journals were used for the seven main bearings and the En 16 crankshaft followed the normal Jaguar pattern, so that the bottom end of the new engine was immensely strong in relation to the forces it had to take.

On top was the Jaguar twin overhead cam head, essentially in unchanged form and differing only in camshafts and carburation. Pursuing the economy theme again, Jaguar deliberately restricted the engine's breathing by using two downdraught Solex B32-PBI-5/s

parameters, Lyons evolved the overall styling, and (remembers Tom Jones) the body designers were left to engineer in between. This was done in conjunction with the Pressed Steel Company of Oxford who applied all their considerable expertise in unitary construction to the project, but even so, the gestation period of the 2.4 is not recalled with particular fondness by those involved.

Firstly, there were economic restrictions and although some £100 000 were invested in the new car, it was in many respects built down to an envisaged selling price. Secondly, great strain had been thrown on the small development staff by the company's racing programme, with the new D-type absorbing large amounts of time which could otherwise have been employed sorting out problems associated with the 2.4 saloon. The year after the 2.4 entered the market, the racing programme was in fact curtailed, and the last factory-built Jaguar to run at Le Mans officially did so in 1956; the cost in terms of lost production and engineering development time was just too great to sustain any longer.

When it appeared, the 2.4's bodyshell was certainly strong enough, even over-engineered perhaps, a common enough occurance in the early days of one-piece bodies when stress engineering in this field was at an early stage – if you weren't quite sure of the stress on a particular component, you made it larger or thicker just in case. This probably accounts for the chunky look of the original 2.4 and 3.4 saloons with their thick screen pillars.

The shell was built up from two perimeter channel sec-

tions, which ran from the very front of the car to the rear wheel arch and spring anchorage on each side, welded to the floor to form box sections. Besides the ribbed steel floor itself, various transverse members joined the longitudinal members, including at the front under the radiator mounting and beneath the front seats, while the whole structure was also tied together by the scuttle and the rear seat pan. Then running diagonally up each side of the engine bay were two more box members, which transferred front-end stress to the scuttle/bulkhead and, via the heavy screen pillars, to the roof as well. On to this composite structure were welded the outer panels such as the inner and outer wings, and the outer sills which themselves formed another longitudinal box section.

The 2.4's suspension design was basically laid down by William Heynes, and at the front, torsion bars were

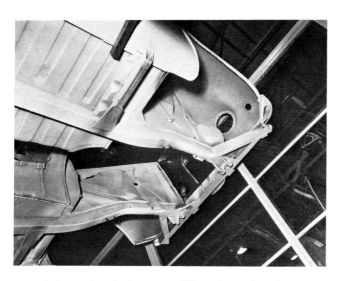

Jaguar's first unitary body was sturdily engineered; underview of front shows integral chassis rails.

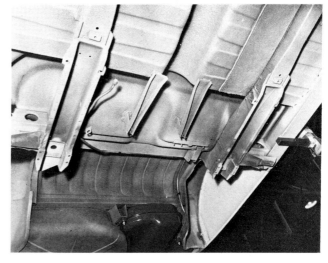

Chassis rails of the 2.4 ended in mountings for the inverted rear springs.

Front end of the 2.4 shell was further stiffened by diagonal box-members running from the bulkhead to meet the chassis rails at the bottom of the engine bay.

Rear end of the 2.4 was not subjected to major stresses, as the suspension was hung from rear bulkhead area. Note spare wheel well pressing and (left) petrol tank in tail.

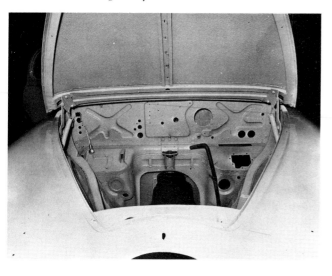

More advanced thinking was seen in the front suspension, a coil spring wishbone arrangement mounted on a subframe to reduce noise transmission. Steering box was also mounted on the separate frame. *Photo: Jaguar Cars*

This picture illustrates well the rubber front mounting of the suspension subframe – no metal-to-metal contact existed anywhere between it and body. *Photo: Jaguar Cars*

replaced by conventional coil springs largely because of space and the complications of anchoring the rear ends of the bars in a unitary shell. Twin, rear-inclined wishbones of unequal length were used, the upper a pressing and the longer, lower wishbone a forging. The coil spring was attached to the lower wishbone, and retained by the hollow steel pillar on which the top wishbone pivoted. Heynes did remain faithful to one characteristic of his original design however, as upper and lower ball joints were still used to accommodate wheel movement and steering. The tubular shock absorber was anchored inside the top of the suspension pillar and ran down through the coil spring to act on the bottom wishbone, which was linked to its opposite number by an anti-roll bar.

One of the 2.4's distinctive features, the separate subframe which carried the front suspension as a detachable unit, evolved along with the suspension design; its major purpose was to insulate the bodyshell from road shocks and noise which might be transmitted by the suspension and to this end it was so designed that no metal-to-metal contact between subframe and body existed anywhere. The final arrangement was the outcome of months of experimentation and research.

The subframe itself was made of a cross beam, with two

arms mounted at right-angles to, and inboard of, the suspension pillars. It was these substantial arms, or extensions, which were used to anchor the assembly to the car. The rear extensions took the main weight and transverse loads through V-shaped rubber-bonded mountings fastened to the car's main channel sections each side, while fore-and-aft location was provided by vertical rubber blocks attached to the front extensions. The composition of these rubber mountings, hard at the rear and softer at the front, was carefully selected to defeat resonance set up by road noise acting on the subframe assembly, though due care was taken to see that the flexibility thus allowed did not interfere with precision of control.

The Burman recirculating ball steering box was also mounted on the front subframe, and was insulated from the steering wheel by two universal joints, while rubber bushes were used for the inner wishbone mountings, the centre section of the track rod, and the anti-roll bar mountings, all to cut down noise and vibration. It was seemingly complex, but it worked at a time when many others were finding it extremely difficult to prevent their unitary shells acting like large sounding drums. That the entire assembly had to be dropped for removal of the sump did not seem too high a price to pay, especially as this was unlikely to be required during the first term of ownership.

Equal if not greater ingenuity had been displayed in the design of the 2.4's rear suspension, though its almost unique, cantilevered axle came about rather through force of circumstances, it seems. Normally disposed semi-elliptic springs were first considered, but without the support of a chassis frame, there were doubts about the advisability of stressing the rear part of the body by mounting a spring shackle on it; finally it was decided to ''avoid a risk area'' by cantilevering the rear axle from mountings located in the main structure forward of the tail, which then only had to carry the luggage compartment, petrol tank and spare wheel.

In any case, the arrangement was very reminiscent of the C-type Jaguar's rear suspension (except that leaf springs instead of torsion bars were used) and of the Traction Citroen before that. These springs were conventional 5-leaf semi-elliptics turned upside-down with their trailing ends attached via rubber bushes to fixed extentions on the axle casing. They anchored to the car inside the rear ends of the 'chassis' rails.

The anchorage here had been very carefully thought

out, and was in two parts. At the centre of the spring, the leaves were fixed together by a bolt which passed through a hole in each leaf, and at the same point, the leaves were clamped between two rubber blocks attached to the car inside the channel member. This located the spring sideways and longitudinally so that it functioned as a lower radius arm, though a given amount of fore-and-aft movement was allowed. Being centrally mounted and flexible, the rubber blocks holding the spring allowed it to rock as loads were applied to the rear of the spring by the axle. This slight movement was absorbed by a thick button-shaped pad at the front end of the spring, solely by compression. Experiments on the road proved that the flexibility allowed by the central mounting of the spring was crucial in eliminating noise which had filtered through the spring/axle attachment point.

Further location of the rear axle was provided by two trailing arms running from the seat pan area to brackets above the axle, operating in rather the same manner as the single arm on the original 1951 C-type had done, to both locate the axle and use its tendency to rotate under power to force the wheels onto the road. They were complemented by an adjustable Panhard rod which prevented sideways movement, though at one stage a simpler A-link

2.4 rear suspension; note central mounting of spring, and axle location by top trailing arm, and adjustable Panhard rod. This is actually a Mk II but the arrangement is much the same. *Photo: Jaguar Cars*

Rear axle of the 2.4, showing brackets for trailing arms on top, and extensions for attaching the springs underneath. *Photo: Jaguar Cars*

arrangement was considered in place of these components.

Girling telescopic shock absorbers with top anchorages adjacent to the wheel arches at the rear of the luggage compartment provided the damping, and like the Panhard rod and trailing arms, these were rubber mounted; nothing on the rear suspension required greasing except the wheel bearings. The Salisbury 3HA hypoid bevel final drive resembled the units used on other Jaguars, but smaller new 15-inch diameter pressed steel wheels were fitted all round, carrying 6.40 section Dunlop tyres.

Brakes were not Girling but Lockheed on the 2.4, though as with the Mk VII, vacuum assistance was provided; drum diameter was 11.125-inch, with a friction lining area of 157sq.in. The front shoes were self-adjusting by means of a bar and friction pads, and each pair of shoes was worked by a single, operating cylinder.

No wonder that with its totally new body, front and rear suspension, brakes, and – to all intents and purposes – engine, the 2.4 was the most ambitious and difficult project that Jaguar had ever undertaken. But they had achieved their aim – with an overall length of 15ft., and a wheelbase of 8ft. 11.375in., the new car was 16-inches shorter in length and 12-inches shorter in wheelbase than the Mk VII, and had up-to-the-minute styling and a

An early stage in 2.4 body design, but right from the start Lyons seemed to know the sort of shape he wanted.

Raised centre of bonnet was obviously discarded as being too fussy; body-colour bumpers, eventually discarded, are often thought to be a modern conception!

View of mock-up without central bonnet swage; motif is Mk VII, grille XK 120. Note side vent, not used in production – wing/body join here might indicate thoughts of hinge-forward bonnet and wings assembly....

Rear of 2.4 mock-up; rear window was made larger for production. Note temporary use of XK 120 reversing light and boot handle.

performance which looked set to be very little less than that of the bigger car. Ready-for-the-road weight was 27cwt., a significant 8cwt. less than the Mk VII, though a good 55% was over the front wheels.

While the car might have been carefully designed to sell at a remarkably low with-tax figure – £1269 for the 'Standard' model and £1298 for the 'Special Equipment' – no short cuts had been taken on quality, and the 2.4 was lavishly equipped with all the refinements which were associated with the marque – walnut veneer dash, cantrails and door cappings, luxurious leather-faced seats (attractive bucket-type in the front), adjustable steering wheel, full instrumentation in the central panel (including an electric clock), twin glove lockers, map pockets in all four doors, two-speed self-parking wipers and vacuum-operated washers, foglamps and automatically engaged reversing light.

The 2.4 as it actually became – an early production 'standard' model without mascot or foglamps; very few of this variant were actually sold.
Photos: Jaguar Cars

The interior was surprisingly roomy too, and in the width of the rear seat only an inch or so was lost out to the Mk VII, and in headroom the dimensions were almost identical, thanks to the unitary body which did not have to sit on a chassis frame. Legroom in the rear of the car was a little restricted, especially if the driver preferred to push his seat right back, but the success of the 2.4's packaging is underlined by the distance between dash and rear seat squab, which was only an inch less than in the Mk VII. For the first time in a Jaguar, one had to step over a fairly high sill and down into footwells.

The 'Standard' model of 2.4 was rarely seen, and its specification lacked a heater, the 5-inch tachometer, folding centre armrest in the rear, screen washers, the twin foglamps, cigar lighter, courtesy switches for the interior rear lighting, and even the vitreous enamel finish on the exhaust manifolds. As only £29 was saved by dispensing with these mostly rather necessary accoutrements, it is scarcely surprising that nearly all 2.4 Jaguars

Above: **High sills were dictated by unitary body design as they contributed strength; sporty bucket seats and polished walnut greeted occupants.** *Photo: Motor*

Left: **The Special Equipment 2.4, with spotlamps and mascot. The vast majority of 2.4s were sold in this form. Note the car's affinity to the XK 140 sports car with its general wing-line and cast grille.** *Photo: Jaguar Cars*

Below: **Rarity – the standard model 2.4, without heater or rev. counter. Space for heater slide control is covered by wood fillet; choke was manually operated as with all 2.4s, by slide control on facia.** *Photo: Jaguar Cars*

were ordered in Special Equipment form.

One additional extra that could be fitted was the Laycock de Normanville overdrive unit, which gave the relaxed overall gearing of 3.54:1 when engaged. When specified, a lower ratio 4.55 axle would be installed, as opposed to the normal 4.27. Top gear mph per 1000rpm with the latter worked out at 17 compared with 21.8 given by the overdrive ratio.

In appearance, the 2.4 was modern without being radical. Front-end styling reflected many XK 140 traits, including the plated, cast-alloy radiator grille, the 'alligator' bonnet, and the rounded sweep of the front wings with their faired-in headlight pods. Unlike any XK though, the sidelights were mounted vertically on the front of the wings in a surprisingly un-Jaguar, after-thought sort of way, and the Special Equipment model was given a leaping jaguar mascot as standard. Mk VII-type horn grilles were let-in to the wings each side of the grille, and big, tough wrap-round bumpers of XK 140/Mk VII pattern were carried.

The 2.4's side elevation was exceptionally smooth, with the front wing line being carried right back in an unbroken sweep at waist level to merge with the rear wing line and then tapering-in towards the rear bumper. Rear wheel spats added to the effect, though the uncompromisingly sturdy windscreen and sidepillars, bereft of chrome decoration, gave the car a rather heavy look. The neat rear quarters, modelled on XK 140 coupe and Mk VII lines, incorporated a useful luggage compartment with a spring-counterbalanced lid (the bonnet was similarly assisted). Tools were now contained in a case within the spare wheel, incidentally, which was covered by a removable lid under the boot floor.

A direct rear view of the car highlighted one of the 2.4's failings – the narrow rear track. This measured only 4ft. 2.25in., compared to 4ft. 6.625in. at the front – in other words, marginally narrower than that of a Morris Minor! This situation possibly resulted from the axle having to conform to body design requirements; it was certainly blamed by many drivers for the 2.4's alleged instability at certain speeds.

Reaction in Great Britain to the 2.4 was of interested enthusiasm, with much attention being paid to its technical novelties. In America, subtleties like cantilevered suspension and rubber-mounted subframes mattered less to the potential owner than sheer performance, and while the quality of the car was universally acknowledged, the saving of a few mpg by virtue of a smaller engine was a factor entirely lost on the average imported car enthusiast there.

"Where the 2.4 Jaguar will fit into the American market is a poser", said *Motor Life*; "its original cost ($3700) is much too high to be considered an economy car... There is a question in our minds, however, as to whether a person who pays upwards of $3700 for a car is interested in economy. It seems that, for the American market at least, the engine could be more highly tuned. Or better yet, the 3.5 liter engine could be installed with apparently very little change. This one change could very well be the difference between the cars' success or failure." Words calculated to strike fear into the hearts of those responsible for Jaguar's distribution in that country!

However, some very valid points had been made, amongst them being that those who wanted economy for its own sake would buy a Volkswagen at a low price to

Rear wheel spats and thick pillars gave the 2.4 a very chunky look. This is the car's Earls Court debut in 1955. Overall length was 15ft, over 1ft 4ins less than the Mk VII.
Photo: Motor

How the 2.4s were built: engine, suspension and transmission would be on a special trolley, and the completed body lowered onto them. Down-draught Solex carburettors were chosen to facilitate the drop. The 3.4's SUs had to be removed for this operation.
Photo: Jaguar Cars

begin with. "Price-wise, it competes with cars like the Olds 98 and Buick Roadmaster", observed *Motor Trend*, "which may or may not be in its favour, depending on how much metal you want for your dollar." *Motor Life* put it much more bluntly: "Our conclusion, and a hasty one at that, is that the only way to save this car will be the installation of the larger engine. People in general, and Americans in particular, who pay that kind of money for a car want more performance and would be satisfied with less economy." Then *Motor Trend* helpfully suggested that you could always fit a D-type head and replace the twin Solex carbs with SUs....

At Coventry, the point was taken. Undoubtedly it had been at the back of Bill Heynes' mind that the 3.4 engine *could* be used in the new compact, but comments, such as have been related, from Jaguar's most crucially important market almost certainly brought the project forward by months, if not years. The 3.4 saloon, devastatingly fast for a luxury four-seater, arrived in September 1957.

Road-testing the 2.4

Not that it is fair to brand the 2.4 Jaguar as being "slow" – far from it, 100mph performance in the mid-fifties was usually the prerogative of stark sports cars, not closed four seaters with interior appointments to rival the smoking room of one of the wealthier London clubs. *The Motor* tried an overdrive 2.4 in July 1956, and it pulled a genuine two-way average of 101.5mph, reaching 60mph in 14.4 seconds – both figures virtually identical to the Mk VIIM with automatic transmission, and marginally slower than the manual version.

As for rivals, there was nothing really equivalent with which to compare it – the Daimler Conquest Century had a similar cubic capacity but conventional overhead valvegear, was over a second slower to 60mph on acceleration, and struggled to top 90mph. Perhaps nearer to the small Jaguar were the lighter Alfa Romeo 1900s, their small twin-cam engines (with Weber carburettors) enabling them to match the 2.4 in top speed if not in acceleration; but they gave way to the slower if better-handling 1290cc Guilietta about the time that the 2.4 was introduced.

In the gears, *The Motor* found that just on 69mph was obtainable on third, and 47mph on second, the latter especially a little low due to the axle ratio fitted to over-drive cars. But the new engine seemed to thrive on hard usage, and would "rev. both freely and continuously" with smoothness and silence. Yet it had lost nothing in flexibility, and would pull from as low as 10mph in overdrive top, albeit at the expense of some pinking on the petrol of that time. Starting was good and warm-up quick, with the driver able to exercise control over cold-start mixture as the Solex carburetters were equipped with a manual choke operate by a slide control on the dashboard.

The transmission was liked by the journal – "it is

The 2.4 received extensive testing at the MIRA proving ground; here a pre-production model undergoes ride evaluation – note amount of wheel travel given. *Photo: Jaguar Cars*

refreshing to return to a vehicle which is essentially meant to be driven", said the writer, though expressing less enthusiasm for the gearlever itself which had an "awkward angle." He also thought that the dash-mounted overdrive switch could have been turned through 90-degrees to make it more usable; this would have made it operate from left to right instead of up and down.

The Motor found that Jaguar's retention of a rigid rear axle was at first sight "flying in the face of progress", as independent rear suspension was already becoming fashionable on fast, expensive machinery. "A very short distance on the road", the magazine went on to say though, "particularly a secondary Continental road, vindicates the system completely, both as to riding comfort and as to roadholding power. On indifferent pave passengers may ride at any speed in comfort equivalent to that given by cars tested by *The Motor* with independent rear suspension. The real achievement of this suspension is that it combines such suppleness with damping which quickly gets rid of the effects of hump-backs or trenches, and allows the car to roll slightly, but not wallow, in a fast corner."

As with the Mk VII, it was felt that the higher of the recommended tyre pressures did little to mar riding comfort but much to enhance the "very controllable handling characteristics' and lighten the steering. This, at 4.5 turns lock-to-lock, was better than it looked on paper "for the turning circle is small, the ratio progressive, and the steering just neutral between under- and over-steering. As a result of this desirable balance, inherently good cornering can be improved by mildly skilful work on the accelerator pedal."

Interestingly, the journal felt moved to comment on the sight of a 2.4 being "cornered in a really enterprising fashion" as viewed from the outside – "...the rear wheels, as seen from a following vehicle, present a rather alarming spectacle, of which no trace is felt from the driving

seat." This was an allusion to the exemplary amount of wheel movement allowed by the suspension, which did a great deal to provide an extremely comfortable ride – but combined with the narrow track did indeed make it seem as if something rather odd was happening on full roll.

Vehicle development engineer R.J. Knight's pioneering work insulating the bodyshell from road noise and vibra-tion had obviously been well done. "The precautions in this case have been most successful" was *The Motor's* verdict, and the writer went on to say that "Whatever the aesthetic appeal of the body shape, it also is extremely effective in reducing noise, so that passengers can and do converse normally at 100mph even with the window open."

As for the brakes, it was noted that the system had been improved in detail since the earliest cars, but that the test car would stop from as high as 90mph "safely and without fade." The servo assistance was higher than that of the Mk VII though, and was thought to be "almost too sensitive" at town speeds. The pendant-type brake and clutch pedals were liked, and so was the seating position.

Fuel consumption wasn't amazingly frugal, 18.25mpg being recorded over the 1830-mile test, which was only a couple of mpg better than the Mk VII and didn't allow a very generous range from the 12-gallon fuel tank. This consumption was improved on vastly by *The Autocar* when they tried an overdrive 2.4 in September 1956, as on that occasion 23.1mpg was achieved overall, which appears to be a little on the optimistic side for a mileage which included performance testing.

While this car's top speed was similar to *The Motor* figure at 102.5mph, acceleration was slightly down with a 0-60mph time of 15.8-seconds; it was also one second slower at 9.6-seconds for the 30-50 direct top gear time, so possibly the car was tuned more for economy; the Mk VII, incidentally, covered the same top gear increment in 7.9-seconds, its extra literage telling in that range.

The manner in which the new 2.4 litre engine gave its power impressed *The Autocar* team greatly. "Mechanical smoothness is matched by the silence of the engine. When accelerating on test runs at full throttle from a standing start, whipping into each higher gear in turn as the rev counter needle touches the red band, high speeds are reached without the slightest mechanical fuss and, although the engine note can be heard, it has a sweet and subdued note. The sound suggests only that the engine wants its driver to know what a willing friend is under the bonnet." Some might regard the last remark as faintly sentimental and even a little out of place in a factual a piece of writing as a road test; but Jaguar owners will realize its truth because they know the bond that tends to grow between the driver and the XK engine over long, fast, hard mileages with that constant, smooth, almost understated surge of power always at command. The XK engine is not perfect – no piece of machinery is – but that it is capable of inspiring affection in its own right is surely

2.4 engine installation; careful mounting ensured that the new saloon was one of the quietest Jaguars yet. Servicing such components as starter motor and dynamo were not much fun, however! *Photo: Autocar*

a characteristic not shared by many power units; one can stand in awe of the musical thrash of a 12-cylinder Ferrari or respect the powerful throb of an American V8, but affection? "Dear old engine..", as Harry Weslake used to say, "dear old engine."

The Jaguar transmission of the period rather brought one down to earth again, however. "...a mite disappointing", reported *The Autocar*, "...and gear selection does not quite match the high engineering standards of the engine. Fast changes can be made up or down, but difficulty in engagement is sometimes encountered when the driver attempts a leisurely change and tries to 'feel' the gear in. This stickiness is noticed primarily when the gearbox is hot." The gearlever placement wasn't liked either.

The 2.4's handling more than passed muster. "Liberties may be taken in appropriate circumstances without upsetting control... At very high speed when the car is forced deliberately to slide a little there is no trace of vice." Again, higher tyre pressures (30lbs. front, 28lbs. rear) were felt to improve response and lighten the steering. Damping was considered excellent (though this was to be a bone of contention with owners of early 2.4 and 3.4 Jaguars) excepting that "at very high speed on indifferent surfaces there is some indecision in the movement of the front of the car...."

The success of Jaguar's engineering department in sound insulation was noted by *The Autocar* too: "The immunity of the occupants from noise initiated by road surfaces is quite astonishingly good" was the comment. Brakes kept up with the car's speed although tended to be jerky at lower rates of progress. The high standard of finish throughout was remarked on, though like *The Motor,* the journal criticised the miss-matching of the wood grain in places. The heater "seemed to have a high

The 2.4 fared well in road tests, even though visibility was not highly rated. This car is fitted with the optional radio – its aerial (at rear of front wing) was retracted using small handle under dash.

Photo: Jaguar Cars

Luggage space was very adequate, with lift-out panel revealing wheel; jack was normally kept clipped to rear panel. Note shock absorber mountings next to wheel arch. *Photo: Jaguar Cars*

output of warmth" but the demisting arrangements couldn't cope with condensation already formed on the screen.

Driving comfort was excellent but visibility was thought capable of improvement, as the nearside front wing couldn't be seen, and the windscreen pillars were described as "unusually thick"; rear view visibility was rated "fair", which really meant 'poor' in the road-test language of the day. Rear seat room wasn't discussed but the "substantial" luggage compartment was, although it was pointed out that luggage had to be removed for access to the spare wheel and tools.

"The 2.4", summarised *The Autocar*, "is one of those cars whose capabilities are appreciated as the mileage mounts. It is quietly very efficient indeed, providing unstinted luxury, fine performance and roadworthiness, and it is offered at a remarkably low price for the high standards and quality construction for which the make is internationally famous."

The 2.4 tested in the States

Meanwhile, Coventry was eagerly awaiting the first North American test reports, and it was *Road & Track* which got into print first, in August 1956. "Like any Jaguar model you can name, the 2.4 sedan is something special, with certain unique features which make it different from all other cars with which one might wish to make comparisons." Most interesting of these features was thought to be the 2.4 power unit, "an engine which is as near 'unburstable' as we know." The car was missing an overdrive but came with the low 4.55 ratio axle, and at the expense of straying into the red sector on the

tachometer, 106mph at 5900rpm was obtained in one direction, with an average of 101mph. It was thought that with a few more miles under its belt, a genuine 105mph two-way average would be approachable. Sixty miles an hour was reached in a brisk 13.1-seconds, over a second better than *The Motor's* time.

This was good enough to be labelled "sports car performance" and even the gearbox failed to arouse strong criticism, though first was thought to be "very low indeed". So far, so good, but how about ride and handling? This was *Road & Track's* pronouncement:

"We felt that the compromise between ride and roll is excellent. Using tyre pressures of 29psi. front, 27psi. rear, the boulevard ride is very little firmer than domestic products. There is some cornering roll, perhaps even considerable by sports car standards, but one of the most remarkable characteristics of this car's handling qualities is its cornering ability. We tried corners faster, and faster, and yet faster. The tires squeal, but we were never able to determine which end 'breaks loose' first. The steering too is deceptive. It takes 4.5 turns lock-to-lock for a 33.5ft. turning circle and there is pronounced understeer. But, on twisting roads the action is quick and, more important, absolutely positive with no vague rubbery feel. Sports car owners will appreciate the combination of road manners and high-speed stability incorporated in the 2.4"

The brakes with their quite strong servo-assistance were probably more in tune with American practice because the tester wrote that "we did not realize there was a booster until after the road test." A good omen was the efficient cooling system, one car being driven through the Mohave desert "under very trying conditions" with no sign of overheating; Bill Cory, the driver, also recorded 25mpg at a cruising speed of 65mph, and *Road & Track* reckoned the car's range to be 17–25mpg. Road noise suppression in the new unitary body was praised, though so far as appearance went, "the bulbous sides and rear end are not universally acclaimed" even though it was admitted that they bestowed "a roomy interior and a low drag factor" (the latter, expressed in pounds at 60mph, was calculated at 122, which was 8lbs. better than the Mercedes 300SL gullwing coupe). The windscreen pillars were considered: "obviously designed more for strength than for best possible visibility."

Road & Track's summary of the 2.4 rounded off an enthusiastic road test well: "We think it is a 'best buy' if you are looking for a compact, safe-handling family car with a durable engine and a sturdy chassis. The sports car performance is a bonus feature – already there, ready to be used, if you require it."

Sports Car Illustrated brought the American reader a test of the new Jaguar as well, in October 1956. Its report was more searchingly critical of the 2.4, but fair and accurate. Acceleration was about the same as *Road & Track* had recorded, at least in the lower ranges, with 60mph coming up in 13.4-seconds, though at the top end this

The 2.4 was well received in the States except for slight reservations about power; most export cars had whitewall tyres as fitted to this home model as an 'extra'. Eleven body colours and six shades of leather could be chosen from.
Photo: Jaguar Cars

Charles Hornburg, Jaguar's dynamic distributor for the west coast of America, on a visit to Browns Lane in the 'fifties.
Photo: Jaguar Cars

4.55 car lost out for some reason, being almost 4-seconds slower to 80mph at 27.2-secs and recording only 99mph flat out (perhaps the driver held it to the 5500 rpm. red line).

Having written approvingly of the car's ride over a variety of surfaces, *Sports Car Illustrated* had this to say on its road behaviour:

> "With an anti-roll bar and 57-per cent of the weight in front, the 2.4 can be expected to understeer, which it does with a vigor that's exaggerated by the somewhat slow steering ratio. You need a lot of helm to hold it into a bend, but only moderate effort. The car as a whole sticks nicely in fast highway manouvres, and it can be very satisfying on fast corners. If it's thrown around more vigorously, however, the steering wheel response becomes delayed and erratic, due in part to the roll angle assumed....
>
> "Taken to extremes, though, the car tends to drift on all fours, and rear wheel slides can be provoked but don't pop up without warning. Cornering on bumpy surfaces is good except at very high lateral G's, when some hopping occurs at both ends of the car. Briefly, the solidity of the car itself isn't always matched by the connection between car and road."

Steering wheel angle, pedal positions (with 'heel and toe' possible) and seats were all liked, so that "the 2.4 controls are sporting but the car's reaction to them are more sedate and sedanlike. It narrowly misses being the perfect machine for the enthusiastic driver who needs family room, but taken strictly as a roomy five-seater, it's exceptionally safe and stable." Also on a practical theme, "interior room for the family is matched by the capacity of the trunk, which is cleanly laid out with the major jacking tools clipped well forward... That jack, by the way, is easy but infinitely boring to operate, since it's designed around an extremely shallow screw thread.''

The 2.4 XK engine received the usual praise – ''a ruggedly precise powerplant'' is how the writer described it. ''Accelerator pumps in the Solexes make up for the plumber's nightmare of manifolding to provide instant throttle response that's expected in a Jag, and this rev-ready eagerness stays there all the way to the top making you wish there wasn't a peg on the tach. Within the visible range there's no shadow of protest or vibration, and the red sector at 5500 is more for decoration than anything else.... We expected a hood full of revs, but we weren't prepared for unusually good low-speed torque for a 150-cubic-incher.''

There wasn't so much enthusiasm over the gearbox. ''The cover of the basically standard Jaguar box has been redesigned to give a mechanically more direct lever control, which somehow manages to have a very vague and rubbery feel. It improves on acquaintance, but the pattern still remains widespread and the knob still evades the wildly groping hand at crucial moments. Jaguar's machine like whine remains in the lower ratios, and is accompanied by slight dog clutch protest if the synchromesh is rushed at all. The indirect gearing is closer to that of the first XKs than it is to the close ratios used in the present 3.5-litre machines, and as a result you're all done

a little sooner in the gears than you would like to be to use that engine to the full.''

Sports Car Illustrated had its own opinion on the subject of extra power for the car, rumour having filtered through that the larger engine might soon be offered, and the proposal, if it had been carried out, would certainly have resulted in a much more 'Alfa-ish' Jaguar that sounds very appealing:

> ''The word now seems to be that the big 3.5 engine will find its way under this hood for the American market, which will dump 51 more pounds where they aren't needed and apply more power when it can't be fully used. We'd much rather see this fascinating short-stroke six developed further, with perhaps an optional C-type head and close-ratio gearbox if more suds are demanded. Those plus stiffer shocks all round would push the 2.4 over the line into the Gran Turismo class and enable it to surprise many a sports car. Even now it's one of the most satisfying small sedans around.''

Meanwhile, production of the 2.4 was building up and teething troubles sorted out – being Jaguar's most technologically advanced car yet, the 2.4 was far from being 'bug-free' as the Americans would put it, with the rear suspension possibly being the most troublesome area. The springs, for instance, could loosen in their channel member to cause knocking noises which were extremely difficult to trace – Jim Stirland, then a Jaguar Service Engineer, was sent out as chief trouble-shooter to

Cutaway drawing by Sydney Porter of *The Motor* shows all the 2.4's main features – cantilevered rear suspension, big hollow sills and integral chassis rails, universally jointed steering column, the Solex-aspirated power unit and wishbone front suspension.

various countries round the world, and recalls trying to solve the mystery with Briggs Cunningham, who by the end of 1955 had been appointed a north-eastern Jaguar distributor. Almost in desperation, Stirland finally suggested that they cut a hole in the of floor the car to see what was really happening, but the idea didn't get a very good reception!

The Panhard rod was also capable of breaking at its outer mounting bracket and, early in May 1956, a reinforcing plate was introduced at this point – an item which could also be fitted retrospectively. The rod itself was given an adjustable end, so that the correct tension could always be arrived at. It was to remain a comparatively weak component all through its production life, however, even in the later Mk II series which used basically the same layout. Dampers were the subject of change too, and eventually the optional stiffer items became standard wear.

Few changes took place in the engine, though a steel sump of similar capacity replaced the more expensive alloy one in November 1956, and earlier, in June of that year, a Metalastic crankshaft damper was installed on the front end of the crankshaft (from engine number BB 2500). Minor changes were made to carburettor settings as well during 1956/57. During the former year, non-overdrive cars were standardised with the 4.27 final drive instead of the 4.55 unit, this mostly effecting export vehicles as most home 2.4s without overdrive were delivered with the higher ratio. A kit for fitting overdrive was introduced too, for those owners who wanted to convert their cars after purchase.

The year of the 2.4 entering production, 1955, had not in fact been a very happy one for Jaguar or for William Lyons. Quite apart from the usual problems in getting a new car under way, the engineering and development departments at the factory had been under pressure due to the D-type racing programme, and even Jaguar's 1955 win at Le Mans was soured by the tragic accident at the circuit when more than 80 people had died. It was a doubly sad occasion for Lyons who suffered a terrible personal loss at the same time, when his only son John was killed in a motor accident in France while travelling out to the race with *The Motor* trophy.

John Michael Lyons was 25 years of age, and after leaving Oundle School he had served a three-year apprenticeship in engineering at Leyland Motors (Sir Henry Spurrier of Leyland was an old friend of Lyons').

Above: Overdrive made for even more relaxed cruising, and could be ordered as an 'extra'. This is the Laycock unit on the 2.4's gearbox. *Photo: Jaguar Cars*

Right: Airflow test on a 2.4 at MIRA – while Jaguar's sports cars (notably the D-type) were built according to aerodynamic principles, with the saloons it was more a case of checking afterwards – styling requirements predominated. *Photo: Jaguar Cars*

Having then completed his military service in the R.E.M.E, he joined the Jaguar company in February 1955 on the administrative side. Those who knew John Lyons described him as possessing all his mother's charm together with all his father's sagacity and sense of purpose. While not devaluing the more important, personal nature of the loss, one can speculate from remarks Sir William himself has made, that Jaguar's future might have turned out very differently had young John Lyons lived to take over his father's position. Lyons must have been rather glad when 1955 came to an end; 1956 was, in recompense, to be a year of achievement, with the New Year's Honours List bringing the news that the founder of Jaguar had been created Knight Bachelor.

A short while before the new 3.4 Jaguar saloon became available, Jaguar acknowledged that some 2.4 owners required more performance from their cars, and accordingly issued a little booklet describing various measures which they could take. The tuning methods outlined in the booklet were divided into three stages. Stage One brought maximum power up to 119bhp at 5800rpm by internal carburettor modifications (26mm chokes, flat type throttle spindles etc) and a straight-through silencer; the engine parts in this case cost £3.8s.0d, the silencer £2.18s.3d. If not already fitted, close ratio gears could be installed in the gearbox (£26.5s.4d), stiffer dampers fitted, and a higher ratio steering box giving a ratio of 15.7 instead of 17.6 could be substituted for the original, this last costing £8.16s.11d exchange.

Stage Two produced 131bhp at 5900 rpm, and meant carrying out the operations involved in Stage One plus the addition of the 3/8-inch high-lift camshafts together with stronger valve springs and a non-standard Lucas distributor. The price of this extra equipment was £18.6s.3d.

Stage Three boosted power to 150bhp at 6000rpm, or about as much as the original XK 120/Mk VII 3442cc engine had produced. It simply involved replacing the standard small-valve head with the new B-type head (complete with inlet manifold and 1.75-inch SU HD6 carburetters) which had been announced with the Mk VIII saloon at the end of 1956. This assembly cost £225.8s.1d including the necessary distributor. Due to the higher torque now produced, either stronger clutch springs or a new clutch assembly was advised. A twin exhaust system was also needed, at the price of £17.1s.10d, which required a repositioning of the handbrake abutment bracket. This twin silencer system could also be fitted to standard or stage one or two cars.

The 3.4 Jaguar

Then the 3.4 saloon came onto the scene, at the end of February 1957. This announcement was a little premature, as Jaguar had been attempting to build up a stock of 3.4 cars in the States so that the all-important dollar customer would not be discouraged by a long waiting list, but after some 200 cars had been sent across the Atlantic, the embargo had been broken and the news

The fire of 1957 was a damaging blow to Jaguar's production, but could have been much worse if heavy equipment had been destroyed. As it was, the cars destroyed were at least replaceable.
Photo: Jaguar Cars

leaked out. Jaguar would also have appreciated a short respite after the serious fire suffered at the Browns Lane works that same month; it caused damage estimated at some 3.5-million pounds, and writing later about it, Sir William said:

"It appeared that it would be impossible for us to produce cars for many months, but the misfortune acted like magic on our workpeople, suppliers, building contractors and fellow manufacturers. We were inundated with offers of help, loan of plant, personnel – in fact anything we could ask for. Our work people 'buckled to', offering to work, for day-rate pay, with shovels and anything they could lay their hands on to clear up the mess.

"Our building contractors brought in many of their competitors and the task of re-building was started within 48-hours of the fire. Tarpaulin structures were erected to provide temporary working protection, and, in exactly nine-days, production on a limited scale had recommenced, and within six-weeks we were back to normal. It was a wonderful experience, and another example of what the people of this country can do when they have their 'backs to the wall.''

Nearly half the main factory had been destroyed, but fortunately no heavy plant had been lost as the fire had mainly effected the service, trim and final test areas. Several hundred cars were lost including a number of 3.4s, but the situation would have been even worse if the fire had reached machinery which might have taken months or even years to replace. That it put paid to a probable return to racing in 1958 was the least of Jaguar's worries.

Returning to the 3.4, it could at once be seen that the new car was much more than simply the 3442cc engine dropped into an unchanged 2.4-litre shell. For a start there was a new, larger radiator grille with narrow slats, a preview of a similar type to be seen on the XK 150 when it was announced three months later, while the full-depth rear wheel spats had gone, to be replaced by cutaway ones. No foglamps were fitted. There was a 3.4 badge on the bootlid, and twin exhausts poked from beneath the rear bumper.

Invisible differences were a larger (10-inch instead of 9-inch) clutch, a new V-type mounting under the gearbox,

A rare colour picture of the new 3.4 Jaguar saloon, photographed at Hickling Broad. Thin slatted grille and cut-away rear spats were the main visual differences. *Photo: Jaguar Cars*

and the Salisbury 4HA rear axle – which in fact consisted of the Mk VIII centre section and heavier gears with 2.4 endpieces. The Panhard rod mounting was also slightly altered because of the new axle. For the first time on the series, an automatic transmission was offered, at first on the 3.4 only; cars so equipped were given a divided propellor shaft with a rubber-mounted central bearing, as the overall length of the Borg Warner box was less than that of the manual gearbox. New front seats of the split-bench variety were fitted when the automatic box was specified.

The full, 210bhp B-type head engine was used complete with HD6 carburetters, though with a new inlet manifold and air silencer; 8:1 compression was standard for most markets, but 7:1 or 9:1 were optional. Modified engine bearers took the extra weight of the 3.4 engine, and a larger radiator block was installed.

Little had been changed inside the car, except that as Borg Warner automatic transmission was now an alternative to the normal Jaguar four-speed box (which could be had with or without overdrive), on cars so equipped a neat "PNDLR" quadrant was visible at the centre of the dashboard under the instruments – a position obviously chosen to suit both left-and right-hand drive cars. The automatic transmission option was not made immediately available for the 2.4-litre car–owners who desired this extra had to wait until the 1958 season. This automatic box was now being made in England too, and was marked "Letchworth, Herts" to distinguish it from the American manufactured boxes which carried a "Detroit, Michegan" label. All automatic boxes fitted to the 2.4 and 3.4 cars had the "Intermediate Hold" facility, and the Salisbury 4HA rear axle with a 3.54 final drive was used – a similar axle ratio was given to the manual gearbox cars, except those with overdrive which had the ratio of 3.77.

Overdrive in particular gave the 3.4 Jaguar a potentially very high cruising speed, as it provided an overall ratio of 2.9:1 – a lazy 4000rpm in overdrive top gave over 105mph! No wonder the American motoring magazines sat up and took notice of the new arrival. "Without a doubt," exclaimed *Road & Track* in its preview, "the most interesting aspect of the 3.4 is its performance...the net result is a sedan which can at least hold its own with all but one or two of our most potent power-packed domestic machines." To those who might think the price was a little high ($4285 list, compared with $3850 for the 2.4 and $5750 for the Mk VIII), the magazine reminded them "that there are no extras when you buy a Jaguar", only a radio, overdrive ($165) and automatic transmission ($250).

Gregor Grant, writing from New York, underlined exactly why the new 3.4 would prove an irresistible package to Americans: "It is as ideally suited to heavy town conditions as it is to highway cruising, and its remarkable acceleration makes it one of the safest cars to drive on the freeways and turnpikes of the American continent... This is extremely important in USA and Canada, where the vast distances involved make 600 to 700-miles in a day fairly commonplace".

Road-testing the 3.4 Jaguar

The Motor published the first full test of the 3.4 in Great Britain, in their April 10 issue of 1957. Probably due to the usual export priorities, the test car was a left-hand drive automatic version. But even when tamed to an extent by such a transmission, the 3.4 turned out to be a very, very rapid machine.

So 60mph was reached from a standstill in 11.2-seconds, 80mph in 17.9-seconds, and 100mph in 30.3-seconds – figures which were better than those of the XK 120, and equal to the XK 140! However, the magazine

was quick to underline the fact that this didn't mean that the 3.4 was "a rip-snorting sports model with a lid on it", but was as refined and as easy to drive as the 2.4. Top speed was a remarkable 119.8mph, while the intermediate ratio provided 81mph, an extremely useful range when overtaking. Enlarging on the car's accelerative powers, *The Motor* continued:

"To drive, the Jaguar 3.4-litre is very much a dual personality car. A light touch on the accelerator pedal will take it quietly and very smoothly away from rest with very little fuss indeed, the engine not rising above 2000rpm, and whilst firmer pressure on the accelerator gives faster acceleration there is nothing fierce about the response. Press really hard on the accelerator pedal, however, and the vast power of the twin-overhead camshaft engine is really unleashed, the automatic gearbox then lets the rev. counter run round to rather more than 5000rpm before making the upward changes from first to second and second to top gears, and the car really leaping forwards."

By the standards of the period, performance of this measure was as *The Motor* said, "fantastic for such a roomy and refined car", particularly as the automatic transmission demanded no particular skill on behalf of

Low angle view of 3.4 saloon illustrates well the wider, narrow-slatted grille which was to appear in similar form on the XK 150 also announced in 1957. *Photo: Jaguar Cars*

the driver in achieving 100mph in half a minute. Nor did the new specification mean a drastic increase in fuel consumption, as an overall 19.2mpg was recorded, with "only a very mild degree of restraint" bringing 20mpg within easy range. The box itself functioned well, though tended to change down and then quickly up again rather frequently, but this was typical of the early Borg Warner transmissions.

As with the 2.4, the suspension dealt with poor surfaces well, though "at speed on some sorts of wavy going the suspension stops come into audible action rather more easily than might be desired by hard-driving owners." Its steering (still over four turns lock-to-lock) was considered "very pleasant" with only a little precision lost through its rubber cushioning against road shocks. The additional power made for a note of caution when it came to handling:

"Cornering at fast touring speeds is, if not absolutely roll-free, at any rate accompanied by only the slightest change of lateral attitude. The driver who seeks to handle this model as a sports car, however, cornering at the limit of adhesion between tyres and road, will find it behaving in rather a less tidy fashion, especially on wet roads when it is exceptionally easy to provoke wheelspin by even quite moderate acceleration."

New Dunlop "Road Speed" tyres had been introduced which were an improvement on the former equipment, but the 3.4's power-to-weight ratio was rather in excess of the state of the tyre-making art in the late 'fifties. It was also definitely even more in advance of Jaguar's drum brakes as *The Motor* was forced to point out:

"Regrettably, the brakes of the model submitted for test fell considerably below desirable standards of performance. Self-adjusting and with vacuum-servo assisted application, they would give a good emergency stop from 100mph, but even a single hard application from high speeds produced some judder accompanied by slight directional hesitancy on the part of the car, and frequent hard brake applications would accentuate these symptoms. The more gentle driver can enjoy light pedal pressures and smooth braking, but a braking system able to withstand harder usage without protest would greatly widen the appeal of this car."

That, for a 1957 British road test, was pretty strong stuff and tantamount to saying that the 3.4 was dangerously underbraked. It had immediate repercussions too, although *The Motor* had been in prior contact with the factory as soon as it had discovered that the increase in speed hadn't been matched by a similar response in the braking department. Editor Christopher Jennings 'phoned Browns Lane to say, quite bluntly, that the car shouldn't be released with drum brakes as they faded far too badly, and that it should be held back until the disc brake installation – a standard fitment on the XK 150 which was due to be launched in May and known to

be on the way for the 3.4 – could be offered on the car.

This elicited an instant response from Sir William who 'phoned back to say that he was sending Heynes down at once to discuss the matter. Basically, the factory's belief at that time was that people wouldn't drive the 3.4 that fast and therefore wouldn't induce the symptoms that *The Motor* was talking about; Jennings remained adamant that they would, and said that as this was the magazine's opinion on the matter, they would have to say so in print. That they did almost certainly hastened the introduction of the Dunlop disc brake on that Jaguar, and both 2.4 and 3.4 customers could (and usually did) specify it by the late autumn of 1957.

This slight altercation with the factory did not mean that *The Motor* condemned the 3.4 Jaguar in its road test – far from it. "Fundamentally, this is a car which has few superiors in respect of providing smooth, quiet and comfortable travel for five people, yet has speed and acceleration of the most remarkable order... a first class express carriage which will be invaluable to the many men for whom, literally, time is money" is how the journal summed up the 3.4. As for detail grumbles, the lack of a map reading light for the driver, no rheostat control for the (conventional) instrument lighting, a heater of "apparently limited power", and combined stop light/flashing indicators were thought to be readily excusable by the incredibly low price of the car (£1242 with automatic transmission but less tax).

Road & Track reported on a manual transmission 3.4 in June 1957, but apart from noting that pedal pressures had been reduced compared with early versions, found the brakes entirely satisfactory, being "applied several times at over 100mph with complete confidence and without the oft-encountered pungent odours." Possibly the standard of comparison was not so high, though!

Despite the use of an absolute rev. limit of 5250rpm instead of the normal red-line 5500rpm in deference to a 1500-mile engine, acceleration times were remarkable. The 3.4 took 10.4-seconds to reach 60mph, and just 17.5-seconds to achieve 80mph, with a standing 1/4-mile of 17.6-seconds. Top speed was reckoned to be a true 120mph, with probably 122–124mph possible after more running-in. "First gear is of course sensational. As tested, with driver and observer, it was easy to get too much wheelspin: 2 long black marks were left in the road for a distance of 50ft. Starts can be effected in 2nd gear with very little clutch slip. On wet roads this is normal procedure. Since second gear can be used up to 68mph (5750rpm) the 0 to 60 test requires only one shift, and this change can be accomplished very quickly."

Of the 3.4 engine installation itself, *Road & Track* had this to say:

"Perhaps the greatest appeal of this car is the tremendous torque and low speed flexibility of its engine... Even in overdrive (2.938) the low speed pulling power is quite good, although the sensible driver does not use this ratio below 40mph. On the highway the dual ratio feature is very useful, as direct drive (3.777) gives excellent passing ability. Or, alternatively, the balked driver can employ 3rd gear and leap past slow moving traffic, moving up as high as 90mph (5250rpm) without entering the 'red' sector on the tachometer. Literally, this is a triple-top-gear machine and with its choice of either 2.94, 3.77, or 4.55 ratios it is a delight to the enthusiast.

That passage also explains admirably why Jaguar never offered an overdrive which worked on any other gear except top – with the torque and power of the XK engine, it just wasn't necessary. The overdrive helped economy of course, a best figure of 23.5mpg being recorded with 70–75mph cruising; worst was a still-moderate 17mpg. Despite an even more marked weight bias on the front wheels (28cwt. distributed 57/43 compared with 55/45 for the 2.4), road-holding was still good: "Handling qualities remain excellent, as reported at some length in our 2.4 test of last August. Alternating between the 2.4 and the 3.4 it is undeniable that the steering of the new car is heavier, but Phil Hill took it for a hot lap around the Playa del Rey 'circuit' (a very rough, winding back road) and commented: 'Imagine trying to do this with an American sedan!'"

Before the end of 1957, disc brakes became an option at £37 extra; these were the earlier type of Dunlop disc brakes with round pads operating on 12-inch discs front and rear to give a total swept area of 552sq.in. Vacuum servo assisted, they worked superbly well and had only one major snag – the wheel cylinders had to be dismantled to replace the pads, which was time-consuming and meant that the system had to be bled each time.

Wire wheels were also offered as an option, and although popular, were not so commonly specified (in this country at least) as the disc-brakes themselves. Of Dunlop manufacture, they came with the smart chromium plated spinners and with either body-colour paint or a chromium plate finish on the spokes and rim. Acknowledging the attraction and worth of these items, in January 1958 Jaguar made kits available so that earlier 2.4 and 3.4 cars could be converted – from drum to disc brakes only, from pressed steel wheels to wires only, or to both discs and wires together. It would cost you £100 for just the brake change, £83 for just the wheel change, or £160 approximately for both together. Owners of the 2.4 would need the cut-away rear spats as well (to clear the spinners), at £4.2s.0d; chrome wire wheels incurred an additional £7.19s.6d.

There was a general sigh of relief when disc brakes were fitted to the 3.4 saloon – its performance definitely required them! No half measures were adopted by Jaguar, and unlike some manufacturers they fitted discs to the rear as well. The handbrake was worked by separate calipers as can be seen. *Photo: Autocar*

Road tests of the disc braked cars quickly showed how worthwhile the new type of brakes were, *Sports Cars Illustrated* enthusing over a 3.4 saloon thus equipped in April 1958. This is what they wrote:

"The brakes were phenomenal: they are, without exception, the finest brakes we have ever found as a production item on a sedan! The four-wheel disc units have stopping power and stamina that repeatedly crash-stop from 60mph, and are impossible to break down or noticeably deteriorate. Our test team really unleashed the stresses and strains. Because of the Jaguar's rapid acceleration, we made ten panic stops from sixty miles an hour in less than 200-seconds!"

This brake test meant repeated zero-to-sixty times in under ten seconds, the average being given as 9.5 seconds in the performance table. The car lapped up this sort of use:

"This engine likes to work at the top half of its range. There's plenty below the 3000 peg, but when the needle starts down the right side of the tach, the muscles of the crouching cat really begin to ripple. The car is deceivingly smooth at high speed, and a glance at the speedo gives quite a shock. All of a sudden you're doing ninety! It's no problem to get up to sixty in second slot, and eighty comes real easy in third. And, with overdrive, there are still *two* gears to go! Cruising speed is whatever you want to do."

While *Road & Track* rated the manual 3.4's gearbox as "a jewel...much improved", *Sports Cars Illustrated* found that it required getting used to, with a long travel between gears and a weak detent spring protecting reverse, which was up alongside the first-gear slot. "Speed shifting is frustrating at first, but after a short time, we knew the box and worked it with dexterity." The non-synchromesh first gear could be selected without a clash by double de-clutching. But the 3.4's capabilities weren't limited to straight line performances only:

"Handling the Jaguar is another pleasure. Tracking on the straights is perfect; it isn't necessary to clench the wheel, but merely to hold it with the tips of the fingers. By boring through a bend under power, you can get the tail to go out, but it only goes out if you want it to, and it's controllable when it does. By applying just the right amount of power you can set up any kind of drift you want, and if you start to get over your head, backing off the accelerator brings the tail right behind the front. Under hard cornering, very little lean is perceptible to observers, and none to the driver. Tire noise is nil, unless you really push the car into very big slip angles. And if you should hit bumps in the middle of your curve, you probably won't even feel it. It's the kind of car that makes you feel you can do no wrong, and chances are you can't, if you use any kind of descretion."

Understandably, the journal had trouble finding anything to compare the car with. "It certainly has no exact

The availability of wire wheels helped both looks and brake cooling; it made the small Jaguar into a true sports saloon, at home on road or track. *Photo: Autocar*

American counterpart, the Fury, perhaps, comes closest. Of course, Jaguar owners expect to *go*, but here's a four-door sedan – family sedan, if you wish – that accelerates and cruises with *very hot* super-stock American sedans, even though the engine is half their displacement."

At home, 3.4s had been available in Britain since May of 1957, and *The Autocar* tried one of the new disc-braked versions, in June 1958. It also differed from *The Motor's* earlier example by having manual transmission with overdrive, and easily matched *Sports Cars Illustrated's* figures on acceleration – 60mph came up in a tyre-burning 9.1-seconds, 80mph in 16, and 100mph in 26; none of these times were much more than a second behind the new and similar-engined XK 150 fixed-head coupe! This wasn't altogether surprising, as unitary construction had enabled Jaguar to keep their latest four-seater down to within a hundredweight of the XK's figure. Progress indeed.

"The attractiveness of the car's behaviour", said *The Autocar*, "covers an exceptionally wide field. As a town carriage it has few peers, while on fast journeys the model's achievement more closely resembles that of the sports racing car than high performance family saloon. The very high rate of acceleration available does not fall off appreciably until after 100mph is exceeded." As an illustration of the huge margin of performance the 3.4 had over contemporary British saloon cars, one can quote other acceleration times – for instance, the 2.6-litre Riley Pathfinder was one of the quicker 'ordinary' saloons, yet

The Autocar's **road test 3.4, with overdrive. It achieved 100mph in 26-seconds, and 120mph top speed. Tower Bridge, London, provides the background in this picture.** *Photo: Autocar*

took 2.7-seconds longer to reach *50mph* than the 3.4 did to reach *60mph,* while its top speed of 93mph was exceeded by 5mph by the 3.4 – in *third* gear. The truly average British family saloon managed 50mph in more like 18 seconds with a top speed of little over 70mph.

Amongst the high-price vehicles, the Bentley S1 Continental was one of the few which could match the 3.4's maximum speed and cruising ability, but even this magnificent car didn't have the acceleration to match – nor was it really comparable to Jaguar's four-seater-compact conception. Armstrong Siddeley made a brave attempt to enter Jaguar's market with the 3435cc Sapphire 346 but it could only manage 100mph flat-out, and anyway, it was almost as large as the Mk VIII. The Daimler Majestic, introduced in 1958, with automatic transmission and disc brakes as standard, again could only just make the 100mph mark (from 3.8-litres), though the rather overlooked Majestic Major of 1959 with its superb 4561cc V8 engine was much quicker and, almost uniquely, could certainly match any standard 3.4 for sheer straightline performance; but its bulk put it into a different category altogether. In Europe, only the Mercedes 300 series had any hope of keeping up with a 3.4 Jaguar, and while they might have scored marginally over the 3.4 in ride comfort due to their swing-axle rear suspension, the lighter British car was quicker in a straight line by a good margin.

This performance did not come at the expense of smoothness or noise, and *The Autocar* noted the quietness and flexibility of the engine, a "pleasant boom' resulting from full throttle work in the gears. Wind noise was well controlled, and "speed appears to be very much less than it is in reality" which could result in corners being approached faster than was the intention!

The gearbox did not escape quite so lightly however, as it was thought that the lever was mounted too far away so that the driver had to lean forward to make a change. Also: "Action of the synchromesh falls short of the standard of the rest of the car. First and second ratios are not always easy to engage when the car is at rest, and quick changes may be accompanied by a grinding noise unless careful and accurate double de-clutching is employed. Ignoring sound effects and the long reach, the mechanism is precise and pleasant to use." The usual Jaguar whine in first gear was remarked on as well.

So far as road behaviour was concerned, the extra weight of the larger engine seemed to have been well accommodated by the revised spring settings "to make the 3.4-litre not only one of the fastest cars on the road but additionally one of the most stable - a car, in fact, to complement a driver's skill." As previous testers found, the car handled much better on higher tyre pressures, though circumspection was required in the wet due to the power available at the rear wheels even with the improved Dunlop Road Speed RS4 tyres fitted. Ride was good even over cobbles, and the steering received approval inspite of strong self-centering action and some heaviness at

On the limit: David McKay explores the roadholding of his modified 3.4 saloon round the Nürburgring after collecting it from Browns Lane. Later the combination competed very effectively in Australian saloon car racing. *Photo: David Lewin*

medium and low speeds – "some fatigue may be caused on long runs at relatively high speed on winding roads."

The brakes of course received unstinted praise – "silent and quite light in operation, they are outstandingly good and come into their own particularly at high speeds." They were also thought to be an essential part of the Jaguar's equipment because "the speed is much higher than that of most other models, and the driver unconsciously makes much greater demands on the brakes in the 3.4... it would be false economy to specify a 3.4 Jaguar without disc brakes." No comment was made on the handbrake, though this was in fact the least satisfactory part of the system.

Visibility was rated as "fair", and it was thought that the location of the instruments could be improved even if it introduced additional complications in production (the central position suited both left-and right-hand drive cars). Interior appointments and quality were approved of, though the heater/fresh air arrangements were not thought clever, and also a considerable amount of engine heat found its way into the car. As for economy of running, *The Autocar* recorded the relatively high overall mpg figure of 16 for their 2121 mile test, but admitted that it was also possible to obtain over 22mpg. Indicative of the car's efficiency was the mpg at 100mph in overdrive top – an impressive 21!

Production changes for the compact Jaguars

In the meantime, both the 2.4 and 3.4 cars had been progressively improved by small changes in specification; the most substantial of these was the standardisation, in September 1957, of the wider radiator grille, all 2.4s from this date thus sharing the same frontal appearance with the 3.4 (from chassis number 907974 and 942465). This entailed new front wings to accommodate the extra width

of the grille, and a modified intake for the air cleaner behind the grille.

February 1958 saw drum braked cars receive a larger servo (from 5.5-inch to 6.875-inch), while disc braked cars were given a cast iron master cylinder instead of an alloy one. About the same time, a progressive bump stop in the form of a tapered rubber block was attached to the turret of the front suspension, working on a bump stop plate fixed to the lower wishbone. The new Dunlop RS4 tyres replaced the RS3 variety in production a couple of months later, with a consequent improvement in wet road grip. The Thornton Powr-Lok differential became available during the summer of 1958 as an extra, though it wasn't widely publicised.

In July 1958, the distinctive 'cut glass' type of overdrive switch with its internal illumination effect (first seen on

A rare under-bonnet snap of David McKay's factory-tuned example, showing the big 2 in SUs; battery has been repositioned in boot for better weight distribution. *Photo: David Lewin.*

From the autumn of 1957, the 2.4 carried the same grille as the 3.4; here Sir William Lyons poses by the 2.4-litre's final trim line. *Photo: Jaguar Cars*

The original 2.4 cylinder head – small inlet valves and 0.312 inch lift camshafts but beautifully finished as with all Jaguar heads.

the Mk VII and XK 140) was replaced by a metal switch similar to that used for the intermediate hold device on automatic cars. Improved dampers were fitted the same month. Even more significantly, the Dunlop 'quick-change' type of disc brake was introduced in January 1959 – identified by their square pads, these brakes had the enormous advantage of the friction-material change being accomplished in a couple of minutes with no dismantling. This occured on the 3.4 from chassis numbers 975688, 990694 (pressed steel wheels) and 975783, 990795 (wire wheels) and on the 2.4 from 913144, 943331 (pressed steel wheels), and 913234, 943343 (wire wheels). At the same time, stronger 72-spoke wire wheels replaced the earlier 60-spoke type, still painted or chromed as desired, while special non-eared hub-caps for the German market were introduced.

On the engine, a half-inch fan belt was fitted from the beginning of 1959 (with pulley to suit), and the vacuum reservoir positioned between manifold and servo (from engine numbers KF 2501 and BC 8075). Lead-indium bearings were fitted to the engine from April 1959 in both 2.4 and 3.4 units. In common with the XK 150 and Mk IX, the front suspension received larger diameter upper ball joints and an increased angle of movement in January 1959. June 1959 saw the substitution of the cable-driven rev. counter for an electric one, operated by a generator running from the rear of the inlet camshaft.

Modifying the 2.4 and 3.4 engines

Ever since the 2.4 was first introduced, some owners tried their own modifications. The obvious thing to do on the Solex-carburetted 2.4 was to install a twin SU set-up,

but as *Road & Track's* Bill Corey found, this didn't necessarily result in the swift increase in horsepower expected.

Both he and the editor of that magazine owned 2.4 Jaguars, and Corey decided to investigate adding some extra urge; this was in 1956/early 1957, some time before the 3.4 appeared. First step was to take a measurement of the bhp at the rear wheels having made sure everything was functioning properly; the figure obtained was 90bhp. "This in itself was quite a surprise, as the usual Mk VII or standard XK with 160bhp engine output seldom exceed this figure. It is evident that the factory rating of 112bhp is quite conservative!" Or more accurate, possibly... Next, the engine was dismantled for balancing, and to Jaguar's credit, only the matching of the pistons could be improved. Combustion chambers were found to be "beautifully machined" as on all the XK engines, but the inlet ports were unfinished and the inlet manifold didn't match the ports in the head well.

Having polished the ports and matched them to a XK 140 inlet manifold, the engine was reassembled with the 1.75-inch SU carburetters. The result? An increase of top end horsepower of only 2bhp! There was a small increase in power at low speeds, but an actual loss in the medium to high ranges. Which goes some way towards proving that factory engineers usually know best, at least at Jaguar. Actually, as Jaguar's tuning booklet on the 2.4 indicated, the best way of going about tuning this engine was merely to modify the existing carburetters and fit the high-lift (3/8 inch) camshafts. Full benefit from the SU carburetters was only really gained when the more efficient B-type head was used. Together with a higher compression ratio of perhaps 9:1 or a little more, this would result in nearly 50% more bhp at the wheels.

Of course, when the 3.4 Jaguar arrived there was less interest shown in tuning the smaller engined car (the art was only properly revived with the coming of pre-1957

Saloon Car racing in Great Britain from 1977). But although the stock 3.4 had an enormous measure of performance by the standards of the day, the temptation to improve it still further was too great to resist, both for racing and road use.

In its period, Mike Hawthorn's familiar British Racing Green 3.4 saloon was about the fastest of its type – as related in the Competition section of this book, Hawthorn's driving of VDU 881 in saloon car races produced some of the most spectacular racing of the 'fifties. The car was modified by the Hawthorn family's own garage, the Tourist Trophy in Farnham, Surrey. Valve sizes appear to have been left standard, but 9:1 pistons were used together with two 2-inch SU car- buretters and a twin exhaust system made up by Tourist Trophy. A competition clutch was also fitted, but inside the car, only a 160mph speedometer betrayed the car's deviation from standard.

Complementing the attentions to the power unit was the stiffening of the suspension all round by fitting an extra leaf to the rear springs and stronger coil springs at the front, with competition shock absorbers. Importantly, rear track was increased by 2-inches through the use of specially made wire wheels, the extra dimensions accommodated by restyled spats. Then finally, the lower final drive of 4.55 was used instead of the standard 3.77. *Motor Racing* magazine reported: "Mike's reason for this is simple; he doesn't like being out-accelerated by 'Kraut cars', referring to a well-known species with an unusual method of door opening".

The combination of the low gearing and the engine modifications described gave the 3.4 a staggering perfor- mance for a saloon car of the late 1950s; no figures were ever taken on this car, it seems, but a reliable estimate of its acceleration would be 0 to 60mph in 8-seconds or less, with 100mph arriving in under 20-seconds. This last representing an improvement over standard in the region of six- or seven-seconds – and, in fact, just about equall- ing Mercedes 300SL times. *Motor Racing* gained some memorable road impressions of VDU 881 late in 1958:

"When it is given a chance, however, the Hawthorn Jaguar really goes! The low ratio gives it tremendous acceleration, especially in second gear, and instead of the forward urge abating as frontal area asserts itself the car hurtles onwards in third and top gears until, at around 5000rpm in top, a flick of the overdrive control 'switches off' a thousand rpm and settles the car into its best, long- striding cruising gait. At this pace the Jaguar is acceptably quiet to its occupants; wind noise is kept to a reasonably low level and the engine gives no indication of stress.

"Christmas traffic, patches of mist, and an unpleasantly wet road made the compilation of performance figures too hazardous to be worthwhile. Maximum speed is something in excess of 120mph (Mike has seen over 130mph), but at this velocity the 3.4 became a little un- stable, due, perhaps, to the undulating road surface.

"In respect of roadholding, the 3.4 can be driven round corners extremely fast...but it really needs a Hawthorn to get the best out of it. For ordinary mortals the combination of a wet road, spinning rear wheels and a sliding tail can become somewhat overawing, particularly as the relatively low-geared steering calls for rather a lot of wheel twirling when correction is required...."

Alas, these words were rather too prophetic, as perhaps it was all too much even for a Hawthorn; for in January 1959 Mike Hawthorn died in his 3.4 on the Guildford bypass. The circumstances of this tragedy – made all the more ironic by Mike's previous announcement of his retirement from motor racing – largely tell the story in themselves. A wet road, a fast bend, the power at the wheels of the Jaguar shod with Dunlop Duraband tyres (superior in the dry to the Dunlop RS4s, but at that stage in their development, unprogressive in the wet) and just possibly the temptation to keep up with Rob Walker's 300SL Mercedes which was in front; one can imagine the sequence of events all too well – the sudden slide, perhaps at three-figures, the armful of opposite lock and a muttered curse – half in annoyance and half in embarrassment – the spray of flying mud and water as the car left the road; and then the tree... Within a few seconds, Britain had lost one of her most likeable and talented young drivers.

It must be part of the Jaguar saloon story that the 3.4 was far ahead of its time in its performance, and that even a standard example demanded a certain respect if its full capabilities were to be explored on public roads. This is far from saying that the 3.4 was intrinsically dangerous, unstable, or merely a little too fast for its chassis – I have driven a 3.4 saloon very quickly for many hundreds of miles without feeling the least bit intimidated (and it was a fast car even by the standards of the late 1970s), but there is just something about its high speed handling which can give momentary cause for circumspection. Lord Montagu sums it up well in *Jaguar – A Biography*, when he tells of his own 3.4: "...my only other criticism concerned a feeling of directional instability at high speed. The car seldom did anything frightening, but I often had the feeling it might..."

There are those who dismiss the car as simply dangerous, but it is possible that they have only sampled a 3.4 in poor condition or with something amiss; like the 2.4, it is essential to make sure that all the suspension components are in perfect order, particularly the Metalastic joints, and not forgetting the front subframe rubber mountings either. Otherwise, the resulting play will certainly give an impression of instability and sloppiness. As a 2.4 owner wrote in 1960 after four years' with his car:

"Essentially the handling of the 2.4 is very dependent upon the state of the rear suspension, and the following points should have careful scrutiny to secure the best performance available:

1) The rear torque arms should be inspected for wear and loosening of their rubber bushings, and if any is detected they should be replaced. Any slight separation of the rubber to metal bonds indicates need for replacement, and inspection must be meticulous to uncover this at times

2) The length of the single rear Panhard rod should be checked and adjusted as necessary, according to the Jaguar factory bulletin on the rear suspension. Exact measurement of this length from specific points as stated in the manual is necessary. The bolting of this rod to the chassis eyehole provided has been known to loosen, and the integrity of this point should be checked as well.

"I have fitted Michelin X tyres which I found to improve the road-holding. Rather than the 6.50 x 15, I fitted the 6.70 x 15 size which appear to offer more road grip. If these are fitted it is necessary to use the tyre pressures suggested by Michelin, and not the pressures for Dunlop. If the latter are used, with less pressure in the rear tyres, a marked understeer will result.

In regard to the front, the following points bear attention:

1) A heavier anti-sway bar, as fitted to the 3.4, can be obtained from Jaguar (C.14035) and should offer some improvement.

2) The steering box sector shaft adjustment should be checked for proper setting of the steering wheel to front wheel transmission of movement, and free play.

3) The square rubber coupling on the lower steering column assembly should be checked for any cracking of the rubber and for firmness of its attachments.

"Koni shock absorbers are a very valuable fitting, either all round or just on the front. Jaguar as well offer stiffer dampers, but I don't believe these are warranted for 20 000 miles as are the Koni units.

"Heavier front coil springs, as fitted to the 3.4, can be obtained from Jaguar and will reduce front end cornering roll. Those with the 'blue streak' will offer less difficulty in fitting, since they require no packing piece."

That comprehensive letter of advice to *The Autocar* followed several from 2.4 owners, all of whom expressed dissatisfaction with the standard shock absorbers whose efficiency only appeared to last between 3500 and 10 000 miles at best. Most agreed that Koni dampers were an ideal substitution, and that make were indeed commonly fitted to Jaguars of all types by their owners during the 'fifties and 'sixties. But that and a rather poor heater were about the only regular grumbles from owners of the otherwise durable 2.4 and 3.4-litre Jaguars; those with the 2.4 appreciated its modest thirst (some reported getting up to 26mpg quite regularly), while the 3.4 driver knew that he possessed one of the fastest four-seaters in the world – a typical opinion is the following from a 3.4 owner in Italy, prompted by *The Autocar's* test of the car in 1958:

"The car is a truly dual purpose carriage, as it proves to be excellent in town yet it has the feel of a *Gran Turismo* vehicle on the open road, where its quite astonishing acceleration and accurate steering make it a joy to drive. The disc brakes are outstanding; I agree with your report that it would be false economy to specify a 3.4 without such brakes. Cruising speeds are what the road and traffic conditions will permit, and anywhere between 90 and 110mph appears to be comfortable; in fact, without looking at the speedometer, which proves to be reasonably accurate, one has little idea that one is actually travelling at such speeds, so stable and quiet is this vehicle."

The writer then went on to describe a trans-continental journey from Milan to London, which inspite of heavy traffic and fog was accomplished at a running average of 56.9mph for a distance of 754-miles; between Brussels and Ostend, one 66-mile stretch was covered at an average speed of 104.1mph.

"I cannot think of any other four-five seater saloon in which I could have driven this distance at such a high average, without fatigue. The car went splendidly, and whenever possible on the autobhan was cruised at 100-110mph. As a result, I was never passed, and was able to leave all opposition.

"Now, after 12,000 miles, my only replacements have been a rubber ring in the brake master cylinder and the packing at the back of the sump, which started to drip oil. The body is quiet, the transmission smooth, and the engine appears to improve in performance as the mileage increases."

The original 2.4 and 3.4 saloons continued in production until superceded by the new Mk II range in October 1959, with little change in the meantime – late modifications to the 2.4 car included a short-stud cylinder head (from engine number 1153), a 12-bladed fan with the fan cowl replaced by a fan shield on top of the radiator block, a more efficient rear hub seal on disc-braked cars, and a shroud fitted to the scuttle vent aperture to prevent water getting behind the instrument panel when the flap was open. These changes took place in June 1959.

These first Jaguar 'compacts' were dated more by their looks than performance, and the Mk II series rectified

Jaguar approved the fitting of a sliding roof to the small Jaguar – this is an export 3.4 so equipped, awaiting shipment.
Photo: Jaguar Cars

their rather heavy, plain appearance in a way which few could dispute as being tasteful and pleasing to the eye. But despite the onslaught of British weather and the motor car manufacturer's usual disregard of corrosion, a large number of 'Mk I' saloons (the factory used that term itself from as early as November 1959) continued in every-day use here until the mid and late 'seventies – only now have the original 2.4 and 3.4 saloons become noticeable by their absence, and at the time of writing in the late 'eighties, the type has still not achieved a high collector's value, being rather overshadowed by the more convenient and, perhaps, better looking Mk II.

But to some, they still hold a great appeal; certainly they have a more compact and manoeuverable feel to them than the Mk II, which seems a larger car altogether inspite of sharing all the Mk I's basic measurements. Possibly it is a function of those thick screen and side pillars, and the sports car bucket seats of the earlier car. In performance, the 3.4 lost nothing to its Mk II equivalent and was in fact marginally quicker in a straight line; on the road, the Mk II was substantially tidier in its handling, though it used very similar suspension arrangements.

The 'Mk I' Jaguar from today's viewpoint

Revisiting a Mk I Jaguar today is an interesting experience, because so far as the 3.4-litre is concerned, it has a completely up-to-date performance – it compares very well, for instance, with the current XJ6 2.9, virtually matching its acceleration and top speed. The advances in handling have been great though, and one cannot begin to follow a modern car of this sort over twisty roads if the other driver knows what he's doing. On fast roads or on motorways though, the 3.4 is still more than a match for most modern cars, a quick flick out of overdrive and full throttle in direct top being enough to leave all but the fastest of saloons (and most sports cars!) behind.

While the Mk I still provides a comfortable ride, the once-admired standards of refinement have been eclipsed by such as the XJ series, and there is an old-fashioned amount of front-end 'crash' over deep ridges and potholes, while on a poor road one sometimes has the impression that the rear axle is getting left behind. There is an old fashioned degree of roll too, and except on wet surfaces or slow bends in the intermediate gears, the Mk I is a determined understeerer – this is especially noticeable with a standard example on the track. Duncan Hamilton recalls that when racing the drum-braked 3.4, full lock could actually be wound on *before* the corner if one were quick enough, the resultant tyre scrub being used in lieu of brakes! The low-geared steering is also inclined to be a disappointment, and makes the car unnecessarily clumsy and tiring to drive over winding roads.

Brakes – well, the cars equipped with discs cannot be greatly faulted, but fade is quite easily induced on the others. This does not necessarily occur under high-speed stop conditions, but it is more likely to be encountered if the car is sprinted between bends with short, frequent applications to bring the speed down for each. There is no real cure, except to slow down or convert the car to discs – the latter being preferable!

It is not quite so common to modify road-going Mk I Jaguars today, but the type has been given a new lease of life in this respect by the recent introduction of pre-1957 saloon car racing. In this very successful branch of club racing, the 3.4 is excluded but the 2.4 is usually a front-runner and it is interesting to note how it has been developed. The rules prohibit major changes to engine or suspension, but with two 2-inch SU carburetters and big-valve C-type heads, these cars are quicker than a standard 3.4; stiffer springs and dampers, plus 6-inch rim wheels to increase the track and provide more rubber (road tyres only are allowed though), enhance the already good handling and elicit praise even from such notable drivers of modern machinery as Gerry Marshall.

The writer has driven one such 2.4 on the road and racing circuit and found the car's behaviour delightful, with only moderate understeer, light steering (despite a high ratio box) and perhaps above all, a superbly smooth, high-revving engine, the sweetest personally encountered. Even a good 3.4 or 3.8 XK engine is inclined to go through a 'busy' phase at about 4500–5000rpm, but the tuned 2.4 unit truly merits the well-worn 'turbine' simile and sounds entirely unstrained at 7000rpm – in fact the writer has unwittingly taken the tachometer needle round to 8000rpm with no ill effects on the engine, or to its apparent distress.

Those owners of Mk I saloons who don't want to race them but would like to see an improvement in handling and performance can quite easily borrow some of these ideas from the racing fraternity. Efficient shock absorbers, stronger front springs and properly adjusted caster and camber angles make for a drastic improvement in response, while (if one can be found today) a high-ratio steering box will also assist in this direction at the expense of a little extra effort being necessary at parking speeds. A steering wheel of a smaller diameter than the standard 17-inch Jaguar one can be fitted with advantage too, provided it is not taken to extremes.

Owners of wire-wheel cars will be able to obtain (or have built-up) slightly wider or offset rims which will help counteract the narrow rear track of the car, though a modification to the rear wheel spats may then be necessary. Wider steel wheels can be built too, but choose a reputable specialist because the quality of the welding will be all-important! At the front of the car, it is possible to fit the stronger Mk II subframe complete with suspension and brakes, while a Mk II rear axle can also be used – though remember to check the axle ratio.

This very sleek two-door coupe design was played with by Jaguar in the early-fifties – styling lent heavily on the 2.4 saloon, but it may have been intended for the XK sports car chassis (note the 16-inch wheels).
Photo: Jaguar Cars

However, it is no good at all carrying out modifications without also ensuring that everything is functioning as the maker intended – all steering and suspension parts, and rubber bushes front and rear including the front sub-frame mountings, should be carefully checked and renewed as necessary; on reassembly, it has been found that best results are obtained by adhering to the manufacturer's workshop manual settings for the front suspension – Bill Heynes knew best!

Bodywork hasn't been mentioned yet, but is likely to cause the Mk I owner more problems and headaches than any mechanical part; as with all unitary construction vehicles, the many closed box-sections encourage condensation and the retention of moisture, and little can be done for a car badly effected except to cut out the rusted metal and weld in new. Unlike mechanical spares, some body parts for Mk I Jaguars are scarce, particularly (at the time of writing) front wings, though it is only a matter of time before 'pattern' parts begin to appear. Those rebuilding their cars are well advised to protect the rebuilt box-sections of the vehicle with some wax-based anti-rust fluid, otherwise it will all happen again in a few years regardless of the mileage covered.

Those not willing or able to rebuild their cars completely should check such points as the rear spring hanger boxes, where the open extension holding the rear spring is an obvious catchment area for mud, which holds

moisture and promotes rot. Jacking points and sills in particular are other areas where the MoT inspector (UK) is liable to carry out an extra thorough inspection.

Modification of the 2.4 engine has been mentioned, but it is perfectly practical to increase the bhp of the larger engine too, provided that the car is sound in suspension and braking departments. The obvious first step in this direction is to fit 9:1 pistons and install 'rich' needles in the standard carburetters, but the former idea is no longer such a good one with the recent decrease in octane rating at the pumps. Two-inch SU carburetters can be fitted but they are unlikely to give much extra power without further changes to the head; the easiest way to increase bhp is to fit an 'E' type straight-port head, and in order to remain with a two-carburetter arrangement (three may require cutting the inner wing) the inlet manifold from a Jaguar 420 or early (pre-XJ) Sovereign can be used, or the complete set-up from a 240 or 340 Jaguar. The head itself is best left alone, or sent to a recognised specialist for modification.

But even completely standard, the original 3.4-litre Jaguar especially, has an undated performance and remains a perfectly practical high-speed touring car. It thus remains true to the original concept of a compact executive express combined with a hint of the sports-car in its make-up – a unique combination, which no Jaguar after the Mk II has ever managed to recapture.

Chapter Eight

The Mk II Jaguar

One of the most impressive sights today is the rapid and purposeful progress of a Mk II Jaguar on a motorway, eating up the miles in the fast lane.

Autocar, April 5, 1963

... motor cars with double-barrelled names seem somewhat expensive when compared with this Coventry-built twin-cam machine

W. Boddy, *Motor Sport,* September 1960

Of all Jaguar saloons, the Mk II was probably the most missed when it left production in the late sixties; it wasn't the very last small Jaguar saloon, but it was the last true *sports* saloon to come from Jaguar. Successive Jaguar four-seaters have been much better cars from a technical point of view, but size has never allowed them to fill the gap left by the departure of the Mk II series.

The Mk II was a superbly executed re-fashioning of the original 2.4 and 3.4 saloons; it retained their major dimensions almost entirely, and thus exactly the same concept of performance combined with compactness, while their looks had undergone an equally subtle re-translation which lost Jaguar no old friends but won them many new. Handling had come in for a big improvement, while there was more power for the 2.4-litre and a new 3.8-litre engine for those who wanted the ultimate in speed. Almost 100 000 Mk IIs were made, which meant that until the XJ6 passed that mark, it was the most successful Jaguar saloon ever.

From the front, it was difficult to instantly tell the old from the new, but a second glance at the revised compact would reveal a new radiator grille with a central rib, spotlights where the air-intake grilles had been, sidelamps on top of the wings XK-style (with flashing indicators taking their original place on the front of the wings), and slimmer windscreen pillars. View the car from the side, however, and no concentration was required to

detect the differences – they were obvious at once. The main door pressings now ended at waist level, leaving slender, chrome-plated frames to contain the door glasses, thus banishing the thick light-stopping pillars which were such a characteristic of the original car. The rear side window frames extended right back behind the door opening, almost meeting the new wrap-round rear window, and they could be hinged open to provide extractor-type ventilation.

So the main improvements to the car's appearance centered around this big increase in glass area – the screen depth had been increased by an inch to 16.5in. while the new door frames allowed an extra 1.25-inch depth and 3-inch width for the front door windows, and a maximum extra depth of 1.5-inches and 6.5-inches width for the rear door windows; the rear screen was no less than 3-inches deeper and 7-inches wider.

Complementing the new side window frames were plated roof gutter mouldings, and neater push-button door handles with improved water sealing. New, larger stop/rear light and indicator lamp housings were in position at the rear of the car, and under the bumper ran a deeper skirt, decorously hiding the petrol tank.

The shape of the car's rear quarters had come under revision anyway, in order to accommodate the wider axle which considerably helped both the car's appearance and its stability. On each side, the axle casings had been extended outwards by 1.625-inch to give a 3.25-inch increase in rear track, which was now 4ft.5.375in. (plus

Right: One of the most admired Jaguar saloons of all time – the Mk II. Thinner windscreen pillars and flashing indicators were amongst the revisions. *Photo: Jaguar Cars*

Below: Side windows now extended back behind the doors, and their frames chromed. This more delicate treatment transformed the look of the car. *Photo: Jaguar Cars*

The new rear window of the Mk II gave a wrap-round effect, and allowed better rear vision; rear light units were larger too. Wire wheels (chrome plated, silver enamel, or body colour) were available as 'extras', together with whitewall tyres. *Photo: Jaguar Cars*

242

0.75-inch if wire wheels were fitted). It still meant that at 4ft. 7in., the Mk II's front track was greater, and this was due, it seems, to an unwillingness to further modify the rear end of the car to accommodate an even wider axle, either for aesthetic or cost reasons. The cutaway-type spats of the 3.4 were retained, secured as before by sprung screw fasteners revealed on opening the rear doors.

These attentions to the rear end of the car were matched by further modifications to the front suspension, again with better handling in view. The same basic arrangement still existed, but to counter roll, both wishbones had been angled downwards to lift the car's roll centre from 0.75inch below ground level to 3.25-inch above, together with increased spacing between the ball joints, brought about by raising the inner pivot of the top wishbone and lowering the ball joint on the bottom wishbone. The increased length of the upper wishbone reduced the effective steering swivel inclination from 7.5-degrees to 4.5-degrees. Together with the new rear axle, all this resulted in a much more manageable and responsive car which felt much more stable at high speed.

Inside the Mk II, all the trim had been redesigned, commencing with the dashboard which set a pattern for many Jaguar models to come; the speedometer and rev. counter had been removed from the traditional Jaguar position in the centre and remounted directly in front of the driver, their place being taken by the four minor instruments, the light switch, and a row of toggle switches which were neatly labelled by an internally illuminated strip underneath. This centre panel could be hinged down in seconds to provide access to the wiring.

Also on the central panel were the ignition and starter button (the two functions still being separated), but the quadrant on the automatic cars was now mounted on the steering column binnacle, where the overdrive switch could be positioned on manual cars. The driver now had a headlamp flasher, this being incorporated in the direction indicator lever, while another innovation was the brake fluid level warning light sited to the right of the driver (RHD cars) on the facia. This system, by Sovy, used a float in the brake hydraulic fluid reservoir, and the light was also employed to act as a handbrake warning indicator when this was applied. The steering wheel itself was totally new, finished in a smooth, shiny black plastic material with a 'half ring' attached to the boss for sounding the horn (instead of a central button), though a white-finished wheel and a wood-rim wheel were options.

Other extras which the Mk II owner could specify were a laminated windscreen at £7.8s.6d, heated rear window (at first without a switch, being operated by the ignition), locking filler cap, rim embellishers, tow bar, childproof locks for the rear doors, auxiliary fuel tank and sliding roof kit.

The driver's and passenger's seats were completely new,

Front suspension on the Mk II was improved by altering wishbone heights to raise the roll centre. Note disc brakes, a universal fitment now. *Photo: Jaguar Cars*

Interior of the Mk II was changed to include picnic tables and a new facia with instruments in front of the driver. Front seats were bulkier and no longer bucket-type. This is an early (1959) example. *Photo: Jaguar Cars*

with deeper squabs and wider cushions offering greater initial comfort (especially to larger men) but not offering the same degree of lateral support as before. In between the seats extended the new console, which covered the top of the transmission hump and rose vertically to house the heater controls and optional HMV radio directly under the central instrument panel. An ashtray was let into the horizontal portion of the console, just in front of the gearlever and its leather gauntlet.

Needless to say, walnut veneer was the finish chosen for the facia and door cappings, with only the central instrument panel differing in having a black leather-grained plastic covering. The front seat passenger had a lockable glove compartment, while the rear seat occupants could use small picnic tables in wood veneer which folded into the backs of the front seats. They also had the use of well designed and nicely contoured combined armrest/magazine holders set into each door trim panel. Leather was used on all seat facings as before, with a high quality vinyl being used for all non-carpeted areas. The boot floor was covered by a shaped Hardura mat, with the spare wheel compartment underneath as formerly.

Jaguar had made an effort to improve the car's heater, which was now rated at 3.9-kilowatts, and additionally

A new feature in the Mk II was the central console housing gearlever, ashtray and, in the vertical panel, heater controls and optional radio (not fitted here). *Photo: Jaguar Cars*

was given with the overdrive engaged, a resounding 125mph mean – this, together with 0 – 60mph and 0 – 100mph times of 8.5- and 25.1-seconds respectively, ensured that this full, four-seater luxury saloon was faster than 80% of all two-seater sports cars. The 11-inch front, 11.375-inch rear disc brakes carried over from the 3.4, and the revised suspension, meant that this level of performance was entirely usable too.

Vigorous acceleration from a standstill no longer produced the axle tramp which could occur with the Mk I saloon, *The Autocar* discovered, largely because of the limited slip differential which was fitted as standard to the 3.8 Jaguars. The full title of the device used by Jaguar was the Spicer Thornton Powr-Lok, and it was manufactured in Great Britain under licence from the Thornton Axle Company of America. Built into the differential unit, its purpose was to transfer torque to whichever roadwheel had the better grip - either due to weight transfer on corners, over wet or slippery surfaces, or through the tendency of the axle to rotate under power and lift a wheel from the ground. The Powr-Lok achieved this through small multi-plate clutches which released the drive to the wheel with the least traction, thus allowing the majority of the torque to reach the wheel with the most grip.

Improved roadworthiness also resulted from the wider rear track, "providing a more stable ride with increased resistance to roll" in conjunction with the revised front suspension. The Mk II was still a strong understeerer though, and "the wide slip angle on the front tyres is clearly seen by an observer" noted the magazine. As before, using the higher recommended tyre pressures assisted the handling and made little difference to ride comfort.

The amount of weight over the front wheels also meant that Jaguar obviously felt unable to offer higher geared steering than 5 turns lock-to-lock, although a high ratio steering box giving 3.5 turns was available as option. Unfortunately, the standard steering box still didn't mean that the wheel was easy to turn during parking, while at higher speeds "there is an increasing need to take bends early and hold the car tight into them, otherwise it may swing wider than intended." Really quick cornering brought further complications:

"Since there is sufficient power to spin the rear wheels quite readily in third gear on wet roads, and because the weight distribution is markedly in favour of the front, care has to be taken to use only light throttle when coming out of bends or away from corners; experienced drivers likely to be attracted by the 3.8 will adopt this technique instinctively.

"...Should the back end slide, lifting the accelerator foot is usually enough to check it at once. Here, however, the low geared steering - 5 turns lock-to-lock with rather slow response around the mid-sector - is at a disadvantage, and it is difficult to apply quickly enough opposite helm to correct a skid at once."

Reclining seats were still an optional extra. Note alloy kick-plates on sill, and screw fastener for spat. *Photo: Motor*

the centre console ended in a duct which led hot air over the propeller shaft tunnel directly to the rear passengers' feet. While this was a step forward, the net result was a heating and ventilation system which was only marginally better than before, and one which was distinctly inferior to those of most American automobiles – and to the majority of European cars as well.

Road-testing the 3.8 Mk II

Early in 1960, *The Autocar* published the first test of the 3.8 Mk II, in overdrive form. The 3.8 engine used was of course similar to that introduced in the Mk IX, and also offered in later XK 150s – though the Mk II version of the 3781cc, 87 x 106mm power unit was fitted with the B-type head giving 220bhp at 5500rpm as for the Mk IX, rather than the 'straight port' triple carburetter head which was a further option on the XK 150, and which was rated at 265bhp.

The most impressive aspect of the 3.8 Mk II was, considered *The Autocar*, "the smooth, silent cruising up to 100mph in overdrive top on auto-routes at home and on the Continent, and the splendid acceleration for quick, safe overtaking, in direct top or third." Maximum speed

Comfort was rated highly, the suspension providing a smooth ride over all but the roughest surfaces and being well damped to prevent pitching; also, "this Jaguar is one of the comparatively few cars in which any size of driver should be able to make himself comfortable" thanks to the long seat travel and adjustable steering column. No means of altering of the seat back angle was yet provided though, and neither were the positions of the pedals (including the accelerator which was no longer of the organ type) thought to be ideal, with heel-and-toe operations being almost impossible. Vision was considered to be much better than before, though the area swept by the driver's wiper was too small. The car's headlights, while not up to its highest cruising speeds, were rated as "powerful."

The back seat passengers found that leg room was restricted if the front seats were pushed right back, but at least access was easy despite the high sill. As for the heater, "a greater heat supply might be expected; it was just sufficient on the test car for comfort when the outside temperature was at freezing point." Luggage capacity was thought good, and the sturdy screw jack mounted at the rear of the boot was approved of; it was also noted that because of the distance the rear wheel dropped on jacking-up, the spats need not be removed to change a wheel.

The test ended with the comment that the 3.8 Mk II had been produced "with a special eye on the American market, and with automatic transmission in mind. Such a model is even better suited to American roads and journeys and offers even better value than its predecessors. The manual change model tested is a very distinguished car; it calls for an experienced driver to take full advantage of its great potential." Possibly a note of warning in that last sentence? The sentiments regarding the American market were indeed correct, and very few 2.4 and 3.4 Mk IIs ever reached that continent. *Road and Track* was about the first North American journal to publish a full test of the Mk II, though the 3.8 they borrowed was slightly unusual as it was a manual gearbox car. "In just 12-years", they began, "the British Jaguar has become virtually synonymous with the term 'expensive foreign car' in the minds of the American public for, if you ask people you meet at random to name one or more imported cars, Jaguar always comes out on top of the list. All this has been done with a meagre advertising budget and fewer than 5000 cars per year available. How was it done? The answer, obviously, lies in the product itself for, in the final analysis, a car of the Jaguar class is bound to be recognised as something out of the ordinary."

Getting down to particulars, *R&T* rated the bigger

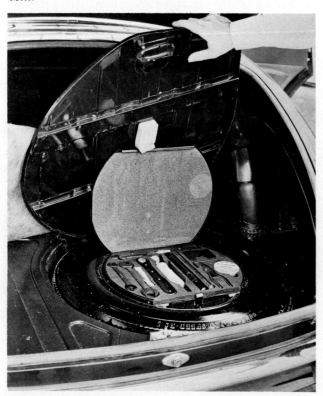

Lift-out panel under boot matting covered the spare wheel complete with its round toolbox – tools included the cam timing plate needed if the valve timing was disturbed. *Photo: Motor*

The early 'sixties saw the opening of a South African assembly plant at East London which built Mk IIs from 'completely-knocked-down' components. This is the first of several thousand Mk IIs to be assembled there.

engine as the most important change – indicative of a different set of priorities on that side of the Atlantic, where the 'horsepower race' was in full swing, with manufacturers offering bigger and more powerful engines at each model change. The 3.8 was well able to keep up though:

"Top speed is pretty academic. Our test car, which, incidentally, belongs to contributor Bill Corey and had 6000 miles on the odometer, has indicated 130mph on an instrument which shows very little error in the upper speed ranges (due to tire expansion at 100mph and up). ...Theoretically, a speed of 146mph would correspond to 5500rpm (in overdrive), but the combination of power available and wind resistance is such that this figure is not attainable. In short, the speed of this car is far above any possible use, but the ability to cruise safely and comfortably at a continuous 100mph is certainly there if road conditions permit. Corey says he drove as above for hour after hour across Arizona and Nevada and got just a fraction under 20mpg in the process.''

The comment on fuel consumption is interesting and was a topic followed up in the test. Confirming the journal's experience with two 3.4s (1957 and 1959) over 34 000 miles (in which the day-to-day consumption never dropped below 19.5mpg), the 3.8 never went below 17mpg, only 2.5mpg worse than *Road and Track* were

getting from a "popular US compact on our staff, with 130 less bhp." And:

A consumption of 23mpg is easily possible, and quite normal, using overdrive and cruising at around 70mph. The automatic version will get 21 to 22mpg under the same conditions, which is identical to the *best* figure we get from the previously mentioned US compact, with a stick shift.''

Road and Track's Mk II had power assisted steering, which did not appear on home market cars until October 1960. The same basic system as used on the Mk IX was employed, with modifications. Firstly, the hydraulic pressure was increased from 650psi to 850psi, while the physical size of the Burman steering box was reduced by a smaller diameter piston (down from 3in. to 2.68in.) and a shorter rocker arm. Then to help steering sensitivity, the

This extravagant exercise was the centrepiece of Jaguar's 1960 New York Show stand – a 3.8 saloon with all plated parts finished in real gold, including the wheels! Estimated value of the car was $25 000, and the model with the car is wearing a specially designed 24-carat gold-thread gown and a Napoleonic tiara containing over 1000 diamonds ... At that time the normal 3.8 Mk II was selling in the States for just over $5000.

rear worm support bearing was changed from adjustable ball to roller, and a full helix of recirculating balls was now used, instead of a half helix. Sealing generally was improved, and a different flow valve setting used in the Hobourn-Eaton pump in view of the greater pressures. All had been carefully engineered so that no modifications were necessary to the front subframe on which the box was mounted, while the only change to the linkages were stiffer steering arms to prevent damage should an insensitive driver turn the wheels against a curb. Kits were later (February 1961 on) issued by Jaguar for those who wished to convert earlier Mk 11s, at a cost of £90.

The installation was a success so far as *Road and Track* was concerned:

"The new power steering is one of the few we have tried that we liked. While the average man driving the previous model felt no need for power steering, many women did object to a slight heaviness, which increased to a considerable force during parking. The new system elimates this objection, and its particular virtue is that it is absolutely impossible to detect when the power comes on. Thus, the oft-encountered lumpiness at either side of straight ahead is not present and, as a matter of interest, several people drove the car without suspecting that it had power steering .... Our only criticism of the steering would be that with power, it could have been made closer to 4 turns lock-to-lock, rather than 5.

The steering was also found to be "very light" during high speed cornering now, and in fact a number of owners would have gone further than the magazine and said that a little assistance could have been traded for less turns, bringing quicker steering and more apparent 'feel' – some preferred the Mk IX's 'power' set-up, with its 3.5 turns lock-to-lock and a little more weight at the rim. But then the required degree of lightness might not have been achieved at parking speeds, or maybe Jaguar thought that they'd simply give the average American driver what he was used to.

The power steering partially disguised the car's good handling, of which *Road and Track* wrote:

"The 'old' cars handled very well for sedans, this feature being particularly appreciated by the driver used to a standard American car. On the other hand, a driver used to any of the more popular sports cars would, generally, dislike the feel of the 3.4 models, particularly the very pronounced understeer when cornering hard and fast. Michelin X tires would completely transform the general feel of the 3.4, but, unfortunately, parking effort went even higher and the car's normally excellent high speed stability decreased. The 3.8 has new suspension geometry with roll center raised from ground level to a point 3.25in. above. Power steering makes it difficult to evaluate this change because rim pull in a high speed bend is now very light. Nevertheless, the car definitely handles better than before and body roll appears to be less, as it should on theoretical grounds.

Comfort was rated highly, and the Mk II showed up all

too well the inadequacies of the home product, which even with the advantage of weight and size could not better the Jaguar:

....everyone who rides in the Jaguar expresses amazement over its comfortable ride. The car is particularly surprising to those people who own and drive nothing but the largest cars. The rear seat room is especially luxurious, thanks to ample legroom, high seat backs and a useful centre armrest which folds out of the way when not required. A particular feature of the riding quality is that it seems so well controlled over rough and wallowing roads. In our opinion, few, if any, cars of this category can keep pace with the Jaguar when the going gets rough.

The test car's manual gearbox came under fire though, not over its manner of operation but its ratios; first gear on the Mk II was lower than previously (12.73 instead of 11.3:1) and the ratios more widely spaced, which wasn't a change approved of. It was noted though, that most Mk IIs coming to the States would be in automatic form, but "while this item takes all the fun out of driving a car such as this, we must admit that the performance is still fantastic and a driver used to, say, a four-passenger Thunderbird, will find the Jaguar a tremendous advance in terms of roominess, accuracy of steering and ability to cruise safely and comfortably at very high speed." To the list price of $4795 (for the manual/overdrive car), automatic transmission would add $100, power steering $130, wire wheels $117 ($278 plated), and locally installed air-conditioning about $700 – a common non-factory extra.

Sports Cars Illustrated also tried the 3.8 manual during 1960. "The Jaguar combines, as no other car does, luxury and performance in a highly usable package. Beneath its leather and walnut skin lurks a heart of highly polished steel and aluminium. When caressed gently at the accelerator pedal, it purrs calmly, propelling this 'gentlemen's carriage' in a smooth, dignified manner. But like a Douglas Fairbanks hero, when hard-pressed it reacts in a violent, soul-stirring fashion. Wheels spin, tires scream with rage and two tons of ironmongery and precision woodwork hurl themselves down the road." Top speed was 125mph, and this came with acceleration which "beats the Ace Bristol or Austin-Healey." As every tester found, "the Dunlop disc brakes are smooth and strong and easily a match for the car's power".

Strong understeer was found, and despite a steering ratio which on paper was "quicker and sharper than a Corvair or Valiant", it was found that "at high cornering speeds the steering seems extraordinarily slow". But inspite of this, the 3.8 was still considered to be a "nimble" car, and all its other attributes were much admired – the "functional" instrumentation which was "in effective and dramatic contrast to the extravagance of the walnut panelling", the visibility, and the "finless fenders" which contributed to a good aerodynamic form and helped return 19mpg "on a traffic-free, gentle run

Wirewheels and whitewalls were almost obligatory for North American Mk IIs. The type was one of the most popular Jaguar saloons ever there, and for several years running was voted 'Best Imported Car.'

from New York City to Bridgehampton and return. If we'd used the full 225 horsepower frequently we would have paid for it, but it's pleasant to realize that unlike the gas-guzzling 'power-pack' the 3.8 can be thrifty when you wish."

This economy bonus was highlighted by *Sports Car Graphic* when it tried a 3.8 in the summer of 1962. "Our acceleration figures were impressive and fuel economy, ranging between 21 and 26mpg, was almost unbelievable." By accident, they also found that the limited slip differential was helpful in off-road situations, the car unditching itself from hub-deep sand in a dried-out river bed, thanks to the traction it provided.

Motor Trend magazine tested the more popular automatic Mk II in September 1961 – while that version was the one usually ordered by the customer, the motoring journals tended to prefer playing with the manual gearbox car because it appealed more to the sporting driver. But even in automatic form, the 3.8 was a fast car. "Performance of the automatic 3.8 compares favourably with that of our better V-8s" wrote *Motor Trend*. "The test car's acceleration times from zero to 30, 45 and 60mph were 4.2-, 7.2- and 10.8-seconds, respectively." Petrol consumption was understandably up on that of the overdrive cars, but still creditable at 15 – 19mpg. Maximum acceleration was assisted by the intermediate hold switch which remained a Jaguar feature, and *Motor Trend* compared its operation with the "2" range in the Chrysler Torqueflite box.

Back in Great Britain, William Body of *Motor Sport* had been casting his keenly critical eye over the 3.8 Mk II, and came away impressed. "One of the best saloon cars in the world", he considered it to be.

"What justification, if any, is needed for this statement? We consider the explanation easy – here is a car capable of 125mph, of devouring a 1/4-mile from a standing start in not much more than 16-seconds, and endowed with a full complement of Dunlop disc brakes which are well able to cope with high-performance of this calibre. Add to this the ease with which this 220 horsepower Jaguar can be driven, the sense of well-being conveyed by its hide upholstery, deep seats and polished veneers, its silent functioning and its very complete equipment, and no-one, surely, will dispute our claim. That such a car can be sold for just over £1,800 is a commercial miracle understood only by Sir William Lyons. Fastidious businessmen and keen motorists can save themselves or their businesses something like £3,000 by bearing these facts in mind, and expensive motor cars with double-barrelled names seem somewhat expensive when compared with this Coventry-built twin-cam machine".

The effortless acceleration provided a clue to the manner in which the car should be driven, thought Mr Boddy: "...there is still little need to wear oneself out hurling it at corners or playing angry bears in traffic. Like a certain well-known big-twin motorcycle it hunches itself up and streaks away from corners and congestion and, with retardation to match, can afford to behave with dignity in adversity. For this reason alone the 3.8 Jaguar is an effortless motor car in which to cover many miles. If its road-holding is bettered in some sports cars or in Continental G.T. vehicles costing fabulous sums, this is scarcely relevant if the driver is in sympathy with the style of driving this Jaguar encourages." The flexibility of the XK engine had "vintage qualities" in being able to run down to 20mph in overdrive top, while the power available was such that "even when motoring determinedly one changes up at around 3500rpm...although it is exceedingly satisfying to have on tap a maximum of 98mph in third gear and as high a pace in the 7-to-1 second gear as many cars stagger up to in third. And there is no finer engine to be behind than the twin-cam, six-cylinder of a Jaguar."

The purchase of Daimler

With these press notices, especially those stemming from America, it was little wonder that in August 1960 Jaguar were able to announce that thanks to record contracts with their USA distributors for 1961, it seemed certain that their exports to that country would be the highest since the company's export drive began in 1947. The need for increased production to meet demand had, in fact, occasioned a momentous move a few months before, when, in May 1960, Jaguar Cars Ltd purchased the Daimler Company Ltd from BSA.

The major reason for this acquisition was the urgent need for more space, and the Daimler works at Radford, Coventry, extended to some 56-acres, with covered floor space of something over a million square feet – this contained not just production lines but a large service department, offices, a big glass-fronted showroom, works maintenance areas and car parks; it more than doubled Jaguar's working area.

Daimler could trace its Coventry beginnings back to 1896, and had built up an enviable name for 'Old English' quality and solidity, with years of patronage by the Royal Family. But it had met with increasing competition during the 'fifties, especially from Jaguar who often seemed able to produce faster, better and cheaper cars than it could, with no apparent loss of quality.

There had been a determined effort in 1959 to re-establish the marque in the luxury car field with a new 4.5-litre V8 engine designed by Edward Turner, a variation of his 2.5-litre V8 engine which was destined for a totally new venture for Daimler, a two-seater sports car. The 4.5 V8 went into the big Majestic Major saloon, a rapid device which could eat a Mk IX for breakfast, while the glassfibre bodied SP250 sports car received the 2.5 V8; both cars were announced in 1959, though the Majestic Major had only just entered production when the take-over by Jaguar was announced. At first, little change was noticeable from the outside after Jaguar had assumed control, with the Majestic and SP250 continuing, but within three years, an interesting marriage had been arranged between the two makes, and an even more intriguing one investigated but not proceeded with. The Daimler commercial vehicle division, mainly centered around passenger buses, was another important aspect of the firm and represented a new field for Jaguar.

Early in 1960, Jaguar announced that they had purchased Daimler, Britain's oldest-established motor manufacturer. At that time one of Daimler's principal offerings was the Majestic saloon seen here.

Mk II production changes

Meanwhile, further refinement of the new Mk II Jaguar had not been neglected and various minor changes were made during the car's first few years of life. To improve cornering behaviour, a stronger anti-roll bar was fitted in February 1961 (previously it had been available to special order), and almost a year before, stiffer dampers had been introduced. In February 1961, forged upper wishbones replaced pressed steel, and August 1961 saw water deflectors for the front hub bearings.

Handbrake efficiency was improved when in August 1961, the mechanism was made self-adjusting; a spring-loaded pawl rotating a toothed nut ensured that the correct disc/pad clearance was always maintained. A kit was made available shortly afterwards so that earlier cars could be converted. A roadwheel change took place in September 1960, when 5-inch rim wheels replaced the

to improve sump sealing, (January 1960), and in June 1962, an O-ring seal was introduced for the rear of the exhaust camshaft cover.

Crankcase pressure also caused problems with the engine breathing arrangements, because oil as well as air tended to get expelled through the breather on the front of the cylinder head. Various breathers were tried, the best experimental technique being simply to make up a new arrangement that looked as if it might work, and bolt it onto the front of the engine and try it (recalls ex-development engineer Ron Beaty). The trick was to find one that separated out the oil without obstructing the escaping gasses too badly.

This type of work would be carried out with an engine on the test-bed, very routine work but sometimes with exciting moments. "I also remember we were using Perspex breathers, to watch the oil collecting", says Ron; "we'd got this 3.8 engine on, a bog standard Mk II, and it

Building Mk IIs: the operation was much as for the 'Mk I', with trimmed and painted bodies being lowered onto the mechanical components. All major internal body pressings were unchanged from the 'Mk I' anyway, the updating process being confined to the outer skin. *Photo: Jaguar Cars*

original 4.5-inch items on cars with pressed steel wheels – the later wheels could be identified by an annular depression around the rim.

No substantial alterations were carried out on the engine, though quite a lot of work went into improving oil-tightness; the twin overhead cam engine was a difficult one to seal, and had a tendency to force oil out of seals and gaskets due to crankcase pressurisation through piston-ring gas blow-by. The rear crankshaft seal was troublesome in this respect, though the original scroll-type seal worked well, except that it could leak if the car was parked on a steep hill with the engine stopped. In December 1961, a crankshaft rear oil seal incorporating asbestos rope in an annular groove was tried. Earlier, a modified crankshaft rear cover assembly had been fitted

must have had a faulty rod or something – we were all bending over the carb side and Bill Wiltshire was standing on the exhaust side, and I heard a noise and I thought, oh, the engine's gone rough, then I looked up and saw Wilky enveloped in flames – oh dear, something has definitely gone amiss... Literally, a rod had come out of the side and taken the whole side of the block with it, and it had gone straight through a door which was 2-inches thick, and was down the drive, outside, about 40-yards away. Wilky was looking at his hand, and he'd got a cut on the back, only a tiny little nick – the rod had gone past him by that much. He was scratching his ear at the time...!"

The final outcome was a breather incorporating a little vertical tower which had vanes cast into it internally, and these collected the oil which then dripped back inside. During 1961, the engine breather was routed so that the gasses were vented into the carburetters instead of the atmosphere, an early 'clean air' requirement for cars exported to California. On 3.4-and 3.8-litre cars, a round paper-element air filter had replaced the oval oil-bath type in May 1960.

Some changes had also taken place in connection with the lubrication system; a modified oil filter, inclined downwards, was fitted in November 1960, and a dipstick tube was introduced in February 1961 to make it easier to replace the dipstick in the sump. A larger oil pump together with a new sump to accommodate it came in June 1961. Drilled camshafts for quieter cold starting were fitted from May 1962, while the 3.8 engine's tendency towards high oil consumption was countered to a large extent in September of that year, when Brico Maxiflex scraper piston rings came into use.

Early and late Mk II engine bays – up until May 1960 an oil bath air filter was employed, after which the round paper-filter type was installed. As with the 'Mk I', engine accessibility was not good.
Photos: Jaguar Cars

On the electrical side, a high-output dynamo became an option in February 1962 – this was commonly used on police Mk IIs – and was standardised in April 1963, type C42 for 3.4 and 3.8 cars, and type C.40L for the 2.4. Sealed beam headlights for right-hand drive cars in September 1962 was a useful substitution, while in October 1963, the centre button of the steering also sounded the horn, as well as the ring. A further change of controls had taken place earlier, when in June 1960 the controls on the upper steering column were re-handed – that is, the flasher/indicator 'stick' went to the left and the overdrive switch (when fitted) went to the right. Jaguar went back to an organ-type accelerator pedal in November 1960, and in the same month, the clearance between the top of the steering column and the facia panel was increased to allow a greater adjustment.

On the dashboard, the 100lb oil gauge went in favour of one reading to "60lb"; this was largely because the earlier gauge had been non-linear, with "60lb" appearing below half-scale, and "30lb" therefore quite close to zero, which made the normal running pressure of around 40lb look dangerously low, which it wasn't. The new gauge only read to 60lb and with more linear markings on the scale, was easier to read and more reassuring; it was adopted in March 1960.

Other detail changes to the interior of the Mk II included a modified telescopic rear view mirror (April 1960), a new type of sun-visor which could swivel to give

The 3.8 Mk II was extremely popular with the police – it had power, space and endurance, and was particularly suited to the new motorway era.

Mk II facia as adapted for police use, with radio telephone installation predominating; while the place of the rear seats might be taken by emergency cones, lights and rescue gear. Contrary to rumour, mechanical specification was standard except for such items as uprated dynamo. *Photos: Jaguar Cars*

protection from sun coming through the side windows too (November 1960) and a spring lid on the gearbox cowl ashtray (also November 1960). The same month too, the side window frames were modified to increase their strength at waist level; this affected the door cappings slightly as well. These frames were again modified in April 1963 to incorporate flocked rubber channel inserts and new window glasses. Rubber buffers were fitted to the outer rear corners of front and rear door sills to eliminate movement of the doors when closed in June 1961, and seatbelt attachments were built in from January 1962. Leg room in the rear was improved by new front seat backs in February 1963, which had scallops at the bottom to give extra foot space. The heater received attention quite early on in production; there had been immediate complaints of unwanted interior heat, and this was partly because (unlike previously) there was no hot water valve built into the system, just a baffle arrangement to direct cool air past the heat exchanger. It didn't work too well, and in July 1960, a water valve was in fact installed, coupled to the temperature control flap in the heater unit and operated by the "Hot-Cold" control in the car.

In hot countries though, this still wasn't good enough as probably due to the somewhat tortuous passage of the air coming in from the vent flap on top of the scuttle, it was impossible to obtain a good flow of cool air. Also, a good deal of heat seemed still to be absorbed from the area of the bulkhead by this meagre volume of 'cool' air, despite the new stop-valve; the fact that you knew that the wretched heater hardly raised the temperature of the interior above freezing when you *needed* warmth made it even more infuriating!

There were two solutions at least, one expensive, the other less so. Those with the necessary $600 plus to spare could have an air-conditioning plant installed – most American manufacturers offered such a device as an option on their top-range models by the early 'sixties, but Mk II owners had to be content with bolt-on proprietary installations. The bulky evaporator units were usually fitted in the luggage compartment, though some could be mounted under the dash. It might be thought that the additional strain on the engine's existing cooling system would be too great to risk this solution (several bhp are required to operate the pump of an air-conditioning unit on full blast) but *Road & Track* was quite adamant that a

properly maintained Jaguar (and that was the secret) had quite enough capacity to cope:

"Overheating of the engine is one thing owners of 3.8 Jaguars need have no fear of, and 3.4 models of earlier vintage fall into the same classification. Mk VIII and IX cars also run exceptionally cool when in proper tune. My old Mk VIII with air-conditioning never overheated under the most severe conditions and we have a number of 3.4 and Mk IX models with air-conditioning operating quite successfully in Death Valley, Calif. Judging from our experience, older Jags can also be made to run cool by applying some of the principles (and parts) used on later models.

Bill Corey went on to suggest the fitting of the later-type water pump in place of the earlier one (on pre-Mk II cars), which required periodic repacking and was less efficient (pulleys had to be changed as well, and the whole conversion cost about $95 then). It was also advised that owners of older cars should get their radiators flow-tested, and the radiator cap pressure tested to 4psi. Jaguar rather experimented with settings for the latter, incidentally, pressurising the Mk II's cooling system as high as 9lbs (early 1963), 7lbs (late 1963) and then 4lbs from May 1964. The water system was further improved when in September 1963, a water pump was fitted to 3.4

Customers in hot climates took to fitting air-conditioning units of their own; here is an installation from Texas housed partially in the transmission tunnel, where the console normally went.

and 3.8 cars which had a 'falling flow' effect above 5000rpm, where previously the water had been circulated unnecessarily fast with an actual drop in cooling efficiency.

The second, relatively inexpensive, solution to the fresh air problem was also suggested by *Road & Track's* Bill Corey, who had tried it out on his 1961 3.8 Mk II. "Remove the kick-panels on either side of the front compartment", he instructed, "and you will find circular access plates which can be removed" – these spaces were intended for radio loudspeakers in the original 2.4 and 3.4 saloons, but as the Mk II had a central console for speakers, it was now possible to put them to another use."With judicious cutting of the side panels and holes, the fresh air intakes, grilles and cable controls from the Corvair can be mounted to replace the removable plates! These Corvair parts are very inexpensive and available through any Chevrolet dealer. When the installation is made, fresh air is introduced either directly from under each fender, or from large tubes leading to the dummy air intakes under each headlamp. In the latter case it will be necessary to replace the 3.8-type grilles with the earlier 3.4 grilles, which are perforated. Properly done, this change permits copious quantities of fresh air for cooling the interior. Don't forget to arrange proper screens to filter out insects, and to provide for water drainage."

An ingenious solution, and better than cutting holes in the front wings as early XK 120 owners often resorted to! These removable plates are, incidentally, very useful for cleaning and rustproofing the cavity formed by the front wing, which can collect debris finding its way past the closing plate in the front wheelarch and thus can quickly cause the bottom of the front wing to rust by holding moisture.

Returning to the theme of detail improvements to the car, other alterations to the Mk II's specification leading up to 1963 included some attention to the transmission – larger diameter propshaft universal joints came in December 1961, and a 3-inch diameter propshaft with sealed-for-life components was made common to all models from September 1963. The 4HA rear axle was standardised by late 1960, which meant that the 2.4 Mk II was no longer the odd one out with the 3HA unit. Axle ratios remained the same.

The tendency of the car to use its full shock absorber capacity was recognised in 1963 by fitting of new gas-cell dampers all round, these being less prone to fade under extreme conditions. Underbonnet changes visible included a polythene brake fluid container (instead of glass) in November 1960, while in the power steering box, a roller type pump replaced the eccentric rotor type. In the engine, modified exhaust valves with an improved steel specification were incorporated by September 1963. The 'short-body' SU fuel pump came in 1961. That the problem of breaking Panhard rod mountings had not disappeared is indicated by the introduction in January

1963 of a reinforcement bracket where the rod attached to the body; this could be fitted retrospectively to earlier cars too, if required.

The 2.5 V8 Daimler

The Mk II range was well established when the first obvious fruits of the Daimler-Jaguar link became apparent in the announcement of a 2.5-litre V8 Daimler using the Mk II shell. This was a very successful deployment of the Edward-Turner designed, 76 x 70mm, 2547cc aluminium engine originally seen in Daimler's own slightly bizarre excursion into the sports car field with the SP 250 of 1959 (which Jaguar kept in production until 1964). It was an extremely good engine, developing 140bhp at 5800rpm, and soon gained the respect of Jaguar's engineering department.

It seems that Daimler themselves had intended to use this engine in a saloon, and but for the purchase of the company by Jaguar, it might well have been seen in (of all things) a Vauxhall Cresta or Velox bodyshell, that car having been eyed by Daimler as a suitable ready-made basis for a new car, suitably retrimmed and re-engined. The project has all the hallmarks of desperation, and Daimler were probably driven to possible solutions of this sort by competition from Jaguar themselves.

Having briefly evaluated the small V8, it was a natural move for Phil Weaver and his men in Jaguar's experimental department to try it in a Jaguar, and the first recipient was a no doubt rather surprised Mk I saloon. The engine was still in its SP 250 form, with a quickly made-up sump to clear the Jaguar's front crossmember and a minimum of work was done to get it installed. The results were interesting, as the car proved to be embarrassingly faster than a normal 2.4 Jaguar....

Prototype Daimler grille being tried out on a Mk II bodyshell; fluting at top was a concession to Daimler tradition. *Photo: Jaguar Cars*

Meanwhile, a great deal of work had been carried out on the Daimler 2.5 V8 engine for a completely different application – as an inboard boat engine. It was completely marinised, with inhibited carburetters, fireproofing, governor control, beautifully designed water-cooled aluminium exhaust manifolds, and even a pump to empty the sump of oil (because draining it in the normal way was, of course, impossible in a boat). But although it aroused quite a lot of interest and was displayed at the Boat Show in London, the project was not continued with.

Then a more serious attempt was made to adapt the V8 to the Mk II bodyshell, and the necessary new parts were designed to enable it to fit neatly into that car's engine bay. It was linked to a normal Borg Warner Type 35 automatic gearbox and apart from a disturbing throbbing which produced an intermittent drumming noise (traced eventually to flexing of the engine/gearbox unit, which is why the bottom plate of the bellhousing is tied to the sump on the Daimler 2.5) the marriage was both convenient and successful. The engine itself had few inherent faults, though it was found that the crankshaft hadn't really enough metal on it for it to be balanced out properly, so for the production engines, the main bearings were narrowed to provide the necessary 'meat'.

While all the prototype engines built up by the development section ran perfectly, ex-Jaguar engineer Ron Beaty recalls a couple of amusing incidents as the first production Daimler 2.5s rolled off the line; first there came alarming reports of a previously unheard-of fault – cracked main bearing caps. This couldn't be reproduced experimentally, so some detective work was embarked on and a discreet walk was taken down the production line.

There it was discovered that an engine fitter was happily applying to the Daimler engine what he'd always applied to the XK engine during assembly – after dropping the crank in, he'd hit the end of it with a lead hammer, then insert a feeler gauge to check the endfloat. Well, the robust dimensions of the XK engine's bottom end took this treatment with no problem, but the small bearing caps on the Daimler unit just couldn't, and cracked. "Confiscate hammer, cure cracked main bearing problem!" says Ron triumphantly. A similar piece of investigation revealed the cause of an unaccountable oil consumption problem that was being reported, where again all attempts to reproduce the condition failed. Then it was noticed that the man fitting the pistons hadn't got a particularly good ring clamp, so while his mate was taking the caps off and fitting the main bearing shells, he was lifting out the scraper ring and cutting off the expander ring so that the piston went in easier! Such are the behind-the-scenes details of engine development work, at least in the nineteen-sixties!

The Daimler engine's design was very sound though; a 90-degree cast iron block was used, with two interchangeable aluminium cylinder heads. The valves were operated by pushrods and rockers from a camshaft mounted high in the centre of the block; motorcycle practice was followed in the arrangement of the valvegear, not surprising in view of designer Edward Turner's motorcycle experience. Turner had designed the twin cylinder engine which was largely responsible for the success of the Triumph motorcycle concern after Jack Sangster had bought it from the Triumph car company, shortly after Jaguar themselves had considered purchasing Triumph. Thus instead of flat-faced tappets which were free to rotate under a convex-flanked cam, the Daimler engine used a round-nosed follower and a straight-flanked cam. Composite pushrods with a duralumin tubular centre section and case-hardened steel ends accommodated expansion of the aluminium cylinder heads. The valve gear matched the engine's free-revving capabilities, with valve bounce not occuring until after 7000rpm.

Several minor changes were made to the unit for installation in the Mk II shell. So that the cylinder heads could be removed while the engine remained in the car, the holding down studs were replaced by set bolts; new exhaust manifolds with rear down-pipes gave the necessary clearance in the engine bay.

Other changes included mounting the water pump centrally on the front face of the cylinder block with split outlets to each bank, and a double-grooved pulley on

Blueprint of the Edward Turner-designed V8 Daimler engine, with centre camshaft working long pushrods.

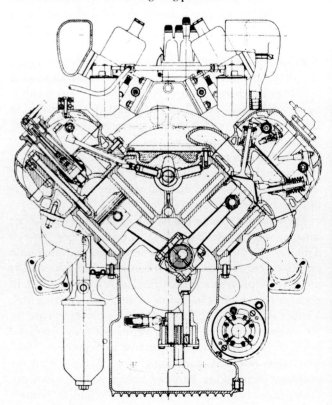

which was now positioned the cooling fan (formerly this was carried on the end of the crankshaft). One groove of the pulley took the drive from the crankshaft via a spring loaded jockey wheel, while the other carried a second belt which drove the dynamo positioned above. A further double pulley mounted forward of the Metalastic crankshaft damper provided the drive to the power steering when fitted. Two 1.75-inch SU carburetters fed the cylinders in a two-tiered arrangement, and these had a new type of air cleaner.

As the new engine represented a 1cwt decrease in weight over the front wheels, changes were made to the suspension as well, with different spring rates and softer damper settings. Less weight also meant lighter steering, though power assistance was still an advantage for town driving. Overall weight was 29cwt, distributed 56.4 percent front, 43.6 percent rear.

From the outside, the obvious difference was the new 'Daimler' radiator grille, incorporating the traditional Daimler fluting; a "D" motif in Mazak was carried on the bonnet in place of the Jaguar mascot. The bootlid carried the "Daimler" name in plated script above the fluted number plate lamp holder, while the legend "Automatic V8" appeared lower down on the lid, adjacent to the offside rear light cluster. "D" emblems were placed on the new hub caps, and in the centre of the rear bumper.

Inside the car, an additional bonus was extra space provided by the Type 35 automatic transmission which was shorter than the box used on the Mk II Jaguars, and gave a less bulky transmission 'hump' in the front. Consequently, the centre console was different, and was not extended between the seats, which also meant that the rear passengers had no heater duct of their own. This enabled the front split-bench seats themselves to be made wider than the individual ones used on even the automatic Mk IIs, and a third person could be installed centrally, at least for shorter journeys. A new design, the seatframe could incorporate an adjustable squab (this remained a surprising extra, as on the Jaguars), with the seat back slimmer altogether and with wider cut-outs at the bottom which gave rear passengers more room; no picnic tables were fitted.

The first V8-engined 'Jaguar' was sampled by *The Autocar* during May 1963. It was indeed quicker than the 2.4 Mk II (judging by Mk I 2.4 figures), with 60mph coming up in 13.8-seconds compared to 15.8-seconds recorded by the *manual* 2.4 Mk I saloon in 1956. The 80mph time for the Daimler was 24.6-seconds, as against 30.6 for the Jaguar, and its top speed was 112.3mpg mean, 10mph quicker than the 2.4. The Mk II version of the 2.4 was no faster than the original as is discussed elsewhere in this chapter.

The Daimler's top speed was recorded at the rather high rpm of almost 6,800rpm, due to the low 4.55 rear axle ratio (4.27 was specified on the launch of the car, but was apparently changed for production). Intermediate and Low ratios gave 70mph and 41mph respectively at 6000rpm, at which engine speed the red band on the rev. counter commenced. Fully automatic changes on full throttle occurred at about 5500rpm, which represented 62mph and 37mph. This gearbox scored over the type fitted to the Mk II Jaguars of that period by giving almost

The Daimler 2½-litre V8 in marine form; Jaguar carried out a considerable amount of development to marinize this power unit, only to cancel the project after a number of production engines had been built.
Photo: Jaguar Cars

full engine braking in each gear range, though it suffered by not having the "Intermediate Hold" switch for retaining or selecting second gear.

Neither was the ratio change on this particular box very good – "it is almost impossible to achieve a smooth upward change from 'Intermediate' to 'Top' except at fairly low speeds and with a light throttle opening. In fact, a thoughtful driver might develop quite a phobia about the nodding of his passengers' heads each time 'Top' comes in. 'Intermediate' engages with quite a bump if one uses the kickdown switch, but almost imperceptibly if the selector is moved from 'D' to 'L' on the overrun." Also, while first gear could be held from rest up to maximum rpm using the selector, it couldn't be regained above about 5mph once a change into "Intermediate" had been made, "a serious nuisance in hilly country when the engine revs in 'Intermediate' have fallen so low that there is little torque." The idea was to avoid a double kickdown from top to low, which could have been dangerous on a sharp bend. Finally, when parked on a 1-in-4 test hill and "P" engaged, a Land Rover had to be employed to tow the car a few inches forward before the transmission lock could be released! Drivers were advised to use the self-adjusting handbrake which was perfectly capable of holding the car on a 1-in-3 slope.

These minor difficulties apart (and they were shared by many automatic transmission cars of the period), the Daimler was liked by the magazine and the engine in particular was thought "sweet and near-silent" at almost any engine speed; though as 100mph represented 6000rpm, the car's natural cruising speed was reckoned to be nearer 80–85mph. Fuel consumption obviously suffered through the low axle ratio too, an overall 17.3mpg being recorded during the test, identical to the heavier and much faster 3.8 Mk II automatic saloon tested by the same journal the month before.

These facts were noted by the factory, and some time later the 4.27 axle did indeed replace the 4.55 with a consequent improvement in economy if at the expense of acceleration – as *The Autocar* discovered when it retested the Daimler 2.5 exactly three years later. Standing start times up to 80mph were within about one-second of the older car's in the lower speed ranges, but at 51.9-seconds, the 4.27 axle began to show with a deficit of 9-seconds to 100mph. Top speed was up by 1mph 'mean', though an impressive 115mph was registered one-way – this was achieved at 6300rpm, which as the journal noted was nearer to the maximum power figure of 5800rpm than before. But above all, it made high-speed cruising a much more relaxed and economical business with 90mph

The original Daimler V8 saloon – few changes except to grille and badging

representing only 5000rpm now; overall mpg was up to 19.3, an improvement of 2mpg. It was now also possible to get more than 20mpg over a long run.

As on the Mk II range, 1965 had seen the improved Borg Warner gearbox fitted with both "D1" and "D2" positions on the quadrant; with "D2" selected, starting could be accomplished in the intermediate ratio which made for more restful motoring and could add to economy when used in town, although adding four-seconds to the acceleration to 60mph compared with the normal time of 14.7-seconds. This latter time was achieved using the manual hold to delay full-throttle changes from 5100rpm to 6500rpm in low and inter-mediate (maximum speeds in these gears now being 44mph and 75mph); maintaining engine revs also helped progress on the road too, as otherwise the car was inclined to feel a little sluggish "particularly at lower speeds". The automatic changes themselves were much smoother than before, and "barely noticeable to passengers."

In other respects, the 'Mk II' part of the car had not dated and *Autocar* reported in generally favourable terms of the car's ride and handling – though the front suspension was considered firm ("even a little harsh and pattery on rough roads"), and on the continent "the occupants become a little too aware of movements of the live axle." Wheel spin was easily provoked in the wet, though "the handling is consistent, so that the driver quickly becomes confident and feels at ease with the car, and if a tail slide is provoked by using the power on corners it is easily con-trolled."

The Daimler 2.5 V8 saloon occupies a unique position in Jaguar's history, because after Daimler's acquisition by Jaguar, it became the only production Jaguar to be marketed as a Daimler *with a Daimler engine*. All the other badge-engineered Daimlers since that time have used either the XK, AJ6 or V12 Jaguar engines with suitable labels on the cam covers. A not-too-serious investigation was made into the possibility of inserting the 4.5-litre Daimler V8 into the Mk II, incidentally, which would have endowed the car with a prodigious performance with virtually no weight penalty; but aside from the problem of mass-producing the 4.5-litre V8, it would have meant new pressings for the internal wing valances surrounding the engine bay of the Mk II bodyshell, an expense which would not have been justified by the low volume sales of the resultant – albeit very exciting – model. The thought of a Mk II variant with an engine producing, as standard, a bhp figure almost identical to that of a 3.4 D-type remains intriguing though!

As it was, the small V8 car slotted very well into the existing Jaguar range in both price and performance. With tax, it cost £1568, compared with £1475 for the automatic 2.4, £1589 for the 3.4, and £1684 for the 3.8; performance fell between that of the 2.4 and 3.4, and the individuality of power unit and name opened up the Mk

II to yet another section of the market. While the car did not, perhaps, have quite the 'bite' which the larger XK engines provided, the V8 power unit was delightfully smooth and quiet; qualities which, combined with most of the Mk II's luxuries of trim and equipment, no doubt appealed to the slightly older and more staid driver who perhaps bought the Daimler. It was never exported to the USA, where the name "Daimler" remains virtually unknown.

Testing the 1963 Mk II

Returning to Jaguar, in April 1963 *Autocar* published a test of a Mk II which incorporated many of the refine-ments brought in for that year; it was a 3.8-litre car, but this time with automatic transmission, unlike the magazine's original manual gearbox road-test car of early 1960. Since that time, Mk II Jaguars had become a more familiar sight, even on British roads: "One of the most impressive sights today is the rapid and purposeful progress of a Mk II Jaguar on a motorway, eating up the miles in the fast lane. Like the nose of a bullet, the rounded frontal shape looks right for high speed, and the sheer velocity attained is usually exhilarating. Over three years have passed since our previous Jaguar 3.8 Road Test...and it is time to reassess."

There was certainly no question of the car having dated, and *Autocar* was at once aware of the "unrestricted visibility" and driving comfort – "few cars today permit one to stretch out as well as does the Jaguar, whose ade-quate seat adjustment allows even the long-legged ample distance from the pedals." The traditional Jaguar feature of the adjustable steering column was once more appreciated, too.

Nor had the car's suspension design become out-moded, despite the introduction of the independent rear suspension Mk 10 since the journal last tested a Mk II. The new Girling gas-cell dampers were thought to "give improved control on rough roads" while the springing was "certainly an excellent compromise in providing the stability for such high performance, coupled with comfort and insulation from bad surfaces expected of a car of this quality. It is especially good over bumps or dips causing large spring deflections, and the recoil is damped out effectively. *Pave* was traversed with unusually little bucketing and bouncing, while a corrugated section, which produces violent shake and vibration in most cars, was taken relatively smoothly." About the only qualifica-tion made was to mention that on ordinary road surfaces "small suspension tremors were felt, as in a car whose tyres are too hard, and the Jaguar felt firm on its springs"; but that was probably preferable to an uncomfortable 'floating' feeling.

Power steering was fitted to this car, adding a total of £66 to its basic price of £1556 (automatic transmission cost another £126 and reclining seats £16). "It certainly reduces the effort needed to hold the car to its line through a fast bend, against the rather pronounced understeer... It is, however, a pity that Jaguar have not taken the opportunity to raise the steering ratio to go with power assistance; at 4.3 turns lock-to-lock the steering is unusually low geared for so fast a car, and there is little response to small movements of the wheel around the straight-ahead position."

The automatic gearbox appeared to work well, though the actual quality of the gearchange wasn't commented on. It certainly suited the car:

> Because of the smoothness and good low-speed torque of its six-cylinder engine, the Jaguar lends itself admirably to automatic transmission. Hustling along secondary and minor roads the driver feels that he is more often holding the car back than he is urging it forward; so quickly does it gather speed that it seems almost to bound away after each hold-up or corner. Similarly; the ability to overtake safely in short distances means that the Jaguar is never delayed for long behind slower traffic. Over the speed range from 30 to 70mph, it takes less than 8 sec for any 20mph speed increment even in top; and the spectacular under-half-minute time for acceleration from rest to 100mph is a measure of the lusty performance."

In fact the automatic Mk II gave away very little to the manual version on acceleration, and the difference in times over a long journey would be neglibile. Compared with the 1960 manual 3.8, *Autocar's* test car with the automatic transmission reached 60mph in 9.8-seconds (manual, 8.5), 100mph in 28.2-seconds (25.1), and covered the standing quarter-mile in 17.2-seconds (16.3). Top speed was 5mph down at 120mph, and probably the automatic car's biggest disadvantage was its lack of that beautifully relaxed overdrive top gear, as with its 3.54 rear axle ratio, it was always cruising at 1000rpm higher (120mph represented 5500rpm).

At this same 'red line' rpm, low gear when held would give 50mph, and intermediate 80mph using the hold switch. In "Drive", the box selected these ratios at 43mph and 74mph respectively, if left to itself on full-throttle acceleration; these latter change-up points represented 5000rpm. While in top gear range the engine was "scarcely heard", the journal reported that "at high revs through low and intermediate, a distinctly audible combination of induction and exhaust noise accentuates the impression of vivid acceleration. With all the windows closed there is unusual freedom from wind noise at speed. This commendable quietness is not spoilt when the rear quarter vents are opened, though the front vents do provoke slipstream shriek."

Surprisingly, overall fuel consumption of the automatic Jaguar was actually better than that recorded by *Autocar* for the 3.8 manual car, at a "commendable" 17.3mpg – despite the advantage of overdrive and a more efficient power train (no torque converter loss), the earlier car had only managed 15.7mpg overall. As a general rule, one would expect the two overall figures to be reversed. Steady-speed consumption tests showed that at 90mph, the automatic Mk II produced 15.5mpg and the overdrive car 17.5mph, further reinforcing the point. *Autocar* did

Many notable personalities bought Mk II Jaguars – here is Lotus Chief Colin Chapman accepting delivery of his new 3.8 from service manager 'Lofty' England; Chapman also raced Mk IIs for fun as well as relying on them for hectic business travel.

notice that whatever the consumption, actual range was limited by the small 12-gallon petrol tank, "so that, within about 170-miles of filling to the brim, the winking 'evil eye' of the fuel warning light reminds the driver that it is time to stop and take out his wallet again." Gentle driving would produce 20mpg though.

Oil consumption was commendably lighter than before, the later road test car returning the equivalent of nearly 4000mpg compared with the 1600mpg of the previous car, thanks apparently to the Maxiflex oil control rings. It was also noted at this point that the car being tried had already covered 52 000 miles – surely making it one of the highest-mileage road tests cars ever supplied by a car manufacturer for a full test, and obviously underlining Jaguar's faith in the durability of their product.

If you weren't happy with your Mk II's range, you could have an extra tank fitted by the works – though this was most often done for competition cars. The auxiliary tank took the place of the spare wheel, which was then carried on what had been the spare wheel lid.
Photos: Jaguar Cars

The 3.4 Mk II

So far we've ignored the smaller-engined Mk IIs in our road test appraisal; this is partly because Jaguar almost always supplied the 3.8 car for 'trial by press', being the fastest and most impressive of the range, while in automatic form, its extra power minimised the effect of bhp lost in the torque convertor. In fact, it seems that a 2.4 Mk II was never released to the major journals for a full test at all – and, of course, the 3.8 was the only model available in the United States anyway. But *The Motor* did sample a 3.4 automatic in the summer of 1961, which makes an interesting comparison with both the original 3.4 Jaguar, and the automatic 3.8 Mk II.

At 30.25cwt, the new 3.4 showed a weight increase of fractionally more than 1cwt over its earlier 'Mk I' counterpart with the same gearbox; it had slightly more weight over its front wheels too, the distribution percentage being 59/41 instead of 58/42. This didn't affect maximum speed at all, the 119.8mph recorded matching the 1957 car to within one decimal place, but acceleration was definitely inferior. Sixty miles an hour took 11.9-seconds to come up, over 0.5-second slower, while at 33.3-seconds, the 100mph time was 3.3-seconds longer than before. Top gear acceleration times confirmed this difference, the 80–100mph increment for old and new cars being 12.4-and 13.3-seconds respectively. Standing quarter-mile time for the Mk II was 18.4-seconds using manual hold, whereas the Mk I covered the distance in 18-seconds dead.

Compared with the 3.8 Mk II, the 3.4 Mk II was significantly slower, although on the road this was rarely noticeable; *The Motor's* 3.8 automatic had reached 60mph in 9.8-seconds, 100mph in 28.2-seconds, and had a

The 3.4 Mk II was quite a favourite — it didn't loose out too much in performance compared with the 3.8, yet was cheaper to insure and was generally more economical on petrol. *Photo: Jaguar Cars*

standing quarter-mile time of 17.2-seconds; maximum speed was only superior to the 3.4-litre car's by about 1mph however, though by pulling into the red a little more may have been possible. Of the three cars, the original Mk I 3.4 had the better fuel consumption at 21mpg overall, compared with 17.3mpg for the 3.8 and 19mpg for the Mk II 3.4 automatics.

As an overall design the Mk II 3.4 was of course a much better car than its Mk I predecessor for everyday use; in its road test *The Motor* called it "a car of brilliant versatility", fitting neatly right in the middle of the Jaguar range which then still included the big Mk IX Jaguar, the advanced two-seater 'E' type (introduced in March 1961) and the 'economy' 2.4 and 'performance' 3.8 litre versions of the Mk II. "While on test a variety of people were invited to comment on it and", reported *The Motor*, "the unanimity of their praise was virtually unprecedented... When price is also considered, it is easy to see why Jaguar competition has been driving one make after another out of existence."

The magazine drew few direct parallels with the 3.8 manual gearbox car which they had already tested, but suspension behaviour and equipment were rated equally highly, except it was thought that the car was "only seen to best advantage on reasonably well surfaced roads", which appears to indicate that ride comfort was not perfect under all circumstances. The automatic box itself

and the power steering were new to the journal though, and rated these comments – of the gearbox: "This is not the smoothest automatic transmission we have sampled; changes of gear are quite evident and alternation between 2nd and top gears sometimes occurs rather easily with small changes of speed or throttle opening, but it is very satisfactory."

The steering was found to still possess a "definite" measure of self-centering, no kick-back and reasonable feel. The usual comment on the ratio being too low was made, "but with such light control very prompt response to any emergency was possible. At speed, there was no trace of instability."

The Motor returned to 3.4 motoring when during 1963, a dark green 3.4 manual overdrive Mk II joined the staff 'long term' fleet; editor Richard Bensted-Smith being the regular user. Explaining the purchase, he wrote as follows: "In the main, I suppose, motoring editors pick Jaguars for the same reasons as other customers. What else, at anything like the price, has the same combination of performance, safety, comfort and (be honest) prestige? An overworked word if you like, prestige is a tool of commerce – and it has more meanings than simple snobbery. Polished walnut fittings may say nothing to you or me (they don't to me), but if the drawing-room atmosphere helps their owner to clinch a business deal they will have earned their keep."

Not, as Bensted-Smith pointed out, that he was usually involved in such activities, but he did "consort with a variety of people, from captains of industry to racing drivers"; hence the Mk II. It was delivered with one 'special order' option – "Carried away with the idea of lightning response, I requested the special-order competition steering box with 1.2 turns less, and suffered for several months of heaving myself into London parking slots. There were other, unexpected snags; an inch or so of free-play in the middle assumed much greater importance, and an average turn into an average side street required too little wheel winding to trip the self-cancelling mechanism of the direction indicators. In the end I gave in and paid to return to normal, which is a lot better than it sounds since (a) ELX's turning circle of 36ft beats the pants off most cars of its size and (b) the progressive steering ratio has a quicker response over the first 15 deg. of wheel movement right or left."

Quite rightly, Bensted-Smith suggested that the real cure for the Mk II's heavy steering lay in weight reduction, which could have been achieved by using the light-alloy block of the racing engine in place of the standard 500lb cast iron one – "but that sort of speculation always brings you back to the astonishing price."

The mechanical failures over the first 12 000 miles were none, if you discount a maladjusted carburettor needle which gave 13mpg for a while (19mpg was a more normal average) and a leaking clutch master cylinder seal. The car did tend to soot up its plugs though, which required ten or fifteen minutes hard driving to clear them after a period of stop-start motoring, and the exhaust tailpipe bracket resisted all attempts to stop it clonking under engine torque.

The gearbox came under fire, although it was hinted that it was only a year or so away from obsolescence. "Forgiving the non-synchromesh bottom gear ...there is still not a great deal of excuse these days for even a very powerful car to demand skill or strength, or both, from the driver who wants to change his own gears. Being built to last, like the engine, the Jaguar gearbox frees up with use at about the same rate as the driver learns to change from first to second without getting frustrated in the middle; but not quickly, or enough." A lighter clutch would have been appreciated too.

Treating the Mk II as a long distance tourer, however, reduced the importance of these items, as a continental trip would show:

"In France, fortunately, gears do not matter very much. Driving prestigiously to Le Mans in June, I rediscovered the great advantage of having a car much faster than you need. Cruising on the great open stretches of N138 between Rouen and Le Mans is scarcely related to mechanical limits when a comfortable overdrive 3.500rpm represents a shade off 100mph and the speed is still within the scope of direct top gear for overtaking. The ride in a laden car travelling fast over a wavy road might be improved by alternative damper setting, and it would certainly be better with independent rear suspension (though quarter elliptics make quite a different device of the live axle), but it is wind noise around poorly fitting window frames which dictates, as much as anything, the choice of touring speed between 80mph and 100mph."

Wind noise appears to vary from car-to-car incidentally, and is very dependent upon the door rubbers sealing properly – any gaps create noise, made all the more apparent by the quietness of the car mechanically. With perfect sealing, a Mk II is still extraodinarily silent at speed, and the writer has travelled in examples which almost rival the XJ at 100mph.

Real invective was saved for the Mk II's heater which came in for a lashing. Having expressed surprise at the car's dynamo keeping up with the current requirements in crawling traffic, with sidelights, radio and heater-fan on, Dick Bensted-Smith continued: "The fan is necessary because the heating system of the Mk II is archaic. For a car of this quality to produce such a dribble of low-temperature air is both ludicrous and a mockery of the neat trunking that taps off part of it for the rear passengers. Summer ventilation suffers likewise from the poor airflow at low speed, though on the open road it can be greatly improved by opening the back quarter-lights".

Radial-ply tyres were tried on this 3.4, a set of Pirelli Cinturatos replacing the original equipment Dunlop RS5s. This seemed to result in better wet-road grip, and quicker steering response, giving the driver "a sense of precise control which is not sent tumbling by the sudden break-away of earlier, steel-banded designs...better roadworthiness has to be paid for, however, and under a variety of conditions from town-pottering to very fast cruising on the concrete section of M1 the ride is now perceptibly harsher and a lot noisier."

Later, Dunlop SP41 tyres were to be offered as an extra on the Mk II series by Jaguar, although owners still argue about the suitability of radials for the car, some maintaining that in addition to a slightly harsher ride (less marked with the Dunlops), steering and suspension parts wear faster due to increased loads, and that the steering itself becomes stiffer. Personally, the writer feels that the much better grip (particularly in the wet) and harder wearing properties of the radial tyre (cross-plies rarely last more than 12 000 miles, radials over twice that distance usually) outweigh any other factor, and found Dunlop SP Sport 185 section radials well suited to his own Mk II 3.8 saloon.

The 2.4 Mk II

The 2.4 Mk II has been rather overshadowed by its speedier brethren, but it had many real qualities. Above all, it probably represented the best value for money of any Jaguar since the pre-war type 1.5-litre, costing as it did barely £1500 (or only just over £1000 basic) and being cheaper to insure and (marginally) to run than the 3.4-and 3.8-litre cars. In an assessment of the car, however, there is no full road-test to refer to, and there is a reason for this – the 2.4 Mk II was the first XK-engined Jaguar not able to reach a genuine two-way-average 100mph!

This fact caused some embarrassment at the works when the first production 2.4 Mk II was tried. Theoretically, there should have been enough power for the car to just about achieve a 'mean' 100mph flat-out, but in practice, it just wouldn't get anywhere near it – something like 94mph was nearer the mark. To make matters worse, a 2.4 had been scheduled to go to *The Autocar* for testing and in desperation, even the main and big-end bearings were loosened off to a minimum torque figure in an attempt to reduce internal friction and hoist the speed; but 98mph was about all that could be obtained, and the magazine never got its road-test 2.4 Mk II.

In the end, all the original power curves for the 2.4 engine were re-checked, and, it seems, those with the engine breathing through Solex carburetters were optimistic for some reason. Confirmation of the car's inability to achieve a two-way 100mph was unwittingly provided by *The Autocar* itself when in 1964 a 2.4 Mk II was tried in the journal's well-known "Used Car Test" series; a well-preserved 26 000 mile overdrive car was the subject, and it returned a mean maximum speed of 96.3mph. So an extra 8bhp or so from the use of the B-type head and 3/8-inch cams were not enough to compensate for the Mk II's extra 1cwt and possibly less aerodynamically efficient shape compared with the

original 2.4: But apart from performance data *The Autocar* provided some useful comments on the character of the 2.4 as well:

"It is not until high performance is needed that one is really conscious of the difference between the 2.4 and the over-3-litre versions. Only then is it appreciated that much more 'engine' has been in use for brisk progress, and less kept in reserve. Even so the 2.4 is a lively car with ample acceleration and speed to please most drivers.

"Optional overdrive is fitted, giving remarkably quiet cruising around the 70mph mark. Rather more effort and noise goes with a motorway 85mph, and given plenty of time the 2.4 is still capable of a true 100mph on the flat in overdrive at 4,550rpm, and gives a mean maximum of 96.3mph. In direct top, the rev counter needle reaches the 5,500rpm red segment at 96mph.

"In both ease of action and efficiency of the synchromesh, the gear box is one of the best we have come across on any Jaguar, and perhaps has benefitted from having less torque through it; but it has a tendency to 'stick' in bottom gear at low speeds. Clutch take-up is smooth and the pedal load is reasonably light. Slight nose-heaviness is noticed on corners; directional stability and steering response on the straight, even in quite strong cross winds, are good. Ride comfort is excellent, and there is extremely efficient damping."

Acceleration figures were taken and the results were as follows: 0–30mph, 5.7-seconds, 40mph 8.5-seconds, 50mph 12.7-seconds, 60mph 17.3-seconds, 70mph 23.8-seconds, 80mph 33.3-seconds, 90mph 49.9-seconds. In Top, 20–40mph took 8.9-seconds and 30–50mph took 9.2-seconds. The standing quarter-mile was covered in 20.8-seconds. All these figures except the 20–40mph time were bettered by *The Autocar's* Mk 1 2.4 tested in 1956, this car reaching 60mph and 80mph in 15.8-and 30.6-seconds respectively, but it is unlikely that the 'used' 2.4 Mk II was

The 2.4 Mk II was more of a home-market model, and was never officially exported to the States. All the usual extras could be ordered for it, though. *Photo: Jaguar Cars*

driven as hard through the gears as the original car was, so the difference may not have been so great.

Purchasers of the 2.4 Jaguar may have saved around £135 on the initial price and undoubtedly paid around 20 percent, or so, a year less for insurance compared with the 3.4, but other running costs were very much the same. Petrol consumption was, in practice, only one or two mpg better, because as *The Autocar* described, the engine was usually working quite hard and nearer to its upper limits than the bigger, lazier 3.4-and 3.8-litre units. As for speed, the 2.4 Mk II could be called slow only in comparison to the far above average performance given by the larger engined Jaguars – amongst other makes of luxury saloon, the 2.4 still represented performance motoring and it took a good car to outrun it, either on acceleration or maximum speed. Owners enjoyed the same high level of interior trim and finish, as there was no differentation between the models in that department.

The Borg Warner automatic gearbox was optional for the 2.4 Mk II as well, but possibly because this diminished both performance and fuel economy, the vast majority of 2.4 Jaguars were delivered with manual transmission – 12 percent or less had the automatic box, compared to more than 20 percent of the larger engined cars.

The B-type head was standardised on all Mk IIs, the 2.4 with Solexes, the 3.4/3.8 with SUs as shown here. In 1964 *Autocar* evaluated 2.4 and 3.4 economy in identical convoy conditions, heavy traffic producing 11/16.3 mpg and motorways 18.6/20.1 mpg in favour of the 2.4. *Photo: Jaguar Cars*

By the end of 1963, the Mk II range had been joined by a new Jaguar, the S-type, which with its independent rear suspension and improved luggage capacity might well have been considered a potential replacement for the Mk II, rather than continuing in parallel production as was the case. But once again, *volume* was Jaguar's aim, and with the S-type sharing much of the Mk II's body tooling, its front suspension and engine, unit costs came down once more; the same applied to its independent rear suspension, which had many components in common with the Mk 10 and 'E' type Jaguars. Even if the Mk II had

been discontinued, the extra number of S-types sold would not have amounted to the *combined* total of Mk IIs and S-types which the factory were producing.

Also, the cars turned out to have sufficiently different characters to justify their separate existences, and to attract customers with different priorities. The Mk II, for instance, continued to attract the sporting driver, the one who required the utmost in performance, and the 3.8 Mk II in particular remained a favourite to the end of its days – Graham Hill drove one long and hard, and when asked why he didn't get an S-type, replied that the Mk II was lighter and therefore faster, and the slightly worse ride didn't bother him. The Mk II was always cheaper as well, especially as there wasn't a 2.4 S-type. But for those who put sheer comfort first, the S-type was the natural choice.

Mk II improvements

Ultimately there was to be a little cross-fertilisation between the two cars, but they always kept their distinct characters. Often in common with the S-type series, minor improvements continued to be made to the Mk II, with the 3.8's oil consumption again being tackled, this time by modified pistons with a chamfer and drain hole below the oil control ring so that oil picked up by the ring could return easily. Two months earlier, in January 1964, a new cast aluminium sump with revised oil pipes and oil pump were fitted to all Mk IIs. The later AUF 301 SU fuel pump, as used on the S-type, was supplied on the Mk II as well from May 1964, and a modified radiator block and fan cowl arrived at the end of the year.

The front suspension received improved wheel swivel grease seals on the top and bottom ball joints in March 1964, these having a nylon washer and bleed hole, the idea being that excess grease passed through the bleed hole and escaped by pushing the nylon washer up, instead of possibly damaging the seals themselves. In practice, a small obstruction could sometimes result in the grease taking the easiest path and exiting through the bleed hole instead of lubricating the ball joint, thereby causing premature wear. The same system was used on the tie-rod joints from that date, and the steering idler assembly was given taper roller bearings. Additionally, grease nipples were introduced to the front hubs on disc-wheeled cars so that it was no longer necessary to dismantle and repack the bearings, and brake disc shields were fitted to reduce the tendency of the inner pads from wearing more quickly than the outer ones.

Perhaps the most important change to occur though was the introduction in September 1965 of the all-synchromesh Jaguar four-speed gearbox, a year after it had made its appearance in the 4.2 'E' type and Mk 10. This gearbox, described in chapter nine, immediately redeemed one of the Mk II's worst features with its light, easy action, much stronger synchromesh (on first gear as

Designs for a new era: sketches for a British Motor Holdings emblem when in 1966 Jaguar combined with the British Motor Corporation to form the new conglomeration. BMC owned Pressed Steel who made Jaguar's bodies and Sir William realised that total independence could not be maintained indefinitely.

well now) and reduced lever travel. A diaphragm clutch came too, with a hydrostatic clutch-operating slave cylinder which compensated for normal wear, though this was deleted in December 1968. Overdrive was still obtainable with the new gearbox of course. The all-synchro box was fitted from the following chassis numbers on:

2.4:	119200 RHD	127822 LHD
3.4:	169341 RHD	180188 LHD
3.8:	234125 RHD	224150 LHD

In round figures, this meant that a couple of thousand RHD Mk IIs of each type, and several hundred LHD, left the factory with all-synchro gearboxes before the car was superseded by the 240 and 340. Needless to say, these late Mk IIs are quite sought-after today. The automatic gearbox and torque converter were revised too in order to improve the change, in June 1965.

Then, in September 1966, came the indignity of plastic upholstery – seat facings from then on were in Ambla, although leather could still be specified at extra cost. The cheapening process was extended to appearance as well; foglights were no longer standard, being replaced by dummy grilles. Jaguar were making sure that, while the Mk II was getting old, it would at least remain relatively cheap.

The last major change to effect the Mk II was the fitting of the Varamatic power steering in July 1967, though this was only seen on a handful of each of the three types because the Mk II was phased out only a few months afterwards. The Marles/Bendix Varamatic steering is fully described in the chapter on the Mk 10, which was the first production car to be fitted with it. As its name suggests, it gave a variable steering ratio ranging from the equivalent

Competitive pricing required some sacrifices of the Mk II; leather upholstery became an extra-cost option, and fog/spotlamps were no longer standard fitments by the autumn of 1966.

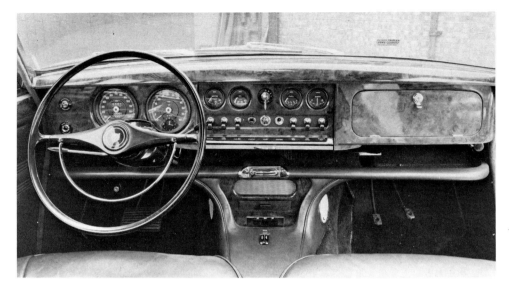

Development of the Mk II might have gone in another direction – towards greater luxury. This is an updated interior produced by the experimental trim shop, after the style of the Mk X or S-type and including parcel shelf, rounded console, and wood inlay for the centre instrument panel. *Photo: Jaguar Cars*

of 4.25 turns in the straight ahead position, to only 2.1 turns by the time the wheels had turned through 16-degrees (or about half full lock); overall ratio was just under 3 turns lock-to-lock, a vast improvement on the previous system's 4-plus turns. A Varamatic-equipped Mk II is a rarity today.

A minor but useful improvement which came in the same month as the new steering was a revised boot lid lock with a new cam, which did away with the embarassing tendency of the Mk II's bootlid to suddenly spring up while on the move.

The 240 and 340 Jaguars

The Mk II proper was made technically obsolete on the announcement of the 240 and 340 Jaguars in September 1967, but new cars were still being sold well into 1968. The slimmed-down, rather more austere 240 and 340 saloons were undoubtedly better and more practical cars in many ways, but some people felt they lacked the 'presence' and character of the Mk II with its assertive bumpers and leather upholstery.

Jaguar's range of saloon cars was, towards the end of

Slimline Mk II: the 340 of 1967 with bumpers of S-type style. Note the new type of hubcap too. At least one 340 was completed to special order with the 3.8-litre power unit.
Photo: Jaguar Cars

1967, becoming rather extended; there was the 420G edition of the Mk 10, the 3.4 and 3.8 S-types, the 420 variation of the S-type which had been introduced in 1966, and all three Mk II models with their different engines - not to mention the 2.5 V8 Daimler version of the Mk II. Much-needed rationalisation was overdue, and, in the form of the XJ6, this was on the way; but not for another year. Meanwhile, the Mk II was given a face-lift, both to modernise it and to keep it competitive in price as new and sophisticated models from other manufacturers began to offer a serious challenge to what was now a 12-year-old design.

Thus the 240 and 340 Jaguars were announced towards the end of September 1967. They looked moderately different from the Mk II, and they *were* moderately different. Instantly noticeable from the outside were the new, slimmer bumpers fore and aft, patterned on those of the S-type. These meant slightly different 'skirts' underneath at each end, while the spot/foglamps were missing from the front, replaced by the dummy grilles like those on the Mk I saloons. New hub caps replaced those used on Jaguars since the Mk V. Inside the car, Ambla plastic took the place of the former leather upholstery, as it had on late Mk IIs when leather became an extra-cost option.

Of the two 'new' models, the 240 was the most technically interesting. Jaguar's engineers had grasped the opportunity to tackle the 2.4's slight power deficiency, and in place of the B-type head was the straight-port 'E' type variety, complete with two HS6 1.75-inch SU carburetters (though with a manually controlled 'mixture' control for cold starting, unlike the 340 which retained the B-type head and auxiliary starting carburetter). A twin-exhaust system was added at the same time, and the result was a very useful increase from 120bhp at 5750rpm to 133bhp at 5500rpm. Bore and stroke remained the same. Improvements in the torque curve came as well, with the peak now 146lb.ft. at 3700rpm instead of

138lb.ft. at the lower rpm of 3000.

Minor engine changes concerned the distributor cap which now had side instead of top entry cables, and a new wax thermostat arrangement which cut off the bypass and thus gave full-flow circulation through the radiator when open. The 240 now had a paper element filter instead of an oil-bath one, and both cars had the latest ribbed camshaft covers.

This enhanced mechanical specification (the all-synchro gearbox was standard as well, of course) was combined with an amazingly low price tag, the basic 240 costing only £1109 without tax, or £1364 with – an increase of only £20 over the original 2.4 of 1956, despite twelve years and a halving of money values! This must enable the 240 to rank as the best Jaguar bargain of all time; no surprise then, that Stuart Bladon of *Autocar* wondered in April 1969 "how long Jaguar can afford to go on producing it." In fact, unbeknown to him, the last 240 had been completed on the 9th of that very month. The 340 was almost as cheap at £1422. In automatic

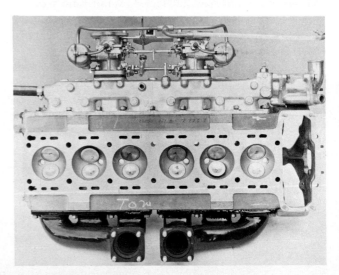

Above: The 240 looked externally just like the 340 Jaguar, but its 2.4-litre engine was given the 'straight-port' cylinder head as used on the 4.2 models. *Photo: Jaguar Cars*

Left: With its new ribbed camshaft covers, the XK engine underwent its biggest change in appearance yet. This is the 240 unit, with two 1.75-inch SU carburetters replacing the Solexes of the old 2.4-litre engine. *Photo: Jaguar Cars*

form, which meant the new Borg Warner Type 35 box, the 240 and 340 actually came with a decrease in price of £16 compared to the previous Mk II 2.4 and 3.4.

The V8 250

Besides the two Jaguars, the Daimler 2.5 V8 was not neglected either in the up-date, and the "V8 250" model was announced a week after the 240 and 340 cars had been made public. Like these, the new 250 had slim bumpers and overriders, and new wheel hubs, but the Daimler retained its foglamps. Mechanically, about the only change to the engine was the provision of separate air filters for each carburetter (previously a single one had been used, positioned over the V-block), giving much easier access to the carburetters, while an alternator was standardised in place of the dynamo. An all-synchro manual gearbox could now be specified if required, with or without overdrive. Marles Varamatic power steering was adopted when power-assistance steering was fitted, the previous type being discontinued.

Inside, the V8 250 now incorporated a style of trim which had previously been seen in the Jaguar 420 (announced in 1966), with a padded roll running across the width of the facia in place of the skull-cracking wooden rail used before, a style continued on the door garnish rails; both door cappings and the vertical side pieces of the dashboard remained in walnut veneer however. Reclining seats were now standard, as was the heated rear window (with warning light on the dashboard alongside the chrome push-pull switch). Total prices for the standard, overdrive and automatic V8 250 cars were £1615, £1660 and £1698 respectively.

Road-testing the 240 Jaguar

Jaguar were now quite confident in allowing a 240 saloon to be tested, *Autocar* publishing their results three weeks before *Motor* released theirs. The former journal tried an overdrive version and while it was found to be considerably quicker than the Mk 1 2.4 tried back in 1956, it was quite rightly pointed out that "what were once very brisk acceleration and a high top speed, can now be matched by several cars with engines of under 2-litres." But at least 100mph was exceeded by a handsome margin, a mean of 106mph being recorded in overdrive top. The sprint to 60mph was achieved in 12.5-seconds, with 80mph coming up in 22.8-seconds.

Unfortunately perhaps, the faster 240 was also thirstier than the 2.4 Jaguars had been, consumption increasing to 18mpg if the engine's willingness to rev was exploited, though a long gentle run did result in 24mpg. The small sacrifice was probably worthwhile though, as "the earlier 2.4 would run out of breath above 80mph and it took a long run to reach maximum speed; by comparison the 240 spurts up to – and cruises at – 100mph with admirable ease and lack of fuss". About the only criticism of the engine was the amount of fan noise above 4000rpm, "which is annoying to a driver who likes to use the gearbox and make the most of the performance."

This 240 was on the optional Dunlop SP 41 radial tyres. "On some sharp irregularities", the magazine reported, "there is the characteristic thump of radials, but Jaguar have done a good job in getting the rubber suspension bushes to absorb most of this. Without testing the adhesion, some of our drivers were not sure they were on radials until they looked, which is a big compliment... It is only by vicious use of the clutch with high revs that the

Old and new V8 Jaguars – the more delicate bumpers of the V8 250 expose more 'skirt' and if anything make the car look higher than the original Daimler V8 model.

back wheels can be made to spin on wet roads and it is impossible to kick the tail round under power."

Thanks to the pruning of bumpers and so on, the 240 weighed the same if not less than the 2.4, turning the scales at 29.4cwt and possessing the most favourable front/rear weight bias of all the Mk II variants – 54.8/44.2. However, it still wasn't enough to counter the type's biggest drawback, the steering – and it wasn't possible to specify power assistance on the 240 either. *Autocar* noted that there was still almost 17cwt (or as much as many smaller cars weighed in total!) over the front wheels, so that steering was both "heavy *and* low geared, which makes parking in tight spaces very wearisome"; it was, however, "quick and very responsive at speed" and gave the car excellent stability in gusty cross-wind situations on the motorway. As for handling, understeer was, as always, the predominant characteristic, and if the tail did attempt to swing out during a tight, second-gear bend, lifting of the inside rear wheel cut back the speed so that understeer once more returned.

The most dated features of the car were thought to be the comparatively high scuttle and shallow windscreen, "especially when peering through the wiper arcs on a dirty winter's day". A minor cause for annoyance was the placing of the handbrake between seat and driver's door, which could get kicked as the driver left the car. It worked very well though, holding the car on a 1-in-3 hill and locking the rear wheels at 30mph used on its own.

Motor published its test at the end of January 1968, the subject being – surprisingly – the 'bottom rung' version of the range, without overdrive. The only extras were radial tyres (£12.12s), heated rear window (£18) and seatbelts (£9. 16s). bringing the as-tested total up to a modest £1405. The car drew what must have been a gratifyingly enthusiastic report for Jaguar to read. It included this paragraph:

> "It is a pity that the praises of the 2.4/240 have been a trifle neglected in the past because the car has much to offer. To begin with, its extremely smooth engine is derived from the larger one by a short throw crankshaft so that it can operate at high rpm at lower stresses. Next there is the price, £1365 for the standard car without overdrive (as tested), and what you get for it. Almost the only cost-cutting expedient adopted in the latest face-lift – and one which few owners are likely to notice – is the use of Ambla leathercloth for the upholstery in place of real leather; in all other respects the 240 remains luxurious and very well equipped."

The lack of an overdrive undoubtedly contributed to an overall mpg of 17.1 – the 4.27 axle replaced the 4.55 ratio on the overdrive cars but was not high enough to compensate for the leisurely 'fifth gear' provided by the Laycock de Normanville device. It also meant that to achieve maximum speed, the engine was taken well into the red sector of the rev counter; this began at 5500rpm which equated with 98mph, so the mean average of

104.8mph was achieved "by considerable over-revving, albeit for no more than a few seconds." The present writer was on the staff of *Motor* at that time, and seems to recall that Jaguar were 'phoned to check that this would be permissible. For this reason *Motor* advised prospective 240 owners intending to use the car for long continental trips to specify the overdrive, well worth the extra £56.

Acceleration was up compared with *Autocar's* 240, as 60mph took only 11.7-seconds as opposed to 12.5, and the 80mph time was faster by 2.3-seconds at 20.5-seconds. These figures matched those of the automatic 3.4 Mk 11 tested by *Motor* in 1961 to within half a second, so the 240 was no sluggard. While giving this performance, the engine was "outstandingly smooth and quiet, better in this respect than most other Jaguars we have tested over the past few years. A subdued breathy hum is its normal song, changing to a satisfying muffled growl if the throttle is opened at, say, 50mph or so in top... Flexibility is another outstanding feature of the engine..."

In view of the general progress made in suspension design during the mid- and late-sixties, it was a little unexpected to find the 240's handling and roadholding praised abundantly; "...all our testers were agreeably surprised at the nimble, responsive handling and the way in which the car could be hustled fast along winding country roads, especially as this agility was allied to outstanding adhesion and roadholding. When 'earholing' on MIRA's test track it was virtually impossible to make the car breakaway in the wet, let alone the dry, the normal behaviour being mild understeer with moderate roll and not much squeal from the SP 41 tyres. It took a sharp second-gear turn, a brutal right foot and a greasy patch on public roads to make the tail swing out, and even then it did so in a gentle and controllable way. Nor was wheelspin easy to provoke, while the live axle...did not hop or tramp." Evidently there was life in the old dog yet!

Needless to say, the exception to all this was the steering. "Despite a steering-box ratio that gives nearly five turns lock-to-lock, the effort required when parking is excessive, and the kindest thing to say of the steering under these conditions is that it develops the muscles." But as previous drivers of the Mk II had found, on the move the car was "quite different", the low ratio not being noticeably obtrusive.

The standard of ride comfort set by the Jaguar S-type and 420 saloons invited odious comparisons with the live-axle 240, but although not rated as outstanding, the test car's ride was still considered "quite acceptable by ordinary standards, being firm and well-damped with a certain amount of pitch and bounce on rough surfaces." Road and wind noise insulation was very good, though opening the front quarterlights or windows provoked a lot of wind roar, this action being "frequently necessary as there is no fresh air ventilation. Even when the engine had warmed up – taking some five- or six-miles of driving

The 240 was relatively cheap to buy and economical to run when new, and happily remains so today; many, such as this well-kept example, are still in active use.

to do so – no warmth could be felt from the heater until some 15-minutes later."

Another old fashioned aspect of the car was the lack of front seat squab adjustment, surprisingly still not offered as standard, and so were the number of chassis points needing grease every 6000 miles – eight in all. Brake performance, as with all Jaguars equipped with discs, could almost be taken as read and gave "firm, progressive retardation at all times." The handbrake gave a very reasonable 0.38g stop but wasn't liked overmuch "because it is very awkwardly placed between the driver's seat and the door, underneath a protruding armrest."

The Jaguar 240 was certainly cheap for what it did and how it did it, but then it needed to be – others were catching-up, particularly now that compact, relatively high-performance cars were coming into vogue. In this country the Rover and Triumph 2000s led the way, the former matching the 240 on price and top speed although not on acceleration (an extra £100-odd bought you the TC version which could). The Triumph – like the Jaguar a

six-cylinder car – also ran the 240 close on acceleration if not top speed, while both the non-Jaguars were much more economical on petrol. They were nicely equipped too and rode and handled well; they probably did take a few sales away from Jaguar, but prestige counts for a lot too, and on that score the Jaguar won every time.

Abroad, ultimately more serious competition came from makes such as BMW, Lancia, and – for different reasons – Volvo. The BMW 2000 saloon gave best to the 240 on maximum speed but easily beat it on acceleration; as a make, BMW were accruing much respect too, but the 2000 was out of direction contention at £1778. The Lancia Fulvia 1.2 GT had the same advantage of a famous name and was good value at around £1300 though it hadn't the room or speed of the 240. Surprisingly, the Volvo 144S virtually matched the Jaguar's acceleration – at least in the lower speed ranges – and could achieve over 95mph; it was leagues behind in refinement though, and cost £40 more.

It needed the resources of the Ford Motor Company to

produce a car which was as fast and at the same time cheaper than the 240; the Zodiac Mk IV matched the 240 on acceleration and top speed and provided much more room and vast acreages of metal all for £1282 – but it was really not in the same ball game when it came to prestige, even if its independent rear suspension gave it a ride very nearly as good as the S-type's. Besides, it more fairly competed with such as Rover's big 3.5 litre saloon, a fast and underrated car in its time.

Autocar investigated the 240 saloon on a long-term basis, running a pre-production example with Mk II-type bumpers from September 1968 to January 1970. It was extremely trouble-free and clocked up 24 000 miles, departing from the staff fleet with its original tyres, battery, brake pads and exhaust system – the SP 41s were not half-worn even then, and had an estimated total life expectancy of more than 35 000 miles. The sole major failures were two clutch replacements, but these were almost certainly due to faulty units as it took an extremely brutal driver to get through a clutch in less than 30 000 miles with any of the Mk II series, and a one-owner car of my acquaintance travelled more than 120 000 miles on its original clutch, despite regular caravan towing.

The regular driver of the car was Stuart Bladon, and as he became tired of the noisy engine fan, had a Kenlowe electric fan substituted, which cut in at about 80 degrees Centigrade – a rise from the normal 70 degrees Centigrade occurred only during a prolonged traffic jam though. One immediate benefit was a rise in top speed from 106mph to 111mph, and it also helped maintain a normal 20-21mpg in fast driving between cities – "it is only in London traffic that there is a disappointing drop to 16 or 17mpg." Oil consumption averaged about 900-miles to the pint.

Particularly without the huge standard pressed-steel fan, the 2.4 engine was quiet and seemingly unstressed – once, a driver forgot to engage overdrive when running at near maximum speed: "None of the three of us in the car noticed that the unfortunate engine was doing 6500rpm at 110mph, the rev counter needle off the scale. Happily it cannot have been for long, and the engine evidently suffered no ill effects. It is a magnificent power unit in every way – smooth, responsive, untemperamental." Normal happy cruising speed was, thought Stuart, 90mph, "since it settles so quietly and effortlessly at this speed" and would still return 20mpg after a motorway journey.

The usual complaint about the heater was made ("the most out-of-date feature of the car"), but the row of identical switches on the dashboard, which some drivers found irritating and occasionally confusing, were approved of, as was the "superb clarity of the instruments...and the pleasing air of quality and refinement about the whole car." The cramped nature of the 240's engine compartment and the contortions needed to reach such items as the adjusting points of the carburetters and distributor aroused much less enthusiasm though – as any 'small' Jaguar owner will confirm!

Road-testing the 340 Jaguar

There were few formal road-tests of the 340 saloon, probably because the 240 caught most of the limelight due to its low price tag. Fortunately for us, though, John Bolster put one through its paces for *Autosport* in February 1968.

The 'economy' specification was noted – "a close inspection reveals that the upholstery no longer comes off the back of cows" – but otherwise Bolster found this manual/overdrive example to perform as well as any 3.4 he'd encountered. The car went from 0-60mph in only 8.8-seconds and reached 100mph in 26.4-seconds – only fractionally more than the original 3.8 Mk II. The 340's maximum speed of 124mph was equally close to that of the overdrive 3.8's, being only 1mph down. It was economical too, averaging around 20mpg.

This 340 was fitted with Dunlop SP41 radial types, which as usual Bolster proceeded to pump up to 35psi for high speed work – "this transformed the steering. Not only did it become far lighter, but the improved responsiveness made it seem higher geared." Nor was there a penalty in the form of road noise from the radials, "except for a slight rumble at low speeds on certain surfaces."

Handling appears to have passed muster, though the understeering characteristics of the car were mentioned in passing, and while stiffer damping would have been preferred by Bolster, "the rear axle does not patter, even under violent acceleration." Heating and demisting were thought "not outstandingly powerful" and better lights would have been appreciated for night driving on the continent – where "one can cruise at 100 or 110mph with little mechanical sound, and the brakes can be used repeatedly from such speeds without any apparent warming up."

Summing up, John Bolster proclaimed: "The Jaguar 340 is a very fast car which is a delight to drive, but is as practical for everyday use as any ordinary vehicle. To the driver and his passengers, it feels, sounds, and looks a very costly car, and everything about it is rich except its price. Once again, I am astonished at the Jaguar miracle of value for money."

The 340 saloon succumbed to progress sooner than the 240; the final example being completed at the end of September 1968 – not many had been built, just 2265

RHD versions and a mere 535 LHD ones. The 240 outlasted its bigger-engined sister by some seven-months, the last of all the Mk II series of cars being built in April 1969, the 3716th RHD to be made; the rarer LHD 240 (only 730 of these were built) had finished production a month before.

The Mk II Estate Car

Back in the late 'fifties, works racing drivers Duncan Hamilton and Mike Hawthorn considered that a Jaguar estate car would be a most useful vehicle, and Duncan – having already had two Mk VIIs converted privately – tried to interest Sir William in the idea, but the 'old man' said he wasn't convinced there was a big enough market for it. So the two D-type drivers decided to go ahead on their own and drew up various plans for an estated based on the then-current Mk I 3.4, with motor racing artist Roy Nockolds being brought in to advise on styling. But then came Mike Hawthorn's death, and the project was postponed.

It was revived when the Mk II entered production, and this time bore fruit – a 3.8 Mk II was converted into a true estate car with opening rear door by Jones Bros. (Coachbuilders) Ltd., to a basic design sketched out by the Nockolds brothers. So, while Jaguar Cars did acquire the car shortly afterwards, the only Mk II estate car was not a direct factory project; it did, however, perform stirling service for the company as a service car, following the works race and rally cars about Europe. Andrew Whyte remembers driving the "County" as it was called, and recalls meeting it during the 1962 *Tour de France,* driven by Mike McDowell and Ted Brookes in its role as support car to the 3.8 Mk IIs competing. Fortunately the car survives today (in private hands), but whether a production Jaguar "County" would have been a commercial success must be a matter for conjecture....

Modifying the Jaguar Mk II

Much of what is written about the Mk I saloon in the previous chapter also applies to the Mk II in this respect; tuning Mk IIs was very popular during the first half of the 'sixties in particular, for road use as well as for racing, with a number of private concerns offering performance parts for the 3.8. Most well known of these was Coombs of Guildford.

Coombs had, of course, considerable experience of making Mk IIs go faster through their racing of "BUY 1", the company's famous 3.8 racing saloon; this expertise was put at the disposal of customers who wished to have their own cars modified – this could be done on a new car supplied by Coombs, or on cars brought in for the purpose. Exactly what work was carried out was up to the

The 'County' Jaguar estate, built by Jones Bros (Coachbuilders) Ltd. Although not a factory project, it was used quite extensively as a works support car during the mid-sixties (in the background, coincidentally, there is a 'Farnham' Ford Zephyr estate, which also was a private venture).

customer, so it is difficult to say what constitutes a 'Coombs Mk II', but the basic specification might read as follows, being taken from a Coombs' invoice of 1963:

"Removing engine and gearbox from chassis, dismantling engine, fitting high compression pistons and machining cylinder head to give 9.5:1 compression ratio, specially balancing crankshaft, conrods and clutch assy., fitting lightened flywheel, dismantling cylinder head for full gas flowing and attention to manifold and valve seats. Fitting open trumpet carburetter intakes. Re-assembling all parts and re-installing engine unit into chassis. Running engine testing and tuning ... £189.10s.0d

Supplying and fitting HD8 2-inch SU carbs
... £40.0s.0d

Supplying and fitting new high ratio steering box giving 3 1/2 turns lock-to-lock
... £20.0s.0d

Making up and fitting cold air intake to carbs complete with polished air spreader
... £35.0s.0d

Supplying and fitting Vari-flow adjustable shock absorbers all round
... £17.10s.0d

Supplying and fitting hand-made silencers with modified tail pipes of straight-through pattern
... £28.0s.0d

Modifying rear wheel arches deleting valances
... £35.0s.0d

Supplying and fitting additional long range 9.4 gallon fuel tank in front end of boot compartment
... £62.10s.0d

Supplying and fitting 'E' type wooden rim steering wheel with centre horn push

Supplying and fitting manually controlled choke switch
... £1.10s.0d

Strengthening rear spring location
... £10.0s.0d

Supplying and fitting high rate front springs
... £14.0s.0d

The above covers many of the popular modifications which keen owners carried out on their Mk IIs; stiffening the front suspension certainly made the car much more responsive to the helm at the expense of only a slight deterioration in the ride. This in conjunction with the

Left: Definitely not a Coombs Mk II – Bob Jankel of Panther West Winds had this Mk II rebuilt to his own specification around 1976, complete with 4.2 engine and wide wheels.

Below: The 'custom' craze has not ignored the Mk II, even though its adherents are more prone to borrowing Jaguar independant rear ends for their projects – this is a pick-up version of a Mk II saloon, seen at a recent JDC rally.

high ratio steering box made the Mk II a much more responsive car to drive even if, as already noted, town parking required considerable effort at the helm!

The Mk II in retrospect

The Mk I/II Jaguars brought the company a level of production undreamed of previously, and in these terms it was the XJ6 of 1968 which was the true successor of the type. But for all its merits and technical superiority, the XJ6 has never managed to quite fill the gap left by the Mk II, almost solely due to its length and bulk; perhaps the two-door coupe of 1975 came nearest to it, but the lack of a true successor to the Mk II is certainly felt by enthusiasts. A new, smaller, Jaguar saloon may be in the company's model programme but at the time of writing it is no more than a twinkle in the eye at Browns Lane. We shall see!

Return to the Mk II accompanied by a late-eighties set of automotive standards and you will take time to adapt – the car looks modestly dimensioned from outside, but drive it and you'll find it vastly less manoeuvrable than the current Jaguar saloon. The steering – quite heavy, yet low geared – will probably be the biggest disappointment, as will be the car's understeering tendencies. The Mk II is not a car to be guided by gentle movement of the wrists; to get the best out of it requires a forceful input from the driver, fairly large movements of the wheel and throttle pedal being needed to overcome the car's initial understeering sogginess. Stiffer front springs and good quality, harder dampers work wonders though, and are to be recommended to the keener driver. Straight line performance and cruising ability is still impressive, however, at least with the 3.4- and 3.8-litre cars.

The fortunes of the Mk II improved markedly as the eighties drew to an end, enthusiasts 'rediscovering' Jaguar's sporting compact with delight; and, with values increasing rapidly (a top-quality restored Mk II can fetch anything between £15,000 and £40,000!) it has become worthwhile at last to invest in proper renovation, a situation which has not yet quite come about for the Mk VII/VIII/IX series, or indeed the Mk X, S-type and 420 – though it must come soon.

In this context one cannot fail to mention the pioneers of total Mk II Jaguar restoration in Britain, the Vicarage Classic Car Company. This West Midlands concern bit on the bullet and advertised rebuilt Mk IIs at a price which reflected the true cost of carrying out such work: in the region of £30,000 upwards. The gamble, if such it was, has paid off with full order books, mainly from overseas customers (who in any case had in recent years tended to spend more on old Mk IIs than did enthusiasts in the home market), though a notable recent customer at the time of writing has been Tom Walkinshaw. For this sort of money you end up with a better-than-new Mk II, incorporating a vast number of new components and, of course, a completely new hide and veneer interior. Interestingly, improvements such as adapted XJ-S power steering, five-speed gearbox and coil-sprung rear axle are optional, in a largely successful attempt to make the old car handle and feel more like a modern Jaguar. Meanwhile, other restoration firms – and countless enthusiasts all over the world – are ensuring the continued survival of this conceptually brilliant Jaguar through their efforts in workshop and garage. So the Mk II is very much still around to be enjoyed by those who appreciate a high-performance, modestly dimensioned, 'family' classic Jaguar.

Chapter Nine

The S≈type and 420 saloons

There can be a few big saloons in which the ride is as good as in the Jaguar S-type and driver and passengers can travel over the most terrible surfaces without having to bother what the wheels are doing.

Autocar, March 19, 1965

As *R&T*'s first long-term road test car, the Jaguar 420 perhaps spoiled us for anything else.

Road & Track, July 1968

The introduction of the Mk X Jaguar in 1961 had the side-effect of making the well-established Mk II saloons look slightly old-fashioned in the suspension department, and ever since the appearance of the big saloon with its advanced independent rear end, there had been speculation that a new, smaller, car might appear with similar suspension to replace the Mk II. Appear it did, almost exactly two years later in October 1963, which means that work must have started on developing the new 'S-type', as it was called, almost as soon as the flagship Mk X had itself been launched.

However, the S-type series did not replace the well-loved Mk II, but instead was intended as an intermediate car between that and the rather gigantic Mk X; larger, and with the relative complexity of independent rear suspension, the S-type was inevitably more expensive and a little slower than the Mk II, thus providing two very good reasons for keeping the latter. As it also used many components from the Mk II, the old argument of unit cost reduction arose again, because dropping the Mk II would not have had the effect of doubling the sales of the S-type. It all appeared very logical.

The S-type was certainly based on the Mk II Jaguar, but it was far from being simply a Mk II with a new front and rear grafted on - even the roofline was different on the new car. But of course the most substantial alterations had taken place aft of the rear seat pan, where a complete redesign of the shell had been necessary to carry the new

suspension - as explained in chapter eight, this part of the Mk II's bodyshell was almost entirely unstressed, with the springs being cantilevered from box members in front of the axle, and it could not therefore be expected to take the independent rear suspension unit without substantial modification.

This strengthening was achieved, and the necessary mounting points provided, by continuing the box sections which had formerly contained the Mk II's leaf springs over the wheel arches and under the boot floor to the back of the car. The floor, double skinned at the rear, was welded to these box sections to form a complete, very strong unit; strength was added to the floor panel by deep ribbing, and through the integral spare wheel well (normally covered by a lift-out section as for the Mk II). This was placed centrally however, and petrol was now contained in two separate tanks installed in the extended inner rear wings of the car, protected from luggage stowed in the boot by detachable trim panels.

Each tank contained 7-gallons, which was a slight improvement over the total 13-gallon capacity of the Mk II's petrol tank which had lived under the floor. Fuel was brought to the engine by a separate electric SU AUF 301 pump for each tank, there being a switch on the dashboard so that the driver could draw from either right- or left-hand tank. The tanks were not interconnected however, which was helpful should one spring a leak! This system also halved the chances of a total fuel supply failure.

The rear suspension itself is fully described in chapter ten, and shared most of the components used in the Mk X and the 'E' type, though unlike the latter no rear anti-roll bar was fitted. The lengths of the driveshafts and lower links were midway between those of the wider Mk X and narrower 'E' type, giving a rear track of 4ft. 6.13in. – just over an inch more than the Mk II thanks to 5.5-inch instead of 5-inch rim steel wheels; wire wheels on the S-type resulted in a track which was narrower by 1.25in.

The latest Dunlop Mk III disc brakes were fitted, inboard of course at the rear, with a self-adjusting handbrake mechanism. As on the other 'independent' Jaguar models, the entire suspension was contained in a sub-frame which was secured to the body by four V-section rubber mountings thus providing an excellent degree of insulation from road noise and vibration. Longitudinal radius arms running from the lower suspension links to mounting points on the channel members in front of the suspension provided fore-and-aft location.

S-type bodyshell prototype – look closely and you can see the joins! These are particularly visible below the rear window and on the rear wings.
Photo: Jaguar Cars

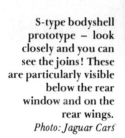

Rolling 'chassis' prepared for a European coachbuilder shows S-type construction well, including the pannier tanks each with its own fuel pump contained within the elongated tail. Outer sill skin has been omitted to show the main wiring harness.
Photo: Jaguar Cars

Upturned view of the S-type's independent rear suspension showing the twin coil-spring/damper units, bridge subframe, and the lower tubular wishbones to which are attached the trailing radius arms and big aluminium hub-carriers.
Photo: Jaguar Cars

The outer body pressings of the car were of course different from the rear door backwards, where the general shape resembled that of the Mk X; as with that car, the wheel cut-outs were very low and the Mk II's detachable spats had gone. Besides holding the wing-mounted petrol tanks, the new dimensions housed a considerably larger boot, the capacity being increased from 12- to 19cu.ft. The rear bumper was of a much slimmer section than the Mk II's, and the rear lights were contained in an extension of the rear wings instead of separate plated housings. The number plate/reversing lamp housing looked similar to the Mk II's but was in fact a different casting, and incorporated the bootlid release. Overall, the S-type was some 7-inches longer than the Mk II thanks to its new tail, but still more than a foot shorter than the Mk X.

The opportunity had been taken to introduce a new roofline, and the S-type's roof panel was longer and flatter than the Mk II's, the extra length being accommodated by a more upright rear window. This didn't actually increase the maximum headroom inside, but did maintain the height much further back, which in conjunction with a thinner, more steeply raked rear seat squab, provided more room for the passengers. The use of a new foam-back Nylon headlining which adhered directly to the steel roof also helped.

At the front of the S-type, a rather more straight forward restyling exercise had been carried out, with no structural changes underneath. The sidelights had disappeared along with their blisters from the tops of the wings, and were now contained at the bottom of each wing alongside separate indicator lights, which were let-in to the wing and followed the curvature round so that they were also visible from the side too. The headlight 'pods' were now extended past the light units to give an eyebrow effect, and the fog lamps underneath were set more deeply into the front of the wings. The radiator grille was modelled on the Mk II's, but had a thicker surround and centre strip. Slim bumpers and overriders matching those at the rear of the car finished off the revisions, which were topped as before by the Jaguar mascot on the bonnet.

Top Left: S-type body mock-up with the revised nose and its cowled headlights, recessed spotlamps, new grille and wrap-round flashers *(á la* Mk X) grafted onto the Mk II shell. *Photo: Jaguar Cars*

Top right: Rear of S-type prototype showing the new rear lights, slim bumpers, and extended boot lid with moulding. *Photo: Jaguar Cars*

Left: S-type prototype next to a standard Mk II, illustrating the frontal differences which came with the new model; under the skin though, engine and front suspension were shared. *Photo: Jaguar Cars*

About the only mechanical change under the bonnet area was the new power steering – at last Jaguar had taken note of the complaints over those unnecessary 4.3 turns lock-to-lock which came with the power assistance on the Mk II. The optional power steering on the S-type – still Burman – had much higher gearing which required only 3.5 turns of the wheel, and had a larger operating ram. An even more interesting advance was the link between the input shaft and the hydraulic valve; this took the form of a torsion bar which introduced a pre-determined load between movement of the wheel and the opening of the valve, increasing the degree of sensitivity at the wheel.

Engine and transmission choice for the S-type was as for Mk II except that the 2.4 power unit really would have been stretched to cope with the extra 3cwt. and so wasn't made available. Customers therefore had the option of 3.4 and 3.8 engines to the same specification as the Mk II, and automatic or manual transmission, with overdrive an optional extra. Final drive ratios were as before too – 3.54 for automatic or the standard manual gearbox, 3.77 for the overdrive cars. Roadwheel diameter remained at 15-inches, but rim width was increased by 0.5-inch to 5.5-inches as already mentioned. Dunlop RS5 covers were the standard tyre fitting, size 6.40 x 15.

The interior of the S-type was still very much 'Jaguar', but leaned more on the Mk X than the Mk II for inspiration, having a shallow but full width parcel shelf under the facia and a new, rounded centre console which contrasted with the sharp angular affair in the Mk II. The actual dash panel and instrumentation was similar to both cars, though with an all-wood finish. As on the Daimler 2.5 V8 launched a year before, the front seats were more of a bench-type than those in the Mk II, almost meeting in the middle. They had a new form of adjustment by swinging links instead of conventional runners, whereby the front of the seat was lowered in an arc and the back raised when the seat was adjusted forward.

Front suspension of the S-type was subframe mounted as for the Mk II, the frame also carrying the improved power-steering box (where this option was specified). *Photo: Jaguar Cars*

Engine bay of a 3.8 S-type – much as for the Mk II with big AC air-filter box. Note power steering fluid reservoir at bottom right, below heater box covered with sound insulating material. *Photo: Motor*

About the only feature lacking in the S-type was fitting of picnic tables in the back of the front seat squabs – "we doubt if the absence of folding tables will worry many owners" commented *Autocar*, probably quite rightly. The front seats were equipped with a reclining facility as

Rear interior of the S-type – note absence of picnic tables in front seat squabs. Room was also increased by a thinner rear seat squab. *Photo: Motor*

standard though, and each had its own centre armrest. Also, with no tables to interfere, the front seat squabs could have open frames which permitted the use of thinner upholstery and thus squeezed another inch or so out of the interior dimensions. Further space was made available to the rear seat passengers by a thinner rear seat squab too, reduced in thickness by 2-inches; it was also reclined a further 1.5-inches back, headroom being maintained by the new roofline and rear window angle. New armrests on the rear doors incorporated both an ashtray and a useful magazine or map pocket.

So that was the S-type. More manageable than the Mk X, more comfortable than the Mk II, it was aimed at yet another group of potential Jaguar purchasers: businessmen, probably, but ones who didn't require either the boardroom space of the Mk X or the lightning acceleration of the Mk II, yet appreciated high performance and the fact that this and the comfort and stability of a good independent rear suspension had now been encapsulated by Jaguar in a body of pleasant design but compact dimensions. Those who bought the new variant soon discovered that little was lost in terms of journey times compared with the ostensibly quicker 3.8 Mk II, yet much was gained in terms of ride quality and handling.

Testing the S-type in America

An important intended market for the new car was, needless to say, the United States, where the S-type's superior ride and increased luggage space could be

expected to appeal very strongly. *Road & Track* formed their opinion of Jaguar's new compact during 1964 and published their thoughts in October of that year. They tested a 3.8 model (the only engine size imported there), equipped with the Borg Warner DG automatic gearbox as most of the S-types were.

The performance figures revealed that the 3.8 S-type almost exactly equalled a 3.4 Mk II in straight line acceleration, given that both cars had the same type of transmission. *Road & Track's* figures from rest to 50, 60 and 80mph were 9-, 11.5- and 20.7-seconds respectively, which compared very well with the times recorded by *Motor's* automatic 3.4 of 9-, 11.9- and 20-seconds for the same speeds – virtually a matching set within experimental error, with perhaps the Mk II having a slight edge towards the top end. It was obviously a case of the S-type's extra power being offset by increased weight (33.3cwt as opposed to 30.25cwt) and, no doubt, a slightly less efficient shape thanks to the headlight 'eyebrows' and longer tail. Top speed of the 3.8 S-type was recorded as 116mph at 5400 on the 3.54 axle ratio, 4mph down on the Mk II's maximum as shown in *Motor's* test of the similarly geared 3.4.

As for the appearance of the car, *Road & Track* had mixed feelings. "We weren't wholly convinced that the proportions of the car are improved by the longer rear end and increased overhang – we always admire the taut, compact look of the 2.4 sedan that came out in 1956 – but certainly the changes that result from the alterations more than make up for it. In addition to the increase in sheer volume...the luggage space is now completely uncluttered

Left-hand drive S-type – the model was quite popular abroad and this example is fitted with the chrome wire wheels which were often specified in the United States.
Photo: Jaguar Cars

S-type facia was a mixture of Mk X and Mk II – centre panel was veneered instead of black leather-grain as in the Mk II, while the new console and parcel shelf also followed Mk X practice. *Photo: Jaguar Cars*

and not even those used to Detroit car trunks would find the difference worth complaining about.'' So practicality wins out. Other than the bodyshell changes, the adoption of independent rear suspension was rated the most important improvement and helped make an outstanding car:

> ''The suspension is very good indeed and the body roll that appears considerable when viewed from the outside is almost unnoticed from the driver's seat as the wheels tend to stay firmly on the ground and the limited-slip differential and the independent rear suspension assure good traction under all but the most hopeless circumstances. It is difficult to fault the handling as the servo-assisted steering is precise, the suspension is superior to almost any sedan you can think of, the power is adequate and the big disc brakes are a pure delight.''

That the car's interior remained strictly traditional Jaguar, though, was definitely approved of: ''The interior of the S-type reflects Jaguar's reputation as a builder of luxury cars. The upholstery is fine English hide, the carpeting is sensually deep and all the facia and window trim is in that perfectly finished walnut veneer that no one has yet been able to duplicate in plastic...'' Likewise, the comprehensive array of properly calibrated dials aroused

admiration and respect: ''... the instrumentation doesn't attempt to offer the driver the sterile comfort of the warning-light world where drivers cannot be trusted to observe and comprehend the meaning of a well designed instrument or gauge.''

The only note of warning sounded in the test revolved, inevitebly, around servicing. ''As we have pointed out before'', the journal wrote, ''Jaguar builds complex automobiles that require expert (and sometimes expensive) service and repair. It seems unlikely that the S-type, sharing so many components with the other models, will be any different in this respect. Extended interval maintenance has been instituted for oil changes (3000 mi) and chassis lubrication (6000 mi), it is true, but no one who buys an S-type should expect it to continue running indefinitely without expert attention.''

Having said that, *Road & Track* closed its test by declaring that: ''At a selling price of **$6000**, the S-type Jaguar, like its companion models from Coventry, must be one of the best buys in the luxury car field – and offers assured driving pleasure to the discriminating purchaser.'' Which is almost as complimentary as its opening epigram: *''When cars with better grace-space-pace are built, Jaguar will probably build them.''*

282

S-type saloon in profile – same wheelbase as the Mk II but seven-inches longer and with more interior and luggage compartment room. Metallic finishes like this metallic "golden sand" were very popular with customers.

Road-testing the S-type at home

In Britain, *Autocar* carried out its first full test of an S-type saloon in March 1965, by which time the car had been given the new and infinitely superior all-synchromesh gearbox – this had been available as an optional extra from December 1964, and was eventually standardised in March of the following year. The car aroused very similar feelings to those displayed by *Road & Track's* writer: "In these days when we are surrounded by plastics and shiny metal it is pleasant to slip back to the days of gracious living and a rich atmosphere of polished woods, leather and deep carpets." The journal went on to define the S-type's character: "The Jaguar S-type is a car which stands on its own, between family transport and executive limousine. It seems tailor-made for the man who likes to drive himself, yet wants a car which will look right anywhere, be it in a farmyard or outside a luxury hotel. As with looks, the Jaguar also has a dual road personality, being able to glide along in crowded city streets or tear down a Route Nationale in under a day for a month in the south of France."

When it came to hard facts, *Autocar* was equally generous with its praise. The gearbox was, of course, rated as a "vast improvement", and the 3.8-litre engine, "now getting on for 17-years old...still performs its duties with terrific urge when needed." This meant 0 - 60mph in 10.4-seconds, 80mph in 17.6-seconds, and the 'ton' in 38.5-seconds – a little slower than an *automatic* 3.8 Mk II, particularly in the higher speed ranges where the Mk II reached 80mph in 16.9-seconds and 100mph in 28.2-seconds. Maximum speed was 121.5mph for the over-drive S-type (rev. limited to 105mph in direct top), which was slightly better than the automatic Mk II but a few mph down on the manual version; at this speed the engine was only turning over at about 4700rpm.

This particular S-type appeared to be very thirsty, recording one of the highest overall fuel consumption figures of any Jaguar road tested up to the early V12 engined cars – 12.8mpg. The consumption varied a great deal, said *Autocar*, with open road or even traffic driving giving around 17mpg, "while hard driving on motorways, with long bursts at well over 100mph, gave a consumption of around 12.5mpg". However, this overall figures does seem a little excessive, especially as *Motor* obtained 15.4mpg overall from the same car (EDU 428C) six-months later. *Road & Track* found that their automatic 3.8 S-type returned 14-17mpg.

The new suspension had certainly improved the ride, although a direct parallel with the Mk II wasn't drawn by *Autocar*. "There can be few big saloons in which the ride is as good as in the Jaguar S-type and passengers can travel over the most terrible surfaces without having to bother what the wheels are doing. The all-independent suspension is not spongy or woolly, yet absorbs bumps, dips and pot holes with almost contemptuous ease. But the driver

never 'loses touch' with the road surface and he remains in complete control. One of the toughest tests on a big car like this is driving on ice and snow-covered roads; provided one does not get too power-happy, the S-type will keep moving when all about are slithering and sliding."

Dunlop SP 41 radial tyres were fitted as standard by this time, "and they give excellent grip. Their radial ply construction does make them transmit small jars and bumps to the chassis, but not to an annoying degree." Power assisted steering was also fitted to the car tested. "The word, 'assisted' is used in its proper sense here, for the system used on the Jaguar leaves the driver in full command of the car, without any sense of being 'taken over' by the hydraulics. At first there is a tendency to use more lock than is necessary to take the car through bends, so light is the pressure needed."

As for interior fitments, the front seats were thought to look more comfortable than they were, largely because they didn't offer much support during fast cornering. But in the rear of the car, "the seats are well shaped with plenty of room for feet to be stretched", so the scrimping and saving of half-inches here and there had paid off. "Furthermore, the rear doors open to expose the whole of the seat, so that exits and entries can be made with dignity."

The instruments and layout of controls was considered "almost ideal", and the new heating and ventilation system appeared to be adequate. "On the centre console,

Interior of an automatic S-type, with console carrying just the heater controls. Note front door trim, with larger map/newspaper flap and smaller grab-handle than the Mk II. *Photo: Jaguar Cars*

below the wide but rather awkward-to-get-at parcel shelf, are the heater controls. Three pushbuttons operate the 'essential services' of the heating – air inlet and heat. A quadrant slide regulates the heat output to a not-very-fine degree. Each side of this quadrant are chromium plated knurled knobs which direct air either to the screen or feet; rear seat passengers have air ducted to their feet from vents under the front seats. A two-speed booster fan is used, and is almost silent on its slow settings." The efficient heated rear screen was much appreciated.

Motor tried the 3.8 S-type in August 1965. Performance testing produced much the same figures as had been recorded in *Autocar* a few months before, with 60mph arriving in 10.2-seconds, and 80mph in 17.1-seconds. Maximum speed was 121.1mph, and as already mentioned, fuel consumption was much better at 15.4mpg overall, with a calculated 'touring' consumption of 19.8mpg. As for the general behaviour of the S-type, *Motor* was more enthusiastic even than *Autocar* had been:

"The ride, probably unexcelled by any other European car, is obtained without most of the disadvantages common to soft springs, for the relatively roll-free cornering ability is of a very high order. With one design Jaguar have proved that independent rear suspension is as suited to the executive saloon as it is to the sporting 'E' type, conferring on each the right properties in the right proportions. ...The car does not set out to be a four-seater 'E' type, and indeed it is not so fast as the lighter 3.8 Mk II, but the extra weight has been well distributed from the outside world, and the overall feel of the car is such that it would probably lose nothing to either on any non-motorway journey and be completely untiring whatever the distance."

About the only deterrent to continuous high speed motoring was, considered *Motor*, the car's petrol consumption. Only at over 100mph did wind noise and some engine noises begin to "rise above an unobtrusive rush." On acceleration, the journal found that as expected the manual gearbox car was considerably quicker than their previous automatic test car off the mark, reaching 50mph in 7.5-seconds instead of 8.5, "and is thus capable of leaving behind all but a few cars of more sporting pretensions. On the average minor road this power is a real advantage for quick safe overtaking on short straights that would leave lesser cars with no safety margin, and the easy swervability of the Jaguar is a useful compliment." As for steady-speed cruising, 3850rpm in overdrive top represented "a particularly effortless 100mph...at which the car is reassuringly steady in both dry and wet conditions, the latter with a long trailing plume of spray which is a tribute to the road wiping properties of the standard Dunlop SP41s."

Once again, the smaller-engined version of a Jaguar model was not released for testing by the major journals, although fortunately we can again thank *Autocar* for putting a used 3.4 S-type through the routine and thus providing us with *some* figures from which conclusions can be drawn. The car in question was a well-kept, low-mileage one owner 1967 example with just over 21 000 miles on the clock and an all-synchro gearbox. It was noted, however, that the engine seemed slightly out of tune, so that it can be assumed that a factory road-test car could have improved a little on the following times – 60mph in 13.9-seconds, 80mph in 25-seconds, and 90mph in 35.3-seconds. Judging from the known

Motor's road-test 3.8 S-type in wintry conditions; with its 'independent' rear end and limited-slip differential traction in such conditions was rarely a problem with the S-type Jaguar.
Photo: Motor

difference between the automatic 3.4 Mk II and 3.8 Mk II saloons to 60mph (about 2-seconds in favour of the latter), one could have expected the 3.4 S-type to reach that speed in about 12.5-seconds – probably a change of plugs and points plus a check on the timing would have regained that 'lost' second or so.

As with the Mk II range, the lack in cubic capacity of the smaller engined model was hardly noticed by the average driver, and even a fast driver would find the occasion rare when he missed the extra 339cc provided by the 3.8 S-type. The same smoothness and flexibility was shared by both 3.4 and 3.8 versions, with little difference in petrol consumption. By any standards, the S-type was a fast car and the only British four-seater car capable of outrunning it was probably the Mk II – a quick survey of the mid-sixties market soon reveals the pecking order in this respect.

Only the far more expensive Aston Martin DB5 could both out-accelerate and out-run the 3.8 S-type, but one would hardly describe the Aston as a full four-seater with 12-inches less leg-room in the back than the Jaguar. The 3.3-litre Vauxhall Cresta was only a couple of seconds adrift up to 60mph but was hardly in the same class as the Jaguar, and anyway could only just make the 'century'; the Ford Zodiac Mk III fell into the same category, so it was necessary to venture abroad to come up with any rival on a performance/space basis. The Mercedes 300SE saloon was magnificently built but could only keep up with the 3.8 S-type in the lower speed ranges, and its top speed was at least 10mph down on the Jaguar's; handling and ride were probably inferior too, and as for price, at £3890 it was no less than £2000 more than the S-type! In Germany though, the price difference was less marked.

To enthusiasts in the United States, the 3.8 S-type's performance was by no means exceptional, although it was easily as quick as the average American sedan. But when it came to the true 'muscle cars' with all the power options, there was no contest; the years extending up to 1968 (when pollution and safety requirements took their toll on bhp) represented the golden age of the accelerative American automobile, and you could buy 'off the shelf' cars which had a truly prodigious performance.

Motor tested the hottest production Ford Mustang available at the end of 1964, one of the still-new 'personal' cars with which the big US manufacturers tried to woo the customer who wanted something a little smaller and more individual than the average sedan. It had almost exactly the same wheelbase as the S-type, but was actually 6-inches shorter overall at 15ft. 1in; the interior was rather more restricted though, and the car could offer neither the luxurious leather comfort of the Jaguar nor its Old English character. The Mustang was incredibly cheap in the States, but the performance of the 'top option' models was firmly in the 'E' type class.

The 271bhp, 4884cc 9:1 cr V8 Mustang could reach 60mph in 7.6-seconds, 80mph in 12.5-seconds, and 100mph in 19.7seconds (the 3.8 S-type took 23.5-seconds to achieve 90mph); the standing quarter mile – the real yardstick by which the American enthusiast judged things – was covered in 15.2-seconds, compared to 17.1 for the S-type. But this was only the beginning – by 1967, cars such as the 375bhp Dodge Coronet and 425bph Dodge Hemi-Charger were returning quarter-mile times of 14.8- and 14.17-seconds straight out of the showroom, which

S-type on a continental cruise – and few other cars in Europe or elsewhere could match it for such activities. Its better ride and greater luggage accomodation made the S-type an even better car than the Mk II for long-distance travel.
Photo: Jaguar Cars

Pleasant re-interpretation of the S-type by Bertone, exhibited in 1966. Group picture shows Sir William with Sergei Bertone and (centre) Dr G. Tarquini at Geneva in 1966 — the car entered limited production under the auspices of the latter and became known as the "Tarquini". Under-bonnet picture shows the car's engine installation, with air-conditioning pump and heat exchanger. Accessability seems much improved over the standard model!

was considerably quicker than the current 4.2 'E' type; and they were almost 17ft. long and weighed up to 37cwt!

To redress the balance a little though, it must be said that in other than a straight line on a good surface, these monsters were extraordinarily inept and often quite frightening to drive quickly over mixed roads, and were almost unusable in the wet. If you ordered the 'heavy duty suspension pack' the ride became very harsh with the whole car shuddering over bad corrugations, and while disc brakes on the front wheels at least were becoming available, they were seldom able to cope with consistently hard braking from high speeds. An S-type or Mk II would feel a real sports car in comparison, able to romp away from the Detroit machines on a road with a goodly number of 60 - 90mph bends.

The standard-engined American family sedan was, of

287

Frua also re-bodied the S-type during the mid-sixties, with a two-door design similar to Bertone's, except for the frontal treatment which dispensed with a recognisable 'Jaguar' radiator grille.

course, generally even worse when it came to 'roadability'; great areas of overhung metal wobbling along on over-soft, under-damped springs with feel-less power-steering of umpteen turns lock-to-lock, and heavily over-servoed brakes which might fade to nothingness after two hard applications from 70mph. 'Primary safety' (the ability of a car to avoid trouble through controllability and roadholding) didn't appear to be a phrase known to the American automobile manufacturer much before 1970. Unfortunately, the vast majority of North American drivers never sampled anything better, and thus had no knowledge at all of the joys of a responsive, sure-footed, nimble European thoroughbred; they were no doubt genuinely puzzled why a few daring individuals risked the drawbacks of an expensive imported car like the Jaguar. To drive the S-type today, with its antiquated power steering and roly-poly suspension, one might look askance at the descriptions "responsive" and "nimble", but a few minutes behind the wheel of a typical 1967 American six-seater would be quite enough to convince the sceptic!

The S-type went through very few changes during its life, and most of these were shared with the Mk II, so the revisions which came in the autumn of 1967 were the first to substantially effect the car. They came at the same time as the transmutation of the Mk II into the 240/340, and with much the same objective – to reduce cost and so make the car both easier to produce and more competitive in price.

The changes were not so marked as with the Mk II; the same mechanical specifications and the "3.4" and "3.8" designations remained (the S-type was the only Jaguar now powered by the 3.8 unit), and the price reductions

were effected by eliminating the twin foglamps which were previously each side of the grille, substituting Ambla for leather upholstery, and changing from pile to tufted carpeting. The standard transmission (non-overdrive) 3.4 S-type now cost £1641 with tax (£108 cheaper), and the standard 3.8 £1741 (£103 cheaper).

The 420 Jaguar

For those whose priority was unashamed luxury, there was always the Jaguar 420 saloon to fall back on, or its even more comprehensively equipped stablemate, the Daimler Sovereign. These had been introduced in October 1966, adding further to a range which already included the three Mk IIs, the two S-types, the Mk X, the 2.5-litre V8 'Daimler', and finally the real Daimlers in the shape of the Majestic Major saloon or limousine; all this at a time when most manufacturers were rationalising their production and "tightening the economic belt" as *Autocar* put it.

The new 420 was based directly on the S-type but was distinguished by an entirely new front end: a completely new bonnet, radiator grille, headlight and front wing arrangement had been installed, the forward-sloping front panel strongly reminiscent of the Mk X. There were changes under the bonnet, too, because the 420 was powered by a new version of the 4.2 XK engine (from which it derived its name), this appearing for the first time with two instead of three HD8 SUs on its straight-port head. These were carried on a new inlet manifold with both water passages and balance pipe cast in. The engine was rated at 245bhp rather than the 265bhp quoted for

Left & bottom left: **The first 420 Jaguar, more or less as for production except that the dummy air vents under the inner pair of headlamps are missing.** *Photos: Jaguar Cars*

The 4.2-litre version of the XK engine, with new manifold and just two HD8 carburettors, went into the 420 and Daimler Sovereign. Mechanically, little else changed.

the Mk X, with about the same maximum torque (282lb/ft) developed at 3750rpm instead of 4000rpm.

The 420 was almost certainly born of frustration over the slow development of the complex and largely all-new XJ6, with Lyons deciding that to fill the gap a face-lift exercise must be carried out on the S-type saloon as soon as possible. Accordingly he designed a new front end which incorporated the forward rake of the front panel, a styling device he was taken with at the time and had first used on the Mk X.

These bodywork alterations, however, entailed a great deal of retooling and this, when linked to the early launch date Sir William had set his heart on, caused all sorts of problems both for Jaguar's own body engineers and those at Pressed Steel Fisher. At first both reported that the retooling was impossible within the timescale laid down, at which Sir William threatened to have the initial run of panels more or less hand-made at Abbey Panels. But thanks to an enormous effort, chiefly by Pressed Steel Fisher, the revised body actually did arrive on time – the

job was remembered for years afterwards at PSF as "the greatest feat of desperate panel design, tool design and tool manufacture we ever achieved"!

Together with its larger air intake, the car was given a more efficient cooling system, with a new crossflow, tube and fin radiator being fitted together with an improved, higher capacity water pump. This gave a much bigger heat dissipation capacity and it also made the fitting of an auxiliary radiator possible for the optional (on LHD cars) air-conditioning plant. The engine fan was the Holset modulated viscous coupling type, which gave a virtually positive drive up to about 2500rpm, and thereafter allowed a progressive slip to develop so that power absorption was minimised and the noise level reduced. The electrics included an alternator as on the other 4.2 cars, driven via its own belt from the crankshaft damper which also served as the pulley wheel for the fan and power steering pump, when fitted.

The 420 Jaguar was probably better looking than the S-type and seemed to fill a niche in the company's expanding model range.

The power steering was the Marles Varamatic variety first seen on the Mk X Jaguar, with its interesting variable ratio reducing the required movement of the steering wheel as it was turned; otherwise Burman recirculating ball remained the standard arrangement for the steering. Brakes were Girling discs (type 72/13) with independent hydraulic circuits for front and rear; Girling had previously taken over the production of these brakes from Dunlop. Transmission options were largely as before, the automatic box being the Borg Warner Type 8 imported from America (as opposed to the Type 35 manufactured at Letchworth for use with engines having less torque than the 4.2); this had the "D1", "D2" positions giving an optional start in second gear.

There was rather more room under the bonnet than in previous Mk II variants, thanks to the Mk X-like front with its wide radiator grille with central rib and four headlamps (the centre pair cutting out when the dipswitch was operated). Two small dummy grilles were positioned either side of the radiator, while the side/flasher units followed S-type practice. Aft of the front wings, the body panels remained identical to those of the S-type.

Inside though, some innovations were evident. As foreshadowed by the 2.5 V8 Daimler saloon of 1962, the facia was now topped by a full-length padded roll of black vinyl, and – a new touch – the clock, formerly incorporated in the rev counter, had been placed in the centre surrounded by the padding. This change from the unyeilding wood facia of the Mk II and S-types was considered to be a useful safety feature, and like the V8

saloon again, was adopted for the doors, though this time in the colour of the internal trim; the door garnish rails kept their walnut veneer however. Instruments were as for the S-type, though the new electric impulse rev counter was used, and the 420 retained a similar transmission tunnel console and heating/ventilation system.

The equally new Daimler Sovereign was identical to the 420 saloon except for some external trim differences – the radiator had the traditional Daimler flutes, this style being continued on the rear number plate lamp housing, and of course "D" for Daimler replaced the Jaguar motif on radiator surround and wheel trims. As for its mechanical specification, the Sovereign was given power steering as standard, and if you opted for the manual gearbox, this would only come with the Laycock overdrive attached.

Of course, you paid more for the 420 models than you did for the S-type cars: the standard 420 without overdrive cost £1930 total as opposed to the basic 3.8 S-type at £1844, while the Daimler Sovereign with automatic gearbox was listed at £2198, only £39 less than the standard 420G (the 4.2 Mk X's new name, bestowed at the same time as the 420's introduction). Jaguar could now offer cars from £1342 for the cheapest Mk II, right up to £2380 for the automatic 420G, seven different saloon cars in all – plus the 4.2 'E' type in open two seater, fixed-head coupe, or two-plus-two forms. Add in the options of standard, overdrive or automatic transmissions and the choice became almost bewildering.

The Daimler Sovereign version of the 420 was sheer badge engineering with nothing Daimler in its make-up except for motifs and fluting on grille; but it attracted those who might not have bought a Jaguar, and outlived all other variations on the Mk II theme.

Road-testing the 420

Autocar published an early road test of the manual/overdrive 420 saloon in March 1967. They found it noticeably faster than the 3.8 S-type, with 60, 80 and 100mph coming up in 9.9-, 16.7- and 27.4-seconds respectively – the S-type took 10.4-, 17.6- and 30.5-seconds to reach these speeds. But it wasn't this reduction in absolute time that was the 4.2 engined car's major advantage, it was "that the much greater torque enables the car to do this more effortlessly. The extra power also shows up better at the top end of the scale. Above 100mph where the S-type's performance is beginning to tail off, the 420 still has acceleration in hand, and takes only 11-seconds to go from 100 to 110mph."

With the 3.77 axle ratio fitted (as it was to all overdrive Mk II variants except the 2.4), it was thought that every gear seemed a little low for maximum performance, but in practice, a lot of gear changing wasn't demanded thanks to the engine's pulling power: "... it is normal to change up at about 3500rpm. Even in overdrive there is surprisingly vigorous performance, and acceleration from 100mph to 110mph, incidentally, is quicker in overdrive than in direct top." The red line was approached (5500rpm) at 110mph in direct top. "The ideal cruising speed seems to be just over 100mph. Top speed, with a one-way maximum of 126mph and 123mph mean, is much the same as that of the 3.8 Mk II, but faster than the other big cars (S-type and 420G)."

In transmitting this power, the clutch was thought "fairly heavy, with quite long travel" and it had a tendency to judder slightly when manoeuvring. But there was no slip, and "the clutch has terrific bite for fierce standing starts and if one wants to be brutal, one can let the clutch in with a bang while the engine is revving at about 4000rpm. The car simply sits down on its rear springs and rockets away with shrieks of wheelspin; but quicker times are obtained by using lower engine speed and more gentle clutch control."

The 420 was, in fact, rather softly sprung, giving "an exceptionally level and comfortable ride, but (lacking in) roll resistance. On winding roads the car seems a little too soft on its springs." Surprisingly, the ride was thought to be better unladen than with a full complement of five passengers; with most cars, the reverse is usually the case. The car was only a fraction heavier than the S-type, at 32.9cwt instead of 32.7cwt, the weight distribution percentage being 53.5F/46.5R. Most of this small increase was carried on the front wheels so understeer was just as predominant as before: "Corners can be taken very fast indeed, though...the power steering disguises the amount of understeer", this last thanks to the Varamatic system's ability to reduce the ratio as the wheel was turned. "Every 420 buyer would be wise to run to the extra cost of the Marles power-assisted steering. The control not only takes the effort out of driving this heavy car without spoiling steering sensitivity, it also increases response on lock."

The 420 wasn't the most economical Jaguar, with consumption varying between 12mpg in London traffic and 17mpg with more gentle driving; fast motorway progress could result in each tankful (7-gallons a side) lasting only an hour. Oil consumption was better than most previous cars however, working out at 2000mpg as opposed to the 3.8 S-type's 1700mpg, and no water was added to the radiator during the test.

The heating and ventilation system with its vacuum operated controls wasn't considered anywhere near perfect by Autocar. "There are still no separate face level inlets, nor any extractors other than the swivelling windows in the rear doors. The heater itself is slow to warm up after a cold start, but considerable thought has gone into the heater controls...rear passengers do not get as warm as those in front. Windscreen demisting could be more effective." The two-speed windscreen wipers cleared "big and well-placed areas" however, and

"excellent illumination for fast night driving is given by 7in. diameter outer lamps for main and dipped beams, and 5in. inner lamps as main beam supplementaries."

Autocar's summary of the 420's merits was typically enthusiastic:

Eagerly awaited since its announcement, the 420 in every way lives up to high expectations. It has an extraordinary dual character in that it can at one moment provide stately, luxurious travel for an elderly party, and behave like a high performance sports car the next. With the extra cost of Varamatic steering included, it just tops the round figure as the best £2,000's worth on the market."

Motor tried an automatic 420 a couple of months later; their introductory paragraph was even more complimentary than Autocar's closing one:

"By any sort of overall scale the Jaguar 420, at £2,200, is little more than a medium-priced car. Yet it seems somehow insolent to apply medium standards to a saloon that for a combination of speed, comfort and safety is as good as any in the world, regardless of cost. Even with the rather jerky automatic transmission fitted as an option to our test car, its quiet, fussless performance is still formidable if no longer quite so fierce and smooth as some competitive American V8 saloons. But the 420 lives in a different world of stability and the worse the conditions, the more conspicuous its virtues become. You can drive at maximum speed – approaching 120mph – in pouring rain without in any way alarming yourself or your passengers, a situation in which other fast cars would feel far from reassuring."

The top speed of this automatic car was 115mph, which apparently disappointed Jaguar – "they were expecting more." But, on the other hand, acceleration was, in part, up on Autocar's manual version, 60mph being reached in 9.4-seconds instead of 9.9, and 80mph in 16.3-seconds as opposed to 16.7 – not much, but one generally expects an

Interior of the 420, similar to the S-types but incorporating such as the central clock mounted in the padded top rail.

automatic car to be whole seconds *down* on the equivalent manual one. This performance was enough to keep the 420 level-pegging with the heavier (37.5cwt) but more powerful 420G automatic saloon previously tried by the magazine. At 15.4mpg, petrol consumption overall was little worse than the 15.7mpg recorded by *Autocar*; that was overall – it ranged from 15 to 18mpg "according to how hard (and where) you drive."

The automatic gearbox itself was not entirely free from criticism, with jerky changes under hard acceleration and rough kickdown changes; it was suggested that due to the engine's copious torque, a lot of motoring could be undertaken with the quadrant lever in the "D2" position, with little loss of performance – about 2.5-seconds on the 0 - 80mph time, for instance. The now-venerable XK engine was still flexible and smooth, but "if you compare it with rival American V8s with which a £2,000 Jaguar must compete, then it is no longer so impressive, especially on performance and smoothness at high revs."

Motor's comments on the 420's ride and handling are worth quoting at length:

"Like the S-type, the 420 has impeccable manners. There cannot be more than two or three cars in the world that offer a better combination of ride and roadholding, two incompatible qualities that usually call for greater compromise than Jaguar have found necessary to make with their refined all-independent suspension. It takes a rough, cambered road, such as you often find in France, to show just how stable and safe this car can be at speed, and a long Continental journey (such as we made on two occasions in the course of an unusually high-mileage test) to discover the real meaning of Grand Touring. Paradoxically, this very English car seemed to reveal all its considerable qualities best when sweeping along the marathon through routes of France.

"At first, we were less enthusiastic about the optional Varamatic power steering fitted to our car. It is pretty quick in response but the variable gearing – higher on lock than around the straight ahead position – calls for familiarisation. Our first impression was that it felt a bit vague for gentle turns or simply for holding a straight line, but that it would respond with unexpected suddeness on a sharper corner. People unused to this characteristic found themselves darting into bends much more sharply than they intended; but with a delicate smooth touch it soon becomes second nature to judge the amount of response to any given steering wheel movement, even though there is no proportional resistance or feel in the system."

Tyres on the 420 were Dunlop SP41 radials which gave "tremendous adhesion" at the expense of some squeal on dry roads; "...even in the wet it is often possible to use full throttle out of sharp corners without breaking the tail away or lifting the inside wheel. Normally there is mild, stable understeer but the rather sudden final degree of modest body roll announces that the back wheels are on the threshhold of a slide. Significantly, not even our faster drivers can recall actually breaking adhesion, deliberately or not, to the extent that opposite lock correction was needed."

The brakes, by this time so good on a Jaguar that they normally only called for a passing mention, did have one

One of the Browns Lane shops in the 'sixties, with S-types and (background) Mk IIs under construction. Here windscreen rubbers and trim parts are being installed.
Photo: Jaguar Cars

fault – while there was virtually no fade, "a 2,000ft descent of the Juras at modest speed with three people plus luggage on board caused such severe juddering that the brakes were practically unusable for 20 minutes. We confirmed this failing in our basic fade test at MIRA (20 0.5g stops from 73mph), when, although the rise in pedal pressure was small, indicating little fade, the onset of juddering after the sixth stop again made the brakes unpleasant to use." The reason was felt to be a compromise in the brake pad material (as with other cars), biased towards long life in the case of the 420, and it was suggested that the customer should have a choice of pads "with a clear explanation of what each type will do."

As for accessories like the heater, *Motor* thought this "quite effective once you have learnt how to use it", with an adequate supply of heat being provided. But it was noted that a number of cheap mass-production cars (the Ford Cortina and Hillman Minx were cited) had superior ventilation arrangements for hot weather. The servicing needs were becoming old fashioned in their extent too, with chassis lubrication to 14-points every 6000-miles, but to assist, the driver's handbook had a "very useful" 28 pages devoted to routine maintenance.

Later that year, *Motor* revisited the car in its Daimler Sovereign form; unusually for the type, it was a 'stick shift' overdrive car. It also reinforced the supposition that in the case of the 420, it made little difference whether a manual or automatic transmission was fitted when it came to acceleration – the times to 60, 80 and 100mph were only improved by 0.2-, 0.1- and 2.7-seconds respectively, the former two times being well within the realms of experimental error. Maximum speed was only up by 2mph as well, and fuel consumption remained around the 15.5mpg mark.

The 420 in America

The 420 was exported to North America, and came up for test by *Road & Track* at the end of 1967. Their verdict was that "the 420 seems to be better adapted to American driving than any Jaguar sedan we've tested before", albeit with a "somewhat vintage body" and an interior layout which was "more classical than functional." Straight line performance was mainly inferior to that recorded by the British magazines, with 60mph being reached in 11-seconds, 80mph in 18, and 100mph in a more respectable 26.9. Top speed was the next to best recorded for a 420, at 120mph (*Autocar* managed 3mph higher). Fuel consumption ranged from 12 to 17.5mpg, quite tolerable by American standards.

Ride and handling were voted "excellent", especially off the main highways: "if you're off the blacktop and onto a patched-up strip of secondary road the wonderful compliance of the suspension and the marvellous directional stability of the car relieves you of any inhibitions about maintaining a high average speed." Of the steering, the Varamatic system was rated alongside the

Finishing a 420 bodyshell – the assembled shell has been lead-loaded and now minor rectification is under way before priming and painting begin. Fit of doors, bonnet and bootlid is checked at this stage too.
Photo: Jaguar Cars

The 420 saloon, last of the Jaguar compacts, in typically English surroundings. The final example was completed in August 1968, although the Daimler version continued for one more year.

Mercedes in accuracy and road feel; road-holding was let down by the crossply Dunlop RS5 tyres which were fitted because whitewall radials weren't available yet. *Road & Track* also noted that the car rode better with two passengers aboard than three.

The new radiator coped well with hot weather motoring – "cruising at a steady 100mph on a sunny 85 deg. day, coolant temperature held at 90 deg.C (194 deg.F) and oil pressure didn't drop from its normal 45psi." The optional air-conditioner (with evaporator mounted in the boot and outlets in the rear parcel shelf) was efficient if not silent and kept 90 degrees Farenheit ambient temperatures at bay.

This same car was retained by *Road & Track* as its first 'long-term' test car, and its progress followed over almost 21 000-miles. Its first trip of any length included 650-miles at 100mph across the Nevada desert and back during a vacation trip. With air-conditioning on, "it did 12.5mpg at 100; not bad at all, and the car was nearly as silent at 100 as at 70. *This* is travelling: 100mph, quietly, stably, safely."

The car's reliability record was judged good if one ignored two unusual faults which came up – a worn and undoubtedly faulty tappet which had to be renewed at 7000-miles; then at 20 000 miles, the overdrive's planetary gears failed, the previous whine building up to "a throaty roar and much grinding." The journal felt that this may have been the large dose of high speed cruising with the overdrive working on its maximum torque capacity; Jaguar didn't agree, and certainly the fault is not a common one.

The crossplies wore out within 12 000-miles – about average for a hard-driven Jaguar – but the replacement Goodyear radials were no more than one third worn almost 9000 miles later. On fitting the radials, "immediately we noticed improved adhesion in the wet; in the dry it was somewhat better too, and we liked the handling feel of the tyres if they were aired up to 30psi all around." The original brake pads still had "ample" material left at the end of the extended test, and when the car departed "it steered, stopped and handled as well as when new" even if a few body-rattles had crept in.

Meanwhile in England, a similar experiment had been continuing at almost exactly the same time, the editor of *Motor* Richard Bensted-Smith having replaced his Mk II 3.4 with a very early 420. During its first year, the record had been marred by quality-control faults more than anything else, Bensted-Smith concluding that "the design was superb but the execution of this early car unduly poor." Updating by the factory brought it into line with the majority of 420s – the throttle linkage was amended to make its action much lighter and more progressive (although with a tendency to go 'over centre' if the driver's foot slipped off the pedal suddenly, allowing it to spring back hard), and stiffer road springs were fitted. "The change has improved handling considerably (especially when combined with tyre pressures about 4lbs higher than the normal motoring recommendation) and made very little difference to ride."

Adjustments were made to the Model 8 transmission which cured some of the jerkiness, but the only mechanical trouble as such was the failure of a ball race in one of the hub carriers on the rear suspension, and the wearing of a steering joint which seemed to be the cause of a front tyre wearing heavily on its inner shoulder – this seems a common fault with 420s and was suffered by an example run by the writer for a good few thousand miles. Tyre wear on *Motor's* car appeared to be heavy anyway, two rear covers being replaced at little more than 16 000 miles. It also got through brake pads more rapidly than its counterpart on the other side of the Atlantic, the fronts being replaced at 12 000 miles and 21 000 miles. The slight leaks from the power steering box, transmission and cam covers were all typical Jaguar nuisances; once, the belt driving the steering pump slackened, resulting in decreasing assistance, but that was easily remedied. Apart from suffering a period at 13.5mpg caused by out of tune carburetters, the average fuel consumption of *Motor's* 420 was 15.4mpg, which tied in exactly with what the road test cars had returned.

However, the writing was on the wall for this most developed version of the Mk II Jaguar – the XJ6 was ushered in on a wave of acclaim in the autumn of 1968. At once, a phased simplification of the rather extended saloon car range began; first victims were the 3.4 and 3.8

S-types, which became obsolete immediately. They'd had a good run, with 11 050 of the former and 15 150 of the latter built during their five-year term of production.

With them went the 420 saloon, one of the rarer 'modern' four-seater Jaguars with only 9800 completed in its short two-year currency. But the Daimler '420' Sovereign lingered on until August 1969, although despite that extension, production only ran to a mere 5850 cars. A discreet gap of three months elapsed before its name was revived for the Daimler version of the XJ6 which was announced in October of that year.

To just a few, the final passing of these cars represented the last of the old-style Jaguars with their opulent walnut facias and heavy, old fashioned luxury and solidity. But all had to admit that the XJ6 was a revelation in ride, handling and sheer silence; and if it *was* bigger, and a medium-sized Jaguar was no longer obtainable, at least the XJ series didn't feel it to drive. Which was some consolation to those who maintained – and who still maintain – that there's a gap in the Jaguar range which should have been neatly and profitably filled by a 1970/80s version of the Mk II or its direct offspring.

Chapter Ten

The Mk X Jaguar

A very soft and "expensive" ride, together with almost sports car stability through fast bends and over rough surfaces, thoroughly justifies the complexity of a superb independent rear suspension.

Autocar, 2 November 1962

Disregarding the frontal treatment, it has a certain resemblance to the 1948 Hudson.

Car and Driver, April 1962

The Mk X saloon was the largest car Jaguar had ever built, and at the time it was also the most sophisticated, bringing a host of new developments to a type of car not noted for introducing advanced motoring concepts to the motoring world. This privilege was usually reserved (whatever the make) for sports cars or small mass-production vehicles, rather than bulky five-seaters in the luxury class. It was as up-to-the-minute as the Mk IX had been outdated, with its all-independant suspension and monocoque body construction, and while the Mk X may not be remembered as the *best* all-round Jaguar saloon, in its time it was one of the most advanced of all British saloons, and very definitely one of the most impressive.

For less than £2500 including tax, the customer obtained a huge car by any but North American standards, and at 6ft. 4in. across it was wider than any other British production saloon including the Rolls-Royce Silver Cloud II; the Mk X was over 3-inches broader than the Mk IX Jaguar it replaced, and also 5.5-inches longer at 16ft.10in. – though it retained the same wheelbase as its predecessor at 10-feet exactly. In only one dimension was it smaller to the Mk IX, and that was in height, where the new car was an impressive 8.5-inches lower at 4ft. 6.75in. The new model was also heavier than the old despite its technically advanced chassis-less construction, weighing in at just over 37cwt ready for the road, against 35.5cwt for the towering Mk IX.

Needless to say, the tried and tested XK engine was installed under the bonnet, but although it was of the same 3781cc capacity as the Mk IX's, it was given considerably more power through the use of the 'straight-port' cylinder head and triple carburetters; in fact, the Mk X had virtually the full 'E' type engine, rated by the factory at 265bhp in 9:1cr form, or 250bhp with 8:1cr – compared with the Mk IX's output of 210bhp with the B-type head and two carburetters.

This was the first use of the straight-port cylinder head on a Jaguar saloon, as until the announcement of the Mk X in October 1961, it had previously appeared only on the 3.4 and 3.8 'S' versions of the XK 150, and on the revolutionary 'E' type which had received its debut eight months earlier in 1961. This cylinder head differed from the earlier types in that the ports were less curved than before, which had the effect of confining turbulance to a smaller region of the combustion chamber and thus improve volumetric efficiency; this change was evolved by Weslake & Co. Ltd. using their well-known airflow techniques.

A new inlet manifold came with this head, three separate aluminium castings each taking one HD8 2-inch SU carburetter; each casting consisted of two tracts so routed that the mixture from each carburetter had the same distance to travel to the cylinder head, despite the grouping of the carburetters together for under-bonnet space purposes. After much experimentation, it was

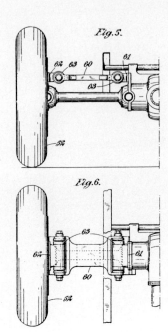

Top left: **The straight-port cylinder head, complete with carburettors and 'equal length' inlet tracts; it first appeared on the XK 150S.** *Photo: Jaguar Cars*

Left: **The 3.8-litre 'S' engine as installed in the Mk X; note the triple carburettors and polished aluminium inlet chamber (rather like a cold-air box) with trunking leading from offside wing.** *Photo: Jaguar Cars*

Above: **Elements of Jaguar's first I.R.S. are present in the system patented by Georges Roesch of Clement Talbot in May 1935, specifically the use of the driveshaft as a suspension component – although here this is shown placed at the bottom, not at the top as on the 'E' type and Mk X Jaguars.**

discovered that these equal-length tracts raised the engine's brake mean effective pressure by 17%. A longitudinal cast gallery linked all three tracts to form a balance duct between them, bolting to flanges on their upper surfaces where a jacket on each allowed engine-heated water to circulate and improve carburation during the warm-up period.

A beautifully engineered rod-and-lever throttle linkage operated the carburetter butterflies; there was no choke control as the usual automatic enriching device was used for cold starting. Cool air was ducted to the carburetters by a flexible trunk from the AC Delco air filter in the right-hand front wing ahead of the wheel arch; this trunking led to a polished aluminium chamber bolted to the carburetter air intake flanges. A new cross-flow radiator and a big, twelve-bladed 16-inch cowled fan provided the cooling (though the latter absorbed some 15bhp at 6000rpm while doing so).

The bottom-end of the engine contained refinements introduced when the original 'S' engine for the XK 150 came in 1958, notably the Vandervell VP2 lead-bronze, indium-flashed main and big-end bearings in place of the previous babbit-lined items from the same manufacturer.

Like the 3.8 XK 150, Mk IX and 'E' type engines, the Mk X's block was dry linered; the sump was cast aluminium, and of a different shape to the 'E' type's because of the lower and more forward position of the Mk X's engine – compared with the Mk IX, the engine in the new car was mounted 2-inches lower.

As for transmission, after development of the car had commenced in 1958, it was not envisaged that it would be sold with anything other than an automatic gearbox – the option of the normal four-speed manual box (with Laycock A type Mk II overdrive if specified) was made available as an alternative only towards the end of development, when it was established that a small but worthwhile demand did indeed exist for the manual transmission. With this box came a Borg & Beck type A6-G 10-inch clutch, hydraulically operated through a Dunlop 0.70-inch diameter master cylinder connected by flexible hose to a 0.875-inch Lockheed slave cylinder; it had a maximum torque capacity exceeding 260lb-ft, this figure being the maximum developed by the engine (at 4000rpm). Effort needed to compress the clutch was 25lbs. The automatic gearbox was the Borg Warner DG unit similar to that used on the Mk IX, complete with the exclusive Jaguar intermediate hold switch. A 3.54 axle ratio was used with this and the standard manual box – overdrive cars had a 3.77 ratio.

The engine and transmission were mounted a little more forward than was the case with the Mk IX, giving more space in the passenger compartment, and the drive was taken to the rear axle by a two-piece static propshaft. Here at the back was one of the Mk X's most technically interesting features, for the car had been given full independent rear suspension. The system used had previously been seen on the 'E' type, but had of course been developed with Jaguar's saloon car range equally in mind ever since experiments had begun seriously in 1955. And ever since that date, one basic type predominated.

This had its roots in the system patented by the Talbot designer George Roesch well before the Second World War, with I.R.S. experiments at Jaguar originating around 1944 when the all-independent lightweight 'jeep', the Ford Prefect-engined 'VB' prototype, had been built. Bob Knight was involved with early road car I.R.S. designs at that time, and first suggested the Roesch type suspension in the late-forties. Essentially this was a double wishbone layout but, unusually, one wishbone was replaced by the driveshaft (the bottom one by Roesch, the top by Jaguar); it was sidelined for a while, then revived when, during the mid-fifties, Lyons considered it was time that the next new Jaguar ought to incorporate independent rear suspension.

Knight produced the first running prototype suspension of this type within weeks, under the direction of Bill Heynes and with draughtsman Frank Wright drawing it up in Knight's office. It incorporated most of the suspension-to-be's major features, including inboard brakes, although later, double wishbones would be tried and the method of mounting the differential experimented with (either direct to the bodyshell, or by means of a sub-frame, this being tried in tubular and pressed steel forms).

Using the driveshaft as the top suspension component remained for the production suspension, however. This brought simplicity to the double wishbone arrangement, which itself avoided the exaggerated camber changes of the ordinary swing-axle and the resultant lack of consistency in handling. Small changes in track occured with the Jaguar system, but generally the wheel remained at the correct angles despite the motions of the suspension itself.

After experiments with a true wishbone having widely spaced inner mountings, a tubular forked lower arm was evolved with two inner Metalastic pivots, and carrying at its outer end the big heat-treated aluminium LM10 hub carrier into which also ran the driveshaft. Fore and aft location was provided by a trailing radius arm attached to the outer end of the lower tubular 'wishbone' and running forward to anchor on the car's floor via a rubber mounting. Damping was effected by two shock absorbers

on each side, each surrounded by a road spring, acting on mounting points attached to either side of the lower suspension member – this arrangement of the damping and springing meant that the forces involved did not exert a turning motion to the suspension component, and dividing them into two (four in all) meant that each individual spring/damper assembly could be made smaller than one large one, saving installation space.

The differential was the 4HU type especially developed by Salisbury Transmission Ltd for independent rear suspension applications; internally, its hypoid gears, differential and bearings were identical to those in the 4HA axle used on the Mk II and other Jaguars, and a Powr-Lok limited slip device was standard. It was rigidly mounted inside a large, bridge-type subframe which was another distinctive feature of Jaguar's independent rear suspension.

Early on in development, Jaguar had mounted the differential straight onto the bodyshell of prototype cars, but this encouraged the transmission of road noise and vibrations, so the idea of a separate frame to carry the rear suspension unit and insulate it from the body evolved; this took the form of a bridge-piece made up of 16swg steel pressings. The differential was bolted solidly to it in the middle, while the coil spring/damper units anchored at the top either side. Inboard disc brakes were used, positioned adjacent to the differential unit; from them ran the driveshafts each with their two universal joints.

The rear brakes used 10-inch diameter discs and 1.625-inch operating cylinders (later increased to 1.687-inch), and because they were so close to the differential unit, care was taken to ensure that the heat generated did not effect the oil seals – though at first the factory were only

Above: **The new rear suspension was developed on earlier Jaguar saloons including 'Mk I' and Mk II cars – one of the latter almost certainly ended up as a quite successful racing saloon, being purchased following its days as a development vehicle by Bill Rigg and then driven by John Harper during the mid-sixties.** *Photo: Harold Barker.*

The inboard rear brakes of the Mk X show clearly in this view of the rear suspension. While unsprung weight was saved, disadvantages were a certain lack of cooling and difficulty of access for major servicing – usually the subframe had to be dropped from the car

The transverse solid beam on which the Mk X's front suspension was carried; note the rubber mount securing it to the bodyshell. Above is an engine mount. *Photo: Jaguar Cars*

The Mk X's front suspension assembly, basically similar to the Mk II's with top and bottom wishbones, and spring/damper top mounting contained in a hollow pillar. This view is from the rear, with anti-roll bar visible on right.
Photo: Jaguar Cars

The rear brakes used 10-inch diameter discs and 1.625-inch operating cylinders (later increased to 1.687-inch), and because they were so close to the differential unit, care was taken to ensure that the heat generated did not effect the oil seals – though at first the factory were only partially successful in this respect and the Viton seals used on the output shaft flanges could sometimes fail in varying degrees. The handbrake used separate calipers on each disc, together with a self-adjusting mechanism.

The whole rear suspension, axle and brake package was detachable in one complete unit contained within the steel bridge-piece. And it was the way in which the bridge was attached to the bodyshell that enabled Jaguar to achieve that uncanny degree of silence and road-shock insulation which the Mk X exhibited; at each outer end of the subframe, two Metalastik V-shape bonded rubber mountings were bolted to reinforced flanges on the car. Both pairs of mountings were arranged at an inclined angle of 90-degrees and there was enough flexibility in the rubber to allow a controlled degree of wind-up of the complete suspension assembly to avoid the transmission of vibration – rather as occurs with a live axle on leaf springs. The trailing radius arm mountings also allowed this movement through the flexibility of their rubber mountings too; on prototypes, the vibration which still persisted was finally dealt with by repositioning the mountings so that the axis of rotation was on the transverse line through the centre of gravity of the whole assembly, one-inch forward of the differential axis. Throughout, there was no direct metal-to-metal contact between the suspension assembly and bodyshell.

The Mk X's front suspension resembled the Mk II's, with top and bottom wishbones and a large coil spring operating on the lower one. But instead of being mounted on a large and comparatively complex subframe as with the Mk II, the suspension assemblies were carried on a single transverse beam; this was an I-section En.16T steel forging 2.125in. deep and 1.625in. wide at its central point, rising to take the suspension pillars at each end – it looked rather like an old-fashioned beam front axle. As with the rear suspension subframe and for the same reasons, it was secured to the body through V-shaped Metalastic rubber mounts, two at each end positioned above the lower wishbone inner pivots.

The front suspension assemblies were made by Alford and Alder; both top and bottom wishbones were forgings, with a steel pressing secured to the lower one to provide a seat for the road spring (rated at 398 lb/in, or at the wheel 108lb/in, this last figure including the effect of the rubber-bushed inner mountings of the wishbones which contributed 23lb/in to the total rate). Ball joints top and bottom were once again favoured. Girling gas-cell telescopic dampers were used, and a 0.875-inch diameter anti-roll bar was fitted.

Although it was one of the biggest cars Jaguar ever produced, the Mk 10 had the smallest wheels of all – 14-inch diameter, with a rim of 5.5-inches taking 7.50-14 Dunlop Road Speed tyres. This meant that space for brakes was limited, and in fact the disc diameters both front and rear were smaller than on the Mk II Jaguar, at 10.75-inches front and 10-inches rear. Normal outboard disc brakes were fitted to the front, operated on by 2.125-inch pistons (later increased to 2.25-inch), and of course the system was Dunlop's Mk II 'quick change pad' type.

The most singular part of the system was the servo which Jaguar used for the Mk X; this was the Kelsey-Hayes booster, originating in the United States and made under licence in Britain by Dunlop; it had first been used by Jaguar on the 'E' type earlier in 1961. A departure from the unit used on the Mk IX and Mk II Jaguars, the Kelsey-Hayes bellows servo exerted a mechanical pressure on the brake master cylinders instead of the more normal hydraulic 'line-pressure.' When the brake pedal was depressed, an air valve was closed and engine vacuum caused the bellows to contract and apply force to the linkage which worked the master cylinders. Should the bellows not function, a direct mechanical link still existed between brake pedal and cylinders.

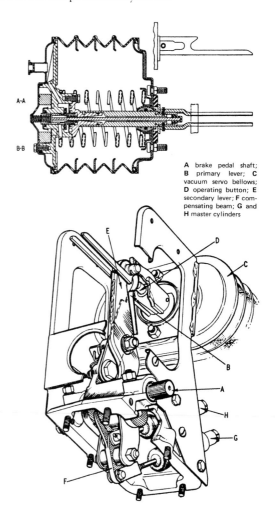

A brake pedal shaft; B primary lever; C vacuum servo bellows; D operating button; E secondary lever; F compensating beam; G and H master cylinders

Diagram of the Kelsey-Hayes bellows servo, showing how it acted mechanically on the two brake master cylinders below.

The unusual-looking vacuum bellows of the Kelsey-Hayes booster, mounted under the bonnet of a left-hand drive Mk X fitted with air-conditioning. *Photo: Jaguar Cars*

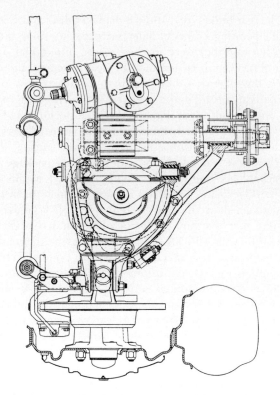

The Burman power-assisted steering box and linkages are shown in this diagram of the Mk X's front suspension.

This system had one advantage in that if the servo had to be removed or repaired, it did not effect the hydraulic system and thus no 'bleeding' was required. On the other hand, the amount of assistance given was not all that great, and also, there could be complaints of delayed response on occasions. The servo itself was simple, tough and long-lasting, thanks largely to the lack of any internal hydraulic circuits to fail or corrode. Twin master cylinders were used with a front-to-rear braking ratio of 66.2/33.8; both had their own transparent plastic brake fluid reservoirs incorporating the usual Sovy low-level warning device. Dividing the braking system in this way was meant to provide a measure of fail-safe braking, but should it be the front half that ceased to work, the rear brakes alone could do only a minimal amount to bring the 40 cwt (laden) car to rest.

Jaguar's tests for resistance to brake fade, fluid evaporation and judder were very stringent and two distinct procedures were carried out. The first involved 30 stops at a mean deceleration of 0.5g from 100 mph at one minute intervals and an 0.5g stop is a pretty severe one, although not in the 'emergency' class. At the end of the 30 stops, no fade, judder or fluid boiling must be apparent. Then, while prototypes were being tested on the continent, it was found that higher brake temperatures were actually obtained when more frequent stops from lower speeds downhill were made. So a second test was instituted, named the "Alpine." This involved 40 stops at an average of 0.5g again, from 50 mph but at half minute intervals, and again, fade, judder and fluid evaporation must not occur. This sort of test was especially important when the car was an automatic, as if the low ratio wasn't selected by the driver, engine braking was relatively slight.

Steering gear on the Mk 10 was power assisted as standard, following the example of the Mk IX. Burman integral power assistance equipment was used, as had already been seen on preceding Jaguars. A Hobourn-Eaton pump was driven from the dynamo at 1.67 times engine speed, with fluid being contained in a 3-pint pressed steel reservoir above; the hydraulic assistance mechanism was contained neatly within the steering box, and both the box and the steering idler were mounted on the transverse beam which carried the front suspension assemblies – this ensured that the steering linkages were unaffected by any deflection of the beam on its 'V' shape rubber mountings, because everything would move together. From lock-to-lock, 4.5 turns of the 17-inch diameter adjustable steering wheel were needed. The steering column was divided, with the upper part mounted on the body; movement between the fixed components and the steering gear was accommodated by a Hooke joint at the lower end and a pot-type universal joint at the upper end.

These particular joints were sealed and didn't require lubrication, but Jaguar did not improve on their usual 2500 mile interval recommended for greasing the ball joints and tie-rods on the front suspension. They even gave a reason for this, saying that with a car as fast as the Mk X, and with steering loads often high with power assistance, it was preferable to lubricate and thus inspect these joints at relatively frequent intervals. The majority of the rear suspension points required greasing at 5000 mile intervals.

All the Mk X advanced engineering features were contained in a one-piece body/chassis structure made by the Pressed Steel Co. Ltd.; all Jaguar bodies were manufactured by Pressed Steel but this was the first one to be made at their Swindon, Wiltshire works. Needless to say, the Mk X bodyshell was one of the largest they produced!

The shell was built from steel pressings, spot welded together; it was assembled from a basic structure consisting of two large box section sills 7-inches deep by 7-inches wide, the floor which incorporated the transmission tunnel and the dashboard/bulkhead at the front and the rear seat pan at the back. The floor area was stiffened by the very large transverse boxes which ran under the front seats. From the bottom of the hollow section front bulkhead ran two members which extended forward to carry the engine and front suspension beam, braced by diagonal pressings coming down from the upper part of the dash, and also by the inner wheel arch panels which were stressed too. The footwells on each side contributed stiffness here as well.

The rear seat pan provided a good deal of the strength at the rear of the car, and consisted of two box section transverse members with a similar depth to that of the main sills which they joined. The rear wheel arch pressings were spot welded to a pressing which ran across the car at the bottom of the seat pan, and underneath, boxed members took the rear suspension assembly. Rearwards from here ran two deep box section members to reach the car tail, forming the sides of the luggage compartment.

The Mk X's body was massively built, with large outer sills, wide crossmembers, and heavy bulkheads. *Photo: Jaguar Cars*

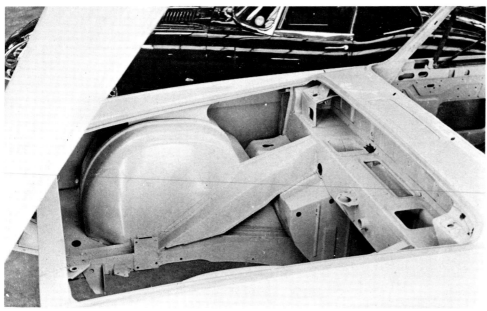

The major engine and suspension stresses were born by two integral frame members, each braced by diagonal sections extending from the front bulkhead (the 'E' type seen in background is, incidentally, 77 RW, the road-test car used by *Motor* to record 150mph). *Photo: Jaguar Cars*

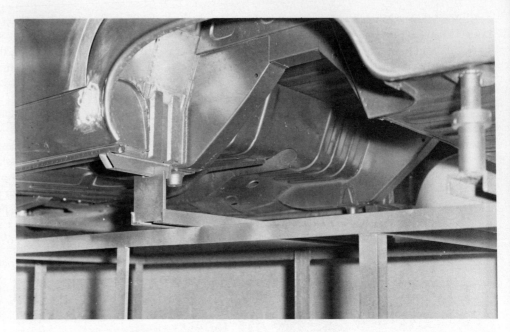

To contain the rear suspension unit, the Mk X bodyshell incorporated arched box-members extending rearwards from the seat pan.
Photo: Jaguar Cars

The rear outer panels of the Mk X were assembled using a technique employed on the 'E' type – the upper and lower body skin panels were joined together by welding out-turned flanges, these being concealed by the rear bumpers on the finished car. The rear wing cavities on each side contained a fuel tank holding ten gallons (ie, 20-gallons total), which left the luggage compartment floor entirely flat. The tanks were made from 20 swg thickness steel and were stitch welded around the flanges; each was secured to its wheel arch by a steel strap. Fuel was sent to the carburetters by a Lucas type 2FP submerged electric pump in each tank, which worked through a rotary impellor driven at a constant 2900rpm to provide continuous flow of petrol; excess being continually returned to the fuel tank via an additional line.

The huge luggage space of the Mk X was kept clear by mounting the fuel tanks in the wings, and the spare wheel was stowed vertically (see depressions on right of floor). *Photo: Jaguar Cars*

The Mk X's door openings were exceptionally wide, having a maximum width of 40.5-in. below the waistline at the front, and 31.5-in. at the rear. This inevitably meant heavy doors, so the pillars and hinges on which they hung were box-section structures of substantial dimensions. To assist the opening of the doors from inside, helical springs were mounted inside the pillars and attached to the front (hinge) face of each door, these being wound up when the doors were closed.

This whole body structure formed an exceptionally rigid shell, having a torsional strength of 8000lb ft per degree measured between the front and rear wheel planes – an extremely high figure for a car of this size. It actually means that the roof section and its pillars were required to contribute virtually nothing to the strength of the assembly, which is quite unusual. In fact, at one stage it was seriously considered styling the Mk X as a 'pillarless saloon', that is, with no middle window pillars at the side of the car above door level – exactly like the XJ coupe to come years later .... There were some regrets when this was not proceeded with in production, but from a practical standpoint, there would inevitably have been problems sealing the glass areas at their joints – a continuous source of difficulty with the XJ coupe.

Years later, the Mk X's enormous waist-line strength was rediscovered when, during the late 'seventies, various enthusiasts and coachbuilders found that the car made an extremely pleasant convertible, complete with power hood (usually employing the basic mechanism from North American convertibles). On driving the Mk X (or 420G) with the roof and all supporting pillars thus removed, no loss of rigidity was discovered with the whole of the vehicle remaining entirely rattle-free and generally unperturbed by the operation. Though no such reserves of strength existed in the much more scientifically designed XJ model which came after the Mk X series.

The usual anti-rust and priming procedures were gone through when the bodyshell arrived 'in the white' from Pressed Steel, the first step being to clean the shell of its protective oil film by a Trico immersion dip. This was followed by a six-stage phosphate process by high pressure jet, and afterwards, the body was dipped to approximately 75 percent of its height in a corrosion-resistant primer, then stoved at 320 degrees Centigrade. Finally a bitumastic sealing compound was sprayed onto the underside of the body.

This all sounds very thorough, and indeed the process used by Jaguar was probably every bit as good as that used by any manufacturer of the day, but it totally failed to provide lasting protection to closed box-sections and mud-trapping cavities in the wings and underside. Indeed, while the techniques of proper rust-proofing had been known for more than 20-years before the Mk X arrived, no manufacturer was to pay real attention to the subject until the mid-seventies – or in many cases much later, if at all. The plain fact is that simple dipping or phosphate treatment is just not enough, and needs to be backed up by the injection of petroleum-based wax-type substances into all closed sections – which is where serious corrosion begins, working from the inside out, not from the outside inwards. The first Jaguar to receive this injection treatment of its major box sections was the Series III XJ saloon of 1979.

After this initial application of primer, undercoating and top coating took place; anti-drum panels were stuck to large floor areas, and one-inch thick felt placed under the carpets. The Mk X adopted the type of headlining with its 0.187-inch sponge rubber backing used on the

'E'type, the material being secured by an adhesive to sound-absorbing material 0.062-inch thick which was stuck to the roof pressing itself; this was simpler and cheaper than the traditional method of installing headlining (as was still being used on the Mk II saloon).

Well aware of complaints about the heating and ventilation systems in earlier Jaguars, the company tried really hard to improve the situation with the Mk X, helped by a 'clean sheet' so far as the bodyshell design

Painting the Mk X – as with all Jaguars at that time, this included a final colour or lacquer coat applied *after* road test, entailing careful masking of lights and chrome trim. This practice was not discontinued until many years later.
Photos: Jaguar Cars

was concerned. The big new dash superstructure therefore has an entirely new heating system built into it, designed by Jaguar's engineers in consultation with Marston Excelsior who supplied the big heat-exchanger matrix. Not one, but two, electric rotary fans boosted the air coming into the car from the flap on the scuttle top. Each of the two outlets had a flap valve that could be adjusted manually to direct air at the feet or body, and two further pipes ran down along the transmission tunnel to the rear passenger's feet. When fresh air was required for ventilation only, it was routed so that it bypassed the heater matrix altogether, so couldn't pick up any heat from that source at all.

With the idea of making the controls as light as possible, Jaguar took the interesting step of making the "off", "air" and "heat" controls vacuum-operated. These took the form of a row of three buttons on the centre console, operating the exterior air intake scuttle flap, the flap valve in the heater unit, and the water valve respectively. The engine manifold depression supplied the vacuum of course, and the system had its own vacuum reservoir, and three vacuum servo units. The passengers could adjust their own supply of heat or air by means of a simple manually operated flap.

Interior furnishing of the Mk X followed traditional Jaguar thinking, with the Mk II providing the main inspiration for the layout of the dashboard and controls. The large diameter 140mph speedometer and rev counter sat in front of the driver, with the usual four minor dials and row of six flick-switches set into a drop-down central panel. Burred walnut was the chief finish and safety padding was still some way off for the big Jaguars, though one innovation was the full-length parcel shelf under the dash. Like the Mk II, the interior was equipped with a large central console but this did not have 'squared-off' lines but instead had rounded edges which merged into the tunnel between the front seats – which were always of the individual type, inspite of the lack of gear lever in the majority of cars produced. For the first time on a Jaguar, the seats had reclining backrests as standard. These seatbacks had walnut-veneer picnic tables set into them, which when opened revealed a full-length vanity mirror as well.

Aluminium tread-plates covered the sills front and rear, while the door window frames were separate chromium plated fixtures rather like those on the Mk II, with that car's feature of rear-door opening quarter lights. Electrically operated windows were a new option,

Unusual picture showing the Mk X's dash and console being formulated in the experimental trim shop. *Photo: Jaguar Cars*

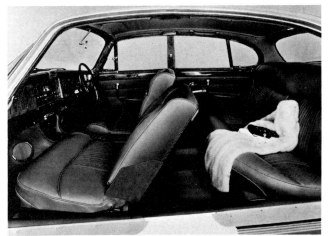

controlled by an individual switch on each passenger door, and by a row of four switches mounted on the central console for use by the driver. The windows now ran in nylon-covered rubber channels which improved draught and water sealing and ensured easy movement of the glass. All the door panel and interior trim was vinyl, except for the Connolly leather seat facings.

We have yet to remark upon the Mk X's appearance. It was very much a departure from previous Lyons designs, though a good number of familiar Jaguar features remained – the plated side window frames for instance, curving round at the rear, a detail used on all closed Jaguars since the Mk V with the exception of the original 2.4 and 3.4 models. There was also something of the Mk II in the tail of the car, albeit in elongated form, and in the rounded profile of the roof. A traditional Jaguar radiator grille was used at the front, but it and the four headlamps were raked forward at an angle. Two round air intake grilles flanked the grille at the bottom, and unlike the Mk II, the sidelights were carried under the outer (7-inch dia.) headlight, and an oblong flashing indicator light 'wrapped round' the corner of the front wing. The big bonnet complete with grille and headlights hinged forward, counterbalanced by looped torsion bars carried adjacent to its bottom-mounted hinges; it was the first saloon Jaguar to have a forward opening bonnet.

The front wing line was carried right along the car at waist level to form the rear wings, which ended in the integral light units containing tail, stop and indicator

The production Mk X trim, with instrument panels resembling the Mk II's except for being wood-finished throughout. Parcel shelf and console were new – this automatic car has electric windows and the control buttons can be seen between the wide, individual seats. *Photo: Jaguar Cars*

Jaguar publicity photograph of the Mk X's interior which serves to show the enormous amount of rear legroom (even if the front seats have been pushed right forward!). The Mk X was considerably roomier than even the long wheelbase XJ saloons, incidentally.

The Mk X had almost limousine-like appointments, such as these large, let-down picnic tables incorporating a full-length mirror. Note too the heater ducts on the transmission tunnel. *Photo: Jaguar Cars*

Sir William arrived at the Mk X's eventual shape by his normal methods. This version shows an upright frontal treatment. Note figure in background carrying an 'alternative' front wing style.

Front view of the experimental shell, with an interesting cowled headlight arrangement on the left, and siamesed headlights plus dummy air vent on the right.

Sir William views the work as the Mk X (code named 'Zenith') evolves; rear view shows chrome moulding absent on production examples, and a Mk IX-type bumper is still carried.

More stages in development: a mock-up Mk X bonnet without its inner headlamp arangement.

Here the characteristic forward slope of the front panel with its twin inner and outer headlamps has arrived. This slope and the Mk X's side 'bulge' may be linked to airflow experiments conducted by Malcolm Sayer on the Mk VII, from which he deduced that they cut down drag.

Virtually complete, with Bill Rankin (left) helping to hold up the background cloth for the photograph. This and previous mock-ups retain what seems to be a detachable rear spat, but this and the chrome waistline didn't feature in the production Mk X.
Photo: Jaguar Cars

lights. The number plate was positioned on the bootlid, topped by a plinth containing the reversing light and number plate light. The bumpers were of much slimmer section than the Mk II's, with a pronounced wrap-round at the rear.

The Mk X was the first Jaguar saloon to appear without detachable rear wheel spats since the old pushrod cars left the scene in 1949. Instead, low wheel arches covered most of the tyre at the top; oval instead of a completely round wheel arches were a feature at the front too, though these were higher than at the rear and coincided with the beginning of a pressed side moulding which was the only relief on the car's expansive side aspect. Here, the panels bulged outwards to give the Mk X its distinctively bulbous appearance, and to make it about the widest British car in production at the time of its announcement in 1961.

The response from observers of the new car was – by comparison with the rave reviews a new Jaguar customarily received – a little cautious, and not always entirely complimentary. The Mk X was always a car which looked at least as big as it was, if not bigger, thanks mainly to those rounded side panels; Bill Boddy described it in *Motor Sport* as "portly", while North American commentators immediately noted its similarity to the 1948 Hudson – "the cars have the same general layout and proportions and the same step-down over the sills" remarked *Car and Driver*, which can't have pleased Jaguar very much. Embarrassed Jaguar dealers in America recognised the affinity too, and began to wonder if this was the first Jaguar they'd really have to *sell*.

Not that it was a large car by American standards, it ranked alongside average-size cars such as the 1962 Plymouth and Dodge, and was actually shorter than the Chevrolet and Ford of that year. No, a 'large' car to Americans was something like the Lincoln Continental, at over 20-inches longer than the Mk X. Those who drove the car soon found that it handled much better than seemed possible, and notwithstanding any initial reservations. Jo Eerdmans, president of Jaguar Cars Inc., reported in January 1962 that distributors had placed

The original Mk X, graceful in its own way, and very much adapted to American motoring conditions and habits.

orders for 4000 Mk Xs, compared with 2500 3.8 Mk IIs – which with orders for 4000 'E'- types as well, produced a total exceeding any previous projected sales figures for Jaguars in the States.

The Mk X did not have a very auspicious start to its production, despite record orders, and Sir William was reported as being "bitterly disappointed" by initial teething troubles – one of the most serious being radiator failure, a fault which was reported in America to have cost the suppliers $500 000 to rectify. The second season of production unfortunately included an extremely severe winter (1963), and the extra quantities of salt on the road showed up further evidence of lack of development when the subframe to body rubber mounts began to deteriorate prematurely – this was cured by using an American bonding agent which was far superior to that being manufactured in Britain at that time. And while Jaguar put a brave face on it, sales figures in the States were not as great as had been anticipated.

However, road tests of the Mk X were generally enthusiastic, and all who sampled the car had to admit that for its size, it performed and handled almost extraordinarily well. An initially sceptical *Road and Track* magazine at last obtained one to try in the autumn of 1962.

They were soon converted: "despite our earlier suspicions, the car turned out to be one of the most pleasing luxury sedans we've ever driven. Actually, we are inclined to put this new car in a rather special category – a true high-performance 'sports' sedan – rather than simply a luxury vehicle, though it is all of that. In other words, the Mk X really has no direct competition except from Jaguar's own more compact 3.8 model." The engine, already considered venerable, was thought to carry its years extremely well, and the automatic transmission "worked well enough, even while going up and down those steep San Francisco hills" with the smoothest shift being obtained under full throttle.

Brakes and steering were liked, although the bellows servo didn't seem to give very much assistance at low speeds; "the power steering was unobtrusive, relayed more road feel to the driver than the majority of these systems do and gave near-perfect control at all times." It was found to be a very silent car too, even with the windows lowered up to 70-75mph, but the Mk X was at its most impressive when its handling and ride qualities were brought into play:

"Almost any car built today will ride smoothly on turnpikes, expressways or freeways, so it was no surprise that the Mk X was smooth on that type of highway. However, getting onto the winding and narrow is the convincer.

We had already noticed that the car handled exceptionally well in a cross wind (a happy combination of weight distribution, centre of pressure, steering geometry and suspension design make this possible) but the forward weight bias gives the Mk X some understeer on winding roads. This is most noticeable on downhill stretches of tight, winding roads or when a curve catches the driver unaware. On fast sweeping curves or any place where the driver can 'set the car up' for negotiating the curve, almost nuetral steer is achieved by a studied manipulation of steering and throttle. Humps, bumps, potholes and ripples in the roadway make no appreciable difference to the ride. We've never driven a car of this type and size that gave any better combination of comfort and handling than the Mk X does. The precise, easy steering and the good handling characteristics resulting from the suspension design make the driver want to drive with more abandon than is really prudent with a car of this size and weight."

About the only inhibiting factor in spirited cornering was the lack of lateral support from the seats, and the wearing of the seatbelts was advised just to hold the occupants in place on the wide expanses of leather.

It might be thought that straight-line acceleration and top speed were not vitally important ingredients with this type of car, but nevertheless, the Mk X offered speed on full measure. *Road and Track's* three-speed automatic

In production – an early batch of Mk Xs line-up outside the Browns Lane office block prior to despatch. *Photo: Jaguar Cars*

reached 60mph in 10.6-seconds, 80mph in 19.3-seconds, and 100 mph in 33.4-seconds, with a standing quarter-mile of 18-seconds dead; maximum speed was an estimated 115mph.

These figures were more or less confirmed when *Autocar* obtained its first road-test Mk X for appraisal – like its North American counterpart, it too had had difficulty in borrowing one from the makers – which may have been indicative of teething troubles, or quite simply no cars to spare due to demand. The car they were lent (8172 RW) was 13 000 miles old and had two Continental trips to its credit, but "there was not a body creak or rattle."

Unlike *Road and Track's* example, this car had an 8:1cr., the standard offering for the home market, 9:1cr being an option. This explained why acceleration was initially slightly down at 12.1-, 20.6- and 33.3-seconds for the 60 mph, 80 mph and 100mph times respectively (though it had caught up towards the end). Top speed was accurately measured though, and found to be an impressive 119.5mph on the 3.54 ratio axle. In other words, the 3.8 litre Mk X had roughly the performance of the lighter 3.4 Mk II, with equivalent transmission. Petrol consumption was higher of course at 14.1mpg overall, with a normal range of 13-17mpg.

The Mk X's power steering was not universally liked. The pump was driven from the rear of the dynamo as can be seen here.
Photo: Jaguar Cars

Autocar confirmed *Road & Track's* impressions on the way the big car handled – "almost sports car stability through fast bends and over rough surfaces ... one can write easily and legibly in the back while being whisked along at high speeds." The British journal, probably more accustomed to the best rack-and-pinion manual steering systems, weren't so taken with the power steering though, which was voted too low geared in the straight-ahead position "and at low speeds lacks the sensitivity that makes for relaxation." It was considered better at higher speeds, but response was still felt to be too slow when entering a fast bend. The brakes were praised without any such reservations though, and gave a consistent 1.0g retardation at every stop for a pedal load of only 60lbs. "They did not make the tyres squeal or pull the car off-course, and there was no fade."

Only one criticism of the car's new suspension was made, and that concerned the damping – "at times one could wish for stronger damping to counteract the slow rate longitudinal 'plunge', as distinct from 'pitch', but this is never excessive." The automatic transmission did not arouse enthusiasm with its tendency to make a "jerky, unwanted change into top when one has accelerated hard in intermediate and then released the throttle, as happens frequently in heavy traffic." It was difficult to dwell on such minor inadequacies when surrounded by such luxury however, graphically described by *Autocar* as follows – "The aroma of good leather pervades the interior, and this with an abundance of timber veneer gives it almost the cosily affluent air of an Edwardian library."

Minor improvements were made to the car soon after it began to reach the market in quantity during 1962, a number being in common with other models in the Jaguar range – the engine had received a new asbestos rope rear crankshaft oil seal by January 1962, drilled camshafts for quieter cold starting in May, larger main bearing cap dowels in October, and better quality exhaust valves around the same time. Gas cell dampers arrived in January 1963 and helped meet *Autocar's* earlier criticism, braking was further improved by larger wheel cylinders (July 1962) and then thicker discs – 0.375 to 0.5-inch – in January 1963 together with a change from Mintex M59 to M33 pad material. The rear subframe mounting position was altered in January 1963, the several changes of rear spring took place with and without aluminium spacers. A power steering pump with 'falling flow' characteristics above 5500rpm was fitted in April 1963, to alleviate high temperature conditions brought on by high speed driving

A useful accessory introduced as an option in April 1962 was the heated backlight; in the Mk X, a feed wire already existed in the harness. Glass could be clear or 'Sundym', and the 5-amp element was live as soon as the ignition switch was turned on – there was no separate switch. The heater controls were altered after the first 318 RHD and 684 LHD cars had been built, so that the scuttle

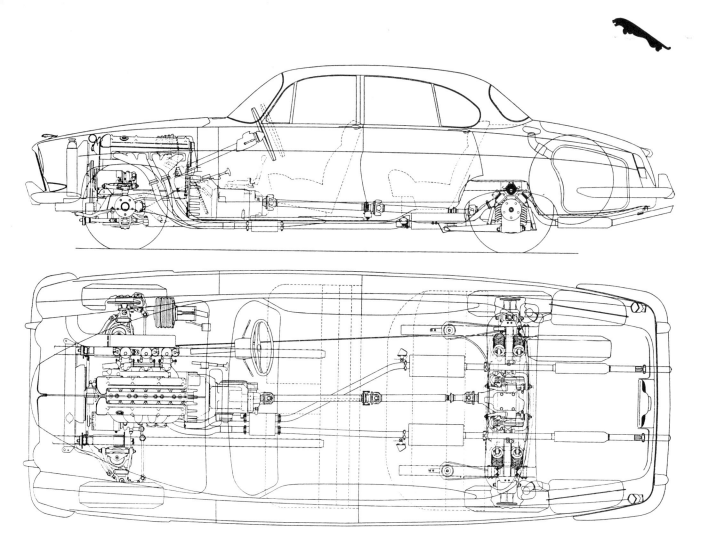

Side and plan views of the Mk X Jaguar, showing how all its major features fit together – from the triple carburettor 3.8 engine at the front to the independent rear suspension unit at the back. Note routing of exhaust system, ending in rear tailpipe silencers.

ventilator flap could be operated independently – thus it could be left closed after pressing the "heat" button until the heating element had warmed up, whereas previously it had opened automatically when "hot" button was pressed ("off", "heat" and "air" buttons now replaced "off", "cold" and "hot" on the console).

November 1963 saw *Motor's* report on an overdrive Mk X, and it was not very complimentary – almost everything except the engine brought some adverse comment or criticism. "If the car cost another £1000 (as it reasonably might) no doubt the sound damping and trim would be much better. Although generally quiet, the engine and gearbox can clearly be heard under heavy acceleration and the decorative woodwork has a skin-deep quality, revealed by close inspection. Like the gracefully bulbous sides that make for thick doors rather than interior space, effect has been placed before function; some people like it, others do not."

Motor thought the 16-year-old engine to be the best part of the car, notwithstanding all the advanced chassis features, with its ability to "pull silkily from 7-to

120mph" and provide acceleration exceeding that of most sports cars. "The engine makes its familiar exciting sound when accelerating hard but at cruising speeds it is cloaked in a subdued and expensive purr that hardly seems to increase with revs. At 60mph the car is extremely quiet – you can almost hear the electric clock ticking – and even at 100mph passengers may converse without raising their voices." Overdrive meant a relaxed 3920rpm at that speed, incidentally.

Criticism of the gearbox was expected with its long travel and whine in first gear, but unusually *Motor* considered that the ride given by the fully independent suspension was "not outstanding" and with a gentle, undulating feel "reminiscent of many large American cars." Roadholding was excellent, but marred by the "absurd lack of lateral support" from the slippery leather seats, and by the power steering. Here, "...the impression transmitted through the wheel when cornering fast is that of driving on a wet road with the front wheels about to break away – a feeling strengthened by the slight but constant correction needed on a long bend. In fact there is usually a great deal of adhesion in reserve – a safety factor of considerable merit. Independently sprung rear wheels accept full power on quite sharp bends without lifting or siding but much greater discretion is naturally needed in the wet when, depending on speed and throttle opening, either the front or the back can be made to break away. Power slides are easy to control; loss of front wheel adhesion tends to send the car off at a disconcertingly straight tangent." Roll was thought exaggerated by the seats but possibly less than expected in a big car, and the turning circle was usefully small at around 36-feet.

Brakes were rated as "exceptional" and immensely reassuring at high speeds. "They are less impressive at low speeds, when sponginess in the pedal gives the impression of momentary delay." This does seem to be a characteristic of the bellows servo – both on the 3.8 'E' type and Mk X, it never gave the instant response associated with conventional line-pressure servos. *Motor* obviously considered that the worst aspect of the brakes was the handbrake which was the pull-out type rather like the Mk V's though not providing a very powerful emergency stop, it could hold the car on a 1-in-3 hill.

The journal felt that the heating and ventilation system suffered from an over-complicated design, "the doubtful policy of more than one manufacturer of expensive cars", with the result that it didn't work as efficiently as the simpler systems on family cars costing a third of the Jaguar's price. In particular, there was no way of con-

The Mk X was the most-tested Jaguar saloon up to that time, with thousands of hard miles being clocked up under arduous conditions both at home and abroad; it was also the most complex saloon Jaguar had yet built. This prototype is disguised with taped-up panels on roof and sides. *Photos: Jaguar Cars*

trolling the amount of hot air delivered (it was all or nothing), and the only way of demisting the screen during slow driving in rain was to use the "prohibitively noisy" high speed setting of the fan. The array of switches and the separate starter button was considered "distinctly unergonomic" and storage space inside was felt to be "meagre" for a large car, although the boot was acknowledged as being "enormous". The four-headlight system gave "exceptional spread and range" and was especially good in fog.

Motor's Mk X was a 9:1cr car, and together with its manual transmission, this made it quicker than *Autocar's* automatic version. The time to 60 mph was cut by 1.3-seconds with a similar advantage being held at 80mph, which came in 19.4-seconds. The 'ton' came up in 32.9-seconds which was less than 0.5-second better, so it appeared that once on the move, the automatic car was little slower in practice. *Motor's* overall fuel consumption was 13.6mpg, with a computed touring consumption of 19.8mpg; in overdrive, almost 25mpg was recorded at a steady 60mph, while at the other extreme, 25-miles cruising at 110mph on the motorway (averaging 101mph) brought the figure up to 12mpg.

The rather disapproving note running through *Motor's* road test caused Jaguar to invite the writer down for "a chat". When the journalist – Roger Bell – arrived, he walked into a room to find virtually all Jaguar's engineers sitting round a long table, and remembers to this day the grilling he received!

There were considerable changes already on the way which would alleviate a number of *Motor's* dislikes, but before the 'new' model arrived, detail modifications were carried out to improve the existing car. November 1963 saw Dunlop SP3 radial tyres (205 x 14 and requiring a new speedometer) adopted in place of the crossplies (*Motor's* road test car must have missed them) and a revised automatic transmission unit with a modified 'anti-bump' main relief valve outer piston to improve the gearchange. January 1964 brought alterations to the cooling system with a new radiator block having a separate header tank bolted on top of the tube-and-fin core; this, together with a re-routing of some water pipes, contributed to increased cooling efficiency and the elimination of air locks.

The same month the halfshaft universal joints in the rear suspension received shrouds, with the joints themselves being made 'sealed' for life shortly afterwards (Jaguar prevaricated here, torn between leaving grease nipples on the joints and seeing them largely ignored during servicing or fitting sealed joints which eventually gave out anyway). March 1964 saw the engine given new pistons with chamfer and drain holes under the oil control ring which collected oil scraped off the bores and returned it to the sump, thus reducing oil consumption further. The first big step in this direction had been the fitting of Maxiflex oil control rings in 1962, which had proved so efficient that a 0.0312-inch hole had to be drilled in the con-rod to spray oil onto the bores because they'd been running too dry. In May 1964, a preset slipper supplemented the timing chain tensioner and took up initial slack to leave the hydraulic tensioner less to do.

On the electrical side, a new distributor was fitted in April 1963 (type 22D6), and in October, the centre horn button was made live in addition to the horn ring. In January twin rectangular foglamps with yellow bulbs

Underbonnet view of the disguised prototype Mk X, apparently fitted with air-conditioning – or possibly a non-standard power steering pump. Quilted sound-deadening material on bonnet was not standard.
Photo: Jaguar Cars

joined those already offered from June 1962 as an option (together with exterior wing mirrors). A line fuse was introduced in the automatic and overdrive gearbox solenoid circuits in May 1964, to protect the wiring should the solenoid fail to cut-out. A limited backlash coupling was fitted to the electric window mechanism in January 1963, to prevent jamming when the windows were either fully open or shut.

Meanwhile, there had been much activity going on at the factory centred around such basic components as engines and transmissions. The horsepower race was in full swing in the United States, and even in Great Britain there were a couple of cars which could challenge the Mk X on acceleration and top speed. One of the latter was the Daimler Majestic Major whose production Jaguar had inherited on acquiring the Daimler company, and which was still being built.

At the heart of the Majestic Major was a superb 90-degree V8 of 4.56-litres capacity and with aluminium cylinder heads; it was effectively a scaled-up version of Edward Turner's 2.5 litre Daimler SP 250 engine, and was notable for its comparatively light weight and tremendous torque – 283ft.lb. at only 3200rpm, compared with the 3781cc Mk X's 260ft.lb. at 4000 rpm. Road tests of the 37cwt car revealed that it possessed a definite edge over a similar automatic Mk X, with 60, 80 and 100mph times of 10.3,- 17.4,- and 30.9 seconds respectively – a margin of around two seconds in each case. Top speed was identical for all intents and purposes, but fuel consumption was actually better. Jaguar's power units division was impressed despite deep loyalties to the old XK engine.

The next step was a natural one – try the V8 in the Mk X and see what happened. Ex-development engineer Ron Beaty recalls the outcome. "It lopped six-seconds off the 0-100mph time, and that was with square-cut exhaust manifolds and an aircleaner you wouldn't put on a lawnmower. It buzzedaround MIRA all day at 133/134mph in the hands of anyone who happened to be about!"

Physically, the engine fitted into the Mk X engine bay with no difficulty, and so theoretically there was nothing to prevent Jaguar following up the 'Mk II' Daimler 2.5 V8 with a prestige Daimler 4.5 litre-engined Mk X; however, the embarassing situation would arise of this variant becoming the quickest saloon in the range, faster than all the four-seaters powered by XK engines. So apparently to maintain Jaguar prestige, the model was not proceeded with. A supplementary (or alternative) reason was that the 4.5 litre V8 was not tooled-up for true quantity production, and it was not worth the company investing large sums of money to expand 4.5 litre production because a new, larger Jaguar engine was already well on the way.

This was the V12 of course; the full story is told in Chapter Eleven, but much of the testing for this power unit was done with Mk X saloons. In particular, the car featured in the experiments which finally decided whether the four-cam V12 or the 'flat-head' single cam per bank engine was to be used. Both types were tried in the Mk X, and top gear acceleration tests proved that the single cam engine had superior torque to the ultimately more powerful four-cam unit lower down the rev band, where it was needed for a road car.

The four-cam V12 engined Mk X was, as can be

A Mk X prototype on test at MIRA, driven in this picture by development engineer Graham Burrows – when sent round the banking, the V12-engined Mk X circulated so rapidly that the full suspension travel was taken up and the tyres burnt the paint off the front wings!
Photo: Jaguar Cars

The first Jaguar V12 engine, with twin overhead camshafts per bank and at one stage seriously considered for a Jaguar road car – the example shown is indeed the SU-carburetted version of the type tried in the Mk X. *Photo: Jaguar Cars*

In 1964 the enlarged, 4.2-litre edition of the XK engine arrived; this is a unit destined for the 4.2 Mk X, with automatic gearbox attached. *Photo: Jaguar Cars*

The 4.2 engine installed in the Mk X; note the alternator and conventional servo (top right) replacing the 3.8's bellows. *Photo: Jaguar Cars*

imagined, quite a devastating machine. This engine was more akin to a slightly de-tuned racing engine than a production unit, giving smooth but unspectacular acceleration "like a 2.4" up to 3500rpm – but then it really took off! Maximum speed was approaching 150mph by all accounts, and this was with completely standard brakes and suspension – "you could put your foot on the brake and the car just carried on!" – remembers Ron Beaty. It became even more frightening when, during investigations into the noise suppression qualities and rigidity of cast-iron as opposed to aluminium, a Mk X was fitted with an iron-block V12 engine weighing well over 1000 lbs, making the car incredibly nose heavy. In fact when driven at high speed around MIRA's banked circuit, the centrifugal force actually pushed the car down on its springs so much that the tyres were pressed against the wings and burnt the paint off! Fortunately, or unfortunately, none of these experimental MK Xs survive....

However, for the production Mk X more power arrived by way of yet another new version of the XK twin cam power unit, which came with a host of other improvements (many carried over onto the 'E' type) in October 1964. Up went the capacity from 3781cc to 4235cc, though in retaining the same exterior dimensions for the cylinder block, considerable rearrangements had taken place inside. Linered as for the 3.8, the bore spacings were altered to accommodate the extra 5.07mm increase in diameter; cylinders numbers 1 and 6 were moved outwards slightly, numbers 2 and 5 remained where they were, while number 3 and 4 were moved closer together. The opportunity was taken to improve water flow around the cylinders by modifying the water jacketing at the same time. Of course the crankshaft was new too to match the different bore spacings, and it had thicker webs for increased strength, rearranged balance weights, and a new crankshaft damper served to break down the torsional frequency of the crank, which otherwise could damage itself at certain revolutions. The connecting rods remained the same, but new pistons carried a chromium plated top ring tapered second ring and multi-rail oil control ring.

The same straight-port cylinder head was kept for the 4.2 engine (time did not permit otherwise), and the fact that the combustion chambers did not quite line-up with the repositioned cylinders was ignored as it made no difference in practice. A new inlet manifold was fitted though, a one-piece casting with an integral balance pipe and water gallery which eliminated steam pockets; three SU HD8 carburetters were still used. The car's entire cooling system had come in for revision with a redesigned tube and corrugated fin radiator, a fan with Holset viscous clutches which slipped at anything over about 2500rpm and consequently absorbed only 2bhp instead of nearer 16, and a speeded-up water pump.

An alternator was fitted to the 4.2 engined cars, and that meant re-routing the various belt drives because the power steering pump could no longer be driven from the back of the dynamo. So the alternator, which ran at twice engine speed, was given its own single-Vee belt running from a groove in the crankshaft damper, while the now-separate steering pump, water pump and fan were operated by another, triangulated belt drive with a spring-loaded jockey wheel to ensure the correct adjustment all the time. To start the car, a Lucas pre-engaged starter motor was now fitted which helped cold starts, as it was not thrown out of mesh by a misfire.

The Mk X's power steering was both new and interesting, and it was exclusive to Jaguar. The Varamatic system, as it was called, had been developed by an Australian named Arthur Bishop from an aircraft nosewheel gear. A report was published on the system by Cornell Aeronautical Laboratories and two years later, in 1958, the Bendix Corporation in America decided to take up the design. Despite excellent results, Bendix failed to find a customer in the States, and so Jaguar became the Varamatic's first user with their Mk X saloon. The Marles Varamatic Bendix power steering (that was its full title) was further developed in Great Britain by Adwest Engineering of Reading.

The name "Varamatic" gives a clue to the principle of

The 'Varamatic' steering box used on the 4.2 Mk X, sharing the cross-beam with the front suspension units. The Jaguar was the first car to use the system, which gave a variable steering ratio.
Photo: Jaguar Cars

the steering – the ratio varied as the steering wheel was turned. Immediately to each side of the straight-ahead position, the ratio corresponded to 4.25 turns lock-to-lock, but by the time the front wheels had turned through about 16-degrees, or about half-lock, the ratio was down to only 2.1 turns. The overall ratio of the new steering was under 3 turns lock-to-lock, compared to almost 4 with the previous system. The varying ratio was given by an hour-glass shaped worm-and-follower arrangement, while the hydraulic assistance was supplied via a rotor valve on the input shaft to a piston within the steering box.

So much for 'go' and 'steer' – the function of stopping had been re-investigated too for the new 4.2 Mk X. The biggest change here was the substitution of the bellows servo for a conventional 'suspended vacuum' servo which gave a direct line-pressure boost; unlike the 'E' type, the brake pedal operated directly on the servo. The braking equipment at the wheels remained the same, except for the Dunlop Mk III calipers which were made out of cast iron instead of malleable iron to cut down bending deflections, and had a larger pad area. The front discs were given mud-shields too. The Mk X's wheel dimensions were essentially unchanged at 14 x 5.5K, but it is worth noting that the 4.2 car's were of a slightly different shape in order to clear the brake pipes.

Finally, the transmission – and here was to be found one of the most important changes of all, for at last Jaguar had gone into production with a modern, all-synchromesh gearbox. It still had a cast-iron case (for rigidity and sound absorbtion) but every forward gear had Warner inertia-lock baulk ring units which positively prevented engagement before synchronisation was complete. Overdrive could still be fitted as an optional extra. Automatic cars were also updated, being given the Borg Warner Model 8 gearbox in place of the old DG unit; the Model 8 was effectively a scaled-up version of the more modern BW model 35 transmission, and had the "D2" position for second gear starts which was shared with the Daimler 2.5 V8 'Mk II' saloon. Fluid temperatures were controlled by a heat exchanger built into the cold return pipe of the engine's cooling system.

The interior of the 4.2 Mk X differed little from that of the 3.8's, only the heater controls having received attention. It was now possible to mix hot and cold air by means of flap valves, but face-level ventilation was still not available. From the outside, the car appeared unchanged except for its 4.2 badge.

The designed purpose of the 4.2 engine was to provide extra torque rather than extra power, and it was rated at the same 265bhp (9:1 cr.) as before – but torque had gone up from a quoted 260 ft. lb. to 283ft. lbs., virtually equalling that given by the Daimler 4.5-litre V8.

Autocar tried the new 4.2 Mk X in October 1964 and found that performance had materially improved. Sixty-miles an hour was reached in only 9.9-seconds, 80mph in

17-seconds dead, and 100mph in 27.4-seconds – better in each instance than the Majestic Major, so one of the objects of the exercise had been achieved! The standing quarter-mile was covered in 17-seconds, while top speed was up slightly to 121.5mph. Particularly noticeable was the improvement in the middle speed ranges, "so that there is more punch in hand after a change up from inter-mediate to top" reported *Autocar*.

The extra urge (it is hard to believe that the increase was confined merely to the torque curve) also narrowed the gap between the Mk X and the fastest of the compact Jaguars, the 3.8 Mk II – the automatic versions of both now had about the same acceleration to 100mph, though the manual 3.8 Mk II still remained consistently quicker throughout. The Model 8 gearbox took advantage of the engine's new pulling power and resisted unnecessary down changes, which made for smoother progress. Nor was there a fuel consumption penalty – *Autocar's* 4.2 Mk X recorded 14.5mpg overall compared to 14.1mpg for the 3.8 road test car.

The new steering was labelled "a revelation", relaxed control being given at high speeds while "on twisting roads, the steering takes so little effort that this big car can be whisked round tight corners with little more than finger pressure on the rim." The actual change in ratio was not thought noticeable by the drivers on this occasion. The Dunlop SP 41 radial tyres, now standard, were squeal-free and roll was described as negligible, but there remained a call for firmer damping, "particularly as, on an undulating road at high speed, there was sufficient verticle movement to compress the bump stops and touch the silencers on the road."

The brakes with their new servo received high praise. "A mere 25lb load on the pedal, scarcely enough to record on the Mintex meter with some cars, gives a near-50 percent stop with this one. Double this pedal load, which is still only the sort of effort needed for a heavy

clutch, scores up appreciably more than 1g retardation, and this heavy car stops all square within 29ft. from 30mph æ under twice its length. The revised heater was thought to perform much better too. "From practically every point of view it is a car which calls for superlatives in its assessment" was *Autocar's* overall verdict.

They had a chance to confirm their first impressions when almost exactly a year later, the journal published a full road test of the manual transmission 4.2 Mk X. Oddly again, it proved impossible to improve acceleration times over the automatic model. "More than the usual number of test runs were made in an attempt to better the 'automatic' times, but it could not be done." Thus 60mph took 10.4-seconds to reach, 80mph 17.1-seconds, and 100mph 29.5-seconds – all slower in fact. The engine could not pull more than 4700rpm in overdrive top, "leaving plenty of margin to cater for downgrades or more favourable winds", that engine speed representing 124mph. The two-way maximum was just 1mph up on the automatic's, at 122.5mph. Petrol consumption was substantially better at 16mpg overall.

The new gearbox contributed much to driver enjoyment:

The latest all-synchromesh gearbox is a great improvement over the superseded unit, and has an excellent set of indirect ratios, such that one is rarely short of a suitable gear for any traffic situation. Movements between gears are quite long, but the gate is well-defined, and the synchromesh quite unbeatable... Second gear, with a useful maximum of 54mph, and third, good for 81mph, are both exceptionally useful for sweeping past slower vehicles....

"Such is the combination of well-bred power, nicely matched ratios, and an easy gear-change that even the most timid driver would find himself pushing the Mk X along very quickly on almost any sort of road, yet at city traffic speeds it is restrained and quiet."

The 4.2-litre Mk X; showing remarkable restraint, no extra chrome or additional modifications were brought in by Jaguar to alter the appearance of the car, so that the very real improvements to its specification remained undetectable from the outside.
Photo: Jaguar Cars

Not that the Mk X could really be regarded as a sports car, as spirited cornering could produce amusing or alarming results – "when driven in a manner not appropriate to its dignity, there was precious little sideways location in these wide seats and one's body tended to slide sideways, leading to involuntary movements of the steering wheel and sudden changes of direction." It was remarked that seatbelts would help check this, "and would have other advantages, as there is no crash padding in evidence, and many sharp and unyielding edges of hardwood on the full-width facia."

Autocar compared the car with others of its type from both Europe and North America which it had tested, and statistically the 4.2 Mk X certainly came out top in most respects. The £2261 Jaguar was quickest in maximum speed, just – the Buick Riviera at the imported price of £3630 being less than 1mph behind. The Rolls-Royce Silver Cloud (£5632) was out of contention at 111mph and so was the Mercedes Benz 300SE (£4086), while the only car to undercut the Mk X in price, the Princess R at £1995, could only manage 106mph. The Jaguar was also the least thirsty of the group, the Riviera being the worst at a little under 11mpg. Brute force told when it came to acceleration though, the Buick clocking a standard quarter-mile time of under 15-seconds, with the Jaguar and Mercedes virtually tying for second place. A similar situation was repeated in the 0 – 60mph stakes, the Buick way out ahead at 7.8-seconds, and the Mk X and 300SE coming next at just over 10-seconds, with the Rolls not far behind. Such aspects as handling and braking weren't discussed, but here the American car would have lost out heavily against the Europeans, amongst whom the Mercedes was probably the more nimble but ultimately

The purchaser of the 4.2 Mk X could specify a new option – air-conditioning. These are some of the major components, including heat-exchanger, refrigeration unit and blower motors, which made up the equipment.
Photo: Jaguar Cars

less predictable than the Jaguar, which possibly also had the best brakes of the bunch.

At the same time that *Autocar* published their 4.2 manual road test, Jaguar announced a new option – air-conditioning. This was *real* air-conditioning incorporating an evaporator unit mounted in the boot, unlike the optimistically described heating/ventilation system detailed in pre-War Jaguar catalogues. Developed jointly by Delany Galley and Jaguar, it worked by drawing warm air from the car's interior through ducts in the rear parcel shelf which then passed through the evaporator unit, to

The rare limousine version of the Mk X, with no outward differences save the interior dividing partition glimpsed through the windows. RAB Cook, then on the staff of *Motor*, borrowed this example from Jaguar for a trip to Scotland.
Photo: RAB Cook

be returned as cool de-humidified air. Freon 12 was used in the refrigeration system, condensed in a two-stage unit mounted below the engine radiator and circulated by an engine-driven compressor. Controls were mounted on a neat crackle-black console above the main heater controls under the dashboard, and they consisted of an on/off switch for the electric clutch on the compressor drive, two variable speed selectors for the twin fans in the evaporator, and a thermostatically governed temperature control. Price with tax was £275.10s in Great Britain, but the expense of the unit plus a lack of knowledge of the very real advantages of air-conditioning even in a country like Britain meant that it is now very rare to see a home market car so equipped. In the States, the unit replaced those manufactured and installed locally.

If air-conditioning was specified by the customer, for whatever market, a modified radiator and larger diameter

fan assembly was added too, in order to cope with the extra load on the cooling system. Then in April 1966, the factory decided that the extra capacity was a good idea anyway, and standardised the arrangement for all cars; it made production simpler as well. The same month, a switch was incorporated in the heated rear window circuit, a plated push-pull device with a warning light alongside, set into the dashboard by the driver. An improved direction indicator switch was fitted too. Britax Autolok inertia reel seatbelts became available in December 1966.

The next big occasion in the Mk X's history came towards the end of 1966, when in October, concurrently with the announcement of the new 420 and Sovereign models, it received a change of name and some minor updating. Largely, it seems, at the behest of American distributors, the big car now became known as the 420G,

Interior of the Mk X (or 420G) limousine, showing the centre partition, cocktail cabinet and even larger picnic tables. Fixed front seats meant less room for the chauffeur. Few of these cars are to be seen these days.
Photos: Motor

Above: The first alteration to the Mk X's external appearance came in 1966, when, renamed the 420G, a chrome waistline and flasher repeater light were added, together with modernised wheel trims.
Photo: Jaguar Cars

Left: A modernised interior came with the 420G name too, with a padded roll and centre clock being added to the facia.

Right: Dignity and size made the 420G an impressive 'official' car; this one served with the British forces in Singapore.
Photo: Joint Services Public Relations Staff

the 'G' apparently standing for 'Grand' though this was never actually specified.

The basic mechanical specification remained exactly the same as before, and the changes which came with the new name were largely visual, and were borrowed from the *decor* which arrived with the smaller 420 series. Except, that is, for the bright metal beading which ran the whole length of the car, commencing at a repeater indicator light which was now set into the front wing a little way back from the outer headlamp. The grille was slightly altered to conform with the 420's, and thus appeared with a central vertical slat.

Inside, Jaguar had obviously taken note of press and customer comments, as the seats were now shaped to give a little more lateral support, and were finished with ventilated leather facings. Like the 420, the wooden top rail of the dashboard was replaced by padded black vinyl as a concession towards safety (and modernity), shaped to include a transistorised clock in the centre. The padded look was transferred to the doors as well, though they kept their walnut cappings. An electric rev. counter took the place of the previous cable-driven instrument, as it had on all the Jaguar range.

After this minor update, the Mk X story held few surprises. Inlet valve-guide oil seals arrived on all Jaguars in March 1967 and helped to reduce oil consumption still further, and solid-skirt Hepworth Grandage pistons were fitted (to 9:1 engines only) from July 1968; a replaceable fuel filter had already been added to the fuel system at the beginning of the year. But development of the 420G itself did still continue, as from the summer of 1968, the front engine mountings were transferred from the bodyshell to the front suspension crossmember beam in order to eliminate possible engine vibrations from being carried through to the body. This was a logical step, as advantage

could be taken of the beam's rubber mountings, and it required no alteration to the crossmember because the bolts holding the steering unit on one side, and the idler unit on the other, were used to take the engine mounting brackets. It did slightly complicate both engine and front suspension removal though, and the revised cylinder block was not interchangeable with the previous engine because of the new mounting procedure.

Then on September 26th 1968, there came a car which made the 420G – and virtually every other luxury saloon in the world – look and feel ridiculously cumbersome and old fashioned. The XJ6 had arrived, and with it a whole set of new standards. But 420G production was to soldier on for almost two-years more, until production of the new saloon had achieved the necessary levels. The last 420G left the factory in August 1970, outlasting every one of the other 'old generation' Jaguar saloons.

A further ironic twist is given to the story in that the Mk X/420G, generally acknowledged to appear the most dated of Jaguar's 'sixties range to modern eyes, could be said to have continued in production up to this very day. For towards the end of 1968, there appeared a 'spiritual successor' to the Majestic Major limousine in the shape of an entirely new Daimler, based on the floor-pan and mechanics of the 420G; it was also nominated the successor to BMC's (as was) big Austin Princess limousine in the new British Leyland Motor Corporation group within which Jaguar themselves had been incorporated that year.

The bodyshell for the new vehicle was assembled by Motor Panels (Coventry) Ltd; to them were delivered the 420G floor pressings, front bulkhead and wheelarches by the manufacturers, Pressed Steel Fisher Ltd. The first step taken during assembly was to increase the length of the shell by inserting an extra 21 inches just behind the

The Mk X Jaguar lives on in the Daimler DS420 limousine by far the largest car made in the British Leyland group

central door pillar, in the form of an extra section of flooring and sill made up of 0.036-inch steel pressings. The new length of sill was made to drop by 1.75 in immediately after the door pillar, for easier entry and exit from the rear seats – the Mk X's large, high sills had always been a little awkward for elderly or infirm passengers to scramble over. To stiffen the elongated structure, a new top-hat section transverse member was welded across the floor where the bracket for the central bearing of the two-piece propeller shaft was mounted underneath.

Under the floor, and running between the existing members front and rear, were spot-welded two longitudinal box sections, 4in. deep and 3in. wide, which increased the beam strength of the shell. All exterior panels were new, and so were the sills, pillars and roof. As the car had a much higher waistline than the 420G, pressings were welded to the existing front bulkhead to increase its height. Through-flow ventilation was built into the car, with slots being placed in the section running under the rear window; being a low-pressure area, air was extracted from the car's interior when on the move. Neoprene valves prevented a reverse flow.

In addition to the normal 420G heater/demister unit mounted under the dash, the rear compartment was heated by an additional Smiths recirculatory unit positioned under the front seat. This took air from the front compartment and discharged it through four ducts

The interior of the Daimler limousine is equipped in typical luxury style, with upholstery in West of England cloth; controls on armrest govern the air-conditioning.

to outlet ports at the base of the division between the front and rear compartments. Rear passengers were given a switch and rheostat control for the auxiliary heater's fan, those being mounted near the left-hand end of the rear seat. Later, fresh air footwell ventilation was added, air being ducted from the horn grilles at the front of the car to outlets in the top corner of each footwell and controlled by "Pull Air" levers.

The 4.2 engine, Model 8 Borg Warner gearbox, and all-independent suspension were standard Mk X/420G components, except for a change of spring rates front and rear to compensate for increased weight; careful attention was paid to damper settings too, in order to obtain the best possible ride. Actual weight was about 43cwt curb, which was 5- or 6cwt more than the normal 420G. Varamatic steering was retained with slight alterations to the hydraulic pressure circuit. Twin petrol tanks of the

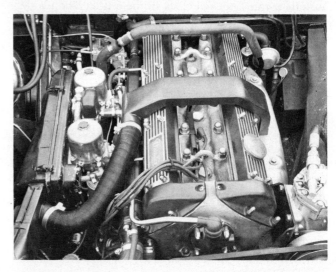

The 4.2 XK engine powering the Daimler limousine, fitted with the crossover emission device.

same 10-gallon capacity remained in the rear wing cavities, each with their own SU petrol pump.

All the mechanical parts were installed by Vanden Plas Ltd of Kingsbury, just off the main Oxford road approaching London, where the complete but unpainted bodies were delivered by Motor Panels. Painting and trimming was carried out by Vanden Plas too, the interior being sumptuously finished in leather and deep-pile carpeting, with folding occasional seats in front of the main rear seating. The Mk X was large enough, but the Daimler Limousine was one of the very few British cars to boast of greater width – 6ft. 6.5in. to be exact, 2.5in. more than the Jaguar. Overall length was 18ft. 10in., and height 5ft. 3.75in.

With its tall, flowing coachwork and big Daimler radiator shell, the Limousine is now a familiar sight outside embassies and international company head-

A very special car – the Daimler Landaulette under construction at the Vanden Plas, Kingsbury Road, plant, a semi-open model announced for very limited, special-order production in 1974.

The Daimler Landaulette, fit for royalty indeed, and the most expensive 'Jaguar' ever produced. It was powered by the standard 4.2-litre engine.

quarters, almost invariably finished in gleaming black with a uniformed chauffeur in attendance. Few more than ten a week were produced, and in 1979 the final finishing just described was transferred to Coventry after the closure of the Kingsbury works.

The Mk X and 420G have, meanwhile, passed into history. Obsolete, their bulk and thirst did not auger well for their survival although petrol consumption apart, they were no more expensive to maintain thań an S-type or 420, and for some reason their bodywork seemed to last better than that of contemporary Jaguars. The type compared badly with the XJ, and to drive a Mk X today æ particularly an early example without the Varamatic steering – one is all too aware of the car's size, a rather over-soft and under-damped suspension, and initial slow response to the helm. But providing the driver can locate himself on the wide seat and summon up the courage to 'cut through' the feeling of imprecision, he will find

unexpected reserves of road-holding and a surprising ability to motor quickly along winding roads.

The car was undoubtedly the most 'Americanised' of all Jaguars, and it was much more suited to the open highways and six-lane turnpikes of North America than the crowded lanes and byways of England. So all in all, it is not surprising to recall the time when it could genuinely be difficult to even give away a reasonable Mk X or 420G – particularly when early XJ6s became obtainable secondhand for reasonable sums. It is only recently that good examples have become relatively valuable, but it may be a fair assumption that because of its very size and lavish equipment, the Mk X and its fellows might eventually become more sought-after (and thus more valuable) than the currently fashionable Mk II saloon, in the eyes of collectors. We shall see – it would indeed be amusing if the oft-derided Mk X had the last laugh of all....

Sir William with a row
of new Mk X Jaguar
saloons, at Browns
Lane. The Mk X was
never his favourite
car, but the type's
undoubted merits are
now being recognised
by the enthusiast and
collector. It will
probably remain the
largest true Jaguar
ever produced.

Chapter Eleven

The First-Generation XJ Jaguars

In our view the only car in the world which rivals the 4.2 litre Jaguar/Daimler for refinement is its 5.3 litre V12 big sister.

Motor, September 22, 1979

Nineteen sixty-eight; a year notable for the introduction of a number of interesting cars from a variety of manufacturers, such as the Ford Escort, all-new and destined to be amongst Ford of Britain's most successful models, the BMW 2002, and by the insertion of the delightful Buick-derived 3½-litre engine into the Rover 2000, the Rover 3500. From Mercedes came another model created from placing a larger engine into a smaller car – the 300SEL 6.3. But the most memorable, and the most significant of all the cars which made their début in 1968 was, almost indisputably, Jaguar's XJ6.

On analysis, there was little that was truly new about the XJ6 – no fancy air, liquid or rubber suspension, no revolutionary power unit or transmission, not even any radically different styling features; yet the small Coventry factory managed to produce a car which at once set a whole array of new standards in ride, comfort, control, handling and silence by which all other manufacturers throughout the world would henceforth be judged. That most of these, even twenty years or more later, are still remarkable, is convincing proof of the Jaguar XJ6 saloon's overwhelming superiority when it made its public bow on September 26, 1968.

In the Jaguar story, the XJ6 is undoubtedly the most significant car since the Mk VII of 1950; but it is a measure of the increased confidence of the company that it was thought unnecessary to write the name of the maker on the front – no mascot either (a victim of North American safety regulations), just a jaguar head medallion set in the radiator grille. The traditional leaping jaguar was present though, in the form of plaques mounted on each side of the car just behind the front wheel arches; at the rear, still no identification, merely the engine size spelt out in plated letters on the vertical face of the bootlid.

The XJ6 was the main component of a rationalisation scheme which was ultimately to result in the XJ series forming the basis of every Jaguar built; but on its announcement in 1968, the new car did not immediately banish all previous Jaguar four-seaters into obsolescence, only the S-types, the 340 and the 420 suffering that fate – and even then, the 420 continued as the Daimler Sovereign. The 420G of course was to remain in production right up to August 1970, emphasising the fact that the new XJ6 was not simply its direct replacement – if anything, the XJ was the direct equivalent of the 420 and S-type, being only 1.25-inches longer than the 420.

Virtually every body component of the XJ6 was new, but its overall shape remained identifiably 'Jaguar', perpetuating a certain look which has characterised the cars ever since the early 'fifties. If first impressions are anything to go by, when I originally saw the still-secret XJ6 at the factory while undertaking the launch photography for *Motor* magazine, it struck me as being a 'squared-off' version of the Mk X, the family resemblance stemming mainly from the forward-sloping nose, and the general sweep of the bonnet and front wings. As an overall shape though, it worked so much better than the Mk X, having none of that car's almost porcine roundness, and possessing a much superior balance of glass-area to body-mass; but perhaps, the most outstanding design feat was the superbly arranged wheel-to-body relationship, and the resulting affinity of the car to the road. The XJ has always managed to convey its tremendous road-holding and handling qualities by the very way it sits on the road, which it appears to grasp and yet flow over at one and the same time. The minimum design life of the car was envisaged as seven years; with very little in the way of major attention to its basic shape, it looks set to treble that life expectancy, still remaining undated and purposeful.

The mechanical make-up of the XJ6 was essentially the mixture as before, but with one or two interesting innovations. Front and rear suspensions were based on Mk X/420 practice, and the XK engine powered the car – this was by now an extremely well-proven design, over 250 000 units having been built by 1968. The steering was a development of the Varamatic system, the brakes were Girling with a new three-pot caliper, a much superior heating and ventilation system was built into the bulkhead, and the interior furnishings were new but firmly in the Jaguar tradition.

The most complex car yet built by Jaguar, the development of the XJ was protracted and often difficult, consuming some four-years and maybe six-million pounds. It was also the first completely new Jaguar since the Mk X, the other saloons introduced in the meantime having been variations of the Mk II. Besides all the usual problems of designing and sorting out a new car, life had been made extra complicated by various regulations imposed by the United States government, and by the parallel development of entirely new engines.

Besides being the most complex Jaguar to date, the XJ6 was also the most refined – and it's worth taking a close look at the refinement of the Jaguar car because it hasn't come about by chance. During the middle to late thirties, and immediately after the war, the better-quality American cars set the standard in isolating a car's occupants from road shocks, noise and vibration (even Rolls-Royce, in danger of being left well behind in the refinement stakes, adopted GM-type independent front suspension, although this, in turn, had been developed by an ex-Rolls-Royce engineer, Maurice Olley!). But with the independently sprung Mk V saloon of 1948, Jaguar for the first time began to match these standards.

This progress was continued at Browns Lane with the XK-engined Mk VII, but it was in the 2.4-litre saloon of 1955 that we first see, in embryonic form, the noise-supression techniques employed later with such success in the XJ6. These needed to be developed because the unitary bodyshell proved much more prone to transmitting noise from the engine, gearbox and road wheels than did a body mounted on a separate chassis, and prototype 2.4s were found to be particularly bad in this respect. While a certain amount could be achieved with sound-deadening materials, it was soon determined that the best course of action was to prevent noise and vibration reaching the shell in the first place.

Main architect of this assault on the refinement conundrum was R.J. 'Bob' Knight who, as Chief Development Engineer, worked under the direction of Bill Heynes. Noise reaching a car's occupants can be defined under three broad headings: structure-borne noise fed directly into the bodyshell by those components (such as engine and transmission, exhaust system, and suspension) which are attached directly to it; airborne noise transmitted to the air by working parts and then picked up by the bodyshell to be radiated to the occupants; and finally, and less importantly, wind noise caused by the air rushing past the car at speed.

A primary defence against structure-borne noise in the 2.4 saloon was the front sub-frame used to carry the front suspension, Jaguar adopting the theory proved elsewhere that if there wasn't a chassis frame to provide a first-stage noise insulator, then why not introduce a local one to do the same job at a key point on the car? But it wasn't quite as simple as that – much work was then needed to arrive at the best method of attaching the sub-frame to the car so that vibratory inputs from the wheels were damped or retuned so that sympathetic vibrations were still not induced in the shell. Considerable calculation and experimentation was needed to arrive at the right solution, because although the softer the sub-frame rubber mountings the better the insulation, they had to be strong enough to locate the frame, too, preventing it from moving in a way that would introduce unwanted steering effects. Furthermore, careful selection of engine mounting types and positions made it possible to tune the engine's pitch resonance to oppose those from wheel bounce, while a crucial factor in the 2.4's refinement was the very low-rate, coil-sprung engine/gearbox mounting. It was also learnt how to tune the rear axle to resonate at a pitch below the usable engine speed in top gear.

As we have seen in the previous chapter, this science was progressively applied to the Mk X which for its new rear sub-frame used a 'vee' rubber mounting similar in principle to that employed on the 2.4's front sub-frame, the 'vee' configuration giving high lateral stiffness to preserve handling but quite low vertical stiffness to counter road and axle noise. At the front, later Mk Xs also used the front sub-frame as an engine mount, another practice continued on the new XJ6. As for airborne noise, the Mk X/420G relied on the extensive use of felt and Hardura, especially on the inside face of the front bulkhead; the XJ6 also used these materials, but in conjunction with a more fundamental approach which included careful attention being paid to the basic design of the bodyshell to reduce airborne noise by means of such design sophistications as a double-skinned bulkhead. The result of all this work, and the fruits of experience going back to the Mk V and the 2.4-litre saloon, was a car which was nothing less than a great leap forward in automobile refinement.

The technical development of the XJ6

To separate engine from chassis development, the latter was commenced using a Mk X as the mobile test-bed for trying ideas out on the road. Originally, the projected new saloon was going to be very different from previous all-independent Jaguars in that the bridge-type subframe for the rear suspension was to be dispensed with, and the individual components mounted directly onto the bodyshell – via the usual layers of rubber, of course. In principle, the layout of the rear suspension was the same as before, with a transverse bottom wishbone and the halfshaft forming the upper link, but in this original scheme the differential casing was fitted with a torque tube or 'nose', doing away with the twin trailing links. The springs and dampers were attached to the body on low-rate rubber mountings.

Prototypes equipped with this suspension handled as well as or even better than cars fitted with the subframe arrangement, but the big snag was a disturbing boom period. For quite some time this was thought to stem from the exhaust system, which in the end was virtually suspended on rubber bands to prove it was being induced by or through the suspension/body mountings. There was

also a mysterious tracking problem, whereby the car wouldn't run true on a straight piece of road, but this was eventually found to be a minor fault in the front suspension geometry.

Chassis engineer Tom Jones then prepared an adaption of the original Mk X rear suspension complete with subframe, suitable for installation in the XJ. The arrangement was examined by Bob Knight and William Heynes. "That's what we'll do, then" said Heynes, and so the XJ received its subframe rear suspension, mounted up under the car behind the rear seat on similar rubber insulated fixings to those used on the 'E' type, Mk X and all the other 'independent rear' Jaguars. The whole suspension assembly was now virtually identical to the Mk X/420G's in appearance, and at 4ft. 10.33in, the track was within 0.33 inch of the 420G's.

Front suspension likewise followed Mk X and even Mk II practice, though with important differences. The suspension units were still mounted on a cross-beam, but on the XJ, this was a large, box-section member instead of a simple forged beam. The method of fixing it to the car was much the same however, vertical loads being sustained by two 45-degree V-shaped bonded natural rubber mountings on the axis of the front wheels, and two large cylindrical rubber bushes on boxed forward extensions taking care of lateral forces. The front engine mounts were also placed on this beam, serving a double purpose – it further insulated the car from engine vibrations, while the mass of the engine itself (80 percent of its weight was carried on these mountings) had the effect of damping road noise coming from the front wheels.

Like the Mk X, the XJ6 used a subframe to carry the front suspension and front engine mounts; but refinement was enhanced by new round mounting-bushes at the front (nicknamed 'six shooters' because of their drilled configuration) and by attaching the dampers directly to the body via specially developed micro-cellular polyurethane bushes.

Photo: Jaguar Cars

Placing the damper outside the road springs allowed a larger unit to be fitted, while mounting the damper directly onto the bodyshell improved the secondary ride (shudder). Note the rack and pinion steering, not used before on a Jaguar saloon.
Photo: Jaguar Cars

Another significant refinement built into the XJ's front suspension was its anti-dive property. This was achieved by inclining the upper wishbone pivot upwards at 3.5-degrees to the horizontal, and the lower one downwards at 4-degrees. Under braking this had the effect of making the suspension upright (or king pin) rotate, which it could only do by pushing the body up, thus resisting dip. This was by no means a new idea (some pre-War cars used the same principle), and it was also possible to achieve a complete cancellation of body dip under braking – or even produce an opposite effect, that of jacking-up the body – but in order to retain braking 'feel', Jaguar felt it desirable to use only 50percent anti-dive (the contemporary Rolls-Royce employed a higher 68percent). But just as importantly, the anti-dive geometry also reduced front spring deflection caused by weight transfer under braking by 50percent, which meant that front spring rates could be reduced by 25percent compared to the 420G, with a consequent improvement in ride.

Also, the Girling Monotube dampers were no longer positioned within the road springs, and their new outboard mounting allowed them greater displacement – 85percent of the wheel travel. Microvon microcellular polyurethane was used for the bushes in the dampers'

upper pivots on the body. New 'Slipflex' bushes were used for the inner pivots of the upper suspension wishbones, and these offered much less resistance to rotation than the Metalastic items used before, with only 1ft/lb of torque being required to rotate the upper arm. Overall, the spring rate at the front wheels was 85lb/in, compared to 108lb/in for the Mk X/420G. An anti-roll bar was fitted as before, acting on the bottom wishbone.

The front subframe carried one other piece of equipment, and that was the steering. This had been specially developed for the XJ6 and incorporated a rack and pinion for the first time on a Jaguar saloon. It was cleverly combined with elements of the Varamatic power assistance mechanism by the makers, Adwest Engineering, principally the all-important rotor valve operated via a torsion bar by the steering wheel. This, together with the inherent directness of the rack, made for a power steering set-up that offered a good amount of 'feel' together with a minimum effort from the driver and a manageable number (3.3) of turns lock-to-lock.

The steering gear was mounted behind the suspension which increased the safety factor, although the steering column incorporated universal joints and a collapsible section as well. The rack mountings were Metalastic pads which allowed a slight movement, thus absorbing road shocks. This movement was accommodated by a swinging link in the lower steering column universal joint.

Brakes on the XJ6 differed from the Girling equipment used on previous cars by virtue of the front calipers, which now had three wheel cylinders, these working two smaller diameter pads on the outside of the disc, and one larger pad on the inside. While this did not produce a greater swept area than before, the effect was to reduce fade and increase pad life. A dual-line braking system was used, in conjunction with a tandem master cylinder and

A view looking up under the XJ's front bulkhead, showing the steering column with its collapsible section and column lock.
Photo: Jaguar Cars

servo which was directly operated by the brake pedal. A dirt shield was fitted to the front discs. The inboard rear brakes were of the normal twinpot caliper type, with a separate handbrake caliper.

When it came to the choice of power units, the situation when development of the XJ began was far from clear, and it was to get more complicated as time went on. A V12 engine was indeed envisaged for future use in the new car, but when the time came for the XJ's body tooling to be laid down, its exact form still hadn't been finally decided – the merits of the racing-type 'four cam' unit was still being weighed against the advantages of the simpler single cam per bank V12, with comparative tests being conducted in long-suffering Mk X saloons. By the car's launch date in 1968, the matter had been resolved in favour of the single cam engine with its better low-speed torque and cheaper production costs – this appeared first in the Series III 'E' type, but not until 1971, and even then there was still a whole year and a half to wait before it was available in the XJ bodyshell.

Inherent in the design of the single cam V12 were 'slant six' or V8 alternatives, using that number of cylinders from the basic V12 and able to be produced on the same tools. In fact the V8 was the favourite of these derivatives for some considerable time, but after prolonged trials in XJ saloons, the feeling grew that it just wasn't smooth enough – it even sounded a bit like a four-cylinder engine, and "it just didn't sound like a Jaguar" as Walter Hassan remarked; he ran a V8 XJ for a considerable time. It was also becoming too complicated, as it lacked the inherent balance of a six or twelve and needed counter-balancing shafts.

There was never any chance of the V12 or derivatives of the same being ready for the initial launch of the XJ, and so the XK engine was the only remaining choice. But even here an orthodox course wasn't followed, for it was the intention to release the XJ with a new 3-litre version of the XK power unit, this being considered sufficient for the car's weight compared to the Mk X at 5cwt less. In fact, it was quite a feasible proposition as the 3-litre version developed around 185bhp, which was only about 5bhp down on that produced by the 4.2 engine; but the problem of low speed torque arose once more, and the 3-litre XJ simply didn't get off the line smartly enough.

Thus it was that the 4.2 XJ6 came into being – a 4.2 engine was commandeered and placed in the prototype XJ shell; it fitted very well of course – except that the bonnet wouldn't close, as the cam covers on the taller block were now too high at the front. The immediate solution for test purposes was simply to cut a hole in the existing bonnet and drive about with cam covers gleaming in the sunshine. As for the production XJ, the bonnet pressing was altered to include the raised centre which is now so much part of the car.

Another little piece of improvisation on the prototype cars revolved around the exhaust system – no-one had

The new saloon was powered by 4.2- or 2.8-litre versions of the XK engine.

thought about making provision for it, and it was a case of having to cut the propeller shaft tunnel to cram the pipes in there... The final production system was dual-pipe, with the unusual feature of a siamese main-pipe section a little way aft of the manifold downpipes to eliminate exhaust 'beat'; the system then continued its two separate paths through two heat-shielded oval silencer boxes in front of the rear suspension, and two larger round ones adjacent to the rear quarter under-panels behind the suspension.

As for the production engines themselves, their specification was entirely conventional; the 4.2 engine was much the same as that used in the 420 Jaguar, with two SU HD8 carburetters rather than the three used for the 420G. (Cars for the North American 'emission' market had twin Zenith-Stromberg 175CDs). Most of the effort had been put into improving the engine's cooling, beginning with a larger impellor for the water pump (turned at a faster rate through the fitting of a smaller pulley), a bigger diameter bypass hose and, in the cylinder head, eliminating the water gallery and circulating the coolant via water transfer holes in the cylinder head gasket – these being made larger on the exhaust valve side to maintain even temperatures. A cross-flow radiator was fitted, with a separate header tank mounted behind the core in order to maintain the low bonnet line; in cars with automatic gearboxes, an oil radiator was built into the bottom of the main radiator. A new 12-bladed plastic fan with a Holset viscous coupling was fitted, the drive being disengaged at 2500 rpm.

The Jaguar 2.8 engine

The 2.8-litre engine (actually 2791.9cc) brought a new capacity to Jaguar's range, and it replaced the 2997cc, 85 x 88m 3-litre unit that originally was to have been the only engine used until the new V12 'family' came into service. With the decision to offer the 4235cc engine as well, torque was no longer quite so important in a smaller engine version so the opportunity was taken to produce the 2.8-litre engine and thus come under the 2.88-litre tax 'ceiling' imposed by a number of European countries. In this form, the bore and stroke were 83 x 86mm.

It could be said that the ancestry of the 2.8-litre engine can be traced back to the 3-litre racing engine developed by Jaguar in the late 'fifties, this being the maximum capacity allowed at Le Mans after the 1957 race, when Jaguar D-types had filled the first four places and secured the marque's fifth win on that circuit. Unfortunately, the 3-litre D-type engine did not always prove to be as reliable as the 3.4 and 3.8 versions, although by the time it was used in E2A – the experimental successor to the D-type entered in the 1960 Le Mans race – it had been developed to give a prodigeous horsepower of somewhere around 315bhp. But with its 'wide angle' big valve cylinder head and aluminium block, it was very different to any production Jaguar engine; about the only feature it shared with the 2.8-litre was the depth of its cylinder block, which dimensionally was Jaguar's normal 'short block' also used for the 2.4 engine.

So it would be more accurate to describe the 2.8-litre as a variant of the 2.4-litre engine, with a slight influence only from the racing unit – for instance, the bore/stroke ratio of the 2.8 was roughly the same as the latter at 1.036:1, compared to 1.035:1 for the 3-litre. It was rated in 9:1cr form at 180bhp gross at 6000rpm, with 182ft/lbs of torque at 3750rpm; the cylinder head was identical to that of the updated 4.2 engine, being the straight-port type equipped with two SU HD8 2-inch carburetters and auxiliary starting carburettor.

The transmission department brought no surprises, though to reduce noise, the helix angle of the constant mesh gears at the front of the four-speed manual gearbox had been increased; a Laycock de Normanville overdrive with a ratio of 0.779:1 was once more available with this box. When overdrive was fitted, a 3.77 final drive ratio was used on 4.2 cars, and a 4.55 ratio on 2.8 models; manual cars without overdrive were given 3.31 and 4.27 axles respectively.

Alternatively, automatic boxes could be specified, Borg Warner Type 35 for the 2.8-litre, and Model 8 for the 4.2-litre; both these transmissions were getting a little long in the tooth now, especially the Model 8, and did not entirely match up to the modernity of the rest of the car. Final drive ratios were originally 3.54 and 4.27:1 for the large and small engines respectively, but in May 1969, all but USA/Canada 4.2 automatics were given the 3.31 axle,

The Dunlop SP Sport E70VR15 radial-tyre especially developed for the XJ6 and used exclusively on the car up until 1979. Wide-section tyres usually create noise but Bob Knight's chassis engineering team successfully overcame the problem.
Photo: Jaguar Cars

and the 2.8 automatic the 4.09 ratio. A limited-slip device was standardised on all the big engined cars.

All cars had 15-inch diameter wheels carrying the largest rim size yet seen on a production Jaguar – 6-inches. These carried the big fat Dunlop E70VR15 tyres specially developed for the XJ and which contributed so much to the car's appearance, handling and roadholding. They had been derived from Dunlop's SP Sport range, and continued to use the 'aquajet' drainage system; wider tyres, particularly of radial construction, are inclined to produce harshness and road noise, but here Jaguar's engineering team under Bob Knight had done a truly masterful job in suppressing these unwanted vibrations, and while others such as Rolls-Royce were more or less forced to continue with crossply tyres, the XJ6 was able to take full advantage of the superior wearing and roadholding qualities of radials. Wire wheels were seriously considered as an option for the XJ, and a set tried on Bill Heynes' own car for a while, but they were never to be offered as a production item.

The XJ's bodyshell

Containing this mechanical package was the steel bodyshell, once more produced by Pressed Steel Fisher Ltd, but not at the Swindon works. At 8500lb.ft/deg. it was even more rigid than the Mk X, though used more support from the roof panel, and was much lighter, weighing 840lb 'in the white.' As the XJ was much lower than previous Jaguar saloons – 1.625inch less overall than the 420 – the problem was to ensure adequate depth in the floor structure without adversely effecting ground clearance or producing an obstructive sill height. The basic method of construction followed the Mk X pattern, with a large number of relatively small pressings being spot-welded together to make the whole.

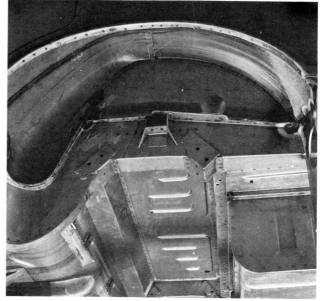

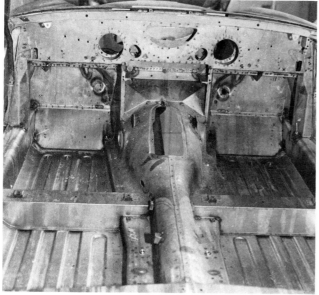

Top left: **Assembling the XJ's bodyshell at Pressed Steel's Castle Bromwich works; here, sections of the main structure (bulkheads and floorpan) are being jigged ready for spot-welding together.** *Photo: Jaguar Cars*

Left: **Air-ducts built into the front bulkhead provided partitions which markedly cut down on airborne noise from the engine bay; deep sills, heavily ribbed floorpan, and deep cross-member contributed to a very strong shell.** *Photo Jaguar Cars*

Above: **Rear end construction; if the slanting rear sub-frame mounting brackets have something of an 'add-on' appearance, it may be due to the original intention not to use a sub-frame and instead mount the suspension components directly to the body.** *Photo: Jaguar Cars*

Large section sills, 'top hat' cross members, and a very substantial front bulkhead combined with floors and door pillars made up the very strong passenger compartment. The bulkhead or dash also used the ducting for the much improved heating and ventilation system as internal bracing between the front and rear walls. From the passenger compartment ran two strong box sections to take the front suspension subframe; they were further braced by the inner wing panels and a box section front cross-member which also acted as the radiator support. At the rear, two box sections ran up and over behind the seat pan to take the rear suspension subframe mountings, after which they met the double-skinned floor of the boot, which was further strengthened by the inner wing panels. Both front and rear sections of the car were designed with the now-required built-in 'crushability' factor,

absorbing the main force of an accident and preventing the car's occupants, in the relatively stronger passenger compartment, from suffering excessive 'g' forces. Approximately 18-inches of controlled deformability was designed into the front of the XJ.

To cheapen repair costs in the case of minor accidents, the XJ's front wings and lower rear wing panels were bolted on to the main structure; removing the latter also revealed the two sealed compartments on either side of the boot which contained the 11.5-gallon fuel tanks. These were filled through recessed caps lying flush with the body panels just inboard of the rear wings behind the rear window. Each tank had its own AUF 303 electric fuel pump mounted under the floor of the boot, with the usual change-over switch and common fuel gauge inside the car.

Interior and equipment

The interior of the XJ6 was clearly a logical development of the trim styles seen for some years in previous Jaguar saloons; a walnut-veneer dash faced the driver, with a padded roll top and bottom, and the two major instruments – speedometer and rev. counter – were set squarely in front of the driver. The four smaller dials were set together in the centre of the dash as before, but the row of switches underneath were now of the rocker variety. A central console rather like the Mk X's contained the heater controls and optional radio, plus the gearlever or quadrant; fresh-air vents were provided at face level now, one at each end of the dash.

For the more expensive models the seat facings were all in Connolly leather of course, and the seats had more pronounced 'shoulders' on both squab and cushion, providing much more lateral support than in earlier Jaguars. The fully-reclining seats themselves were developed by the Slumberland Group, using a miniature version of their 'Posture Springing' system, and apart from contributing to one of the most comfortable seats installed in a motor car, this system had the additional advantage of being 10percent lighter than conventional springing. The door trims and other non-wearing surfaces were in plastic; the front door panels contained combined armrests/map pockets reminiscent of those used in the *rear* of the Mk II Jaguar, while the back seat passengers had similar facilities. Pile carpeting over a thick layer of felt covered the floor, and the nylon headlining was fixed directly to the roof as in the 420.

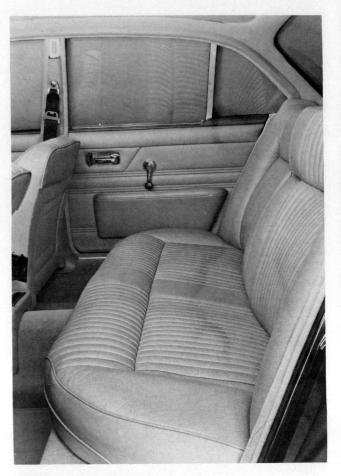

Rear seats in the XJ had shaped squabs and (of course) Connolly leather facings. Note lack of provision for head restraints on front seats in this early car. *Photo: Jaguar Cars*

The convenience of a hinge-down panel for the central instrument cluster was a feature carried over from earlier Jaguars. This picture also shows the central console with its heater controls, optional Radiomobile receiver, and (in this instance) the automatic gearbox quadrant. Knob replaced leaping jaguar badge on air-conditioned models.

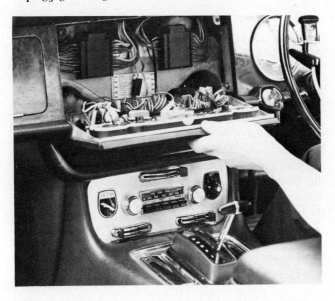

Electrically operated windows were optional, operated by small switches in each door, or independently by a bank of switches set into the forward face of the large glove locker which sat between the front seats.

The heating and ventilation system in the XJ deserves a paragraph of its own, because Jaguar had really tried hard. Engineered by Delaney Galley of Barking, the unit was capable of 5.5kW output at a difference in temperature of 180 degrees Farenheit between the ambient air and the coolant, with a maximum airflow of 160cu.ft. per minute. The desired temperature was selected by the driver, after which a heat-sensing unit would automatically regulate the temperature of the air entering the passenger compartment. The volume delivered could be independently adjusted for each side of the front compartment and for the separate duct to the rear. Part of the system's success was due to the extractor effect of the slot which was set below the rear window inside the car, and which allowed stale air to pass through a one-way flap to the low-pressure area outlet concealed between the bootlid and body. A full air-conditioning unit was an optional extra, specially designed to fit into

Many export cars were ordered with the new, optional Delanair air-conditioning system which was specially designed for building into the XJ. It was, however, only marginally capable of dealing with the hottest climates.

the existing heating system without taking up room in the boot or interior.

The standard 2.8-litre car wasn't quite so lavishly equipped as the 4.2 version; it had Ambla instead of leather upholstery, no rear seat centre folding armrest, a modified console with no provision for rear heater ducts, simplified armrests, no pockets in the rear doors, and no power steering, although you could specify that as an option. This car was something of a 'loss leader' and very few were produced. A de luxe edition of the 2.8 was available though, and this followed the 4.2 car in almost every respect except for the engine. All three XJs represented incredible value for money, and when the time came for the car to be sampled by press and public, they could scarcely believe that such a stupendous car could be offered at the price – the most basic 2.8 was a mere £1797 including tax, and the 4.2 manual/overdrive £2314. The most expensive in the range was the automatic 4.2 at £2397.

A brief comparison with other makes on sale at the same time will bring home this value-for-money factor very strongly – the noisier, less comfortable, slower and generally less refined Rover 3500 Coupe was only £44 cheaper than the XJ6 4.2 automatic, while for marginally less performance, the XJ6 2.8 de luxe undercut it by getting on for £300! Saloons of anywhere near comparable performance and quality from abroad were priced right out of the market, with the 300SEL Mercedes retailing at £5624, the Lancia Flaminia 2800 at £3029, and the Oldsmobile Cutlass at £3612. In overseas markets, the XJ6 was still highly competitive, even if it didn't undercut local opposition (if there *was* anything remotely comparable) by quite so much.

Road-testing the 4.2 XJ6

Autocar published its first test of the XJ6 in June 1969,

the subject being an automatic transmission 4.2 and thus representative of the vast majority of XJ6s built (only a comparatively small number were ordered with the manual gearbox, and virtually none were made during the first year of production). The waiting list for an XJ in Great Britain (and in many other countries) was months long, so the test was read with extra interest by everyone – particularly impatient would-be customers. Unfortunately, it only served to whet their appetites even further....

Speed the 4.2 XJ6 had in full measure, but that wasn't the single most outstanding feature of the car. *Autocar* got it right when it proclaimed: "Now we are entering a new era", for the XJ combined so many qualities that it was immediately elevated above virtually every other car in the world. "From our company chauffeur who merely took the test car through city streets to a drive-in car wash to our most blasé tester, everyone was impressed immediately with the completely out-of-its-class ride and silence. With certain qualifications we would say it is the smoothest and quietest car we have ever driven or been driven in. And that includes cars in the multi-thousand pound bracket like the Rolls-Royce and Mercedes 600. And after detailed discussions our test staff agreed that the handling was, if anything, better than that of the 'E' type and certainly unmatched by anything in the saloon car class."

The car's ride qualities were superlatively good no matter what the surface: "On smooth roads one would easily believe that there was some springing medium other than steel, so gentle are the vertical disturbances. On rough stuff, particularly on the kind of torture like a badly-filled level-crossing, it seems to make little difference, and while passengers look horrified and

Motor's road-test car, one of the original, hand-assembled cars; it achieved a maximum speed of 124mph in overdrive top. *Photo: P. Skilleter, 'Motor'*

335

wince, the driver can storm across without reducing speed because the car barely tremors." Very sharp edges produced a little bump-thump, "but it is very well insulated." Genuine continental *pavé* produced equally impressive results, while 100mph cruising could be maintained on D-class minor roads without fight or kick-back through the wheel.

At these speeds, the sheer silence of the car became truly apparent. This same 100mph cruising speed produced "no wind whistle, no engine noise, no road roar and no transmission whine." About all that could be heard was, at low speeds, a faint hiss from the power steering occasionally and a slight wheeze from the vacuum brake servo in traffic. The XJ's handling elicited the following eulogy:

"Like the ride, the handling and road-holding of the XJ6 are superb. It really feels as if each wheel is hugging the road surface the whole time... On the few occasions we felt inclined to thrash the car through open country lanes at high speed, there was always far more cornering power than we could use.

"In balance, the XJ6 is as neutral as one could wish for. It hugs each curve equally at the front and rear, and the front wheels will always turn more, without understeer, to tighten the line. This latest Adwest power-assisted rack and this application deserves the highest praise possible for its positive feel, quick response and light effort. We could not fault it on any count."

Unlike those in the 420G, the XJ6's seats held their occupants securely and were easily adjusted by a full-width bar running under the front edge of the seat. Other details and improvements were noted, such as the banishing of the separate starter button and the old rotary light switch (the latter replaced by a double tumbler switch), the plated bezels to the instruments (not universally liked, incidentally), the substitution of the ammeter by a voltmeter, the vanity mirror in the glove locker not in the passenger's sun-visor, the hazard-warning flasher switch and the standard (on 4.2 cars) heated rear window. Passenger comfort in the rear was excellent though a little warmth penetrated the floor from the intermediate silencers, as it did the luggage boot – which was low but long and deep enough for "several large suitcases." The spare wheel lived under the carpeted boot floor.

When the journal did return to the subject of performance, it could report a top speed for the car of 120mph, with acceleration to 60mph and 100mph in 10.1-seconds and 30.4-seconds respectively – excellent, although down slightly on the figures recorded for the triple carburetter 4.2 Mk X, which was 1 or 2mph faster in maximum speed and could better the 0 – 100mph time by 3-seconds. So the manual gearbox 3.8 Mk II saloon, which was faster still, remained the quickest Jaguar saloon made, although it had been obsolete for some years by 1969. But straight-line figures do not tell the full story, and in practice the XJ was by far the quickest car over any appreciable distance, by virtue of its outstanding roadholding qualities – never mind its vastly better ride and insulation from road, transmission and engine noise.

The XJ6 was no lightweight – *Autocar* found that it weighed 32.4cwt distributed 52.8/47.2 (front to rear) – but it was some 4cwt on the better side compared to the Mk X and less than 2cwt heavier than the 3.8 Mk II automatic. This helped fuel consumption to an extent, and 15.2mpg was recorded overall after the gruelling eight-day, 1300 mile test – slightly better than that returned by the 4.2 Mk X. Economy was not the automatic XJ's strong point

Stages in XJ evolution: this very curvaceous prototype represents Sir William's earlier thoughts on a Mk X/420G replacement, and carries a number of 'E' type characteristics like bonnet bulge and motif bar.

Slant-eyed look, rather like the Gordon Keeble, was an early feature of this exercise; windscreen looks the divided type but almost certainly wasn't.

This more finished stage exhibits a sill-finisher, and a novel place for the sidelight – between the headlight units.

Below: Most XJ-orientated feature of this prototype is the roof and window pillar arrangement, plus the kick-up over the rear wheel; otherwise the two-door layout places it more as an intermediate step between 2-plus-2 'E' type and XJ-S.
Photos: Jaguar Cars

however, although in practice somewhere around 17mpg was nearer the average obtained by most owners, unless they consistently motored in London traffic. Oil consumption with this particular car was average at 900 miles to the pint.

Motor got into print with their first XJ6 test in May 1969, a month before *Autocar*; the car was a manual gearbox version.

The impression which the new Jaguar made on *Motor* was profound: "We believe that in its behaviour it gets closer to overall perfection than any other car we have yet tested, regardless of price. If not faultless, it is impossible

After-thought: almost as soon as the XJ6 was in production, this revised front end mock-up was created as ideas for a face-lift were investigated; but when it did finally arrive, Series 2 did not adopt the horizontal grille approach.

Below: **This full-size mock-up shows the lights set into the bonnet panel, but the radiator grille is still very much like the Mk X's.**

Above: **Then it is modified to dispense with the heavy chrome top bar...**

...and modified to give a flatter profile which is now very similar to the final product. Here, experimental bodyshop engineers position the new section.

Meanwhile the rear end of the car has been more or less finalised *(above)*, with the familiar 'lift' over the rear light units — Sir William has been accused of borrowing an Alfa-Romeo device here, but it is simply the round tail of the previous exercise 'chopped' *(right)*, the section revealed giving exactly this shape.

The fullsize bodyshell mock-up coming together in the more secret recesses of Browns Lane; note the wire wheels, abandoned as a production option only at quite late a stage.

Almost certainly this is the first XJ body assembled from production parts, one of some half-dozen cars built-up by hand for extensive testing. Note absence of raised moulding in bonnet – scheduled for a 3-litre 'short-block' engine, the height of the 4.2 power unit eventually used for production hadn't been allowed for! *Photo: Jaguar Cars*

Experimental interior of one of the first running XJ6 saloons – compare the many differences (like woodrim wheel, different instrument layout and switch clusters, console, etc) with the actual production interior.

341

to charge it with any significant criticisms, even when judged by absolute standards, and its tally of top marks makes impressive reading."

Thanks to the great efficiency of Jaguar's four-speed all-synchromesh gearbox, this car was considerably faster on acceleration than the automatic, reaching 60mph in a rapid 8.8-seconds, and 100mph in 24.1-seconds – times which few two-seaters could match, and generally quicker than Jaguar's own 3.4 XK 150 sports car of a few years before. The mean maximum speed was 124mph, recorded in overdrive top, and first, second and third gears gave 35-, 53- and 73mph respectively at 5500 rpm – compared to the 53- and 87mph provided by the intermediates in the automatic gearbox. Overdrive also assisted fuel consumption, the car returning just over 20mpg at 70mph as opposed to the automatic's 18.9mpg. Overall there appeared to be less in it, at 15.3mpg, but *Motor* reckoned 20mpg was 'on' with care.

Cruising at 70mph in overdrive top meant that the engine was turning over at 2700rpm ("little wonder that you can't hear it'''), the extra gear providing a relaxed 26mph per 1000rpm; unlike previous Jaguars, the XJ6 had the overdrive switch in the handle of the gearlever, as with Vauxhalls of the time. The gearchange itself was thought pleasant, if a little notchy, with the clutch's heavy 45lb weight camouflaged by a good angle of attack. A

faint whine was detectable from the intermediate gears, especially third, and the final drive was not entirely silent either.

The XJ6's handling was described as "uncannily good" – a phrase that was to crop up over the years when words were needed to convey an impression of the XJ's behaviour.

"The steering (one of the best powered systems we have tried) is responsive, accurate and very light – perhaps too light for our taste as the variations in resistance, so vital for road feel and thus the detection of impending front end breakaway, are really too small to notice. In this respect, we still prefer the slightly less assisted ZF system of the NSU R080 and Aston Martin DBS which, real or artificial, does transmit some sort of message to your hands from the tyres and allows a firmer hand-hold and, on twisty roads, cleaner straihtening up.

"The car just floats round corners with such enormous reserves of adhesion that the driver's nerve will invariably be lost before the grip. We had to try much harder and faster than usual to discover that the initial mild understeer doesn't, as you might expect, build up to a total front-end slide at the limit – at least, not on a dry road – but that the tail drifts gently out. This seems to apply both under power and on the overrun if you lift off in mid corner."

As with any powerful car, the throttle needed to be treated with a little more respect in the wet, "especially on

An early XJ6 Series 1, showing off its feline character in a suitably wild setting. *Photo: Jaguar Cars*

Amongst the many accolades which came its way, the XJ6 captured *Car* magazine's 1968 'Car of the Year' award; the trophy was designed by Bill Towns, who was responsible for the Aston Martin DBS shape.

roundabouts and slippery town streets. Similarly, the car can understeer straight on during a fast trailing throttle approach (even under power sometimes). Perhaps it is because the car normally instills such confidence that any sudden loss of adhesion – and it does tend to be pretty sudden – catches you unaware''. Roll on corners was slight, helped by the wide track, and the brakes appeared

to be easily up to the speeds attainable and withstood the 20-stop fade test from 85mph well – although on another occasion ''we twice detected fade – or at least a noticeable rise in pedal pressure – during heavy braking from high speeds''; rear wheel locking during ''really vicious braking'' from high speeds sometimes occured as well.

Under the heading of ''Comfort and Control'', the journal voted the XJ6 ''one of the most comfortable cars we have ever tried'', and went on to describe why: ''The ride is more stable, but less boulevard, than that of many softly sprung cars; the resilience is there but none of the wallowy swell. Only a sharp hump taken at speed catches it out, the normal millpond float suddenly being disturbed by a rather sickly sinking as the suspension uses up its long travel. Even when the car sinks to the bump stops, though, it doesn't scrape its belly on the road like the last 420 we tried. ''Road noise and tyre thump had been suppressed so well despite the use of the massive radial tyres that *Motor* considered it was going to cause many other manufacturers (''some illustrious ones amongst them'') to think again about suspension and noise suppression. ''British and best'' was how *Motor* summed up the XJ6.

It was not until May 1971 that *Autocar* was able to report on a manual version of the 4.2 XJ6. As expected, it was considerably quicker than the automatic car reaching 60mph in 8.7-seconds, and 100mph in 27.5 seconds, with 123mph being recorded in overdrive top – at 4470rpm, still below the 5000rpm red line. Petrol consumption was only marginally better at 16.5mpg, possible because the manual box encouraged even more spirited use of the car though *Autocar* considered that 4500rpm was a realistic limit through the gears as ''considerable harshness is evident at anything above this, especially when lifting off''.

The acceleration of the car was certainly good, being quicker than the BMW 2800 to 60mpg by 0.2-seconds, and beating the Mercedes 280SE to the same speed by as much as 2.5-seconds. The manual XJ was also the fastest

The XJ6 was born into the era of safety standards and barrier tests; the car passed the statutory 30mph collision test with flying colours.
Photo: Jaguar Cars

to 100mph, the Mercedes lagged behind by over 12-seconds. The Rolls-Royce Silver Shadow was also slower throughout, as was the Chevrolet Impala (60mph in 9-seconds; 116mph top speed). Over the standing quarter mile, the Jaguar more or less tied with the BMW at 16.5 seconds and was quicker than the rest. The German car was significantly more economical though, recording 21.4mpg overall, while the Mercedes managed 17.5mpg which was better too. The Rolls-Royce and the Chevrolet could only obtain an average of 12.2 and 10.3 miles, respectively, from each gallon.

Two years had not caused *Autocar* to alter its opinion of the XJ's other merits – ride, handling, quietness and refinement: "If there is a car capable of matching it on all these scores, we have yet to find it." About the only major grumble was the stiffness of the clutch, which made traffic driving tiring; the all-synchro gearbox was thought to have rather lengthy lever movements but the synchromesh "copes well with all but the most brutal hand-ling." The brakes showed a very slight trace of fade during tests at MIRA, but on the road their behaviour could not be faulted. While some others considered the steering too light, *Autocar* continued to praise it as "among the best we have tried."

The unfortunate *Road & Track* magazine in America did not get to try an XJ6 of any description until early in 1972, or well over three years after its introduction. Their impression of the car varied a little from those of their opposite numbers in Britain – yes, the XJ was outstanding, a true sports saloon indeed, but there were a few things ...

"A strange and wonderous car, this XJ6. It's one of the most beautiful sedans in the world, and certainly one of the best-handling, best-riding ones...elements of greatness to be sure. Its styling, inside and out, is master-ful – combining elegance, graciousness and tradition with a look and feel of speed and sportiness in a way absolutely no other car even approaches. But in some respects – rather important ones – it seems to have been designed in a vacuum; it's as though the designers refused to look around them and see what everyone else is doing these days. Is it British pride, or simply British insularity, that lies behind the XJ's ergonomic backwardness? The XJ is a good car, make no mistake, but it's maddeningly short of what it could be if it were designed as competently all the way through as its suspension and exterior bodywork are."

The particular aspects of the car which *Road & Track* were sniping at were the switchgear ("look-alike, feel-alike") and the lack of column-mounted stalks for such functions as windscreen wipers and washers, plus the (wait for it) ventilation system. This still wasn't up to coping with high ambient temperatures even with the optional ($549) air-conditioning unit fitted – the blowers were not capable of "giving the blast of air we get in domestic cars for rapid summer cool-down" and there was no provision for the conditioning of fresh air, as the unit worked on a recirculatory system.

One can detect that these relatively minor grumbles were in a way more upsetting than such fundamental shortcomings as an old-fashioned engine and transmission. The 22-year-old XK engine was labelled one of the XJ's "vintage" features, not really bad – "just below the general quality level of the car", being "rough and noisy" under full power from 3500rpm upwards and sounding busy and strained at highway cruising speeds (when there was quite a lot of wind noise too, which makes one wonder if this particular car wasn't a little below standard in these respects). However, it was admitted that it was pretty well the equal of Mercedes new V8 engine when it came to performance. The Model 8 gearbox (well known on domestic products) was also at its best during gentle driving, and did not match up to the best recent designs, though Jaguar had actually dealt with that complaint, having adopted the new Model 12 box in June 1970 – *Road & Track's* test car was some months old.

Surprisingly, the brakes fell short of usual Jaguar standards in that fade appeared to set in, with a 29 percent increase in pedal effort necessary after six 0.5-g stops from 60mph; while in normal driving, the brakes did not pull evenly, and in an emergency 80mph stop, a rear wheel locked up.

In America, the XJ6 saloon had to wear the 'Nordel' overriders to meet the 5mph impact regulation introduced in that country.

On the credit side, the magazine rated the XJ6's handling as "slightly better than the BMW (Bavaria) and much better than the Mercedes (280SE 4.5)", with no tyre squeal and great controllability. "Lifting the throttle in a hard turn produces a gentle tail-out transition, one that is usable by an expert driver and not dangerous for a non-expert." The Adwest steering was considered a little too light and with less feel than was ideal – a significant comment coming from an American magazine, even if it was European-orientated.

Considering that the car was an automatic with all the current emission control equipment, including Zenith-Stromberg carburettors and the cross-over heating which used the exhaust manifold to heat up the mixture, it performed well and wasn't too far behind the British road-test automatics. It took 10.7-seconds to reach 60mph, and 34.1-seconds to achieve 100mph; maximum speed was down to 115mph. All quite respectable for an engine rated at 168bhp at 4500rpm. Fuel consumption with "normal driving" was put at 15.2mpg, efficiency being diminished by the enforced use of emission equipment

Meanwhile in Europe, others were having trouble getting the new Jaguar; the home market was, of course, rather used to long waiting lists for Jaguars and resigned itself to a year-long queue – or a $1000 premium over the list price to jump it via the blackmarket. Others were not so patient, and in May 1970 some 20 irate Swiss businessmen and women expressed their feelings by actually flying from Zurich to London and paraded outside BLMC's Berkeley Square headquarters with banners decrying their 14-month's wait. Lord Stokes emerged, took them all to lunch, and said he was pleased that people actually wanted to buy their products so badly.

Something like 600 XJ6s were thought to be on order in Switzerland at that time, and as a Jaguar spokesman said at the time of this well-publicised demonstration, it was heartening that in view of the exotic machinery available to the Swiss they should feel so strongly about wanting a Jaguar. Some 529 Jaguars, mostly XJs, had been delivered to Switzerland since production of the new car had got underway in the first half of 1969. By the end of 1970, overall production figures ran like this: 7000 RHD 4.2 XJ6s, surprisingly less LHD versions at 4180, 5100 RHD 2.8 cars, and 3120 LHD 2.8 examples. Some 19 400 cars in all, a drop in the ocean compared with world-wide demand, and that was despite inflation causing steep price rises at regular intervals.

Motor magazine had to wait 10-months for the 'long-term' 4.2 XJ6 it purchased, largely, thought editor Charles Bulmer, because they'd specified a manual gearbox car. It was run for a pleasantly trouble-free 18 000-miles and showed its tremendous capacity for silent, high speed crusing, especially on the continent where 110mph could be maintained for miles on end.

One such journey showed a running average of well over 80mph for 460-miles across Germany from the Austrian to the Belgian frontiers in heavy summer weekend traffic, with the car still returning 17.7mpg. "It is difficult to think of any other car in the world", commented Charles Bulmer, "which can compare with it for carrying four people across Europe with maximum comfort and speed and reasonable economy." About the only disappointment was the fresh-air ventilation system, which wasn't up to coping with warm climates.

Actual faults were few; a mysterious clicking or pinging noise from the rear end was never tracked down (two years later the factory cured the trouble by replacing the steel rear hub spacer with a phosphor bronze one in production), a leaking clutch master cylinder seal, a slight water leak from the cylinder head gasket which virtually cured itself after the head nuts were tightened down, some brake roughness (cured by new pads), and the failure of the heated rear window switch.

Much head-scratching was caused by steering shimmy and high speed vibration, until changing the tyres round gave a clue to the cause, though it was a bit more complex than simply out-of-balance wheels - eccentricity of the tyre or tyres was the culprit, and the offside front one was over one-eighth inch out. "Obviously this is a serious problem with very high speed tyres. Periodic rebalancing is desirable to keep the tyres in shape but even then they may distort after prolonged very high speed motoring and become virtually unusable long before the tread is seriously worn." Otherwise the XJ's rubber was very long lasting, the set on 'Motor's car having an estimated life of over 30 000-miles.

The 2.8 litre XJ6 was never given the honour of a full road-test by a major journal in this country, because Jaguar never released an example for this purpose. In any case, the model did not have a particularly happy history – sales were lower than expected, for it seemed that once again Jaguar had underestimated the market capacity for the top range cars, and even in countries where the 2.8-engine capacity would result in cheaper tax and insurance for the owner, the preference was still for the 4.2-litre car. Added to this, reports began to filter through to Browns Lane of extraordinary cases of serious piston failure in the 2.8-litre XK engine.

Jonathan Heynes, son of William Heynes (by this time Vice-President, Engineering) was the first to confirm these reports, after visiting a Belgian distributor on a trouble-shooting mission – sure enough, there was a 2.8 engine complete with a well and truly holed piston. This was not a unique occurance either, but mystified the factory because they were not at once able to duplicate the fault experimentally; nor could any material defects be found in the components. Eventually the cause was discovered to be "residual metallic ash deposits" which built up on the combustion chamber, valve and piston surfaces and caused detonation, which under certain conditions would burn through a piston. Apparently the exhaust valves were too close to the pistons in the 2.8-litre engine, and it was this that was the cause of the problem.

It has also been suggested that inadequate cooling of the cylinder bores (because of the thickness of metal round the smaller diameter cylinders) caused the pistons to 'pick-up' on the cylinder walls, with consequent breakages.

This had not come to light during Jaguar's own extensive pre-production tests of the 2.8 XJ engine because, it seemed, the build-up of these injurious deposits only occured on cars driven slowly at relatively low revs; even then, piston failure might not follow, unless the car was subsequently driven at high speed and wide throttle openings. In other words a 2.8 driven constantly fast – thrashed, in fact, like a test car – was least likely to be effected, which explains why experimental road testing had not discovered the fault before cars were released to the public. Although revised pistons were fitted from June 1970 (engine number 7G.8849 on), there was little the factory could do except advise careful removal of all deposits from the engines affected, and the resetting of the static ignition timing to 6-degrees BTDC, which was found to postpone the onset of detonation at wide throttle openings.

In all other respects the 2.8 was an excellent car, with all the virtues of the larger engined XJ at a lower initial cost. Silence, ride and handling were up to the same standards, the last two maybe even fractionally better due to the lesser weight of the short-block engine. As for performance, the 2.8 was by no means a slow car, and there was roughly the same relationship between the 2.8 and the 4.2 litre XJs as there had been between the 2.4 and 3.4/3.8 Mk II saloons. During normal driving the loss of almost 1.5-litres was not too noticeable; fast driving being required to reveal a lack of reserve power com-

pared with the larger engined car. Maximum power was developed at the high engine speed of 6000rpm, so when full performance was required, the gearbox needed to be used and the revs kept up. This in turn didn't exactly help economy, and just as with the 2.4 Jaguars of earlier years, there was little point in ordering a 2.8 XJ in order to save on petrol costs – 1 or 2mpg extra was about all that could be hoped for.

While the XJ 2.8 was indeed never independently tested here, Jaguar themselves did take full sets of figures with the car at MIRA, and as far as can be established, they are properly representative of the type. On acceleration, the overdrive 2.8 saloon was consistently faster than the lighter 240 overdrive Jaguar, with 60mph and 80mph times of 11.0 and 19.3-seconds. 100mph was reached in 35-seconds, or about 5-seconds more than the automatic 4.2 XJ took to reach the same speed. Probably more noticeable in day-to-day driving was the slower pick-up in top gear though; 30-50mph took 8.7-seconds for the 2.8 car, but only 6.9-seconds for the overdrive 4.2. Likewise, 60-80mph was covered in 6.8-seconds by the 4.2 car, while the 2.8-litre took 9.8-seconds.

The automatic 2.8 was of course slower still, 60mph being reached from a standstill in 12.6-seconds, 80mph in 21.9- and 100mph in 39.9-seconds; its maximum speed was 113mph, compared with 117mph given for the manual car. One market at which the 2.8 was aimed was West Germany, and here at least it *was* tested, including by *Auto Motor und Sport* in a comparison test with arch rivals on the luxury car scene – the BMW 2800, Fiat 130, Mercedes 280SE and the Opel Diplomat. All had automatic gearboxes, including the XJ 2.8.

Frankly, the Jaguar didn't fare too well. For a start, it was by far the most expensive at 26 496DM, over 3 500DM more than the next costly, the Mercedes 280SE; and it had the highest running costs. Against the other cars, it was also marked down on performance (although the car tested seemed slower than average) and roominess. Only in looks and in the success of its suspension did it clearly show superiority. Of 'riding comfort', *Auto Motor und Sport* wrote:

> "In this the Jaguar excells and is way ahead of its competitors; here it can make up most of the points lost so far. It is no exaggeration if we put the Jaguar one class in front of its competitors. The suspension takes up all the unevenness of the road in an excellent way even at slow speeds making the Jaguar feel all softness. Good comfort at low speeds has been bought at the cost of bad shock-absorbing conditions sometimes at high speed but the XJ6 proves to be way ahead even at high speeds...."

At the end of the test, however, things had evened out and in the magazine's marking system, only 5-points separated the first and last cars – the Opel with 332 and the Jaguar with 327. "The five competitors are very much

About the only way to identify the smaller engined XJ6 was by its '2.8-litre' badge carried on the bootlid.

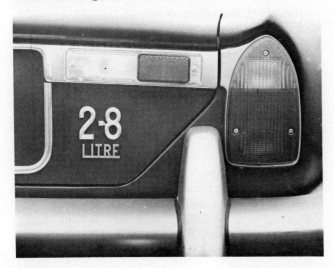

different and each has a character of its own. But none can be definitely regarded as the best or the worst. Rejection or attraction can depend on very personal arguments: whoever is fascinated by the shape of the Jaguar will hardly be satisfied with the Fiat and he who is enthusiastic for the BMW engine will not look at the Mercedes or Opel.''

Even though the 2.8-litre saved the German motorist paying extra road tax, its advantages did not in the long run outweigh such disadvantages as a power deficiency and a lack of reliability, and the last 2.8-litre XJ6 was completed in May 1973.

The Daimler Sovereign

Daimler, in the meantime, had not been allowed to fade away; the '420' Sovereign remained in production until August 1969, and then, after a decent lapse of two months, the model name was reissued on the XJ6 body. The new Daimler Sovereign was announced on October 9 1969, and it was identical to the Jaguar except for a fluted 'Daimler' radiator (gaining the car its nickname, by the irreverent, of 'the crinkle-cut Jaguar'), badging, and (as with the previous Sovereign) a number of extras incorporated as standard – such as overdrive on the (few) manual transmission versions. It was available in both 4.2 and 2.8 form. With the substitution of the new Sovereign for the old, all links with the previous generation of Jaguar saloons were cut – from now on, every production Jaguar and Daimler saloon would be XJ based. True, the Mk10-based limousine soldiered massively on, but it was hardly a production car in the sense that the XJ series was.

Interior equipment of the Sovereign was as for XJ6; this picture shows one of the first Sovereigns, lacking a head-restraint facility. *Photo: Jaguar Cars*

If there had been any passing regrets at the factory over the departure of a 'compact' saloon from the range, they were soon forgotten in coping with the overwhelming demand for the XJ – and if anything, thoughts would be turning to increased inches for the car, instead of the other way about.

Production changes to the first XJs

While the basic XJ formula had been right from the start (save possibly the 2.8-litre engine's pistons!), detail improvements were constantly being made from the moment the car entered production. Early cars often suffered from petrol fumes (not a fault altogether unknown on earlier Jaguars either), largely cured by new filler caps incorporating an anti-surge flap, while in March 1971, SE HS8 carburetters were fitted which included a new automatic enriching device for cold starting and improved warm-up. In the suspension, stiffer front and road springs and revised anti-roll bars and mountings came early in 1969, together with modified front spring pans to provide better tyre clearance – though this did not altogether cure the problem, and in October 1970 modifications were made to the front wheel arch flanges which finally did. Mudflaps were made an option from August 1969.

Early XJ6 front seats did not have provision for head restraints, but this was rectified by August 1969 – the restraints themselves were optional, and black plastic plugs were fitted in the sockets when they weren't specified. Inertia-reel seat belts could be fitted from then on too. In November 1969, heat shields were fitted between exhaust and body under the front passenger compartments, while 1970 saw quite a rash of interior improvements – fresh air footwell vents using inlets cleverly situated over the headlights, improved door

Better fresh-air ventilation was provided for the XJ series in 1970, through ducts let into the headlight 'peaks'; the flow was controlled by a lever inside. *Photo: Jaguar Cars*

locks, scuttle vent grille changed from bright chrome to satin chrome to avoid glare (both these in April), new interior mirror (May), non-reflective bezels fitted to the instruments in place of the rather gaudy plated finish seen before, and the transference of the toolroll and jack from the spare wheel compartment to the boot itself. October saw new aluminium door tread plates incorporating the name "Jaguar" – the only place on the entire car where the maker's name appeared!

A number of minor changes were made to the engine, (including quieter running camshafts in November 1969, improved engine mountings, and the standardisation of the emission-type exhaust manifolds on all engines in March 1970) but the most important – so far as possible consequences were concerned – was the re-introduction of the old type of camshaft sprocket adjuster plate in place of a new one which had been tried for a while; this latter item had proved to be something of a disaster, as it had lobes in place of vernier teeth and could strip, resulting in a loss of camshaft drive with consequent havoc to the valve gear. This substitution was carried out retrospectively on earlier cars too. A visible underbonnet change was a new brake fluid reservoir positioned on the inboard side of the brake booster, instead of at the rear, this being affected in July/August 1970. An improved crankshaft rear oil seal was fitted in April 1971 to the 2.8-litre car.

Not much was done – or was needed – to alter the car's appearance though side and flasher lamps to meet EEC regulations were introduced in March 1970, and stop/tail lamps to similar requirements in August; the changes were hardly noticeable though. Nor was the three-piece rear bumper which came in March 1971, the two wrap-round side members meeting the central section behind the overriders.

More significant was the new automatic gearbox which arrived on the 4.2 XJ during the first half of 1970. This was the Borg Warner Model 12, and it replaced the elderly Model 8, though was really a tougher, more developed version of that box; its capacity for much higher torque input (up to 40 percent more) than given by the XK engine immediately provoked speculation as to the possible imminence of the much-talked-of but still secret new engine from Jaguar. The advantages of the revised gearbox included part-throttle down changes (you didn't necessarily have to floor the throttle and operate the kick-down switch to obtain the intermediate ratio while in Drive), and a better over-ride control. Instead of the P-R-N-D-L selector, the Model 12 had a P-R-N-D-2-1 layout with no detent between 2 and 1. Ratios remained the same, and so did full-throttle performance. The 2.8-litre car stayed with its already more up-to-date Model 35 box, though it was modified to incorporate a self-adjusting front servo in October 1970, cutting out a routine maintenance task.

Production of the XJ6 had been steadily increasing

The Borg Warner Model 12 automatic gearbox arrived in 1970, together with a new quadrant giving a choice of 'D1' or 'D2' instead of just 'low' gear.

from 140 a week during the build-up year of 1969 to some 450 a week by early 1970. At the end of that year, Jaguar announced that more XJ6s had been made than any other single model in previous ranges over a 12-month period. But long waiting lists remained, and low-mileage used XJs continued to fetch 'new' prices. By September 1971, over 50 000 XJ6 and Daimler Sovereign saloons had been built, of which more than 28 000, or 56 percent had been exported. Weekly production was now up to 650-units, with North America receiving about 100 of that total, and inroads were at last being made on the backlog of orders. The new Series III 'E' type, with its 5.3-litre V12 engine, was selling well too, and on the roads around Allesley village, the observant were noticing that certain factory-registered XJs had a rather different exhaust note and a distinctly quick turn of acceleration away from the lights ...

Building the XJ6: a completed bodyshell (followed by a Series 3 'E' type) enters a drying oven after receiving a coat of primer.

The body-mount line, with completed bodies being lowered onto engine and front and rear suspension assemblies – much the same procedure as Jaguar originally introduced for the 2.4 'Mk I' saloon in 1955.

With all mechanical components in place, the third and final production line saw the remaining items of trim and minor accessories installed. Then came road-testing, rectification as necessary, and final paint inspection before despatch.
Photo: Jaguar Cars

When during the early sixties Jaguar began to think seriously about a completely new range, it was chiefly with racing applications in mind. The prospect of competing at Le Mans once more had become attractive, and the XK engine, with its old fashioned long stroke, had really been developed up to its practical limits for long-distance racing. A new engine could also take advantage of the larger, 5-litre, capacity limit for sports prototypes at Le Mans. It was envisaged that a de-tuned road version of this unit would be suitable for powering production Jaguars – a reversal of the original engine philosophy of 1948, when the XK power unit was built purely for road-going use, and only afterwards developed into a supremely successful racing engine.

The 4991cc, 87mm x 70mm prototype V12 engine which stemmed from this thinking had twin overhead camshafts on each bank of cylinders, and closely followed XK design features in principle, though with significant differences, such as a shallower combustion chamber depth, an included valve angle of 60-degrees instead of 70-degrees, and a downdraught inlet port, as engine bay space precluded sidedraught ports as with the XK. This engine produced 502bhp at 7600rpm, though further development finally increased this to a massive 802bhp at 7600 rpm.

Simultaneously, production versions of the engine were being developed and these easily met the first of the original design requirements, which specified an engine which in production form would give the same power as the best achieved by the XK engine in full racing trim – around 330bhp. It was less successful in meeting other parameters, particularly those which required the new engine to be reasonably cheap to make, and to fit into the bodyshells of existing models without structural alterations. Both fuel injection and carburetters were tried, and test engines fitted to Mk X saloons for road evaluation. Then came the final decision not to re-enter motor racing, inspite of a superb mid-engined and potentially highly competitive sports racing car (the XJ13) having been designed, built and tested.

This of course meant a reassessment of the whole power unit situation, as top-end power immediately became much less important than a healthy supply of low and middle range torque, which is the requirement of a road car. While experiments continued with the original four-cam engine, a completely new design was gradually evolved which would be cheaper to produce, and be quieter and more refined that the 'racing' engine. Coventry Climax (part of Jaguar since 1963, and bringing Walter Hassan back into the fold) had previously developed a 'flat head' design, and this was investigated using single-cylinder experimental engines with encouraging results.

These showed that the single-camshaft, flat-head

Above: **Jaguar's first V12 engine, with** *four* **overhead-camshafts; this wet-sump example (racing versions were dry-sump) is shown bereft of carburettors – with all ancilliary equipment it was indeed a bulky mass to accommodate, and in the end it never saw the engine compartment of an XJ saloon.** *(Below)* **Its place was taken by the simpler, flat-head, V12 engine developed afterwards and first used in the 'E' type.** *Photos: Jaguar Cars*

layout was superior to the traditional Jaguar/Weslake hemispherical, twin overhead camshaft design in every respect up to 5000rpm. A full-size engine was then built which gave very similar results; this was of slightly larger capacity than the four-cam engine because there was no longer any necessity to remain below 5litres, so the bores were enlarged from 87mm to 90mm, giving 5343cc. The advantages of the single-cam, flat head engine over the twin-cam per bank layout are summarised by Walter Hassan as follows:

a) the basic head is simpler and cheaper. There is a considerable weight advantage (16 lb. per head assembly)
b) weight and cost are reduced by using a single chain drive with four sprockets compared with four chains and twelve sprockets. The noise level is lower and the drive smoother with twice the number of cams on each shaft.

c) the smaller bulk of the single-cam box permitted the use of a low-mounted twelve-cylinder ignition distributor and space for an air-conditioning compressor between the cylinder heads. Providing space for auxiliaries on the twin-cam engine would have been a formidable problem.

d) the overall width across the valve covers, and more importantly across the exhaust manifolds, is less; the latter is critical for large wheel lock angles in conjunction with wide tyres to obtain a smaller turning circle.

Saying goodbye to the classic configuration of hemispherical combustion chambers and twin overhead camshafts was not easy, and it required a practical demonstration before the matter was resolved to William Heynes' satisfaction at least. Two Mk Xs were prepared, one with the four-cam engine, the other with the flat-

head V12; on driving these it was very obvious how much better the flat-head engine pulled from low revs, scoring heavily on top gear acceleration until well over 5000rpm. This factor, combined with cost and space considerations, overwhelmed any lingering objections, and from then on it was all systems go for the single-cam engine.

Of course, the one basic premise remained – it was still a V12. This configuration had been chosen for a mixture of practical and prestige reasons; that a large number of Jaguars were sold in the United States, and that V8s already dominated this market, made it very sensible for Jaguar to be different and appear with a V12, taking advantage at the same time of the V12 'mystique' built up by such true exotic cars as Ferrari and Lamborghini. Then practically, the V12 has also equal firing impulses

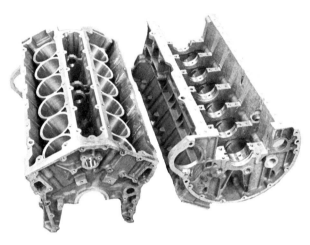

Top and bottom views of the production V12 engine's aluminium block, in finished machined form. Right-hand view shows the considerable depth of 'skirt' – the cast-iron XK block ended at the centre-line of the crankcase.

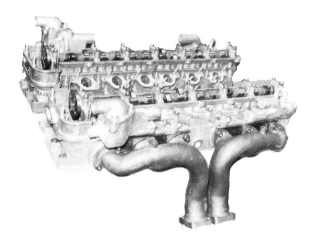

V12 heads assembled but with covers removed to show the single camshaft per bank; inlet ports are visible on farthest head, and exhaust manifolds on nearest. These are actually from a Series 3 'E' type engine, but little was changed for the saloon installation.

The aluminium cylinder heads of the V12 engine, before machining. Farthest casting shows the 'flat-head' design, with six sets of inlet/exhaust ports (without valves at this stage, of course)

The V12 engine is usually only seen installed, and obscured by all the plumbing and accessories that surround a modern power unit so that the 'V' formation of the cylinders is almost completely hidden. However, this view of a stripped block and heads displays it very well.

along each bank of cylinders, and unlike the V8 is inherently free of out-of-balance forces, making it an extremely smooth power unit.

The production V12 had an aluminium crankcase, not known before in a road Jaguar though seen in the D-type and competition 'E' type; it also differed from the XK engine in having a skirt extending 4-inches below the crankshaft, to increase beam stiffness and the rigidity between cylinder block and transmission housing. The 'open deck' alloy block also saved 116 lb. compared to a cast iron one, which was actually made and tested because of fears concerning bearing rumble (unfounded as it turned out). Cast iron was still used for the seven main bearing caps, and the prefinished liners were a light push-fit into the block.

Major items such as crankcase and cylinder heads were already being tooled up for as development was continuing with combustion chamber shape, now even more important because of increasingly severe emission control regulations coming into force. The engine's basic dimensions were in fact decided before Walter Hassan and Harry Mundy were completely ready to say that these were their final requirements, but work had to begin on the lengthy and expensive business of producing the major tools on which the engine would be manufactured if any sort of deadline was to be met. As it was, production was some two years behind the date originally envisaged, the launch being postponed at roughly six-month intervals, not the least because of the time needed to meet emission regulations.

The new V12 engine was a centre of attraction wherever it was displayed. Here the famous Mme. Joska Bourgeois, Chairman of Jaguar's Belgian importers, describes the engine to H.R.H. Prince Albert of Belgium (centre), together with M. Jacques Mounier, managing director of the Belgium Motor Company S.A.

Originally, the piston crown was of the Heron form, with cutouts for the valves, but later a simple, shallow bowl-in-piston crown was settled on. Compression ratio commenced at 10.6:1 but was later reduced to 9:1 in the search for a cleaner exhaust, with provision for 7.8:1 ratio later on for use with 91 octane lead-free fuel. Emission considerations also ruled out the use of the Lucas mechanical fuel injection system used on the later D-types and many other racing cars because the metering could not control the fuelling accurately enough, although it gave excellent maximum power and torque figures. The day appeared to be saved when Brico Ltd. developed an electronic fuel injection system, but just as it was being satisfactorily installed, Brico cancelled its production plans, leaving Jaguar with no alternative but to continue with carburetters.

Because bonnet height restricted the space available, the four Stromberg 175 CD emission control carburetters used were placed outside the 60-degree 'V', with 11-inch induction pipes leading to the ports; had suitable British-made downdraught carburetters been available for mounting within the 'V', the designers would almost certainly have used them. Camshafts were still operated by chain in a single stage layout with a special tensioner jointly developed by Jaguar and Morse – belts would have increased the engine's length, and anyway Jaguar's experience of them was not very extensive so they elected to stay with the medium they knew.

The new engine's ignition system was quite advanced, using a completely new design by Lucas based on units developed for racing engines. It employed their OPUS (Oscillating Pick-up System) device which used an electro-magnetic pick-up and solid-state switching, instead of the more fallible make and break mechanism; wear problems were eliminated, and ignition timing remained constant, which was a very important factor in controlling exhaust emission levels.

The big centrally-positioned distributor of the V12 engine, which worked in conjunction with the OPUS solid-state ignition system. Note as well the long inlet tracts leading to the ports. *Photo: P. Skilleter*

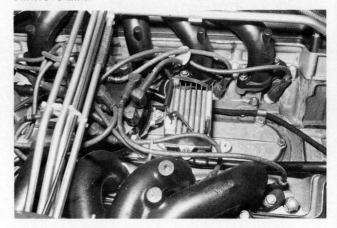

As installed in the XJ saloon, the engine gave 265bhp net at 6000rpm, a figure considerably more honest, it should be said, than the 265bhp gross which used to be quoted for the old 3.8 and 4.2 straight-port engines. But while obviously intended for the XJ series, the new V12 made its bow in a revamped edition of the 'E' type, which appeared as the Series III in March 1971. Rather as the original XK engine had received a useful 'try-out' period in the XK 120 sports car, so the V12 production line could be 'run-in' using the 'E' type as a pre-XJ test bed.

The assembly of the V12 engine took place at what had been the Daimler factory at Radford, and some $3 000 000 had been spent on the tooling-up programme. Automation of the procedures involved was considerable, with many operations carried out on automatic transfer equipment such as the three Archdale machines with a total of 57-stations which handled the single most complex aluminium component, the cylinder block; these cost £850 000. Machinery for the aluminium cylinder head cost a further £700 000 installed, and included a 42-station Huller transfer machine. The extensive use of alloys meant careful handling of components, and equally careful testing afterwards. Final machining of the cylinder head face wasn't carried out until all other work has been completed.

The new shop also included an aluminium small-components section, where such items as the manifolds, tappet blocks, sump, camshaft covers and water pump housing were machined after their arrival from the foundry. The crankshaft was in EN 16T steel, and underwent a complex series of operations, with main and big-end bearings being finished to an accuracy of 0.0003-inch. The actual assembly of the engine was carried out on an electrically driven 52-stage track with the block contained on a cradle which could be swung to various positions.

One of the three Archdale machines which Jaguar invested in for V12 engine production, for the finishing of the aluminium blocks.

Part of the engine-build line, with V12 blocks being fitted up with various parts.

Nearby, various sub-assembly sections built up the cylinder heads and the crankshaft/clutch/flywheel assembly, which afterwards was balanced as a complete unit. Finally, the standard Jaguar practice of bench-testing was carried out on each completed engine before it was taken by lorry to the Browns Lane works, some three miles from Radford. Initial output when the XJ12 arrived in July 1973 was estimated at 200 units a week, 100 of these going into the 'E' type, but the assembly line itself had a total optimum capacity of approaching 1000 units over an 80-hour (two-shift) week. The machinery was also designed so that alternative configurations and capacities could be produced on the same equipment, such as V8 and straight-six variants of the '12'.

While it was indeed intended that the XJ saloon would one day get a new engine, it was far from being built around the production V12, as the major engineering features of the car had been determined long before the V12 engine design had been finalised. Thus it was still quite a shoe-horn job to insert the new power unit in the XJ shell, with a number of dummy engines and ancilliaries in wood being used to determine the final installation – certainly, if the original twin-cam design had been retained, the task would probably have turned out to be completely impossible. It wasn't the bulk of the engine itself that was difficult to accommodate, so much as the large number of ancilliary components which a modern power unit has to carry these days, and the complex plumbing of the cooling arrangements.

An engine bay crammed full of 5.3-litres of hard-working machinery creates other problems too, of which heat dispersal was the greatest. While the V12 'E' type had bonnet louvres to help keep down underbonnet temperatures, Jaguar obviously considered that such alterations to the XJ were not appropriate, so they concentrated on other ways to counteract the heat – which was aggravated by pollution control equipment on North American cars where the exhaust manifolds were injected with air to promote additional combustion of hydrocarbons (the pipes could glow red-hot), and also by the extra loads imposed by air-conditioning plant when this was specified. So high could underbonnet temperatures rise that the battery was given its own cooling fan, enclosed within the battery container. True, the battery could have been placed at the rear of the car, but this would have needed extra lengths of expensive cable and additional time on the production line to route it (though on the XJS, that's where it ended up).

This is how the V12 power unit looked when mounted in the car; the four Stromberg carburettors are visible, fed by cool air ducted from the nose via AC filters. Note the central capston for the throttle linkage. As further equipment was added, so the XJ's engine compartment became even more crowded.

Even the basic water cooling system was complex; the cross-flow radiator, lacking the mixing effect given by the header tank of a vertical flow radiator, had to be divided horizontally into an upper 36-tube section and a lower 80-tube one, to maintain even temperatures in both cylinder tanks – the water from both banks met in the upper section, with the total flow then passing through the lower 80-tube section, which incorporated a transmission oil heat-exchanger. A generous four gallons of coolant were used, pressurised at 13psi, and a four-blade Airscrew Weyroc electric fan supplemented a 17-inch diameter engine-driven fan – the latter with a Torquatrol viscous coupling which allowed slip above 1700rpm. The electric fan ran continously on air-conditioned cars when the compressor clutch was engaged, otherwise cutting-in at 90 degrees Centigrade and out at 86 degrees Centigrade. It was still possible to fit a Bray engine heater, an adaptor being incorporated on the water pump housing.

Heat shielding by stainless steel guards protected the steering rack and engine mountings, while the exhaust downpipes themselves were double-skinned to reduce noise; heat shields also protected the bodyshell from heat as the exhaust pipes ran the length of the car. Silencing was basically as for the six-cylinder car, and was effective enough to make it difficult to distinguish the exhaust note from that of the XJ6 unless you listened carefully!

High underbonnet temperatures generated by a large engine in a relatively small space prompted Jaguar to fit an extractor fan to the battery box, to prevent excessive evaporation of the distilled water! *Photo: P. Skilleter*

The V12 power unit as fitted to the XJ differed in minor respects to that used by the Series III 'E' type. The XJ's front suspension crossmember meant that the water/oil heat exchanger built into the front part of the sump could not be used, and instead a conventional twin-tube oil cooler was mounted below the radiator. The overall state of tune was the same though, and the XJ also shared the very efficient throttle capstan mounted to the rear of the 'V' which gave the accelerator pedal its smooth and progressive action.

The XJ12 itself; no outward changes except for a new radiator grille with vertical-only slats – a simpler and possibly more attractive design than the XJ's cross-hatched style – and, of course, badging. But the XJ12's performance was virtually unmatched by any other full four-seater in the world. *Photo: P. Skilleter, 'Motor'*

The engine weighed 680lb, or about 80lb more than the XK six-cylinder – a moderate increase, but disturbing most of the extra 123 lb over the front wheels compared with the XJ6, and altering the weight distribution slightly too, which now became 53.8 percent front, 46.2 percent rear instead of 52.8/47.2. To compensate for this, front spring rates were increased slightly, more so on the air-conditioned cars due to the additional weight of the compressor pump and heat exchanger. Ventilated front discs of a similar pattern to those already installed on the V12 'E' type helped the braking system cope with the extra loads and speeds involved, and a Kelsey Hayes brake balance valve reduced any tendency for the rear wheels to lock – it distributed pressure equally between front and rear circuits at low pedal pressures, but increased that on the front at higher pressures. Servo assistance was provided by a Girling Supervac with an additional vacuum reservoir of polypropylene mounted underneath the right-hand front wing.

Dunlop once again provided the tyres, based on the original E70 SP Sport covers developed for the XJ6, then uprated with a nylon casing for the Series III 'E' type, and now incorporating a steel breaker strip in view of the XJ12's higher weight and cruising speed potential. Rim size remained at 6-inches, but wheels with improved ventilation were fitted as standard; the final drive remained at 3.31 and a Powr Lok differential was standard too. The car was only available with automatic transmission though, which had always been the case so far as the North American market was concerned (with only 17 percent of XJ6 customers elsewhere specifying a manual gearbox). The Borg Warner Model 12 box was used, as had been adopted for the XJ6 some time before. Little had changed inside the car, new armrests, incorporating hand holds as already fitted to the Daimler Sovereign models and black pvc trim on the centre console being about the only noticeable differences, though the driver was aware of the new 7000rpm rev

XJ12 interior: again, few changes, with only the 7000rpm rev. counter and "V12" badge on the console giving the game away. The 12-cylinder car had a manual choke, controlled by lever under dash on left.

Seating arrangements in the XJ12 were as for the six-cylinder car, though for a luxury vehicle appealing to the executive, the rather small amount of rear legroom was becoming noticeable. Armrests on doors now incorporated grab handles, plus a switch for electric windows where fitted.

Discreet "XJ12" badge under the reversing light was a potent status symbol in 1973, but soon escalating oil prices affected even the luxury-car market and demand for the big-engined Jaguar dropped sharply.

counter. Externally, the extra six-cylinders were proclaimed in a very low key manner by an XJ12 badge on the rear (with "Jaguar" written, at last, on the opposite side), and a black and gold plastic inlaid V12 badge on the centre bar of the new radiator grille with its neater vertical slats. But for all that, the writer does recall that the XJ12 seemed always to be immediately noticed by other road users and pedestrians alike when driven about shortly after its introduction. Even the value for money factor was still there, total list price in Great Britain being £3725 – only a little more than a third of the price of the cheapest Rolls-Royce ...

Unhappily, the July 1972 launch of the XJ12 coincided with a fortunately quite rare strike at the Browns Lane plant, apparently timed to destroy the impact of the new model; for a while, only three XJ12s were openly on display outside the factory, the writer having assisted in the 'liberation' of one of them during a photographic visit to the plant. This of course served to lengthen the already long waiting list, but when production was resumed later on in the summer, for once the home market received the initial production – possibly because it would then be easier to monitor any teething troubles which might crop up with this most complex of all Jaguars.

Road test cars were also slow coming through, and the writer and Robert Danny had fun scooping the national motoring press by publishing the first-ever XJ12 road test, in the *Jaguar Driver* magazine of November 1972. While a fifth wheel was not available, considerable care was taken in calibrating the largely accurate speedometer and the acceleration figures obtained were generally within a fraction of a second of those recorded later by *Autocar* and *Motor* – significant only in that it proved that a standard XJ12, selected at random (it was actually hired from Guy Salmon!), was perfectly capable of duplicating the performance given by the official factory road test vehicles. No special preparation there!

Also unveiled in July 1972, but only to the press at a surprise ceremony at an XJ12 reception near London Airport, was the Vanden Plas version of the Daimler Double-Six (the mechanically identical twin of the XJ12 announced one month after). As the curtain was lifted, a superbly finished and equipped saloon was revealed, but more interesting than its high level of luxury appointments was the fact that its wheelbase had been increased by 4-inches to give more space in the rear compartment. The Daimler Double-Six Vanden Plas saloon, to give its full title, was officially announced on September 26 1972, and it immediately became the most expensive Daimler or Jaguar at £5363.

On test – the XJ12 whose performance was measured by the author and Robert Danny in 1972; selected at random, it returned the same figures as the factory's official press cars did in the hands of *Motor* and *Autocar*.
Photo: P. Skilleter

The Vanden Plas XJ

The Vanden Plas version was arrived at by allowing a normal Double-Six to pass down the production line at Browns Lane, where it received all its mechanical components and its first colour coat, but no interior trimming. It would then be taken to the Vanden Plas premises at Kingsbury, vinyl roof covered by a glass fibre protector, and all exterior accessories and chrome masked off; the original paintwork would then be flattened, and three more coats applied and baked on. The remainder of the car's equipment would afterwards be fitted, and the interior retrimmed to an even higher standard than normal. After a final inspection and road test, it would be ready for despatch to the dealer.

Rear legroom had always been a little marginal in the XJ series, at least for a big luxury car, and so it was not surprising that at the 1972 Motor Show in October, long wheelbase versions of the normal XJ6, XJ12 and Daimler models too were to be seen on the Jaguar stand. There is evidence to suggest that the lengthening of the wheelbase was a fairly sudden decision, and a reaction to the successful marketing of the roomier Mercedes models. Eventually, the long wheelbase car would supplant the normal wheelbase variety altogether, but as yet, the XJ6L and XJ12L were available as additions to the existing range, together with the lengthened Daimler which was known as the Sovereign LWB. The extra 4-inches added 1.5 cwt to the weight and one-second to the 0-100mph acceleration time, but seemed not to effect the car's hand ling

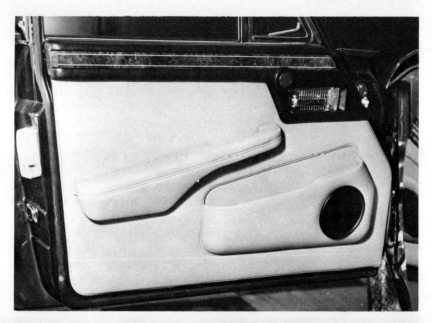

A higher level of trim distinguished the Vanden Plas cars, with plushier door panels incorporating a wood garnish rail.
Photo: Jaguar Cars

XJ 6-L interior: the long wheelbase cars had enough room in the back to satisfy almost everybody.
Photo: Jaguar Cars

Longer is better – the first XJ to appear with the increased wheelbase was the luxury Vanden Plas Daimler Double-six announced in September 1972; some time later the longer wheelbase was adopted for all the range as the increased amount of room in the rear was very useful. *Photo: Jaguar Cars*

By October 1972, long wheelbase versions of the normal six- and twelve-cylinder Jaguars had been announced; this is an XJ 12-L. The extra four-inches seemed scarcely to affect performance or handling. *Photo: Jaguar Cars*

Autocar managed to obtain a normal wheelbase XJ12 at the beginning of 1973, and published its first test of the type in March. Maximum speed was a resounding 146mph, and petrol consumption an equally resounding 11.4mpg ... Performance was, in fact, almost up to V12 'E' type standards, and far ahead of virtually any other genuine four-seater production car in the world. Sixty-miles an hour was attained in 7.4-seconds (10.1 for the automatic 4.2), 80mph in 12.2-seconds, and 100mph in 19-seconds dead. In barely over half a minute, 120mph would be on the clock, and the standing quarter-mile was covered in 15.7-seconds. As for the maximum speed runs, 148mph was obtained in one direction, the rev counter reading 6550rpm or just into the red; this and the fact that at 100mph the engine was turning over at 4350rpm led *Autocar* to express the opinion that a higher final drive than the standard 3.31 ratio might be less wasteful of fuel.

Not that high engine revolutions were really noticeable other than by watching the tachometer. "In terms of mechanical quietness", recounted *Autocar,* "the XJ12 represents the nearest approach yet to a car in which the only sensation of having a propulsive unit under the bonnet is that of speed and acceleration. It is not only the exceptionally low noise level, but the complete absence of any vibration or harshness as well, which makes the car so fantastically docile and effortless. Extra pressure on the accelerator brings response simply in acceleration without any accompanying power roar or exhaust noise."

The Model 12 automatic gearbox coped with the new power very well, and in the test car held the intermediate gears to 5700rpm and 6000rpm (higher than the figure in the handbook, and 500rpm more than given by the 1972 car tested by the writer); this represented 63mph in first and 102mph in second, and these gears could be obtained on the kick-down at anything below 30mph and 81mph respectively. Holding the intermediates manually to 6500rpm only improved the acceleration times by one-second at the most. The automatic changes were very acceptable, but *Autocar* did remark on the selector itself: "It seems quite illogical that there is no safety notch to prevent the lever from being moved forward accidentally from Drive to Neutral, although there *is* a notch between Drive and Intermediate positions. The change down to Intermediate, which is made frequently for negotiating roundabouts, for example, is needlessly awkward, and it is all too easy to then draw the selector too far back, into the Low position. However, first gear will not engage, even if selected, above 20mph on a closed throttle".

Other criticisms concerned the ventilation system, which suffered from an inadequate throughput due, apparently, to a lack of extraction – opening a window improved both the fresh air flow and the heater output, though doing this of course destroyed much of the car's quietness at speed. While the heater's temperature

The XJ12 was not without minor faults; *Autocar* did not like the lack of a detent between "Drive" and "Neutral" on the selector, thought the heater output poor and would have preferred stalk operation of the wiper switch.

control seemed to work well, the fan was noisy. It was also thought that while the layout of the centralised switchgear became familiar with use, the car was really due for a more accessible wiper switch. The reduced capacity of the petrol tanks (down to 10-gallons a side in order to comply with a safety requirement) and the increased thirst combined to seriously reduce the range of the car compared with that of the XJ6, and unfortunately the V12's petrol consumption proved to be almost as much of a talking point as its performance. It could increase as much as 8mpg in heavy traffic or when run at maximum speed, though when the overall consumption was considered – between 11 and 12mpg – and measured against the performance offered, it was really not excessive and only 3 or 4mpg worse than an automatic XJ6.

Motor's 12-cylinder road-test saloon was the Daimler Double-Six, mechanically identical to the *Autocar's* XJ12 and also with the normal wheelbase. The magazine was embarassed by the car – once more, the Coventry firm had produced a winner to join their long list of superb cars and once more, superlatives were required to describe it. The uncanny silence of the vehicle, and the

Motor's road-test **Daimler Double-six,** *en route* to the Geneva motor show with Tony Curtis at the wheel and then-editor Charles Bulmer about to sample the back-seat ride. *Photo: P. Skilleter, 'Motor'*

enormous performance particularly above 100mph, impressed *Motor* as much as they had *Autocar*, while the acceleration figures were, if anything, fractionally better than the latter's – 11.8 seconds to 80mph, and 18.5 seconds to 100mph.

The maximum speed of this car was down, though; 135.7mph mean was obtained, with a best one-way speed of 140mph exactly. The author worked the watches for this exercise when returning from the Geneva Motor Show with Tony Curtis (currently editor of *Motor*), and remembers the occasion mainly for its sheer lack of drama – the car was almost boring for its lack of noise and total stability at such rates of progress. The discrepancy of 10mph between our figures and those of *Autocar* is way beyond experimental error, and subsequent findings make it appear that almost certainly *Motor's* figure in this instance is the most representative of the Double-Six or XJ12.

The XJ12 (or Daimler Double-six) would pull well over 6000rpm given suitable conditions; here, *Motor's* Daimler shows 6300rpm at an indicated 151mph on an only slightly optimistic speedometer. True 'mean' speed recorded by the writer and Tony Curtis was 135.7mph on level ground. *Photo: P. Skilleter, 'Motor'*

Motor's overall fuel consumption figure tallied with *Autocar's* at 11.5mpg, which the journal thought compared well with the slower, heavier and larger Rolls-Royce Silver Shadow at 11.3mpg, and the slightly faster Maserati Indy at 12.5mpg – in other words, size for size and mph for mph, consumption was as could be expected and little was lost in the way of excessive internal friction from 12- instead of 6- or 8-cylinders. The fuel consumption graph also showed that little extra petrol was burnt through cruising the car at between 100 and 120mph instead of at (say) 70mph; or conversely, there wasn't an awful lot to gain if you drove an XJ12 slowly! It wasn't thought that the average Daimler (or Jaguar) owner would be too concerned about running costs, but that he or she might be by the poor range of about 240-miles. "We feel that without much sacrifice of acceleration this range could perhaps be improved a little – and the engine revs usefully lowered – by the adoption of slightly higher gearing. A five-speed manual gearbox would be even more effective". This last remark was an oblique reference to the excellent five-speed box which had indeed been developed by Jaguar behind the scenes, but was destined never to reach production.

The transmission came in for criticism by *Motor*, the journal considering that it didn't match the standards set by the Chrysler Torqueflite or the GM box as refined by Rolls-Royce engineers. Like *Autocar'*, they also found that kick-down into first didn't occur above about 25mph; nor did part-throttle changes take place from top to Intermediate with the Model 12. The power steering was not considered beyond criticism either and was discussed in detail:

> "... we are bound to record our belief that the car would be far easier and more pleasant to drive if its power steering had the proper resistance and feel characteristics. We have no quarrel with the directness of the system fitted which requires 1 turn for a 50ft circle and 3.1 turns for a lock-to-lock movement, though the turning circle is poor compared with that of competitors like the Mercedes 280E. What we dislike is the excessive lightness of the steering which calls for extra concentration at high speeds in cross winds and makes it difficult to aim the car accurately in corners, let alone to sense reduced adhesion on slippery patches. Both Jensen and Aston Martin use exactly the same Adwest Pow-a-Rack steering system but, as we've said many times before, eliminate all these defects completely by choosing settings which require a minimum force at the wheel rim of around 8lb for a parking manoeuvre on a dry metalled surface. As a result their steering arrangements are indistinguishable from good manual systems while remaining light enough to be operated by any woman – Jaguar, please copy.

While the car's general handling was rated very highly, it was also felt that there was room for improvement here, namely "a certain lack of roll damping which allows the car to lurch into its final roll attitude, making it a trifle untidy and unbalanced in esses." Probably Jaguar took a

CVC 448K again, this time on the No. 2 circuit at MIRA with Rex Greenslade at the wheel during *Motor's* road-test.
Photo: P. Skilleter, 'Motor'

conscious decision to sacrifice a very small amount of 'swervability' in order to obtain the best possible ride, and one must agree that this is what most customers would rather have. The writer has driven a modified XJ12 with wider tyres and carefully chosen, stiffer springs and shock absorbers, and can vouch for the fact that the car certainly can be made to handle much more like a sports car; but this is not really the market at which Jaguar were or are aiming.

The new ventilated discs eradicated all traces of judder and fade which *Motor* had previously experienced on the XJ6 under "fast driving on twisty roads or an alpine descent at reasonable speed". At the wheel, *Motor* echoed *Autocar's* sentiments about the lack of stalk controls, and commented as well on the poor through-put of the heater and fresh air ventilator. Finally, it was noted that the Daimler required quite a lot of servicing, with the greasing of 17-points being needed every 6000-miles, while the 'major' service at 12 000 miles demanded that the wheel bearings must be greased – all a bit old-fashioned for 1973.

What was it like to own the original XJ12? *Autocar* were discovering via a car bought from Henlys by the journal's former Managing Director in March 1973. The first 8000-miles didn't present a very brilliant picture, with delivery faults including a seriously distorted laminated windscreen ("it is amazing that such a fault could ever have passed the factory inspection"), a poor fitting driver's door, strong smell of petrol in the boot, excessive loss of coolant, a noisy speedometer, several areas of poor paintwork with undercoat showing, transmission selector not working, the leaping jaguar badge missing from one side and the nearside badge fitted on the offside ("hence the animal running backwards!"). However, only the coolant loss proved difficult to rectify – it was at last tracked down to the overflow pipe, which disgorged as much as half a pint of coolant in four miles. A catch

Fastest fire-tender in the world? Jaguar presented this pensioned-off XJ12 test car to the British Racing Drivers' Club for use at Silverstone circuit. Even fully equipped with Chubb extinguishers and foam cylinder, it proved capable of keeping up with the back-markers as it followed competitors round for the first lap. *Photo: P. Skilleter*

bottle was fitted and all was well. The smell of petrol was cured by replacing the underfloor petrol pipes with new ones of a different material.

Then at 5300-miles the final drive unit was replaced under guarantee due to leaking and becoming noisy, a new clock was fitted, and the boot lid seal replaced. Within a further 3000-miles, a rattle was traced to a loose generator flange, and a leaking rear damper pad had to be replaced; the final drive sprang another leak and a seal was replaced, and earlier misfiring after use in traffic was cured by modifications to the OPUS electronic ignition system (this was a fairly common occurance with early V12s, both in the 'E' type and saloon – it could be sooted plugs or the ignition system, and was tackled by uprating the voltage from the coil, different plug leads, non-porous rotor arm, and modified amplifier for the distributor).

The fuel consumption record was interesting, particularly as the period covered included the first major oil crisis to hit this country since Suez. It was noted that rigid observance of the 50mph limit brought in made little difference to the fuel used, and in fact the car was marginally more economical when allowed to cruise at 70mph than it was at 50mph. Overall consumption for

the first 7838-miles was a respectable 13.2mpg, with a best figure over a total of 379-miles of 14.6mpg, recorded during a long motorway trip with the speed kept down to 70mph – that surely represents about the very best an XJ12 owner could ever expect, with carburettors.

Inevitably, the V12 Jaguars and Daimlers (and even the 6-cylinder ones) invited comparison with 'the best car in the world', and the writer was involved when *Motor* put the point to the test and conducted a side-by-side evaluation of the Daimler Double-Six Vanden Plas saloon and the current Silver Shadow in May 1973. Predictably,

perhaps, the Daimler scored on driver appeal and the Rolls on finish and comfort – though only marginally so. "To us, the delightfully smooth performance of the Daimler's 5343cc V12 engine, which gives the car a top speed of over 130mph and 120mph plus cruising, is rather more important that a perfect finish under the wheelarches." On the other hand, rear seat passengers in the Shadow enjoyed a better ride and more room, even though the Vanden Plas was of course the LWB version of the XJ.

Interestingly, noise readings from inside both cars at

The 'Series 1' XJ12 saloon, powered by one of the best production engines ever made

various speeds and over various surfaces were taken at MIRA, and scientifically evaluated. The Shadow was the quieter car at speed, wind noise being the same at 90mph in the Rolls-Royce as it was at 80mph in the Daimler; but over a noise generating surface, the positions were reversed and the Daimler was superior.

Few people would buy either car for sports-car motoring, but when pressed near the limit on a corner, the cheaper car behaved best. "The Daimler has better roadholding and it is more neutral in its handling than the understeering R-R", the latter understeering to the extent that the front tyres "tended to scrub very rapidly, causing a drastic reduction in tyre life..." But *Motor* considered that the Shadow's better weighted power steering provided more 'feel' than the Daimler's which felt a little "unconnected" and made for unease near the limit. The brakes on both cars were excellent and seemed immune from fade, with the Daimler's vented discs not suffering the "disquieting throbbing noise" which appeared when slowing the Shadow from high speed. Fuel consumption averaged between 11 and 13mpg for both cars, and it was the effect of this on range rather than on wallet which *Motor* thought would be a little worrying to potential owners.

While there was (and is) no substitute for the Rolls-Royce radiator grille as a motoring status symbol, the XJ more than acquitted itself well – almost miraculously so when its price of £5363 was taken into account against the Shadow's £10 403. Its greatest advantage over the Rolls-Royce was probably its high-speed cruising ability – maybe 120mph – which was some 4 or 5mph above the other car's *maximum*, and the short time it needed to achieve such speeds; 100mph was reached from rest in 19.8-seconds, with the Shadow trailing well behind at 38.1-seconds.

The Series 2 XJ

At the Frankfurt Show on September 13 1973, Jaguar unveiled the results of their efforts to even further improve the XJ series; and certainly, the Series 2 Jaguars as they were known, met nearly all the minor criticisms which could formerly be levelled at the XJ saloons. They were joined by an entirely new model, a 2-door version of the normal wheelbase car named (according to engine type) the XJ6C and XJ12C – from which, inevitably, it became known as the 'coupe' Jaguar, which strictly

In 1973 came the Series 2 XJ range, which brought many detail improvements; XJ6, the new two-door model, and Daimler Sovereign are grouped together here. *Photo: P. Skilleter, 'Motor'*

speaking it wasn't. The Daimlers also received the Series 2 treatment, and there appeared a Daimler Sovereign 2-door also with either the six or twelve cylinder engine – though Jaguar took care to emphasize that none of the new 2-door Jaguars or Daimlers were yet in production, and would not generally be available until early 1974 (an optimistic pronouncement as it turned out – the 2-doors were not offered for sale until April 1975).

The Series 2 cars certainly looked different; a new, higher, bumper line at the front was the obvious change, now 16-inches above the road to comply with rather futile American requirements for 1974 aimed at achieving similar bumper heights (the rule makers had apparently forgotten about suspension deflection which could create a height differential of a foot or more under braking ...). The overriders had become 'underriders', flanking the now-prominent rectangular air intake under the bumper, while perforce the original radiator grille was now somewhat shorter than before, and (apart from a V12 badge) was common to XJ6 and 12. New all-plastic sidelights, claimed to be longer lasting and easier to replace, were now below bumper level. Lighting at the back was much the same except for a repositioned number plate lamp, directly above the plate now to meet new regulations.

From a technical standpoint, though, the XJ had altered even more, with substantial changes to the interior of the bodyshell in the region of the front bulkhead, and an array of new features designed to make the car easier to live with. The bulkhead alterations were necessary because of the complete re-think of the heating and ventilation system which had taken place, indicating the importance of such an item in a modern car.

The whole principle of the heater unit had been altered – it became an air-blending unit instead of a water-valve controlled heater, which enabled instant variations of temperature to be made and, just as importantly, the set temperature would be maintained regardless of the speed or temperature of the incoming air. The throughput of the heater unit was also increased, this and not a lack of extraction having been the main cause of inefficiency before, resulting in slight stuffiness at times. The new controls were operated by an electric servo-motor and a series of nylon cams and gear trains, except for the main water valve controlling the supply to the heater matrix and the air distribution flap, which were still operated by engine vacuum.

Considerable effort was also expended on the air-conditioner unit, so essential in most North American

The 'Federal' version of the Series 2 XJ 6-L, with the new full-width 5mph impact bumpers fitted to all Jaguars exported to the states.
Photo Jaguar Cars

USA specification cars carried black rubber bumpers at the rear too, along with auxiliary reflectors and repeater flasher lights on the sides of the wings. *Photo: Jaguar Cars*

To accept the new heater and refrigeration unit, a major redesign of the front bulkhead was necessary. Formerly it had been hollow, incorporating much of the air ducting in its construction. For the Series 2, a single skin panel was used in order to make room for the new assembly – but any possible decrease in sound deadening that this substitution caused was more than compensated for by the amazing attention to detail which Jaguar's development engineers paid to the way it was installed and used. A full width asbestos shield was mounted on the engine side to provide the initial heat resistance necessary, while on the cockpit side, the bulkhead, footwells and transmission hump were given shaped covers of Oldfield bitumen and felt, and Hardura pvc foam. A new light alloy pedal box was necessary, and clutch and brake pedal housings were sealed with a flexible boot, with a cowl sealing the aperture for the steering column.

and equatorial territories. Complaints of an inadequate supply of refrigerated air resulted in a unit which could supply 300 instead of 200cu. ft per minute of cool air, rigorously tested by Jaguar's engineers themselves who took a car to the Arizona deserts, and compared it against the unit in a Cadillac.

Even more ingenious was the method adopted in dealing with the penetration of the bulkhead by all the

The revised air-conditioning system fitted to the Series 2 Jaguars was extensively tested in such diverse places as Arizona and the Arctic Circle (or very near it!). But maybe not enough time was spent in Californian traffic jams because there were some complaints of engine overheating after hours of crawling along under a baking sun with the air-conditioning on full blast ...

367

wires, control cables and pipes; the usual failure-prone grommets were discarded, and instead Jaguar imbedded multi-pin sockets in the bulkhead wall, one on each side, into which plugged all the wiring. Also, heater and refrigeration liquids used rigid tubes sealed into the wall, with flexible pipes clipped onto these at each end. This also had the convenient effect of making the electrics and hoses easier to service or repair.

These changes were largely unseen, but substantial differences were visible at once on opening the door of the Series 2 and looking inside. Still real leather and polished walnut, but now all the minor instruments lay in front of the driver, each side of the large speedometer and rev. counter. In place of that row of ten switches in the middle of the dash was the new central ventilator for the heating/air conditioner, and now such vital controls as

Right & below:
Very worthwhile improvements had taken place inside the XJ Series 2, including a completely new, modernised dash – although the incorporation of the two major instruments in a plastic moulding was thought by some to look cheap; these views show a manual left-hand drive car, and a home-market V12 automatic.

Long awaited – a stalk control for the windscreen wipers and washers; no 'wiper-dwell' facility yet however. New light switch is just visible in the background.

Stricter requirements for pollution control continued to come in, and some were incorporated in home-market cars too – such as the exhaust-heated inlet manifold shown on this 1974 European-specification 4.2 engine, with the crossover trunking from the exhaust manifold. *Photo: Jaguar Cars*

wiper and washers were transferred to clearly marked stalks. The dipswitch was no longer floor mounted, the function being taken on by the stalk which operated the indicators and flasher. Mixture control for the V12 cars was still manual and situated under the dash. Electric windows were standardised, except on the normal wheelbase XJ6 where they remained optional; the console control panel for the electric windows now had a cut-out switch, which was designed to prevent children opening the rear windows when they shouldn't.

The parcel shelf was missing from under the dash, but in recompense, the passenger's glove compartment was now of a usable size, with the lid incorporating the vanity mirror. Front door armrests were bigger, and the grab handles "made easier to grab" as *Autocar* put it. In the rear, the single ashtray behind the central air outlet was replaced by ashtrays in each door, because cigarette ash was apt to get blown away before the ashtray could be reached with the former arrangement. The Series 2 also had a centralised locking system, the door locks being worked by solenoids, unlike Mercedes who used vacuum operation.

A new steering wheel was in evidence, with a large padded centre which when pressed anywhere sounded the horn. The driver was also faced by new technology in the form of fibre optics, used to replace some four separate bulbs illuminating the two heater/air conditioning controls, and the light and ignition switches; the light conducting cables ran from a single bulb to these points, the first time they'd been used on a British production car, and developed by Jaguar and Lucas in conjunction with H.V. Skan Ltd of Solihull. Space saving and ease of bulb replacement were the greatest advantages.

Under the bonnet, most of the changes concerned the six-cylinder cars, which were fitted with a new air-cleaner and thermostatically controlled exhaust heated air intake system as for the North American cars (though without air-injection), reducing the power output to 170bhp DIN at 4500rpm. These engines were also provided with a new

Clayton Dewandre single-tube oil cooler; transmission oil was cooled by a heat exchanger on the side tank of the radiator (the V12 retained its Marston oil cooler and transmission oil cooler under the main radiator). The six-cylinder cars had the fan-cooled battery container fitted as well. The XK engine was at last rid of the flexible section in the exhaust system, and instead the downpipes merged into a 23-inch length of double skinned pipe which then split and continued to the silencers. The V12 engine was now rated at 250bhp due to pollution controls, but torque remained unaffected at 301ft. lb. at 3500rpm. Ventilated front discs were now standardised throughout the range.

The two-door XJ

The new two-door Jaguars aroused great interest, and considered a definite step in the right direction by those who thought Jaguar were becoming too 'executive'; and certainly, the 'coupe' with its dashing, pillarless styling might seem to appeal to the younger company man (most cars in this class being purchased by companies). Wheelbase, length and external roofline were all as for the normal wheelbase saloon, but instead of four doors, two were installed, each 4-inches longer than the normal saloon's front door. There was no central pillar, and both door and rear side windows could wind down out of sight, leaving a completely glassless side aspect which was most attractive.

To allow the rear side window to disappear required some clever thinking on Jaguar's part, and as it was lowered, it tilted itself forward to miss the rear wheel arch. Unfortunately – and this was a supplementary reason why the car was a long time coming into production – Jaguar found it extremely difficult to achieve a wind-tight seal between side and door window glasses, inspite of a tensioned pulley arrangement which kept the side windows under pressure when up. High speeds were apt to cause low pressure areas which sucked the seals apart, the resultant wind noise being very noticeable due to the high standards of quietness inherent in the car otherwise.

The two-door XJ was given a black grained vinyl roof covering, and this helped to disguise the slight extra width of the rear pillar which had needed this reinforcement to meet roof-crush resistance regulations. Despite the missing centre pillar, the roof was still an integral part of the stress-bearing structure of the car, which was further stengthened in two-door form by an additional boxed post behind the door shut face pillar. Inside, no legroom was lost over the four-door models, although access to the rear seats, via the tip-forward squabs of the front seats, was slightly more awkward. The inertia reels for the seatbelts were neatly concealed behind the trim panels each side of the rear seats; and while the Series 2 cars were generally some 80lb heavier than the Series 1 range, the two-door was actually 50lb lighter, which was to be applauded. It is probably due to Sir William himself that Jaguar persevered with the 'coupe' and eventually marketed it, because it was one of his favourites; now out of production, it is already regarded as a 'classic'.

Above:
Based on the short-wheelbase saloon, the 'coupe' didn't have over-generous leg room in the rear, and to obtain access to the back seat, the front seat passenger had to be displaced while the seat squab was tilted. But it was still a very practical four-seater, and more useable in this respect than the XJ-S to come.
Photo: P. Skilleter, 'Motor'

Below:
Two-door centre console showing the switches for operating the electric windows – including the 'disappearing' rear side glasses. *Photo: Jaguar Cars*

Left:
The inertia-reels for the seatbelts were housed in the rear trim panels in the two-door cars. *Photo: Jaguar Cars*

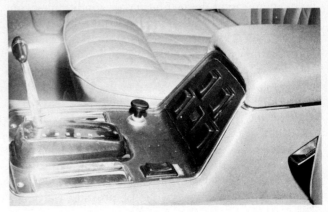

Most different of the Series 2 cars was the two-door version, with its distinctive 'pillarless' construction. *Photo: P. Skilleter, 'Motor'*

The beautifully balanced lines of the two-door XJ complimenting those of the Trident.

Talking of obsolescence, the writing was on the wall for the 2.8-litre, and the 'basic' version – if it ever existed – had been officially discontinued in March 1972. While the piston burning problems had been overcome to some extent, Jaguar announced that the Series 2 version of the car would only be offered in certain countries abroad, namely Belgium, France, Greece, Italy and Portugal. Even then, production only continued until July 1973 after which it ceased altogether, largely unnoticed. Since then, a number of cars have been converted to 4.2-litres privately, or have taken advantage of the 3-litre conversion using a different crankshaft offered by Forward Engineering of Hampton-in-Arden, Warwickshire, where ex-Jaguar development engineer Ron Beaty also supplies enlarged and/or modified versions of the 4.2 and 5.3 engines.

Also departing from the scene in September 1973 were the normal wheelbase XJ12 and Daimler Double-Six cars, which thus never appeared in Series 2 form. Neither were the existing normal wheelbase XK engined models destined to last a great deal longer, being phased out themselves at the end of 1974 in favour of the more sensibly proportioned long wheelbase bodyshell. So to summarise Jaguar's 1973/74 range:

6-cylinder (4.2-litre)	Jaguar XJ6 and Daimler Sovereign	Four-door, normal wheelbase
	Jaguar XJ6L, Daimler Sovereign (LWB), Vanden Plas 4.2-litre saloon	Four-door, long wheelbase
	Jaguar XJ6C Daimler Sovereign 2-door	Two-door, normal wheelbase
12-cylinder	Jaguar XJ12L, Daimler Double-Six (LWB), Daimler Double-Six Vanden Plas	Four-door, long wheelbase
	Jaguar XJ12C, Daimler Double-Six 2-door	Two-door, normal wheelbase

As mentioned, the two-door cars were prototypes only at this stage, and did not become available until the spring of 1975. By this time, Jaguar had tackled the embarassing petrol consumption of the 12-cylinder cars by returning to fuel-injection, which they now managed to get in production thanks to Lucas and Bosch. But the petrol shortages of 1973/74 also prompted Jaguar to take another look at their 6-cylinder engine which had much greater potential as an economy unit for the range.

The XJ 3.4

Thus in April 1975, the capacity of 3442cc once again figured in Jaguar's catalogue, with the coming of a new economy version of the XJ and Sovereign; although the capacity was the same as that of the original XK engine of 1948 (and last seen in the 340 which left the scene in September 1968 with the coming of the XJ itself), it was not the old 3.4 block revived. Instead, Jaguar had used the same 83 x 106mm bore and stroke in a strengthened and improved version of the 4.2-type block, with its offset bores; the new 3.4 engine also used the straight-port head of the 4.2 series, together with similar SU HS8 carburetters with automatic cold-start enrichment, and was rated at 161bhp DIN at 5000rpm – just 1bhp more than was quoted for the first 3.4 engine. The car was available with manual or automatic (Model 65) transmission with overdrive standard on the former; a 3.54 final drive ratio was used with both these transmissions, instead of the 4.2's 3.31. The smaller engine was not available in the 2-door models.

Economy didn't stop at the engine; the Jaguar XJ 3.4 and Daimler Sovereign 3.4 as they were known were given narrow-pleated cloth-trimmed seat facings, using an anti-static strain-resistant polyester material with a cropped-pile surface in sand, jade, garnet, navy or black. This could also be specified as a no-extra-cost option on 4.2 and 5.3 cars too, when it came with matching cloth interior door panels. The new 3.4 models were priced at £4794 on the home market, compared with £5136 for the cheapest 4.2, which was a useful saving; there was no longer any differentation in cost between automatic or manual overdrive cars.

While from March 1979 each car in Jaguar's range become known by its capacity (that is, XJ 3.4, XJ 4.2 and XJ 5.3), in the United States they were still called simply XJ6 and XJ12 – this was because the 3.4 engined car was not sold there, and so a capacity identification wasn't needed.

Fuel-injection for the V12

As for the V12 engined cars, the adoption of fuel-injection from the end of April 1975 – initially on the two-door models only – brought the double advantages of added economy plus extra power, with the DIN figure going right up to 285bhp again, developed at 250rpm lower than previously at 5750rpm. The system had been originated by Bendix, developed and engineered by Bosch, then jointly adapted by Lucas and Jaguar. The main reason for choosing fuel-injection was for its ability to deliver a very precise fuel/air mixture to the combustion chamber, thanks in this case to the Bosch system's electronic control unit; the right fuel mix delivered at the right time ensured economy, flexibility and performance,

Above:
The XJ 3.4 – economy with six-cylinders for the XJ range came in 1975, with an engine based on the 4.2 block but with the traditional bore and stroke of 83x106mm. Moderate driving produced well over 20mpg. *Photo: P. Skilleter*

Below:
Also in 1975 came the new option of cloth seat-facings for the XJ, an upholstery finish that was standardised on the 3.4 models. *Photo: Jaguar Cars*

Left:
The 3.4 engine in the XJ hardly looked any different to the 4.2, and was still fed by twin 2-inch SU carburettors; it was rated at 161bhp. *Photo: P. Skilleter*

and just as important, enabled the engine to meet tougher anti-pollution regulations through its increased efficiency and the ability of the electronic injection system to maintain the correct state of tune over many thousands of miles.

The electronic control unit which was the heart of this received data from sensors in the engine and ancilliaries, computed the engine's fuel requirements and transmitted the appropriate impulses to the injector solenoids. An independent cold start injector on each inlet manifold supplied the fuel initially until the engine temperature caused a change over to the main system, which could adjust itself automatically according to the coolant and air intake temperatures. A single high pressure pump brought the fuel (at 28psi) from the twin 10-gallon tanks.

The fuel injected Jaguars had a "Fuel Injection" badge placed under the name "Jaguar", as did the similar Daimler models, to distinguish them from the carburetted XJ12 and Double-Six saloons which were phased out later in 1975. Additionally, all 5.3 models were now distinguished by a black vinyl roof and chromium side-strip on the bodywork, and could be fitted with light-alloy road wheels by GKN Kent Alloys as an extra-cost option – these couldn't be fitted to other than injection models because of an alteration to the front brake calipers. A higher axle ratio was used too, 3.07 instead of 3.31, which further helped economy.

For the first time, Jaguar offered a light-alloy road wheel as an optional extra; rim width remained at 6-inches

The fuel-injected 5.3 saloons, when announced later in 1975, had a new livery – vinyl roof and chromium waistline strip. *Photo: Jaguar Cars*

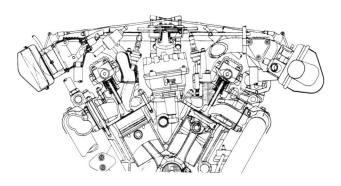

Biggest change for the V12-engined cars in 1975 was the adoption of fuel-injection, initially on the two-door cars; the injectors sprayed directly into the inlet manifold, and no major changes were made to the engine's layout.

Above:
The new fuel-injection system was rigorously tested before its introduction, during which Jaguar's engineers carried out high-altitude tests at the famous Colorado, N. American speed hillclimb toll road at Pike's Peak (which already had a Jaguar connection, Bobby Unser winning there on six successive occasions driving a Jaguar-engined special).

Below: The V12 engine fitted with fuel-injection, with an aluminium collecting chamber taking the place of the carburettors; the injectors can be made out on the inlet tracts within the 'V'.
(Left) An 'emission' 5.3 'injected' engine installed in a left-hand drive car.
Photos: Jaguar Cars

Not announced publicly but introduced at the same time on the injection cars were a number of modifications to improve the already excellent handling. These included a revised steering rack with an 8-tooth pinion, revised anti-roll bar, new vertical link assembly, a change in castor angle, new steering arms and revised upper wishbones. Then the V12 engine received a revised rear main bearing side seal, for improved sealing between the bearing cap and cylinder block.

Finally, a new Daimler model joined the range; this was the Vanden Plas version with the 4.2 engine, not previously available in this most luxurious and expensive of the entire Daimler/XJ spectrum (the Vanden Plas Double-Six was now £8044).

Road-testing the XJ3.4

Autocar tried the most genuinely different XJ model during the Autumn of 1975, publishing a road test of the 3.4 in September. They called it "an intelligent compromise between performance and economy", going on to describe the behaviour of the new 3.4 engine as follows:

"The first and most obvious point about the 3.4 litre engine is that it is remarkably smooth and refined, certainly more so than its bigger brother. Only when taken beyond the 5,000rpm mark does it start to sound and feel even remotely rough. On the other hand, for those used to the 4.2 litre, there is no doubt the smaller engine lacks the punch, especially for the driver too lazy to change down. If one is to make consistently rapid progress, much more use must be made of the gears, helped by the higher rev limit. The gear ratios are very well chosen and the lowering of first gear has opened up no obvious gap. Maxima in the lower gears at the red line are 36, 62 and 85mph. This is good spacing, and for the press-on driver second gear proves ideal for minor roads and third for A-road overtaking."

Top speed was virtually the same in either direct or overdrive top, the former giving 115mph and the latter a "more relaxed and stable-feeling 117mph in reasonable conditions"; 100mph was still thought a "very comfortable" cruising speed. When it came to comparing the figures with those of the 4.2 tested in 1971, the point was made that a reduction in compression ratio and other changes to meet de-toxing regulations meant that the current 4.2 was probably not as quick as it used to be. Thus the gap between the 3.4 and 1971 4.2 of 6mph in top speed and 2.2-seconds in the acceleration to 60mph (the 3.4 recorded 10.9-seconds) was probably exaggerated. But where the missing cubic capacity was really felt was in top gear acceleration, with the 3.4 taking 9.5-seconds to cover the increment 30-50mph compared with the 4.2's

Thanks to minor suspension and steering improvements brought in since the early XJ, *Motor* considered that the 3.4 handled even better than previous models. *Photo: P. Skilleter, 'Motor'*

6.9-seconds. Contrary to expectations, perhaps, the 3.4 also weighed more than *Autocar's* 1971 road test 4.2, by almost one hundredweight at 33.2cwt.

It was still a fast car in general terms though, even if slower than the lighter 3.4 Mk II saloon of days gone by, and there was certainly some improvement to report in petrol consumption. This was now down from around 15mpg to 17mpg, with more than 21mpg obtainable with gentle driving; steady speed cruising at 80mph still returned over 20mpg, and at 100mph the figure was 15.4mpg.

All the new Series 2 features were appreciated, and the extra wheelbase "has made a tremendous difference to the amount of room inside"; the cloth seats were liked and "stayed comfortable throughout the extremely hot and humid weather of the test period." The slightly more weighted steering was approved of, and "the 3.4 certainly gave the driver a better idea what the front wheels were trying to do, self centering was better, and there was no longer any tendency to wander slightly because the driver, unawares, is not holding the wheel absolutely still."

Much of *Autocar's* findings were supported by *Motor* when they published their test of the 3.4 manual during the same month, though the power steering was still considered too light; the journal pointed out that Mercedes, who also sold large quantities of cars to the States, found it reasonable to give the driver a little more work to do, with a concomitant increase in the feeling of controllability. Other than that, the worst characteristic of cornering was the early onset of tyre squeal from the big Dunlops. Interestingly, two of the staff who had tried automatic 3.4s decided they liked these better than the manual version, especially with the newer Model 65 gearbox (fitted to 6-cylinder cars from December 1973) which gave smoother changes than the old Model 12. Of details, the parking 'dance' of the wipers was found annoying, but the quartz halogen headlights were thought superb. And despite all the redesigning, *Motor* did not award the heating and ventilation system full marks due to a poor through-put of cool air and a lack of versatility.

In spite of weighing as much if not rather more than the original 4.2 XJ6, the XJ 3.4 fared well in road tests; 100mph was reckoned a comfortable cruising speed, with 117mph available in overdrive top.

The XJ5.3C road-tested

The first and long-awaited road test of the much more exciting XJ 5.3C came towards the end of 1975, *Autocar* publishing theirs in November. The 285bhp fuel-injected car surged to a maximum of 147mph, although due to an increase of around 2cwt and higher gearing did not quite match the acceleration figures which *Autocar* recorded with their original XJ12 road test car of 1973 – the 'coupe' was about one second down more or less throughout the range, reaching 60mph in 8.3-seconds, 80mph in 13.1-seconds, and 100mph in 19.9-seconds; standing quarter-mile time was 16-seconds exactly. But economy was markedly better, the injection car returning an overall consumption of 13.8mph compared with 11.4mpg of the carburetted version, and frequently gave over 15mpg when driven gently. This also increased the car's range usefully, which went up from a little over 200-miles to nearer 300.

The practical aspects of 'coupe' ownership in no way spoilt the car, *Autocar* considered, with rear seat room "really generous" despite the smaller wheelbase, and the side window sealing now being largely successful although "it cannot be said that the problem has been completely solved since there is certainly some wind noise."

As for the XJ 5.3C's general behaviour on the road, *Autocar* thought that it was better than before:

"By a steady process of development, the ride of the XJ series had been refined to the very highest standards and one is very hard put indeed to find cars to rival it. Perhaps at high speed, the Mercedes 450 range is fractionally better, but at low speed, the Jaguar is measurably better than this German rival and in fact, one would find few opponents to a claim that the Jaguar offers the best ride in the world. There is absolutely no sensation of float or pitch and the very worst undulations or irregularities of road surface are soaked up without sound or sensation reaching the car's occupants... Compared with earlier XJs, the current car has heavier steering (or should it be 'less light') and this helps to avoid the slight lurch that used to accompany turning into a corner....

"Handling on wet roads is a revelation bordering on the magical. That a car of this weight and size can be hustled along at undreamed of speeds on streaming wet surfaces is quite extraordinary and it goes without saying that it inspires confidence in driver and passengers alike. Aids in this are the limited slip differential and the extremely smooth power delivery which helps to avoid sudden unsettling tendencies, which might break the adhesion of the rear wheels."

Autocar once more criticised the gearchange and the "dangerous" lack of any safety notch to prevent the selector lever from going beyond Drive to Neutral, but an

Road-tests of the V12 two-door XJ immediately revealed the benefits of fuel-injection, as the consumption figures improved fairly dramatically – over 15mpg was now quite feasible. *Photo: Jaguar Cars*

Left:
XJ12C interior, windows down; no 12-cylinder XJ besides the XJ-S was offered with manual transmission, although a few private conversions have been carried out using Jaguar's 4-speed box as fitted to the 4.2 XJ6.

answer to this was on the way in the form of an entirely new automatic transmission which was then being evaluated by Jaguar. The journal also regretted the lack of an optional manual gearbox: "Having tried a car with a 5-speed manual gearbox we can only hope that Jaguar have it in mind to widen the appeal of the model by its adoption", though this was to be wishful thinking.

Motor had to wait rather longer before putting a 2-door XJ through their road test routine, though benefitted by sampling a car (PWK 513R) with the new General Motors' Turbo Hydramatic automatic gearbox introduced to the 12-cylinder XJ range in April 1977. And while attempts to obtain a maximum speed were frustrated, this car was considerably quicker off the mark than *Autocar's* had been; with the latter's figures in brackets, the times were 60 mph in 7.6-seconds (8.3), 80mph in 11.8 (13.1), 100mph in 18.4 (19.1), and 120mph in 30.5 (32.0). The standing quarter-mile was covered in 15.7-seconds, 0.3-seconds faster than *Autocar's* XJ5.3C. Top speed, judging from the car's accelerative powers at 140mph, was estimated at being between 145 and 150mph.

Even for some exotic sports car, such figures would have been exceptional; coming from a very genuine, four/five-seater saloon produced in reasonable numbers and which could be serviced in any big town, it was nothing less than amazing. "Nor are these figures achieved at the expense of frantic wheelspin, snatched changes and frenzied engine revs; the car simply wafts forward in a totally undramatic surge with only a faint hum from the engine even at maximum revs."

Fuel consumption was up though, *Motor* recording an overall 11.9mpg (possibly the electronic fuel injection had been 'tuned' for power rather than economy?), reducing the range to 200-220 miles once more. The GM Hydramatic gearbox was approved of though, with the changes virtually undetectable at small throttle openinge, "and even at full throttle it is more a change in engine note that tells you that something has happened." Kickdown was sometimes slightly jerky however, "but the

Increased sophistication arrived when the GM Hydramatic gearbox replaced the Borg Warner box on the V12 saloons, with gearchanges becoming even smoother.

most disappointing facet of its performance is the reluctance to kick down to first at any speed above 15mph." And *Motor* felt that the steering was *still* too light, even though the car's handling was otherwise as good as ever.

The journal then went on to spell out what it considered to be the Jaguar's most outstanding trait:

"Were we to single out the one aspect of the car that puts it firmly in the contention for the title of 'best in the world' it would be refinement. The engine is never, even at full throttle and maximum revs, more than a distant hum. On most surfaces there isn't any road noise (though occasionally a bump-thump can be heard faintly) and, though wind noise (noticeably from the top of the passenger's window and the bottom of the driver's window) starts at 70mph, it is very faint and gets no worse as speed increases until above 120mph when the passenger's window opens out slightly with a noticeable increase in roar. To achieve this with any car is excellent; to do so with a pillarless coupe is almost miraculous. To put it all into context, the Coupe is the only car we know in which the radio can be set at 30mph and doesn't require adjusting right up to 120mph....

To sum up, the XJ5.3 Coupe is a marvellous piece of modern engineering. It is, in our experience, the most refined car made today, travels indecently quickly yet so smoothly and quietly that high speeds are the norm rather than the exception, while being utterly tractable at the other end of the scale...on the whole the Jaguar gets closer to perfection than any other we know, which makes it something of a bargain at £10,000."

Rivals to the car were few, with some being disqualified on the grounds of sheer cost – like the slower Rolls-Royce Corniche 2-door at £33 134, the far less refined Maserati Khamsin at £17 960, the Bristol range starting at £20 000, and the less roomy, noisier but faster Aston Martin V8 at £17 000 for the cheapest. Of the others, the Mercedes 450SLC ran the Jaguar close in overall ability but wasn't so sure-footed (and cost almost £4000 more) the BMW 633CSi equalled the XJ's performance and handling in most respects, and managed to return 20mpg while doing so – though again this was rather outweighed by a £14 799 price tag – while the new Lotus Elite 503 gave even more miles to the gallon, was quicker in the lower speed ranges, but had cramped rear seating and a doubtful every-day use capability, even though it was only £3 more than the 5.3C at £10 109. While a few North American cars might qualify on sheer acceleration, none could approach the Jaguar's refinement under all conditions, or equal any of the Europeans when it came to handling and roadholding; in fairness though, it must be said that they were cheap compared to the imports on their home-ground.

Testing the 5.3 injection saloon

Even more comfort – at least for rear seat passengers – was provided by the XJ5.3 *saloon*, and with very little, if anything, lost in the way of performance compared with the two-door car. That the longer car gave virtually nothing away to the shorter one except possibly in looks was underlined by *Autocar's* test of September 1978.

Weight-for-weight, the fuel injected V12 Jaguar saloon was calculated by *Autocar* to be as efficient as a Porsche or Lotus; despite performance testing (a suspiciously fast 147mph top speed was recorded) the magazine achieved 13.2mpg.

At 36.5cwt, the four-door XJ was a mere 14lb. heavier than the 'coupe' tested by the same magazine in 1975, and its acceleration was distinctly better, virtually equalling the faster 2-door tried by *Motor* in 1977; 60mph came in 7.8-seconds, 80mph in 12.6-seconds, and 100mph in 18.8-seconds. Top speed was the equal of that recorded for any XJ saloon at 147mph mean, and the overall petrol consumption was reasonable at 13.2mpg – in fact *Autocar* computed that, weight-for-weight, the XJ5.3 was pretty well as efficient in this respect as the 2.7-litre Porsche and the 2-litre Lotus. And the fuel-injected engine was much more responsive to 'nursing' of the throttle than the previous carburetted V12, and could return 16mpg if required.

Despite the passage of ten-years since the introduction of the XJ, handling and roadholding were still rated as exemplary and the steering too light... For enthusiastic driving, the full load tyre pressures of 29/30 instead of 28/26 were thought to improve the car's behaviour "at a small price in its famous suppression of road noise and, less so, in ride quality." This last was still impressive: "The Jaguar ride is perhaps the best ride compromise achieved by *any* manufacturer, because it does not seem to get caught out. Take off at 90mph on an unforeseen hump and the car lands extraordinarily comfortably, unlike some supposedly more advanced hydropneumatic designs. And it rides with very little road noise – there is some, but less than any rival."

Only minor items of equipment marred the car in *Autocar's* eyes, and these only stood out because the rest were perfectly satisfactory. A 'press-to-zero' trip would have been better than the 'twiddle' sort, while an intermittent wipe facility was a strange omission on a £14 000 car – and the Lucas wipers themselves with their "quaint little step-changing dance" were "extraordinarily out of date" and should have been completely self-parking. *Autocar* also would have expected a car of the XJ's price to have a variable seat height (although seat comfort was very good as it was), and the "noisy solenoid" central locking system was complex and didn't include the boot lock in its operation (unlike the Mercedes system).

The GM box behaved well but *Autocar* still didn't like the selector which had an unnecessary detent between Drive and Intermediate, but none between Drive and Neutral – Mercedes again set the standard there. In Drive, the box in this car would however readily kick down to first at up to 38 mph, and into second at up to 86mph; using the selector, the driver could hold the intermediate gears to 6500rpm, which gave 65mph and 109mph. The lack of an optional manual box was mourned, as, said *Autocar*, it would allow full use to be made of the V12 engine's incredible flexibility, and reduce fuel consumption. The Rover '77mm' 5-speed box which by then had become available for the XJ3.4 could not handle the 5.3 power unit's torque, and all hope of Harry Mundy's "superb" 5-speed gearbox which had

XJ 5.3 saloon with the optional cloth interior; *Autocar* could only fault its road-test car on minor items of equipment, which were now lagging behind the opposition – but virtually every point was to be met by Jaguar in the next update of the XJ range.

been in existence at the works for years ever 'entering production' had been given up.

Autocar compared the XJ 5.3 with such rivals as the BMW 733i, Mercedes 450 SEL, Aston Martin V8 automatic, Rolls-Royce Silver Shadow, and the recently obsolete Ferrari 365GT4 2-plus-2 – noting that while the Jaguar still offered tremendous value for money, (now £12 436), its price was now 47% of the contemporary Rolls-Royce as opposed to only 38% in 1972... The magazine thought that the Mercedes was closest to the XJ on all counts, once the sports-car appeal of the Ferrari and Aston was discounted, and the snob-appeal of the Shadow; but that "without doubt, it is the Jaguar which dominates overall."

The Jaguar XJ-S

Even by the end of the 'sixties, it was realised at the factory that the life of the 'E' type could not be extended indefinitely, and although in Series III form with the V12 engine it developed into a refined and still-modern sports car, the practical limit for further modification had been reached. The high standard of heating and ventilation now demanded even of sports cars could not be met without a basic redesign of the car's bodyshell, and while the huge bonnet and front wings assembly was ideal 'crushable material' for the head-on barrier tests which had since become mandatory, there was no hope of the boot-mounted fuel tank meeting the 30mph rearward barrier test scheduled for 1976.

A new sporting Jaguar was therefore needed, and it was sensible for this to be based on the existing XJ saloon so that suspension, engine and even a good deal of body engineering and development costs could be minimised. Really, this was only a reversion to Jaguar's approach to the subject in the late nineteen-forties, when the XK 120 was basically a short-chassis version of the Mk VII saloon. Unfortunately though, Jaguar's design staff of 1970 did not have the same freedom of action that they enjoyed twenty-years before, thanks largely to incoming American Federal Government automotive regulations.

At this time, just when the main concept of the new car had to be finalised, it was universally considered that these regulations would sooner or later prohibit open cars. Subsequently this was held to be an infringement of the freedom of the individual and open cars were – and still are – able to be sold freely on the American market; but the draft proposals were not thrown out until 1974, by which time Jaguar with the as-yet unnamed XJ-S, Triumph with the TR7, and many of the big Detroit companies, had all shelved plans for conventional open top models.

The retention of the closed roof also caused an adjustment of emphasis at Browns Lane, which now shifted from what had been a more sporting role for the new car, to one of even greater refinement, quietness and sophistication; indeed the XJ-S ended up as the flagship of the entire Jaguar fleet, with an elaborate specification and such items as full air-conditioning as standard, and inevitably a long way from being a replacement for the 'E' type – which for the forseeable future at least, would appear to safely hold the honour of being the last open-two-seater Jaguar built.

The XJ-S used the platform of the original 108.8 inch wheelbase XJ as its starting point, but with a number of important differences – such as the wheelbase itself which was even shorter at 102 inches. This was achieved by moving the rear suspension assembly forward under the rear seat pan which was also shorter than the standard XJ's. As before, most of the stressed steel panels were in 22-gauge rather than the more common, lighter 24-gauge material used on most other British Leyland cars, and the assembly was made even stronger by increased triangulation of the front bulkhead and engine compartment sides in line with the front screen pillars, thus making better use of the cabin superstructure. Ahead of the radiator ran a horizontal cross tube, with a diagonal one bolted across bracing the sides. At 720 lb. the basic platform was usefully lighter than the XJ saloon's, by about 100lb.

Incorporated in the front and rear ends were new impact-absorbing 5mph bumpers, standard on all cars whatever the market; they used "Menasco" struts for the first time on a European car, which absorbed an impact rather in the way that a normal suspension damper would, except that silicone-wax was the hydraulic medium, this being forced by the piston through small ports in the chamber. Afterwards, the wax would return to the chamber over a period of about 30-minutes, returning the bumper to its original shape.

The petrol tank mounting was completely different on the XJ-S, the wing mounting of two individual tanks being abandoned and a single 20-gallon tank being positioned across the rear suspension arch, well inboard of damage sustained in a rear-end collision. It was given a small separate collector tank or sump positioned underneath the now rear-mounted battery to eliminate surge problems, and from which the immersed 28psi Lucas petrol pump drew. Alongside the battery and also mounted across the car was the upright spare wheel with its plastic cover – rather like the arrangement in the Mk X boot, except that there the wheel was carried to one side. A thoughtful detail in the boot was the pair of flexible louvres in the floor, intended to extract stale air from the deep, 15cu ft luggage compartment.

Extremely thorough measures were taken throughout the car to match or exceed the standard of quietness set by the XJ saloons; the engine bay itself was designed to reflect noise away from the passenger compartment, and of course the same inter-bulkhead connections were made by plug and socket. Inside, specially moulded sound-deadening material was used extensively, plus extra touches like a coiled fuel pipe contained within a larger foam tube to cut down pump noise.

Suspension front and rear was XJ, with suitable modifications to cater for the slightly reduced weight of the XJ-S, which at 34.75cwt was about 2cwt less than that of the XJ 5.3 saloon – front spring rates were 90lb. per inch compared with 92lb. per inch for the saloon, the rear 125lb. per inch instead of 154lb. per inch. The later 8-tooth steering rack used by the XJ 5.3 since the spring of 1975 was adopted, but 3.5 instead of 2.5 degrees of caster was given to provide better self-centering and feel. The new 0.875-inch diameter anti-roll bar also standardised on the V12 cars since May was fitted at the front, and – exclusive to the XJ-S – an anti-roll bar of 0.562 inch diameter was incorporated in the rear suspension too. The alloy wheel first offered on the 5.3 saloons was standard on the XJ-S, with its 6-inch rim and ventilation slots.

The engine and transmission was as for the saloons, the injected 285bhp version of the V12 power unit being standard and driving through the Borg Warner Model 12 automatic box, though a single propshaft was used. But

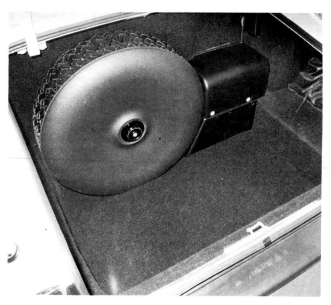

Top left: XJ-S bodyshell, based on the short wheelbase saloon platform but with the rear bulkhead brought forward. *Photo: Jaguar Cars*

Top right: Underside view of the front end of the XJ-S , showing the integral chassis 'legs' projecting from the front bulkhead to carry the engine/suspension subframe. *Photo: Jaguar Cars*

Above: The front subframe and suspension used on the XJ-S – basically as for the XJ 5.3 saloon, including the ventilated disc brakes. *Photo: Jaguar Cars*

Centre left: Engine bay of the XJ-S was shaped to reflect noise away from the interior. *Photo: Jaguar Cars*

Left: Boot area was rearranged for the XJ-S, the petrol tank being carried across the rear suspension instead of in the wings; spare wheel has plastic cover and so has the battery next to it. *Photo: P. Skilleter*

one concession to the 'sporting' aspect of driving the car was the option of Jaguar's four-speed manual gearbox, though not many customers specified it. In either case, the 3.07 Powr-Lok differential was fitted, and new steel-braced type tyres especially developed by Dunlop to give an effectively even higher speed rating than before due to a cooler-running tread. Testing was carried out at Jabbeke, Belgium, Jaguar's old record-breaking haunt.

Cars bound for California's peculiar climate were more afflicted with anti-pollution controls than those delivered elsewhere, and because of greater exhaust recirculation, had the total power output reduced to 244bhp at 5250rpm, and 269lb.ft. of torque at 4500rpm. To compensate for any lost acceleration, a lower 3.31 axle ratio was fitted, which together with the decreased efficiency of the engine must have made the California-specification V12 Jaguars rather thirsty machines.

Much thought had gone into the interior layout of the XJ-S, and it was not simply a rearranged XJ inside. New seats were in evidence, the front pair having a special seat cushion made up of two separate components, a softer centre piece and a firmer outer surround, which gave better lateral support. Leather was used for the upholstery facings, and hidden inertia reel seatbelts were standard. The instrument layout was almost entirely new, and dominated by a battery of no less than 18 warning-lights monitoring various functions from brake circuits to stoplight bulbs; a fault, if detected, would light-up a red or an amber light – red meant stop at once and investigate, while amber meant check when convenient.

Speedometer and rev-counter were housed behind the steering wheel and remained easily read, with white lettering on a black surface; unfortunately, in the opinion of some, they were surrounded by cheap-looking plastic bezzles with a painted silver outline. Between them were entirely new vertical instruments which indicated fuel level, water temperature, oil pressure, and battery condition, and, besides their format, they differed from previous ones by working through a variation in the magnetic field between three opposing coils; this gave a greater degree of accuracy, and more important, reacted quicker to any alterations. Stalk controls similar to the Series 2 Jaguar saloons worked dipswitch, indicators and flasher, wipers and windscreen washers (surprisingly, still no intermittent-wipe facility), while illuminated push-on, push-off switches controlled minor functions.

The V12 fuel-injected engine as installed in the XJ-S, complete with air-conditioning plant which was a standard feature. *Photo: P. Skilleter, 'Motor'*

Interior of the XJ-S differed from the saloons in many ways, including seats and instrument panel. Handbrake dropped down out of the way after it was applied. *Photo: P. Skilleter*

Rear seat area in the XJ-S was pleasantly trimmed but really suited only children over long journeys. *Photo: P. Skilleter*

XJ-S instruments included new vertical indicators monitoring water, oil, fuel and voltage; the black plastic surround was not universally admired. Note battery of warning lights above the dials.

Headlights had been specially designed for the car by Cibié to fit in with its streamlined shape, with the optical unit containing two wide, independent reflectors, each equipped with a halogen bulb to give dip and main beam; the units were faired-in to the car's long nose. Peculiar thinking on the part of the North American authorities precluded the use of these powerful lights in that country, and so cars for this market were given an ordinary four-headlamp GEC tungsten lighting system– which some people thought looked better, but which gave a dismal light output compared with the Cibié units.

To stop this most luxurious of two-plus-twos (and Jaguar gave its top speed as 150mph plus), the same ventilated 11.18-inch front discs and 10.38-inch plain rear discs were fitted as used on all XJ saloons by then, with four-piston calipers working on the big front discs. Servo assistance was by a Girling in-line tandem servo mounted on the pedal box, using vacuum assistance from a reservoir located under the front wing. A divided circuit was of course still used. Jaguar claimed that the XJ-S could accelerate to 100mph and stop again in just over 20 seconds. The handbrake was applied in the normal way,

but the handle would then drop back to the floor out of the way beside the seat – a more satisfactory arrangement than the under-dash umbrella system even if at least one subsequent road-test found it to be less efficient when its effect was measured.

The most controversial aspects of the new car were, jointly, its overall concept and its appearance. Many people were still eagerly expecting an 'F-type', a genuine successor to the late-lamented 'E' type which had ceased production in February 1975 – an open wind-in-the-hair sports car with less refinement but even more urge and elemental appeal than the incredibly smooth, 'soft' closed two-plus-two which actually appeared. Nor were the looks of the XJ-S universally acclaimed, and it was probably the first Jaguar of all not to have received automatic rave reviews in the American motoring press over its appearance; ironically it was almost too 'American' in this respect, following the lines of the Camaro – a handsome car in its own right, but that was hardly the point to the American European-car enthusiast, who justifiably wanted pure European (Jaguar) looks.

Alloy wheels and 5mph-impact bumpers (which worked extremely well) were all standard features of the XJ-S. Body shape was basically Malcolm Sayer, Jaguar's aerodynamicist. *Photo: Jaguar Cars*

While not everyone's favourite, the XJ-S certainly has a degree of poise; rectangular light units on home-market cars were by the French manufacturers Cibié. *Photo: Jaguar Cars*

At a time when Jaguar were under pressure by corporate-minded British Leyland executives, the traditional Jaguar logo above the rear number plate on the XJ-S was almost an act of defiance ...

No-one, on either side of the Atlantic, argued that the XJ-S didn't achieve what it had set out to do – which was to ferry two people, their luggage, and an occasional extra two passengers across country in the shortest possible time and in the greatest comfort, quietness and safety conceivable. This the XJ-S did superbly – but there remained lingering doubts as to whether it was really the right car for the times, and whether Jaguar would not have been better advised to have produced something a little smaller, a little more economical – and rather cheaper. Roger Bell of *Motor* described the XJ-S as "a magnificent anachronism."

There had also been speculation about whether the new Jaguar would be mid-engined, this configuration being highly fashionable for sporting cars of the mid-seventies; the rumour had also been given substance when the existence of the mid-engined, four-cam V12 racing prototype, the XJ13, was publicly revealed in 1973. But quite rightly, Jaguar maintained that placing the engine behind the driver had little to commend itself for a road car, reducing space and making it very difficult to isolate noise and heat from the car's occupants, in return for minimal or non-existent roadholding advantages. The superb handling of the XJ-S itself proved the point, and Jaguar's refusal to follow fashion has since been endorsed by such competent manufacturers as Porsche and Lotus who have also produced exceptionally good front-engined designs which have excelled in roadholding and handling qualities. Having the bulk of the engine in front of the passenger compartment would also assist in the more severe barrier tests which were being predicted.

While the wheel-to-body relationship of the XJ-S was clearly XJ, the treatment of the remainder was definitely new, particularly at the rear. 'Flying buttresses' ran down from roof level either side of the boot to the tail, giving the XJ-S its distinctive profile. These had not been seen

before on a Jaguar, although they had been tried during at least one experimental re-styling of the 'E' type 2-plus-2 towards the end of the 'sixties'.

At the front, the nose had to accommodate the large, black rubber 5mph impact bumpers, which it did tolerably gracefully. Under the nose was a narrow but effective spoiler, which in conjunction with an engine undershield was found in wind-tunnel tests to reduce lift by 50 percent and drag by 10 percent – perhaps surprisingly, the XJ-S was a more efficient shape than even the Series III 'E' type and the wind tunnel drag figures for the XJ6, XJ-S and 'E' type were, with frontal areas in brackets, as follows: XJ6 0.48 (19.8sq.ft); 'E' type 0.455 (17.8sq.ft); XJ-S 0.39 (19.8sq.ft). Possible even more surprising is the fact that the XJ-S actually had a shorter wheelbase than the V12 'E' type by 3-inches, and contrary to appearances was only about 4-inches longer when the earlier car was equipped with its Nordel 5mph impact overriders.

Aerodynamics figured in the design of the car's shape from the very beginning, when Sir William Lyons worked with Malcolm Sayer, the man previously responsible for the appearance of the C-, D- and 'E' types; alas Sayer was to die prematurely in 1970, after producing some of the most enduring and beautiful sports car designs ever. The bodyshells for the XJ-S were made at British Leyland's Castle Bromwich factory on new tooling and press shop machinery, installed for the purpose; this was part of a £6.5-million investment in the XJ-S, which included a new 2000ft track at the Browns Lane assembly plant, alongside the existing saloon and coupe lines.

Initial production was scheduled to be 60 cars a week, with the intention of building-up to nearer 150 a week, almost as much as the peak production of the less complex 'E' type had been at 170 cars per week. North

Some aspects of XJ-S body design can clearly be traced back to previous stillborn prototypes – for instance, the front-end treatment of the two-door experimental car dating from the first half of the 'sixties carries the basic XJ-S bonnet/wings relationship. *Photo: Jaguar Cars*

There was little chance that the successor to the famous 'E' type would be mid-engined – the nearest road-going Jaguars to that concept of weight distribution were these scale-model design exercises by Malcolm Sayer, based loosely on the XJ-13 theme. *Photos: Jaguar Cars*

The other distinctive feature of the XJ-S's bodywork, the 'flying buttresses' at the rear, was first tried on this 2-plus-2 'E' type update which was never proceeded with. *Photo: Jaguar Cars*

America was expected to take 75 percent of this output, the remainder going to Australia and Europe where British Leyland saw the XJ-S tackling markets traditionally held by exotic supercars like Ferrari. But it seems as if its styling, combined with the psychological effect of occasional oil shortages, made these projections a little optimistic particularly where America was concerned.

The fact that governments were now finding it politic to demonstrate that oil was a finite commodity had effected sales of all the big-engined Jaguars. In September 1975 when the XJ-S appeared, XJ saloon production was down from 900 a week to 750, of which no less than 600 were six-cylinder models!

This ratio of 4.2 to 5.3 models with its heavy bias to six-cylinder cars was almost certainly not that envisaged four- or five-years before, when it was probably reasonably assumed that the twelve-cylinder engine would gradually become the mainstay of production, perhaps supported by a six- or eight-cylinder derivative of the new power unit; home market demand for the XJ12 dropped dramatically during the first oil crisis of 1973/74 and the day was virtually saved by the faithful old XK engine, and as the 'eighties drew nearer, even American manufacturers were at last showing signs of abandoning their "size is beautiful" philosophy and producing smaller and more economical cars – perhaps fearful that

otherwise their customers would turn to the rising tide of much more frugal foreign imports.

However, there will always remain a market for the best and the fastest, and the first road tests of the XJ-S confirmed that it definitely fell into that bracket. At £9608 it was not cheap in the sense that the simpler 'E' type had been in its day, but it still undercut any other manufacturer offering even a vaguely similar model. *Autocar* tried a manual gearbox example (no overdrive was offered because none was available that could accept the torque output of the 5.3-litre V12). "Opinions may differ over how good-looking the XJ-S body is. Over its effectiveness as a means of carrying two people, plus two smaller people behind, in safety at speed, and of insulating them from bumps and noise, there is no doubt."

When it came to straight-line performance, the XJ-S at 34.8cwt carried 18 percent more weight than the 1971 V12 'E' type two-plus-two but only just under 5 percent more power; this explained why the newer car couldn't quite match the older one in sheer acceleration, though the gap was very small – 60, 80 and 100mph times were 6.9; 10.8- and 16.9-seconds, for the XJ-S, and 6.8-, 10.6- and 16.4-seconds for the 'E' type. Top gear acceleration times were also in favour of the 'E' type, which covered 30-50mph in 5.9-seconds and 90-110mph in 8.3-seconds, the XJ-S figures being 6.7-seconds and 8.8-seconds; axle ratio was the same 3.07 in both cases.

Overhead view of the XJ-S shows its lines to good advantage; visibility through the rear window is, in fact, quite good. The flying buttresses were not merely ornamental but were included for aerodynamic effect. *Photo: Jaguar Cars*

The XJ-S was the only V12 XJ-variant to be offered with manual transmission – and even that option (rarely exercised by a customer) was withdrawn in mid-1979, although a few cars were completed with the four-speed box to special order after that date. *Photo: Jaguar Cars*

A superior shape told in the maximum speed runs though, and the manual XJ-S achieved an excellent 153mph, 11mph more than the closed V12 'E' type (and matching the speed set up by *Autocar's* fastest run in a six-cylinder 'E' type which almost certainly had been slightly tuned by the factory). At this speed, the engine was running at 6200rpm which was beyond peak power, developed at 5500rpm, so *Autocar* concluded that really the XJ-S was undergeared. "Assuming conservatively that 285bhp would propel the XJ-S at 155mph, a simple calculation shows that it would take a rise in overall gearing at 29.2mph per 1000rpm, provided by the final

drive of 2.69 and 1 instead of the current 3.07 to 1. Such a step up in gearing – 12.4 percent – could be achieved by an overdrive, which on motorways would further improve fuel consumption and range." As we have said, no suitable overdrive existed, but Jaguar were already experimenting with two-speed rear axles – which may well come into production one day...

With a manual gearbox version of the fuel-injected V12 to experiment with, *Autocar* were at last able to sample (and measure) the enormous flexibility of this magnificent power unit. This quality was demonstrated in a graphic experiment suggested by Jaguar:

"With the engine warm but switched off and the car at rest, the gearlever in top, the left foot out of the way, and the right foot holding the accelerator at about one-fifth of its travel, the car can be propelled forward from standstill on the starter motor. Neither rev counter nor speedometer needles will have begun to move off their stops (which are at zero) when the first pulses of each 445cc cylinder are felt – the speed is about 3 or 4 mph – and the engine smoothly, so smoothly, takes over. It must be emphasised that the period for which you feel each pulse is very short; smooth pulling begins at about 40mph. In 25-seconds you have passed 60mph, in 40-seconds you are doing 100, in 50-seconds 120 and in just under 70-seconds, 140mph. Power required to overcome drag is exceeded by power delivered to an almost straight-line degree over most of the acceleration in top..."

The absence of a torque-converter also had its effect on fuel consumption, because overall fuel consumption despite all the performance testing and high speed runs, came out at 15.4mpg; this compared very favourably with

XJ-S at speed on the MIRA banking; independent road-tests showed a top speed of 153mph for the manual gearbox version, making it a faster car than the Series 3 'E' type.

the 13.8mpg of the admittedly heavier automatic 5.3 coupe. Maximum speed work produced 10mpg or a little under ("reasonable in the circumstances", and even motoring which included cruising at between 90 and 120mph returned 14mpg; gentler driving gave 17.8mpg, while *Autocar* thought that 20mpg was quite attainable under easy conditions, which could give the car a theoretical range of 400-miles from its 20-gallon tank.

When fully enjoying the performance, the driver could detect some engine noise, as the car wasn't *completely* silent:

> "Driven hard, revving this extraordinary engine high, does make the power unit audible inside the car, but not in the way one expects from other differently admirable V12s. It is an imposing sound, hard to describe, rising excitingly but not loudly, the voice of great, continuing acceleration kept down, never raucous, even at the top end ... Wind noise becomes noticeable to some extent from 80mph, and more so further on, only slightly marring the car's otherwise totally relaxed 120mph cruising ability ... Road noise is remarkably low, both in bump thump and road roar ..."

Handling complemented the performance, though feel through the steering wheel was considered slight, even if the steering was a little heavier than on the XJ saloons and seemed to self-centre more readily, But it was "superbly accurate, with no mentionable lost motion, and no wander. Side wind stability is also good. You might not expect from a 53.3/45.7 percent front/rear weight distribution to find the best of traction, yet it is so. The for-once inaudible Powr-Lok differential is one reason." The grip given by the new Dunlop Super Sport tyres was "most reassuring" in the wet or dry, and thanks largely to the exceptionally smooth throttle control, the XJ-S was "easier than many less powerful cars to drive safely on ice." The tail could be provoked into a slide, "but you have got to be fairly abusive". The ride was rated on par with the saloons and "gets better still as one goes faster." Little could be said about the brakes because they were "superb", returning over 1.0g maximum retardation and resisting fade well. The handbrake on this car was perfectly efficient "and gave better-than-average retardation on its own."

From the driving seat, the arrangement of controls were generally liked, though "some of us missed the traditional Jaguar round minor instruments." The only major criticism made was the lack of a fast enough wiper setting, the 60 strokes a minute given being inadequate during heavy rain, with 80 strokes (as on a Porsche) really being required. The absence of an intermittent wipe setting was also felt. The front seats were found very comfortable, but predictably, in the back "a 6ft adult will request those in the front to move forward for the sake of his legs, and head, which must be stooped to clear the roof."

The Delanair heater and air conditioning unit regulated the selected air temperature well and didn't need constant adjustment, and the usual air-conditioning tendency for the screen to rapidly mist up on first starting up could quickly be cleared by turning the control to de-mist. The Cibié lights have a "very useful" dipped beam and a "flood of light and a good range" on main beam. "Overall, the Jaguar XJ-S is superb", summed up *Autocar*. "With very few exceptions, when you compare it with very nearly all its competitors, it is not only still competitively priced, but a completely sorted motor car, giving the highest satisfaction. Jaguar have really done their development work, and one can appreciate why it took so long to appear. We envy those who can find a place for this most covetable car."

When *Motor* published its test a couple of weeks after *Autocar*, they came to much the same conclusion; acceleration figures taken of a similar manual-gearbox car were fractionally better (60mph in 6.7, 100mph in 16.2-seconds), although weather conditions forclosed on a proper) maximum speed run. But it wasn't so much the figures themselves which impressed *Motor's* team but the way in which they were achieved: "There is no temperament, no fuss or bother, no abrupt change, no 'coming on the cam', in fact none of the characteristics which are oftenthe hallmarks of cars with equal or better performance but with more highly tuned and stressed engines."

The gearbox – still the same four-speed unit which had come with the 4.2 engine in 1964 – handled the power very well, although like *Autocar*, *Motor* detected a slight stickiness in the change. The power steering was felt not to be up to the standard set by Mercedes or Aston Martin. On corners: "The handling is exemplary and the car always feels well balanced and safe. You have to be cornering very hard before the normal mild understeer changes to predictable and controllable oversteer under power. Lifting off or braking in a corner simply tightens the line without any drama. When the tail does break away – and that requires a fair amount of throttle – the XJ-S can be untidy in that, possibly due to the limited slip differential, poor steering feel or a slightly too stiff anti-roll bar, the rear end tends to lurch round."

In this respect, *Motor* considered that it possible for the Mercedes "and some of the more expensive exoticars" to behave even better, but only at limits which few owners were ever going to reach. The brakes gave a deceleration of 1g in the *wet*. ("some cars cannot even achieve that in the dry") and showed no signs of fade during the brake test of 20 stops, one-minute apart, from a speed of 100mph. On this car, the handbrake only managed 0.22g but may have been faulty as *Autocar* recorded 0.38g.

Comfort for the driver and front seat passenger was good but room behind was not so generous. "Not only is leg and footroom severely restricted with the front seats anywhere near their rearmost position (a situation rarely likely to occur) but even for short people headroom is

A closed test-track was really needed to explore the XJ-S's handling to this extent! A Jaguar test driver enjoys himself on MIRA's ride-and-handling circuit. *Photo: Jaguar Cars*

limited and width is just about adequate due to intrusive armrests – but shoulder width is reasonable. The bench seat itself is well padded and reasonably comfortable but you sit noticeably higher than those in front, the cushion is short, and you have to adopt an upright position". But *Motor* did point out that the Jaguar was not unique in this respect, passengers in the faster Aston Martin V8 and the aging Jensen Interceptor ("plus many others") suffering in the same way. "The Lotus Elite again shows how it can and should be done" (at £8153 the 503 Elite was cheaper too, although rather slower in a straight line and with a reliability record worse than early Aston Martin V8s).

Motor's XJ-S was not so economical as *Autocar's*, possibly because less time was spent steady-speed cruising where the car was perhaps at 'its most efficient; overall consumption was 12.8mpg, with a computed 14.4mpg 'touring' figure – 1mpg down on *Autocar's* overall total. This was on par with the heavier injected 5.3-litre saloons and only a little better than the original XJ12 running on carburetters. "Much the same result could be achieved with less weight, capacity or complication, and thus better fuel consumption" thought *Motor*, citing the Elite again; but there is evidence to suggest that it is the very weight and bulk of the Jaguar that helps it attain the unmatched

The XJ-S in North American form, with the twin headlight units being the most obvious change although extra emission equipment under the bonnet made it a slower car than European-specification cars.

This is a 1975 emission engine in the XJ-S; breathing restrictions resulted in a noticeable loss of performance, and top speed was probably down by some 15-20mph.

degree of silence and refinement that it offers.

In America, *Road & Track* tested the XJ-S with the 'emission' engine which showed a distinct loss of performance compared with the home market car. The times to 60 and 100mph were 8.6- and 22.2-seconds (2.1- and 4.7-seconds down on *Autocar's* results, which is quite a lot), with a standing quarter mile of 16.5- rather than 15.2-seconds. But most interesting to record are Bob Tullius's impressions of a stock road-going XJ-S which *R&T* prevailed upon him to drive round the Road Atlanta, Georgia, circuit during a comparison test with Group 44's racing version (described elsewhere in this book):

"Even though it's a street car, this car does what it's supposed to do. It doesn't understeer a whole lot and it doesn't oversteer a whole lot; in fact, you can get it to do a broad slide which is quite unusual for a stock street machine. It handles much like a race car if you can interpolate the difference between the need for a race car to be stiff and the street car to be soft. The only real difference between it and the race car is the throttle application. With the street car you can stand on the throttle and it won't spin the wheels and send you roaring into the woods somewhere. When the car goes into a corner it tends to understeer just a bit until you get the throttle on and then it gets up on its haunches and does a little broad slide or the tail hangs out a little. It's exactly like the race car only softer and gentler."

Tullius also commented on the aerodynamics of the XJ-S which with some misgivings were left standard on the prototype racing XJ-S. But it turned out that Jaguar had got their sums right, and even the production spoiler was retained. "At an indicated 130mph on the back straight there was absolutely no indication that the speed was affecting the stability", said Bob Tullius of the road XJ-S, while as for the racing version, "at Daytona I could effortlessly drive up and down the banking at 180mph." So even at its maximum of 150mph-odd, the standard XJ-S is functioning well within its designed limits.

1977 Production changes

Nineteen seventy-seven brought modest cosmetic changes to the XJ-S. The radiator grille, previously finished in black, was given a bright finish and correspondingly the rear panel on the bootlid was now body colour instead of black, with satin chrome on the rear light infills on each side where the matching black finish used to be. On the side of the car, the central door pillar now had a black finisher in place of a chromium one, "to emphasise the horizontal lines of the car" in Jaguar's own words.

These revisions came in the autumn of 1977, but earlier in the year Jaguar had quietly begun to use the General Motors Hydramatic 400 automatic gearbox in all the 12-cylinder cars, in place of the Borg Warner Model 12 box. This was a conventional three-speed epicyclic design coupled to the engine by a torque converter but gave what Jaguar termed "a more sporting response" to the throttle, changing down sooner than the Model 12 and kicking-down to the next ratio at higher speeds. The selector also allowed the driver to hold first and second (both slightly lower geared than previously at 1.48 and 2.48 instead of 1.45 and 2.39) until the red line, and the automatic changes were slightly smoother than before. Rolls-Royce used the same gearbox with subtle changes engineered by their own transmission people, and Jaguar's unit was 'tuned' to the V12's torque and rev bands.

All four-door saloons were also affected by an addition to their specification, which took the form of the four-speaker Phillips AC460 mono radio/stereo cassette player being made standard on the Jaguar/Daimler range. This meant that the only factory-fitted audio option was the Phillips AC860 FM *stereo* radio combination unit. Finally, no-one was dismayed to find that from autumn 1977 too, the bright bezels round the instruments were replaced by a non-reflecting black finish on all cars, including the XJ-S.

Above: **The XJ-S changed little after 1977, when the radiator grille was changed to a bright finish, and the side-pillars to matt-black.**

Left: **Underbonnet view of the 1979 XJ-S engine, looking even more crowded...**
Photo: Jaguar Cars

It was during 1977 that the last 2-door Jaguars and Daimlers were built; these beautiful and comparatively rare variants of the XJ range were 'retired' because of the wind-sealing problem already mentioned, and in the cause of rationalisation – for every coupe produced, one less XJ four-door left the factory to help meet the demand which (usually) outstripped supply. Some commentators (*Autocar* included) had rated the 2-door above the XJ-S as the best all-round 'sporting' Jaguar, as it possessed most of that car's speed, had more practical rear-seat accommodation and was arguably better-looking; but in the end, the XJ-S won.

Rarest of the 'coupes' was the 5.3 engined one, a mere 604 RHD example being made and only 1269 LHD. The last two-door Jaguars were completed in November 1977.

Fuel-injection for the XK engine

Meanwhile, work had been going on at Browns Lane to update the XK engine. While the loss of performance occasioned by the anti-pollution gear demanded by the authorities in America (especially California) was not too serious for the V12 Jaguars, which had such a huge performance to begin with, it was beginning to affect the six-cylinder cars quite badly. "Air injection and exhaust gas recirculation took a lot of the sparkle out of the performance and made the car thirstier", said Harry Mundy, by then director of power unit and transmission engineering So in May 1978, the XK engine too went over to fuel injection.

The XJ 4.2 (the 3.4, not sold in the States, remained on SUs) was given the Lucas/Bosch L-Jetronic system equipped with a feedback control from an exhaust sensor and a three-way catalytic converter. This converter oxidised hydrocarbons and carbon monoxide while simultaneously reducing the nitric oxides, turning these three pollutants into harmless water, carbon dioxide and nitrogen. Its efficiency was determined by the proportion of fuel and air being burnt by the engine, as tiny variations from the ideal could result in gases which would stop the catalyst from working properly. This was the reason for the exhaust sensor placed between engine and catalyst, which caused the electronic injection control unit to adjust the mixture as necessary.

This worked so well that Jaguar were able to raise the compression ratio from a low 7.4:1 to 8:1; they also installed larger inlet valves, the first time these had been

The XJ 'coupe' was phased out during 1977, mainly to provide more room for building the saloon models. Cars like the one illustrated – a Double-six two-door with the optional alloy wheels – are now becoming collector's pieces, although worry about fossil fuels prevented a rise in value for some years. One Vanden Plas Double-six 'coupe' was completed, incidentally, but it was never a catalogued model.

increased from 1.75-inch since the XK engine had appeared in 1948. The diameter chosen was a well-established one however, for the 1.875 inch inlet valve size had been used in 1954 on the D-type sports racing car. The injected version of the 4.2 engine developed a much healthier 176bhp even in full emission form instead of 161 bhp, yet had a cleaner exhaust. A further spin-off from this development was that a single specification engine now sufficed for the entire market, whereas before different specifications had been required for California and for the rest of North America. This made production, and service, much simpler.

Petrol consumption was improved as well, the official EPA combined city and highway fuel consumption figure being 16-miles per US gallon with the injected XK engine, against the previous California and Federal cars' figures of 14mpg and 15mpg respectively. A year later, the fuel injection 4.2 engine had been standardised for the home and European market too – along with many other changes.

The biggest alteration to the XK engine since its enlargement to 4.2-litres in 1964 came when in 1978, electronic fuel-injection was installed; previously only competition versions of the XK power unit had been so fuelled. Initially the injected engine was offered in the United States only.

The 1977/78 Series 2 saloon, little changed in its last years apart from minor alterations inside. This is a September 1977 six-cylinder European market car.

The Series 3 XJ6 could well be termed the 'unintended Jaguar' because, very much like the Mk V saloon of 1948, it came about only because of unexpected delays with its successor. Had XJ40 proceeded according to plan in its early days, then the Series 2 XJ, or a close derivation of it, would have fulfilled the role of Jaguar's mainstream saloon until the emergence of XJ40 in the showrooms. But when it became clear that politics and other complications would extend the new saloon's gestation period, another facelifting excercise was deemed essential to modernise the XJ6 and so carry it well into the eighties.

Series 3 arrived on 28 March 1979, the fruits of a £7 million investment by Jaguar. The changes did not extend to the basic engineering of the car, but rather were aimed at updating and augmenting its ancillary equipment, which, never particularly advanced, had fallen even further behind the opposition. Nevertheless, Jaguar had not stinted in their revision of the XJ range, which underwent its most comprehensive and far-reaching update of all.

"The new range is intended to be evolutionary, not revolutionary", said Bob Knight at the launch; and he was right of course – under the skin, the XJ remained as before; a great complement to a design which had celebrated its tenth birthday. Indeed, the car was still the match of virtually any other four-seater regardless of price in handling, roadholding and performance; only in terms of ancilliary equipment and luxury 'extras' could the XJ be thought to have slipped behind the times, and it was this that the Series 3 was intended to make good.

Of the bodyshell changes, the new roofline was probably the most noticeable, giving the car a sleeker look and the occupants greater headroom. The front windscreen pillars were inclined an extra 3-inches from the perpendicular to achieve this effect, and towards the rear, the roofline was raised to give rear seat passengers more space, ending in a flatter backlight with no sacrifice in parcel shelf space; both laminated front and toughened rear screens were now fitted by thermal adhesion which decreased the likelihood of leaks and, because the glass now formed part of the body structure, increased the shell's torsional rigidity. Tinted glass was standard on all cars except the 3.4, where it was an optional extra.

In fact the entire glass area had been increased by virtue of extra depth, giving the car a leaner appearance especially side-on, enhanced by the removal of the front quarter-light post and the crisper, less rounded profile of the new roof panel itself. The roof had also been reduced in width a little, increasing the curvature or 'tumble-home' of the side windows to the waistline, which remained as before except that under the rear quarter-light the sweep of the bodyline had been straightened before it met the characteristic 'lift' of the rear wing top panel. While these revisions to the bodywork were generally well-received, it is a little sad to note that, for the first time, an outside styling consultant had been retained by Jaguar to assist in the redesign – Carrozzeria Pininfarina of Turin.

Optional was an electrically operated sunshine roof. Like all previous Jaguar sunroofs, it was a flush-fitting metal panel, and retracted into the space between

The Daimler Sovereign edition of the Series 3 range, also sporting the new front bumper; this car is fitted with the headlight wash/wipe as well. *Photo: Jaguar Cars*

The XJ range was markedly improved with the coming of the Series 3 cars, with crisper lines and much improved ancilliary equipment, more inclined screen pillars and a deeper glass area all round contributed to a more modern, 'airy' look.

Side view of the Series 3 shows the optional sunroof, and the 'straightened-out' bodyline under the rear side window.

headling and roof. It was operated by a double cable which was linked to an electric motor in the boot, underneath the parcel shelf, and controlled by a console switch which allowed full or partial opening of the panel. This was the first time that an opening roof had been fitted to an XJ by Jaguar – or even officially approved as a proprietary 'extra'.

Below the car's waistline, many minor changes of detail had taken place; door handles were now flush-fitting for safety and styling reasons, operating on a lift/pull flap principle. The leaping Jaguar badge on the side panels behind the front wheels was retained, silver for the XJ3.4 and 4.2, gold for the XJ5.3; all V12 cars carried a double coachline, while the 4.2 cars were given a single one – only the 3.4 had no such decoration at all.

Black bumpers distinguished the Series 3 cars at the front; for North America these incorporated 5mph impact absorbing beams, though for virtually all other markets these weight and cost adding structures were omitted. The bumper bars were covered by wrap-around black injection mouldings and decorated by a brightwork capping.

The front bumpers now contained the recessed indicator lights, and the sidelights were now incorporated in the outer headlamps as the new wider bumpers took up the previous position of the side/indicator light units. The radiator grille was new, the grid pattern of the bars being replaced by neater vertical slats and a centre rib, much more like the original XJ12 grille. The Jaguar head was still carried on the top piece of the grille, gold on black

for the six-cylinder cars, and gold on bronze for the XJ5.3 – though no longer a V12 motif underneath. Daimler grilles remained much as before, with the fluted top piece and "D" symbol.

Rear bumpers were similar-pattern black too, and fog guard lamps were carried in the bumpers themselves instead of underneath (though not for the USA). New lamp clusters which were slightly similar to those on the XJ-S gave a larger area of illumination and incorporated the reversing lights which were formerly mounted on the bootlid either side of the release. Here, a re-designed number plate lamp housing and boot handle were installed, the flatter, wider housing covering the width of the number plate and containing the bootlatch, again similar to the arrangement on the XJ-S. Rear badging for the Series 3 car was as follows: "Jaguar" on the left, and "XJ6 3.4", "XJ6 4.2" or "XJ12 5.3" on the right; "Daimler" on the left, and "Sovereign 4.2" or "Double-Six 5.3" on the right as appropriate. Vanden Plas cars were identified by the coachmaker's name on the right, and "Daimler 4.2" or "Daimler Double-Six" on the left. In America though, the cars remained simply "XJ6" or "XJ12", as there was no 3.4 variant to complicate the issue.

The Series 3 road wheels remained at 6K but were given new stainless steel wheel trims which left the wheel nuts exposed, thus making wheel changing easier because the sometimes awkward task of levering off the trims was avoided. Alloy wheels were still an option on all cars including the XJ3.4, except the Vanden Plas Daimlers.

Then came a whole host of refinements and improvements to the XJ's specification which put the car firmly in the 'eighties. First there was the Cruise Control; this aid to long distance driving on motorways or freeways maintained a driver-selected speed up hill and down dale, being instantly cancelled by a touch on the brakes – though the cruise control computer memorised the previously set speed, and on pressing of the "resume" rocker switch, the car automatically returned to its cruising speed. Switching off the ignition automatically wiped-out the setting. The device only worked in top gear and above 24-28mph (depending on axle ratio), and could only be specified on automatic 4.2 and 5.3 models, though it was standard on these cars for the North American market – indeed there were no 'extras' at all for cars destined for the States, as they came with everything!

Jaguar's already comfortable seats were improved still further by the new advanced lumbar-support seats introduced in the Series 3, whereby the driver and front seat passenger could shape the squabs to match their spines by means of control knobs positioned on the inside edge of each seat – the squab shape could be altered by as much as 1.5 inches in this way. This facility was standard throughout the range, but optional was the electrically controlled front seat height adjustment, a rocker switch on the outer corner of the seat causing the seat cushion to

Before it entered production, Jaguar ran a check on the new sliding roof in the wind-tunnel to evaluate the effects of an open space on the airflow. *Photo: Jaguar Cars*

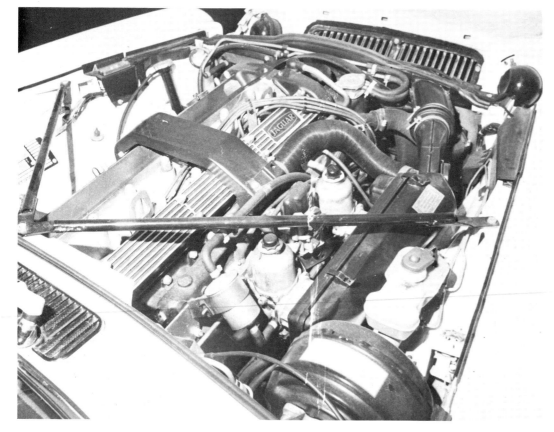

Above: **This view of the Series 3 shows the re-designed rear-end detail, including the matt-black badging, numberplate lamp housing and boot handle, and 5mph-impact bumper.**

The tightly packed engine compartment of the Series 3 XJ 3.4; it retained its SU carburettors unlike its sister 4.2.

be raised or lowered through an arc of nearly 2-inches. It was an extra cost fitment to the driver's seat on all cars, except the Daimler Vanden Plas saloons where it was standard on both driver's and passenger's seat.

Additionally, the height of the seat backs was raised by 1.5 inches for extra support, and the head restraints modified to move the pad nearer the back of the head. New seat-back map pockets were fitted to all models, and the front seat inertia reels were now hidden in the centre door pillars to give more space for rear seat passengers and to generally tidy up the interior. Provision was also made for the fitting of three-point inertia reel seatbelts to the outer rear seating positions in the back, and a manually adjusted lap belt for the centre rear seat position – these belts were standard fitments for USA, Canada and France. New moulded headlinings with recessed sun visors were specified (with glass fibre noise insulation underneath the lining), and a larger interior rear view mirror installed to give better rearward visibility.

Carpeting was new, deep pile and with a softer and more luxurious feel; it also contributed towards sound deadening. Grey was re-introduced as a Jaguar/Daimler carpet colour to replace dark blue, the other colours being from a choice of russet red, light brown and black. Windscreen wiper operation had received its long-awaited update on the Series 3 – at last an intermittent wipe position was added, giving a six-second delay between each sweep of the blade, and a modern automatic parking operation included, the depth of the sweep increasing when the wipers were switched off by the stalk control. The 'flick-wipe' action was retained as well, making the system one of the most versatile seen on any car.

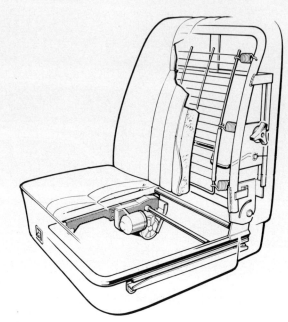

The new electrically-controlled seat mechanism allowed automatic adjustment of seat height, while the side adjustment knob altered the seat squab shape to suit any back.

The new seats and deep-pile carpeting in the Series 3 XJ.

The same stalk controlled another new facility – the headlamp wash/wipe, standard on Daimler Vanden Plas cars and optional on all other Series 3 models. When the windscreen wash button was pressed, the headlamp wash/wipe cleaned the outer lamp lenses, which were flat, though it worked only when the headlamps were actually on. A new, larger reservoir, common to both windscreen and headlamp washers, was fitted under the left-hand front wing in the engine compartment, holding 7-litres of fluid compared to the 1.7-litres held before; as the take-off pipes for screen and lights were at different levels, when the screen washers ran dry some 0.85 litre remained for use on the headlamps, acting as a reminder for the owner to top-up.

The control column stalks (wipers and indicators/lights) were also contraposed to conform with proposed international regulations on standard controls, while all facia instrument switches and dials were now marked with symbols instead of words, again for international recognition; the wheel itself was given a re-styled spoke for better instrument visibility. New instrument graphics included mph *and* kph calibrations on the speedometer.

New warning lights were added to the instrument panel centre strips, one warning of low coolant level, and another that the rear foglights are illuminated. Furthermore, all Series 3 cars were given a bulb failure warning light, located in the speedometer face. This lit up whenever one of the sidelights or brake lights failed, or if

there was a stoplight fault. Radio receiver and cassette tape player equipment was as for later Series 3, though now an electric rise-and-fall radio aerial was standardised having an advanced delay mechanism built into the automatic aerial control system which prevented the rise and fall of the aerial while the engine was being started.

Another built-in delay circuit was now adopted for the interior lights, which meant that at night time, when the doors were shut after entering the car, two interior lights stayed on for 10-15 seconds to give the driver time to locate the ignition key switch and fasten his seatbelt. This too was standard on all cars. The heated rear window also had its own timing memory; it could be switched on or off manually as before, but now, after being left on for about 15 minutes, the heater would switch itself off, thereby saving any drain on the battery. Again it was fitted across the range.

The Series 3 was easier to live with in respect of its locking arrangement too, and more thief-proof. A simplified three-key system was used – an ignition key, a service key which would unlock only the doors and petrol filler cap (not the boot when closed by the centrally locking, in which circuit it was now included), and a master key which would centrally lock the doors and boot but only electrically unlock doors; it would also unlock the boot manually.

Standard on Vanden Plas and USA specification cars was the new electric control exterior rear view mirror on each front door, adjustment being by two small joy-stick

The wash-wipe mechanism on the Series 3 Jaguar cleaned the outer headlight glasses, and was standard on Vanden Plas cars and optional on the other models

The comprehensive updating of the XJ's dashboard and minor controls was generally welcomed; the wiper stalk now gave a delayed action sweep of the blades, new warning lights were added, and symbols replaced words on all controls.

controls within easy reach of the driver; as standard, the remote control adjustment was carried out manually, both in vertical and horizontal planes. Night-time visibility was improved by the standardisation of quartz halogen headlights on all Series 3 cars except the 3.4, where it was an extra-cost option. These had the added advantage of needing only the bulb changed in the event of a failure, instead of the entire tungsten sealed-beam unit as before.

In the boot, Jaguar once more treated even the tools aesthetically, as these were now contained in a neat 'briefcase' with handle clipped to the boot sidewall; the case was made from moulded plastic, and rather like the arrangement in the Mk II, contained padded slots for a variety of tools including wrench, plug and other spanners, pliers, screwdriver, spare bulbs and fuses.

Interesting to relate, Jaguar were apparently not satisfied with their previous almost unmatched standards of silence and improved the XJ's sound deadening even further. This was achieved by even greater attention to the placing of vacuum formed mouldings of rubber and foam in the door panels, bulkhead and propeller shaft tunnel.

As already intimated, few mechanical changes came with the Series 3. Fuel injection on the 4.2 six-cylinder was standardised, complete with OPUS electronic ignition. In home market form, the engine developed just over 200bhp at the lower rpm figure of 5000 – or in other

The Series 3 XJ 4.2 was equipped with the electronic fuel-injection system which had already seen service on American-market XJ6s for a year

A pleasing touch on the Series 3 was the neat 'briefcase' for the tools, kept in the luggage compartment.

words, as much as the triple-carburetter 3.8 litre Mk X 'E' type engine ever did, unrestricted by any anti-pollution devices. Fuel was now supplied at the higher pressure of 36psi, this uprating also applying to the 5.3 injection system. Although one difference between the two systems was that on the six-cylinder injection equipment, the sensor, which fed the electronic control unit with information, now measured the airflow in the manifold and not the air pressure. The airflow was found to be much more critical to the precise timing of injection into the manifold, which from then on took place as two squirts in place of one. On the V12, a bimetal strip instead of a wax capsule thermostat now cut out the special cold-start injector when the engine attained its running temperature.

An interesting new economy feature on the 4.2 engine was the overrun fuel cut-off. This came into effect when the accelerator pedal was released, the fuel supply to the engine being stopped until the revolutions dropped to 1200rpm. Like the 5.3's, the 4.2's injection system was a sealed unit so far as the owner was concerned, and any faults needed the special test equipment of Jaguar and Daimler franchise holders.

The 4.2 injected engine was further quietened by a simple modification to the air cleaner, whereby induction roar was reduced by the removal of the hot-air flap which was necessary for carburettor fuel control, though drivers of early injected six-cylinder cars noted that a certain degree of extra noise was made by the new version of the XK engine, which seemed to produce a more 'sporty' note on hard acceleration.

Certainly the additional response from the trusty old six-cylinder appeared to invite a more vigorous driving style, especially when the Rover SD1 5-speed gearbox, introduced on Jaguars at the 1978 Motor Show, was fitted. This weighed 30lb. less than the old four-speed box plus overdrive, which was a step in the right direction, although the net result wasn't quite the same – a similar 3.54 rear axle ratio was fitted, but the new gearbox 5th gear gave only 25.8mph per 1000rpm compared with the previous overdrive's 27.5mph per 1000rpm which was enough to make cruising slightly less relaxing. It also effected economy slightly, and, if full use of the injected engine's new power and response was employed, Series 3 4.2 drivers found that their overall fuel consumption was not very different to that of the normally aspirated Series 2 car.

The adoption of the 5-speed gearbox also signalled the death-knell of the last manual transmission V12 Jaguar, for manufacture of the Jaguar four-speed box ceased, and the XJ-S could only be supplied in manual form up until stockpiled supplies of this gearbox lasted. While few owners in fact ever specified manual transmission on the XJ-S, its final abandonment was a cause for regret as no longer could the V12 engine's fabulous flexibility and smoothness be fully exploited.

Although the XJ-S was largely unaffected by the introduction of the Series 3 saloons, a revised version was to follow. This XJ-S interior, with wood veneer and other modifications, inspired the XJ-S HE furnishings of 1980.

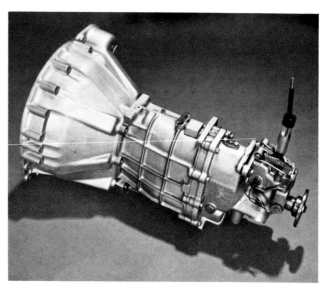

The Rover 5-speed gearbox as used by the XJ6 since the end of 1978; it was considerably altered by Jaguar's engineers before installation to reduce noise and to enable it to fit, with a new casing and new linkage

Road testing the Series 3

The first British road-test of the extensively revised new XJ was published by *Motor* in September 1979. "More grace, pace and space" was the magazine's summary, although adding by way of qualification, "some traditional shortcomings remain." Given that the car's handling and road-holding were as good as ever (except for a slight deterioration, the journal felt, in straightline stability at high-speed), the item which made the biggest impression on the road-test team was the fuel-injection power unit. "Without question, the XK engine is more efficient with the new injection system than it was on carburettors", said *Motor*, after recording an overall consumption figure of 15.7mpg (including testing and very hard driving) which compared with 13.7mpg returned by a Series 2 4.2 tried the previous year. Even better, the computed 'touring' consumption worked out at 19.3mpg, "which we feel many owners will approach, if not better".

Performance had obviously improved too, although the issue was confused by gearing – the Series 2 tried in 1978 had a 3.31 rear axle ratio, while the latest car was fitted with the (free-option) 3.07 axle. "However, a measure of the improvement in the engine's efficiency is that the acceleration from rest to 70mph is virtually unchanged, depsite the longer-legged gearing, and from then on is significantly better." Thus 60mph was reached in 10.5-seconds, 70mph in 13.5-seconds, and 100mph in 28.4-seconds – the latter time being 2.6-seconds less than the Series 2 4.2.

Both these Jaguars were automatics, the Series 3 having an updated version of the Borg Warner Model 65 box which "in most circumstances ... offers an excellent blend of responsiveness and unobstrusiveness." Though major complaints here were that the box refused to kick-down into first over about 30mph, and that the change-up point from first to second was "unnecessarily slow", which made the car feel "irritatingly sluggish" when, for example, accelerating out of a roundabout. The manual hold could be used, though to overcome this problem.

In maximum speed, the injected 4.2 automatic was much quicker than any previous automatic six-cylinder Jaguar saloon, 128mph being recorded by *Motor* on a trip to limit-free West Germany, and it was pointed out that even more performance – especially in acceleration – would be provided by the five-speed manual gearbox cars, which the journal thought would attract about 50% of buyers – a much higher percentage than had previously ordered manual Series 1 and 2 cars. In fact the much improved economy of the fuel-injection 4.2 engine had the effect of cutting sales of the 3.4, which, remaining on its two 1.75-inch SU carburettors, was hardly any more frugal on petrol and gave a considerably poorer performance.

Autocar tried a similar 4.2 Series 3 car at the end of 1979, publishing its findings in December of that year. Performance was much the same as *Motor's* example, and the magazine pointed out that in particular, the previous 90-110mph time of 32.3-seconds had been "virtually halved" to 16.2-seconds. A mean maximum speed of 127mph was reached, with a best one-way speed of 130mph (at 5250rpm, indicating that the car was "just about ideally geared"). And besides a better performance and greater economy ("with consideration owners should easily average between 18 and 20mpg"), another benefit of fuel-injection was the easy starting and an "utterly hesitation free" warm-up driving period.

Unlike *Motor's* car, *Autocar's* XJ had the Pirelli P5 tyres which were fitted to most Series 3 as standard (Dunlop Sports were still available as an option). "Better handling response is claimed for the new Pirelli P5s", said the journal; "however they undoubtedly generate more roar and rumble than the ... exceptionally quiet-running Dunlops. This is particularly noticeable over ridged concrete or coarse and uneven surfaces." But despite this and a slight increase in wind-noise and some "rumble and thump" through the bodyshell, *Autocar* still considered the XJ to be "a surprisingly quiet and peaceful car to ride in."

Most of what *Autocar* did have to grumble about concerned the automatic transmission selector – it still had the "inexplicable" detent between "2" and "D", but none between "D" and "Neutral", which meant that having moved the "delightfully slender" lever sideways to overcome the detent, it would be easy to shoot straight past "D" into "Neutral". Similarly, the lack of a detent between "D" and "1" could allow the lever to go from "D' to "1" at much too high a road speed (although an

inhibitor in the gearbox would prevent actual engagement). So it was not possible to slide easily between "D" and "2" (for overtaking for instance), but was possible ("for the unfamiliar, or nervous driver") to get the wrong (or no) gear with potentially disastrous results. Borg Warner, incidentally, stated afterwards that it was up to the car manufacturer to specify what arrangement the selector mechanism, took, so this rather silly state of affairs was down to Jaguar....

What of the opposition? *Car* magazine investigated this aspect when it conducted a searching comparison between the Series 3 5.3 and the latest Mercedes range ... The latest Jaguar was driven to Stuttgart where comparisons were made between it and the 500SE from Mercedes' new and latest S-class – essentially a generation ahead of the Jaguar, having been designed when the XJ series had already been in production four-or five-years.

The increased importance of fuel economy and the advances made in construction techniques since the XJ6 was 'laid down' in the first half of the 'sixties was evident in weight alone – although almost 1.5-inches longer than the Jaguar and higher and wider the 500SE actually weighed 673lb *less* than the Series 3 5.3. And it was powered by a new 3.8-litre 92x71.8mm V8 engine with one overhead cam per bank, giving 218bhp (DIN) at 5500rpm which, up to three-figure speeds, left the 12-cylinder Jaguar well behind. That wasn't all – this engine was backed up by an equally new 5-litre V8 giving 240bhp (DIN), enough to give the car the same performance as that bestowed by the old 6.9-litre unit used in the previous S-class.

Despite these products of a "fabulously wealthy company, fabulously staffed and equipped", the Jaguar equalled the Mercedes' handling and roadholding, was quieter and more refined, and its V12 engine silkier than either the 3.8 or 5-litre Mercedes power units. And at really high speeds it seemed to have a faster response to the accelerator than even the larger-engined Mercedes, and at least as good a top speed. The Mercedes undoubtedly scored in many other important ways though, being more aerodynamic and more frugal, 12 000-mile service intervals (6000 for the Jaguar), better put together, and "full of really thoughtful and useful touches." "But", wrote Mel Nichols for *Car*, "is it a *better* car than the Jaguar?"

"The Jaguar is still, overall, the more refined; it has a link with the past and with a British style of quality and excellence that stands out positively in today's world and which prevents Mercedes, for all its time advantages, standing as clearly the best car in the world. With all due respect to both of them – and it is no trouble to accord both that respect; they are different in their ways but they are both superb – we suggest that they must share the best saloon in the world pedestal. Neither eclipses the other; but, despite their few flaws, they each eclipse all their opponents."

Road & Track sampled a Series 3 in September 1980 and reckoned that it "upholds the tradition well" though the magazine expressed puzzlement at some of the minor alterations which appeared to them to be change for the sake of change. Some drivers felt that the reshaped front seats were less comfortable, and this car displayed more wind noise than previous test cars. A sign of the (petrol conscious) times was their description of the 4.2 engine as "big", although it was rated smooth if not completely silent. The 0–60mph time of this car was actually one second down on that recorded previously by their injected XJ6L Series 2, but as a slight fuel injection fault was acknowledged (raising consumption from the expected 15-16mpg to 13.5mpg) possibly the car wasn't quite up to scratch.

Overall the car was liked, but once more *R&T* felt obliged to qualify their approval by saying that because the make "is haunted by a reputation for poor quality control and indifferent service ... our praises have to be tempered with our reservations". Such was the feeling of the time, and it was inevitably keeping many Americans from buying a Jaguar; as *Car & Driver* remarked in its road test of the Series 3 (having described the car as "slick as the inside of Faye Dunaway's dressing gown"!), "A lot of this bad repute is myth .... but it's a powerful myth, reinforced by just enough truth to keep it at the front of our minds."

Overall, Jaguar had succeeded where some were fearful they might fail – improving and visually updating the XJ in a way which did not spoil its innate balance and good-looks, or unnecessarily altering its character simply to meet the whim of some corporate marketing executive. Public and dealer reaction alike was enthusiastic, although the supply of cars did not initially support the heavily promoted launch of the Series 3 – while 3.4 and 5.3 models appeared to be in fairly good supply, the popular 4.2 was not; the choice of colours was limited at first too, white, yellow or red being about the only hues available until the new Castle Bromwich paint shop came into operation.

This was a very ambitious, £15.5-million complex which was heralded as the most technically advanced in the UK, and was housed on two working levels covering some 500 000 square feet. The Series 3 Jaguar was in fact the initial reason for the construction of the plant, though its siting at Castle Bromwich, Birmingham, was not without controversy – there were doubts concerning the feasability of transporting completely painted shells to Browns Lane without damage, and without the traditional Jaguar procedure of not applying the final coat until the last road-test and checking operation had been carried out.

The paint used was the latest thermoplastic acrylic with proven long-life gloss, and some very attractive new metallic shades became available on a Jaguar for the first time, including platinum metallic, chestnut metallic,

cobalt blue metallic, and quartz blue metallic; black and Sebring red were optional to special order. Just as importantly, wax injection was now carried out on all major box sections of the Series 3 bodyshell, a much overdue step in the combating of body corrosion – though in this respect Jaguar were no worse than many other prestige (and bread-and-butter) manufacturers who up until very recently have apparently been unconcerned about the otherwise inevitable body deterioration after three or four years.

The Series 3's production career, 1980 – 1986

Beset though it might have been with quality control problems, Jaguar was still able to respond to the market, and in a conscious effort to lower the threshold of Jaguar ownership, announced a revised specification 3.4 saloon in October 1980. This was priced at £12,750, £500 cheaper than before and allowing it to compete directly against the Mercedes 280E. Little was sacrificed in the way of luxury, though the radio was cheaper and its aerial had to be operated by hand. As previously, cloth upholstery was standard and automatic transmission would cost you an extra £200, but the 3.4 owner could always upgrade his car by ordering such options as alloy wheels, headlamp wipe/wash, air-conditioning, electric seat adjustment and electric sun roof.

Previously, in May 1980, it had been decided that the 3,000 mile service was unnecessary, and for all cars for 1981 the 6,000 mile service was extended to 7,500 miles, and the 12,000 mile service to 15,000 miles. North American service schedules had been so based from somewhat earlier.

It was the V12-engined cars that received attention for 1981, with dramatic results in the market place as the news spread – the big bogey of the V12, its fuel consumption, had well and truly been cut down to size. It all stemmed from a visit to Harry Munday's power units department by a young Swiss engineer named Michael May, who had been invited to expand on his radical ideas on combustion chamber design. Later, he brought his modified VW Passat to Browns Lane for evaluation, experimental engines were built, and, impressed, Jaguar opted to become the first manufacturer to put May's theories into production. These centred round a special two-chamber combustion arrangement with the inlet valve recessed in a collecting zone, and the exhaust valve located higher up in a 'bathtub' combustion chamber into which projected the sparking plug. A swirl-inducing ramp connected the two chambers, the mixture being pushed by the piston from the inlet valve zone to the combustion chamber on its compression stroke. This gave a low-turbulence, concentrated charge around the sparking plug, which enabled rapid and complete burning of a very lean, highly compressed, mixture.

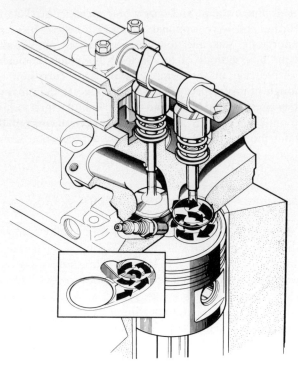

Principle of the 'May' head used on the HE Jaguars and Daimlers: compression stroke introduces swirl in the 'fireball' combustion chamber. Inset shows the underside of the swirl pattern.

HE engine bay; the V12 Jaguars now had a 20mpg potential, and in normal use returned similar figures to those of the pre-injection XJ6.

Up until then, the V12 engine's combustion chamber had been formed by the piston crown, but fortunately there was enough depth in the cylinder head casting for one to be created there. Flat-topped pistons replaced the originals, giving a 12.5:1 compression ratio. A new high-power amplifier, twin-coil ignition system provided the more powerful spark needed, while the latest type of Lucas digital electronic fuel injection was reprogrammed to suit the lean-burn characteristics of the engine.

It had cost £½ million to alter the cylinder head plant at Radford to mill chambers in the previously flat head casting, but the results were fiercely worthwhile. The new HE ('High Efficiency') saloons could record 15mpg on the official urban cycle consumption test, as opposed to 12.5mpg previously; steady speed figures were (with the 'old' car's in brackets) 26.8mpg at 56mph (21.2mpg), and 21.5mpg at 75mph (18.2mpg). Browns Lane were not tardy in pointing out that the big Mercedes saloon, the 500 SEL, returned an inferior 14, 24.4 and 20.2mpg on the same test.

The effort to revive the fortunes of this basically magnificent car continued with emphasising its exclusivity and top-of-the-range status. This was achieved by new paint finishes unique to the XJ12 HE (as the new model was badged), plus a chrome waistline moulding. Alloy wheels were standardised and given a silver-enamel finish, and included in the basic specification were electric

sunroof, twin electrically-controlled door mirrors, and headlamp wipe/wash with new, heavy duty pumps. No suspension changes were made but the new Dunlop D7 tyres featured, their 215 section helping to provide better handling and straight-line 'feel' than the previous 205 section covers. Unlike the XJ-S HE announced at the same time, however, the HE saloon rim width stayed at 6in.

The Daimler Double Six received similar attention, though as part of a policy to give the Daimler marque a greater identity of its own, the Double Six wasn't given alloy wheels as standard but instead it featured seats with electrically-controlled height adjustment, carpets which extended onto the lower parts of the 'A' posts, deep-pile footrugs for the rear compartment, detachable rear seat headrests, and smooth leather fluting of the seats instead of embossing. The Daimler individual-style rear seats were retained.

Then Jaguar really went to town on the Double Six Vanden Plas; air conditioning had always been standard but now there was also cruise control, even plusher seating, and inlays to the veneered door fillets. The Daimler 4.2 Vanden Plas received similar treatment.

As for the other six-cylinder cars, the biggest mechanical changes concerned cooling: an 18-inch, viscous-coupled fan of a type used on the V12 cars was fitted, now thermostatically controlled so that its slip was in direct relationship to the coolant temperature as well as engine revolutions, while for the first time on a Jaguar six-cylinder road car, an oil cooler was made standard.

To counteract sometimes misleading indications of coolant level portrayed by the coolant header tank, a larger, clear plastic tank was situated higher up in the engine bay; this also improved the flow. Both six- and twelve-cylinder cars now enjoyed low-maintenance batteries needing only an annual check.

Increased safety was the reasoning behind the change of automatic gear selector on all automatic cars (the GM400 on the V12s, and the Borg Warner 66, an updated version of the 65, on the 'sixes'). This moved the detent from its illogical position between D and 2, placing it instead between D and N. You could now shift the selector between D and 2 as quickly as you liked without the danger of over-shooting into neutral or even reverse.

The five-speed manual gearbox remained the standard fitment on the 4.2 car, however, though it was specified by only about 15 per cent of drivers. Tinted glass, quartz halogen headlights, and a combined radio/cassette player were, along with leather trim, the items which set the standard 4.2 saloon apart from the standard 3.4. This latter remained the lowest-priced Jaguar though it, too, included electric windows, central locking, childproof rear locks, adjustable lumbar support for the front seats, cubby-hole light and door-open guard lights in its specification. Unique to Daimler models, however, was a reversible bootmat (rubber on one side, carpet on the other) while all saloons now sported a colour-keyed heel mat in the driver's footwell, moulded with the Daimler script or the Jaguar name and symbol as appropriate.

For 1983 Jaguar not only revised some aspects of the cars, but changed the name structure, too. In October 1982 it was thus announced that the Daimler name would be dropped for the European market, replaced instead by

A new model name for Jaguar arrived with the 'Sovereign' badge; it denoted high-specification versions of the 4.2-and 5.3-litre Jaguars – this is the Jaguar Sovereign 4.2, fitted with the new perforated wheels.

a 'new' saloon, a high-specification car to be called the Jaguar Sovereign. Yes, the borrowing of the traditionally Daimler model name was a little confusing, but the reason for dropping the Daimler marque in Europe (it had never been sold in the USA) was given as confusion on the part of the customer, especially in Germany, home of Daimler Benz (later this reasoning was reversed, and Daimlers were reintroduced in Germany to take advantage of the commonality!). The Jaguar Sovereign soon became available on the home market as well.

As for the existing model line-up, the most obvious changes concerned their interiors. The new centre console caught the eye first, its upper part vacuum-formed and including the switch panel and a storage tray; both upper and lower switch panels were given figured walnut veneer (Jaguars) or burr walnut veneer (Daimlers). The analogue clock or trip computer, when fitted, were moved to the upper console, and badges denoting the marque were introduced on the centre of the lower console. Meeting a small criticism was the thicker-rimmed steering wheel, there was a new horn push for the Daimlers, and a new panel with black grained finish carried the radio and heater/air conditioning controls. The front seats were improved by internal stiffening, and a new fine-line pattern Raschelle material adopted for the 3.4 and (optionally) for the XJ6 and XJ12. Headlining colour was now standardised as Limestone whatever trim colour was specified, and Daimler and Vanden Plas cars received larger areas of wood finishes on the doors.

In the boot, Daimlers were equipped with a liner to tidy up its appearance, and on all the cars the previously discontinued attaché case tool container was reintroduced. Mechanical changes consisted of only detail refinements and improvements, which continued to be introduced all the while as Jaguar's persistent quest for quality continued unabated.

The revised automatic gear selector used on Series 3 cars from 1981 which prevented the accidental selection of 'N' or 'R' from 'D'. Central locking panic-button is below.

From the outside, the XJ12 HE looked the most altered in that it had been given new 'perforated' alloy wheels; for £543 you could also specify them on your new 3.4 or 4.2 XJ. Daimlers retained the previous spoked alloy wheels, which were standard on the VDP 5.3-litre car. The 'leaping cat' side wing badges were restyled, the silver-on-black six-cylinder grille badge was commonised on all Jaguars, and the chromium centre bonnet strip was discontinued which entailed a small change to the Daimler grille. The Daimlers carried a bright side-moulding, while the Jaguar 3.4 now sported a single coachline as opposed to the 4.2 and 5.3 cars' twin fine-line coachlines. The 1983 model 3.4 was finally equipped with quartz halogen headlights, the last XJ model this side of the Atlantic to be so.

The Jaguar Sovereign came to the home market for the 1984 model year. Looking very distinguished with its perforated alloy road wheels, it carried electrically-controlled door mirrors, while its interior specification was much upgraded – standard were front seats with electrically controlled height adjustment, trip computer, rear headrests, rear reading lights and seat belts, passenger footwell rugs, air conditioning and carpeted boot. For this you paid £18,495 against £15,997 for the normal 4.2 – but the Sovereign cost almost £1,000 less than the Vanden Plas variant it replaced.

There was a V12 equivalent too: the new Jaguar Sovereign HE. This replaced the XJ12 and edged the V12 saloon even further up market. Its equipment (which included all the six-cylinder Sovereign's accoutrements, plus cruise control, headlamp wipe/wash, and a better radio/cassette player) ensured that it equated more with the 1983 model Double Six HE which had retailed for £21,372; so while at £20,995 it was dearer than the old XJ12, it still represented good value.

The XJ6 3.4 was now even better value; its price had been maintained for three years and so remained under the British £14,000 business-car tax bracket. The 4.2 saloon had only increased by 1 per cent over its 1980 price, too, compared with rises of 14 per cent suffered by Mercedes and BMW. This contrasted with the dark years of the late seventies when under BL influence the Jaguar price was 'milked' for short-term gain; now, the old value-for-money ethic was reasserting itself, thanks to much improved productivity and sales.

There were now just two Daimlers left in the range, not counting the big limousine: the Daimler 4.2 and the Daimler Double Six, priced at £22,946 and £26,965 respectively. Extra equipment included front fog lamps, electric steel sunroof, spoked alloy wheels, individual rear seats, cruise control and walnut door casing inserts. So by price and specification they were at the top of Jaguar's model range.

Mention was made of the Daimler limousine; this had quietly continued in production in a corner of the Browns Lane works, built on a 'cell' principle with the same

The Jaguar Sovereign HE, part of the six-car line up for the 1984 home market; the Vanden Plas badge would now only be seen in the USA.

The Daimler Double Six continued for 1984, with spoked alloy wheels and extra equipment; the HE badge was dropped though – the V12's new-found economy no longer needed emphasising.

Jaguar Sovereign 4.2 interior; note the inlaid veneer door cappings, though 'separate' rear seats remained exclusive to Daimler.

group of men responsible for virtually the complete build of one car. Between two and five a week were being made, and during 1984 Jaguar offered the car as a 'mobile office'. If so desired the limousine would be delivered with a range of built-in office equipment such as radio telephone and printer, TV monitor, video recorder/player and radio/cassette player. Installation of the complex electronic systems was delegated by Jaguar to outside firms. Other features of the new model – built to special order only – were individual (non bench-type) front seats, armchair-style rear seats, electrically-controlled sliding glass division, inter-com between front and rear compartments, and more normal items such as central locking, electrically operated windows, Sundym glass and a rear window blind. A fully-equipped Daimler limousine cost £49,000.

Meanwhile those who had waited in vain for a full road test of the five-speed Series 3 were pleased when in January 1984 *Autocar* went into print with exactly that, the only British journal to do so within the lifespan of Series 3. Contrary to the odd rumour about the durability of its gearbox, the car withstood the usual standing-start and maximum speed runs without fault, though gunning the car off the line without the damping effect of the torque converter certainly highlighted the tendency of the sub-frame-mounted rear suspension to tramp during wheel-spin starts! This same lack of cushioning effect by a torque converter also transmitted very much more faithfully what the magazine termed "the famous XK top-end crankshaft vibration", another indication that the venerable old engine was in some respects behind the times – and more particularly behind the opposition in

The XJ6 3.4 saloon continued the meanwhile, still on carburettors and inclined to be forgotten – except by those who took advantage of low-threshold Jaguar motoring. For 1986 a new wool blend tweed upholstery was specified, and the top of the central console was given a veneered finish (this latter applied to all the 1986 saloons as did the plated seat adjuster bar just visible).

this respect. But it still gave the big car an energetic performance: a 0–60mph time of 8.6-seconds was not bad for a 34cwt saloon, while the 128mph achieved in top was the highest ever recorded for a standard Series 3 by an independent authority.

The test car was fitted with the 3.31 final drive ratio, and *Autocar* felt that it could have pulled the optional 3.07 to give better economy and more relaxed cruising. As for the success or otherwise of the five-speed box installation, the clutch pedal was considered heavy and its positioning less than ideal – maybe an indication of insufficient

Of the Series 3 range, only the Sovereign V12 was to survive beyond 1987; this is one of the last 1986 cars, sporting the 'Sovereign' twin coachline.

The Jaguar Sovereign 4.2 with which Series 3 XJ6 production was to end; the last car of all has been retained by Jaguar for posterity.

Greater quality pushed Series 3 XJ6 sales to new records in the States, but there were penalties – Jaguar were the first company to be fined for failing to achieve the minimum Corporate Average Fuel Economy level (CAFE) and in the last year of Series 3 production, around £5m penalties under CAFE and an additional £16m gas guzzler tax were incurred. (Compare this picture of a 1986 Jaguar Vanden Plas with that of a US-spec. XJ40).

development by Jaguar. But if you could live with this aspect, the ability to choose exactly which gear you wanted when you wanted, plus the undeniable 'poke' of the injected 4.2 engine, made the Series 3 manual car as much a sports saloon as any XJ6 had been. There was a petrol consumption bonus too; *Autocar* recorded an overall figure including testing of 18.3mpg, compared to the 16.8mpg returned by its 1979 Series 3 4.2 automatic.

By 1985, Series 3 was, in a sense, living beyond the grave – had circumstances been different, its place would by then have been taken by XJ40. Nevertheless, it was thriving as never before and almost each month, new records for XJ production were set. Nor did Jaguar slacken in its efforts to improve and broaden the appeal of the car worldwide even though barely a year remained before, in six-cylinder form at least, it became obsolete.

Cockpit of the North American 1986 Jaguar XJ6 interior, showing the greater areas of wood veneer on the final Series 3.

The changes announced on 13 September 1985 were to be the last major batch of improvements to Series 3 before its demise. Virtually all were centred around increasing the aura of luxury, especially from the driving seat. Starting with the 3.4, a new wool-blend tweed cloth supplanted the velour upholstery used previously on the centre panels of the seats, the herringbone pattern setting a trend which would be continued in XJ40 when it arrived. Four colour options were available and the new material was standardised on the XJ6 4.2 saloon; the Daimlers and the Jaguar Sovereign continued with leather though the new cloth upholstery could be specified as a no-cost option.

All 1986 saloons were given burr or figured walnut (according to model) panels extending to the top of their centre consoles, and veneered wood also now surrounded the gear lever or selector base. The XJ6 3.4 and 4.2 cars were given Vanden Plas-style veneered insets to their door tops. Rear seat belts, electric door mirrors and tinted glass all became standard on these cars. 'Discreet' chrome trim to the front seat adjuster bars, radio speaker surrounds and locks and lock plates contributed to a lighter, more interesting look to the interior. Stainless steel tread plates, with, of course, either the Jaguar or Daimler name incorporated, featured now on all saloons.

British Racing Green was added to the range of colours, plus three others: Steel (blue), Windsor Blue, and Curlew (brown). These were accompanied by single or twin coachlines on Jaguar saloons and by a chrome strip and single coachline on Daimlers. Badging was simplified with engine capacities now deleted, and having done its job, the 'HE' badge was dropped from the 5.3-litre Jaguar Sovereign.

In America, Leonia's '1986' announcement came a month later. The saloon range consisted of just two models, the XJ6 sedan and the Vanden Plas; the latter equating to the European Sovereign in specification, and carrying virtually every conceivable 'extra' as standard equipment. It was noted that the leather upholstery included a new colour, magnolia, while the Vanden Plas could be delivered with black paintwork, or Silver Sand, Antelope, Cranberry or Sage Green metallic finishes. A trip computer was standard across the range. The suggested retail price for the XJ6 was $32,250, and for the Vanden Plas $35,550, both at port of entry, and represented fine value for money especially as the American dollar was beginning to weaken. And, as always, customers were reminded that very little in the way of extras needed to be specified, unlike some other makes where much that was standard on a Jaguar had to be paid for separately.

Then it was very gratifying for Jaguar Cars Incorporated to be able to report, at the same time as announcing the 1986 model range, that Jaguar had achieved fifth place among all cars in the 1985 J.D. Power Consumer Satisfaction Index. The Power survey was

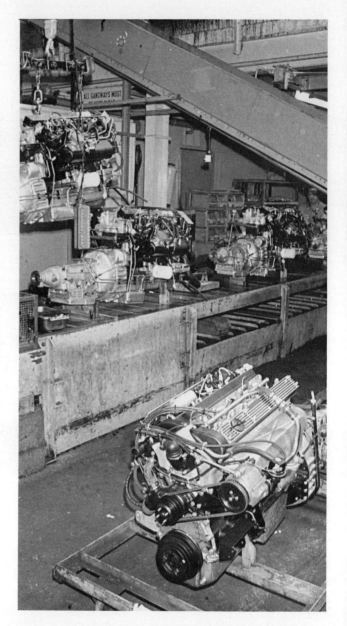

By the spring of 1987 the last Series 3 XJ6 had been built, and the XK engine was out of series production. These are 4.2 injection units, complete with automatic gearboxes, at Browns Lane awaiting fitment – but near the beginning of Series 3 production, in 1979.

acknowledged as the most authoritative study of US car buyers and their perception of their car and the capabilities of the selling and servicing dealer.

This position in the Index would have been almost unimaginable five years before; it was as if (in UK terms) a Skoda had been voted 'Car of the Year'. In fact five years previously Jaguar had been at the bottom of the table, and the progress to fifth place was concrete evidence that Jaguar's devotion to improving the quality of its cars and the dealership which sold and looked after them was really working.

Series 3 variation – the estate conversion of the 4.2 saloon by Avon Stephens of Warwick resulted in a practical and quite good-looking vehicle; a number were produced during the early 1980s.

V12 XJ-S coupe, 1979 to 1987

Meanwhile the XJ-S had to a great extent been left alone; 1979 did indeed see the last production manual gearbox XJ-S off the line, this being a squadron blue car (VIN JNAEW2 AC 101814), though it is probable that one or two special-order examples were completed shortly afterwards. There were no distinct 1980 models but pending the introduction of the 'May' head on the V12, the latest Lucas/Bosch digital electronic fuel injection system was fitted to the XJ-S. This decreased fuel consumption by a couple of mpg – from around $13\frac{1}{2}$ to nearer $15\frac{1}{2}$mpg – and slightly higher bhp/torque figures were quoted – 300bhp at 5,400rpm and 318lb/ft torque at 3,900rpm.

In the USA, the substitution of a three-way catalytic converter for the previous air injection/exhaust gas recirculation equipment allowed the big engine to breathe a lot better, quoted bhp rising from 244 to 262. Economy improved to around 14mpg assisted by a higher (3.07 instead of 3.31) axle ratio while the extra power and torque reduced the 0–60mph time by a whole second, to 7.8-seconds.

Nevertheless, the XJ-S remained unfashionably thirsty in all markets and this, together with Jaguar's blighted reliability record, had seen sales crash from a best of 4,020 units in 1976 (this included 143 manual cars), to a

disastrous 1,131 in 1980. Discontinuation was being actively discussed at Browns Lane and the model's final chance was the 'May' cylinder head.

The announcement of the 'HE' range of V12 Jaguars came on 15 July 1981, and it was soon discovered that under most conditions the lean-burn, high compression technology worked. A little extra power meant that a higher (2.88) final drive could be fitted, and while the previous official 'urban-cycle' fuel consumption figures had showed 12.7mpg, the HE registered 15.6mpg. At steady speeds the improvement was even more dramatic, with 27.1mpg instead of 21.9mpg being shown at 56mph. Certainly, the 20mpg XJ-S was now a genuine possibility, a bench-mark figure Jaguar had set great store by.

These improvements were confirmed independently by road test, *Motor* trying an XJ-S HE in October 1981 and finding it 21 per cent more economical than its previous XJ-S. Commented the journal, "it is now possible to achieve an astounding 22mpg at an average (over 650 miles) of more than 62mph". Alas, these benefits were not so striking in the USA where emission regulations demanded catalytic converters to reduce carbon monoxide, hydrocarbon and nitrogen oxides to carbon dioxide and nitrogen. This meant that a Federal XJ-S might return as little as 10mpg during fast driving, while it was considerably less accelerative than its European counterpart; 0–100mph might take 21-seconds as opposed to 17 for a UK-spec. model.

Hopes had been fading for the long-term future of the V12
engine, but the arrival of the 'HE' models sounded a note of
optimism. The XJ-S could now return 20 mpg-plus.

The revised XJ-S was announced in July 1981, boasting new
wheels, a redesigned interior – and the all-important 'HE'
badge. *Photo: P. Skilleter*

But the XJ-S HE didn't just incorporate technological
improvements; there were many visual changes. New,
domed alloy wheels with 6½-inch rims and a Jaguar head
in the centre carried Dunlop D7 tyres, and the bumpers
gained Series 3-style bright plated cappings. The scuttle-
mounted heater/air conditioner intakes were now in a
black finish, as were the wiper arms, and all cars gained
US-type flasher repeater lights on the sides. A twin,
tapering coachline ran down the car, and the badging had
been changed; like the V12 saloons, the XJ-S now
boasted a prominent 'HE' badge at the rear, while the
bonnet carried a unique antique-finish Jaguar head
medallion.

Perhaps even more important were the interior
revisions. Jaguar had quite clearly got it wrong originally,
and disapproving comments about the car's sombre,
black facia unrelieved by the warmth of wood veneer had
been received at Browns Lane almost since the day the car
was launched in 1975. But to revise a car's facia and dash
is an expensive undertaking and, almost perpetuating a
vicious circle, no doubt Jaguar were unwilling to spend
significant sums on a model which at one time looked like
being on the way out. That is speculation, but what is not
is the confirmation by customer feedback (from the States
especially) that the XJ-S interior was not perceived as
being either pleasant or 'Jaguar'. The customer did not

Almost as important as the 'new' engine was the XJ-S HE's revised interior – at last equipped in proper Jaguar fashion with plenty of wood veneer. Steering wheel was now leather-bound Series 3 style.

want modern, BMW style sporting austerity, he wanted walnut and leather.

This message had in fact been taken on board at Jaguar some years earlier, and various new trim combinations were evolved by the experimental trim shop (unusually one of these exercises escaped, the car being bought by then Jaguar Driver's Club chairman David Harvey). The final production result was a complete upgrading of the XJ-S interior; first and foremost, wood veneer was installed on the facia, centre switch panel and door cappings, while leather replaced vinyl on the door casings, centre console and rear quarter trim panels; all combined to produce that rich, 'English luxury' appearance that had served Jaguar so well on most models it had produced over the years.

But Jaguar didn't stop there, and many Series 3 modernisations were carried over to the XJ-S. Prominent was a new leather-bound steering wheel, improved central locking allowing both doors to be locked by either of the interior or exterior locks on each door (the central console door lock switch was in consequence

discontinued), a timer-linked rear window heater element was added, better electric window switches arrived, there was now a courtesy light delay, and Vanden Plas-style red guard lamps were set in the door pockets. Then the wiper blade sweep was altered to clear a greater area of screen, a delay wipe facility was added, and there were revised instrument and switch graphics. For the new interior you could choose from a new range of colours, while in the boot, the spare wheel and battery box were now carpeted and a Series 3-type courtesy light was fitted.

All this investment in the XJ-S must have been something of an act of faith by Jaguar at the time – but then, most things at Browns Lane were during the early eighties! Soon, however, the quality drive took effect and, spearheaded by vastly better built Series 3 saloons, Jaguar's sales lifted – and the XJ-S's with them. Soon, from being bottom of the class, the V12-engined XJ-S became Jaguar's star performer and not only won a reprieve from possible extinction, but appeared set to enjoy a career that would actually outlast, by many years, the saloon car range from which it had sprung.

The XJ-S 3.6

The arrival of a new engine from Jaguar is a rare event. Up until 1983, only two pure-Jaguar engines had been seen, the XK and the V12 units (discounting the earlier push-rod engines as Standard-based), with the twin overhead cam XK powering by far the greatest number of Jaguars and being made in, as we have seen, 2.4, 2.8, 3.4, 3.8 and 4.2 litre forms. But magnificently though the XK engine had served Jaguar since 1948, the end of its production life could not be postponed indefinitely.

The reason for this could be detected to some extent from behind the wheel; even in its latest injected form the engine was definitely not happy at over about 4,500 rpm when compared with modern 'sixes'. But the 'rev. limit' problem (due mainly to its long stroke) was only one of many: it was heavy, some of its design features would not meet Jaguar's desired 150,000 mile durability targets, and the method of its production was old-fashioned.

Nevertheless, when money was short in the mid-seventies there was a serious investigation into substantially revising the XK engine instead of building an entirely new power unit. This included a lighter, simplified, XK block and a new four-valve cylinder head (to which project Walter Hassan had devoted a good deal of thought prior to his retirement in 1972). A number of prototype engines were built but a hard look at the XK engine's build facilities – which the new version was designed to utilise – underlined the fact that they were now very old and in any case would be incapable of producing the volumes intended for the new power unit. So it was commonsense to spend no more time and money on the XK engine and its facilities, but instead to design an entirely new power unit. Even then the story is not a simple one, the new engine being heavily influenced during its early design stages by the other existing Jaguar engine – the V12 – and by diesel engine proposals. The V12 had been designed from the outset with the possibility of six- or even eight-cylinder derivations being built using the same facilities, and indeed the original power unit scheduled for the 1973-concept XJ40 was just such a 'slant six' offshoot. It became apparent, however, that the V12 transfer line did not after all lend itself to the building of a six-cylinder derivative, particularly after intended volumes had been revised upwards substantially. So with that avenue blocked, and the XK update also impractical, it was rather a case of back to the drawing board ....

Harry Mundy, one of the architects of the AJ series of engines; he retired as power units chief in March 1980, well over three years before the new engine went into production in the XJ-S. *Photo: P. Skilleter*

The AJ6 engine underwent a punishing programme of tests; here is a radio-equipped 3.6 XJ-S at rest while undergoing durability running on the vast, circular Nardo high-speed circuit in Italy. *Photo: Paul Walker*

The family of engines which grew out of this, in effect, third attempt to find a new Jaguar power unit bore a passing resemblance to aspects of both the V12 and the still-born updated XK project. The 3.6 engine reflected the four-valves-per-cylinder approach of the latter, while the 2.9 was allied even more with a half-V12 'slant six' ancestry and inherited the 5.3-litre engine's bore spacings, valves and camshafts, and eventually the high compression 'May' combustion chambers, too. The 3.6's pedigree was further influenced by the possible need for a diesel version, hence its 91 x 92mm bore and stroke dimensions were intentionally those of the Mercedes automotive diesel engine, due to Harry Munday wishing to play safe and use known technology. In addition, Jaguar were able to draw on experiments carried out on a four-valve version of the V12 dating from 1971, while familiar features retained from the XK concept were of course chain-driven overhead camshafts (two for the 3.6 six, one for the 2.9) operating the valves via bucket tappets. The new engines shared the same basic block, which had originally been designed as a die-casting with free-standing iron liners exactly like the V12 (the '2000' series) but changed for production to a closed-deck design using thin-wall shrink fit dry liners (the '3000' series). This method saved on die-casting tooling costs and reduced weight by a useful 3.8kg. The block skirt was

Just as the first XK engine was seen in a sports model, so Jaguar's engine for the 1990s first appeared in a sporting model. This is the all-aluminium 3.6-litre engine in the 1983 coupé.
Photo: P. Skilleter

A manual gearbox hadn't been seen in an XJ-S since 1979. Otherwise, the 3.6 coupe's interior reflected that of the HE model which continued in parallel production.
Photo: P. Skilleter

The 3.6 coupe retained the normal XJ-S profile, complete with flying buttresses, and was most readily identified by its '3.6' boot lid badge. *Photo: P. Skilleter*

extended well below the crankshaft centre line (unlike the XK) to increase the rigidity of the block, while the material chosen was aluminium. Experience within the industry of aluminium six-cylinder engines was not great but the weight advantages persuaded Jaguar that the use of this alloy was essential.

Once more seven main bearings supported the crankshaft, and the crank pin diameter of 52.98mm was identical to that of the 4.2-litre XK engine – a generous size which allowed Jaguar to use a nodular cast iron crank rather than a steel one. Cast iron being 9 per cent lower in density than steel meant that it suffered less of a penalty in terms of crankshaft torsional resonant frequencies, which can be a problem with straight-six engines. In fact Jaguar found that there was a lot to learn about six-cylinder crankshafts, in spite of having used them for thirty years already, and fresh research by the Cranfield Institute of Technology undertaken since the early seventies was drawn upon.

The 3.6's four-valve cylinder head was an aluminium sand-casting in LM25, the two inlet valves inclined at 24 degrees from the vertical and the two exhaust valves (slightly smaller than the inlets) at 23 degrees into a pentroof combustion chamber. The two overhead camshafts ran directly in the cylinder head, and while a two-stage belt drive for these was seriously contemplated, this would have increased the overall length of the already quite long engine. A single-stage belt drive was considered, too, but this would have increased engine height due to the need for a larger camshaft sprocket, so a two-stage chain drive of the type Jaguar had so much experience of was adopted.

Conventional 'H' section forged connecting rods were used, very carefully balanced, and cast aluminium pistons with circumferential steel struts. Stroke on the 3.6 engine was virtually square with the bore at 92mm; the 2.9, not seen until the advent of XJ40, used a shorter stroke (74.8mm) which necessitated a different crankshaft casting. The smaller engine also incorporated the same May 'fireball' combustion technology as the V12 HE engine already described.

Fuel injection was mandatory due to the need for accurate calibration of the mixture essential for optimum economy and for when emission equipment was used. As first announced the Lucas/Bosch P digital system was used for the 3.6 in conjunction with a 9.6:1 compression ratio. This contributed to a power output of 225bhp at 5,300rpm and 240lb/ft of torque at 4,000rpm which compared very favourably with the old 4.2-litre's 205bhp at 5,000rpm and 236lb/ft of torque at 3,750rpm. The new engine also weighed in at 430lb compared with 553lb for the 4.2 (and, incidentally, 640lb for the V12). Thus did Jaguar achieve its aim of increasing power output by 10 per cent while reducing weight by 20 per cent (the 2.9 litre engine, announced some time later and exclusive to XJ40, produced 165bhp at 5,600rpm or about 4bhp more than the 3.4 XK unit).

Development of the new AJ6 ('Advanced Jaguar') engines ran in parallel with, but in earlier days not necessarily interlinked with, XJ40, the car they were intended for. In February 1979, after postponement of the latter's launch and strangely in parallel with what had occurred around thirty years before when the Mk VII was delayed, the decision was taken to divorce AJ6 schedules from XJ40 and allow it – or the 3.6 litre version – to go onto the market in a sports model first. The 3.6 engine was released for production in August 1983, and in the autumn of that year came the announcement of two new Jaguar models: the XJ-S 3.6 and the XJ-SC 3.6.

The big news was the engine, of course; everybody knew that it was destined for the much-leaked new Jaguar saloon and so its technical details were examined with relish. But significant in its own way was the cabriolet variant, for while the XJ-S 3.6 retained the normal XJ-S profile, the SC marked Jaguar's return to open air motoring. An open version of the XJ-S – coded XJ28 – had been toyed with years previously at Browns Lane but the project in a new form was revived within four months of John Egan arriving in 1980 (the year in which an AJ6-engined XJ-S first ran, incidentally).

The new XJ-S was not a true convertible (such a beast was, for the moment, being left to outside specialists) but followed the 'targa' approach having fixed side rails and a centre cross-bar; you obtained your open air by getting out and removing the two roof panels secured by locking devices sunk into the interior roof lining, and putting them into a storage envelope in the boot. Then you could either drop the rear 'hood' or take off the glass fibre 'half

The AJ6-engined XJ-S also came in cabriolet form and was a considerably more glamourous car; with roof panels removed and rear hood down, it *almost* gave true open-air motoring.
Photo: Jaguar Cars

A new profile: the cabriolet (this is the V12 introduced in July 1985) provided an opportunity to "get rid of the flying buttresses" as one factory man put it; as they were outside Browns Lane, opinions were divided inside about Malcolm Sayer's famous styling device! *Photo: P. Skilleter*

hardtop' should that be fitted (the latter did not last all that long as an accessory, though). The result was a very pleasant open-roof motor car, even if the process of making it so was rather more long-winded than the 'three catches and pull it back' operation carried out from the driver's seat on an XK or 'E' type!

The cabriolet conversion of a normal XJ-S shell was initially carried out in rather a complex manner, a body minus roof and rear deck being taken from the Castle Bromwich works to Park Sheet Metal at Exhall who removed the buttresses, strengthened the floorpan with an additional cross-member and installed the centre cross-bar (this contained a steel roll-over bar, as did the cant rails over the door apertures). It was then taken back to Castle Bromwich for painting, then to Browns Lane for the installation of mechanical components, trim and road test, then off to Aston Martin Tickford at their new Bedworth factory for the hood and Targa arrangements to be fitted. Finally, the much-travelled car was

transported back to Browns Lane for checking and quality audit before being despatched to a dealer. No wonder that in later years the process was simplified, with the trim work being taken on board at Browns Lane.

Both open and closed cars had the 225bhp 3.6 four-valve engine, plus a further novelty in the form of a manual gearbox – not seen in a production XJ-S since 1979. This time it was not of British manufacture but German, being a five speed Getrag unit; by all accounts a ZF automatic gearbox was scheduled for XJ57 but development work had taken longer than expected, hence the substitution of the Getrag. No matter – both were already part of XJ40!

As for interior appointments, while the 3.6 coupe had conventional XJ-S furnishings, the cabriolet had no rear seat but a luggage shelf instead which, by virtue of a couple of lids, did duty as a locker, too. This was thought to be a safety measure; should the car overturn, unbelted rear occupants would most surely have been thrown out.

Chassis changes were few: softer front springs (329lb/in instead of 423lb/in) compensated for the lighter engine, while a slightly thinner front anti-roll bar – just 1/16in smaller diameter at 0.811in – and the discontinuation of the rear anti-roll bar were the only other changes. Project engineer Paul Walker found that the XJ-S was very sensitive to anti-roll bar changes and this was all that was needed to produce a more responsive car without interfering with the handling/ride balance.

More difficult was engineering the AJ6 engine installation. It fitted all right, but the big battle turned out to be refinement. To be frank, at higher revs the new engine could be harsh and noisy – raucous, almost. 'There were some fairly vicious ones about,' admitted a senior Jaguar engineer some years later when things had been sorted out. Road tests of the 3.6 in the UK (it was not exported to the USA) generally reflected a liking for the overall concept of XJ57, but on occasion were downright damning of the engine installation. Certainly, my fears after driving an early example at the time were for XJ40 – how was the Series 3's legendary refinement to be maintained in the new saloon with an engine like that up front?

Nevertheless, the car returned a good performance; *Autocar* recorded a maximum of 141mph for their coupe which thanks to its manual gearbox, reached 60mph as quickly as their previous road-test twelve-cylinder XJ-S had done, in 6.7 seconds. The 'ton' was reached in 19.7 seconds, four seconds down on the V12 but matching the capabilities of a late-model 4.2 'E' type. All very commendable, given the fact that the new car had to make do with, in effect, half an engine!

But the car did feel more of a sports car than its V12 cousin, largely because the driver could always specify the right gear for the right occasion; in particular, the performance gap left by the automatic gearbox's refusal to kick-down under 30mph was overcome, and 'B' road driving became considerably more enjoyable. Economy was better, too; consumption ranged from 17½ to 25mpg according to driving style. Criticism of the 3.6's refinement was taken to heart at Jaguar – but they already knew there was a problem in that area. The basic strength of the engine was never in doubt, for major components rarely failed during development. Recalls Trevor Crisp, who succeeded Harry Munday as chief power unit engineer: "You know, we've never broken a crankshaft in the whole of the test programme. The only time we've broken a crankshaft was when someone knocked one over one day – it fell in half!" But there was a long, hard road to tread before the refinement factor was overcome.

Much was done at the manufacturing stage; balancing tolerances were tightened, and bearing clearances brought down to modern tolerances. The crankshaft damper, timing ring and pulley were balanced as a unit, instead of singly. A lot of time was spent on overcoming piston noise; even more on the valve gear. The chain

Both six- and twelve-cylinder cabriolets employed these bags in the boot to contain the lift-out roof panels; seen on the floor is the envelope used to cover the furled hood. *Photo: P.Skilleter*

As were their closed counterparts, the 'cabrios' were beautifully trimmed. This is the V12, automatic as all multi-cylinder Jaguars had been since 1979. *Photo: P.Skilleter*

drives were quietened through changes to the tensioners, the base circle diameter of the camshafts was increased to stiffen them further against the loads imposed by the twelve sets of valve springs, and the cam profiles modified to reduce valve lift by 4 per cent (this lost 2 or 3bhp but increased torque). And finally, the bucket tappets they operated were lightened through a change of material from cast iron to squeeze-cast steel.

These modifications were progresssively introduced on the 3.6 engine and all were incorporated into XJ40's engine from the start. In fact the new saloon benefitted enormously from the AJ6's three-year production run in the XJ-S; had it been launched with the engine in its 1983 'raw' state one cannot imagine that it would have displayed the refinement that it did – with predictable consequences in the market place.

No rear seats in the cabriolet XJ-S, just a luggage shelf with a lid each side covering a shallow locker. TWR, however, did offer a rear seat conversion. *Photo: P.Skilleter*

Meanwhile the original, 5.3-litre XJ-S came in for minor attention, and for 1984, cruise control, a trip computer, an improved stereo radio/cassette player with digital tuning, and headlamp wash/wipe were all standardised (such items were extra on the 3.6-litre cars). Already its sales were on the upturn after their low in 1981 of 1,131, the 1983 total being 4,808, and at the end of 1984 it saw another big leap to 6,028. This resurgence was due mainly to John Egan's quality drive – the car had always been widely admired but now confidence in its reliability was returning.

On 17 July 1985 came the announcement of a further new XJ-S model: the expected V12 Cabriolet. "With the introduction of the V12 Cabriolet, Jaguar has created one of the world's fastest open top cars," said the factory's press release, and indeed, performance hardly differed from the mechanically identical 150mph-plus XJ-S V12 coupe which of course continued as the mainstay of the XJ-S range. Internal layout of the new car mirrored that of the 3.6 cabriolet, with a fully carpeted luggage area instead of seats in the rear. Externally the car was identified (apart from its Targa features) by XJ-SC badging on the tail, and at £26,995 it was just on £3,000 more than the V12 coupe.

The earlier cabriolets had suffered slow sales largely because of the somewhat tortuous path they had to take during assembly. Even Jaguar admitted that they had to quote "unreasonably long" delivery dates for these special-order cars. Only 11 had been completed in 1983, and 178 in 1984. So during 1985, while the shuttling back and forth to Park Sheet Metal continued for the body shell modifications, at least after being painted at Castle Bromwich the car went to Browns Lane and stayed there for its cabriolet roof to be fitted.

Cabriolet production, however, remained low whatever engine was specified; then in September 1985

came news of 1986 improvements, which for the XJ-S were minimal. With Tom Walkinshaw's XJ-S cars having won the European Touring Car Championship it was perhaps appropriate that Jaguar should introduce British Racing Green to the colour charts, this being applicable to the saloons as well as the XJ-S. External badging was altered, too, with the 'HE' badge on 5.3-litre cars being replaced by a 'V12' one. Also on the V12 XJ-S, burr walnut replaced burr elm though the latter was continued on the six-cylinder models, which were now upholstered in wool blend tweed cloth. Both were given upgraded audio systems, all received additional plating inside to brighten the interior. It was also noted that the XJ-SC 3.6 was now on sale in France, at a tax-paid price of 307,900 francs, or around £25,650. Americans had to wait until April 1986 before getting their hands on a Jaguar cabriolet – which predictably was just the V12 version.

During 1987, changes and improvements of a more substantial nature arrived for the XJ-S. In February automatic versions of the 3.6-litre coupe and cabriolet were launched to further augment the XJ-S's sales progress; 1986 had seen 8,820 cars sold, predominantly V12s, and it was felt that an automatic option on the 3.6 would increase its appeal in some quarters. This time, engineering the change was not difficult as Jaguar were able to utilise the experienced gained with the ZF four-speed box in the new XJ6. The 'J' gate remained exclusive to the saloon, however. Also from the XJ6 came the car's superior engine management system, giving the car better economy and improved driveability. The 0–60 time of the automatic 3.6 XJ-S was quoted as 8.1 seconds, or just 1/2 second slower than the manual version.

At the same time Jaguar further showed its commitment to the continued development of its prodigal son by announcing a whole host of interior updates for the XJ-S. All gained heated door mirrors and bright-finish stainless steel door tread plates (etched with the Jaguar name), while the V12 was given electrically-heated

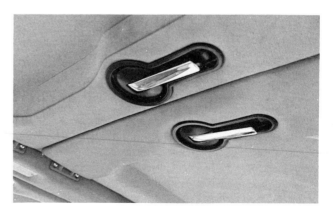

The cabriolet's roof panels were detached by pulling down these central overhead handles. You then had to stow the panels in the boot, so obtaining open-air motoring was a premeditated rather than a spontaneous act. *Photo: P.Skilleter*

XJ-S successes on the track brought back modified Jaguars to the road; TWR offered a bodily and mechanically uprated XJ-S as did other concerns. This is the Lister XJ-S, produced in association with Brian Lister of Lister-Jaguar fame.

Other 'privateers' sought not performance but other forms of exclusivity; this is Lynx Engineering's true convertible XJ-S, photographed in prototype form at least seven years before Jaguar announced their own. *Photo: Graham Bigg*

front seats for both driver and passenger, controlled by timer and thermostat; these seats were also equipped with an electrically-operated lumbar adjustment, whereby an electric motor was used to inflate or deflate what Jaguar rather unglamorously described as a "lumbar support bladder" in the seat squabs. The new seats could be specified on the 3.6-litre models as an extra-cost option. Controls for the seat heating and lumbar support devices were mounted on the side of the new centre console, which now incorporated burr elm veneer on the 3.6 and

burr walnut on the 5.3. All console switchgear was redesigned too. Seat belt buckles were now mounted on the seats themselves, allowing them to be adjusted with the seat for improved comfort.

Externally, both the V12 and straight six cars were given a locking fuel filler cap, thus reducing the number of keys from three to two (cabriolet models already had an externally mounted cap). Then the introduction of an automatic version of the 3.6 litre car meant a change of cruise control unit. Both automatic and manual 'sixes'

The 'official' XJ-S Convertible made its bow in a low-key launch at the Geneva Show on 1 March 1988. It had been a long time coming – FEPs had been running shortly after John Egan arrived at Browns Lane – but was another component in Jaguar's highly successful plan to promote the XJ-S as a sports model alongside XJ40. In traditional Jaguar style the fabric hood was fully lined; in addition it boasted power operation and a rigid heated rear window. The interior maintained the current XJ-S luxury approach and the specification included the Teves anti-lock braking device which was standardised throughout the XJ-S range from February 1988. Project engineer for the new convertible was Ken Giles. (The object adjacent to the bootlid on this export car contains the high-level brake lights demanded by North American regulations.)

could now be fitted with the Hella system which allowed higher and more stable cruising speeds, and faster acceleration on the command to resume the chosen speed; it operated on 'D' and '3' on automatic cars, and on all five gears above 25mph on manually equipped versions.

The dramatic revival of the XJ-S's fortunes – very much mirroring that of its parent company – was underlined when in August 1987 Jaguar announced a notable landmark: the 100,000th Jaguar V12 engine had been built. Moreover, 49,371 of these had left Browns Lane in XJ-Ss, more than in any other single model; and, at the same time, the 50,000th XJ-S itself had been completed during 1987, as 3,837 AJ6-engined cars could be added to the V12 total. For a car which had faced extinction six years before, this was a remarkable performance.

The 1988 XJ-S range incorporated some exciting new advances. Jaguar demonstrated that it was not deaf to the pleas from enthusiastic drivers for crisper response from the XJ-S (maybe it was also a case of not allowing the sporting model to fall too much behind the new XJ6 in terms of handling), and a number of changes were made to the 3.6's suspension and steering, and modifications incorporated to provide a more sporting interior. On the other hand, the model range was decreased; while the V12 cabriolet remained for the time being, the 3.6 open

A true Jaguar variation on the XJ-S theme – a one-off long wheelbase experiment (circa 1987) offering greater rear legroom and an alternative roofline. The brainchild of Jim Randle, it wasn't to enter production however.

car did not survive into 1988.

Considerable work had been done on the 3.6's suspension: front spring rates were increased from 69.5 lbf/in to 96.6 lbf/in, and the rear spring rates from 134.3lbf/in to 180lbf/in. In addition, a larger diameter

(0.875in from 0.811in) front anti-roll bar was fitted, upping the rate from 107lbf/in to 152lbf/in, while the previously discontinued rear anti-roll bar was replaced (0.971in dia. and 300lbf/in). These changes were designed to reduce body roll and improve bounce and pitch control, enabling the car to get the best from the Pirelli P600 235-60VR 15 low-profile tyres now specified (on 6½in rims). Boge dampers, "carefully tuned to the car's suspension characteristics" completed the suspension package. Response was further tautened by redesigning the steering rack mounting bushes for increased lateral location, and by revalving the power steering to decrease the level of assistance by 17 per cent. The steering wheel itself was given a thicker rim, to go with new 'sports' seats. These incorporated side bolsters for better lateral support and, as standard, were upholstered in hard-wearing wool cloth. All-leather seats could be obtained at extra cost, as could (still) the electrically-heated, lumbar support seats.

The XJ-S V12 cabriolet ceased to be built after the end of 1987, and indeed no orders had been taken for it since the autumn. So ended the cabriolet line of Jaguars, probably without too many regrets at Browns Lane – they had been complex to build and the true convertible XJ-S, announced in 1988, was a more satisfactory car. Meanwhile the closed-coupe V12 XJ-S continued alongside its 3.6 counterpart. Its suspension and steering remained for the time being unmodified, though the sports-style seats were adopted along with the new thicker-rimmed leather-covered steering wheel. Optional, at no extra cost, were the 3.6-style alloy sports wheels with their wider, lower profile, tyres; the distinctive 'starfish' alloy wheels remained exclusive to the V12 XJ-S. Externally, new, slightly bolder twin coachlines were featured.

So there were, even more clearly, divergent lines of development established for the XJ-S, at supremely smooth, silent and effortless V12 Grand Tourer, and the 'sports car' 3.6 with its enhanced turn-in and (if required) manual gear selection, each meeting the requirement of different types of customer. The XJ-S looks set to continue in production at least until the much-rumoured true Jaguar sports car (XJ40 based) makes its appearance in the 1990s.

Jaguar management in the XJ era

On March 3 1972, fifty-years after joining William Walmsley to form the Swallow Sidecar Company, Sir William Lyons retired from his position of Chairman and Chief Executive of Jaguar Cars; to many at the factory, it hardly seemed possible – Browns Lane without the presence of Sir William.

He was succeded by 'Lofty' England who had joined Jaguar as service manager in 1946, assuming responsibility for all service and spares activities while still managing to run Jaguar's successful race and rally pro-

grammes. Lofty had been appointed Assistant Managing Director in 1961, Deputy Chairman in 1967, and thereafter progressively took over the management of the company from Sir William; these were years which saw Jaguar achieve record production levels.

Lofty himself was not that far from retirement, however, and with this in mind, BL brought in Geoffrey Robinson as Managing Director in September 1973. He then proceeded to introduce to Jaguar ideas he had applied at Innocenti, BL's plant in Italy best known for its locally-assembled Minis and 1100s. England himself retired in February 1974 after 27 years with Jaguar, leaving the field clear for Robinson who – no doubt in a large measure due to the tutorage of Lofty – did appreciate that Jaguar was not just another car assembly plant:

> "There are two aspects of Jaguar that make it different from any other motor company. They are the engineering and the way it is sold, in that order. The engineering must be different, must be separate. The Jaguar is a very personal car. The XJ6 from an engineering point of view is the personal car of Bob Knight (then Jaguar's technical director). It is 'his' car, for although the styling was always the responsibility of Sir William, the structure of the car, the engineering of its chassis was always the responsibility of Bob Knight. We must do nothing to upset the close personal identification of the car with our engineers. That is much more vital to the success of Jaguar than the imposition of any theoretical organisational structure on the engineering or any other department..."

To this extent Robinson appreciated the essential 'spirit of Jaguar' and its vital need to remain, but while he also realised that Jaguar's engineering resources had been underfunded, his major goal became increased production – which is probably why, during his relatively short term in office, he never really got to grips with the growing quality problem. Then in April came the Ryder Report and with it the news that Jaguar was to lose its own board (it was, indeed, going to have a 'theoretical organisational structure' imposed on it); amid almost emotional scenes at Browns Lane – it is very rare for British shop stewards to organise a demonstration in favour of their company's chief executive! – Geoffrey Robinson resigned.

The vacuum that was left was filled in essence by Bob Knight, whose position was ratified in 1978 when (following Sir Michael Edwardes' appointment to BL the year before) he was made Managing Director of Jaguar. But much of his time was spent retaining his engineering department's independence from BL and the quality of the product failed to improve greatly. The decade ended with the launch of the Series 3 in 1979.

When the first edition of this book went to press in February 1980, Jaguar was going through its darkest days; in the grips of BL, its component parts were being torn from it and only Engineering – the heart of Jaguar –

stood aloof and unsullied, protected (from what could almost be described as the malice of those who wished to submerge it in the corporate mass) by a confusing defensive web woven by managing director Bob Knight. The only light at the end of the tunnel seemed to be Sir Michael Edwardes' resolution in solving BL's labour and management problems, and his statements in favour of Jaguar, Rover and Triumph having greater independence within the JRT Group – itself a hastily-conceived conglomeration with no readily identifiable purpose. Sales of Jaguar cars were tumbling worldwide, due to build-quality and morale, which were at an all time low. Browns Lane had been turning out more cars per month in 1958 than they were doing early in 1980.

Then, in March 1980, John Egan accepted (at the second time of asking) an invitation by Sir Michael to come and run Jaguar. He arrived in the middle of a strike, but went and talked to the men who, if not totally convinced, accepted that his was a genuine commitment to the company and returned to work. In the following months John Egan spent an immense amount of time getting to know how Browns Lane and Radford operated, what its people thought, and what the problems were. Unusually, he also took care to learn about Jaguar's past, its previous triumphs and failures, in short the ethos of the place. Especially, he talked to Sir William, for to John Egan, history was not bunk and what had succeeded in the past must surely succeed in the future – given that the root cause of Jaguar's problems could be identified and put right.

Several factors must have become apparent to John Egan during those months: firstly, that the products – the XJ saloons and the XJ-S – were superb in terms of basic design and function; secondly, that Engineering contained talent in abundance and was quite able to continue designing and developing equally brilliant models; thirdly, that the build quality of the existing cars bordered on the appalling; and fourthly, if someone didn't solve the problems then Jaguar would cease to exist within a year or two. Sir Michael had underlined that.

As for the problems, it was a question of priorities. Production had dipped, but was the answer simply to make more cars? That had been the policy of Geoffrey Robinson to be sure, in slightly easier times, before he resigned in protest at the abolition of the Jaguar board. No; John Egan looked beyond the figures and came to the conclusion, within almost weeks, that the underlying cause of Jaguar's malaise was not the product itself – that, he was convinced, remained a world-leader – but in the way it was made. It therefore followed that if the cars were to be built properly, and that potential customers *knew* that they were being built properly, then the innate qualities of the XJ range must surely bring success, a rising sales pattern, and the profits needed to carry Jaguar safely into the future.

He was right of course. Before 1980 was out, the major problem areas had been identified and assigned either to board members or to managers, and the first Japanese-style 'quality circles' established whereby groups of workers, with their managers, would discuss what they were doing and how improvements could be made.

The immediate concern was quality of the bodies and paintwork stemming from the Castle Bromwich body assembly and paint factory, which was not directly under Jaguar's control. Next was the long-term quality problem of components bought from outside suppliers – they were often shoddy and so was the attitude of the companies (not all British) that made them. Not that those already at Jaguar were unaware of this; even the shop floor workers "knew they were fitting rubbish to the cars" as one manager said later. Jim Randle, who in 1980 became director, product engineering, after Bob Knight's retirement, recalls what happened.

"To be perfectly honest it wasn't until John Egan came that we had any push with the suppliers, to change the situation. I'd written specifications long before John Egan came, trying to get bad components put right – particularly things like the steering gear – but we could not get any movement from the suppliers, they were just not interested. But John really forced the issue. And that really turned the tide on quality.'

Forcing the issue meant issuing an ultimatum: improve your product or loose the contract. Most suppliers saw the light; a few didn't, and were dropped. On the production line, redundancies had to take place; there were too many people building too few cars, and what appeared to be cruelty in the short term was essential for Jaguar's survival long term. Later, more people than ever would be on the payroll, and making four cars a person a year instead of two. Dealers were not excluded from the quality crusade, and those that didn't like, or ignored, Jaguar's new, serious approach to quality and service at all levels, or were unable or unwilling to provide the correct facilities, were dropped from the network.

John Egan travelled to America, too, and met some very dispirited dealers. Their collective income had halved over the past few years, and anyway, no one relished selling obviously substandard cars to people – they are inclined to come back and tell you about them. But until then, no one at Coventry appeared to have time to listen to or to appreciate their tales of cars which didn't steer properly, whose electric windows would open only two inches, whose central locking wouldn't. So when John Egan stood up and, without prompting, actually *listed* the faults they thought nobody knew or cared about at Jaguar, their relief was almost touching. And when Egan announced that Jaguar had now invented the round tyre, he received nothing less than shouts of glee ...

Sir William Lyons,
Founder and
President of Jaguar
Cars, at his
Warwickshire home
with Lady Lyons;
after his retirement
in 1972 he spent
much time
innovating and
perfecting new
techniques on his
farm, interspersed
with quite regular
visits to Jaguar.

It took a little time to arrest Jaguar's downward momentum. To their credit the BL board granted the necessary funds to make XJ40 a production reality. Jaguar certainly couldn't have funded the project alone and, indeed, 1981 saw the stricken company record a loss of £36.3 million for the year, plus its lowest-ever production total (a little under 14,000 vehicles) since 1957. But that year proved to be the worst. In 1982, 21, 934 cars were delivered; in 1983, 27,331; in 1984, 33,355; while all-time records for sales in the vital North American market were beginning to be set – and broken – regularly. In addition, Jaguar regained control of its sales, marketing and public affairs departments. Politics were

still involved, although this time constructively, and at the very highest levels, for the Conservative government, idealogically committed to the privatisation of hitherto public companies (which Jaguar had become when the Government had taken responsibility for BL and all its parts), saw that the successful return of Jaguar – now spectacularly recovered – to the private sector would be a fine endorsement of their philosophy.

Accordingly, preparations went ahead with almost frantic haste for the structuring of the company with this end in view. Following a profit of almost £50 million forecast for 1983, Norman Tebbit for the Government confirmed that the sale by BL of Jaguar would take place

During his career at Jaguar, which lasted from 1944 until 1980, Bob Knight (left) was possibly the world's leading passenger-vehicle chassis engineer. He is seen here talking to ex-works driver Stirling Moss and Geoffrey Robinson, during the time of the latter's managing directorship of Jaguar.

in 1984. The flotation, in August 1984, was of course wildly successful (the shares proved almost equally popular when, later, they were listed on Wall Street). But it is well to remember that while in the long run privatisation was the only correct and fair outcome for Jaguar, the timing of the flotation was entirely political, and that through sound business practices, and the perception, flair and commitment of John Egan, Jaguar had already pulled itself out of the mire.

The original XJ6 series in retrospect

It doesn't seem all that many years ago when it seemed almost inconceivable that any car – Jaguar or not – could significantly better the XJ6 as a luxury car package. There were other great cars that were faster, handled better, were brilliantly styled, and provided as much or even

more prestige. But no other individual car offered such a *blend* of all these qualities, many of which were perceived as incompatible within the industry – ride and handling, for example, or refinement and speed. To the end of its days, the XJ6 remained the yardstick by which all luxury cars were judged. But subtley, that XJ6 yardstick shifted; for maybe twelve or fifteen years, it was a question of how near competitive marques could *approach* the Jaguar's combination of virtues, but increasingly during the 1980s, it became a case of how many of the XJ6's standards could be *exceeded*. This was because by the mid-eighties, BMW and Mercedes in particular had equalled the score in many departments, especially in terms of ride/handling compromise, BMW's new 7-series in particular being consistently rated the superior driver's car. In short, towards the end of its career the XJ6 was relying increasingly on its beautiful looks and unique Jaguar ambience for its conquests, and no longer on

There was a slight chance that the XJ-S Spyder by Pininfarina, introduced in 1978, might have been put into limited production had funds been available; it was based on an ex-factory development car, with the standard body cut off and the floorpan strengthened. The new bodywork, in steel for the single prototype built, seems to have successfully integrated more traditional Jaguar curves with a modern shape, although wind-tunnel tests shows excessive high-speed lift which means that the front end would need to be slightly modified for production. To many enthusiasts, the XJ-S Spyder would have been the answer to the dream of an open Jaguar, and it may well point the way ahead to a Jaguar Sports Car of the future.

sheer, unmatched technical ability.

To an extent the same applied to the XJ12; its multi-cylinder engine was as magnificent as ever, but its XJ6-based chassis was showing signs of ageing. This was brought home to me when, a couple of years before the XJ6's obsolescence, I borrowed a current Daimler Double Six from the factory and conducted a convoy-run comparison test with an immaculately preserved and maintained short wheelbase XJ12, vintage 1973. The results were illuminating: contrary to expectations the earlier car handled better than the later, with less roll, more precise cornering and greater controllability. The latest version, though faster and slighly quieter, felt underdamped and

was distinctly unhappy at being asked to change direction rapidly, as through an 'S' bend at speed. Undoubtedly, this slight inferiority was due to spring and damper rates remaining unchanged, despite the extra weight bestowed by the longer body and greater level of equipment.

The original XJ12 felt a true sports saloon, while the later car seemed much less sure of its identity, and it was difficult to know how to judge it: as a limousine or as a sports car. It had failings in both roles, yet was still a unique mixture of them both, and in this the contemporary Series 3 XJ6 shared. By 1986, the Series 3 was still a wonderful car to drive and own, but its standards were now yesterday's, and it had become clear, even to the

The Pininfarina Jaguar XJ12 of 1973 — a one-off styling exercise on a standard XJ12 platform which, apart from more obvious differences, provided a larger area of glass which did point the way ahead. *Photo: Tim Parker collection*

Meanwhile in England, H.R. Owen also commissioned a special XJ, this one designed by Chris Humberstone of SAC designs; built largely of aluminium by Williams & Pritchard, it was called the Owen Sedanca de Ville after the well-remembered Rolls and Bentley chassis rebodied by H.R. Owen before the War. The rear window lifted up and the luggage area disclosed could be increased by folding forward the rear seat squabs.

most ardent admirer of the Series 3, that XJ40 *was* necessary ...

As we have seen, though, the Series 3 underwrote the new car and made it financially possible for Jaguar to go forward into the 1990s; as John Egan said at the time, no manufacturer could ask more of its outgoing model. It may also be sad that the valiant old XK engine has left volume production (it continues in the limousine), but it, too, has enjoyed a magnificent career spanning almost thirty years. That Heynes/Hassan/Baily masterpiece has certainly served Jaguar well.

The Series 3 XJ6 bowed out in May 1987, on, as we have seen, very much a high note. The last car of all was a Jaguar Sovereign XJ6 automatic, chassis no. 477824, and it came off the final line on 10 May 1987. Since the late sixties, at least, Jaguar had begun to appreciate the value of retaining or acquiring examples of its more significant models, and 477824 has joined various other road and racing Jaguars and Daimlers in the company's Jaguar Daimler Heritage Collection; it can usually be seen today on display in the Browns Lane showroom, the last Jaguar saloon of all to be powered by the XK engine – if you except the Daimler-badged Mk X-based limousine which is set to continue in production almost indefinitely.

The final *customer* XJ6 to be delivered was 477823, and that was despatched to Los Angeles on 1 May 1987; it was a Jaguar XJ6 automatic, left-hand drive, of course. All this was rather fitting; Jaguar retaining the very last (and home-market specification) XJ6, and America, where the type most dramatically staged its remarkable comeback, taking to its bosom the final car actually to be delivered. I wonder if that Los Angeles customer knew he was driving around in a little piece of Jaguar history?

Meanwhile, the story of Series 3 itself has not ended, as production of the V12-engined car continues on what had been the XJ40 pilot-build line, just a few a day being assembled at Browns Lane. Outdated in some respects maybe, especially when compared with the new 3.6 XJ40 (which is little slower and whose handling, is on a higher plane altogether), but with the considerable asset of its superb Jaguar V12 engine it is not entirely outclassed or outmoded. It is no secret that during the early 1990s a long wheelbase XJ40 will appear with that same power unit, but until then the XJ12 has much to offer.

In fact, I'll leave the Series 3 story with a little anecdote. Just before this new edition went to press I was talking to some Jaguar men over lunch at Browns Lane, and they were discoursing on which of the current Jaguar range they really liked best, as individuals. Some considered the XJ40 to be the only choice, others still rated the XJ-S. But at least one leaned back and said, "Do you know, for a long trip, when you don't want hassle, when you want the ultimate in comfort, there's still nothing quite like the XJ12. It's just a lovely old car." Which is, surely, rather a nice note on which to end this chapter of Jaguar history.

The ultimate production Series 3 XJ6, receiving its farewell from the workforce. It has been retained by Jaguar.

Chapter Twelve

The XJ40

XJ6 is not perfect. But it is several thousand pounds cheaper than the competition, handsome, enjoyable to drive, and arguably the world's most comfortable car.

Motor, Oct 11, 1986

No previous new Jaguar had ever been quite so vital to Jaguar's survival as was XJ40 during its development; nor had any previous new model experienced such an extended nativity or been developed against such a background of turbulent political, financial and leadership changes. For while its origins can be traced back to 1972, the XJ40 (or 'new' XJ6, as it would be called) did not appear on the market until 1986, and the intervening years witnessed no fewer than four managing directors, the near-extinction of the Jaguar company, and finally its almost miraculous recovery which culminated in its return to full independence as Jaguar Cars plc.

The eventual replacement for the 1968-launched XJ6 was far removed, however, from the original XJ40 proposals of the early 1970s, and in broad terms it could be said that XJ40 had two starting points. The first was in late 1972 when 'Lofty' England, who had just succeeded Sir William as chairman and chief executive, schemed out with Bob Knight the basic specification of a replacement for the XJ6, which was then still in its 1968 guise but with a 'Series 2' update in the pipeline.

There was no particular pressure on Jaguar's management at this time to come up with a new model. The year before a record 32,589 cars had been delivered and the company appeared to be in fine condition, even if vague doubts were beginning to accumulate about the long-term affects of BL's control. Indeed, a new model in these

circumstances was almost a luxury, and not the necessity that the XJ6 had been in the days when the 420G was turning in such disappointing sales figures.

Writing fourteen years later in *Australian Jaguar* magazine, Lofty made it clear that at this stage the new car was intended to share a significant proportion of the Series 2 XJ6's engineering. This was quite logical, the XJ6 having been launched only four years previously and with no rival looking likely to surpass it in any major respect for a number of years to come. So that while a substantially new bodyshell was scheduled (it was to be wider, with higher door apertures for easier access, more interior space, an extended front body section to meet possible stiffer crash tests, flatter roof panel, and reduced windscreen curvature adjacent to the front pillars to lessen wind noise) the existing floorpan and front and rear suspension sub-frames were scheduled for re-use.

The recently-launched V12 engine would have powered the car as an option to a smaller capacity 'slant six' offshoot made on the same tooling, while intended transmission systems included a new automatic gearbox by Borg Warner incorporating an overdrive and a new five-speed Jaguar manual gearbox. A two-speed axle arrangement was also under development for use with either manual or automatic gearboxes.

The styling of the car was undertaken by Jaguar's body styling department under the direction of Lofty England and Bob Knight, with chief body engineer Cyril Crouch

F.R.W. 'Lofty' England, who with Bob Knight commenced the XJ6 replacement project in 1972, seen here with Ian Appleyard.

advising on structural and production aspects. The resulting quarter- and full-scale styling models were early instances of the use of clay models by Jaguar. In Sir William's day of course, such prototypes had always been fashioned life-size from painted metal. But the same men who had previously interpreted Sir William's ideas were involved in the new project, and the final proposal was intentionally Jaguar-looking in many respects. Nevertheless, it was, Lofty relates, turned down by Lord Stokes and John Barber of BL when presented to them in October 1973, Barber considering it not to be different enough.

From then on there were more and more political intrusions on the XJ40 project; Geoffrey Robinson was appointed chief executive, and with the encouragement of John Barber, commissioned Pininfarina, Bertone and Ital Design to style their ideas of a new Jaguar within the engineering parameters given to them. The results were viewed at Browns Lane during 1974 alongside developments of the in-house car. Lofty England retired early and left them to it. No decisions had been made when Robinson himself left in April 1975 after publication of the Ryder Report, and by 1976 the new Jaguar was, apparently on the insistance of Spen King, being termed 'LC 40' rather than XJ40 – at least by the Leyland Cars men.

Heavily involved in maintaining his engineering department as a unique Jaguar function, Bob Knight (made managing director in title only during 1978) still found time to progress XJ40 development and took just as much interest in its styling as in its engineering. But there is no doubt that the political and financial atmosphere as the BL giant blundered on delayed the finalisation of an XJ40 concept by some years. As it was the BL factor came near to sinking the whole company as, along with morale, quality dipped sharply towards the end of the 1970s,

followed by plunging sales as confidence in the product waned. It was only Jaguar Engineering that contrived to remain unsullied by the onslaught, thanks to Bob Knight. As his successor Jim Randle is quick to emphasise: "In many respects he made sure the company was whole, and although many of the other functions like finance and purchasing went, the engineering did not go, and as a result the company could be restructured. We all owe Bob a great deal and I don't think anyone here forgets that."

James Randle, who had joined Jaguar from Rover in 1975, had been playing an increasingly major role in XJ40's development in his position as director, vehicle engineering, under Bob Knight and played a key role in returning the new car's styling to the straight and narrow (or, rather, the reverse as he sought to reintroduce a more curvaceous 'Jaguar' line into the styling philosophy). He worked a good deal with George Thompson and Chris Greville-Smith of Jaguar's styling department (which had been run since 1963 by Douglas Thorpe). "I think it was 1978 or '79 when I got George to just start to look at *Jaguars;* to try and make it *look* like a Jaguar, putting some of the Jaguar features there – like the grille as we know it, and the haunches in the rear wings," recalls Jim Randle.

This was really the birth of the 'phase 2' XJ40, and by this time the idea of using anything at all from the 'old' car had been dropped. It was to be 'all new' with no carry-over of either body or mechanical components.

By the time John Egan arrived in April 1980, the format of XJ40's major components had been finalised with Pressed Steel Fisher of Swindon already working on some body tooling. But it was still not certain that the final go-ahead would be given. "When we put the car to the BL board in May 1980 we weren't at all sure we were going to get it!" recounts Jim Randle. "I don't think anyone here really thought we were going to get it. They thought XJ40 was just a myth and it wouldn't happen, it had been talked about for such a long time. I don't think some people believed it until we got one running, and that was July 1981!" But the concept was approved by the BL board in the summer of 1980, followed in February 1981 by approval of the initial £77.92 million required to make it a reality. Within months the first prototype was running.

During the course of this immensely long and fraught gestation period the basic XJ40 *concept* had changed but little; but as already indicated, such was not the case with its engineering. The timespan had been enough for entirely new suspension and braking systems to be designed and evaluated, in conjunction with a completely new bodyshell, all taking advantage of much new technology which simply hadn't existed in the early seventies. In addition, any 'desperation factor' to get the new model into production, which might have been present during Series 3's blackest days in the late seventies, began to recede as John Egan's quality drive resulted in a leaping sales graph. This happier state of affairs bought time and

During the Robinson era Italian coachbuilders were solicited for XJ replacement ideas and a variety of shapes were viewed at Browns Lane in June 1974. Nearest the camera is Ital Design's Guigaro interpretation, then a more speculative Guigaro design next to Bertone's offering.
Photo: Jaguar Cars

allowed the post-approval time-table to be wound down, providing extra time for extended testing and fine honing of XJ40's functions; so while there was still no room for complacency, at least there was no need to panic either. XJ40 was to enjoy a natural birth, not an induced one.

Concept and specification evolution

For the duration of Sir William's own, absolute, rule at Jaguar it is difficult to formulate an analysis of how individual models were conceived other than that they stemmed from the great man himself; or, if the car had in some way been inspired by another, it was Sir William who dictated *what* it must achieve even if he left his engineers to work out the *how*. To put it bluntly, the search for each new Jaguar occurred because it seemed a good idea at the time – and, indeed, with very few exceptions each new model proved to be exactly that.

In the XJ40's very earliest stages, immediately after Sir William retired, this state of affairs still obtained. It seemed a logical and sensible idea to begin work on a successor to the XJ6, and so work did begin. "There were no analyses, submissions or clinics, no feasibility studies. It was all done on the backs of envelopes," is how one old campaigner put it years later. He was being intentionally simplistic; of course there *were* parameters laid down for new models in those days, but in both depth and in orders of priority they differed immensely from those drawn up for what in effect was the second attempt at getting XJ40 under way, during the late seventies and into the eighties. By that time things had become very much more scientific, and Jaguar had to abide by the new 'world' rules of the game or go under.

The principal objectives in force when the BL board were presented with the XJ40 programme in May 1980 are listed by Jim Randle as follows:

1. To reduce manufacturing complexity and thereby improve productivity and quality.
2. To improve reliability through improved standards and procedures.
3. To improve economy through low weight, improved aerodynamics and improved engine and engine management and transmission management systems.
4. To achieve a better performance and to maintain the car's position in the luxury sector by at least equalling its predecessor in style and refinement.

As can be seen, productivity, quality and reliability feature high on the list; style and refinement follow later. This is not to say that the latter were regarded as unimportant, simply that Jaguar now knew that first and foremost, the car must function reliably. Customer expectation in this respect had greatly increased since the company had launched its last major new saloon, and the days had passed when the customer might put up with an underdeveloped car because it looked so good or was so cheap. The new durability target was, in fact, 150,000 miles or twelve years of normal motoring without major component failure, and a halving of faults occurring in the first year of warranty compared with Series 3.

So the aim was to build in reliability to XJ40 from the very start, and that began with defining the performance requirements of bought-in components much more stringently. While XJ4 (as the original XJ6 was coded) component suppliers would produce parts *they* considered suitable, this time Jaguar laid down in great detail how that part must perform and explained in detail how the item was going to be used on the car.

In addition, aircraft-style 'failure modes and effects analysis' of working parts was brought in for XJ40 at both the design stage and with the hardware itself; this explored, by computer projection and by actual test, how a component might fail, what would happen if it did, and how the potential for failure could be eliminated. This

James Randle, engineering architect of XJ40, at play *(centre)* at an ETC round with *(right)* Tom Walkinshaw. Randle not only oversaw the new car's engineering evolution, but was instrumental in returning its styling towards a more traditional approach.
Photo: P. Skilleter

analysis was applied particularly stringently where safety was at stake. Improved serviceability was recognised as another important parameter at the design stage, in addition to ease of production, so that once on the road, the car would be serviced and repaired more quickly and more easily.

Jaguar's engineering division, and Jim Randle in particular, had been all too aware of the effect that shoddy components from suppliers was having on Series 3 reliability, and thanks to John Egan's back-up (see Chapter 11) not only managed to turn the situation round on Series 3 but also ensured that XJ40 would start life with an inherent reliability far higher than any previous Jaguar. This was not only desirable, but vitally necessary if the new car was to succeed in world markets. Everyone knew that if it failed, so too would the company. But as one Jaguar engineer put it, "good durability and reliability cannot be developed. They are achieved through sound and comprehensive design practices". Something similar applies to the success of the car's overall design, too. In comparing the genesis of XJ4 and XJ40, Jim Randle says: "We've got better equipment to do the testing nowadays, we've better software so that we can do the analysis. However, there's no real substitution for the intellectual power which has to be applied to the original design – that hasn't changed. What we have now

Phase two of XJ40 styling returned to a more Jaguar shape which, if not so radically different, blended the best of the old with features new to the marque. Importantly, Sir William was at hand at every formative stage to contribute ideas, particularly on the all-important detailing, and is seen here examining a late prototype XJ40 at Wappenbury with Jaguar stylist George Thompson; the date is 1983 or 1984.

This was termed 'IRS 3'; instead of radius arms, 'A' brackets were used but as these were mounted on the two-speed axle unit, when this feature was dropped the design was no longer viable. Inboard disc brakes were retained at this stage.

An early outboard brake experiment on what was basically still an S3 suspension. The linkage attached to the modified hub carrier was designed to provide an anti-lift effect.

This suspension was the direct forerunner of XJ40's, incorporating as it did the 'pendulum' device which allowed independence of fore/aft and longitudinal stiffnesses within the suspension. Note outboard brakes.

is tools; the brainpower hasn't changed". Certainly, XJ40 displays much original thinking, as indeed, XJ4 and many previous Jaguars have done in their eras.

One area where this application of intellect is particularly evident is in XJ40's rear suspension. The Series 3 rear suspension was still superior to that used on many rivals but as already recounted, even for the original XJ6 an improved system was sought and very nearly fitted. Since then experiments had continued with a variety of different systems, all intended to meet the three major objectives required for a luxury car, defined by Jaguar as a) isolation of the vehicle's occupants from road disturbances, road noises, axle noise and power unit vibration and noise, b) safe handling, so that even a non-skilled driver can enjoy high levels of response and cornering power combined with total predictability and c) durability and reliability. In designing such a suspension the engineer is faced with a constant battle between compliance and what is termed parasitic steering – that is, while the softest possible bushes and mounts are needed to kill vibrations from the road, the wheels must still not be allowed to deflect in a way that will 'steer' the car. Much research went into resolving these conflicting factors and into the incorporation of anti-dive and anti-squat characteristics. Many new suspension systems were built and evaluated, including on the road, using adapted XJ4 'simulators'. Some of these suspensions were based on improving the existing I.R.S; one design, for example, replaced the radius arm with a Watts linkage. Another, more radical, approach used a lower wishbone with an 'A' bracket replacing the radius arm; this "showed much promise" but the 'A' bracket and the front arm of the wishbone were mounted on the two-speed axle casing, and when this was dropped from production plans, the

whole system had to be abandoned. Then much work was put into a 'compliant wishbone' which allowed the hub, mounted on the end of co-axial tubes, to rotate. This produced "exceptional" refinement and was attractively simple, but with the rotational freedom came bump steer so it was reluctantly abandoned.

Early on, experiments had been carried out siting the brakes not adjacent to the differential, but outboard on the hubs. While in theory this increase in unsprung weight should have affected ride and handling, this was not detectable in practice, and as there were great gains in serviceability and performance (no longer would the axle oil seals 'cook'!) outboard brakes were from then on a confirmed XJ40 feature.

The search for controlled compliance continued though, and success was finally achieved through the use of a unique 'pendulum' system devised by Jim Randle. A lower wishbone (fabricated from two large pressings) carried the hub and outboard brakes, in conjunction with the drive shaft acting as the top member. But the inner mounting of the wishbone was unconventional in that its rubber-bushed fulcrum shaft was mounted on a pendulum arrangement at the front, and on a cross tie-bar at the rear, all designed so that a good degree of fore-and-aft movement of the wishbone was allowed, but very little lateral (across the car) travel. This produced a very high level of refinement as noise and vibration ('bump-thump') caused by the tyres striking protuberances on the road were absorbed as the tyres 'rode back' with the impact. Yet because of the high lateral control, Jaguar's obsession with the eradication of rear wheel steer was satisfied.

In addition, the wishbone's inner fulcrum was angled down 8 degrees to give 19 per cent anti-dive and 69 per

Single coil spring/damper units were chosen for the new I.R.S.; cast aluminium upright carries hub and outboard disc brakes, with (new to Jaguar) a drum arrangement to provide a more efficient handbrake. The outboard brakes were found to increase refinement by moving the wheel bounce mode frequency away from that of the bodyshell; nor did the change affect handling.
Photo: Paul Skilleter

cent anti-squat properties, and a single coil spring/damper was fitted each side, the latter incorporating rebound and bump stops. As required, the damping system at the rear could also incorporate suspension height control, through the use of hydraulically-pressurized struts.

At the heart of the system was the axle assembly, to which was attached the pendulum at the front and the tie-bar at the rear. This illustrates another precept espoused by Jaguar; that wherever possible throughout the car, mass should be used as a noise and vibration attenuator. The vehicle has to carry large lumps of metal, like the engine and axles, so why not use them? So the loads fed inwards from the wishbones met the mass of the final-drive unit.

The science was continued in the mounting of the suspension system to the body. The axle was attached to a pressed steel subframe which took the main loads outboard to the body's longitudinal box sections, its rubber mountings – thanks to the positioning of the spring damper units – taking all suspension loads. The addition of a pair of inclined links at the rear merely controlled wind-up of the system under braking and acceleration, an effect already partly countered by a

downthrust at the differential nose occurring during weight transfer – again due to the positioning of the spring damper units on the body.

This may sound complex, and to a degree it is, but the decision had been taken to commence design work with a clean sheet of paper, and if optimum results were to be obtained with such a system, then that's what would go into production (there's a story told in engineering about an even more complex suspension devised by Bob Knight which used a multiplicity of struts, of which he joked that he was trying to produce something the Germans wouldn't understand how was held up!). Some aspects of the rear suspension were, in fact, similar to the stillborn design eventually rejected for XJ4, but the latter did not possess important XJ40 features such as its wishbone compliance.

The car's front suspension was not so radically different; XJ4s already incorporated anti-dive geometry and shared a subframe with the engine mounts (using mass as a noise/vibration attenuator again), and as it worked well, in principle it was carried over to the new car. But this was not done without much experimentation with the subframe and its method of mounting. Front, back and triangular mounting systems were built and evaluated, this resulting in the one major change evident, which was to face the pitch control arms rearwards instead of forwards, so that they could anchor onto a stiffer part of the bodyshell adjacent to the front bulkhead. Also, a tie-bar was introduced across the subframe to brace the front wishbone pivots, while the sub-frame beam itself was much simpler, consisting of two major pressings. All fulcrums and mounting points on the beam were designed to be machined after assembly, to ensure the greatest accuracy and eliminate

the need for adjustment of camber or steering rack height during build. The spring damper units still mounted direct to the body, but within each Boge damper was additional rebound progression, which reduced stresses on the wishbones. An anti-roll bar once more connected the lower wishbones via short drop-links.

The influence of tyres on handling and refinement is great, and for XJ40 Dunlop and Michelin jointly developed a new TD cover designed to allow low vertical stiffness for the best ride comfort, but retain a flat tread area during cornering for maximum grip. Of 220 section, the tyre's profile was low at 65 and of course it was VR rated allowing 130mph cruising speeds.

A notable feature of the tyre was its resistance to dislodgement from the wheel rim should a puncture cause total deflation. The TD tyre bead was locked in a groove in the specially designed wheel which, if the tyre lost its air, prevented the bead rolling off into the wheel well and allowing the rim to dig into the road surface. In addition, a sealant gel carried inside the tyre casing became liquid above a certain temperature and sealed small punctures and resisted destruction of a flat tyre for long enough for the car to be driven to a garage.

The car's steering was mounted on the front subframe and, also like Series 3, used a power-assisted rack and pinion, with the pump now driven not by belt, but via a chain and skew gear off the timing chain. Turns lock-to-lock were 2.8 which gave a reasonable turning circle of 40ft 8in.

Crucial to the car's refinement was its bodyshell. This was designed from first principles, not only to ensure adequate strength with minimum weight, but also to 'build in' refinement. A car bodyshell, with its multiplicity of panels, box sections and metal thicknesses,

Front dampers mount directly to the body so the correct specification of the top bushes was vital. By attaching them to the body, the dampers also controlled the shake movement of the front suspension beam as well as fulfilling their conventional role.

Bodyshell assembly at Castle Bromwich. Complete, the shell weighed 295kg compared with 380kg for Series 3. Note space for the 19.6 gallon fuel tank above axle line, where it was more protected than were the pannier tanks of Series 3.

is an incredibly complex-sounding device and while, as we have seen, suspension systems are designed to insulate it as much as possible from road and mechanical noise, nevertheless many vibrations do get through to it – and with XJ40, it was Jaguar's aim to quantify what was happening to the shell, and modify its design so that a minimum of resonances were set up.

This pioneering work was carried out in conjunction with the Automotive Engineering Centre at the University of Birmingham, and involved an analysis of the shell whereby the structure was excited at a particular spot and the frequency responses measured at a large number of points all over the shell. This was repeated until a complete 'picture' of the shell had been built up, showing how mass and stiffness were distributed throughout the body, and how these could be redistributed to improve refinement. This is something of an over-simplification of a very complex operation, but the end result was a

significant contribution to the car's exceptionally low noise levels.

Structurally, XJ40's shell followed existing Jaguar/Pressed Steel Fisher patterns with large sill sections either side of the braced floorpan; boxed extensions ran forward from the front bulkhead to carry the front suspension beam. But much new thinking went into its manufacture, commencing with the final clay model. This was 'digitised' and a hardwood model produced by a computer-controlled Wadkin CNC machine tool – the first time Jaguar had produced such a model other than by hand. A glass fibre mould was taken so that mock-up GRP models could be made for reference and minor styling changes, after which the next stop was to investigate the reduction in the number of body panels. This would not only simplify and speed up assembly, but would also reduce the number of press tools and assembly jigs required, resulting in significant cost and time savings.

XJ40 did, in fact, end up with 425 panels compared with Series 3's 558; an oft-quoted example is the new car's monoside, which involved only 13 dies compared with Series 3's 55 – and it was stronger too. As many of the press tools as possible were made direct from the computer data base, although because only the skin panels had been digitised, this meant that the internal patterns and tooling were produced conventionally. All the press tools were made by Austin Rover's press shops at Swindon, those for the skin panels being finished to a high standard by hand. Swindon also made the steel pressings which then travelled to Jaguar's body assembly plant at Castle Bromwich where they were jig-welded and then painted.

Corrosion resistance was considered right from the beginning, with zinc-coated steel being specified for vulnerable areas such as box sections and sills, while certain skin panels were of one-side coated Zintec steel. After assembly, bodywork seams were sealed before priming by immersing the negatively-charged bodyshell in a tank of positively-charged paint. The underside is protected by a coat of thick sealant.

For exterior paintwork, Jaguar adopted 'clear over base' technology, not just for metallic colours, but for solids as well. Quality of finish was enhanced through the use of de-ionised compressed air to remove static electricity and dust from the body as it passed through the booths. Air-conditioning was employed, while a recently introduced colour oven incorporated a dark radiation 'heat up' zone which achieved a rapid curing of the paint's surface film which minimises damage from dust fall-out. Before the bodies were transferred to Browns Lane all internal cavities were flooded with hot wax as a final rust preventive.

While Series 3 cars, particularly late models, had a vastly increased resistance to corrosion compared with Series 2, for XJ40 even more stringent standards were applied. It was decided the car had to meet the Canadian Anti-Corrosion Code, which involved a 12-week cycle of tests including mud and salt sprays, endurance running over rough gravel roads, and prolonged exposure to a 100 per cent humidity atmosphere. This was designed to equate to six years' use in Canada's harsh climate, and was originally devised by Triumph. Sample bodies were afterwards sectioned and every cavity and panel examined inside and out. It would appear, therefore, that in later years XJ40 owners will not have to endure the misery of holed sills and wings, and decaying cross-members, that is the lot of many second-hand Series 1 and 2 owners!

As for XJ40's final shape, we have already seen how it was gradually guided away from the crisper but less

'Jaguar' style into which it had drifted. These new curves furthered its evolutionary look and while, on announcement, the clear family resemblance to the Series 3 was a disappointment to some who had looked forward to a more radically modern Jaguar saloon, it was a relief to those American dealers who, having by 1986 at last persuaded many of their fellow-countrymen to take the Jaguar saloon seriously, were somewhat terrified at the prospect of re-educating them to an entirely different-looking car!

Retaining the Jaguar look did mean sacrificing the ultimate in aerodynamic efficiency, though much was done to reduce drag wherever possible. Using data collected from wind-tunnel studies it was found that the Series 3's typical nose-forward stance and its headlight peaks were the biggest contributors to the drag figure. So for XJ40, the forward slope of the radiator panel – as we have seen, a feature quite possibly originating from Malcolm Sayer's studies on the Mk VII – was lessened, a top to bottom radius introduced on the front corners, and the headlight eyebrows removed. At the rear a small lip was included in the bootlid pressing, a separate spoiler to reduce rear end lift not being considered acceptable on a Jaguar, while a discreet front spoiler contributed the necessary characteristics at that end of the car.

By these methods the target of bettering the Series 3 Cds (drag coefficient plus frontal area) figure was achieved, XJ40 recording 0.762 and Series 3 0.849. Of equal or even greater importance was the new car's cross-wind stability remaining the equal of Series 3 and bettering that of the immediate competition. Straight-line stability has always been a characteristic of the Jaguar car, nearly all models displaying a remarkable resistance to deflection at speed – for example, during buffeting caused by passing heavy lorries on motorways – a virtue that adds much to the enjoyment of driving the car and of considerably more practical use than a slightly better Cd figure to be quoted in an advertisement!

The interior design of a Jaguar is almost as important as its exterior styling; the latter might attract you to the car, but it is the seductiveness of the interior furnishings which make you want to get in and try it. With XJ40, Jaguar had to tread a wary path between the need to incorporate modern instrumentation and controls and the necessity to retain the Jaguar ambience. At first, the tendency was to update and modernise a little too much, and it was the direct result of a pre-launch clinic in the US – where potential Jaguar customers were asked to view a number of cars and give their opinion – that XJ40's interior was quite substantially revised. This was because the 'customers' had almost unanimously preferred Series

The engine management systems control both fuelling and ignition by microprocessor with information received from sensors monitoring every key function of the engine. (J.C.)

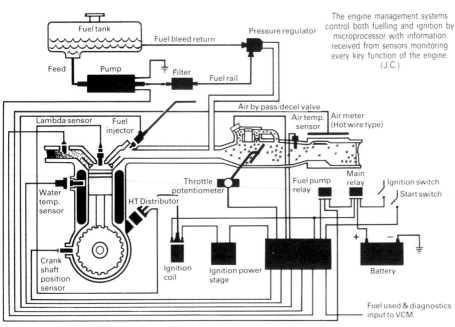

While the 3.6 AJ6 engine had previously been seen in the XJS, the single-cam version was unique to the new saloon. With its 'May' combustion chambers and reduced capacity, economy was Jaguar's aim; like the 3.6, its construction was all-aluminium.

Layout of the engine management system developed jointly by Lucas and Jaguar for the four-valve 3.6-litre engine; important elements included the hot wire type air mass flow meter and mapped digital ignition; the latter replaced the conventional mechanical bob-weight advance mechanism.

3 to XJ40! Back at Browns Lane, the hourly-graded personnel who'd made the prototype trim just said "told you so"; they had maintained all along that what they were making wasn't Jaguar, and indeed, the Daimler/Vanden Plas versions of XJ40 did afterwards incorporate suggestions from the trimshop workers.

So as it appeared for production, XJ40 featured traditional wood veneer and leather hide in rather more generous quantities than originally intended – and of course was the better for it. But nevertheless high technology was present, too, and while round dials still portrayed speed and engine revolutions, vacuum fluorescent bar graph displays indicated fuel, battery level voltage, oil pressure and coolant temperature. Moreover, warnings of low levels were indicated by a colour change, and finally by a flashing ring that would indicate, for instance, that the car was nearly out of fuel.

Also completely new was the Vehicle Condition Monitor, a microprocessor controlled unit which could display vital information about the car's working parts; up to 34 functions could be monitored. Using a 32 x 32 dot matrix grid display, the monitor could, by way of symbols, indicate such things as brake failure, worn brake pads, low coolant, seat belt not fastened, door or bootlid opened, bulb failure, washer fluid low and so forth. If the warning was urgent, an amber or red frame lit up round the grid.

After launch, there were one or two criticisms about the vacuum displays and the monitor not being in keeping with Jaguar's traditional image, or being unpleasant to look at. But those at Jaguar pointed out that instruments are present solely to inform and there was no way anyone could miss a warning from the new type of display, whereas many drivers (especially women and the less

An SDV on test in Arizona; by the end of the pre-launch programme some 16 locally recruited drivers, quite a large proportion of them women, were working a two-shift system.

Low temperature operation testing in Canada; Jaguar's permanent facility there was in Timmins, Ontario, used for the winter months of November to April. This SDV carries the lift-off glass-fibre disguise panels used prior to launch.

mechanically-minded) would often fail to notice a needle moving to the wrong end of the scale on a conventional instrument. All sorts of additional equipment was specified on the new models as the Jaguar saloon was brought up-to-date with a vengeance – including such items as heated windscreen washer nozzles, heated mirrors and door locks, and central locking which also closed windows or sun-roof if open. (see Appendix for full details.)

Heating and ventilation were of a new generation too, all mechanical control linkages and flap valves being eliminated and replaced by rotary barrel valves operated by DC motors. Side window demisting viaducts in the doors featured, too. The air-conditioning unit was extremely sophisticated, variably controlling humidity as well as temperature, and incorporating solar heat compensation, whereby a sensor on top of the dash measured sunshine and directed the air conditioning microprocessor to switch in extra cooling accordingly.

To operate the complex new instrumentation and all the other electrical functions on the car (some 200 in all), Jaguar adopted low current earth line switching. This enabled each electrical device to be switched by a lightweight command cable carrying only five volts and the few milliamps usually required to issue orders to an intermediate transistor-based device. This system saved around 50 per cent of normal wiring harness weight. Then to improve reliability (and the electrical system of a car is historically its least reliable aspect) great efforts were made, in concert with suppliers, to develop better relays and switches. The latter employed precious metals and bounce-free contacts within hermetically sealed cases to protect them from contamination. Pass-out requirements ranged from the ability to complete from 150,000 to as much as 2,000,000 operations in some applications!

Connections too can be a source of unreliability; for XJ40, Jaguar evolved a range of aircraft-standard multi-pin connectors with 'positive mate anti-backout systems'

Many engineers were involved in the XJ40 development and test programme; this is Peter Taylor, one of Jaguar's ace 'sorters' who helped fine-tune XJ40's handling and ride characteristics.

September 1986, and Sir John Egan addresses the dealers at the trade preview at Browns Lane.
Photo: A.J.A. Whyte

First public showing of XJ40 was at the Paris Show, 8 October 1986. Left to right in this picture are Stephen Perrin (Marketing Director), John Morgan (European Operations Director), Roger Putnam (Director, Sales & Marketing) and Barry Thrussell (Service Director).
Photo: A.J.A. Whyte

The two faces of XJ40: XJ6 models carried individual round headlamps, Sovereigns rectangular type. Grilles were identical. (For the record, car on left is no. 500289, on right no. 500306).

446

which would either latch or reject. Then the wiring itself was upgraded when it was found that under extremely cold conditions the insulation could crack.

For the new car came a new engine, and the need to develop a new range of power units at the same time as an all-new model threw considerable strain on Jaguar's engineering resources, which by the late-seventies were heavily under-funded (perhaps they had always been so). However, again thanks to successive decisions putting back XJ40's launch, the power units were signed-off before the car, and as recounted in Chapter 11, the 3.6 engine was given the much-needed benefit of low-volume production in the XJ-S well before XJ40 itself appeared. This trial run proved to be vital. As it first appeared the new twin-cam 3.6 was somewhat behind even the old XK engine in refinement, and might have been a positive disaster for Jaguar had it been installed in XJ40 in that condition. The basic components such as the block and the cast crank never broke or gave trouble, but, as one senior engineer put it, "refinement turned out to be the big one". Much development work was carried out on the chain drives, the pistons and the valve gear, and to such good effect that when installed in XJ40, both the 3.6 and the previously unseen 2.9 single-cam engines received high praise for their smoothness and refinement. But up to that time it had worried a lot of people both inside and outside the factory!

The development of the 3.6-litre four-valve twin ohc AJ6 engine is described in Chapter 11; the 2.9-litre AJ6 engine used exclusively in XJ40 at the time of writing also had its origins in the V12 engine, and dates back to the earliest XJ40 proposals when, during the 'Lofty' England era, it was intended as an optional power unit to a V8 derivation (the V8, deemed inappropriate for a Jaguar in any case by some, proved unreliable and tended to break its crankshaft due, it seems, to an inherent unbalance.

Cat's tails: bootlid incorporated a slight spoiler lip and more conventionally-shaped rear light units than Series 3s. The general effect was variously likened to Rolls-Royce or Mercedes. Rear screen was flush-mounted to reduce drag.

Strong elements of Series 3 remained in XJ40 styling, the characteristic forward-sloping nose being reduced but given an even more thrusting grille; also noticeable was the change to a single wiper arm.

The 2.9-litre engined XJ6; the 'haunch' over the rear wheels – a Jaguar styling trademark since the XK120 and Mk VII – was retained but lower-body mouldings had been seen on no previous Jaguar.

XJ6 five-speed interior; this car is lacking extras such as electric seat adjustment. Dash layout with binnacles is shared with other models though.

Although some tooling for its manufacture was put in at the Radford works, it had been shelved by 1976). The 2.9 engine therefore shared a number of features with the V12 including the bore spacing, 'May' head and 12.6:1 compression ratio, cylinder head porting, valves and camshaft. It used the same aluminium block and 91 mm bore diameter as the 3.6 engine but a different crankshaft gave a shorter, 74.8 mm, stroke and a V12-type single overhead cam operated just two valves per cylinder. The Bosch EZ-F programmed electronic ignition system was specified, this providing the necessarily changing advance curve to match closely the detonation limit in the high compression 'lean burn' head. Output is listed at 165bhp (DIN) at 5,600 rpm, or 4bhp more than the 3.4-litre XK engine.

XJ40 arrived with two transmission options: a ZF automatic gearbox or a Getrag manual one. The former was selected by Jaguar after consideration had been given to Borg Warner and GM alternatives, and provided three speeds plus an 'overdrive' fourth. With the selector in 'D' top gear did not come into play until the accelerator was lifted from the floor (rather like the old automatic overdrive system used on Mk 2 Ford Zephyrs and Zodiacs), and for additional economy the gearbox incorporated a lock-up clutch within the torque converter, as indeed had the Borg Warner gearbox first fitted to Jaguar's original automatic saloon, the Mk VII.

The most novel external feature of the gearbox was its selector, which was an exclusive Jaguar design. This featured the now-famous 'J' gate, which placed the 'automatic' modes – Park, Reverse, Neutral and Drive – on one plane, and the manual override modes – Drive, 3 and 2 – on the other. Soon nicknamed the 'Randle handle' by the more humorous element of the motoring press core, the device certainly fulfilled its intended function, which was to avert the real danger of overshooting the desired mode and inadvertently selecting Reverse instead of, for example, Neutral. More than one driver has achieved this with the conventional gate on Series 3, locking the rear wheels and giving themselves a fright!

Final drive gearing differed according to which engine or gearbox was fitted; the 2.9 manual gave 26.6mph per 1000 rpm in top, or 25.5mph in automatic form. For the 3.6, higher gearing provided figures of 28.3mph and 29.5mph. For comparison, the old Jaguar four-speed box in overdrive top had given 27.5mph per 1000rpm, and in fifth gear, Series 3 had provided a rather lower 25.8mph with the 3.31 axle ratio. All the new cars, but particularly the 3.6 versions, therefore gave relaxed cruising at 70mph. Indeed, in automatic form the 3.6 engine was turning over at a mere 2,400rpm at that speed, and for maximum fuel economy, US market 3.6 cars were even higher geared. A limited-slip differential was standard on Daimler models and optional on the others. Much attention was paid to the mounting of the engine and gearbox in the car, once more in the name of refinement. As with XJ4 (and, indeed, the late Mk Xs) the engine was carried on bobbin-type rubber mounts seated on the front suspension beam, positioned so that the mountings were placed at the point where the engine/gearbox unit tended to bend most (and therefore vibrate). As the engine was not vertical, account had to be taken of this in the stiffness and angle of the rubber used for right-hand and left-hand mountings.

The rear (gearbox) mounting also called for considerable thought as space for it was limited, yet it was the only such mount to be fixed directly to the body. A co-axial spring arrangement, vaguely reminiscent of the mounting used for the 2.4-litre saloon's gearbox, was employed with a polyurethane ring providing lateral control. In practice this was found to produce a very high degree of noise attenuation, particularly over the 3,000 – 4,000rpm speed range.

XJ40's braking system saw a radical departure from past Jaguar road car practice, as a conventional vacuum servo had been discarded in favour of assistance provided by an engine driven hydraulic pump. This was driven from the front of the engine and delivered up to 1,500 psi via a relief valve which, according to demand, either allowed the hydraulic mineral oil to recirculate around the pump or enter a nitrogen-filled pressure accumulator. This latter could store enough energy if the

The celebrated 'J' gate which separates park and reverse from manual selection of '2' and '3'; surround is rubber, presumably to minimise vibration and noise. This XJ6 boasts electric seat controls (mounted on side of console).

XJ6 2.9 and 3.6 cars featured herringbone-pattern cloth upholstery as standard – leather was an extra-cost option. The seats were developed in conjunction with Loughborough University to combine comfort with location; all models featured a gear-driven lumbar support mechanism in the front seat squabs.

Rear seats, XJ6; the aim throughout the car's interior was to employ traditional craftsmanship where it could be seen, and modern technologies where they could be invisible. Under the cloth or leather, cold-cure polyurethane foam was used in place of Series 3's more complex foam and spring casings assembly.

Unique: no previous four-door Jaguar had appeared with a side window behind the rear doors.

engine stopped to provide between eight and 20 retardations, far more than is allowed by a normal vacuum booster.

The brakes themselves were operated by normal synthetic/vegetable hydraulic fluid and featured 11.6in ventilated discs at the front, and 10.9in solid discs at the rear, these incorporating a separate cable-operated handbrake drum each. Most importantly, for the first time Jaguar offered anti-lock braking, too, standardised on the Daimler and Sovereign models and optional on the XJ6. The Bosch system used features a sensor on each wheel which feeds information to the anti-lock processor. This assesses which wheel is about to lock, whereupon it stops any more brake pressure going to that wheel. If the wheel still decelerates the pressure to it is released entirely. As the wheel then speeds up again, the sensor notes this and starts an electric motor which pumps fluid back to the brake on a cycle of between two and eight times per second.

The system also incorporated a 'yaw control' facility which could compensate for widely differing side-to-side braking effort by initially reducing braking pressure on the 'good' wheels as well as the one about to lock, allowing the driver progressively to apply steering compensation.

As can be seen, XJ40 was by far the most complex Jaguar ever to be built, and while stringent component specification and rig-testing provided a head-start in reliability over previous models, it was still essential for every aspect to be thoroughly tested on the road.

Initially, and well before any XJ40 prototypes as such were built, individual suspension systems and other major components were tried on simulators, Series 3 cars

converted to accept XJ40 parts. The results were quantified alongside those obtained from static rig tests, of which there were 94 in-house and 384 used by suppliers.

From simulators the next stop was to build Semi-Engineered Prototypes, or SEPs. These were purpose-built cars with bodies made from hand-beaten, hand-assembled panels and were used to prove the basic layout of the new model and its major components. The first of five SEPs (recalled by the then vehicle proving engineer Norman Dewis as a somewhat raw machine) was driven in July 1981, to be followed by twenty Fully-Engineered Prototypes. FEPs still employed hand-assembled shells but the panels were made on 'soft' limited-run tooling and thus were much more representative of the production car to be.

The final prototype phase was represented by SDVs or Specially Designated vehicles. Broadly speaking they equated to what were termed pre-production cars in XJ4 days, being assembled from production parts, and they were used for purposes in addition to testing, such as catalogue photography. Between 1983 and mid-1986 some 400 SDVs were constructed on a pilot-build line which Jaguar laid down for the purpose. This line proved a tremendously worthwhile investment for it enabled Jaguar to train operators and assess the most efficient method of building the new cars, so that when the actual production line was put in, it was substantially snag-free. Afterwards the pilot-build line was turned over to assembly of the low-volume XJ12.

The FEPs and SDVs were subjected to the most rigorous testing, this mainly the province of Vehicle Proving, a sort of in-house critical customer. XJ4 had also undergone a test programme but although severe by Jaguar's standards then, was certainly inadequate and it was only thanks to a combination of good basic design, a small but highly dedicated team of engineers, and customers prepared to put up with a less reliable car, that Jaguar largely got away with it. No such chances were taken with XJ40.

Of all their achievements with XJ40, Jaguar's engineers seemed most proud of their enhancement of the XJ's legendary ride/handling compromise – to drive, the car is immensely confidence-inspiring, resulting in higher average speeds for less effort compared with Series 3.

Sovereign, with elegance from previous generations: Mk VII saloon and Glamis Castle; all photographed during XJ40's UK press launch in Scotland. Like its sisters, D34 BRW (no. 500306) was assembled on the XJ40 pilot-build line in the summer of 1986.

'Sovereign' badge replaced 'XJ6' on back panel of the luxury variant, but type of gearbox fitted was not signified. Fog warning lamps were built into bumper which retained some traditional Jaguar chrome plate.

Individual seats, picnic tables, pleated magazine holders, centre console, and veneer surrounds to electric window buttons on door grab handles all contributed to the higher level of luxury enjoyed by Sovereign rear passengers.

Besides the hundreds of thousands of miles clocked up at the MIRA and Gaydon test grounds in Britain, and on British roads, extensive testing was carried out overseas, too. The earliest overseas tests involved FEPs running from Jaguar's Timmins, Ontario base in Canada, a succession of FEPs and SDVs then being subjected to the rigours of the Canadian winters where the temperature can drop to – 56°C. In contrast, a million miles of testing was completed in the often baking heat of Australia, 104,000 miles were completed in the Oman, while a large base was established at Phoenix, Arizona in the USA. From there, using up to sixteen drivers (mostly recruited locally, and including a good number of women), some 1¼ million miles were clocked up by XJ40 prototypes. High mileages were also covered on the heavily-trafficked, pot-holed roads of New York, too.

High-speed endurance testing was mainly carried out at the Nardo proving ground in Italy. This was as much a test of engine and transmission as anything else, and the target set, and achieved, for the new AJ6 engine was 25,000 miles on a high-speed (virtually flat-out) test cycle there. In total, prior to launch over 5½ million miles of testing had been accumulated by pre-production XJ40 cars.

XJ40 was announced on Wednesday, 8th October 1986, seven years after the go-ahead for the car in its final form had been given. The first surprise was the name – XJ6. But the logic behind the choice was indisputable: it emphasised the continuity of the Jaguar saloon car (reflected too in the new XJ6's evolutionary styling), and above all traded on the unique, world-wide acclaim and respect that the name 'XJ6' had acquired since 1968. It

would, surely, have been foolish to have thrown that advantage away.

As launched for the UK market that day, the model line-up looked like this: there was the XJ6 2.9 with the single-cam, two valves per cylinder, 91 x 74.8mm, 2,919cc engine developing 165bhp at 5,600rpm, and the XJ 3.6 which had the twin ohc, four valves per cylinder, 91 x 92mm, 3,590cc engine developing 221bhp at 5,000rpm. Both cars used the five-speed Getrag manual gearbox; the four-speed ZF automatic gearbox was an extra-cost option as were other mechanical refinements such as ride levelling, anti-lock braking, a limited-slip differential, and cruise control.

Then there were the Jaguar Sovereigns, which were a continuation of the theme established with the later Series 3 whereby the previously 'Daimler' model name was

For the UK and parts of Europe the Daimler name was marketed alongside that of Jaguar; the car possessed the highest specification of any XJ40 and was available in 3.6-litre form only.

The new car was launched in the USA during the early spring of 1987. Early examples tended to be criticised for insufficient performance and, by the autumn of 1987, as the car was more than meeting its target fuel economy, the final drive had been lowered and the compression ratio raised to produce better acceleration.

applied to luxury-equipped Jaguars. Thus the Jaguar Sovereigns arrived with automatic transmission, anti-lock brakes, ride levelling, cruise control, air-conditioning and eight-way electrically-adjustable leather seats all as standard.

Finally, Daimler had not been excluded from the model line-up, at least for Great Britain and parts of Europe, and not surprisingly represented the flag-ship of the new range. Amongst its unique features, not available on the other cars in the range, were individually-shaped rear seats (a hall-mark of previous XJ Daimlers), leather trimmed door castings and centre console, burr walnut veneer with deep wood facia, passenger footwell rugs, and burr walnut picnic tables for rear passengers. Outside a chrome body side moulding was featured. Mechanically, the car was identical to the XJ6 3.6 Sovereign with the automatic gearbox standard and the five-speeder a no-cost option.

One additional model, seriously considered during the XJ40 project's earlier years, was absent from the catalogue. This – in direct contrast to the Daimler just described – was a base 'executive' version of the XJ6. This is worth examining because it illustrates the conditions and doubts under which the new car had to labour even after its major units had been signed-off for production. The design of a down-market XJ40 derivative was set in hand towards the end of 1981. It should be remembered that the atmosphere at Browns Lane was very different then for the company had just endured one of the worst years in its history with world sales down to 14,000 cars, and doubts were creeping in about the viability of the luxury car market itself. Was the XJ40 as specified really going to be the right car? Would it be too expensive and too thirsty to achieve good sales, especially in the United States where the indiginous motor industry was still down-sizing fast? As one Jaguar engineer relates, "it was by no means a sure-fire thing that XJ40 was the right product, and it was felt there might be a need to bolster it with a down market version".

By that time, of course, the car's overall dimensions (it was $1\frac{1}{2}$in longer than Series 3) had long been fixed, but it was thought that cost and weight could still be pared away by reducing its secondary specification and using lighter, cheaper materials for some of the trim. As a 'body in white', XJ40 was already 41kg lighter than the 336kg Series 3 in a similar condition, and its new rear suspension was a little lighter than Series 3's, too, but these gains were more than offset by the extra equipment the new car carried – and had to carry, because the luxury-car customer now expected far more than did his counterpart in 1968.

In practice however, down-grading the car proved to reduce neither cost nor weight sufficiently to make the exercise worthwhile. This, combined with increasing confidence as the luxury car market improved generally, and the dramatic Series 3 sales improvement in particular,

sunk the 'XJ6E' (my description!) for good. This eventually was much to the relief of the engineers involved – 'cheapening' a Jaguar is not a very rewarding exercise.

Another possible variant which didn't appear in October 1986 was a 12-cylinder XJ40, and again, its non-appearance serves to highlight Jaguar's thinking, only this time, much earlier in the car's evolution. For during the middle and late seventies, Jaguar, along with a number of other manufacturers, were fairly convinced that because of the market's then-current obsession with fuel economy, a big multi-cylinder engine could no longer be justified in commerical terms; but in addition, there was the sinister possibility, likelihood even, of BL's forcing Jaguar to fit the Rover V8 engine. The result was that XJ40's engine bay was designed so that a 'V' engine just wouldn't fit ... Times change though, and it is no secret that XJ40 is being re-engineered so that the all-aluminium V12 engine can be used (it will probably feature a longer wheelbase, and four-wheel-drive).

Finally, the inclusion of a diesel-engined model in the XJ40 range was under serious consideration at one stage, in response to the rush by North American manufacturers to offer such power units. But as this fad began to pass (helped by, in some cases, some very unsatisfactory diesel installations) so too, did the apparent need for Jaguar to offer the same, and deliberations about both diesel versions of the AJ6 engine and the use of Italian-made VM diesels (turbocharged versions of which were tested by Jaguar) were wound down. Jaguar are, however, continuing to keep abreast of diesel developments should such engines ever again appear necessary.

Leading up to the car's UK launch, Jim Randle, XJ40 project engineer Malcolm Oliver, and other members of the staff gave a notable presentation to the Institute of Mechanical Engineers in London on the development of XJ40. The presentation was remarkable not only for the erudition of the lectures but also for the appearance of XJ40 itself in the Birdcage Walk, Westminster head-quarters of the Institute. It was manoeuvred in, on its side, using a specially constructed frame. Many equally spectacular presentations followed, for both European and American dealers, with the first major press launch being near Dunkeld in Scotland. There, from a hotel base, the world's press sampled XJ40 over a demanding route through the Scottish Highlands.

The public announcement of the car in October made headlines – after all, Jaguar had been 'news' for some time now, the company's imagination-grabbing recovery over the previous few years being upheld as a shining example of what *could* be achieved by British industry when its management, workforce and suppliers got their act together. The razzmatazz surrounding the company's privatisation had further established the name Jaguar as a media buzz-word. One newsworthy feature latched onto by both the specialist and non-specialist press was the new car's price tag: the XJ6 2.9 manual retailed at £16,495 and

New XJ6 styling was favourably received in the States. although *Town & Country* considered that its execution seemed "a bit timid", and also preferred the European composite headlight arrangement. XJ40 spearheaded Jaguar's attack on Mercedes position in the United States – the German firm had sold 99,314 cars there in 1986 as opposed to Jaguar's 24,464.

'Federal' XJ6 Sovereign facia; the aura of quality impressed but as at home, there were reservations about the fluorescent displays ("this gaudy arrangement may be fine for Cadillacs", one journal opined, "but this, after all, is a Jaguar"). No-one appeared to doubt the effectiveness of the scheme's message delivering capabilities though.

US-spec. Sovereign XJ6 interior; as Graham Whitehead, president of Jaguar Cars Inc., said of his company, "we deal in wood, leather, and chrome" and there was certainly a generous measure of the former two materials in the new car's furnishings, with enough of the latter to add sparkle. The old formula was just as successful for Jaguar as it had always been.

An important feature of XJ40 was low maintenance and electronic fault detection, the latter through the Jaguar Diagnostic System. Connected to the car, it takes the operator through a logical investigative procedure and, after finally identifying the fault, prints out the analysis and the least expensive repair.

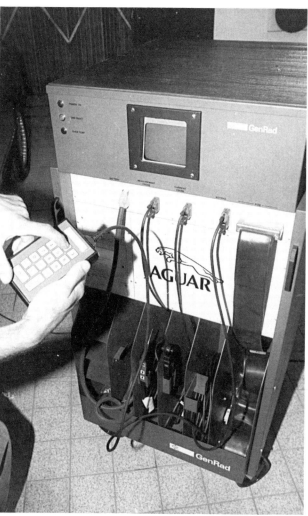

it was pointed out that this undercut the unfortunate new Rover 800 Sterling which in top spec. guise sold for more than £18,000. In reality the two were very different cars with the Rover being, perhaps, the most competent car that the rest of BL had managed to produce for many years. The most expensive XJ40 was the Daimler at £28,495.

XJ40 on road test

Initial press reviews of the car were good; the reasoning behind the car's evolutionary styling was appreciated and the totally modern equipment was approved of, with the occasional exception of the solid-state minor instruments. But, as with most Jaguars, it was driving the car that sold it – metaphorically so far as most of the press were concerned (to their sorrow!).

Autocar boasted of publishing the world's first full road test of the new XJ6 in its Vol. 170, number 3 issue on 15th October 1986. The car's road behaviour did indeed receive high praise; the damping was considered to provide "a near magical ride/handling compromise" the car remaining "gloriously controllable" on poor surfaces, while its stable understeering condition could only be modified into an oversteering attitude by applying excess throttle at low speeds, or lifting off the power and then re-applying it on higher speed corners. "It remains controllable throughout such antics and is possessed of a beautiful high speed balance for a front-engined car" stated the writer. The engine received accolades too, *Autocar* commenting on its "inviting charms" and "free revving nature". The gearbox installation was approved of with the Getrag's change being rated "delightfully positive" even though "not the lightweight thing you find in so many smaller cars of today". The positioning of the clutch pedal was noted to be better than that of the manual Series 3, where heel and toeing had been almost impossible.

There weren't many criticisms: the new-shape boot was thought only adequate, and the horn note not up to the car's status, but that was about it. The performance was certainly admired: 60mph came up from rest in 7.4 seconds, 100mph in 20.6-seconds, and the maximum speed in top was 137mph. Acceleration in fourth didn't always quite match Series 3's incidentally, which possessed a slight advantage up to the 50-70mph increment, which the new car matched at 7.7-seconds. Thereafter the later XJ6 pulled away at an increasing rate, with 90-110mph being bridged in just 8.3-seconds compared to the injected 4.2's 13.6-seconds. Overall petrol consumption came out at 20.7mpg, slightly down on likely rivals but better than the Series 3 manual's 18.3mpg.

Motor published its first XJ40 test just before the close of 1986, the subject being the 'entry level' XJ6 2.9. The journal noted that the Rover Sterling and the Granada/Scorpio Executive were more expensive, but also pointed out that both of them had similar internal dimensions, and would get you across Europe quicker and more frugally than the 2.9.

The new Jaguar gave a "disastrously bad" 16.8mpg overall during the test, which was only 0.5mpg better than the last V12 XJS they'd tried. The computed touring consumption of 27.1mpg sounded more reasonable though, and as most owners of the car found, was a better clue to the sort of mpg the 2.9 was capable of in practice. Why? Because most 2.9 owners tended to drive considerably less quickly than magazine road testers, and the high compression, 'May' head did tend to return good consumption under part-throttle conditions.

On the other hand, the car's road-holding and handling brought high praise, related in glowing prose that reminds one of original XJ6 road tests. "There is an uncanny grace and balance in the way it can string together a series of demanding sweeps, and the bumpier the road the more remarkable its reserves of poise appears... In short we know of no other large saloon that will live with the XJ6 on really rough roads, much less one that's as forgiving on the limit." Ride comfort received similar praise: "If there's a hump, the Jaguar flattens it. If there's a dip, the Jaguar fills it in. It glides over rough surfaces with consummate control – it doesn't float, it doesn't pitch." Low-speed ride was rated as knobbly, however, except for back seat passengers; "the rear seat ride is uniformly superb". So Jim Randle's rear suspension really worked! Summarising the 2.9, *Motor* said: "In this car the miles simply melt away, involving

the driver only as much as he wants to be involved. It handles better than an S-class Merc yet rides more smoothly and quietly than a Rolls-Royce".

Later, in May 1987, the same journal reported on the Sovereign 3.6 automatic. Ride, handling and brakes all scored highly, but the steering was felt to be unresponsive in the straight-ahead position, and still too light (later it was found that some cars had left the factory with incorrect castor settings). The magazine was also "unconvinced" by the vacuum-display minor instruments, felt that the build quality showed the results of John Egan's quality drive but wasn't quite up to Mercedes/BMW standards of finish, and that in this context, under the bonnet "the untidy pipe and cablework is an opportunity lost".

Petrol consumption at 17.3mph was actually an improvement over the figure recorded for the 2.9 but significantly down on the BMW735i's 20.1mpg. Acceleration was rated as good (0-60mpg in 8.4-seconds) and top speed reasonable (131.9mph). But as in the journal's comparison test with the BMW carried out earlier, it was felt that the German car was "more consistently brilliant", although not equalling the 3.6's "typically Jaguar ambience".

Meanwhile the new car's production was proceeding smoothly, and despite the change-over from Series 3 to XJ40 assembly at Browns Lane, the build rate of new Jaguars was actually increased. By the end of December 1986 Jaguar were able to announce a new weekly production record of 1,026 cars, mostly XJ40s, which brought the year's production total to a record 41,437 vehicles, compared with 38,500 the year before. Broken down, this meant that 32,385 saloons had been completed, 4,000 of which were the new model, and 9,052 XJ-S cars. A second assembly track came into operation during the spring of 1987 and during the first three months of the new year, sales were again at a record level, but still constrained by the factory's inability to meet demand. In the UK, the waiting list was up to two years and low-mileage 'used' XJ6s were changing hands at £2,000 or £3,000 up on list price. Shades indeed of the months following the launch of the first XJ6! Accolades gained by the new car included the British 'Top Car' award in November 1986 and the Queen's Technology Award in April 1987.

Also in the spring of 1987 was the all-important American launch. In contrast to the situation which had all too often occurred in the past, this time Jaguar had contrived to get stocks of the new car to the dealers at the same time; this resulted in an all-time sales record for Jaguar in May 1987, 20 per cent up on the previous May, with 2,304 cars being sold in the USA, 312 in Canada, 837 in the UK and 2,944 in continental Europe. Not that there weren't teething troubles; in May the factory issued a recall involving some 4,800 cars due to some cars losing their brake servo assistance because of foreign matter in the brake fluid – the fault of a supplier. Then in July, 1600

European-specification XJ6 on the continent; Germany represented Jaguar's biggest potential market on its side of the Atlantic and bolstered by the success of the XJR8 in vanquishing Porsche to win the 1987 World Sports Car Championship, and a re-organised German sales organisation, Jaguar look set to make a determined onslaught on Mercedes Benz's homeland.

The three graces – *left to right,* Daimler 3.6, Jaguar Sovereign 3.6, and Jaguar XJ6 3.6, all in 1988 form. Tower of London and Tower Bridge provide a patriotic background.

AJ6-engined cars (some XJS were included) fitted with cruise control and sold during the spring were recalled for replacement of a micro-switch which, if it failed, could inhibit automatic cancellation of the cruise control on depression of the brake pedal. Earlier there had been puzzlement amongst some due to the more than anticipated sensitivity of the car to sidewinds. This was traced to faulty alignment equipment at the factory which had been setting the front wheel castor at 5.5 degrees instead of 3.5 to 4.5 degrees, and any owners who thought their cars had poor high-speed stability were invited to bring their vehicle in for checking.

At the half-year point Jaguar could claim more records. 23,663 cars having been made, 7 per cent up on the same period in 1986, with 50 per cent more cars being sold in the UK than in the previous period. European sales were also up markedly; only those in the USA had dipped (by 12.9 per cent) due to the run-out of Series 3 and the later introduction of XJ40 there.

Changes announced for the 1988 season were few. Heated door mirrors – already standard on Sovereign and Daimler models – were added to the XJ6's catalogued specification, the Sovereigns received standardised alloy wheels with nave plates and exposed wheel nuts, and all Daimlers now arrived with heated door locks and rear sun blinds. Finally, a new audio system styled to integrate with the centre console was specified, the 'built in' condition also rated as a deterrent to thieves; it gave an improved sound quality and now possessed additional features such as an automatic tuner memory store facility. The cassette storage arrangements were revised at the same time, and the new system was standard on Sovereign and Daimler cars and optional on the XJ6.

The birth of XJ40 had been drawn-out, beset with many difficulties – a good proportion not of Jaguar's own making – and resolved only at the expense of much effort and dedication. But any doubts that might have been lingering at Browns Lane up until the launch on the suitability of the car were dispelled within weeks as the initial enthusiastic reaction of the customer and the press was consolidated as the months went by with ever more orders. A mediocre reception for XJ40 would have spelled disaster for the whole company; the near-rapturous one that actually occurred was no more than was needed to put in place, as Sir John Egan stated in his annual report, "the foundations of a very fine business". To him, and his team at Jaguar, XJ40 represented not the end of a project, but the beginning of a new era.

Like any brand-new car, the first-year production XJ40s did suffer some teething troubles and, for a while, the now largely bug-free Series 3 XJ12 was, perhaps, the most reliable car to issue from Brown Lane. The new XJ6's electrical system – perhaps the most revolutionary feature of the car – did not initially match the reliability standards Jaguar had set for it, and there were some reports of inconsistent quality of dampers and the ride

levelling system. Then in February 1988, Jaguar issued a recall involving some 11,000 XJ6, Sovereign and Daimler cars sold on the home market due to 'isolated' instances of a fixing bolt failure on the front suspension's lower spring pan (if one did fail, the car would settle on one side but without any loss of control). However, most of these teething troubles were production-orientated and once the build-lines were themselves 'run-in', then XJ40's inherent reliability could surface and today, the type must be one of the most dependable luxury saloons on the market.

Certainly, the first full year's sales figures emphasised the success of the new model, and 1987 saw Jaguar achieve its fourth consecutive annual sales record, a total of 46,612 Jaguars and Daimlers having been sold worldwide (compared with 40,971 units in 1986 – which, of course, also included a number of Series 3 XJ6 cars). Of this total, 17,539 were XJ6s sold in the USA, a figure which would have been bettered had more cars been available. That country also took 5,380 XJSs, which at 10 per cent up on the previous best was also a record.

But the most significant news from Browns Lane in early 1988 was the 10 February announcement about the formation of Venture Pressings Ltd. This new company had been set up jointly by GKN Sankey and Jaguar to supply all major body pressings for the Jaguar/Daimler range by 1991. At last, Jaguar were to extend their manufacturing autonomy to body pressings, too, and the establishment of Venture Pressings was seen as the last major step in Jaguar's progress to full independence. Understandably, with the fate (and ownership) of Austin Rover in question, Jaguar were concerned over possible complications with their bodyshell supplies in future years. The plant was at Telford, where an estimated £35m was to be invested in equipment and project costs.

XJ40 was quickly pounced upon by independent 'go-faster' specialists; this is a saloon equipped with skirts and spoiler by TWR. The Wiltshire-based Janspeed concern were offering a turbocharger installation by 1987, giving the 3.6 engine nearly 300bhp and a 0 – 100mph time of 16.2 seconds, while AJ6 Engineering of Stockport produced a 4.3 litre conversion, achieved by boring the cylinders to 99.2mm diameter.

Part Two

The S.S. and Jaguar
saloons in competition

Introduction

Jaguar's involvement in motor competition began with touring cars.

In the beginning, there was no *sports* car; there was the Swallow *side*car, which achieved some success in trials and races in the 'twenties. The Swallow-bodied Austins started a trend of success in *concours d'élégance* which was taken up strongly by the new S.S.marque, with its immediate charm, in the early nineteen-thirties. The S.S. motorcar soon ran the risk of a reputation for 'all looks, no go'.

Getting the S.S. range into production at all was rather a nightmare. The S.S. II on the unmodified standard chassis didn't present too many problems; but the original S.S.I gave all kinds of trouble – as one might expect from a company making its first complete motorcar – and production didn't settle down until the revamped 1933 model was on the line. Parallel with development of the better-proportioned 'second attempt' coupe came the equally-attractive if more orthodox four-seat tourer, announced slightly later, in the spring of 1933. This was the model with which the competition story begins.

All S.S. models were then referred to by the press, very loosely, as 'sports cars'. After all, to define a sports car is a traditionally dangerous activity, and who is to say that any car designed to give pleasure is not a 'sports' car? Williams Lyon's aim was always to give his cars a look that was pleasing, anyway.

Nevertheless, in his original master-work *(Jaguar Sports Cars,* also published by Haynes), Paul Skilleter was in my opinion right to identify the first two-seater S.S. – the "90" of 1935 – as his proper starting point; surely there is just as much of a merger of touring and sports car principles in today's XJ-S, as there was when that 'short-chassis S.S.I' appeared?

In the way that Jaguar sports cars and sports-racers are linked with particular events – Le Mans, Reims and Sebring, for example – Jaguar saloons and tourers have *their* special associations. The Monte Carlo Rally and the Tour de France come to mind immediately. However, this competition narrative begins with an event that has brought success to Jaguar sports *and* touring cars in great measure over the years – the Alpine Rally, one of the longer-lived classic mountain tests.

Andrew Whyte

Chapter Thirteen

The International Alpine Trial

It all began with the Austrian Alpine Trials of 1910 to 1914. These continued after the war until 1929, when an 'international' label was acquired with France, Germany, Italy, Switzerland, and Yugloslavia all becoming involved at different times; and it was *truly* international, not only in its variety of competitors but also in its organisation. Each year it was the responsibility of a different national club receiving assistance from the clubs through whose territory the event passed.

France was in charge for 1933, and Nice was chosen as the finishing point. It had been the intention to begin the trial at Munich, but politics intervened and the start was moved to Merano in the heart of the Italian Alps.

A particularly satisfactory feature of the organisation was Monsieur Perouse's refusal to incorporate the traditional secret check. Instead all controls had printing clocks in competitors' full view. The cars themselves could be altered in certain respects, but basically had to be production sports or touring cars of which at least 50 examples must, theoretically, exist.

The two major awards to be gained in the International Alpine Trial were an Alpine Cup (teams) or a Glacier Cup (individuals). It was not possible to win both cups; nominated one-make teams and individual entries ran in separate categories within five classes for 1100cc, 1500cc, 2000cc, 3000cc, and over 3000cc cars. Only if a team car dropped out were the surviving members eligible for an individual award.

Four SS.I. four-seater tourers were prepared for the 1933 event. The three official team cars had large Union Jacks on the bonnet, and were painted red, white, and blue. This patriotic touch, however, gave many Continental observers the impression that the drivers must be Italian, German, and French, whereas the crews were in fact British!

The red car was handled by Symons/Wright, the white one by Needham/Munro, and the blue by Miss Allan/Mrs. Eaton. All had won Glacier cups previously, and were competition drivers of proven ability.

Humfrey Symons was the original *Grande Vitesse* of *The Motor;* an accomplished journalist, he later wrote for various national newspapers and for *The Autocar.* In addition to a fine rallying career he undertook a number of record-breaking drives across the Sahara and finally (just before World War II in which, as Flight Lieutenant, he was to lose his life over Dunkerque) broke the England-to-the-Cape record in an incident-fraught journey with the famous Wolseley 18/85 saloon *Voortrekker;* his Alpine co-driver James Wright, was a Brooklands MG driver. Charles Needham, a Manchester clothier, achieved success in rallies well into the post-war years, his name being associated particularly with Invicta, the marque with which he gained a Glacier Cup in 1932.

The third member of the S.S. team, Miss Margaret Allan, was one of the greatest women drivers in trials, rallies, and races. Probably her most memorable feats were achieved with Richard Marker's enormous Bentley which wore an ungainly Parry Thomas body picked up by Marker at a Thomson and Taylor sale, and which startled Brooklands spectators. (They found it difficult to believe that the diminutive figure behind the wheel could be in control of such an awe-inspiring beast as it bounded round the concrete bankings). Miss Allan was to marry former Riley trainee Christopher Jennings, later editor of *The Motor*.

Entered in the individual category was former boat-builder Georg Hans Koch, S.S.'s Viennese distributor, a keen sportsman who excelled in boats, motor cars, and on skis. In 1926 he won an Alpine award driving an 18/36 Standard. He was the only Austrian selling British cars during the economic crisis and, after World War Two, he and his wife became British subjects, to help facilitate travel between Austria and the UK. They were a wonderful team; after her husband's untimely death she ran the

Above: **The 1933 Alpine team at Swallow Road, with the cars of Symons, Needham and Allan ready for the company's first serious attack on a continental 'classic'.**

Right: **The Merano** *parc ferme* **during the 1933 Alpine; spare-wheel mountings were special of course – normally a single spare was carried at the rear.**
Photo: Autocar

Jaguar business in Vienna for many years.

The fifth S.S. entry was Austro-Hungarian – Count Orssich's S.S.I coupe. (Orssich was to achieve good results at Le Mans in 1937 and 1938 with the streamlined Adler).

The four factory-prepared cars were collected from the Holbrook Lane works by their respective drivers, and run-in on the way to the start, It was therefore a leisurely trip, and Symons – acting as unofficial publicity representative – had time to photograph the team crossing some of the passes that were to form part of the competition.

With the starting point moved from Munich to Merano there was no easy warming-up section, and the first day consisted of a circuit of the Dolomites, including the Monte Giovo (both directions), Falzarego and Pordoi passes, the latter being timed. There was no works representative to look after the cars and although the

R.A.G. carburetter people did send one man, he could do nothing in the face of chronic head-gasket failure which was to occur after new, untried high-compression cylinder heads were fitted at Merano, as a last-minute effort to gain badly needed power. Margaret Allan and Colleen Eaton lost a good half-hour on the first day due to carburetter trouble and their progress, particularly down the Monte Giovo as they strove to make up time afterwards, impressed onlookers greatly!

All the S.S.s got back to Merano successfully, but the team cars, at least, were already showing signs of their aluminium cylinder heads warping. Symons used up forty-minutes of running time on the second morning by changing the cylinder head gasket, but did not have time to warm up the engine before screwing the nuts down finally. Inevitably the joint gave way on the first pass, the Stelvio, but Symons got the car over the top and was able to coast down the other side to Bormio. Here he found

Count Peter Orssich's S.S.I. coupé in action during the 1933 Alpine; it proved more successful than the tourers. *Photo: Autocar*

The three S.S.I. team cars posing on the Stelvio – obviously photographed by Symons judging by the empty seat in number 18.

Pigé-Leschallas's A.C. being repaired, which was fortunate as this car was a sort of unofficial team-mate. (Leschallas's co-driver, Hugh Eaton, was the husband of S.S. team-member Colleen Eaton.) As the A.C. and the S.S.I. had both had enough, they continued together, Symons' car spending most of the time on the end of a tow rope, having finally expired on the next pass, the Bernina.

Margaret Allan's car did not last much longer, and retired with the same trouble while attempting the

Albula, another of the passes to be crossed en route to the second night's resting place, St. Moritz. Needham, however, managed to keep going despite water leaks, on the run over the Julier and San Bernardino to Turin where, on the fourth day, he was able to cure the trouble with a leak-stopping compound. Although the final stages from Turin to Grenoble and Grenoble to Nice included many high passes, and with the steering of his car becoming progressively stiffer, Needham reached the finish to be placed 8th in the 2-to-3-litre "individual"

Failure – the cars of Symons (18) and Allan (20) join the A.C. of Pige/Leschallas for repairs at St. Moritz, having been put out of the running by head gasket failure. *Photo: Mrs. M. Jennings*

Koch and Orssich (6th and 11th respectively in their class) and, beyond, one of the Bugattis that beat them.

class. Koch, an individual entry from the start, did well to make 14th best performance out of 121 starters, and take 6th position in that class, being beaten by four Bugattis (three of them supercharged) and a Hotchkiss. Orssich's coupé was 11th. In the 2-to 3-litre team event, Hotchkiss won easily from Daimler-Benz; the latter team had been well behind the S.S.s on the first day, and this was no doubt some consolation to Coventry,

Although hardly an auspicious opening gambit by S.S., they certainly did not disgrace themselves. The 1933 Alpine Trial had been a particularly hard one. Five S.S.s had started and three had finished, Koch's being the best-placed British car in its class.

It is worth noting that all expenses were paid by the competitors themselves, the cars alone being loaned free of charge. Margaret Allan and Humfrey Symons coaxed their cars down to Nice and were nursing them home again afterwards when, with no more gaskets or heads available, Miss Allan's car finally refused to function. Consequently a send-man-with-head telegram was despatched to Coventry; Miss Allan and Mrs. Eaton came home slowly in the Symons/Wright car – an understandable action, since they were footing the bills. It was some time before the car was collected, as Mr. Lyons was

indisposed at the time and no-one else felt they had the authority to send for it.

*   *   *

S.S. returned to the Alps in 1934 and this time they met with a measure of success. On this occasion the event was run by the Germans, who kept changing the stringent regulations and making them difficult to interpret. The closing date for entries was extended, and then the R.A.C. was inundated with enquiries from prospective British entrants who had not received their paperwork. The political situation was worse than ever, and a limit of £28 per person was placed on everyone entering Germany – enough perhaps, provided no emergencies arose. British competitors were, as in 1933, assisted by the presence of Captain Atkins of "Autocheques", who followed the event with a Carter Paterson lorry to carry all surplus baggage, never failing to reach the halting places at the end of each stage. All the same, it was quite a worrying situation financially.

Once again, five S.S. cars took part. Symons and Miss Allan, who had been so unlucky the previous year, drove MG and Lancia respectively; but Needham remained

Sydney Light was indeed a remarkable personality. During the 1930s he was regarded as something of a playboy, who spent most of his time as a weekend yachtsman or driving in rallies. His true character emerged however, a few years later. Although he could well have been commissioned he chose, in 1939, to become an "Able-bodied Seaman Light, Merchantile Marine". It was in this role that Sydney Light was awarded the George Medal for his brave conduct in the North Atlantic in 1940. The citation read: "Seaman Light's ship was torpedoed at night. He took charge of one of the boats, and after ten-days of privation, weariness and danger, they sighted a British ship. His courage, leadership, self-sacrifice and stout heart saved not only his own crew, but the sixteen men whose boat he had towed." (In addition to his own boat load of ten faithful to the marque and took with him Harry Gill from the S.S. works. Although 'works blessed', two of the three team cars were privately-owned 20hp S.S.I. tourers, driven by Needham and S.H. Light. Harry Gill had given himself a fright when one of the rally cars was stolen one night, in Coventry, before the rally.

men, he had also taken in tow, and shared supplies with, a drifting lifeboat from a Canadian ship).

Way back in 1934, however, Light was busy rallying his S.S.I. and, prior to the Alpine of that year, he had already had quite a successful run in the Monte Carlo Rally.

Mr. and Mrs. A.G. Douglas Clease were using an S.S.I. tourer regularly during 1934, and this car – the one they used as members of the Alpine S.S. team – was later the subject of a very favourable 20 000 mile report in *The Autocar*.

The official team was augmented by the 20hp S.S.I. tourer of F.W. Morgan and a Coventry-registered S.S.II. tourer driven by the well-known racing driver Norman Black – both these cars being entered in the individual category.

There were 122 starters, including 45 from Britain. For the first three days none of the S.S.s lost marks. The first day's run was from Nice to Aix-les-Bains via the Col de la Cayolle and the Col d'Izoard; the Galibier was blocked, so everyone had to go round by the Lautaret and the Glandon. Overheating was still a problem, but containable. Next day's route took off up the Isère valley and

The 1934 Alpine gave S.S. Cars something they could talk about – this is a page from their 1935 catalogue (although the S.S. team was actually third in its class, not second as the caption says here).

SOME RECENT ACHIEVEMENTS

The silver gilt plaque won by the SS Team in the International Alpine Trial, 1934.

S. H. Light, first in the unlimited open class at the Monte Carlo Rally Concours de Confort, receiving his award.

Car No. 52, driven by F. W. Morgan —winner of an Individual Class award— negotiating one of the numerous hairpin bends in the Alpine Trial.

The SS Team which gained 2nd place in the 2000 3000 c.c. class in the International Alpine Trial.

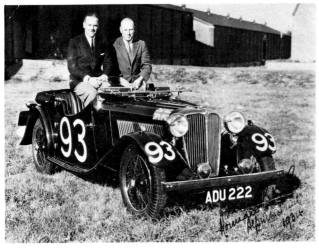

into Italy via the little St. Bernard then on into Switzerland via the big St. Bernard, and finally over the Col. du Pillon to Interlaken. Main passes on day three were the Grimsel, Furka, Splügen and Maloja. Day four from St. Moritz to Venice was the killer.

Actually, it was the Stelvio that undid the S.S.s. They had managed to do three days 'clean', but just did not have the performance to keep their schedule up through those forty-eight hairpins – although Douglas Clease said very nice things in print afterwards, pointing out that the S.S. tourers were "standard models with full four-seater bodies and big wings. Not with light bodies and small close-fitting wings as so many of the German cars were." (His car weighed 27.5 cwt.)

Top: The crew that slept in! Black and Harveyson with their S.S. II photographed at the Coventry works.

Left: Sydney Light with his S.S.I. on the 1934 Alpine Trial. *Photo: Motor*

Below: Harry Gill takes Needham's S.S.I. through a village during the 1934 Alpine. *Photo: Autocar*

On a dusty road, heading for Bassano del Grappa, Sydney Light went off the road, due to a puncture, damaging the car enough to lose maximum marks for the day. Needham 'cleaned' the *autostrada* speed test near Padua, but Clease (with ignition trouble) and Morgan dropped ten marks each.

Disaster befell Norman Black and Reuben Harveyson who missed their fifth morning call, and made no attempt to continue with their S.S. II tourer.

The final day – Zagreb to Munich over the Turracher Hohe – was uneventful apart from concern about the recent fighting, and the alarming enthusiasm of a Nazi welcome into Germany. ("We just hoped it was all a bad dream", John Dugdale wrote, much later. He had covered that Alpine for *Autocar*).

Despite their problems, the S.S.s won a Silver-Gilt Alpine plaque, gaining 2630 marks despite Light's crash. Maximum marks (3000 per team, or 1000 per car) were gained by the Talbots and Adlers, so the S.S.I. team had to be content with third place in their (2-to 3 litre) group.

In the individual competitors' 2-to 3-litre groups Morgan finished 4th equal, with 978 marks – best performance by an S.S. behind Carrière's Hotchkiss (1000 marks), Vial's Hotchkiss (999) and Legré's Panhard (995). For this performance Morgan, deservedly, gained a Silver-Gilt Glacier plaque.

The 1933 and 1934 Alpine Trials had taught S.S. a lot at relatively low cost to themselves (thanks to the enthusiasm of private owners) and their reputation.

There was no 1935 rally; and in 1936 it was Tommy Wisdom who was to show everyone the way – driving the new S.S. 'Jaguar' 100 sports car to a Glacier Cup and best performance overall.

Indeed (as recorded in Paul Skilleter's book, *Jaguar Sports Cars*) the Alpine Rally was to become the happy hunting ground of the S.S.100 and XK 120. The idea of a special cup for individual competitors losing no marks was continued post-War, the "Alpine Cup" (the old name for an unpenalised team prize) replacing the "Glacier Cup" title of the nineteen-thirties.

'Bobby' Parkes and Arthur Senior (3.4) before the start of the 1959 'Alpine', at Marseille's old port.

Eleven Alpine Cups have been won by Jaguars, no fewer than five by the great Ian Appleyard. The last two were, however, won by touring models and thus merit mention here. The French crew of José Béhra and René Richard and the Englishmen Bobby Parkes and Geoff Howarth took 3.8-litre Mark II Jaguar saloons on the 1960 Alpine, and each won a *Coupe des Alpes*. They were third and fifth overall, out of only six *coupe* winners – the others being an Alfa Romeo, an Austin-Healey, a Mercedes Benz and a Citroen. Béhra/Richard won the touring category. John Cuff drove Hugh O'Connor Rorke's modified 3.4 'Mark I' as though possessed, and put up best time of the day in the Monza high speed test; this crew did not finish the rally, however. For Bobby Parkes, of Small and Parkes (the "Don" friction material people), his *Coupe des Alpes* was really the culmination of many years of effort in rallying, including several very successful seasons in B.T.R.D.A. star events with an XK 140. Later he changed to a 3.4 saloon with which he would have won a *Coupe* in 1959 had he not driven *too quickly* up the Stelvio; so Parkes' 1960 Alpine Cup was particularly hard-earned and well-deserved.

1961 was even tougher, with only three cars getting through 'clean'; none was a Jaguar, but Peter Jopp and Sir Gawaine Baillie did win their poorly-supported class in a 3.8.

There was still a Jaguar presence in the 1962 and 1963 events, though the Alpine and the marque were becoming incompatible as, every year, the stages tightened and rally cars began to need more and more specialised preparation.

Bobby Parkes returned in 1962 with his 3.8 rally-cum-race car overloaded with a two-man crew of George Humble and Roy Dixon; they holed the sump early-on, then did the same thing to a piston during the speed test at Monza.

1963 saw the interesting 'one-off' entry of Dan Margulies in a 3.8-litre saloon, accompanied by one of Britain's top navigators, John Brown. Things started off quite well, and they made a good climb up the long and mainly fast Mont Ventoux stage. A traditional habit in racing and in rallying was to hold the bonnet on to its catches by the simple expedient of passing a hooked strap round the tail of the leaping jaguar bonnet mascot and

Parkes missed a *Coupe* in the 1959 'Alpine' by *exceeding* the required speed in one test (but the following year he won a *Coupe* with a 3.8 Mk II).

Peter Jopp stamps his route card at Schilpario *en route* to his 1961 Alpine class win in a 3.8 Mk II

Roy Dixon removing the 'leaping jaguar' from the bonnet of 'Bobby' Parkes' 3.8 (SRC 999) at scrutineering for the 1962 Alpine Rally at Marseilles, as required by French road regulations. Rear view of third crew man, George Humble.
Photo: Andrew Whyte

securing each end through the top of the grille. Some countries – France and Belgium come to mind – never allowed Jaguar to supply Mk IIs with mascots because of national regulations, and I remember scrutineers insisting on their removal by visiting competitors. Whatever the reason Dan Margulies, who had done a hectic 1955 season of road racing in a 'C'-type with Graham Hill but was not a regular Jaguar competitor, had not got very far into the 1963 Alpine when the bonnet jerked on to the first catch at high speed and (being rear hinged) snapped up and off its mountings in a trice! This was not the only problem, however, and the Margulies/Brown Jaguar retired early on the second day with major braking

trouble after a hectic night's motoring ... and that, really, is where the Jaguar Alpine story ends.

The 1933 and 1934 Alpines had been the rallies in which S.S. Cars had learned its first sharp lessons about arduous competition motoring. The successes of Jaguar cars regularly from 1936 through to 1960 suggest that they were lessons well-learned. When it came to the time that any serious rallyist needed constant attention from service crews, however, Jaguar as a company did not join in, for their products were becoming less rather than more appropriate to rough and tumble of the modern-style rally.

Early morning in a French Alpine village, and the impassive villagers have obviously seen dust and stones fly many times before! Dan Margulies and John Brown – Andrew Whyte's predecessor at *Motoring News* – hustle towards retirement on the 1963 Alpine (the bonnet is in the boot, having detached itself at speed).
Photo: Motor

Chapter Fourteen

The Monte Carlo Rally

Jaguar performances in the most famous of all rallies, the "Monte" were consistently outstanding during the nineteen-fifties. Twenty-years earlier, however, a low-slung S.S. could hardly have been expected to compete seriously with the rugged Hotchkisses and Renaults or the sporting Ford V8s and Delahayes that dominated the great trans-European winter trek.

This is not to say that the S.S. was unable to cope with a long journey on normal roads. S.S. had been a marque in its own right for only just over a year, though, when V.A. Prideaux Budge of Camberley set off from the John O'Groats start of the 1933 Monte Carlo Rally.

As they waited at Folkestone to board the *Autocarrier*, Budge and his two co-drivers posed confidently, leather coated, by their 20hp 1933-style S.S.I. coupe with its scuttle-mounted spotlamp and a union jack above its rally-plate. Unfortunately they didn't get far into France before damaging the front of the car after skidding on an icy and partly-blocked bend. What with getting the axle straightened, renewing several broken spring clips, and checking the steering and brakes, far too much time had been lost for there to be any real hope of ultimate success. Nevertheless, Prideaux Budge went on to reach Monte Carlo, within the time limit – thus assuring the first S.S. to take part in the Monte a finisher's plaque. Budge was finally placed 58th and by no means last. Back home he spoke highly of the car which gave him "no mechanical

trouble whatsoever", and praised the mechanic at Bouttencourt-les-Blangy who had done the afore-mentioned impromptu repairs in an hour and twenty-minutes for the equivalent of 17/6d.

The *Concours de Confort* was really the forte of the S.S. in the Monte Carlo Rally. Sydney Light's S.S.I. four-seater tourer was a class winner in the 1934 event.

In 1935 Hon. Brian Lewis had similar success in a similar car, beating a Delahaye and a Mercedes Benz; Sydney Light was a class runner-up to the overall *concours* winner, Pascoe (Talbot), using one of the newly announced S.S.I. Airline saloons. Lewis and Light were 54th and 64th in the rally proper; two other S.S. cars finished even further down the order.

1936 saw Lewis take second place in his *concours* class with the latest S.S. Jaguar saloon. Best S.S. result in 1937 was Harrop's 29th in the general classification; in 1938 Willing's 3.5 was first of all competitors in the *concours* but only 42nd in the rally itself.

At last, in 1939, the marque achieved a place on the Monte leader board. Accompanied by George Mongoletsi and William Currie, Jack Harrop brought a 3.5 litre saloon through strongly from Athens to finish tenth equal and to achieve best British car performance despite several off-course excursions in bad weather.

It was not until the third post-war event, however, that Jaguars again became serious contenders. The underrated Irishman, Cecil Vard, was still getting good results (in

Sydney Light takes his S.S.I tourer through the final test of the 1934 Monte Carlo Rally but ...

... Light's first prize was won in a *concours* class.

Lyons (right) and the Hon. Brian Lewis at S.S.'s front door before the 1935 Monte.

Below: Best SS performance in the 1937 Monte was by Jack Harrop, who finished 29th in the general classification – this is almost certainly his car; note twin spare wheels as on the 'Alpine' tourers. *Photo: Autocar*

J.O.H. Willing collects the *Grand Prix d'Honeur* **in the 1938** *Concours de confort.*

Porsches) well into the nineteen-seventies; back in 1951 he gained fame by bringing his Mk V Jaguar home an excellent third behind a 4.5-litre Delahaye and a Ford V8. Wally Waring (who was to succeed Ken Wharton as British trials champion that year) came 9th also in a Mk V.

Centre: **Jack Harrop and his crew check in at Salonika during the 1939 Monte.**

Right: **William Currie (left), Jack Harrop and George Mangoletsi (right) pose below the Acropolis, Athens, before making best pre-War SS Jaguar performance in a Monte Carlo Rally; the year is 1939.**

One of the most adaptable of drivers, excellent in driving tests and on special stages during over 20 years of rallying, Cecil Vard swoops up the ramp of the Monte Carlo GP circuit to take a superb 3rd place in the 1951 rally with his Mk V. *Photo: Autocar*

The 1952 Monte was more of a lottery than ever. Already its marking depended far too much upon "regularity" and "autotest" driving. This time it was the weather. Blizzards affected different sections of the entry in different ways. It was, nevertheless, a famous British victory when Sydney Allard's P-type Allard saloon – the only car to get through from Glasgow unpenalised – went on to win from Stirling Moss in a Sunbeam Talbot 90. There were no other British drivers in the top twenty. However in this the first major event for the new Mk VII, French-crewed Jaguars finished 4th (René Cotton), and 6th (Jean Heurtaux). Best British-driven Jaguar was Bertie Bradnack's very bent Mk VII (45th). The three next best Jaguars were all driven by Jaguar agents – Ian Appleyard (taking a Mk VII on his first Monte, 53rd), Reg Mansbridge (94th in a Mk V), and W.H. Wadham, co-driving a Mk VII with Waring (156th) – each out of serious contention because of the snow. Waring and Wadham had the consolation of winning their class in the *concours*, ahead of

the vast straight-eight Hooper-bodied Daimler which, driven by Tommy Wisdom and Lord Selsdon, had somehow ploughed its way into the top fifty in the general category – surely one of the more remarkable of Monte feats? Raymond Baxter and Gordon Wilkins in a factory-loaned Mk VII (LWK 343) ran out of road and time.

It had taken the French to uphold Jaguar honour in the 1952 Monte Carlo Rally. By 1953 more and more enthusiasts – mainly British – were taking part in the Monte lottery. This time the weather was kind, and the event (as I am afraid it often did) became a farce. More than half the entry (including 14 out of 19 Jaguars) completed the road section unpenalised, and an impromptu braking and acceleration test was held, simply to whittle down the field to one hundred for a final regularity test on the Col de Braus. Accuracy with a stop-watch rather than driving skill settled the outcome, and it was very much to Pat Appleyard's credit that her husband Ian's Mk VII showed only three-seconds of inaccuracy over the whole test. Unfortunately for them, the very experienced Gatsonides (Ford Zephyr) was only two seconds 'out' and they had to be content as runners-up! Cecil Vard was placed fifth in the now-obsolete Mk V, and Mk VII's came 8th, 11th and 15th driven by Donald Bennett, René Cotton and Ronald Adams respectively. Appleyard, Vard and Bennett shared the prize for the three highest-placed cars of one make.

By 1954 the consistently successful Jaguar drivers were beginning to emerge and be noticed when it came to the works lending-out Mk VIIs for the most famous motor rallies. Cecil Vard at last gave up the Mk V, and took the well used grey Mk VII (LWK 343) to finish a consistent eighth with co-drivers Arthur Jolley and Frank Bigger. Vard and Ronald Adams (Mk VII) were outstanding in the test on the Monaco Grand Prix circuit. Adams (with

Right: **Only 18 competitors got to Monte Carlo unpenalised in 1952; best Jaguar was the Mk VII of René Cotton of France (co-driver L. Didier), seen here at prizegiving.**

Below: **Another excellent performance in the 1952 Monte – a particularly tough one – was that of Heurtaux and Crespin of France in their Mk VII (Heurtaux was to be killed driving a C-type in a hill-climb).** *Photo: Louis Klementaski*

Ian and Pat Appleyard, accompanied by the bearded Louis Klementaski, spent a lot of time off the road in 1952, and finished 53rd. The next year as a twosome, they very nearly won. *Photo: Autocar*

The Appleyards' Mk VII may have come close to winning the 1953 Monte Carlo Rally, but Cecil Vard's was perhaps the most memorable performance. Having had a fruitless run in 1952 with a Lagonda, he returned to his old Mk V for 1953 – and finished 5th! No wonder he and Arthur Jolley looked happy afterwards!

Desmond Titterington) had led the rally after the regularity run from Gap to the principality, ahead of Louis Chiron (2.5 Lancia Aurelia GT). Inevitably, Chiron was quickest in his home town, with a best lap of 2-minutes 20-seconds; Adams was next (2-minutes 24.6-seconds) but he and Vard were handicapped down to 6th and 8th respectively in the final order. Charles Lambton's Mk VII won a *concours* award. An official team of Mk VIIs was entered for the 1955 event – Adams (PWK 700), Appleyard (SUM 7), and Vard (PWK 701), being nominated. Vard was heavily penalised at a secret check; Appleyard hit a rock and, later on, came to rest, creating a mammoth geyser as the result of a blown engine core-plug while on the mountain circuit; and Adams hit a parapet as a result of brake fade! The latter lost Adams only a few places and he finished 8th. Vard made a marvellous recovery from 84th after his penalty, to 28th

at the end, whereas the Appleyards dropped back from 11th to 83rd. Perseverence won the day, however, and the Jaguar trio did succeed in taking the nominated team trophy, as no other team got as far round the mountain circuit as they did. A Norwegian crew took first place in the rally (Sunbeam).

Just as it was beginning to look as though Jaguar cars were destined to be the bridesmaids of Monte Carlo, never brides, success finally came their way in 1956. Ulsterman Ronald Adams and PWK 700 – the dark green Mk VII he had used the previous year and that Jimmy Stewart later drove at Silverstone – teamed up with Dublin Jaguar racer Frank Bigger and Lisburn rallyman Derek Johnston (a former Circuit of Ireland winner); and a brilliant and thorough crew they made. With Adams driving for most of the trickier bits, but otherwise working to no specifically pre-arranged plan, the Irish

Above and below: **The Appleyards in the 1955 Monte before and after their Mk VII blew a core plug! Despite not completing that final mountain circuit, they were winners (with Adams and Vard) of the Faroux Team prize.** *Photo: Ian Appleyard*

Mk Vs were still at it in 1954 – here is the car of J.A.D. Lucas and L.H. Handley on the way to a 'finish' with snow tyres and shovel on the roof. No longer could the car hope to do well, though. *Photo: Motor*

After finishing 15th, 6th and 8th with Mk VIIs in the previous three rallies, Ronald Adams and his crew gave Jaguar an outright victory at last in 1956. *Photo: Motor*

483

threesome headed the field in a virtually trouble-free fair-weather run. Extra satisfaction came from beating Schock's Mercedes-Benz into 2nd place; Reg and Joan Mansbridge of Lincoln were 45th; Vard finished well down, but helped Mansbridge and Adams to give third in the team event to Jaguar.

The winning car was flown by Silver City Bristol freighter from Nice to Blackbushe, where the cameras and pressmen were waiting. Frank Bigger was quoted as saying the car ran "like a bird" and had "not the slightest whisper of brake trouble". Shortly afterwards, John Bolster tested the car for *Autosport*, and confirmed the braking powerful and fade-free.

With no 1957 rally (following Suez) and a new set of mystifying regulations for 1958, Jaguar cars stopped lending cars for rallies. The works continued to show an interest by advising competitors, doing a bit of preparation work, and having a factory representative in attendance; at least, as far as Dover!

The large Jaguars were of no further interest to rally drivers now that the 'compact' 2.4 and 3.4 had arrived on the scene; there were thirty Jaguar entries (mostly 3.4s) in the 1958 Monte – more than any other single make! 'Lofty' England clearly felt the competitors needed moral support, although some of the traditional Jaguar drivers were now in other makes – notably Adams in a Ford,

Above: In the late 'fifties, privateers could still enjoy the Monte, even it it was virtually their only competitive event. Vernon Cooper was one of the regulars – seen here between Luc and Langogne in the 3.4 he shared with Geoff Barker in 1959. They were 56th (about halfway down the field). *Photo: Maurice Rowe, Motor*

Raymond Baxter, flanked by 1956 'Monte' winners Ronald Adams and Derek Johnston (both from Lisburn, Co. Antrim), talks to Dubliner Frank Bigger (left)

George 'Bobby' Parkes isn't in this picture of the 1959 Faroux Team Prize winning 3.4s. His car (OKY 450) was co-driven to 8th overall by Arthur Senior and Geoffrey Howarth (right); Eric Brinkman (left) took John Cuff (arms folded) in YBP 33 to finish 37th. In the middle is the Philip Walton/Michael Martin car (GTY 7) which finished 9th overall and second (to Parkes) of all the Glasgow starters.
Photo: Motor

Bigger in an Austin, and Vard in a Simca. (When Vard's car crashed, it was towed to a garage by England's Jaguar, which must have been some consolation to the Irishman who had done so well, so often).

Force of numbers did not help the Jaguars; for 1958 was a difficult year, with plenty of snow and a 1000km final test out of Monaco. It could have been a good event but secret checks spoiled it. A special 'GT' Renault Dauphine won. Best Jaguar was the wire-wheeled 3.4 driven by Carris and Beziers of Monaco; they were second in class and 24th out of 59 classified finishers.

In 1959 there was again a large contingent of Jaguars, and Bobby Parkes's 3.4 won the Group 1 touring class, co-driven by Arthur Senior and navigated by Geoff Howarth. The Jaguar 3.4s of Parkes (8th overall), Walton (9th), and Brinkman (37th) won the nominated one-make

team prize. Coltelloni's Citroën was the rally winner.

There were not so many Jaguars taking part in 1960, and none qualified for the mountain test. Mercedes had a field day; Walter Schock (who had finished second to the winning Jaguar in 1956) was victorious for Germany. Still, there *was* a Jaguar connection. Two Jaguar apprentices, Roger Stephens and David Corbett, borrowed a Sunbeam Rapier and finished 37th!

In 1961, "the year of the small cars" (when a Panhard won), Eric Brinkman and Philip Walton finished well down (104th and 130th!) in their Jaguars, but Walton had the pleasure of winning the optional Mont Agel hillclimb easily with his 3.8. By now it was possible to work out who should be winning rallies on scratch, for the "special stage" had come to stay. It is perhaps interesting that the great René Trautmann (Citroën), although fastest over

the stages, was handicapped down to 19th.

The modernisation of the Monte began in 1962 when performance was rewarded by outright victory for Erik Carlsson (Saab), who repeated his success the next year. Even then a trickle of Jaguars would still appear – but the days of the privateer, especially in a relatively large and heavy saloon car, were gone. No longer was crossing Europe in winter an adventure to savour; and while rallying became a more specialised form of competition, the Jaguar concept of producing more sophisticated road cars became more specialised than ever, too.

Thus, by the mid-nineteen-sixties, Jaguar cars and motor-rallying had lost anything they ever had in common .... Yet there *were* drivers who kept on trying. An example was the extremely quick Lancashire driver, John Cuff, who took a 3.8-litre Jaguar saloon on the Monte as recently as 1966 only to become one of ten competitors – including the true winner, Timo Makinen (Mini-Cooper 'S') – to be disqualified for 'infringements' related to interpretation of regulations about dipped headlamps! To add that a French car won that rally would be a very political remark!

Above: **Michael Wallace of the Jaguar service dept. on duty at Dover during the 1961 Monte Carlo Rally. It wasn't a good year for Jaguars in this event, but this 3.8 (driven by Phil Walton) went on to win the 'bonus' timed climb of Mont Agel afterwards.**
Photo: Andrew Whyte

Right: **John Cuff (3.8) in the 1966 'Monte', at Dover. Lighting arrangements caused him to be disqualified.**
Photo: Richard Taylor

Chapter Fifteen

The R.A.C. Rally

Today, the R.A.C. Rally is one of the finest and best-organised in the world, with straightforward timing and tough special stages – mostly by courtesy of the Forestry Commission. On the other hand many years have passed since you could reasonably enter your everyday car and, without doing it or your bank balance too much harm, take part quite seriously in Britain's top motor rally; now, it would seem, there is more entertainment to be had from spending equivalent sums driving out to Britain's parks and forests, to watch highly-paid professionals taking much greater risks than you would personally. Modern rallying was summed-up, for me, in 1979 by the action replay of a Ford Escort 'ditch-hooking' and rolling onto its roof right under the BBC camera's eye, during a special-for-television competition between ace rallymen watched by millions – at home!

Britain's first R.A.C. rally took place in February 1932, and was hardly calculated to set the adrenalin running. The top places went to cars with fluid flywheel transmission which proved unbeatable in the slow-driving (!) eliminating test at Torquay – and therefore in the rally as a whole, which was won by Colonel Loughborough in one of the first Daimler-built Lanchesters. Second came J. Mercer's sleeve-valve Daimler Double-Six driven by an extremely tall twenty-year old, just ending a Daimler apprenticeship; his name was Raymond England. Forty years later he was to become Chief Executive of Jaguar Cars Ltd.

Young 'Lofty' England was too preoccupied to take much notice of three new cars taking part in the same event. Like most of the entry, they had normal friction-clutch transmission and stood no chance in the 'creeping' test. Their performance capabilities would not have helped much had the test been one of speed, either. They were called "S.S.", and one of them was entered by the late Edward Huckvale (Swallow's secretary, an ex-Singer man); the others by Douglas Clease of *Autocar* (this was the first of many rallies in which he drove S.S. cars) and the Countess of Drogheda; and even she of the very special colour schemes didn't pick up a *concours* award. Huckvale's widow and sons don't think he ever went in for a rally, so perhaps he was simply the official entrant. Nevertheless, it makes this event the company's first involvement with competitions (apart from the early sidecar days); and it was in the following twelve-months that much of the thinking was done that led to better performance, and to the S.S. company eventually designing and building its own power units. At the time, the youthful 'Lofty', with fourteen-years as a racing mechanic and war service still to come, can hardly have been guessing that he would ever control the fortunes of one of Britain's most successful post-War racing teams, or that these ill-proportioned coupes represented the evolution from Swallow to Jaguar.

The R.A.C. Rally continued in its weary way for several years, and most other road events followed the same

According to the results published in the *Standard Car Review*, 'plaques' in the 1932 RAC Rally were awarded to V. Budge, E.F. Huckvale, and H. Scott-Jones, all in S.S.Is. As this was the first-ever event for S.S. cars, it should be stated that the 'Huckvale' car was probably a factory entry for A.G. Douglas Clease; and that a C.E. Moy was also due to start in an S.S.I, but it is not certain that he actually did! However, it is pretty certain that the car in this picture is that of Kathleen, Countess of Drogheda, but the flat-hat makes it appear that she got someone else to drive in the final tests at Torquay! *Photo: Autocar*

A.G. Douglas Clease with his 'long term' S.S.I tourer in the 1934 RAC Rally., He always ran the latest S.S. in this event, and in 1933 he had driven a wireless-equipped S.S.I coupe. *Photo: Autocar*

Above: This is almost certainly A.H.G. Hooper's S.S.I saloon in the 1935 RAC Rally; he won a first class award. Note Tommy Wisdom looking on, with inevitable cigarette. *Photo: Autocar*

Left: Clease in the latest model as usual − Coventry registered too, if not a 'works' entry. Clease won a first-class award with this rare S.S.I drophead in the 1935 RAC Rally, which finished at Eastbourne.

The RAC Rally was becoming quite competitive by 1937, when there was also a 'general classification' to establish a real winner! The 1937 event was won by Hanah's SS Jaguar 100 sports car. One of the other 'Jaguars' taking part was I.W.H. Thompson's Coventry-registered OHV SS Jaguar tourer, seen here in a hill-start test at Hastings (Count T. Heyden's Delahaye awaits).

pattern – a series of monotonous runs from different starting points to a seaside resort, followed by a few manoeuvres and *concours d'elegance et confort* on the prom. (Contemporary advertising and reporting add to my 'cocktails-at-seven' impression). One should not, perhaps, be too cynical, for *concours* are still taken very seriously, especially among one-make car clubs!

The art of driving in the R.A.C. Rally began to mean more in the late nineteen-thirties, when S.S. 'Jaguar' 100s did particularly well. The event was revived in 1951, with Ian Appleyard doing exceptionally well in Jaguar XK sports cars – best performance in 1951 and 1953, 2nd in 1956, 3rd in 1952 – but never competing in it with a saloon. (It is, I think, a noteworthy aside that in his first-ever rally – the Lancashire Automobile Club's 1947 Blackpool event – Appleyard drove a 3.5-litre Jaguar *saloon* . For the record, he was second in his class and 44th overall).

Jaguar saloons fared well in their classes in the R.A.C. Rally for nearly ten-years. J.C. Smith's Mk V was third in the over-2500cc closed car class in 1952, despite the presence of more modern cars such as Jaguar's own Mk VII maid-of-all-work (LWK 343) on loan to Tommy Wisdom, who did not figure in the results, although he was quickest in class on the timed ascent of Rest-and-be-Thankful.

In 1953, Denis Scott took a Mk VII to 10th overall and a class win. A year later J. Ashworth's Mk VII was also 10th, but only second in class.

The 1956 'R.A.C.' marked the debut of the compact Jaguar 2.4 saloon and, with Ian Hall navigating, Bill Bleakley drove a superb rally to take the over 2-litre class and gain 4th overall. 'Suez' prevented a 1957 event from happening, but in 1958 Brian Waddilove won his class in a 2.4 while Brinkman, Sopwith and Rowe were 1st, 2nd and 3rd in the large saloon class, all in Jaguars.

Above: **Three Mk Vs chase an Austin A90 Atlantic round Silverstone during the first post-War RAC Rally in 1951.** *Photo: Autocar*

Right: **Tommy Wisdom gave the Mk VII its RAC debut in the 1952 event. He is seen during a test at Blackpool and (inset) waiting to clock-in at Onich shortly after making BTD in his class at Rest-&-Be-Thankful; he was not placed in the final results, though.** *Photos: Motor and Andrew Whyte*

Above: **Best RAC Rally performance for a Mk V was J.C. Smith's third in class in 1952; a few drivers went on competing with them after this however, including R.W. Blackhurst seen here at Prescott in 1954.**

Left: **The last good international 'place' for the Mk VII occured in the 1958 RAC Rally, when Tommy Rowe (at the wheel) and Tom Dooley came third in their class, behind the 3.4s of Eric Brinkman and Tommy Sopwith. Rowe bought the car (OVC 69, with which Ivor Bueb had won at Silverstone in 1956) from the works, and rallied and raced it successfully. This picture was taken on another rally at about the same period.**

1959 was the catastrophic year when a key road became blocked by snow, and the rally and its organisation were reduced to a shambles. Bobby Parkes's 3.4 saloon finished fairly well down the field but fifth in class.

Never again has the R.A.C. Rally sunk so low; indeed it rapidly improved its international status and style from 1960, when Erik Carlsson scored the only clear round in the first international British rally to feature special stages (if only a few) as well as some very 'tight' navigation. René Trautmann, who might have secured the European rally title, took his Citroen through a Yorkshire wall and out of the rally – leaving that year's Championship to Walter Schock of the Mercedes team which withdrew and went home to Germany pursued, metaphorically, by catcalls for not bothering to finish. Their departure made no difference to the remarkable performance of Jack Sears and Willy Cave in a 3.8 Mk II Jaguar, a compact car compared with the old Mk VII, but still hardly suitable for

tight schedules on narrow and twisting roads – or cross-country 'killers' like Monument Hill overlooking Loch Awe in Argyll. It was here that Carlsson's Saab, navigated by Stuart Turner, hopped and scrabbled over the ancient track to make sure of the only penalty-free run. Sears's Jaguar crunched from rock to rock, but survived this test with the loss of only two-minutes. These, plus a minute lost on the first night, were the Jaguar's only 'road' penalties. Sears and Cave ended the rally well ahead in their class and a terrific fourth in the whole rally beaten only by Carlsson's 'clean' Saab and the Austin-Healeys of Sprinzel and the Morley brothers, each with two minutes' penalty.

It had been a rousing end to a period of great success for Jaguar cars, sports and saloons, in Britain's premier rally. Now the event was committed to going "off the roads" and into the forests – no place for Jaguars, which failed to figure in the R.A.C. in 1961 (when John Casewell's 3.8 was a brave forty-ninth out of eighty-two finishers) or subsequently.

Chapter Sixteen

The Tour de France

As the R.A.C. Rally approached the end of its suitability for Jaguars in 1960, another highly individual international rally was developing as if tailor-made for the Coventry marque.

When the name *Tour de France* is mentioned, most people "think bike". The *Tour de France Automobile* was, however, a superb motor rally, combining tight-scheduled road sections with circuit races of up to two hours' duration each, and speed hillclimbs in the Pyrenees, Massif Centrale, Vosges, Alps – and once even of Corsica. It was created by the *Automobile Club de Nice* with help from the sporting newspaper *L'Equipe* and trade sponsorship, for it was a costly project. Jaguar XK120 sports cars were well-placed class winners in the first two events, Hache being 5th on 'scratch' placing in 1951 and Berthomier 4th the following year.

The first Jaguar saloon to win its class in the Tour was a Mk VII driven by Novelli and Guido in 1953. No Jaguars featured in the 1954 event, but it should be noted that a Frenchman called Consten finished 11th in a Triumph TR2. Following the disaster at Le Mans, there was no Tour in 1955; but it was revived in 1956 when famous racing drivers filled six of the first seven places. Fon de Portago and Ed Nelson (who were to lose their lives in that final, tragic, Mille Miglia only a few months later) won in a Ferrari 250.

From 1957, the Tour Auto took on a new format with two separate classifications – GT and Touring – and therefore two outright winners, although the marking system was the same for both; so you could still calculate an 'imaginary' general classification. The format remained the same until 1964, and Jaguar cars dominated the touring category for virtually the whole period. Ferrari 250s (latterly GTOs) always controlled the GT event.

It took several years for the Jaguars to start winning, however, In 1957, the Franco-Brazilian Hernano da Silva Ramos led for much of the rally in one of the new Jaguar 3.4-litre saloons before retiring and leaving the field open to a battalion of Alfa Romeos. Earlier the Da Silva Ramos/Monnoyeur car had been overtaken by the similar Jaguar of Jopp and Baillie; but the Britisher's lead had been shortlived, as a burst tyre took the car down a wooded bank at the Rouen circuit, and it was fortunate that no-one was hurt in the ensuing fire. Another 3.4, the earlier leader, retired too; driven by Consten and Renel.

For 1958, Da Silva Ramos switched to Ferrari and came third in the GT competition. Consten teamed up with Jean Hébert to give Alfa Romeo (and Hébert) their second successive touring category victory. Peter Jopp and Sir Gawaine Baillie (3.4) could manage only third place among the 'tourers'. Two other Jaguar 3.4 s had been put out while leading – first Sopwith and Goldthorpe whose car collided with a taxi, and then the Whitehead half-brothers whose car went off the road with tragic consequences.

Jaguars had done well in the first two *Tours Auto* (1951 and 1952) – but it was not until the third (in 1953) that a Jaguar touring car figured in the results. Novelli and Guido (and, it seems, A.N. Other) won their unmodified saloon class, and were certainly dressed for the job!

Peter Whitehead had raced successfully in the nineteen-thirties and 'forties, mostly in ERA and Ferrari cars; he had brought the C-type across the line first in the great Jaguar Le Mans victory of 1951; he had co-driven the D-type to *its* first race win, too, in the 1954 Reims 12-hour. Later in their careers Graham and Peter Whitehead often shared the wheel in long-distance events, and in 1958 their four-year-old Aston Martin DB3S was second at Le Mans. They had not been so fortunate in the Tour de France. In 1957 they had shared the wheel of a brand new Jaguar XK 150 fixed-head coupe in the vain hope that it could compete with the GT Ferraris and they had retired early with brake trouble. A 3,4 saloon in the touring category was their obvious choice for 1958. Peter Whitehead was in the passenger's seat when the car went into the rocky chasm that took his life.

Graham Whitehead went to France again for the 1959 Tour; his co-driver was Peter Riley. They had been lying second when forced to retire after a collision in fog. Da Silva Ramos returned to a 3.4 and the touring category that year and, with Estager, romped away from a gaggle of Alfa Romeos and maintained his lead to the finish. The name Consten did not appear on the 1959 results list, but it was to return with a vengeance! For four-years, from 1960 to 1963, Bernard Consten and Jack Renel were to

drive steadily but very fast to win the touring category outright.

From 1960, the 3.8-litre Mk II replaced the 3.4 as 'top tourer', and Consten and his white cars became legendary for their thorough recces, always followed by regimented progress in the rally-proper. From 1959 Jaguar Cars came to recognise the value of winning the Tour and gave increasing support to Consten and other Jaguar participants – especially the British ones – in preparation, technical advice and service throughout the nine-day event. When I was covering the Tour (as *Verglas* of Motoring News) in 1962, the Jaguar 3.8 "County" one-off estate car was frequently seen, thoroughly overloaded and with the tailgate taped up to keep out exhaust fumes, being driven hard by Michael MacDowel or Ted Brookes from the works.

France had always been an important market for Jaguar. The Tour while not providing the world-wide publicity of *Les Vingt Quatre Heures du Mans,* became an event worth winning; and so those vestiges of a 'competition' department remaining at Browns Lane concentrated their efforts upon this one endurance event during this period of the early nineteen-sixties. Most of the old racing team members worked in the experimental or service departments – many still do! – and preparation

The Baillie/Jopp 3.8 on the Montlhery banking *en route* to second in the 1960 'Tour'.

The 1959 'Tour' winners were Nano da Silva Ramos and Jean Estager in a 3.4, although the car in this picture is the Baillie/Jopp 3.4 which did not finish. The location is Montlhery.
Photo: Motor

Two of France's greatest touring car competitors – Bernard Consten (left) and Jose Behra (sitting on the 3.8 in which they had recently won a *Coupe des Alpes*) at the start of the Reims race in the 1960 *Tour de France*.

A Superb shot of the 1960 'Tour' winner Consten on the Col de Braus.

Consten looks on casually as a wheel is changed before the Col d'Aubisque climb in the Pyrenees on the way to victory, during the 1961 'Tour'. *Photo: Motor*

work for private owners continued to involve both areas. After all, even when Jaguar's racing activity had been at its most intensive, in the nineteen-fifties, 'Lofty' England had organised the programme from within Jaguar's existing facilities – *not* created a completely new department. This policy had added to a feeling of involvement in the company, and its progress, by virtually every Jaguar employee.

England's job, first and foremost, was that of Service Manager. By the early nineteen-sixties, however, he was moving quickly into the top echelon of management although he continued to control competition policy, it was the job of former Cooper works driver Michael MacDowel to attend to the immediate needs of serious private entrants in serious events. He covered the Tour three times for Jaguar Cars before leaving to join John Coombs, their distributor for Guildford. He returned to active competition motoring, too, and became British hill-climb champion; today MacDowel is a director of the Coombs organisation.

In 1962 MacDowel found himself at the centre of a controversy which was brewing-up over the fitting of 2-inch SU carburetters to the two 'British' Jaguars, whose crews were apparently the only ones to have correctly interpreted "Appendix J", as regards carburetter type. Consten, his plans laid with military care, was naturally put out as he watched Jack Sears (in Claude Lego's 3.8) and the familiar team of Baillie and Jopp build up a comfortable 1-2 position in the touring category. Soon Consten was his cool smiling self again, and not without reason.

Walking in from a vantage point on the splendid Charade circuit above Clermont Ferrand, I soon found out why the two leading Jaguars had suddenly gone missing. First I saw the flattened remains of Lego's bright

red Mk II lying by a cafe doorway. Sears had had the 'door closed' upon him while overtaking a Citroen, and it was fortunate that he had been thrown out while the car was rolling – for the cockpit had become very small! Further on, I came upon Sir Gawaine Baillie's car which had suffered a puncture on a fast up-hill bend, sailed over a bank, and landed in a heap on a road below. I considered Baillie and Sears lucky to receive only slight injuries.

After that, of course, Consten controlled the pace for the third successive year despite having the 1.75-inch carburetters, and any ill-feeling he may have felt was soon dispelled by the extra attention he got from the 'County's' crew after the favourites had fallen.

Although they couldn't spare the same amount of time as Consten, Jopp and MacDowel did spend a considerable time in reconnaissance, on behalf of Sir Gawaine

Top left: Jack Sears lost his lead in the 1962 'Tour' when the errant Marang's Citroen 'closed the door' on him while being lapped during the Clermont Ferrand race – the car was owned by Claude Lego. *(Above)* The factory tender-car, the one-off 3.8 'County' estate, overladen as usual, at Reims. Its crew was Mike MacDowell and Ted Brookes. Then *(left)* is the final race of the 1962 'Tour' at Reims, where René Richard beat José Rosinski. Final order of the whole 'Tour' (with Jaguars 1, 2, 3, 4) was Consten, Rosinski, Richard and Andre Chollet, all of whom are seen here. *Photos: Andrew Whyte*

1963 was Consten's fourth and greatest 'Tour' victory. Here he out-accelerates the Galaxies of Henri Greder and Peter Jopp at Le Mans. Both passed him, as usual, but then ...

... Greder spun into the sand at Terte Rouge, and spent the rest of the rally recovering (to seventh place at the finish). Annie Soisbault passes in her 3.8.

Baillie who was unlucky never to win the Tour – although he and Jopp did come second to Consten in 1960 and 1961. Ted Brookes of the experimental department had started covering the Tour in 1959, often travelling in company with Baillie's own mechanic. He remembers, in particular, the forceful driving of Da Silva Ramos.

For 1963, Consten's car was prepared in France, and Brookes was sent there to help. (In the days of Le Mans, Brookes had usually worked with the Belgian Jaguar team; today he is superintendent of the Jaguar experimental workshop.) It was reasonable, by then, for anyone to suppose that American cars would run away with the Tour; and Jaguar's competition side (handled, then, by Christopher Leaver – later, by Roger Woodley – both ex-apprentices) was, more than ever, an adjunct to the Customer Service function, rather than a major aid to likely winners of races or rallies. No-one really expected victory this time, but Brookes's visit to Paris was certainly an added guard against failure for the methodical Consten, who was now happy to use 2-inch carburetters.

Eternally second, Sir Gawaine Baillie finally gave up racing and rallying Jaguars, which certainly had not brought him all the success he deserved. Unfortunately, his new 7-litre Galaxie was no kinder to him.

The 1963 Tour was tougher than ever, with twelve-hours of racing on nine different circuits, seven timed mountain climbs, and some extremely 'tight' road work, much of which had to be undertaken at night; total distance was over 3600-miles.

As usual, Ferraris were to dominate the GT event. In touring, however, the Jaguar drivers were threatened not only with increasingly-quick opposition from Alfa Romeo, but no fewer than three of the vast 7-litre Fords which (with the Ford Lotus-Cortinas) were already prising short-distance international touring car racing from the Jaguar grip.

Nevertheless, Consten took an immediate lead at the climb of Les Trois Epis near the Strasbourg start, followed by the Galaxies of Greder, Ljungfeldt, and Baillie. Bo Ljungfeldt's car blew-up in the Nürburgring race, where Greder and Baillie overtook Consten; he knew better than to try to get his 3.8 anywhere near the flying Fords which disappeared into the distance at the very fast Spa and Reims circuits, too, So slight did he feel was the risk, Consten even allowed Jean Rolland (Alfa) to beat him at Reims.

Consten 'split' the Fords at Rouen; then Peter Jopp won the race at Le Mans for Baillie, while rally leader Henri Greder spun into the sand backwards at Tertre Rouge on his last lap, scoring maximum penalties. Rolland broke his Alfa's engine.

As the rally moved south the courses became trickier and the weather wetter. Despite a spin in the rain at Pau, Consten's Jaguar soon began to threaten the leading Baillie/Jopp Galaxie, which ripped its sump plug out on a level crossing and retired during the next night section. On that section Greder lost twelve-minutes while Consten lost only one, yet again evidence of this Frenchman's

The weather wasn't helping Baillie and Jopp to keep their lead in the Galaxie on the tight Pau circuit. Consten and Soisbault have taken up their final positions as they go through the station hairpin. Also 'in shot' are Roger de Lageneste (Fiat) and Paddy Hopkirk who was to finish third in the Touring catagory in this 1963 'Tour' behind the two Jaguars. Shortly afterwards the big Ford retired, having lost its oil – violently!

1964 'Tour': the Ford Galaxie is joined by four Mustangs – but still Consten outguns them at Reims! Eventually though, he had to let two of them stay ahead. *Photo: Motoring News*

The 1964 event was the last 'Tour' for five years; here Consten's Jaguar (*en route* to third place) leads the *Coupé des Dames* winning car of Louisette Texier (formerly Annie Soisbault's co-driver) and Marie-Louise Mermod through typical 'Tour' country (the girls 3.8 finished 6th in the 'Touring' class). At least Consten had the consolation of, yet again, taking the best aggregate times over all the timed climbs of the mountains he knew so well!

extraordinary ability neither to panic nor to blow an opportunity.

Although Greder in the surviving Galaxie made great efforts to regain the lead, Consten continued to turn in best performances in the hillclimbs, and gave Jaguar their fifth (his and Renel's fourth) successive Tour victory, with the similar car of French girls Annie Soisbault and Louisette Texier – also players of a waiting game – in second place, and Paddy Hopkirk's fighting Mini-Cooper 'S' (with superb night navigation from Henry Liddon) third, and winner on handicap. Eleven touring cars were classified, out of sixty-one starters, so it was another superb result for Jaguar; Greder managed to bring the Galaxie up to seventh place at the finish. John Sprinzel (co-driver with Andrew Hedges in an MGB which crashed out of the rally in the Pyrenees) described that Tour as "just about the best motoring all-rounder in the world" – despite a broken rib and severe bruising!

I have often felt that the *Tour de France Automobile* was underrated as a severe test, and have dwelt on it at length here for that reason. It was the event in which any observer, less biased than I, could see just how universal a high-speed touring car was the Jaguar 3.8-litre Mk II.

1964 marked the end of an era for the Tour and for Jaguar. In GT, Ford power struck in Cobra form – but at the end it was Ferrari in business as usual. In Touring, Baillie's Galaxie retired gloriously but expensively while leading a race at Reims. Four compact new Ford

Mustangs were there to take its place. Two of them lasted the distance, and it was the crew of Andrew Cowan and Peter Procter that broke Jaguar's five-year domination.

Yet again, the incredible Consten (with Claude Leguezec) took the "mountain championship" for best aggregate performance in the hillclimbs, but his Jaguar was finally placed an honourable third behind the two remaining Mustangs that had outpaced it on the circuits and kept up well on the road sections. For the second year, too, the Jaguar of Louisette Texier (partnered this time by Marie-Louise Mermod) won the touring category ladies prize.

The 'double-event' *Tour de France* was doomed; the cash had run out. For four-years it was forgotten.

In 1969 one of the greatest, yet relatively unsung, long-distance rally-drivers of his time, Bernard Consten, became president of the French motor-sport federation – which immediately came to the aid of the *A.C. de Nice*. The first of the revived Tours was, not unnaturally, a Porsche benefit in Touring *and* GT! Four-years is a long time ...

In the early nineteen-sixties, the *Tour de France* was the one event that led to specific work being done to improve the Jaguar Mk II saloon – especially in the mundane areas of mountings, attachments, and general bracketry. These improvements were very much to the advantage of the customer when the more sophisticated developments – the 3.4S, the 3.8S, and the 420 – were introduced.

Chapter Seventeen

A European Rally Championship

I t took self-discipline and a car that was either very strong or very fast (or a bit of both) to do well in the *Tour de France* which was, to my mind, the ultimate in traditional-style rallying. By this I mean the kind of rally privateers could enjoy. They could treat their cars as carefully or as harshly as they chose, and accept the consequences. I regarded it as a worthy 'successor' to the Alpine, and I believe that the marque's remarkable success in these two events is directly related to the character of the Jaguar car itself.

Before the 1939-1945 war, S.S. and Jaguar touring cars hardly featured in international rallying, apart from the Alpine and Monte Carlo results already recalled.

Although rallyist Mike Couper and writer Rodney Walkerley borrowed a 3.5 litre Jaguar saloon from the works in 1946 to do their own private Monte Carlo 'rally' (subsequently reported in *The Motor*, of which Walkerley was Sports Editor), the only classic rally to get going again quickly after the war was the Alpine. The Monte was not revived until 1949; but as fuel restrictions eased and car production recovered, rallying quickly grew in popularity to a level never previously reached.

1951 saw Jaguar sports cars winning the fabulous Liége-Rome rally (Johnny Claes and Jacques Ickx of Belgium) as well as the R.A.C., Tulip, and Alpine events – all won by Ian Appleyard who would have been European rally champion had there yet been such a competition!

In 1952, the Appleyards still used the famous XK 120 (NUB 120) in The Alpine and the R.A.C., but turned to a Mk VII for the Tulip Rally – finishing second overall to Ken Wharton's Ford. Ian Appleyard was still clearly Britain's best rally driver, but victory in the Liége and good placings in the Sestrière and Travemünde rallies put Helmut Polensky of Germany ahead of Appleyard at the top of the unofficial international rally league. Porsche cars won three major rallies, and Allards two so – despite a consistent season, with four second places including Appleyard's Mk VII success in the Dutch event – Jaguar cars did not end the year on quite such a resounding note.

Ten classic rallies were counted as qualifying events for the European Touring Championship which was finally launched in 1953, and, by the end of May, Appleyard was firmly in the lead, thanks not only to his second R.A.C. Rally victory in the XK 120 but two outstanding performances in the MK VII – 2nd in the Monte Carlo and 5th on the Tulip. As the season progressed, Helmut Polensky and his co-driver Walter Schlüter put in some stirring performances, and a rare crash which damaged the Mk VII's steering badly in the Norwegian qualifying event did not help Appleyard's chances. (A 'local' Mk VII, driven by Haaken Mathiesen and Per Stefferud, was best in the three special stages, and placed 13th overall).

Polensky and Schlüter ended the season with 74 points scored from four of the ten events, driving FIAT, Lancia, and Porsche. The Appleyards had gained 80 points (50

You could enjoy your motoring in different ways in the Britain of the 1930s – you could decorate your S.S.I saloon and just sort of stand there ...

... or you could try a local trial in your S.S. II ...

... or (like A.P. Smith and his 2.5-litre SS Jaguar seen here in Derbyshire) take off your front bumper, and do a proper national rally.

from XK scores, and the other 30 with the Mk VII) in five events.

It really did look as if Ian Appleyard was champion, and a photograph and eulogistic editorial were published in the Earls Court motor show edition of *Autosport*. A week later, editor Gregor Grant reported sadly that : "In common with the majority of Continental newspapers, *Autosport* fell into the error of awarding Ian and Pat Appleyard the 1953 European Touring Championship. Apparently scoring was on the basis of best performance in any four of the ten qualifying rallies ..."

So, the British Jaguar crew had to forfeit twelve points

and what would have been an historic title – but then Jaguar have never taken much notice of championships of any kind. In any case, Ian Appleyard had known the rules all along. He bore no ill-will, and regarded Polensky and Schlüter (who had also retired while leading the Liége) as worthy champions.

Appleyard then announced his retirement from regular rallying after seven years of outstanding results, nearly always in Jaguars. He did, of course, drive in several more rallies, the last time being in 1958. (Then he and Bill Bleakley took a 3.4 on the Tulip, only to drop out with recurring loss of the exhaust system!)

Ian Appleyard's first Mk VII (PNW 7) gave him second place in the 1953 'Monte' (*above*) and the fifth in the Tulip ...

... but his crash on the Norwegian (*left*) probably cost him the 1953 European Championship.

The Mk VII was a popular and successful car in the Tulip Rally, but it's not surprising that this one didn't feature in the 1954 results, judging by the level-crossing technique! *Photo: Autocar*

With his departure from the scene Appleyard's ability became especially evident by its absence! Apart from the 1956 Monte Carlo and 1959 Tulip, no more European Championship rallies were to be won by Jaguars.

Best result of 1954 was a class win and 4th overall by the Mk VII of Boardman and Duckworth in the Tulip Rally. At home, after finishing third in class in the Scottish Rally, E.R. Parsons (Mk VII) was declared outright winner of the M.C.C. Round Britain Rally, navigated by Mrs. J.G.M. Vann.

1955 was a lean year for Jaguar in rallying altogether but Boardman's Mk VII did win its class in The Tulip again, co-driven this time by Whitworth – and, of course, there was that rather lucky Monte Carlo team prize for the Mk VIIs. The outright Monte win for a Mk VII was, naturally, Jaguar's 1956 highlight; but the new 2.4 saloon's fourth place in the R.A.C. Rally was a notable debut that year, and marked the arrival of a Jaguar saloon that was competent and not too heavy either.

The best Jaguar result in 1957 rallying occurred when Mrs. 'Geordie' Anderson, accompanied by Jaguar racer Bill Pitt and Jim Abercombie, won her class in the 10 500-mile Round Australia Rally with a Mk VIII of all things! It was an exceptional performance; the Jaguar was beaten by six Volkswagens, which had a highly-organised service network throughout, but it finished ahead of every other competitor. Jaguars have not often featured in economy events, but it is interesting that Mobilgas included an automatic transmission class in the Australian Economy Run of 1958 – and that a Mk VIII Jaguar won it, driven by Dunning and Cash.

Although a Greek-driven 2.4 was second in its class in the 1958 Acropolis Rally, the highlight of that year was when two unknowns, Donald and Erle Morley, took their private 2.4 to a class victory, and best British performance (8th overall) in the Tulip Rally.

The Tulip had become the Morley's annual holiday. A new 2.4 had been ordered for 1956 but it didn't come in time, so the brothers had borrowed their father's Riley Pathfinder and took fourth place in their class. With the Jaguar 2.4 they had come third in class in 1957. After the 1958 class-win the 2.4 was replaced, and 1959 saw the twins setting off for Holland with a brand-new 3.4 saloon.

Donald Morley's 2.4 on the way to 8th overall, a class win, and best British place in the 1958 Tulip. In this Zandvoort race, the nearest Zephyr is Hoogoven's. *Photo: Motor*

That 1959 Tulip was one of the toughest ever, and the regulations went as far as to suggest it would be won on the road, rather than the subsidiary tests! The organisers were very nearly right; on the run from Noordwijk to the South of France and back, bad weather certainly looked like ensuring that no-one would maintain the set average speeds between each control. In the end rain and mist helped to reduce the number of 'clean sheets' to five. Erik Carlsson (Saab, 5th), Rob Gorris (Porsche, 4th), Peter Riley (Ford Zephyr, 3rd), Keith Ballisat (Triumph TR 3, 2nd) and first – with a total of 166 out of a possible 170 points from the tests – the Morley brothers (with Barry Hercock) in the 3.4!

After surviving several sections on which they had clocked-in with only seconds to spare, the Morleys' only real incident happened in the Vosges mountains as they were tiring towards the end of the rally. In their haste, after overshooting a junction, they reversed into some rocks. This may have led to breakage of the Panhard rod bracket (by no means unheard of on Jaguars!), which was their only mechanical trouble. This was welded at Eindhoven by the mechanics of N.V. Lagerwij's of the Hague, Jaguar's Dutch importers.

Donald Morley made quite sure of victory by winning his race at the Zandvoort circuit. Second in the class was Eric Brinkman (3.4) with Coventry man Frank Ward fourth – despite co-driver Gerry Cooper rolling Ward's 3.4 on to its roof-lamp and out of the race, right in front of the grandstands, while doing battle with a Chevrolet Impala!

"Maybe Lofty's paying your expenses", Marcus Chambers joked, on the boat home, and the Morleys just smiled back. In fact, they were given a celebration lunch at the works. "Jaguar put the car right", Donald Morley tells me, "and I ran that 3.4 for six years." Meanwhile, Chambers sent the popular and unassuming brothers an invitation to join his Abingdon team – which they did; but they never signed a contract! On the other hand, their rallying was to be free from now on, and they were about to enjoy six seasons of brilliant success – mostly in the fearsome (but surely, not "big"?) Austin-Healey 3000 with which they invariably put up best individual Tulip Rally times and very nearly won an Alpine *Gold* Cup –

Above: **Donald Morley steps into his 3.4 to complete the job he set out to do, and *(left)* romps away from the rest of his class to win the 1959 Tulip Rally. It was this fine win that got the quiet Suffolk-farming Morley brothers the BMC works team place that would bring them fame on a par with that of Ian Appleyard.**

In the same race at Zandvoort, Brinkman and Cooper sandwiched Steunebrink's Chevrolet Impala in a spectacular battle. Cooper (third in this picture) rolled Ward's 3.4 out of contention. Steunebrink was to become a Jaguar enthusiast himself and, driving a 3.8, was to finish second in class in 1960 and finally win his class in the 1961 Tulip Rally.

Plaut and Heinemann of Germany scoring a victory for the 3.4 in the over-1.6 Touring class of the 1959 Sestrière Rally.

M. Lloyd and P. Walker, 2.4, on the 1959 Coronation Safari. They did not figure in the results, but this shot made a lovely cover for the Jaguar apprentices' magazine!

Gerry Flewitt and his class-winning
2.4 in the 1959 Scottish Rally, at
Invergarry. *Photo: Andrew Whyte*

before quietly returning to their Suffolk farms full-time. The Morleys were always fond of the Jaguar marque, and would have liked to see the E-type developed into a rally car of the kind that could do very well in the Liége or the Alpine. (Donald Morley has now been an XJ owner for many years).

The face of rallying was certainly changing by 1960. Nevertheless, the introduction of the Mk II, with 3.8-litre engine option, gave Jaguar a new lease of life that year.

As well as consolidating their position as 'the cars to beat' in the *Tour de France,* the smaller Jaguar saloons gained five class wins in 1960 European Championship rallies. Helped by a non-saloon class victory in the Tupli (by the XK 150'S' of British stalwarts Eric Haddon and Charles Vivian), the Jaguar marque was rated second only to Austin-Healey among British-made cars in championship events. Austin-Healey had eight class wins – including a fantastic outright victory by Pat Moss and Ann Wisdom in the Liége – Jaguar had their six, Triumph five, and Sunbeam four.

In 1961, however, Jaguar's European Championship class-wins came down to two; in 1962, just one; and in 1963, the whole Championship rally structure changed – the trend towards a *World* Championship of rallies had begun.

Non-championship successes kept popping-up however; for example, there were many other high-speed rallies in France besides the *Tour de France* – like the *Picardie* and the *Rallye des Routes du Nord* – in which the Mk II throve. The international Circuit of Ireland, with its fast closed-road sections, was also good Jaguar country, although the marque never won it outright. In 1961, Bobby Parkes (3.8 MkII) and John Cuff (modified 3.4, with Hugh O'Connor-Rorke) each won their classes.

As the character of rallying and rally-cars changed, Jaguars became a decreasingly familiar sight – as did larger cars generally.

For a brief period, the big American Fords showed well: Henri Greder and Marcial Delalande took a Ford France-entered Falcon Futura Sprint to victory in the touring section of the Tulip Rally of 1963. Tulip scoring was based on 'class improvement' which is unfair in that the strength or weakness of the opposition, in your class, directly affects your own marks towards a general classification. For example, the Morleys (driving for BMC) made best 'scratch' performance in their Austin-Healey 3000, but failed to win the GT section simply because of the retirement of someone in another class! Anyway, the Frenchmen romped home in the touring

'Bobby' Parkes was one of the first regular 'mainlanders' to compete in the Circuit of Ireland rally; he won his class with an Austin-Healey in 1960, and again in 1961 with his 3.8, seen (right) just before assaulting one of Ireland's greatest special stages – the Tim Healy pass. Here, co-driver Geoff Howarth shares a quick thirst-quencher with the crew of the 'official' works/army Vauxhall, which was navigated into second place in the same class by Second Lieutenant Andrew Whyte, RASC! *Photo: Andrew Whyte*

Swedes Lundberg and Lindström (3.8) at the Spa circuit – one of the tests in the 1963 Tulip Rally. They were second in class.
Photo: Andrew Whyte

Navigated by the late Barry Hughes – a glass-blower by profession, but also one of Britain's best 'spare-time' co-drivers – the John Sprinzel 3.8 Jaguar makes its way to third in class in the 1963 Tulip Rally.
Photo: Andrew Whyte

Below: One of Britain's best-known rallyists, John Sprinzel, photographed during a pre-Tulip (1963) visit to the Coventry works service department (it was the only time he drove a Jaguar in an international rally).
Photo: Andrew Whyte

category, and took the big saloons class from the Swedes Lundberg and Lindström in a 3.8-litre Jaguar saloon. Third in that class came Britain's John Sprinzel and the late Barry Hughes in another privately-owned Jaguar 3.8 – a virtually standard car that gave no trouble at all, whereas the winning Falcon needed a lot of attention from a host of service crews, including a new rear axle.

That is something that needs reiterating: all Jaguar's success, or otherwise, in competition has been related to the basic reliability of the vehicle. It must be said that Jaguar showed enthusiasm when it could – like when Bob Berry and Alan Currie from the works used their Mk VII tender car to try and keep a pass open during a Monte blizzard in the early 'fifties. The company never contemplated more than nominal help, and often that had to come from the dealer network rather than the factory itself. Entrants in rallies might get the factory to service their cars but, apart from a nice letter of good cheer from

'Lofty' England or PR-chief Ernest Rankin, that was usually *all* they got from Coventry – they were on their own!

The rally car and the preparation it receives has now moved as far away from everyday motoring as today's Le Mans winners. Commercialism and the media have popularised rallying into becoming a 'Superstar' sport – but the budgets of today's rally teams (never mind inflation) could not have been provided by Jaguar Cars at any stage of the company's development.

For the 'shoestring' assistance given to (say) Consten or the Appleyards – let alone other rally crews without their track-record or their association with Coventry – Jaguar's return from international rallying in terms of good results must have represented incredible value for money. As with the World Sports-Car Racing Championship, one cannot help feeling that, with a little more planning, Jaguar cars could have won a few championships – but then, in racing as in rallying, Jaguar always went for a limited programme and individual wins. Tempting they might be, but championships were never to become a Jaguar priority.

Chapter Eighteen

Marathons, M.P.H. and Monza

Before moving on to pure racing – which Jaguar was to dominate for so long – it is important to ensure that certain less specific, yet competitive touring car happenings are recorded.

It is already clear that *concours* were the forte of Swallow-bodied and S.S. touring cars in the nineteen-thirties – apart from the odd class win in rallies like the Scottish and the Welsh. All the same, the S.S.I. tourer's performance was quite respectable, as shown by Needham's 50.2-seconds for the 1000-yard ascent of Shelsley Walsh hill in the beautiful Teme valley, still one of Britain's best motoring venues, and by Leather's Brooklands lap time of 79.05mph during a one-hour speed trial in 1934.

It was the S.S. Jaguar 100 2-seater that was to take most of the laurels, over the years that followed.

Best pre-War result for a Jaguar saloon was Harrop's tenth-equal in the 1939 Monte, as previously recorded; then shortly after the war, Rodney Walkerley and Mike Couper hatched their plot – involving a similar 3.5-litre saloon – to create their own private Monte, as there was still no official one! Couper was a St. Albans motor-businessman and successful competition driver. Walkerley was sports editor of *The Motor*, better known as "Grande Vitesse". They borrowed the car from the works and, apart from some short cuts due to shortage of petrol coupons, more-or-less followed the familar route from Calais to Bordeaux, then inland as far as Lyons before heading south again to Monaco. January 1947 was snowy

all over Europe, and the pair did well to average more than 25mph for the journey – including fuel and meal stops.

They frightened themselves several times, trying to keep up impossible averages over snow-covered *cols* and, reading between the lines it is apparent that the long, low saloon was hardly ideal for such games and grateful for the softness of the adjacent snowdrifts! Nevertheless, the adventure was completed with the car virtually unmarked. "We never had the slightest trouble with any part or component", Walkerley declared in the three-part article that followed, "and no tool was touched from start to finish."

Anthony Noghes and his committee of the A.C. de Monaco had apparently given up Couper and Walkerley for lost, and treated them to a gala banquet that would have done credit to a real Monte.

Five years later a similar car set off on a similar route but for a quite different purpose. *This* 3.5-litre saloon had been built in 1949; but it had just been back to Coventry for a rebore and major service. Behind it there followed an Alperson Streamline Sprite caravan. The route remained similar only as far as Bordeaux.

Martin Lumby, Publicity Manager of the Caravans International group told me the background to it. "The caravan 'industry' was then rather a jungle, and some makers foisted on to the public a load of rubbishy old boxes-on-wheels under the name of 'caravans'. Even among the 'honest' makes the poor buyer had little hope

Right: One of the few consistently successful S.S.I drivers was Charles Needham. Here he is winning his class on the 1934 Scottish Rally (with Dornoch Firth beyond).

Below: 10 000-miles around the 'Med' with a 3.5-litre Jaguar and a Sprite caravan at an average of 30mph and 16mpg – quite a demonstration, in 1952!
Photo: Martin Lumby

of sorting out one from the other." Sam Alper, the young boss of Alperson Products Ltd., had a flair for promoting the caravans he made, and became famous for the stunts he dreamed-up. One of his first was also one of the longest and toughest of all – to encircle the Mediterranean in one go!

Sam Alper, Graham Hoare, and Martin Lumby, set off on 2nd April, 1952; they travelled for thirty-four days and visited agents for another seven; and they clocked-up 10 000-miles just before driving on to the boat home on May 12. For the whole trip they had averaged just under 30mph (excluding stops) and very nearly 16mpg.

Lumby was associate editor of *Caravan and Trailer Trades Journal* at the time, but he prepared reports on the journey for more than one publication. In *The Motor* he wrote of the Jaguar's need for better ground clearance. "Our Dunlop tyres on the car were still the original set and on the van they had been changed half-way round; there had been two punctures on the car and one on the van. The worst troubles on the car were the failure of one of the fuel pumps in Greece and the rev. counter in Jugoslavia. The rear springs had weakened and the tail end was an inch or two lower than when we started." On the return leg through Greece the exhaust was damaged so badly, during a four-hour run in which thirty-miles were covered, that they were forced to do what most other motorists did: they put the outfit on a train. Later, still in Greece, the heat was nearly too much for the Jaguar, which boiled three times in one day.

It was a good demonstration for Sprite Caravans, as the company was to be called; and for Jaguar, despite (or because of) its being two models obsolete!

Sam Alper is now chairman of Caravans International which includes Eccles, about whom I cannot resist quoting a cautionary tale told me by Martin Lumby. "Every year in the '50s brought new teams of undergraduates seeking sponsorship to drive to some outlandish spot. In one massive 'con' of this kind the perpetrators charmed a car out of another Coventry manufacturer and from Eccles they got a 12ft. caravan adapted to float, carry girder-type bridges, be pulled by oxen, and even be lifted clear of the jungle or swamp by balloon! It was called the Pan-American expedition and was to run from Alaska to Tierra del Fuego. They shipped to New York, did a spot of high living and sold everything, never to be heard-of again. The only publicity was a scandal story in, I think, the *Sunday Pictorial*."

In the motor industry, one often felt regret when turning-down ideas for promotional projects that are 'different'; but one was likely to sleep better! In any case, Jaguar Cars Ltd. was never famous for instant philanthropy.

Incidentally, Martin Lumby is a past winner of the British Caravan Rally, although not with a Jaguar. The marque *has* featured in the results, however, and I have seen for myself the speed with which an XJ6 is able to tow

L. Muncaster's XJ-6 making best time round Snetterton during a British caravan rally!

a caravan round the Snetterton circuit, albeit in a series of rather alarming six-wheel slides.

In terms of sheer maximum speed, it was expected that the Mk VII would be the first Jaguar saloon to exceed 100mph in standard form. In competition it was verified first by motoring scribe Tom McCahill at the 1952 Daytona speed Trials; then in April 1953, Norman Dewis took a well-tuned Mk VII along the Jabbeke highway in Belgium at 121.704mph. (This effort was incidental to running a C-type up to 148.435mph, which Jaguar claimed as a world production car record).

Record-breaking over longer distances was something Jaguar had experienced with the XK 120's one-hundred-miles-an-hour-for-a-week run at Linas-Montlhéry in 1952; but as far as Jaguar saloons were concerned it was the oil company Castrol that took the initiative in this field.

March 1963 saw a silver-grey 3.8-litre Jaguar Mk II, registration number 7116 VC, arrive at an unusual location – Monza! The hard winter of 1962/3 had affected Italy badly, and snow had been cleared away from the famous circuit only a few days before the Castrol-Jaguar team moved in.

The car had been prepared in the Jaguar Service department, mostly by Ron Bromage and Peter Chambers who were to be fitters-in-charge in Italy assisted by Castrol personnel and Jaguar apprentices Brian Jacques and Clive Martin. Team management was in the hands of Jimmy Hill, Castrol's competitions chief, with 'Lofty' England on hand to advise. The presence of Ferrari held up proceedings and the whole affair nearly didn't get off the ground at all, for the 3.8 (laden to over 35cwt!) soon broke one rear axle tube, and then another! The huge centrifugal force generated every time the car thumped and banged its way round the aging concrete banking could spell only structural disaster. Had there been an

Above: Tom McCahill underlined the Mk VII's 100mph potential at the Daytona Speed Trials in February 1952, returning 100.9mph – the fastest stock saloon car speed ever recorded up until then on the famous Florida beach. This was inspite of heavy winds and a soft surface; a standard XK 120 open two-seater recorded an average of 119.8mph at the same time and was the fastest standard sports car.

Norman Dewis, Jaguar's chief experimental test driver, takes good old LWK 343 along the Belgian motorway at over 120mph in 1953. *Photo: Jaguar Cars*

Jaguars can prove *economical* in competitions, too! This 3.4 won its class in the 1958 Rhodesian Mobilgas Economy Run, averaging 35.59mpg; this performance was backed-up in 1959 when J.B. Scott's 3.4 – seen here on Bwlch-y-Groes – averaged 34.20mpg in the British Mobilgas event.

opportunity to practise properly on location, things might have been different. As it was, the attempt was called-off while all unnecessary weight was removed and yet another axle fitted.

This time there was no mistake. The team of experienced drivers – Geoff Duke, John Bekaert, Andrew Hedges, Peter Lumsden and Peter Sargent – set off again and took four international Class C (3 to 5-litre) records, all at well around 107mph.

Very unfortunately, because the circuit had been booked in advance (and, of course, because the Castrol team were now behind schedule) the Jaguar had to be called in after just four-days.

Suddenly, after the night-and-day drone of the 3.8 engine and the even louder thunder of rubber beating concrete, there was silence – but not for long. Soon after the champagne had been poured over the Jaguar's bonnet, and paraphernalia removed to the paddock, the silence gave way to a harsh crackle as the Zundapp team got down to their business ... You had to queue-up, if you wanted to use Monza!

The four-day average speed of 106.62mph., including scheduled stops every three hours, showed that the 3.8 could have gone on and beaten the 100mph for-a-week figure easily.

As it was, after official verification of the engine

The flag falls at Monza, March 1963. *Photo: Andrew Whyte*

This sequence of pictures shows the terrific hammering which the suspension of the 3.8 underwent on Monza's far from smooth banking – and this went on for 10 000-miles! *Photos: Andrew Whyte*

Right: Team leader Geoff Duke infuriates rather than enthuses John Bekaert with his somewhat informal pit-signalling! *Photo: Andrew Whyte*

Below: Routine pit-stop at Monza: Dunlop's Vic Barlow checks tyre temperatures and wear, while Clive Martin of Jaguar checks oil; beyond him (in flat hat) is project organiser Jimmy Hill of Castrol. *Photo: Andrew Whyte*

specification, I was given the task of getting her to the show on time! The 'high' axle and XK exhaust (the nearest things to major departures from standard) made the night run down the Rhône valley from Brig to Martigny a truly memorable one. Next day, after several press demonstrations, the Jaguar was put on display in Geneva's exhibition hall, to become star attraction of Jaguar's traditional prime site there.

So favourable was public reaction that the problems were soon forgotten, and Castrol and Jaguar came away from the exercise with the feeling that it had all been worthwhile – the event, perhaps, consciously going some way to countering the rapidly approaching American threat in British touring car racing.

Travel and champagne stained 3.8 takes pride of place at the Geneva Show, 1963.
Photo: Jaguar Cars

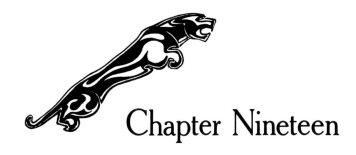

Chapter Nineteen

Silverstone in VIIs

While civilian business and pleasure were taking their first steps after World War II, Britain's motor-manufacturers were finding their feet, too – and the sure way of getting into production quickly was to revive what you had been making in the nineteen-thirties.

If your company was new to car-making, then of course you had to start from scratch; and Donald Healey, always something of a human dynamo, was just about the quickest off the mark. In 1946 he was producing sporty Riley-engined cars and was soon entering them in competitions. Most distinctive and original in its appearance was the Elliott-bodied Healey 2-door saloon which possessed an extravagance of line worthy of a Paris coachbuilder yet managed to retain compact dimensions and balanced proportions. I still find it a most attractive-looking car.

In contrast to Donald Healey and his small works twelve-miles away in Warwick, William Lyons had problems more akin to the mass-producer. S.S. Cars Ltd. had been heavily engaged on War work; in peacetime they needed relatively high output.

In 1945 the name "S.S." was dropped but, for the next three years, the 'Jaguars' that rolled along the wooden floors and down the ramps of the Holbrook Lane works were virtually the same as their pre-War counterparts. In 1948 came the Mk V – a great car but clearly an interim model, with its running boards and its Weslake-Standard engine.

It was the Mk VII – introduced in 1950, in full production in 1952 (following the move to Browns Lane) – which brought Jaguar Cars right up to date and into the 100mph class.

From almost every point of view, related to Jaguar's historical development, the Mk VII represents the cornerstone of the company's rise to greatness.

Racing hardly played any part in the Mk VII's life – except at one venue, and that was Silverstone. The XK 120, the C-type, and the D-type – *they* were the cars around which Jaguar's competition prowess was to be built.

Of all the circuits tried-out or proposed after the War, Silverstone soon emerged as Britain's motor-racing heart. It went 'international' in October 1948 with Formula One and 500cc races, and the same basic menu again in May and August 1949 – but at the latter meeting, sponsored by the *Daily Express*, there was an added attraction. Billed as a production car race, it attracted a mixture of sports and saloon cars – and it was won by a Jaguar XK 120. While they ran together it was inevitable that a sports car would win, and for May 1952 it was decided that it was high time to have a saloon car event in its own right.

Healey's lightweight Elliott body had already been superseded by much heavier Tickford coachwork of considerably less character. (I suppose it must have been quieter and more refined). The lone Healey entry was, naturally enough, an Elliott saloon and, with Ken

Wharton at the wheel, it made best official lap in practice, in 2-minutes 16-seconds.

Stirling Moss in the works-entered Jaguar Mk VII could manage only 2-minutes 18-seconds – officially 2-minutes, 19-seconds – a respectable enough time when you realise that it was about fifty-percent heavier than the Healey. The car was prepared in the service department at Coventry and fitted with an engine and close-ratio gearbox built and tested in the engineering experimental department. It incorporated one-inch diameter torsion bars, 'export' shock absorbers, 4.27 to 1 axle, 17.6 to 1 (XK 120) steering and XK 120 exhaust system. Brakes were unmodified, and the car was tested at Lindley (the motor industry test track near Nuneaton) a week beforehand.

The 1952 *Daily Express* meeting was the first to use the

Above: There was virtually no pure touring car racing pre-War, but there *was* great variety to be found at Brooklands! This strangely grouped field includes two SS Jaguars and many other makes to fascinate the thirties historian. *Photo: Autocar*

Right: Stirling Moss takes the chequered flag to start Jaguar's run of victories in the Silverstone touring car races; Moss also took fastest lap in this 1952 event. *Photo: Motor*

Jaguar boss William Lyons – soon to be *Sir* William – at Silverstone with Stirling Moss, who scored so many good Jaguar victories, including the first two touring car races (1952 and 1953 in LWK 343).

Above: **Close-up of Moss driving determinedly in LWK 343, to finish 3rd in 1954 – after rocking the car to free the starter. (Lucky it was a Le Mans start!).**

Top: **Bertie Bradnack finishing fourth in Silverstone's first touring car race, 1952.**

Centre: **Stirling Moss, winning again in 1953.** *Photo: Guy Griffiths, courtesy Jaguar Cars.*

new start and finish location – just after Woodcote Corner, where "it all happens", still! From the Le Mans-type start, Moss made his usual quick getaway in LWK 343 which had already taken part in the Monte Carlo and RAC Rallies, and was to become the hardest-worked of all Mk VIIs. Wharton drove the Healey very well but, inexplicably in view of his practice time, could not get very close to Moss, who pulled away at an average of nearly a second a lap. Sydney Allard in his Monte-winning P-type Allard saloon couldn't get near the leaders, but finished third ahead of Bertie Bradnack's Mk VII Jaguar – which finished fourth and was the last non-lapped car. It had moved ahead of Gerry Dunham's Alvis and Tony Crook's Bristol after a slowish start, for the Bradnack frame was not designed to run fast! The Moss Jaguar averaged 75.22mph and made fastest lap. Leslie Johnson was due to have started in a Mk VII, but didn't.

Thus began ten years of Jaguar wins in Silverstone touring car races.

In 1953, Moss did the same thing with the same car – but slightly slower, for there was no competitive Healey this time, and only two cars (Grace's Riley nearly a minute behind, and Dunham's Alvis) completed the seventeen laps.

By 1954, the Silverstone saloon car race was becoming an established favourite, and although disappointed that the newly-announced D-type would not be present (Jaguar were determined not to have their Le Mans preparations interrupted) the *Daily Express* and the B.R.D.C. were grateful for the more-competitive-than-ever list of touring car entrants.

The regulations referred rather loosely to "special Series" touring cars, and Jaguar took the opportunity to prepare two Mk VII entries, LWK 343 for Stirling Moss and LHP 5 for Tony Rolt – as well as provide assistance for Ian Appleyard, whose own new Mk VII (SUM 7) completed the officially-entered Jaguar team. Ronald Adams brought *his* Mk VII, but Charles Goodacre's threatened new Armstrong-Siddeley Sapphire did not materialise; however, the opposition was strong, headed by a very serious team of newly-announced Daimler Conquest Century saloons.

Ken Wharton's Daimler led away but it was Lyndon Sims's Riley 2.5-litre that swept through Woodcote in the lead on lap one, chased by Appleyard's white Jaguar, Wharton's Daimler and Crook's Lancia Aurelia. Moss had been held up at the start with a jammed starter, but was already carving through the field. Sims spun away Riley's chances early in the race, and Rolt moved forward to take up station behind Appleyard. Crook spun the Lancia on lap 5, to be rammed by Wharton's Daimler. The only other challenger, Gerry Dunham (Alvis), spun away fourth place.

In 1954, Ronald Adams finished 5th, beaten by three other Jaguars and Reg Parnell in one of the impressive Daimler Conquest Century saloons – seen here harrying the Adams Mk VII ...

...but 1, 2, 3 over the line was the impressive trio of Appleyard, Rolt and Moss. *Photo: Autocar*

This left the 200hp Jaguars 1, 2 and 3, with Appleyard winning from Rolt and Moss – the latter driving in a disciplined manner to ensure Jaguar took the team prize. All three lapped in in 2-minutes 16-seconds, although Moss and Appleyard had done 2-minutes 14-seconds in practice. Adams was fifth. Appleyard averaged 75.55mph and Reg Parnell 73.74 to finish 4th in the leading Daimler.

There were big changes in Jaguar's racing team for 1955, and these were reflected in the Silverstone touring car entry. Duncan Hamilton and Tony Rolt continued to be regular D-type Jaguar partners; but Stirling Moss and Peter Walker had left the team – Moss to drive for Mercedes-Benz and Walker to Aston Martin because he had not turned up for team selection testing. The other regulars Ken Wharton and Peter Whitehead left for other reasons; Wharton had never been considered because he had already had taken on competition managership of Daimler without telling Jaguar, and the steady and gentlemanly Whitehead had bowed-out and gone to race in Australia, realising that he was unlikely to be selected again. The new men were Don Beauman, Mike

In 1955, Hawthorn replaced Moss as Jaguar team leader – but it was the same old Mk VII he drove to victory from Jimmy Stewart in PWK 700 (the car that was destined to win the next 'Monte'!) *Photo: Autocar*

Third in 1955 was Titterington (PWK 701) but Appleyard (SUM 7) had to retire with severe overheating. *Photo: Autocar*

Jimmy Stewart, driving to second place behind Hawthorn in 1955. *Photo: Motor*

Hawthorn, Jimmy Stewart, and Desmond Titterington – and it was the last named trio that formed Jaguar's official Mk VII team, although Appleyard was there again as an individual entry.

That morning, the sports car event had been a great disappointment for Jaguar, Hawthorn having broken the lap record and led from early in the race until the 36th of 40 laps; he had then dropped to fourth after his D-type's top hose had blown. (He'd been passed by Parnell and Salvadori in Aston Martins, and Rolt's D-type Jaguar. Hamilton and Titterington had finished 5th and 6th).

So, as the lunchtime touring car race got under way, it was clear that the Jaguar team meant business. So smartly did they get away that Titterington had time for a spin on lap three and to get going again without losing fourth place. Appleyard retired at two-thirds distance in a cloud of steam. Hawthorn passed the chequered flag in LWK 343 just two-seconds ahead of Jimmy Stewart in PWK 700 which was destined to win the next Monte Carlo Rally. Titterington came in third, all on his own, to complete Jaguar's second almost-copybook team prize performance. Fourth was the versatile Wharton now driving a Ford Zephyr with a Raymond Mays conversion!

The Jaguar team's new 'No 1' fresh from his victory in the Florida 12-hour race, took two lap records at Silverstone that day – 1-minute 49-seconds (96.67mph) with the Jaguar D-type and 2-minutes 10-seconds (81.06mph) with the Mk VII. It is interesting to note that the best Formula One laps in that afternoon's International Trophy race were by the 250F Maseratis of Peter Collins and Roy Salvadori in 1-minute 47-seconds.

Before the 1955 season was much older, Jaguar had to find two more recruits. Jimmy Stewart decided to retire from racing altogether after hurting himself in a couple of unfortunate accidents (not in works Jaguars), although he *did* compete in the odd hillclimb later on; and poor Don Beauman had a fatal crash in a single-seater Connaught in Ireland; so the annual Jaguar line-up at Silverstone for the International May meeting included another two new names in 1956.

There was something else different, too – for Jaguar had announced their new compact saloon, the 2.4, and here were three of them making their race debuts ... but the Mk VIIs were on hand, just in case! They were entrusted to the new team members, Ivor Bueb and Paul Frère.

The new cars were certainly impressive in practice, Mike Hawthorn circulating in 2-minutes 7-seconds; but after surging into the lead the new 2.4 retired when a valve spring broke with only a couple of laps completed, Jaguar dealer John Coombs had to call in for water in *his* 2.4, and Duncan Hamilton's 2.4 was losing over a second a lap to the leaders... The leaders? 'Deposed' Jaguar team driver Ken Wharton was at it again, now using an Austin Westminster with Weber carburetters, and all manner of other Austin-Healey-type modifications to challenge the Jaguars. This year he nearly did it, too! – but for Bueb who managed to keep the bulky Mk VII *just* ahead of the flying Austin for the 20 laps. Bueb and Wharton shared a new lap record (2-minutes 9-seconds), Hamilton did 2-

Strange bedfellows – Tommy Rowe's car flanked by Dalton's Aston Martin DB3S and McKenzie's Bentley at Silverstone for the 1958 AMOC relay race. *Photo: Andrew White*

Jaguar's own Bob Berry raced and rallied this lightened Mk VII to good effect. It was made up of an experimental works vehicle, and is seen here somewhere near the Welsh border one night in 1959.

The Mk VIII and IX rarely if ever figured in racing – basically because the 'new' compact Jaguars could do the job so much better (after 1956). Here is the works Mk VIII demonstrator, however, being driven fully-laden and with aplomb as a course car at a contemporary Brands Hatch meeting. *Photo: Andrew Whyte*

The big Jaguars did re-emerge in 1975 for the first of the now-popular "Pre-1957 Saloon" races; the winner, appropriately at a Jaguar Driver's Club meeting, was Michael Rouse's modified Mk IX (no. 46) – but only just, from Bob Meacham's 2.4 seen nearest the camera. The former Bob Berry car can also be seen on the extreme left of the picture, driven by the late Christopher Sturridge. *Photo: Andrew Whyte*

Historic saloon racer Graig Hinton, seen here at Silverstone where Mk VII race history commenced 25-years earlier! He was awarded the title "Jaguar Driver of the Year" in 1976, and in the 1980s was introducing Americans to such activities, having settled in Florida.

The aluminium-bodied Mk VII as it is now − Bob Berry obtained the lightweight bodyshell (the only complete one to be assembled) and used it on a progressively modified chassis − although a subsequent owner has added the peg-drive D-type wheels. It is now kept, in superb order by the Sturridge family. *Photo: P. Skilleter*

minutes 10-seconds *en route* to third, while Frère brought the Monte-winning Mk VII home fourth ahead of Jo Bonnier's Alfa Romeo.

Autosport's John Bolster was unusually acid in his technical appraisal: "I decline to comment on the so-called touring cars", he said. "When regulations permit bonnets full of Weber carburettors, racing cylinder heads, and so forth, the thing can only become a farce."

Within a year the 2.4 was supplemented by a 3.4 – a natural recipe for success which spelt the end for the Mk VII as a racer. Its successors, the Mk VIII, Mk IX and Mk X paved the way for today's highly refined XJs; but they were big, heavy road cars and, as such, were fortunately never seen in serious motor races.

Twenty-years on, as we shall see, the *really* big cats did prowl once more. In the interim, the lightweight Mk VII hybrid of Bob Berry provided exciting dicing for the crowds and embarrassment for the opposition in British club racing in the late 'fifties. Having, in effect, a wet-sump D-type engine did help; but this alloy-bodied monster was quite a tractable 'street machine' and Berry even did the odd rally with it. (Privately pensioned-off, the 1956 Silverstone winner, OVC 69, also saw action in races and rallies to brighten its twilight years, driven by Cheshire enthusiast Tom Rowe).

Since the mid-'seventies, 'classic', saloon car racing has provided genuine nostalgia, and today's race-going enthusiasts are being reminded just how entertaining a bravely-driven Mk VII can be to watch. Historic car specialist Graig Hinton was the chief protagonist until the early 1980s, when he moved to Florida and continued his racing mainly in a Mark II 3.8; he races for the sheer fun of it, much as (I like to think) people did in 'the old days'.

Chapter Twenty

UK domination ~ the `compact racers´

The versatility of the compact 'integral' Jaguars – the 2.4, the 3.4, and their Mk II successors – has been referred to previously.

In racing, even more convincingly than in rallying, they added much to the sporting image that had been built up around the Jaguar name. The fact that the cars were not works-entered – although success breeds success, and factory experience and help were therefore often sought and usually willingly given – probably assisted rather than hindered Jaguar's reputation.

There was still an official works team, however, at Silverstone in May 1956, when Duncan Hamilton brought the new 2.4 over the line third, as previously described; and it was with a factory 2.4 that Paul Frère won the 10-lap (88-mile) special series touring car race on his national circuit (near Spa, Belgium) at over 96mph a week later.

On October 13 that year came the official announcement: "Jaguar Cars Ltd., after very serious consideration announce their withdrawal from the field of international racing and other competitive events ... the information gained as a result of the highly successful racing programme ... has been of the utmost value... Nevertheless an annual racing programme imposes a very heavy burden on the... engineering division which is already fully extended in implementing plans for the further development of Jaguar cars... Whether the Company will resume its racing activities in 1958... must depend on circumstances."

Then two crises followed in quick succession. In November 1956, for the first time in its history, Jaguar Cars had to go on to a four-day working week, because of petrol restrictions in Britain and on the Continent. The return to full-time working in late January was the prelude to crisis number two. On the evening of February 12 1957, fire gutted a large proportion of the Browns Lane Works. Production barely stopped and, as if to emphasise the company's determination to survive, they announced the 3.4 a fortnight later.

Fortunately the *Daily Express* Silverstone meeting was put back from May to September so preparation of cars for Hawthorn, Hamilton, and Bueb – now privateers! – was not affected unduly; but it was just as well that the factory was not trying to operate an official team, what with all its problems. On the day, the 3.4s of Hawthorn, Hamilton, and Bueb screeched and yawed their way around to take the first three places. The new car could hardly fail! Archie Scott-Brown's 3.4 had been close to Hawthorn's to start with, but retired (brakes!). Disc brakes were needed urgently with this sort of performance, and very soon they became a production option. Hawthorn averaged 82.19mph and Ron Flockhart, driving John Coombs's 2.4, did 76.19mph to finish 5th – but he was just beaten in his class by veteran Riley driver Harold Grace. Jack Sears was sixth in an Austin Westminster and third in class; Sears' day was to come.

Above: Debut for the 3.4 at Silverstone, 1957, a year in which regulations were tightened, so cars were allowed fewer mods. (left to right) Hawthorn, Hamilton, Bueb and Scott-Brown dash for their cars. Next in the line is Harold Grace's Riley Pathfinder and Ron Flockhart's Coombs 2.4 beyond it. *Photo: Motor*

Right: Hawthorn takes the 3.4 Jaguar to its first win, despite sorely tried drum brakes.

Archie Scott Brown (TBM 2) lost his brakes in 1957 and retired from second place, after lapping Tom Bridge's Borgward.

With plans afoot for British touring car race championship, the team of Tommy Sopwith, Sir Gawaine Baillie and their 3.4-litre Jaguars began a series of sweeping victories around the country, starting at Brands Hatch on Boxing Day 1957 where Sopwith won easily but Baillie only just managed to keep MacKay (supercharged Ford Anglia)) and Scott-Brown (1900 Alfa Romeo) at bay. "The race of the day", *Autosport* called it, and referred to tyre smoke coming from Sopwith's car on every corner. This would have been *oil smoke* in fact – and, with the 3.4's tremendous roll angle, this was to become a familiar sight as high cornering forces pushed oil out through the breather pipe and on to the exhaust.

Sopwith was the regular winner throughout 1958, Baillie usually winning when Sopwith ran into trouble such as brakelessness at Aintree. Duncan Hamilton beat

them both at Whit-Goodwood, driving John Coombs' 3.4; and at Silverstone where it had all started, Hawthorn and Sopwith gave the crowd just the duel they wanted to see – a pair of 3.4s racing at close quarters, on the limit. Hawthorn knew how to please people but made sure he crossed the line first! Flockhart was third in the Coombs' car.

There was a second chance to see the 'tourers' on Silverstone's long circuit that year, when another race was held on Grand Prix day. Sopwith led from pole position – it was a grid start; seatbelt sense was coming in – ahead of Briggs Cunningham's star sports-car driver, Walter Hansgen. Just after half-distance Sopwith lost his nearside rear wheel and Hansgen, already close behind, inherited a big lead (over Baillie) to take an easy victory in TWK 287 – the Coventry-registered 'Coombs' car.

The great American driver Walter Hansgen used the first (Coventry registered) 'Coombs' 3.4 to win with ease at the 1958 Silverstone GP meeting, after Sopwith lost a wheel.

The great double-act – Hawthorn and Sopwith playing to the gallery at Silverstone in 1958. On one lap, Sopwith took an unofficial line at Stowe *behind* the barrier...

...emerging with foot still hard down to chase and overtake Hawthorn by the time the two 3.4s came round again. However, it was Hawthorn who finally crossed the line first in VDU 881 (note JDC badge). *Photos: Tom March*

The Championship drew to a close in October, at the season's final, wet, Brands Hatch meeting. Sopwith won again and Jack Sears as usual won his class in the Austin A105, so the pair finished with equal points. Marcus Chambers, who was beginning to get real results from BMC's Abingdon competition shop, laid on two Riley One-Point-Fives for the 'shoot out' – two five-lap match races with a car-swop in between. Sopwith won the first, by 2.2-seconds; Sears won the second by four, and thus became the first BRSCC British saloon car champion – but only just!

A week later, on October 11 1958, Tommy Sopwith won the Snetterton one-hour race for GT and special series saloons – then hung up his helmet for good; conversely his great rival Jack Sears, who came in nine-seconds later in an Austin-Healey 100/6, was to continue racing for many more seasons – often at the wheel of Sopwith's Jaguars!

1959 started sadly with the death of Mike Hawthorn in a road accident, driving his 3.4. That season Ivor Bueb took over Sopwith's role as *Equipe Endeavour* team leader, backed up by Sir Gawaine Baillie; Roy Salvadori became John Coombs' regular Jaguar driver. At the big Goodwood, Aintree and Silverstone spring meetings, the order was Bueb, Salvadori, Baillie each time. That summer, in the Formula Two *Grand Prix des Auvergnes*, Ivor Bueb crashed his BRP Cooper-Borgward and was killed. Twice a Le Mans-winner in Jaguars, and master of the later Lister-Jaguars in any weather, Bueb's death was another extra-big blow to motor-racing.

Salvadori and Baillie both won races after that and, although the 3.4 was still king, the most consistent class winner Jeff Uren (Ford Zephyr) who took the Championship.

Following its introduction in October 1959, with 3.8-litre engine optional and wider rear track, the Jaguar Mk II saloon took over as top tourer in racing from the 3.4; but successful rivalry between the Coombs and Sopwith teams meant that no individual Jaguar driver would become British Saloon Champion.

Baillie winning at the Boxing Day Brands meeting of 1960 – the new Mk II had first raced at Goodwood on Easter Monday when Salvadori beat Sears, although both finished after Moss in a DB4 Aston Martin (it was a closed car race). Baillie, though, had the honour of being first outright race winner in the 3.8, when he beat Doug Uren in a similar car at the BRSCC Spring Meeting at Snetterton. *Photo: Motor*

Pattern for 1959: Bueb (in Sopwith's 3.4) beating Salvadori (in Coombs' 3.4) at Goodwood. No longer did Silverstone have 'full rights' for big-time saloon car racing in Britain! *Photo: Autocar*

The main Jaguar 3.8 winners in 1960 were Salvadori, Sears and Baillie, with Colin Chapman of Lotus Cars taking a one-off victory in what 'Lofty' England called a "Coombs demonstration." (It worked, apparently, because Chapman bought a 3.8 Mk II for himself soon afterwards!).

A third team – Peter Berry Racing – came on the scene, providing saloon car fun for Bruce McLaren, John Surtees, and Dennis Taylor; but their 3.8's were beaten during 1961 by the Coombs (Salvadori) and Sopwith (Mike Parkes and Graham Hill) cars. Key race of that year was at the traditionl Silverstone May meeting, when Dan

Above: **A nice win for Salvadori over Moss at Silverstone, May 1960 (Moss was having a rare drive in an *Equipe Endeavour* 3.8). Photo: Tom March FRPS**

Left: **Second Silverstone win for 6 PPF – Colin Chapman gets across the line at the 1960 July GP meeting just ahead of the 'Endeavour' car, driven this time by Jack Sears.**

Above: **Big game! – and the first warning (May 1961, Silverstone). Dan Gurney feeds on the power and the 'newcomer' Impala holds off the snapping Jaguars, which might not have caught it if it hadn't lost a wheel.**

Right: **Mike Parkes follows Jack Sears (the eventual winner, after Bob Jane's retirement) past K. Bell's upturned Vauxhall VX 4/90, during the Aintree British GP meeting of July 1962.**
Photo: Autocar

Gurney out-dragged all the Jaguars which found themselves being challenged seriously for the first time ever. Gurney's vast Chevrolet Impala was able to accelerate away comfortably on the straights, but Graham Hill's Jaguar would close under braking and through the corners. Nevertheless, Gurney certainly had the race under control; then his nearside rear wheel came adrift and stuck inside the wheel-arch, causing the Chevrolet to grind to a halt only a few laps from home. It *might* be said that Hill's 3.8 won by default – but it did break the touring car lap record at 92.11mph (1-minute 54.4-seconds), and made the American work quite hard.

In his first World Championship year, 1962, Graham Hill became the leading light in Jaguars, with saloon victories at Oulton Park, Goodwood, Aintree, Silverstone, Mallory Park, and Suetterton – now driving for John Coombs now only in saloons but in the car that was to be the prototype for the 'lightweight' E-types.

Mike Parkes had wins at Snetterton and Brands Hatch for Equipe Endeavour; and Jack Sears finished just ahead of Parkes in the other Sopwith car at the British GP meeting on the Aintree circuit. In this race Bob Jane (of whom, more anon) got away first, then weaved all the way down the straight. After five laps he spun the Coombs 3.8 just in front of Sears and Parkes and was never able to catch them; finally Jane retired with overheating and 'pommie' lectures on 'British behaviour'. His technique of 'repelling boarders' was seen in one press photograph above the caption "Jane's Fighting Style", which seemed apt.

Not only were the professionals racing Mk II Jaguars; there were more and more opportunities at club and national level for saloon car drivers such as Peter Sargent, Albert Powell, Peter Woodroffe, Vic Parness, Bill Aston, Chris McLaren, Peter Dodd, Mike Pendleton, John Adams and many more. Hardly surprising, then, was Coombs of Guildford's introduction, in May 1962, of a properly-marketed 'go-faster' conversion kit for the Jaguar saloon. Nine-to-one pistons, gas-flowed head, long-range fuel tank, manual choke control, 'high' steering box ratio, and straight- through exhaust were among the features. A fully-modified 3.8 with 2-inch SU carburetters provided claimed figures of 0 to 60mph in 6.9-seconds, 0 to 100 in 16.2 and, the standing-start quarter-mile in 14.7-seconds. Indeed Coombs' tests showed their car to be quicker up to 110mph than the standard E-type.

The American menace had not gone away, however, and it was a Coombs Jaguar driven by Roy Salvadori that quelled it.

Alexander Engineering made a determined onslaught on Jaguar's domain by preparing a pair of Chevrolet Chevy IIs for Peter Sachs and Charles Kelsey. On the whole, they had a disastrous season, but – not to be left out of the record books – Kelsey became the first driver actually to topple Jaguar in saloon car racing.

It happened at the National Brands Hatch meeting of May 1962. Salvadori, by far the fastest in practice, held pole position; Sir Gawaine Baillie was there alongside him. Also on the front row of the grid were Kelsey (Chevy II) and Dodd (Jaguar).

Kelsey made a great start, and Salvadori had to tuck in behind the American – and that's how the position stayed. Even when lapping tail-enders, Salvadori could not get the Jaguar's nose far enough in front to stay there; the course would straighten-out, and off the big V8 engined machine would gallop! No matter how strongly he may have felt he could stay ahead if he got there, the frustrated Salvadori must have realised that, with its straight-line performance and well-sorted suspension, the Chevy could not, reasonably, be expected to move aside for him – but it did seem a very wide car that day! A new lap record was not much consolation to Salvadori as he crossed the line in second place, well ahead of Baillie and Dodd; Jaguars 2nd, 3rd and 4th. It had happened!

Jaguar enthusiasts were relieved a fortnight later at Crystal Palace when Salvadori warded-off Kelsey's advances. That must have been Salvadori's most satisfying result of the year.

First major defeat for the Jaguar saloon came at Brands Hatch in May 1962, when Salvadori (3.8) had to be content to 'sit on the tail' of Charles Kelsey's Chevy II. At Crystal Palace (shown here) he was not going to let the same thing happen a fortnight later, and is seen pulling clear of Kelsey at Ramp Bend, while Sears shapes up to pass the Chevy and take second place. Baillie (far left of picture) had to be content with fourth. *Photo: Motor*

Alexander's Chevrolet *did* have another national win – at the September Crystal Palace meeting – but the Jaguars were up at Oulton Park that day, and Peter Sachs (who had been 2nd to Hill at Snetterton) simply had to make sure not to lose his line under braking to keep ahead of the buzzing Ford Anglias of Peter Ashdown and Chris Craft. A hollow Chevy victory? – maybe! – but a final warning that, in short-distance racing at least, the Mk II's days were numbered. In longer events, the Jaguar remained invincible.

October 1962 saw *The Motor* promote a new event, a six-hour race for Group 2 saloons – that is to say, simply, cars which could be modified, but within a strict if not always clear framework of rules that prevented the specification from getting unrealistic; you could still associate them quite closely with what you might go out and buy from your dealer.

The race was held at Brands Hatch, and produced that last of the big Coombs *v* Sopwith battles. Mike Salmon and Peter Sutcliffe kept the Coombs car ahead for over 100 laps, but Mike Parkes and Jimmy Blumer took the Sopwith 3.8 ahead after making quicker pit-stops. Five-hours' racing completed, and the leaders were still close together – then Salmon came in to retire with front wheel-bearing failure, so Parkes was able to slow down and let Peter Lindner and Peter Nöcker of Germany catch up slightly in their 3.8. The winning Jaguar covered 171 laps in the six-hours, the runners-up did 167 laps. Very impressive in third place (164 laps) was the Mini-Cooper

of Denny Hulme and John Aley; Aley, incidentally, was Britain's leading promoter of a saloon racing championship for Europe, which was inaugurated in 1963.

Above: **Pitstop for the Salmon/Sutcliffe 3.8 entered by Coombs for the 1962 6-hours race; note auxiliary tank in boot being filled. Salmon (fastening helmet) prepares to take over from Sutcliffe.** *Photo: Motor*

Below: **Start of the 1962 *Motor* 6-hour race. The winning car (no. 1, JAG 400) was driven by Michael Parkes and James Blumer.** *Photo: Motor*

The Motor's road-test team, being directly associated with the six-hour race, tried the two successful Jaguars afterwards. They found the German's car gave "an impression almost of opulence", and retained the normal 1.75-inch SU carburetters. The winning car was "much starker and seemed to have undergone the six-hour ordeal much more successfully than the German one." Its more obvious modifications included twin 2-inch SU carburetters, special oil breathers for engine, gearbox and rear axle, perspex rear and side windows, and a lightweight battery. It ran on 7.00 x 15 Dunlop racing tyres inflated to over 50psi (reduced to 40 for the test);

Lindner's car wore 6.50 x 15 tyres. On both cars the clutch had deteriorated during the race, and acceleration times were not easy to obtain. Those they got produced 0 to 90mph figures of 16.7- and 17.8-seconds, the winner's being the better time. Both had high ratio steering and stiffer suspension which were highly praised. The Sopwith car could be "guided with precision whether complete adhesion between the tyres and the road have been maintained or not."

The Motor's conclusion was that "while substantially 'same-as-you-can-buy', these are nonetheless exciting racers."

The Lindner/Nöcker second-place 3.8 joins other competitors for the *Motor* road-test team to try out after the 1962 race. *Photo: Motor*

Engine compartment of the Lindner/Nöcker 3.8: less modified than the winning car, it used 1.75-inch SUs, albeit with ram pipes and a cold-air feed. Note the twin-pipe engine breather. *Photo: Motor*

Graham Hill stayed with the Coombs team for 1963, while Salvadori 'changed colours' for the metallic bluey-green of Tommy Atkins' neatly presented team, consisting of a Cooper Moncao and two Jaguars (a lightweight 'E' type and a 3.8 saloon). Salvadori began by beating Hill in the wet at Snetterton; but Hill won his other two races that day, driving BRM and 'E' type Jaguar, so had little to complain about. Salvadori gave best to Hill at Oulton Park, and was then disqualified for having oversize wheel rims; he was beaten again by Hill at Goodwood and Aintree in April.

Then came Silverstone, where not a year since 1952 had passed without a Jaguar taking the saloon car honours.

Now it was not a Chevrolet but a Ford Galaxie (entered by Jeff Uren for John Willment's organisation) that unleashed almost twice as many horses as the Jaguar in the direction of Copse corner at flagfall. The driver? – none other than Jack Sears, who was able to take things easy after creating a new lap record, and still average 91.77mph for the race. Salvadori brought the Atkins 3.8 home, more then 20-seconds adrift, at an average of 90.38mph.

Oulton Park, Spring Cup meeting, April 1963. Up goes the one minute signal for (left to right) Bill Aston, Mike Salmon, Roy Salvadori and Graham Hill.
Photo: Andrew Whyte

Goodwood Easter Monday, 1963 – Salmon leads Hill, but not for long! After the leaders come Salvadori, Dodd, Aston and Pendleton.
Photo: Andrew Whyte

Defeat at last! Roy Salvadori does the best he can at Silverstone (May 1963), but Jack Sears is a long way in front with the Willment Galaxie. Salvadori was now driving for C.T. Atkins, and this 3.8 was declared the victor a few weeks later in the second *Motor* 6-hour race at Brands Hatch, where Denny Hulme was to be Salvadori's co-driver.

It was just the beginning! At Aintree later in the month, Sears won as he pleased, nursing the huge Ford's tyres and moving ahead of Mike Salmon (3.8 Jaguar) only when it seemed advisable. Even at Crystal Palace the Sears Galaxie had an easy victory, although Salvadori and Hill were able to finish ahead of Sir Gawaine Baillie who had now acquired one of the monster Fords. On the same day, Whit-Monday, Mike Salmon wisely took his Atherstone Engineering ex-Coombs 3.8 Jaguar (BUY 12) to Goodwood – and won. At least that Ford couldn't be in two places at once!

On went Sears, despite all sorts of niggling problems; the Galaxie was so fast, it was never fully extended. At Snetterton he won despite fumes from a broken exhaust getting into the cockpit; he had time to hang his head out of the window. At the Silverstone GP meeting Sears and Baillie came 1st and 2nd, with Mike MacDowel having a rare outing in a Coombs 3.8 to finish third.

At Bank Holiday Brands, Sears and Baillie retired, but World Champion-elect Jimmy Clark had a go in a Galaxie, so it was Hill second, Salvadori third once again in the Jaguars.

The second Brands Hatch six-hour race (held in the summer this time) was a different story.

Things started badly when John Willment instructed team manager Jeff Uren to withdraw the Galaxie, because of a couple of discrepancies between the photographs on the form of recognition and what the scrutineer saw on the car. Both parties – the R.A.C. and the entrant – stated their arguments logically. The sad thing was that the public was deprived of seeing the year's quickest saloon in action on race day. Just imagine, too, the idea of *removing* rather than adding roll-cage bars! – that was what had to be done at Crystal Palace a few weeks earlier to comply with the homologation scrutineer's ruling! On the other hand, how would that Galaxie have got on in the US Federal crash test procedure, had it been required then?

There had been a clash with the US Grand Prix in 1962; this year there was no such clash and several GP drivers came along including Jack Brabham and Dan Gurney in a Galaxie entered by Alan Brown. The old Jaguar partnership of Baillie and Jopp was there; but they had the Galaxie now. A third Galaxie was driven by Col. Merton Lucia, USAF, and John Sprinzel – one of Britain's best all-round *small* car drivers! Jack Sears and Bo Ljungfeldt drove a Willment Ford Cortina GT in place of the Galaxie and were probably very glad they did!

The main Jaguar teams were there – Salmon and Sutcliffe with the former Coombs car, Hulme and Salvadori driving for Tommy Atkins, Lindner and Nöcker from Germany, and several others – but no entry from the 1962 winners, Equipe Endeavour.

Most of the race was run in pelting rain, and the Jaguars soon moved into the lead after Gurney spun off (hardly surprising with Firestone rain tyres on the front and harder Goodyears at the rear!) and Baillie had been reeled in on lap three first by Salmon, then by Lindner, who was 'grass-cutting' for much of the time, as in 1962!

Three Galaxies on the front row – Brands Hatch 6-hours, 1963. But the big Ford V8s were out of luck, and the Jaguars won again.

Salmon and Sutcliffe drove a fine race and a close-running thing turned-into an easy victory, when Denny Hulme came in to change a wheel twenty minutes from "time". Victory turned sour at scrutineering when the 3.8's inlet valve diameter was found to be 47.6mm (the form said 44.45!) and Hulme and Salvadori became the lucky winners having covered 165 laps at 72.62mph *and* put in the fastest lap. This promoted Lindner and Nöcker (3.8) to 2nd, and Sears and Ljungfeldt (Cortina GT) to 3rd – whereas the gallant Galaxies were left floundering. Sir

Michael Salmon leads the 1963 6-hour race in the rain, only to be disqualified. Following him through the murk is the Lindner/Nocker 3.8 – third on the road, but second after the Salmon/Sutcliffe car's disqualification for having oversize valves.

Gawaine Baillie and Peter Jopp worked hard for their 7th place; Brabham and Gurney were 9th, and Lucia and Sprinzel 23rd.

Throughout the later nineteen-sixties and even during the nineteen-seventies, there remained a thread of enthusiasm which kept a Jaguar presence in club racing while Ford and BMW took over the leading saloon car roles in international level racing, with some intervention from the Chevrolet Camaro. Even Jackie Stewart was once a driver in the winning Mk II team for a club relay race at Oulton Park, I remember!

It is a rather strange quirk of 'fair-play' that, at the time of writing, the only compact Jaguar eligible for the British classic saloon car race championship is the early type of 2.4 – the only one that never had an international race victory in the UK!

This limitation seems to make for close racing, and there is a tinge of nostalgia every time these cars come out and squeal their way round Britain's circuits; and the similarity remains, right down to the last little niggle over whether or not the rule book really means what it says!

Left: After the big Fords came the little Fords! The Lotus-Cortina represented a new breed of sports saloon and had little difficulty in disposing of the heavier Jaguars, as is being demonstrated in this May 1964 Silverstone race. *Photo: Motor*

Below: Agreed! – Jackie Stewart only borrowed this *road* 3.8 to drive around in New Zealand during a Tasman series, but he *did* once race one at Oulton Park, winning a team event in his early days!

Of all the names to crop up amongst Jaguar saloon racers in the late 'sixties and early 'seventies, the most frequent is that of Albert Betts. A fine preparer and driver, Betts often surprised his opponents with his 3.8-engined 'old body' car. Best result against up-to-date opposition was probably in the 1967 BRSCC "Festival of Saloon Car Races" at Snetterton. The big race was of two-hours duration, and Betts led initially from Geoff Breakell in Tom Clapham's Alfa-Romeo GTA. After two-hour's racing (including a spin), Betts' old Jaguar finished second to the Alfa and ahead of the Lotus-Cortinas of Willy Kay and Henry Hotham. *Photo: P. Skilleter*

The old Coombs 3.8 was one of many Mk IIs adapted to take modern wide wheels in the 'seventies — this is Tony Strawson at Silverstone. *Photo: P. Skilleter*

Throughout the 1970s, Risca Garages of Wales were producing race-winning 3.8s for club events (this is Tony Williams at Silverstone). By the mid-eighties, complete fields of Jaguar compacts were racing again, albeit in more standard forms. *Photo: P. Skilleter*

As for the 'Mk I' saloon, that still wins in "Pre-1957" saloon car racing; here Bill Pinckney, driver of the most successful 2.4 in 1977/79, receives the factory's "Jaguar Driver of the Year" award for 1977 from Sir William Lyons. On the left is John Fitzpatrick, from another era of Jaguar saloon car racing. *Photo: Jaguar Cars*

Chapter Twenty-one

Racing around the World

Energy and interest shown by the importer have been the main factors in the racing of Jaguar touring cars outside Britain. By far the most successful of those energetic people was the importer for Germany, whose story comes later on in this chapter.

Racing of Jaguars in the large North American market has, in the main, been the province of sports cars such as the 'D' types that won at Sebring, Watkins Glen and other famous courses – thanks to sportsman Briggs Cunningham, who held responsibilities for Jaguar in the east, and worked closely with the importing company Jaguar Cars Inc., which was run by Johannes Eerdmans (a Sir William 'discovery'). There were sedan races of all kinds – from Lime Rock's 'Little Le Mans' to the amazing high-speed stock cars that are still a USA speciality. As the 'D' type became obsolescent, Eerdmans preferred to remain associated with racing through the Alfred Momo-prepared Cunningham-team Lister-Jaguars that became top-cats in American sports-car racing for several seasons in the late 'fifties, when Jaguar was beginning to build a big name for itself abroad.

On two specific occasions, however, the opportunity to race Jaguar saloons was taken. These were international races, in that they were held as added attractions at the first two World Championship Grand Prix meetings ever held in the USA – at Sebring, Florida, in 1959 and at Riverside, California (1960) – and the Jaguars won easily.

Briggs Cunningham's leading driver Walter Hansgen

and 'rooky' Phil Forno were provided with a 3.4 each for the Sebring compact race of two-hours duration. Hansgen managed to do thirty-one laps and record fastest lap with ease, but second place went to the Moody-prepared V8 Studebaker Lark of Curtis Turner, which was reaching over 125mph on the main straight and not rolling as sharply as the Jaguars through the bends. Forno's Jaguar was the only other car to complete 30 laps. 'Fireball' Roberts did 29 laps in another Lark, while Art Riley (Volvo) and Ed Hugus (Chevrolet Corvair) covered 28. Seventh, on 27 laps, was the late-lamented Pedro Rodriguez at the wheel of a PV544 Volvo.

British cars were more dominant in the poorly-supported thirty-lapper run in conjunction with the second USA GP meeting of 1960; but with only one American car present (a Falcon which finished four laps down in sixth place) it was a hollow victory. Walt Hansgen and Augie Pabst managed to make a race of it, swopping places regularly in their twin 3.8 Mk II saloons; Hansgen took the flag by half a second and Peter Harper (Sunbeam Rapier) reeled off 29 laps to finish third. Not a memorable race, unfortunately! Everett Martin of Jaguar Cars Inc., didn't even consider publicising this Jaguar win despite the importance usually attached to *any* success at *any* Grand Prix meeting. Riverside just made no impact at all, with few spectators – and only a move back east to Watkins Glen in 1961 saved the USA Grand Prix from financial doom.

1er Casablanca. Alger
1er Classement General
Pneus "Dunlop". Graissage "Mobiloil".

This signed photograph appears to be dated "Casablanca 10th April 1947", but the signature is unreadable. It was sent to "SS Cars" (didn't the owner know the company had changed its name?), *"en souvenir de ma victoire de la grand épreuve Alger-Casa-Alger 2,600 kilometres sur voiture SS...1er Casablanca-Alger, 1er Classement General, Pneus 'Dunlop', Graissage 'Mobiloil.'"* If anyone can tell us more, please write – in case we can add to the caption for a future edition!

John Clarke of Johannesburg was the first S.S. distributor in South Africa, from the early 1930s, and must have sold this S.S.I tourer originally. It was later stripped and raced locally by F. Allen. Perhaps this was the first instance of an S.S. touring car racing abroad?

The Mk V was too early for the British touring car race 'boom' which began in 1952. It was being raced abroad in 1950 though! Here one heads a pack which includes Lancia and Ford Zephyr, chasing an Australian Holden – in Australia of course.

The *Carrera Panamericana Mexico*, 1950 – a frightening 2178-mile six-day race over Central America for 'stock' saloons; this Mk V driven by Jay C. Chamberlain and Jorgen Thayssen of Los Angeles was the only Jaguar running, and dropped out after the third leg when in 53rd position out of 131 starters. The event was won by an Oldsmobile, although Alfa-Romeos driven by Felice Bonetto and Piero Taruffi finished well up.

Walter Hansgen romps away with the 'compact' race that accompanied the 1959 USA GP at Sebring, in a works-prepared 3.4.

Australia always catered for saloon car racing on a national scale and many of the top drivers used Jaguar 3.4s and 3.8s to good effect – none more so than Robert Jane who, with the help of his friend and racing mechanic, John Sawyer, spent several years developing his 3.8 Mk II. His first appearance with it was at Lowood, Queensland, in 1961; he retired when a rear spring pulled out of the structure.

"Our rules, being somewhat different to F.I.A ones, allowed us to develop the cylinder head, with larger valves and ports; also three 45 DCOE Weber carburetters with our own manifold, and special camshafts to our own timing. At one stage we bored a 3.8 block out to 4.2, but this was not much good; later we bored the block 2mm (after perfecting low-temperature welding of the block) and used a crankshaft also stroked 2mm; we modified the sump and had an electric pump taking oil from it through two air coolers then back to the sump again – independent of the filter system. A great deal of work was done on the suspension and brakes. This, I think, was the car's best point as it could outbrake any touring car." That, in Bob Jane's own words, is the essence of probably the world's most powerful (well over 300bhp) Jaguar six-cylinder saloon which, through 1963 and 1964, won just about every race for which it was entered. Jane's greatest rival at that time was the equally forceful Norman Beechey who ran a Chevrolet Impala in 1963, and a Holman and Moody-powered Ford Galaxie as well as a highly modified Holden S4 in 1964 – but, somehow, Jane's Jaguar was always there, virtually unbeatable. Jane's records show that he won 38 races in succession at one stage!

Bob Jane in action at Catalina Park, Katoomba, during a NSW championship event.

Things were getting a little strained by 1965, when Jane passed Beechey (now Mustang-mounted) and was leading him by 100-yards just as the Jaguar's engine failed for the first time in two-years; the two fighters shared fastest lap at Warwick Farm, New South Wales, that day. Jane went on racing the Jaguar for as long as he had a reasonable chance of winning.

For the second year running, Bob Jane won the saloon car race at Australia's GP meeting and Sandown Park, Melbourne (1964). Norman Beechey's Holman & Moody Galaxie chases vainly.

Bob Jane's amazing Mk II holds Brian Muir's Holden at bay during a Warwick Farm, Sydney event in 1964. Jane had first raced the Jaguar in 1961, and won the Australian Touring Car Championship of 1962 and 1963; clutch trouble dropped him to 3rd in 1964.
Photo: Spencer Martin

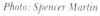

David McKay and his Jaguar 3.4, scoring one of many wins in Australia. McKay became Australia's first touring car champion, in 1960. His two 3.4s were later raced successfully by Bill Burns and Ron Hodgson (other great 3.4 users down under were Bill Pitt and Ian Geoghegan who came 1st and 2nd in the 1961 Australian Touring Car Championship race).

One typical Jane *v* Beechey battle took place at Sandown Park, Melbourne, in May 1962 when Beechey's Chevrolet blew-up in practice and he reverted to his veteran Holden for race day. In the end, the Holden blew its cylinder-head gasket but had been passing the Jaguar on bends before that. Bob Jane had four wins on that day alone with the white Jaguar. One of them was in the Ron Flockhart Memorial Race prior to which showers of rose petals fluttered down from three Royal Victorian Aero Club aircraft, in tribute to the memory of the former Jaguar driver who had been killed locally in an air-crash not long before.

Bob Jane also raced an 'E' type 'lightweight' which he owned for years and a 'D' type Jagur which had the rare distinction of being broken-into one night, not many years ago, and driven out (literally) through Jane's showroom window, fortunately with less ultimate damage than there might have been.

Before Bob Jane 'took over' Australian touring car racing, David McKay, Ron Hodgson and Bill Pitt had all enjoyed their share of success in Jaguar saloons; and there was encouragement from Bryson's, the importers, as well as Anderson's (the Brisbane Jaguar people) for whom Pitt worked.

Bob Jane had several successes in New Zealand too, but, in general, the noteworthy touring car races there were for more-or-less true production cars, and from 1963 New Zealand had its own endurance event – the Wills 6-hour. This was held on the tight Pukekohe circuit near Auckland, and the first one was led initially by the Ward/Richards 3.8-litre Mk II Jaguar. John Ward soon had to come into the pits with "rear suspension trouble" – the Panhard-rod bracket, one imagines – and lost half-an-hour.

John Ward's 3.8 leads NZ's first long-distance touring car race, at Pukekohe 1963. Ward lost a lot of time in the pits, but was to win the same race two years later.

Meanwhile the only other Jaguar was holding off a concerted attack from Bill Thomasen's Mercedes-Benz 220SE. Former New Zealand Saloon Car Champion, Ray Archibald, the South Island Jaguar distributor, had brought his Coventry-prepared 3.8 Mk II across Cook Strait to team-up with his North Island colleague, Tony Shelly, better-known as a promising Lotus single-seater driver. Archibald's Jaguar racing experience was considerable, and during an hour or so while it was raining, he pulled away from Thomasen. Nevertheless the Mercedes hung on to second place until just over an hour to go, when a rear brake cylinder failed. Brakes were most people's biggest problem and the Ford Zodiac of Robbie Franicevic and Steve Borich which inherited second place

The Archibald/Shelley car takes over the lead at Pukekohe 1963.

Pitstop for the victorious Mk II at Pukekohe.

had very warped discs by the end. Kerry Grant and Frank Hamlin were third in the new Ford Cortina GT; the Jaguar won by four laps.

Hot on the heels of the Cortina GT in the terms of new car announcements came the Ford Lotus-Cortina, and it was soon winning races where the Jaguar opposition was dying-out or where larger Fords or Chevrolets were too ungainly. Incidentally, Bob Jane had won Australia's first endurance race for unmodified locally-assembled saloons, driving a Cortina GT with Harry Firth in the 1963 Bathurst 500-miler and he transferred to a Lotus-Cortina in 1964, for races in which his Jaguar was not eligible. The second New Zealand six-hour event provided a one-two for the new Fords, too. Jim Palmer and Paul Fahey (Lotus-Cortina) were the 1964 winners, in an event that no Jaguars contested.

The 1965 and 1966 Pukekohe six-hour races showed just how useful the Mk II Jaguar still was, when major modifications were not permitted.

1965 saw Ray Archibald team-up with Ernie Sprague but their leading 3.8 lost a lot of time in the pits with a damaged wheel-stud, and John Ward reversed the 1963 situation by moving into the lead. Ward, with co-driver Rod Coppins, held off a strong Alfa Romeo challenge (headed by Ross and Syd Jensen) to win for Jaguar. Archibald and Sprague managed to pull back to third in class in this, the first New Zealand event ever to include night racing.

The 'old firm' of Ray Archibald from Christchurch and Tony Shelly from Wellington was back together again for 1966. Ernie Sprague and David Simpson were leading during the fifth-hour, when the similar 3.8 Jaguar of Archibald/Shelly passed them in pouring rain and drew away to win. 1965 victors Ward and Coppins did not finish as high up the field this time, but contributed enough to ensure that Jaguars won the team prize.

Thus Jaguar 3.8s won New Zealand's premier event three times in four-years. In fact, the 1966 Pukekohe six-hour was the very last major endurance event to be won by a Jaguar saloon, at a time when the model was obsolete and the XJ6 much more than just a rumour.

There were other Jaguar saloon successes, however, all of which helped to keep up a Jaguar sporting image around the world. For example, in January 1962 Jaguar's agent in Argentina, José Millet, sent a surprise cable to the Coventry works, reporting victory for the Mk II in a new event – the 500-mile production touring car race on the Buenos Aires Autodrome. After nearly eight-hours of racing Rodriguez Larreta ('Larry') and Jack F. Greene had covered 204 laps in their 3.8 – one more than the Menditeguy/Cupeiro Alfa Romeo.

Former Grand Prix exponent Carlos Menditeguy had been fourth quickest in practice behind the drivers of three Jaguars, one of which had engine failure, driven by the Pesce brothers, while Reyes and Salerno dropped back to finish fifth in the race behind two more Alfas. The Jaguars consumed tyres at a great rate on the short twisty autodrome course. Had the Argentine Sports Car Club had their way – a 12-hour race over the old road circuit – it might have been a more convincing win. As it was, after 'Larry' had built up a good advantage (more than a lap in the first hour), the leading Jaguar cruised around just quickly enough to balance pit-stops against tyre wear, yet keep the Alfas at bay.

In the Far East, Jaguar saloons showed well in short 'supporting features' at meetings such as the Macau and Malaysian Grands Prix on several occasions, but in South Africa there was more opportunity to show the marque's prowess over long distances. There Ian Fraser-Jones and Chris Griffith shared a 3.8 saloon very effectively, and

Above: **Pukekohe 1966 – Archibald and Shelly on course for victory again, this time in the wet!**

Right: **The winning Jaguar crosses the line at Pukekohe, 1966! Second were Sprague and Simpson in another 3.8, while in third place, holding off a strong GM and Ford challenge, was the Alfa-Romeo Giulia TI of Ron Moore and Ray Thackwell.**

particularly in the 1962 Kyalami nine-hour race where they won on handicap and were sixth overall (winner on scratch being the GTO Ferrari of David Piper and Bruce Johnstone).

Easter 1963 saw the same car and crew win the Durban combined 6-hour/400-mile touring car race with an Alfa Romeo T1 second a long way behind. Rain and wind accompanied this race, so it was no fun for the Jaguar drivers when something fell off the spectator's bridge and

shattered the windscreen soon after the start.

Apart from North America, Continental Europe has always been Jaguar's most important export market, although only rarely has the potential been realised. Germany is a case in point, where conditions should be ideal for selling high-speed luxury cars. A fine road system (in general) and an affluent business world have helped Mercedes-Benz, BMW and even Opel maintain high positions among the world's great touring cars.

Motorcars have a very hard life in Germany, and top-class service back-up – a priority in any country – is absolutely essential in the land of the *autobahn*.

A young businessman with garages in Frankfurt, Wiesbaden, and Düsseldorf recognised the effort needed to do his job of carving a niche for the compact Jaguars, despite the fact that they offered the ideal combination of features for motoring in his country. With some advice and assistance from Coventry, but mostly by his own enterprise, he helped put Jaguar well and truly on the European map. His name was Peter Lindner.

Lindner began competing with his 3.4 litre saloon in rallies and races in the late nineteen-fifties, but it was when having one of his rarer outings in an Aston Martin DB4GT (Lindner sold Astons and Lotuses, too), that he met Peter Nöcker for the first time. While Lindner had the publicity angle to think of, Nöcker raced his Mercedes-Benz 300SL purely as a hobby, his own

business being to do with ready-mixed concete.

It was Nöcker who persuaded Lindner to concentrate upon racing, and thus began a partnership that was to prove outstanding in saloon and GT events for Jaguar throughout Europe over a three-year period, starting with the Nürburgring six-hour race of 1961, which they won in the Lindner 3.4 (a feat they were to repeat in a 3.8 in 1962 and 1963). Lindner himself won his class in every race he entered in 1961, thus becoming the national combined GT and touring car race champion. In the 12-hour race at Nürburgring, however, the 3.4 had its only major trouble, when the clutch and the steering column mounting broke; yet the 3.4 still won its class.

The longest races which Lindner ever contested and won were the 12-hour touring car events held at the Nürburgring in 1962 and 1963. In the first of these, Hans-Joachim Walter – better known as reigning European Rally Champion for Porsche – co-drove with

Lindner's line-up for the 1962 Nurburgring six-hour race! Peter Nocker stands by his car (centre), arms folded.

Lindner and Nöcker winning the 1962 Nurburgring six-hour. Second was the similar 3.8 of Schadrack and Baumgartner.

555

Lindner (Nöcker not being available) and their 3.8 Jaguar led all the way, winning by over half a lap from the Cabella/Lizzano Flaminia coupé. Retirements included the Schadrack/Degner 3.8 (which had lain second) for unspecified reasons. The winning Jaguar averaged over 70mph including all stops. Jaguars were 3rd and 5th and took the team prize.

Main opposition in the 1963 twelve-hour came from a pair of Fiat-Abarth 2.3-litre coupes. Lindner and Nöcker led for five-hours; then their 3.8 was stopped for thirty-seven-minutes – equivalent to about 3.5 laps of the fabulous circuit that twists up and down for fourteen-miles through the Eifel forests – while the Panhard rod mounting was repaired. For a time, the Jaguar's 'recovery' seemed to mean very little until, with Lindner at the wheel, as the last lap came, it was noticed that the British car was barely half-a-minute behind the Frère/Bianchi Fiat! Too late, Paul Frère realised the danger; Peter Lindner used all the road, as well as some of the banks and hedges he knew so well, and swept into the lead to wild acclaim, the Jaguar crossing the line with an advantage of just over two-seconds! On his last lap, Lindner had broken the record with a shattering 10m.33s., an average of 80.77mph – fully earning his nickname 'King of the Ring' – comparing very favourably with a practice time of 9m.58.4s. with his new lightweight 'E' type a few weeks earlier and 9m.37.9s. a year later (by which time that ill-fated beauty had acquired Malcolm Sayer's aerodynamic improvements and other factory modifications).

Realising the great possibilities of doing well on Mercedes-Benz's home ground, Jaguar's 'Lofty' England had agreed (back in 1961) to the preparation of three Mk II saloons for racing by the Lindner organisation. Together with four cars for Paris distributor Charley Delecroix (for the use of Bernard Consten, Robert Dutoit, Claude Lego and José Rosinski in high-speed French rallies such as the Tour de France), these three machines were the subject of a specification prepared in January 1962 by Jaguar chief designer Claude Baily for action by Michael MacDowel within the regulations permitted for the various events in which the owners planned to take part.

All seven were wire-wheeled 3.8-litre Mk II overdrive saloons with left-hand high-ratio steering, and each bodyshell was checked and additional welding added where it seemed advisable to do so. Boots (trunks) were modified to accept auxiliary tanks, and bucket seats and laminated windscreens were fitted. The engines were built up with gasflowed heads, fully polished crankshafts, and twin SU 1.75-inch HD6 carburetters with a cut-out switch to over-ride the (normally automatic) choke. The compression ratio chosen was 8.3 to 1; this was considered the best compromise between reliability and performance in the endurance events. Reinforcement of mounting points plus careful preparation – these were the keynotes of the

factory's involvement; the service department did the work that could not be done as easily in the production shops. Being an importer, too, Ray Archibald was able to arrange to have a project specification for *his* car, to race in New Zealand. This was prepared by Baily in mid 1962; and copies of the schedules were made available, for reference, to other distributors such as Millet in Buenos Aires – as guidance for their own preparation work.

The three Lindner cars were painted Opalescent Dark Green, trimmed in beige leather, and looked very businesslike. Unfortunately none of the drivers Lindner found ever matched his or Nöcker's skills at the wheel, although Schadrack and Baumgartner were runners-up to their team leaders in the 1962 6-hour race at the Nürburgring where it was announced that the next year's event would be the German contribution to a new championship – the *Europa-Pokal Für Tourenwagenrennen*

Yes, Europe was to have a touring car race championship from 1963; and it was the German *Automobilclub Saar*, that co-ordinated the first regulations with the various national clubs that wanted to take part.

With the cancellation of the Brussels meeting planned for April 1963, the Championship did not get under way until June when – on the same weekend as the 24-hours of Le Mans, Jaguar's favourite lair of the nineteen-fifties – the 1963 Nürburgring six-hour race took place.

There were entries from several Italian and German factories, most notable being the presence of the great Mercedes-Benz driver, and Walter's successor as European Rally Champion, Eugen Böhringer in a 300SE which went round the Eifel Mountains in 8m.37s.; Peter Lindner put his Jaguar in pole position with 8m.35s., however, and despite the presence of back-up cars of both marques, the race was to be dominated by the two front-runners – Lindner/Nöcker (Jaguar) and Böhringer/Glemser (Mercedes). Lindner was first away as the flag fell, and Böhringer was 3.1s. down at the end of lap one. In a big effort around half distance, the Mercedes ran off the road trying to catch up, and damaged a wheel. It continued, but finished over half a lap behind the Jaguar – Lindner and Nöcker winning at record speed.

It was a fine demonstration by Böhringer, who had just won the Acropolis rally and would shortly take his second successive victory in the *Marathon de la Route* in a very busy season of rallying and racing. Mercedes obviously wanted him to be European Champion in both types of event that year! However, Nürburgring still belonged to the Jaguar men.

The first *Europa-Pokal*, or European Touring Car Race Championship for Appendix J FIA approved Group 2 cars, was divided into eight classes, the highest capacity class being over 2.5 litres. Points were awarded not to cars but to drivers, and if there were two or more, each driver was still to be awarded full points. The best five results were to count and had to include at least one of two nominated mountain climbs. If the same people kept

Start of the opening race of the first European touring car race championship, which Peter Nöcker was to win for Jaguar. The starting of competitors in groups seems a good thing, in view of the severity of the Nurburgring. In the big car classes, it began with four Jaguars *versus* four Mercedes, plus a pair each of Lancia and Alfa.

Several seconds later, and Bohringer's Mercedes is tucked in behind Lindner's Jaguar. The Lindner/Nöcker Jaguar went on to win.

One of the finest Jaguar racing shots of all time, taken by H.P. Seufert, as Peter Lindner builds up his lead over the Mercedes at Nürburgring during the 1963 six-hours. Lindner always seemed to be wedging himself against the door on left-handers, but even the 'set-up' Jaguars rolled quite a lot, so maybe it's not surprising (the personalised numberplate reads: "Wiesbaden – Peter Lindner – 1").

winning their classes, the Nürburgring result was to be the tie-breaker – so Lindner and Nöcker had got off to a good start!

For their next event, the German Jaguar pair chose the Brands Hatch six-hour race, in which they had finished second in 1962. Again they finished second (as related in the previous chapter), but gained maximum points, as the race winners had not entered for the European Championship.

August brought what turned out to be the crucial event – a touring car race at the brand new Zolder circuit in Belgium, a late addition to the list of qualifying events, replacing Brussels. It was crucial because Lindner and

Nöcker drove separate cars, and because Lindner didn't make it round the first corner and entangled his Jaguar in some fencing. This left Nöcker in a reasonably comfortable lead. He won by fourteen-seconds from John Sparrow's 3.8. Incidentally, Sparrow stayed on and won a race at Zandvoort a week later.

Now Lindner's job was to ensure that his team mate would get maximum marks in the remaining European Championship competitions, as well as maintain the lead he now had in the German Touring contest. For example, Nöcker won a national race at Hanover airport that September, and next day made best touring car ascent of the Timmelsjoch in Austria to gain his hillclimb points! It was all very hectic, for a week later came the final European round – a four-hour race through the streets of Budapest. Three Lindner Jaguars were taken, and they finished first, third, and ninth overall.

Peter Lindner built-up a lead sufficient to exchange places with the ultra-careful Nöcker, who simply had to 'hedge his bets' between the cars. Tilo Schadrack trundled the third Jaguar round in third place in the class, just in case anything should happen to the other two – the Mercedes team having already given up trying to win the series. It had been a real team effort, ensuring that the name of Peter Nöcker – coupled with Lindner and Jaguar – would go down in history as the first European Touring Car Race Champion. Shortly afterwards, Nöcker became Touring Champion of Germany, too.

A remarkable drive in Budapest was put up by Jochen Neerpasch, Talbot's competitions chief, then driving a Volvo. His final placing in the European Championship was tenth. Behind Nöcker came Wolf Dieter Mantzel (DKW F12) and Hubert Hahne (BMW 700), both driving works cars; Rob Slotemaker was fourth in a Downton Engineering Mini-Cooper 'S' followed by Tom Trana in a works Volvo for Sweden, all being class winners. Other class winners were Gosta Karlsson – whose Saab finished sixth, closely followed by the similar car of Bjorn Rothstein in a closely-contested category – Luigi Cabella (Lancia Flaminia) eighth, and Leo Cella (Lancia Flavia) ninth. What is not clear to me is what happened to the points amassed by, say, Peter Lindner himself? Presumably only the best individual marks of any pair of drivers counted; or perhaps only Nöcker was nominated?

Architect of Jaguar's success in the 1963 European Touring Car race championship, and many other victories throughout the continent, German importer Peter Lindner was tragically killed in his 'E' type during a race in France in 1964.

Final of the 1963 Championship, with the victor, Peter Nöcker's 3.8, thumping over Budapest's cobbles ahead of Peter Lindner's similar car – Lindner ready, given any sign of trouble, to hand over to Nöcker, to ensure victory in the Championship.

Anyway, the important thing was that the driver of the fastest car was the overall winner, which is always the most satisfactory result!

Such an achievement today would be greeted with delight by Jaguar enthusiasts around the world. In fact, it was a very badly publicised contest throughout, and to finish the first Championship in far-off Hungary was hardly conducive to Monday morning headlines – no matter how good it may have been for *entente*.

As it was, Jaguar Cars – on the verge of introducing the 'softer' S-type saloons – had reached the stage of not being very fond of the 'boy-racer' and 'get-away car' image, acquired over an eight-year period by the compact saloons, and now beginning to rub-off on the larger Jaguars. There was also the co-incidence of Bernard Consten's Jaguar overcoming the Ford Galaxies in the Tour de France, on the very same day as the Budapest race. Sponsored not only by Shell but by *L'Equipe*, the French 'International' was reported daily – although not on the same scale as its two-wheel namesake. The best way for Jaguar's management to find out how the Tour was going was to get the duty apprentice ('on loan' to Henly's Piccadilly showroom) to nip out to a good London newsagent around mid-morning and pick-up *L'Equipe* with all the previous day's results recorded in full detail.

Very much to the disadvantage of the Lindner organisation, too, was the fact that the Frankfurt Motor Show was held just too early for the German Jaguar achievement to be the theme of their display.

In 1964 the *Europa-Pokal,* now officially recognised by the FIA, followed a similar pattern, but with the best seven results (out of ten events), to count, including two hillclimbs. The Broadspeed 1275cc Mini-Cooper 'S's of John Handley and Ralph Broad (of whom more anon) did well in their class; but the Championship winner, driving a works Mini-Cooper 'S' in the *1000cc* category, was Warwick Banks – a result that helped make-up for the way his Formula Junior team mate Jackie Stewart was overshadowing him so often! Böhringer led a team for Mercedes-Benz, his best win being in the Nürburgring six-hour race where he found no serious opposition, Lindner having turned his attention to Le Mans for his first and only appearance there. This season Lindner and Nöcker had forsaken saloons for a few selected races with the lightweight Sayer 'E' type, which boasted the most powerful of XK engines – a 3.8-litre fuel-injected alloy unit developing 344bhp, failure of which caused a lengthy pit-stop and eventual retirement in the French classic. Poor Lindner died in an horrific accident with that 'E' type in pouring rain at Montlhéry that autumn; he had worked hard to build Jaguar's and of course his own reputation in Germany, and no-one has managed to emulate him yet – although the full weight of British Leyland very nearly did so, fifteen years later, as I shall relate shortly.

John Sparrow drove his 3.8 in Europe several times in 1964, but with no real success. At home, he finished thirteenth in the BRSCC Saloon Car Championship (in which Chris McLaren's similar car came a creditable fourth) the easy winner being Jim Clark's Ford Lotus-Cortina.

From 1964, isolated Jaguar successes did occur in

John Sparrow raced this ex-Jaguar experimental department car in Europe with some success after most Jaguar saloon car racers had packed up or moved on to other makes. His best result was probably at Zandvoort in 1963, although this picture was taken at Brands Hatch.

Above: In action for the cameras for the first time, at a dreary-weather Silverstone test-day for the benefit of the press in March 1976 *Photo: P. Skilleter*

Below: Originally, without its spoiler, the car looked good from the rear. Its prime purpose was to promote the *Corporation,*. however, and its appearance was changed several times to try and emphasise this idea. Note the obsolete "XJ12C" badging in this March 1976 view. *Photo: P. Skilleter.*

that they often needed nursing through the long races, the 'old' CSLs were still having things their own way in the European touring series! Broad is also certain that it would have taken very little extra effort for BL to present the new XJ-S for approval by the international racing federation; at the time one of the rear interior dimensions was said to be just too small for the car to be accepted as a Group Two saloon; rather than risk a long haggle over this matter, Broad and BL plumped for the saloon shape.

So, co-incidental with the XJ-S's public announcement, BL commissioned Broad to design and build a racing Jaguar, based on the XJ5.3C ("C" stood for coupe, although the model had a silhouette identical to that of the original short-chassis XJ saloon), and soon one of the attractive two-door bodyshells was delivered quietly from Coventry to the back door of Broadspeed's workshop at nearby Southam.

One might have imagined that such a small company had enough to do, running BL's official British championship-winning Triumph Dolomite team, but Broad re-orientated his business to concentrate on the new challenge.

After its first race (the 1976 TT) the car was brought to Coventry for a second time – to be shown to Jaguar Driver's Club members attending their AGM. Ralph Broad (right) and driver Andy Rouse (left) talk to JDC Chairman David Harvey.

What Broad did was virtually to design a new motorcar, and he had to put in a great deal of development work. The engine was bored out 0.6mm, bringing the capacity up from 5343 to 5416cc, and the specification included 12 to 1 compression pistons and other components from Cosworth Engineering. Broad's own modifications to the sump (which had to remain wet, to keep within the regulations) were considerable, involving a system of chambers and baffles to counteract oil-surge under extreme conditions. At least three engines were destroyed in circuit testing before the car ever raced. Lucas mechanical fuel injection took air from a specially designed ram-effect plenum chamber. The Jaguar close-ratio gearbox was coupled to a single plate clutch, hydraulically-operated to ensure a high clamping load with reasonable pedal pressure.

The car was already bristling with oil and water pumps and radiators when, after barely six-months work and with much more to be done, the car and the programme were announced. Leyland and the public were itching for results; Broad's infectious enthusiasm had caught their imagination; his desperate need for long and concerted experiment had not. With the launch of the car came the announcement that it would be contesting its very first race at Salzburgring – less than a month away, on Easter Sunday 1976!

The 1976 European Touring Car Championship opened with a four-hour race at Monza which Ralph Broad attended, to size-up the opposition. There he saw the Stuart Graham/Reine Wisell Chevrolet Camaro make fastest lap and lead the race by 38-seconds only to retire near the end with excessive pad, belt, and water consumption, plus a blown petrol pump fuse. He saw four German Zakspeed Ford engines fail due to oil surge, and he saw a Belgium-entered BMW win with ease. He returned to England and persuaded BL to postpone 'his' Jaguar's debut until the Mugello race near Florence in May. It had been a miserable spring so far, with hardly any opportunity to test in dry weather. "I am determined not to prejudice this long-term race programme for the sake of one event", he said, and, as it was such short notice, the Leyland team's Group Two Broadspeed Dolomite Sprint was sent to Austria more as an act of good faith than for any other reason. Derek Bell and David Hobbs retired at Salzburgring, the Triumph breaking a rocker. The German Fords failed again and this time Belgian BMWs were first and second. At Mugello and at Brno in May it was the same story – but now there were rumours that the Jaguar could well meet not only BMW but Mercedes opposition at the Nürburgring in July.

At home there was speculation as to who would replace Steve Thompson, one of four contract drivers, who signed-off in mid-season; and still the Jaguar was not considered raceworthy. A principal reason for this was the international sporting commission's refusal to admit water-cooling for the large disc brakes which were overheating badly during testing. When a radical change

During 1976, the underbonnet appearance was quickly tidied-up from this...

...to this!

The four-pot Lockheed calipers installed on the racing coupe; the car's weight strained its braking capacity to the limit.

(from a four to two caliper system) began to be effective, oil surge and other difficulties emerged. Even the road wheels and hubs had to be redesigned; the original wheels had been distorting and 'working' on the hubs, causing breakages resulting from high cornering forces. Such basic problems with a lightened but still very heavy car brought home to BL management the need to listen to a basic Ralph Broad dictum: "Develop one thing at a time; develop two or more at once and you are lost."

A red herring was the idea of taking part in the non-championship 24-hour race at Spa, to make up for missing Nürburgring and to get in some racing miles. The Jaguar missed both. Chris Craft was nominated to replace Steve Thompson. In August, with Broadspeed's own development driver Andy Rouse driving, one of the two Jaguars now being worked upon crashed through the catch-fencing at Becketts – Silverstone's slowest corner – when a wheel broke-up due to fouling.

August 1976 also marked the debut of an XJ in racing – but it was not the Broadspeed car!

At Mosport Park, Canada, Bob Tullius of Group 44 – another team well-known for meticulous race preparation – fielded a Jaguar XJ-S backed by BL's North America subsidiary and Quaker State Oil. The Jaguar qualified fastest in its class, and was well ahead in the SCCA production car race when it dropped to fifth as an oil cooler gave trouble. The Broad project was still having oil problems too; the original detergent oil had turned frothy and very hot. Broad had then gone to a non-detergent oil, which ran so cool that the camshafts were damaged. Now, an oil was being developed that operated at around 85 degrees Centigrade – thus this was just another example of the frustration and expense that surrounded the whole British exercise.

While the American XJ race debut had been on a low key, there had to be a fanfare when – at last – one Jaguar was entered for the Tourist Trophy, Britain's qualifying

round in the Championship in September. British Leyland wanted something back for the investment so far, and Broad's compromise was to agree to a common purpose – to put the Jaguar on pole position and to see it lead the race at Silverstone, Broadspeed's local circuit.

With special qualifying Dunlop tyres, Derek Bell put the car on the front row with a 1m.36.72s. compared with the Belgian Pierre Dieudonné whose 1m.38.69s. was fairly easily quickest of the BMW times. Bell led on the first lap of the race itself, to shouts of delight from the large crowd of enthusiasts who had come to see *their* eagerly awaited 'Big Cat' – the semi-official nickname the racing XJ had been given.

Streaking through from the third row, Gunnar Nilsson (on loan to the Belgian Luigi team as pacemaker) brought

Right & Below: Leyland Competitions Chief John Davenport (left) and Ralph Broad confer during the traumatic practicing at the coupe's first 1977 race. Down to one car already, they send John Fitzpatrick out just before the end of the session...

...to get in his 'flyer' of a lap!
Photo: Andrew Whyte

his BMW alongside Bell's Jaguar as they came past the pits for the second time. Nilsson moved ahead for three laps, but Bell was determined to prove the Jaguar's performance. The car's handling soon began to deteriorate due to an unfortunate mixture of tyre types, but Bell kept up a spectacular show for as long as possible, losing the lead on lap nine. Then a tyre went soft and disintegrated as Bell was making for the pits. Five laps were lost before Bell was back in the fray for twenty more laps, creating a new official Group Two record of 1m.38.50s.; then David Hobbs took over at the first refuelling stop, but only six laps later he lost a wheel at Becketts Corner when a driveshaft failed – supposedly weakened by the effects of the puncture and the flailing tyre. BL boss Alex Park was there, and declared himself ''absolutely delighted'' with the Jaguar's first outing, describing its failure as ''simply bad luck''. Before the race BL and Broad had said that this would be the car's only appearance in 1976; afterwards Park confirmed that the development programme would continue through the winter, with the 1977 European Touring Championships as the goal.

The 1976 championship went to Pierre Dieudonné and Jean Xhenceval (brother-in-law of Belgian team chief Luigi Cimarosti) with the all-conquering 3.2-litre BMW CSL; they'd won at Silverstone after the Nilsson car had lost time while a leaking fuel pump was repaired.

That winter, former Daimler apprentice David Hobbs – a great Jaguar fan – accepted a BMW offer he couldn't refuse. That left Derek Bell and Andy Rouse in the Jaguar team, and two places to fill. The Chris Craft plan came to nothing; the new team members were John Fitzpatrick and Tim Schenken, two respected names in motor-racing

– a disappointment to several drivers who would have relished a BL contract including Stuart Graham, winner of the two previous TTs (and, by the way, son of the great two-wheel TT rider, Les Graham). Former journalist John Davenport was brought in to become BL's Competitions director, very largely because of the Triumph TR 7 assault on rallies – Davenport's speciality! (He is one of Britain's most successful co-drivers).

Although Bob Tullius had won his class second time out with the XJ-S at Lime Rock, Connecticut, the SCCA finals at Atlanta, Georgia, produced a first lap spin and then retirement with fuel feed trouble – but not before he had qualified fastest. Winter 1976 saw the Group 44 XJ-S shed 240lb. in weight (to 2860lb.), for Category I of the 1977 TransAm Series in which the American Jaguar had been entered.

Round One of the 1977 European Touring Championship came in March, and two Jaguar XJ5.3Cs reported to Monza in a new version of the red, white, and blue Leyland Motorsport colour scheme; they had new nineteen-inch diameter Dunlop shod wheels (thus scotching a rumour that Goodyear might be brought in), and an unsightly spoiler was fitted to the boot-lid.

Potentially a good race lay ahead, for not only were the two Jaguars faced with the Belgian BMWs (including one that had been sold to Italian millionaire sportsman Martino Finotto) but a greater menace in the form of another 3.2-litre BMW, beautifully prepared by the Bavarian engineering company, Alpina.

Both marques suffered from oil starvation, and the Monza paddock during practice seemed littered with 6-cylinder BMW and 12-cylinder Jaguar engines in various stages of undress.

Fitzpatrick and Quester at the front of the Monza grid. On the second row are the BMWs of Dieudonné/Xhenceval and the winners Facetti/Finotto – BMW number three, and the only big car to finish.
Photo: Andrew Whyte

It was in the front-runners' interests to make a success of Group Two, and Old Pros Ralph Broad and Burkhard Bovensiepen of Alpina worked hard together, even utilising a German scheme for improving oil circulation in engines that were being starved under braking for the chicanes which have made Monza a slower circuit than (say) Silverstone.

There was only one replacement engine for the two Jaguars, and it went into the Fitzpatrick/Schenken car simply because theirs had been the first to come to grief in practice. Fitzpatrick had best time with a calculated 'flyer' of a lap, but was still less than a second ahead of the experienced Austrian driver Dieter Quester in the 340bhp Alpina BMW which (like the Belgian entries) was right on the 1050Kg. weight limit. The Jaguars had shed a little weight since 1976; no figures were disclosed, but it had been done in part by deleting power-assistance from the steering; the Jaguars were overweight at around 27cwt, and that situation could never be altered appreciably, no matter what wizardry Ralph Broad and his team might weave; all his team's big problems stemmed from that.

Fitzpatrick was left by Quester in a ragged rolling start, but the Jaguar – perhaps 550bhp of it – reached the chicane first, and drew away from the BMW, which lay a comfortable second for twenty-one laps, after which it retired with a recurrance of cylinder head gasket failure which had damaged two Alpina engines in practice; so Vittorio Brambilla never got a drive. John Fitzpatrick came in for a routine pit-stop after just over fifty-minutes with the Jaguar looking and sounding wonderful, and well in the lead. Schenken took over, but within two laps he was back; the oil pressure had dropped and not climbed back, as he braked for a chicane; not even the combined efforts of two of Europe's finest 'fettlers' were able fully to overcome the dire effects of wet-sump lubrication! John Davenport of BL was to make it a priority, from then on, to get that regulation changed! Only one BMW lasted the race, but it won with ease.

Broad continued to work on improving the bearing starvation problem, and testing went on unabated at Silverstone, Goodwood, and even the brand new Donington whenever there was something to test. Bell lost a wheel at a Silverstone session.

Round Two at the Salzburgring was an unexpected disaster, for practice had been relatively trouble-free, and the Jaguars were first and fourth on the grid. Quester led away in the Alpina BMW which he was sharing with Gunnar Nilsson, but was passed by Schenken, then by Rouse. Rouse then led while Schenken retired after only eleven laps with driveshaft failure. The same thing – shearing of the outer flange – happened to Rouse, still leading after twenty laps; he had to come in to the pits after a stone had gone into the radiator, and that was when the failing flange was noted. This time the Alpina car ran well, and earned its runaway victory.

Rain and snow had added to the misery of spectators and the Broadspeed team. Former Jaguar chief 'Lofty' England didn't say very much; he simply whisked Ralph Broad off to his retirement home in the mountains nearby, for a few days' much needed rest.

The Alpina BMW moved ahead of the Broadspeed Jaguar shortly after this picture was taken at the rolling start, but Fitzpatrick was first again by the chicane, never to be overtaken until the pit-stops began. *Photo: Andrew Whyte*

Interior of the first 'competition coupe' – smaller wheel, no carpets, but still some walnut veneer; not that one saw any *production* V12 coupes with a stick shift... *Photo: P. Skilleter*

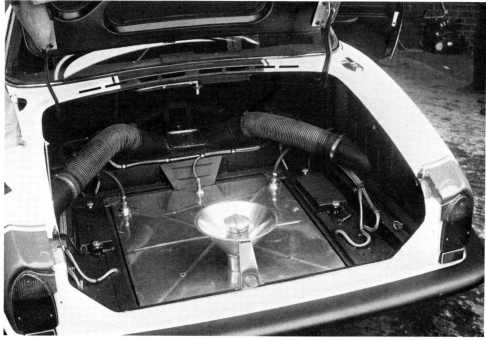

Large petrol tank let into the floor of the coupe, early on in development. Flexible tubing ducts hot air away from the inboard rear brake discs – always a problem to cool with the bridge-type system of mounting the rear suspension used by Jaguar.

The transporters moved south to Mugello and waited while new driveshafts were being tested at the Jaguar works in Coventry. BL managment insisted that the cars should be raced only if the tests proved satisfactory. Andy Rouse waited patiently for news, hoping to fly out with the driveshafts; the Broadspeed boys had the cars ready and scrutineered down in Italy; but no news was bad news! The Jaguars were packed away once more, without turning a wheel on the circuit.

Burkhard Bovensiepen was disappointed when Quester put a connecting rod through the side of his BMW's engine, giving victory at Mugello to the Luigi cars. He was even more disappointed at the lack of opposition, and withdrew his car from Round Four (Enna, Sicily) a fortnight later when told the Jaguars would not be there. A rather daunting prospect anywhere in Italy is the prospect of legal action in the event of a racing accident, and this was one very good reason why the Broadspeed transporters set off, not south, but northbound from Mugello. Down in Sicily, Belgian BMWs had another field day.

If anywhere was Jaguar territory in the summer of 1977

If the Jaguars were going to win anywhere, they should have done it on the very fast Brno circuit, where they are seen sandwiching the Alpina BMW of European Champion-elect Dieter Quester

The coupes reached well over 170mph on the Brno course – virtually as much as was recorded by the all-out-racing D-types on the Mulsanne straight at Le Mans in another era. Aerodynamics had been checked back home in MIRA's wind-tunnel. *Photo: Jaguar Cars*

it was surely Czechoslovakia's long fast Brno road circuit – and there were the two British cars sharing the front row at last! Averaging about 115mph for their best 6.8-mile practice laps, the Jaguars were reaching well over 170mph on the fastest sections of the course. Two days of Goodwood testing had reassured BL and Broadspeed about the latest driveshaft flanges.

After one race lap, Bell led Fitzpatrick, and both were pounding away from Quester's and the other BMWs. On Lap Two, Bell came into the pits with a burst oil-delivery pipe; he went out again after a long halt caused by faulty diagnosis, but soon the gearbox seized and he gave up after fifteen laps. Fitzpatrick had a high-speed blow-out, possibly caused by debris, which tore away the offside rear of the bodywork. As the mechanics struggled to replace damaged rear suspension parts, they must have wondered what else they had to do to get the V12 Jaguar to finish a race... Well, quite a lot! At its final pitstop amidst blue oil smoke, the Fitzpatrick/Schenken Jaguar was given a liberal squirt from a fire extinguisher, allowing the clutch facings sufficient grip for one more lap. Eleven laps behind the winner, third in class, and sixteenth overall – not a memorable result, and even Fitzpatrick's unofficial record lap in 3m.31.4s. did not appear on the results sheet.

Nürburgring, scene of so many long-distance race-wins for Jaguar in the past, was the next stop for the V12 team, where a long and relatively trouble-free training session was held on the way back from Brno to Southam. The long-awaited (and expected) acceptance of dry sumps for Groups Two and Four found Broadspeed unready, and in early practice one of the cars ran a bearing as if to remind the team that its engine lubrication problems were not over. The other car had to have an engine change, too, after a gudgeon pin had moved. Then the oil problem recurred; another engine-change for Fitzpatrick and Schenken! The Bell/Rouse car overheated because of a blow-hole in a casting; a cylinder-head change! In final practice, one car had a misfire and the other needed a new fuel-metering unit. It had been a shattering pre-race experience for the British team, and the likelihood of finishing seemed further away than ever.

The 5.3 coupe at an early test session at Silverstone, showing its Leyland colours of blue and white – rather than the sober British Racing Green of its forebears from Coventry. But for all the tribulations surrounding the car's track career, it aroused great interest wherever it appeared and increased spectator attendences at every Championship round at which it performed. *Photo: P. Skilleter*

The Jaguars were in the heart of serious "selling country"; and to achieve success at Nürburgring always adds prestige, for the 14.2-mile circuit is so demanding.

Jaguar's early racing days had not brought many good results from the Coventry marque's rare visits there, whereas some of Aston Martin's greatest triumphs had occurred at the classic German circuit. Best placing (in the 'fifties) for a Jaguar in Germany had been when Roy Salvadori and Ian Stewart in an *Ecurie Ecosse* C-type came second to the Ascari/Farina Ferrari in the first-ever Nueburgring 1000-Kilometre race (1953). The early 'sixties', however, had been wonderful years for Jaguar saloon cars, thanks to the late Peter Lindner whose exploits at the Ring have been recorded previously.

Now, in 1977 a completely new team from a completely different organisation was pitting its resources against those swoops and switchbacks with Jaguar motor-cars – and BL Germany were out in force, to promote, hard.

John Fitzpatrick rose to the occasion as usual to take one car round in 8m. 30.3s, best practice time – without even getting a proper flying start to the lap! Bell and Rouse had to make do with a third row position; being on the grid at all was a relief, and they were to adopt a new policy for their race – simply to set a fairly low average speed and to drive steadily.

Fitzpatrick was left to decide how to tackle the race, and as he set off in the lead it seemed probable that he would retain it for a lap; not even *he* expected to return a mere 8m. 29.8s. later, having averaged 100.46mph to record fastest race lap from a rolling start! It was twelve-seconds before Quester came by with the Alpina BMW in second place, and Fitzpatrick said afterwards he had *not* put everything into that lap, even wondering on the long finishing straight if some incident had held up the field behind him! He had time to wonder, for the Jaguar's engine failed again on lap two.

Both coupes in the pits during practice at Nurburgring, where the Broadspeed men spent every night and day working on one engine or another.
Photo: Andrew Whyte

John Fitzpatrick straps himself in, having gained pole position at Nurburgring, prior to breaking the lap record (at over 100mph average) and, as usual, retiring!
Photo: Andrew Whyte

Bell and Rouse drove a fine controlled race, and if it had not been for an unscheduled stop to change the rear wheels one of which was bent, and another to collect just enough fuel to complete the four-hour race ... ah! if! Gunnar Nilsson had taken over from Quester and, as the race progressed, he was having to contend with low oil pressure and actually coasted the BMW during the final stages. All the other quick BMWs were in trouble, too, and so the surviving Jaguar *did* seem to be in with a chance. The popular Nilsson, fresh from his Belgian Grand Prix win for Team Lotus, was too canny to let victory slip away, however, and the Jaguar was still nearly 2.5 minutes behind when the BMW took the chequered flag with twenty-seven laps completed. Third, a lap down, was one of the fast 2-litre Zakspeed Fords which had been quick to reappear on the scene as soon as dry sumps were permitted.

Delight at coming second was tempered in the BL/Broadspeed camp by the knowledge that opposition had been in such mechanical chaos, too! Everyone was pleased for the jolly Swede, Gunnar Nilsson; it was to be the last victory for the brave young man who was to create an international cancer treatment campaign shortly before his own death the following year.

At Zandvoort in August, the Alpina BMW and one of the Jaguars appeared with dry-sump lubrication for the first time; the Fitzpatrick/Schenken car soon had one of the new twin Cosworth scavenge pump drives break, as well as having faults in the gearbox and final drive. It qualified fifth fastest, while the wet-sump car of Bell/Rouse managed third. For the first time BMWs dominated the grid. Rouse managed to bring his car through from the second row to lead at the end of lap one and for seven of the next twenty, until a rear wheel

puncture sent him into the pits. He recovered to run third, until the final drive began to disintegrate, a tooth jamming in the special differential oil pump – which the gallant Broadspeed men replaced, although all hope for the race was already lost, Schenken having brought in the dry-sump Jaguar for the first of four scavenge-pump drive changes. Toine Hezemans shared Quester's third win of the year.

The Nürburgring result *might* have led BL to continue sponsorship of the Broadspeed Jaguar project for another year. The Dutch event that followed it now sealed the project's fate.

Ralph Broad moved on to Silverstone six-weeks later in the knowledge that, no matter how well his V12s might do in the Tourist Trophy, his Jaguar team would not be racing in 1978.

This did not prevent a tremendous effort being made for the first anniversary of the car's debut, and one of the biggest improvements came with the fitting of rear tyres with stiffer sidewalls. These helped the Jaguars – now producing a reputed 570bhp – make the two fastest practice laps, Rouse being quickest in 1m.36.05s. (nearly 110mph average) – but Quester, using qualifying tyres, was only just behind.

It turned into the best race of the series; but the wishes of a huge crowd of enthusiasts (most of whom hadn't seen the Jaguar for a year) were not sufficient to overcome a tactical problem that could be solved only by finishing races – the problem of pitstops. Simply, throughout the season of three-to-four hour races, the BMWs could manage with just one pitstop for fuel and a driver-change; the Jaguars would need at least two stops, despite an improvement in fuel consumption since the project had begun.

Rouse leads Schenken and Quester into Copse corner on lap one of the TT.

Schenken is ahead on lap two. Note how, on rformance, the Alpina car is the only BMW to provide any real opposition at all: the others are already trailing.

Soon after, Schenken half-spins on oil while Rouse goes through waving "bad luck."

Schenken recovers quickly, but Quester's BMW storms past into second place.

Rouse leads Quester, and Schenken begins to catch up.

Rouse continues to scythe through the field while, lights ablaze, Schenken draws level with Quester in front of the grandstands. How the crowds loved it; the serious trouble had yet to intervene!

577

Early leader Tim Schenken half-spun and later crashed his dry-sump car (now with an improved scavenge pump drive) out of third place at Becketts when a front hub sheared. Rouse was leading Quester when he handed the Jaguar over to Derek Bell after 38 laps.

Bell was able to regain and increase the Jaguar's lead to 27-seconds in a wonderfully responsible stint to lap seventy-five; but the BMWs had had all their pitstops and, after the Jaguar had taken on fuel, oil, water (for the brake coolers) and one new front tyre, Rouse was faced with the task of making up over twenty seconds in the thirty laps that remained. It looked possible ...

Then the rains came! Dark clouds had been threatening all day, with light drizzle from time to time; now the fine rain became heavier, steadier – not enough to create proper puddles, but quite sufficient to make the rubber and oil soaked track even greasier. The gap came down to under a quarter of a minute, then 'hung' there. Rouse, slicing through whole bunches of slower cars, now caught occasional glimpses of the bright green Alpina BMW that had challenged so hard all year. Now it was being driven by Britisher Tom Walkinshaw, tip-toeing round, well briefed by his pit. Several laps from home, however, Walkinshaw got the fright of his life when the BMW skated on to the grass at nearly 150mph coming out of Abbey Curve; luck as well as skill brought him back on course for victory. A lap later he was able to breathe easily. There, hard against the barriers, lay the Jaguar; it had caught the same patch of oil and Rouse's brave drive came to an alarming but relatively undamaging end.

Being classified fourth behind three BMWs and creating a new Group Two lap record in 1m.36.98s. (108.84mph) was no consolation and (apart from a sense of fairplay to the Belgian organisers) it is very difficult to know why the Broadspeed transporters very soon were on their way to the tight Zolder circuit for the last act of the tragedy to be played out, a week later.

To complete the story: the Jaguars qualified second and third in Belgium after an engine-change for the dry-sump car and tyre trouble. Fitzpatrick led briefly with Bell third, but these positions became second and fourth until the agony began again. Fitzpatrick had a puncture then retired with a broken valve spring. The second car had gearbox seizure. Only after this reminder of a relentless saga against overwhelming problems did the official announcement come from British Leyland. Ralph Broad remained resilient to the end, pointing out that the cars had had to become heavier again with every little modification to make them stronger or more reliable. He and his team had done the best they could. "We were beaten by weight" he said in a terse interview.

The last two rounds of the Championship took place in Spain and Portugal, the French event being cancelled. They were BMW battles, of course, and four different drivers were in with a chance of becoming champion – the consistent Belgians Dieudonné and Xhenceval, Italian veteran Carlo Facetti (who had campaigned Alfa Romeo early in the season), and the imperious Austrian, Dieter Quester. In the end it was the Austrian who took the honours for the very professional Alpina team whose 3.2-litre BMW CSL had been the only car to compete with the Jaguars on pure performance, and had overcome some similar problems in doing so. Helped by five different co-drivers, Quester had five wins, a second, and a fourth. Quester's 'second' happened at Estoril, and Alpina's success was soured by a silly accident as Quester's co-driver – Umberto Grano who had broken with the Luigi team after a row about tactics – killed a pedestrian who tried to cross the track as the race drew to a sad close. (Grano was to become Champion in 1978).

Perhaps the most remarkable aspect of the Broadspeed effort was the way in which all the Jaguar drivers backed one another and the team. Their morale, loyalty and self-control showed that they had been correctly

Andy Rouse making the big effort at the Silverstone TT in September 1977, attempting to catch Walkinshaw's BMW; but it all ended against the Armco...

chosen and their skill (and pleasure) in driving the XJs had been a highlight for the spectators

In its short career the Broadspeed Jaguar XJ12C had competed in eight races and led them all. It had qualified fastest five times; yet out of fifteen opportunities it had genuinely finished only three times – second in Germany, fourth in Britain and sixteenth in Czechoslovakia.

The comradeship in Group Two, while the Jaguars were racing, was a pleasant aspect of 1977 and it came about through mutual respect and a desire for the European series to be a success. Subsequently AMG of Stuttgart entered several races with the long-rumoured Mercedes-Benz 450SLC, fitted with automatic transmission; it did no better than the Jaguars, but did it quietly, then disappeared even more quietly. Had the Jaguars become a really serious threat, it seems likely that someone would eventually have made discreet enquiries as to whether any XJ5.3s had actually been built with manual gearboxes for customers ...

Later a South African BL dealer prepared an XJ5.3 four-door saloon for racing, but, fortunately, it did not get much publicity. Apart from the 'XJ-8' – a 'Super-Saloon' racer of a few years ago, powered by an American V8 engine, which won several events – there have been no other serious attempts to race the XJ12.

The XJ12 saloon competition story should not be closed without mentioning the special two-door racer built as an almost undrivable road-car for "John Steed" in the *New Avengers* television series, or the short-wheelbase four-door which was given by 'Lofty' England many years ago for use as a high-speed fire-tender. The latter still causes favourable comment as it swishes round, quickly and quietly at the back, for the first lap of most Silverstone races.

A dealer entered this modified XJ5.3 four-door saloon in the touring car race that went with the 1979 South African Grand Prix. It was not a success!
Photos: LAT London

Postscript

Racing the 'saloon shape' Jaguars opened the BL/Broadspeed project to criticism from several points of view. Apart from anything else, the image of (perhaps) the world's smoothest and most refined car being turned into a roaring, spectacular monster did seem to some people to make very little sense in promoting British Leyland as a whole, *or* Jaguar specifically.

The *XJ-S* coupe was another matter altogether, for it was different in concept from all previous Jaguars and *looked* different too! Jaguar engineering in Coventry even devoted some time to creating an XJ-S for racing; but it was a desultory project and, although some of the former works racing mechanics are still at Browns Lane, they know what it would take to go racing again ... and it is generally realised (if not stated) that there just could not be *more* money around for *more* motor-racing!

In any case, as mentioned earlier, Group 44 of Virginia were preparing an XJ-S for an ideal race series in North America where sales of Jaguars in earlier days helped bring prosperity to the Coventry firm, and where – as in any strong market – every marque still has to work hard to preserve its reputation.

Browns Lane did investigate competition modifications for the XJ-S although the project did not develop into a serious one; this is an airflow test on a spoiler fitted to a standard car. The limited information gained from this project – which coincided with the Broadspeed activity – was passed on to Australians John McCormack and John Goss when they made separate visits to Jaguar in the early 1980s.
Photo: Jaguar Cars

The clinically spotless Group 44 workshop at Herndon, Virginia.
Photo: P. Skilleter

Together with Joe Huffaker and Lee Mueller in the West, Bob Tullius of the eastern Group 44 team had enjoyed more than two years of E-type racing (1974 to 1976), winning several Championships and getting to know the Jaguar V12 engine very well.

For 1977 and 1978 Tullius used his experience to develop the XJ-S for the TransAm Category One Championship. (Category One is for "cars prepared to Sports Car Club of America Production and Sedan specifications.") In 1977, the Group 44 XJ-S achieved five Category One wins from ten meetings, and Tullius amassed enough points to win the Driver's Championship.

The 1978 results were even better, bringing this V12 racing story to a happier conclusion. Not only did Tullius again take the honours, but the Jaguar did what it had just failed to do a year earlier – win the manufacturers' prize too!

The racing V12 engine in the XJ-S, as modified by Group 44 for the 1976 season. *Photo: P. Skilleter*

A determined Bob Tullius heads Porsche opposition during a *sorte* with the XJ-S in late 1976.

Bob Tullius and his XJ-S in 1977, when he won his driver's division of the TransAm Championship.

Tullius's greatest achievement with the XJ-S came in 1978, when he was champion again — but also managed to put the Jaguar ahead of strong General Motors competition in the manufacturers' category as well.

Biggest success on the publicity front for the XJ-S in the States was undoubtedly its victory in the very illegal "Cannonball" dash of 1979; this semi-regular event organised by Brock Yates involves 3000-miles of motoring right across North America, in defiance of speed limits. The Jaguar averaged more than 87mph (the maximum speed limit in most States is 55mph!) and finished ahead of Mercedes, Pontiac Trans-Am and Corvette opposition, crewed by Dave Heinz and Dave Yarborough.
Photo: Roger Bell

The clincher, at Mexico City's Ricardo Rodriguez autodrome in November, gave Tullius his seventh victory in a row ahead of all the Corvettes, Camaros and Porsche 911s. He even took a back-up car for the last two rounds, to be driven by his chief engineer (and co-driver in longer races) Brian Fuerstenau. In the penultimate race at Laguna Seca, California, Fuerstenau came third, but in Mexico he hit oil, spun, damaged a wheel and later had a stub axle break – yet he was still classified eighth. The second car was entered late in the season, simply to safeguard Jaguar's lead in the manufacturers' standings, and final victory over Chevrolet was sweet.

Lightened and very well-prepared, the Group 44 cars could not be modified as much as the XJ12s used in European racing nor were the races, in general, nearly as arduous. Despite (or because of) this fact Tullius's success meant that advertising and publicity for Jaguar's most sporting model could include the catch-phrase "Thundering Elegance" to link performance with luxury in a way that would have been inappropriate for the saloons, even if the European challenge *had* succeeded – but of course *that* programme had been aimed to boost the *corporate* image of British Leyland, not the Jaguar marque as such.

In 1979 came what might be considered the most significant of all XJ competition successes, in an event that catches the enthusiast's imagination.

Certainly not 'Thundering' – more like lightning – was the elegance with which a standard Jaguar XJ-S glided some 3000-miles from Darien, Connecticut, to Los Angeles in 32-hours and 51-minutes to beat the previous coast-to-coast record by over three-hours.

This was not quite the irresponsible action it might seem to be; David Heinz of Florida and David Yarborough of South Carolina rarely exceeded 100mph as they cruised quietly and in air-conditioned comfort across the great continent. This unique event, the "Cannonball Dash" was organised by motoring writer Brock Yates who won the first one himself in 1971 (with Dan Gurney and a Ferrari Daytona).

Yates thought-up the idea to demonstrate that fast-driving can be safe on America's superb inter-state roads with their ridiculous 55mph limit. There is, of course, no publicity beforehand. After the 1979 'race' was over, however, there is no doubt that few potential buyers of 'drivers' cars' in the USA remained unaware of the special capabilities of the Jaguar motor car for very long.

This unobtrusive, docile, black cat had slunk across

their land at an average speed of 87mph!

In 1979-80 Tullius ran a limited programme for the V8 Triumph, but the Jaguars sat silent. It looked as if BL could back Tullius no more, and he considered entering the world of historic Jaguar restoration and preparation for a while; Group 44 was pared to a token force.

Prospects for Jaguar looked bad. Even during John Egan's first year, not everyone was sure whether the marque would be allowed to survive. Michael Edwardes, the head of BL, had warned that Browns Lane could be closed down unless a dramatic improvement was made in the marketplace. *Sir* Michael and *Sir* John can, of course, look back with satisfaction on the early eighties which gave Jaguar a new lease of life, whereas Triumph as a marque went to the wall. BL in North America had little to offer a critical and demanding public that is well aware that an attorney is only a phone call away, if that.

Britishers Graham Whitehead and Michael Dale were far too professional to allow BL's problems to deter them. So it was that as the other marques fell by the wayside, Jaguar began to take their sole attention. As the marque's North American importers, they provided the catalyst between Tullius and Egan. The immediate result was the chance for Group 44 to create a 'silhouette' XJ-S for the top Trans Am category of 1981. Tullius won three races outright and was runner-up in the championship.

From August 1982 to July 1987, now based in new premises at Winchester, Virginia, Group 44 raced their Jaguar V12-powered XJR-5 and XJR-7 mid-engined prototypes in the Camel GT series, winning nine races outright in that period; *and* they took the Jaguar name back to Le Mans for the first time in twenty years. But 1987 saw a parting of the ways for Jaguar and Group 44.

Group 44's XJ-S experience was absorbed in several areas, not least in Australia where, early in 1980, the BL parts organisation Unipart announced that it would promote its name and its wares by racing XJ-S. As the first edition of this book closed for press, there were plans for Australian Group 1 *and* 5 and, therefore, probably *two* cars painted in the familiar red-white-and-blue Unipart style ... a reminder of the patriotic 1933 Alpine SSs and 1949 Silverstone XK120s!

The project was in the hands of John McCormack, who always appeared to go motor-racing in an impressively individual way; and it seemed the budget was there. Motor racing is well covered on Australian television, the year's highlight being the 1000km autumn marathon of Mount Panorama, normally the province of Ford and GM. Jaguar's Vehicle Engineering Director, Jim Randle, is known to have been impressed by McCormack and to have provided technical help and advice from the Jaguar storehouse of experience. At this point in the first edition, I wrote: "If the next edition of this book can include the story of the Jaguar that beat the Holdens, it will be thanks to McCormack's quiet initiative as well as Unipart dollars...."

Well, unfortunately, John McCormack was injured in a road accident soon afterwards, and that project never really got off the ground. (The former McCormack car was still enjoying club-level success in the mid-1980s, however, driven by Mark Trenoweth who was elected Jaguar Driver of the Year, 1986.) On the other hand, another Australian – John Goss – picked up what he could from both Tullius and McCormack and made his own XJ-S bid. It was not a successful one, and Goss had to put up with a lot of ribbing from a hard-hitting local press. Before long, though, a Jaguar *would* beat the Holdens: but not in a way I predicted.

Touring car racing was still a sore point in Europe as far as Jaguar was concerned, and few people paid much attention when the FIA announced a new premier formula for 1982 – Group A.

The idea was to give the word 'touring' more meaning, by restricting wheel rim widths and fuel capacities according to a sliding scale related to engine size, and above all to ensure that the cars *looked* basically like their showroom equivalents. To date (beginning of 1987 season, and a new World series) it has worked well, despite the inevitable hiccups, with a variety of manufacturers taking interest.

The most interested Britisher back in 1982 was Tom Walkinshaw, a Scots businessman and racing driver of keen financial mind and prize-fighter physique. He looked at the regulations and he looked at the XJ-S; then he spoke to John Egan and Jim Randle. "You go racing in Europe," they advised him. "Come back empty-handed and it'll be your show and your bad luck. Win something and we'll back you." Early 1982 brought its problems, but by June the lone black TWR Jaguar XJ-S with Motul and Akai backing was showing stamina as well as speed ... and stamina was necessary in the European Touring Car Championship, as always. Minimum race distance was decreed at 500km; minimum time (the alternative measure) was three and a half hours.

The Brno Grand Prix of 1982 gave the Jaguar marque its first major victory in Europe since the days of the late Peter Lindner and his champion co-driver Peter Nöcker back in 1963. Soon afterwards, Charles Nickerson ("Chuck Nicholson") as his driving partner, Walkinshaw won the classic Nürburgring six-hour race ... on the old *Nordschleife,* of course. A second car was prepared and, although both crashed out of the Belgian 24-hour race, one-two successes were scored at Silverstone and Zolder before the season was out. The Italo-German team of Umberto Grano and Helmut Kelleners (BMW) took the ETC title, followed by Walkinshaw in third and "Nicholson" fourth. These performances were followed by Jaguar's announcement that it would recognise the TWR Jaguar team officially and share the sponsorship with the French Motul Oil company.

1983 saw the two-car team win five ETC races, and Walkinshaw take a close second to Austria's Dieter

Tullius's crew chief for many years, Lawton Foushee, with the tube-framed XJ-S lookalike which brought Group 44 back into contention with three victories in 1981. *Photo: Jaguar Cars Inc*

The first year in Europe for TWR and Motul was 1982, when this picture was taken at Silverstone. As yet, the Jaguar company was staying out of the picture.

Photo: Jaguar Cars Ltd

TWR Jaguar chief mechanic Kevin Lee *(left)* with Tom Walkinshaw and the team manager, Paul Davis. *Photo: Andrew Whyte*

Dunlop tyre technician Bill
Mack (facing camera) sits in on
a Walkinshaw-Davis-Lee
discussion, Brno 1982.
Photo: Vladimir Havranek

First victory for the XJ-S in
Europe: the
Walkinshaw/"Nicholson" XJ-S
sweeps through Bosonohy
village en route to success in the
1982 Brno GP. *Photo: J Reinhard*

Hero of Donington Park in atrocious conditions was Martin Brundle, who shared the winners' rostrum in 1983 with John Fitzpatrick and Enzo Calderari. Following here is the great Hans-Joachim Stuck (Schnitzer BMW).
Photo: Jaguar Cars Ltd

The three green-with-white Jaguars wave their aerials at an ETC interloper (Volvo turbo) at Monza; first round of the great 1984 season. *Photo: J. Reinhard*

Greatest win of the great 1984 season was by Walkinshaw, Percy and Heyer in the 24-hours of Francorchamps.
Photo: Jaguar Cars Ltd

stone, had to be replaced; they still finished third. The Allam/Dickson Jaguar had retired early on, having ingested part of a headlamp glass in a first-corner clash. This situation left Armin Hahne and none other than John Goss carrying the Jaguar banner, which they did to the end, despite a collapsed seat and the attendant problems of remaining in full control at speed!

"King of the Mountain" Peter Brock (Holden) had looked like coming second but he was sidelined near the finish, and it was the Schnitzer BMW of Roberto Ravaglia and Johnny Cecotto (entered by Australian superstar of the sixties Bob Jane) which split the Jaguars. It should go on record that Garry Willmington and Peter Janson came fourteenth at Bathurst in 1985, a worthy effort for a car with minimal backing, *and* that Bathurst would prove to be the Group A XJ-S's twentieth (and final) victory.

Walkinshaw hoped to return to Bathurst in 1986, but could not strike a deal with the Jaguar importer, upon whom he had relied the previous year; instead he took two cars to Fuji for the November race, supported by Win Percy, Armin Hahne and Denny Hulme, the latter's first race in the Jaguar car for many a year, though he had

recently won the TT again, driving a Rover. On this occasion, both Jaguars led – but both retired. There must be an element of risk in racing only once a year.

Group A requires new homologation of cars every so often. Jaguar decided not to re-homologate the XJ-S, but TWR was given a month's dispensation, and took the two XJ-S's to New Zealand for races at Wellington and Pukekohe in early 1987. Tyre and differential trouble put them out in the first race, but Hahne and Percy scored a strong second place at Pukekohe on 1st February, to sing the Jaguar's Group A swansong after five illustrious years.

The work done by Tullius and Walkinshaw on Jaguar's behalf has been inestimable in its value; they turned an unlikely car, the XJ-S, into a race-winner at a time when success in racing was seen as crucial to the business revival Jaguar needed so badly, and when Jaguar's own engineering resources had to deal with far higher priorities. This led to prototype racing, with TWR's "Silk Cut Jaguar Team" winning the Group C World Championship of 1987 and running Jaguar's Group C *and* IMSA programmes in 1988 – leaving another Jaguar saloon car racing era to history.

Brakes	Girling rod-operated
Gearing	1st – 19.18:1
	2nd – 11.80:1
	3rd – 7.06:1
	Top – 4.86:1
Tyres and wheels	Dunlop '90' 5.25 x 18 covers on 18in Dunlop knock-off wire wheels

Performance

Standing start

0 – 30mph	6.6 sec
0 – 50	17.0
0 – 60	25.1

Max. speed 71.7mph

Speeds in gears: 1st – 20mph
2nd – 32
3rd – 57

Overall fuel consumption: 25-27mpg
(*The Autocar* July 8, 1938).

Top gear	
10 – 30mph	12.5 sec
20 – 40	12.7
30 – 50	14.5

SS Jaguar 2.5-Litre Saloon 1938 – 1940 all-steel

Engine

Cubic capacity	2663cc
Bore and stroke	73 x 106mm
Valves and valve gear	Overhead pushrod
Compression ratio	7.6:1
Cylinder head	Cast iron
Carburettors	Two SU 1.375
Max. power	105bhp at 4600rpm (approx)

Chassis

Weight	32cwt
Dimensions: Wheelbase	10ft
Track – front	4ft 6in
rear	4ft 8in
Length	15ft 6in
Width	5ft 6in
Height	5ft 1in
Suspension: Front	Beam axle, half-elliptic leaf
Rear	Beam axle, half-elliptic leaf
Steering	Burman Douglas worm-and-nut
Brakes	Girling rod-operated
Gearing	1st – 16.20:1
	2nd – 9.5:1
	3rd – 6.16:1
	Top – 4.50:1
Tyres and wheels	Dunlop '90' 5.50 x 18 covers on Dunlop 18in knock-off wire wheels

Performance

Standing start

| 0 – 30mph | 4.7 sec |
| 0 – 50 | 10.6 |

Top gear	
10 – 30mph	9.8 sec
20 – 40	9.5

0 – 60	17		30 – 50	9.4
0 – 70	25		40 – 60	10
			50 – 70	13 (Approx)

Standing quarter-mile: 20.6 sec
Max. speed: 87mph
Speed in 3rd: 70mph
Overall fuel consumption: 19mpg
(*The Motor* June 20, 1939)

SS Jaguar 3.5-Litre Saloon 1938 – 1940 all-steel

Engine

Cubic capacity	3485cc
Bore and stroke	82 x 110mm
Valves and valve gear	Overhead pushrod
Compression ratio	7.2:1
Cylinder head	Cast iron
Carburetters	Two SU 1 1/2in
Max. power	125bhp at 4500rpm approx

Chassis

Weight	32cwt 3qr
Dimensions: Wheelbase	10ft
Track – front	4ft 6in
rear	4ft 8in
Length	15ft 6in
Width	5ft 6in
Height	5ft 1in
Suspension: Front	Beam axle, half-elliptic leaf
Rear	Live beam, half-elliptic leaf
Steering	Burman Douglas worm-and-nut
Brakes	Girling rod-operated
Gearing	1st – 13.45:1
	2nd – 7.9:1
	3rd – 5.12:1
	Top – 4.25:1
Tyres and wheels	Dunlop 'Fort' 5.50 x 18 on Dunlop 18in knock-off wire wheels

Performance

Standing start:
0 – 30mph 4.1 sec
0 – 50   9
Standing quarter-mile: 19.4 sec
Max. speed: 91.8mph
Speed in 3rd gear: 76mph
Overall fuel consumption: 18-20mpg.
(*The Motor* May 31, 1938)

Top gear		
10 – 30mph	7.4 sec
20 – 40	7.8
30 – 50	8.5
40 – 60	9.5
50 – 70	11 (approx)

SS Jaguar 2.5-and 3.5-Litre Drophead Coupes 1938– 1940

As for saloons except:

Weight	33.5cwt (34 cwt – 3.5-litre) approx.

SS Jaguar 1.5-Litre Drophead Coupe 1938 – 1940
As for saloon except:
Weight   27.5cwt approx

Jaguar 2.5-and 3.5-Saloon and Drophead Coupes
As for pre-War series except:

Engine
Compression ratio   6.9 or 7.6:1 (2.5-litre); 6.6 or 7.2:1 (3.5-litre)
Max. torque   136lb/ft at 2500rpm; 184lb/ft at 2000rpm
                                                      (3.5-litre)

Chassis
Gearing (3.5-litre, figures for 2.5-litre in brackets)   1st – 14.41:1 (15.36)
                                                         2nd – 8.28:1 (8.82)
                                                         3rd – 5.74:1 (6.12)
                                                         Top – 4.27:1 (4.55)

Performance
3.5-litre Saloon
Standing start: Standing start
0 – 30mph   5.3 sec   10 – 30mph   9.8 sec
0 – 50   11.9   20 – 40   9.6
0 – 60   16.8   30 – 50   10.3
0 – 70   25.6
Max. speed: 91mph
Speeds in gears: 1st – 27mph
                 2nd – 46
                 3rd – 67
Overall fuel consumption: 16 – 18mpg.
(*The Autocar* March 19, 1948)

Jaguar 1.5-Litre Saloon and Drophead Coupe
As for pre-War series except:

Engine
Compression ratio   6.8 or 7.6:1
Carburetter   Horizontal SU on new manifold
Max. torque   97ft/lb at 2500rpm

Chassis
Gearing   1st – 19.23:1
                                                      2nd – 11.84:1
                                                      3rd – 7.08:1
                                                      Top – 4.875:1

Jaguar MkV 3.5-Litre Saloon and Drophead Coupe

Engine
Cubic capacity   3485cc

Bore and stroke	82 x 110mm
Valves and valve gear	Overhead pushrod
Compression ratio	6.75:1
Cylinder head	Cast iron
Carburetters	Two SU 1.5in
Max. power	125bhp at 4250rpm
Max. torque	

Chassis

Weight and F/R distribution	33cwt, 51/49 (34.5cwt approx Coupe)
Dimensions: Wheelbase	10ft
Track – front	4ft 8in
rear	4ft 8in
Length	15ft 7in
Width	5ft 9in
Height	5ft 2.5in
Suspension: Front	Independent, wishbones, torsion bar, anti-roll bar
Rear	Live axle, half-elliptic leaf
Steering	Burman recirculating ball
Brakes	Girling hydraulic (2LS front)
Gearing (4.30 ENV axle; figures for 4.27 Salisbury code in brackets)	1st – 14.5:1 (14.41)
	2nd – 8.52:1 (8.28)
	3rd – 5.87:1 (5.74)
	Top –4.30:1 (4.27)
Tyres and wheels	Dunlop 6.70 x 16 covers on 5K x 16in bolt-on pressed-steel wheels

Performance

4.30:1 axle ratio

Standing start		Top gear	
0 – 30mph	4.9 sec	10 – 30mph	8 sec
0 – 40	7.1	20 – 40	7.8
0 – 50	9.9	30 – 50	8.9
0 – 60	14.7	40 – 60	10.1
0 – 70	20.4	50 – 70	11.9
0 – 80	31.4	60 – 80	19.3

Standing quarter-mile: 20.2 secs

Speeds in gears: 2nd 46mph
                 3rd 67

Overall fuel consumption: 18.2mpg.

(*The Motor* April 5, 1950)

Jaguar MkV 2.5-Litre Saloon and Drophead Coupe

Engine

Cubic capacity	2663cc
Bore and stroke	73 x 106mm
Valves and valve gear	Overhead pushrod
Compression ratio	7.3:1
Cylinder head	Cast iron
Carburetters	Two SU 1.375in
Max. power	102bhp at 4600rpm
Max. torque	–

Chassis

Weight and F/R distribution	32.5cwt (34cwt approx, Coupe)
Dimensions: Wheelbase	10ft
Track – front	4ft 8in
rear	4ft 9.5in
Length	15ft 7in
Width	5ft 9in
Height	5ft 2.5in
Suspension: Front	Independent, wishbones, torsion bar, anti-roll bar
Rear	Live axle, half-elliptics
Steering	Burman recirculating ball worm-and-nut
Brakes	Girling hydraulic (2LS front)
Gearing (ENV and Salisbury)	1st – 15.35:1
	2nd – 9.61:1
	3rd – 6.21:1
	Top – 4.55
Tyres and wheels	Dunlop 6.70 x 16 covers on 5K x 16in bolt-on pressed-steel wheels

Performance

Approx. as for 1945 – 1949 2.5 litre Jaguar saloon

Jaguar Mk VII Saloon

Engine

Cubic capacity	3442cc
Bore and stroke	83 x 106mm
Valves and valve gear	Twin ohc 0.312in lift; inlet dia. 1.75in, exhaust 1.437
Compression ratio	8:1 (7:1 optional)
Cylinder head	Aluminium alloy, hemispherical combustion chambers
Carburetters	Two SU 1.75in H6
Max. power	160bhp at 5200rpm (150bhp at 5200rpm, 7:1)
Max. torque	195lb/ft at 2500rpm

Chassis

Weight and F/R distribution	34.5cwt, 53/47
Dimensions: Wheelbase	10ft
Track – front	4ft 8in (4ft 8.5in, post-May 1952)
Track – rear	4ft 9.5in (4ft 10in, post-May 1952)
Length	16ft 4.5in
Width	6ft 1in
Height	5ft 3in
Suspension: Front	Independent, wishbone, torsion bar, anti-roll bar
Rear	Live axle, half-elliptic leaf
Steering	Burman recirculating ball worm-and-nut
Brakes	Girling hydraulic servo assisted (two trailing shoe front)

Gearing

Standard:	Automatic:	Overdrive:
1st – 14.4:1	Low – 21.2 to 9.9:1	1st – 13.6:1
2nd – 8.48:1	Inter – 13.1 to 6.12:1	2nd – 7.96:1
3rd – 5.84:1	Top – 4.27:1	3rd – 5.5:1

Top – 4.27:1

Tyres and wheels

Top – 4.55:1
O/D – 3.54:1

Dunlop 6.70 x 16 covers on 16in 5K (5.5K from late 1952)
bolt-on pressed-steel wheels

Performance
160bhp, 8:1cr
Standing start:

	Standard trans	O/D trans.			Top gear	Direct top, O/d trans.
0 – 30mph	4.6 secs	4.4 sec	10 – 30mph	7.9 sec		8.1
0 – 40	7	–	20 – 40	7.8		7.8
0 – 50	9.8	9.9	30 – 50	7.9		7.9
0 – 60	13.7	13.6	40 – 60	8.3		8.6
0 – 70	17.5	18.7	50 – 70	8.6		9.5
0 – 80	23.9	25.7	60 – 80	10.4		12.6
0 – 90	34.4	35.8	70 – 90	16.5		

Standing quarter-mile: 19.3 sec
Max. speed: 101mph (102mph overdrive)
Speeds in gears – 1st 30mph   28mph (overdrive)
            2nd 51   46
            3rd 74   70
Overall fuel consumption: 17.6mpg (17 – 24mpg overdrive)
(*The Motor* April 16, 1952)

Jaguar MkVIIM Saloon

Engine
Cubic capacity	3442cc
Bore and stroke	83 x 106mm
Valves and valve gear	Twin ohc 0.375 lift; inlet dia. 1.75in, exhaust 1.437in (C-type head optional, exhaust dia. 1.625in).
Compression ratio	8:1 (7:1, 9:1 optional)
Cylinder head	Aluminium alloy, hemispherical combustion chambers
Carburetters	Two SU 1.75in H6 (2in H8 optional)
Max. power	190bhp at 5500rpm (8:1)
Max. torque	203lb/ft at 3000rpm

Chassis
As for MkVII except:
Weight and F/R distribution   34.75cwt 54/46 (with overdrive)
Gearing
Standard: Automatic: Overdrive (alternatives)
1st – 12.73:1   As for MkVII
2nd – 7.47:1   1st – 13.56:1 (15.35)
3rd – 5.17:1   2nd – 7.96:1 (9.015)
Top – 4.27:1   3rd – 5.5:1 (6.22)
                                        Top – 4.55:1 (4.55)
                                        O/D – 3.54:1 (3.54)

Performance

Overdrive Saloon, 4.55 axle (automatic figures in brackets)
Standing start:
           Overdrive   Top gear
0 – 30mph 4.5 sec (4.8)   10 – 30mph 6.9 sec

0 – 40	6.9 sec			20 – 40	6.8 sec
0 – 50	9.8	(10.1)		30 – 50	7.6
0 – 60	14.1	(14.3)		40 – 60	8.7
0 – 70	19	(19.3)		50 – 70	9.4
0 – 80	26.5	(26.8)		60 – 80	11.1
0 – 90	33.4	(38.6)		70 – 90	20.6

Standing quarter-mile:19.5 sec (19.7)
Max. speed: 104.3mph (100)
Speeds in gears: 1st – 29mph (39)
                 2nd – 50
                 3rd – 73
Direct top – 100
Overall fuel consumption: 18.8mpg. (18.5)
4200(Overdrive figures: *The Motor* Sept 7, 1955; automatic figures, *The Autocar* May 11, 1956)

Jaguar MkVIII Saloon

Engine

Cubic capacity	3,442cc
Bore and stroke	83 x 106mm
Valves and valve gear	Twin ohc 0.375 in lift; inlet valve dia. 1.75 in, exhaust 1.625 in
Compression ratio	8:1 (7:1 optional)
Cylinder head	'B'-type, aluminium alloy, hemispherical combustion chambers
Carburetters	Two SU 1.75 in HD6
Max. power	210bhp at 5500rpm
Max. torque	216lb/ft at 3000rpm

Chassis

As for MkVIIM except:

Weight and F/R distribution	36cwt, 53/47 (automatic)

Performance

Automatic Saloon, 4.27 axle.
Standing start:

0 – 30 mph	4.4 sec
0 – 50	8.7
0 – 60	11.6
0 – 70	15.2
0 – 80	20.2
0 – 90	26.7
0 – 100	35.7

Standing quarter-mile: 18.4 sec
Max. speed: 106.5mph
Speeds in gears: Low – 46mph
                Int. – 72
Overall fuel consumption: 17.9mpg
(*The Autocar* January 4, 1957)

Jaguar MkIX Saloon

Engine

Cubic capacity	3781cc
Bore and stroke	87 x 106mm
Valves and valve gear	Twin ohc 0.375 in lift; inlet valve diam. 1.75 in, exhaust 1.625 in
Compression ratio	8:1 (7:1 optional)
Cylinder head	'B-type', aluminium alloy, hemispherical combustion chambers
Carburetters	Two SU 1.75 HD6
Max. power	220bhp at 5500rpm
Max. torque	240lb/ft at 3000rpm

Chassis

As for MkVIII except:

Weight and F/R distribution	35.5cwt, 56/44
Steering	Burman recirculating ball worm-and-nut, power assisted
Brakes	Dunlop disc, 12.125in dia. front, 12in dia. rear, servo assisted
Gearing (automatic); manual as for MkVIIM	Low – 21.2 to 9.86
	Int. – 13.2 to 6.14
	Top – 4.27:1

Performance

Automatic transmission

Standing start:

0 – 30mph	4.2 sec
0 – 40	5.9
0 – 50	8.5
0 – 60	11.3
0 – 70	14.8
0 – 80	18.6
0 – 90	25.9
0 – 100	34.8

Standing quarter-mile: 18.1 sec

Max speed: 114.3mph

Speeds in gears: 1st – 48mph

2nd – 80

Overall fuel consumption: 13.5mpg

(*The Motor* October 8, 1958)

Jaguar 2.4 Saloon

Engine

Cubic capacity	2483cc
Bore and stroke	83 x 76.5mm
Valves and valve gear	Twin ohc 0.312 in lift; inlet valve diam. 1.75in, exhaust 1.437in
Compression ratio	8:1 (7:1 optional)
Cylinder head	Aluminium alloy, hemispherical combustion chambers 'B-type head optional
Carburetters	Two Solex downdraught 24mm; SU optional

| Max. power | 112bhp at 5750rpm (8:1) |
| Max. torque | 140lb/ft at 2000rpm |

Chassis

Weight and F/R distribution	27cwt, 55/45
Dimensions: Wheelbase	8ft 11.375in
Track – front	4ft 6.625in
rear	4ft 2.125in
Length	15ft 0.75in
Width	5ft 6.75in
Height	4ft 9.5in

Suspension: Front — Independent, semi-trailing double wishbone, coil springs, anti-roll bar

Rear — Cantilevered live axle, parallel radius arms, Panhard rod, half-elliptic leaf springs

Steering — Burman recirculating ball worm-and-nut

Brakes — Lockheed Brakemaster hydraulic drum, vacuum assisted; Dunlop disc, 11.375 diam, optional from late 1957

Gearing

Standard:
4.55:1 axle ratio until June 1956, then 4.27:1 (in brackets)

Overdrive – 4.55
1st – 15.35:1
2nd – 9.01
3rd – 6.22
Top – 4.55
(O/d – 3.54)
(1st – 14.4:1)
(2nd – 8.46)
(3rd – 5.84)
(Top – 4.27)

Automatic
Low – 21.2 to 9.86
Int – 13.2 to 6.14
Top – 4.27

Tyres and wheels — Dunlop Road Speed 6.40 x 15 covers on 5K x 15in bolt-on pressed steel wheels (5K x 15in knock-off wire wheels optional)

Performance

Overdrive, 4.55 axle Saloon

Standing start

0 – 30mph	4.6 sec
0 – 40	6.9
0 – 50	11
0 – 60	14.4
0 – 70	19.9
0 – 80	28.6
0 – 90	39.1

Standing quarter-mile: 24.6 sec
Max. speed: 101:5mph
Speeds in gears:
1st – 28mph
2nd – 47
3rd – 68.5
Direct top – 93.5
Overall fuel consumption: 18.3mpg.
(*The Motor* July 25, 1956)

Direct top gear

10 – 30mph	8.2 secs
20 – 40	8.4
30 – 50	8.6
40 – 60	8.7
50 – 70	9.9
60 – 80	14.7
70 – 90	19.7

Jaguar 3.4 Saloon

Engine

Cubic capacity	3442 cc
Bore and stroke	83 x 106mm
Valves and valve gear	Twin ohc 0.375 in lift; inlet valve diam 1.75 in, exhaust valve 1.625 in
Compression ratio	8:1 (7:1, 9:1 optional)
Cylinder head	'B-type', aluminium alloy, hemispherical combustion chambers
Carburetters	Two SU 1.75 H.D.6 (2 in HD8 optional)
Max. power	210bhp at 5500rpm (8:1)
Max. torque	216lb/ft at 3000rpm

Chassis

As for 2.4 except:

Weight and F/R distribution   28.5cwt, 57/43

Gearing:

Standard:	Overdrive:	Automatic:
3.54 axle ratio (close ratio in brackets)	3.77 axle ratio	3.54 axle ratio
1st – 11.95:1 (10.55)	1st – 12.73 (11.23)	Low – 17.6 to 7.08
2nd – 6.584 (6.20)	2nd – 7.012 (6.597)	Int – 10.95 to 8.16
3rd – 4.541 (4.28)	3rd – 4.836 (4.561)	Top – 3.54
Top – 3.54 (3.54)	Direct top – 3.77 (3.77)	
	O/d – 2.933 (2.933)	

Performance

Overdrive, 3.77 axle ratio saloon (automatic figures in brackets)

Standing start:			Top gear	
0 – 30mph	3.1 sec	(4.5)	20 – 40mph	7.1 sec
0 – 40mph		(6.5)	30 – 50	6.7
0 – 50	7	(8.7)	40 – 60	6.9
0 – 60	9.1	(11.2)	50 – 70	7.5
0 – 70	12.4	(14.2)	60 – 80	7.7
0 – 80	16	(17.9)	70 – 90	8.5
0 – 90	20.5	(23)	80 – 100	9.8
0 – 100	26	(30.3)		
0 – 110	34.6			

Standing quarter-mile: 17.2 (18)

Max. speed: 120mph (119.8)

Speeds in gears: 1st – 36mph (43)

                 2nd – 67 (81)

                 3rd – 97

                 Direct top – 119

Overall fuel consumption: 16.0mpg, normal range 15 – 22 mpg (19.2)

(Manual figures: *The Autocar* 13 June, 1958. Automatic figures: *The Motor* April 10, 1957)

Jaguar MkII 2.4 Saloon

Engine

Cubic capacity	2483cc
Bore and stroke	83 x 76.5mm

| Max. torque | 240ft/lbs at 3000rpm |

Chassis
As for 2.4 and 3.4 Mk II except:

| Weight and F/R distribution | 30cwt, 56.5/43.5 |

Performance
Overdrive, 3.77 axle, (automatic figures in brackets)

Standing start			Top gear	
0 – 30mph	3.2 sec (3.6)		10 – 30mph	6.7 secs
0 – 40	4.9	(5.3)	20 – 40	6
0 – 50	6.4	(9.8)	30 – 50	6.1
0 – 60	8.5	(9.8)	40 – 60	5.7
0 – 70	11.7	(12.9)	50 – 70	5.9
0 – 80	14.6	(16.9)	60 – 80	6.3
0 – 90	18.2	(21.3)	70 – 90	7.7
0 – 100	25.1	(28.2)	80 – 100	9.7
0 – 110	33.2	(37.0)	90 – 110	15.5

Standing quarter mile: 16.3 sec (17.2)
Max. speed: 125mph (120.4)
Speeds in gears – 1st: 35mph (50)
2nd: 64 (81)
3rd: 98
Direct top: 120
Overall fuel consumption: 15.7mpg (17.3)
(Manual: *The Autocar* Feb 26, 1960; Automatic: *The Autocar* April 5, 1963)

Jaguar 3.8 MkX Saloon

Engine

Cubic capacity	3781cc
Bore and stroke	87 x 106mm
Valves and valve gear	Twin ohc 0.375 in lift; inlet valve diam. 1.75 in, exhaust valve 1.625 in.
Compression ratio	8:1 (7:1, 9:1 optional)
Cylinder head	'Straight port', aluminium alloy, hemispherical combustion chambers
Carburetters	Three SU 2ins HD8
Max. power	265bhp at 5500rpm
Max. torque	260lb/ft at 4000rpm

Chassis

Weight and F/R distribution	37cwt 1qr, 53.4/46.6
Dimensions: Wheelbase	10ft
Track – front	4ft 10in
rear	4ft 10in
Length	16ft 10in
Width	6ft 4in
Height	4ft 6.75in

Suspension
As for S-type saloon

Steering	Burman recirculating ball, power assistance standard
Brakes	Dunlop discs, 10.75ins front, 10ins rear, Kelsey Hayes vacuum servo

Gearing:

Standard:	Overdrive:	Automatic:
1st – 11.954:1	1st – 12.731:1	Low – 17.6 to 8.16:1
2nd – 6.584	2nd – 7.012	Int – 10.95 to 5.08
3rd – 4.541	3rd – 4.836	Top – 3.54
Top – 3.54	Top – 3.77	
	O/d – 2.933	

Tyres and wheels — Dunlop 7.50 x 14 RS5 covers on 5.5K x 14in bolt-on pressed-steel wheels

Performance

Overdrive Saloon, 3.77 axle (automatic figures in brackets)

Standing start:

			Direct top gear	
0 – 30mph	3.6 sec (4.9)		10 – 30mph	8.9 sec
0 – 40	6.1	(6.7)	20 – 40	8.8
0 – 50	8.4	(9.1)	30 – 40	8.6
0 – 60	10.8	(9.1)	40 – 60	8.5
0 – 70	15	(15.1)	50 – 70	9.3
0 – 80	19.4	(26.3)	60 – 80	9.4
0 – 90	24.8	(26.3)	70 – 90	9.9
0 – 100	32.9	(33.3)	80 – 100	13.6
0 – 110mph	–	(44.9)		

Standing quarter-mile: 18.4 sec (18.5)

Max. speed: 120mph (119.5)

Speeds in gears: 1st – 35mph (51)
2nd – 60 (82)
3rd – 90
Direct top – 107mph

Overall fuel consumption: 13.6mpg (14.1mpg).

(Overdrive: *The Motor* November 3, 1963; Automatic, *Autocar* November 2, 1962)

Jaguar 4.2 MkX Saloon

Engine

Cubic capacity	4235 cc
Bore and stroke	92.07 x 106mm
Valves and valve gear	Twin ohc 0.375 in lift; inlet valve diam 1.75 in, exhaust valve 1.625 in
Compression ratio	8:1 (7:1, 9:1 optional)
Cylinder head	'Straight port', aluminium alloy, hemispherical combustion chambers
Carburetters	Three SU 2ins. HD8
Max. power	265bhp at 5400rpm
Max. torque	283lb/ft at 4000rpm

Chassis

As for 3.8 car except:

Steering	Burman recirculating ball, Varamatic power assistance standard
Brakes	Dunlop disc, 10.91in front, 10.375in rear, Dunlop vacuum servo assistance

Gearing:

Standard:	Overdrive:	Automatic:
1st – 10.76:1	1st – 11.46:1	Low – 17.0 to 8.5

2nd – 6.98
3rd – 4.70
Top – 3.54

2nd – 7.44
3rd – 5.00
Direct top – 3.77
O/D – 2.93

Int – 10.33 to 5.16
Top – 7.08 to 3.54

All-synchro box; Powr-lok diff. standard; SP 41 radial tyres

Performance

Overdrive Saloon (automatic figures in brackets)

Standing start:

0 – 30mph	3.9 sec	(4)
0 – 40	5.8	(5.6)
0 – 50	7.9	(7.2)
0 – 60	10.4	(9.9)
0 – 70	13.6	(12.8)
0 – 80	17.1	(17)
0 – 90	22.5	(21.9)
0 – 100	29.5	(27.4)
0 – 110	36.5	(40.3)

Top gear:

20 – 40mph	7.5 sec
30 – 50	7.4
40 – 60	7.5 sec
50 – 70	7.6
60 – 80	8.2
70 – 90	9.4
80 – 100	11.6

Standing quarter-mile: 17.4 sec (17)
Max. speed: 122.5mph (121.5)
Speeds in gears: 1st – 35mph (47)
2nd – 54   (76)
3rd – 81
Direct top – 107
Overall fuel consumption: 16mpg (14.5)
(Overdrive: *Autocar* October 8, 1965: Automatic, *Autocar* October 16, 1964)

Jaguar 420G Saloon

Specification and performance as for 4.2 MkX.

Jaguar S-Type 3.4

Engine

Cubic capacity	3442cc
Bore and stroke	83 x 106mm
Valves and valve gear	Twin ohc 0.375in lift; inlet valve diam. 1.75 in exhaust valve 1.625in
Compression ratio	8:1 (7:1, 9:1 optional)
Cylinder head	'B-type', aluminium alloy, hemispherical combustion chambers
Carburetters	Two SU 1.75in HD6
Max. power	210bhp at 5500rpm
Max. torque	216ft/lb at 3000rpm

Chassis

Weight and F/R distribution		32cwt, 53/47
Dimensions:	Wheelbase	8ft 11.5 in
	Track – front	4ft 7.25in
	Rear	4ft 6.25 in
	Length	15ft 7in
	Width	5ft 6.25 in
	Height	4ft 7.75in

Suspension	Front	Independent, semi-trailing double wishbones, coil springs, anti-roll bar
	Rear	Independent, lower wishbone/upper driveshaft link, radius arms, twin coil springs
Steering		Burman recirculating ball worm-and-nut, power assistance optional
Brakes		Dunlop disc, 11ins front, 11.375in rear, vacuum assisted

Gearing:
As for 3.4 MkII; all-synchro box adopted from September 1965, optional from December 1964 – see 340 for gearing.

| Tyres and wheels | Dunlop RS5 6.40 x 16 or SP 41 185 x 15 covers on 5K x 15in bolt-on pressed steel wheels (5K knock-off wire wheels optional) |

Performance
Overdrive Saloon – used car test

Standing start		Direct top gear	
0 – 30mph	4.1 sec	10 – 30mph	9.5 sec
0 – 40	7	20 – 40	9.5
0 – 50	9.6	30 – 50	9.7
0 – 60	13.9	48 – 60	10.1
0 – 70	18.4	50 – 70	11.1
0 – 80	25	60 – 80	12.9
0 – 90	35.3	70 – 90	16.9

Standing quarter-mile: 19.2 sec
Overall consumption: 14 – 17mpg
(*Autocar* November 19, 1970)

Jaguar S-Type 3.8

Engine
Cubic capacity	3781 cc
Bore and stroke	87 x 106mm
Valves and valve gear	Twin ohc 0.375 in lift; inlet valve dia. 1.75 in, exhaust valve 1.625 in
Compression ratio	8:1 (7:1, 9:1 optional)
Cylinder head	'B-type', aluminium alloy. hemispherical combustion chambers
Carburetters	Two SU 1.75 in HD6
Max. power	220bhp at 5500rpm
Max. torque	240ft/lbs at 3000rpm

Chassis
As for 3.4 S-type except:

| Weight and F/R distribution | 33cwt 53.5/46.5 |

Gearing:
As for 3.8 MkII; all synchro box adopted from September 1964, optional from December 1964 – ratios as follows:

Overdrive
1st – 11.46:1
2nd – 7.389
3rd – 5.01
Direct top – 3.77
O/d – 2.93

Performance

Overdrive Saloon, 3.77 axle, all-synchro gearbox; automatic figures in brackets

Standing start			Direct top gear		
0 – 30mph	3.6 secs (4.5)		20 – 40mph	6.8	
0 – 40	5.5	(6.4)	30 – 50	7	
0 – 50	7.5	(8.5)	40 – 60	7.3	
0 – 60	10.2	(11.8)	50 – 70	7.7	
0 – 70	13.3	(16.5)	60 – 80	8.3	
0 – 80	17.1	(20.9)	70 – 90	10.7	
0 – 90	23.5	(26.6)			
0 – 100	31.8	(34.3)	80 – 100	14.3	

Standing quarter-mile: 17.1 secs (18.3)

Max. Speed: 121.1mph (116)

Speeds in gears: 1st – 37 (40) mph
2nd – 57 (72)
3rd – 84
Direct top – 111

Overall fuel consumption: 15.4mpg (15.3)

(*Motor* December 5, 1964 automatic; August 14, 1965 O/drive)

Jaguar 420 Saloon

Engine

Cubic capacity	4235cc
Bore and stroke	92.07 x 106mm
Valves and valve gear	Twin ohc 0.375in lift; inlet valve dia. 1.75in, exhaust valve 1.625in
Compression ratio	8:1 (7:1, 9:1 optional)
Cylinder head	'Straight port', aluminium alloy, hemispherical combustion chambers
Carburetters	Two SU 2ins HD8
Max. power	245bhp at 5500rpm
Max. torque	283ft/lbs at 3750rpm

Chassis

Weight and F/R distribution		33cwt, 55.5/44.5
Dimensions:	Wheelbase	8ft 11.75in
	Track – front	4ft 7.5in
	rear	4ft 6.5in
	Length	15ft 7.5in
	Width	5ft 7in
	Height	4ft 8.25in
Suspension:		As for S-type saloon
Steering		Burman recirculating ball, Varamatic power assistance optional
Brakes		Girling disc, 11in front, 11.375 rear, vacuum assisted

Gearing:

Standard:	Overdrive:	Automatic:
1st – 10.76	1st – 11.46	Low – 4.80 to 2.40
2nd – 6.97	2nd – 7.44	Int – 2.92 to 1.46
3rd – 4.70	3rd – 5.00	Top – 2.0 to 1.0
Top – 3.54	Direct top – 3.77	
	0/d – 2.93	

| Tyres and wheels | Dunlop RS5 6.40 x 15 or SP 41 185 x 15 on 5.5K x 15ins bolt-on pressed steel wheels (5.5K x 15in wire wheels optional) |

Performance

Overdrive Saloon, 3.77 axle; automatic figures in brackets

Standing start:

				Top gear	(direct top)
0 – 30mph	3.1 secs	(3.5)		10 – 30mph	6.9
0 – 40	5.2	(5.2)		20 – 40	6.3
0 – 50	7	(7)		30 – 50	6.3
0 – 60	9.9	(9.4)		40 – 60	6.4
0 – 70	12.6	(12.3)		50 – 70	6.5
0 – 80	16.7	(16.3)		60 – 80	7
0 – 90	21.3	(21.6)		70 – 90	8.4
0 – 100	27.4	(29.8)		80 – 100	11
0 – 110	38.5			100 – 110	19.2

Speeds in gears: 1st – 36mph (50)

2nd – 56   (78)

3rd – 83

Direct top – 110

Standing quarter-mile: 16.7 sec (17.5)

Max. speed: 123mph (115)

Overall fuel consumption: 15.7mpg (15.4)

Overdrive: *Autocar* March 2, 1967; automatic: *Motor* May 6, 1967)

Jaguar 240 Saloon

Engine

Cubic capacity	2483 cc
Bore and stroke	83 x 76.5mm
Valves and valve gear	Twin ohc 0.375 in lift; inlet valve diam. 1.75 in, exhaust valve 1.625 in
Compression ratio	8:1 (7:1 optional)
Cylinder head	'Straight-port', aluminium, hemispherical combustion chambers
Carburetters	Two SU 1.75 in HS6
Max. power	133bhp at 5500 rpm
Max. torque	146ft/lbs at 3700 rpm

Chassis

As for Mk II 2.4 except:

Dimensions: Length	14ft 11in
Gearing:	Overdrive 1st – 12.19:1 2nd – 7.92 3rd – 5.78 Direct Top – 4.55 O/D – 3.54
Tyres and wheels	Dunlop RS5 6.40 x 15 or SP 185 x 15 on 5K 15in bolt-on pressed-steel wheels

Performance

Overdrive Saloon, 4.55 axle

Standing start

0 – 30mph	4.1 sec
0 – 40	6.3
0 – 50	9.3
0 – 60	12.5
0 – 70	16.4
0 – 80	22.8
0 – 90	31.0
0 – 100	44.8

Standing quarter-mile: 18.7 sec

Max. speed: 106mph

Overall consumption: 18.4mpg

(*Autocar* Jan 4, 1968)

Top gear

10 – 30mph	8.7 sec
20 – 40	8.3
30 – 50	8.3
40 – 60	8.4
50 – 70	8.7
60 – 80	8.7
70 – 90	11.5
80 – 100	14.1

Speeds in gears: (at 5500rpm)

1st – 35mph

2nd – 63

3rd – 73

Direct top – 107mph

Jaguar 340 Saloon

Engine

Cubic capacity	3442 cc
Bore and stroke	83 x 106mm
Valves and valve gear	Twin ohc 0.375 in lift; inlet valve diam. 1.75 in, exhaust valve 1.625 in
Compression ratio	8:1 (7:1 optional)
Cylinder heed	'B-type', aluminium alloy, hemispherical combust on chambers
Carburetters	Two SU 1.75in HD6
Max. power	210bhp at 5500rpm
Max. torque	216lb/ft at 3000rpm

Chassis

As for 240 except:

Weight and F/R distribution	30cwt, 59/41
Gearing	

As for MkII 3.4

Performance

Overdrive, 3.77 axle

Standing start:

0 – 30mph	3.5 sec
0 – 50	6.9
0 – 60	8.8
0 – 80	16.6
0 – 100	26.4

Standing quarter-mile: 17.2 sec

Max. speed: 124mph

Speeds in gears: 1st – 36mph

2nd – 60

3rd – 85

Direct top: 115mph

Overall fuel consumption: 17-22mpg

(John Bolster, *Autosport,* February 16, 1968)

Jaguar 4.2 XJ6 Saloon

Engine

Cubic capacity	4235cc
Bore and stroke	92.7 x 106 mm
Valves and valve gear	Twin ohc 0.375in lift; inlet valve diam. 1.75in, exhaust valve 1.625in
Compression ratio	9:1 (8:1, 7:1 optional)
Cylinder head	'Straight port', aluminium alloy, hemispherical combustion chambers
Carburetters	Two SU 2in HD8 (type HS8 from March 1971)
Max. power	245bhp at 5500rpm
Max. torque	283lb/ft at 3750rpm

Chassis

Weight and F/R distribution	33cwt 1qr, 52/48
Dimensions: Wheelbase	9ft 0.75in
Track – front	4ft 10in
rear	4ft 10.5in
Length	15ft 9.5 in
Width	5ft 9.25in
Height	4ft 6in
Suspension: Front	Independent, semi-trailing double wishbones, coil springs, anti-roll bar
Rear	Independent, lower wishbone/upper driveshaft link, radius arms, twin coil springs
Steering	Rack and pinion, Adwest power assistance standard
Brakes	Girling disc, 11.8in front, 10.4in rear, Lockheed vacuum servo

Gearing:

Standard:	Overdrive:	Automatic:
1st – 10.38:1	1st – 11.04:1	Low – 4.78 to 2.39
2nd – 6.74	2nd – 7.18	Int – 2.9 to 1.45
3rd – 4.92	3rd – 5.23	Top – 2.0 to 1.0
Top – 3.54	Direct top – 3.77	
	O/d – 2.94	

Tyres and wheels	Dunlop E70 VR-15 SP Sport covers on 6K x 15in bolt-on pressed-steel wheels

Performance

Overdrive Saloon, 3.77 axle (automatic figures in brackets, 3.31 axle)

Standing start:			Top gear:	
0 – 30mph	3.1 sec	(3.9)	20 – 40mph	6.3 sec
0 – 40	4.6	(5.5)	30 – 50	6.5
0 – 50	6.6	(7.6)	40 – 60	6.4
0 – 60	8.8	(10.1)	50 – 70	5.9
0 – 70	11.3	(13.4)	60 – 80	6.8
0 – 80	14.7	(17.8)	70 – 90	7.6
0 – 90	18.8	(23)	80 – 100	9
0 – 100	24.1	(30.4)		

Standing quarter-mile: 16.5 sec (17.5)
Max. speed: 124mph (120)
Speeds in gears: 1st – 35mph (53)
(at 5,000rpm   2nd – 53   (87)
for manual car,
5,500 auto.)   3rd – 73

Direct top – 101
Overall fuel consumption: 15.3mpg (15.2)
(Overdrive: *Motor* May 10, 1969, Automatic: *Autocar* June 12, 1969)

Jaguar 2.8 XJ6 Saloon

Engine

Cubic capacity	2791.9cc
Bore and stroke	83 x 86mm
Valves and valve gear	Twin ohc 0.375in lift; inlet valve diam. 1.75 in, exhaust valve 1.625in
Compression ratio	9:1 (7:1, 8:1 optional)
Cylinder head	'Straight port', aluminium alloy, hemispherical combustion chambers
Carburetters	Two SU 2ins HD8
Max. power	180bhp at 6000rpm
Max. torque	182lb/ft at 3750rpm

Chassis

As for 4.2 saloon except:

Weight and F/R distribution   32cwt 3qr, 51.5/48.5

Gearing:

Standard:	Overdrive:	Automatic:
1st – 12.5:1	1st – 13.32	Low – 10.2 to 20.41
2nd – 8.14	2nd – 8.67	Int – 6.19 to 12.38
3rd – 5.93	3rd – 6.33	Top – 4.27 to 8.54
Top – 4.27	Direct top – 4.55	
	O/d – 3.54	

Performance

Overdrive Saloon, 4.55 axle (automatic figures in brackets, 4.09 axle)

Standing start:			Top gear:		
0 – 30mph	3.8 sec	(4.9)	10 – 30mph	8.7 secs	
0 – 40	6	(7.2)	20 – 40	8.7	
0 – 50	8.2	(9.3)	30 – 50	8.7	
0 – 60	11	(12.6)	40 – 60	8.7	
0 – 70	15.2	(16.3)	50 – 70	8.9	
0 – 80	19.3	(21.8)	60 – 80	9.8	
0 – 90	26.4	(29.9)	70 – 90	11.6	
0 – 100	35	(39.9)	80 – 100	14.9	

Standing quarter-mile: 18.1 sec (19.2)
Max. speed: 117mph (113)
Fuel range: 16–20mpg (15 – 19)
(Data: Jaguar Cars)

Jaguar XJ12 Saloon

Engine

Cubic capacity	5343cc 60 deg. V12
Bore and stroke	90 x 70mm
Valves and valve gear	Single ohc per bank, 0.375in lift; inlet valve diam. 1.625in exhaust valve 1.360in

Compression ratio	9:1
Cylinder head	Two flat-face, aluminium alloy
Carburettors	Four Zenith 175CD SE
Max. power	253bhp (DIN) at 6000rpm
Max. torque	302lb/ft (DIN) at 3500rpm

Chassis

As for 4.2 saloon except:

| Weight and F/R distribution | 35cwt, 53.8/46.2 |
| Brakes | Girling disc, 11.18in vented front, 10.38in rear, Girling Supervac 100 servo |

Gearing:
Low – 4.80 – 2.40
Int. – 2.90 – 1.45
Top – 2.0 – 1.0

Performance

Standing start:

0 – 30mph	3.1 sec
0 – 40	4.4
0 – 50	5.9
0 – 60	7.4
0 – 70	9.6
0 – 80	12.2
0 – 90	15.2
0 – 100	19.0
0 – 110	23.9
0 – 120	31.0

Standing quarter-mile: 15.7 sec
Speeds in gears (at 6500rpm): Low – 63mph
Int. – 102mph
Overall fuel consumption: 11.4mpg
(*Autocar* March 29, 1973)

Jaguar 4.2 XJ6 & XJ6L Saloon Series 2 (XJ4.2 from May 1975)

Engine

As for Series 1 except:

| Max. power | 170bhp (DIN) at 4500rpm |
| Max. torque | 231lb/ft at 3500rpm |

Chassis

As for Series 1 except:

Weight (XJ6L)	34cwt
Dimensions: (XJ6L):	
Wheelbase	9ft 4.75in (from October 1972)
Length	16ft 2.75in
Brakes	Girling disc, 11.18in ventilated front, 10.38 in rear

Gearing
1st – 10.72:1 instead 10.38 from April 1975

Performance

As for Series 1.

Jaguar XJ6C (XJ 4.2L from May 1975)

Engine
As for saloon

Chassis
As for saloon except:
Weight	33cwt 1qr
Wheelbase	9ft 1in

Other dimensions as for Series 1 normal wheelbase saloon

Performance
As for Series I 4.2 Saloon

Jaguar XJ12L Series 2 (XJ 5.3 from May 1975)

Engine
As series 1 XJ12 except from May 1975 fuel injection instead of carburetters
Max. power	285bhp at 5750rpm
Max. torque	294lb/ft at 3500rpm

Chassis
As for Series 1 XJ12L.
Gearing
GM Turbo Hydra-Matic gearbox ratios as follows:
1st − 5.95 to 2.48
2nd − 3.55 to 1.48
Top − 3.07

Performance
XJ 5.3, 3.07 axle
Standing start:
0 − 30mph	3.3 sec
0 − 40	4.8
0 − 50	6
0 − 60	7.8
0 − 70	9.7
0 − 80	12.6
0 − 90	15.7
0 − 100	18.8
0 − 110	24
0 − 120	31.2
0 − 130	42.9

Standing quarter-mile: 15.7 secs
Max. speed: 147mph
Speeds in gears (at 6500rpm): 1st − 65 mph
                                              2nd − 109
Overall fuel consumption: 13.2mpg
(*Autocar* September 9, 1978)

Jaguar XJ12C (XJ 5.3C from May 1975)

Engine
As for Series 2 XJ12/XJ 5.3 saloon

Chassis

As for Series 2 XJ12/XJ 5.3 saloon except,
Weight and F/R distribution   36 cwt, 55/45
Dimensions   As for XJ6C

Performance

XJ 5.3C, 3.31 axle
Standing start:

0 – 30mph	3.2 sec
0 – 40	4.4
0 – 50	5.9
0 – 60	7.6
0 – 70	9.4
0 – 80	11.8
0 – 90	14.4
0 – 100	18.4
0 – 110	23
0 – 120	30.5

Standing quarter-mile: 15.7 secs
Max speed: 148mph (estimated)
Speeds in gears: 1st – 60mph
(at 6500rpm)   2nd – 100
Overall fuel consumption: 11.9mpg
(*Motor* April 30, 1979)

Jaguar XJ 3.4 Saloon

Engine

Cubic capacity   3442cc
Bore and stroke   83 x 106mm
Valves and valve gear   Twin ohc 0.375 in lift; inlet valve diam. 1.75in, exhaust
    1.625 in
Compression ratio   8.8:1
Cylinder head   'Straight port', aluminium alloy, hemispherical
    combustion chambers
Carburetters   Two SU 1.75in HS6
Max. power   161bhp (DIN) at 5000rpm
Max. torque   189lb/ft at 3500rpm

Chassis

As for Series 2 XJ6L saloon except,
Weight and F/R distribution   32cwt 3qr, 53.3/46.7
Gearing:
Overdrive (standard fitment):   Automatic (BW Model 65):
1st – 11.45:1   Low – 4.80 to 2.40
2nd – 6.75   Int. – 2.90 to 1.45
3rd – 4.91   Top – 2.0 to 1.0
Top – 3.54
O/d – 2.75

Performance

Overdrive Saloon, 3.54 axle (automatic figures in brackets)

Standing start:

0 – 30mph	3.7 sec	
0 – 40	5.4	
0 – 50	7.8	(9.2)
0 – 60	10.9	(11.9)
0 – 70	15	(16.6)
0 – 80	19.8	
0 – 90	27.3	
0 – 100	37.9	

Standing quarter-mile: 18 sec (18.6)

Max. speed: 117mph (115)

Speeds in gears: 1st – 36mph
2nd – 62
3rd – 85
Direct top – 115

Overall fuel consumption: 16.7mpg

(Manual: *Autocar* September 27, 1975; Automatic: Jaguar Cars)

Top gear:

10 – 30mph	11.9 sec
20 – 40	10.6
30 – 50	9.5
40 – 60	9.8
50 – 70	10.7
60 – 80	1.7
70 – 90	13.8
80 – 100	18.4

Jaguar XJ-S GT Coupe

Engine

Cubic capacity	5343 cc, 60deg. V12
Bore and stroke	90 x 70mm
Valves and valve gear	Single ohc per bank, 0.375 in lift; inlet valve dia. 1.625in, exhaust valve 1.360in.
Compression ratio .	9.0:1
Cylinder head	Two flat-face, aluminium alloy
Fuel injection	Lucas
Max. power	285bhp (DIN) at 5500rpm
Max. torque	294lb/ft (DIN) at 3500rpm

Chassis

Weight and F/R distribution	34cwt 1qr, 54.3/45.7
Dimensions: Wheelbase	8ft 6in
Track – front	4ft 10.5in
rear	4ft 10in
Length	15ft 11.75in
Width	5ft 10.5in
Height	4ft 2in
Suspension	As for XJ saloon, except rear anti-roll bar
Steering and brakes	As for XJ 5.3 saloon.
Gearing:	
Manual gearbox:	Automatic:
1st – 9.94:1	1st – 14.68 to 7.34
2nd – 5.85	2nd – 8.92 to 4.46
3rd – 4.26	Top – 6.14 to 3.07
Top – 3.07	
Tyres and wheels	Dunlop SP Super steelbraced 205/70 VR 15 or Pirelli P5 205 VR covers on 6K x 15 in GKN Kent Alloy bolt-on wheelscovers on 6K x 15in GKN Kent Alloy bolt-on wheels

Performance

Manual transmission car, 3.07 axle (automatic figures in brackets, 3.07 axle)

Standing start:

0 – 30mph	2.8 sec	(3.2)
0 – 40	3.8	(4.5)
0 – 50	5.1	(5.9)
0 – 60	6.7	(7.5)
0 – 70	8.4	(9.5)
0 – 80	10.5	(11.9)
0 – 90	13.4	(14.7)
0 – 100	16.2	(18.4)
0 – 110	20.2	(23.1)
0 – 120	25.8	(30.4)

Top gear:

10 – 30mph	7.5 sec
20 – 40	6.8
30 – 50	6.6
40 – 60	6.8
50 – 70	6.9
60 – 80	7.1
70 – 90	7.2
80 – 100	8
90 – 110	8.6
100 – 120	10.3

Standing quarter-mile: 15 sec (15.7)

Max. speed: 153mph (142)

Speeds in gears (at 6500rpm): 1st – 50mph (64)

2nd – 84 (108)

3rd – 116

Overall fuel consumption: 12.8mpg (14).

(Manual: *Motor* February 21, 1976; Automatic and manual max. speed, *Autocar* May 28, 1977, and February 7, 1976)

Jaguar XJ 4.2 Series 3 Saloon

Engine

Cubic capacity	4235cc
Bore and stroke	92.07 x 106mm
Valves and valve gear	Twin ohc 0.375 in lift; inlet valve diam. 1.88in, exhaust valve 1.625in.
Compression ratio	8.7:1 (7.8:1 USA)
Cylinder head	'Straight port', aluminium alloy, hemispherical combustion chambers
Fuel injection	Lucas electronic
Max. power	200bhp at 5000rpm (176bhp at 4750rpm USA)
Max. torque	236lb/ft at 2750rpm (219 lb/ft at 2500rpm USA)

(NB: above engine also fitted to USA Series 2 XJ 4.2 from May 1978)

Chassis

Weight and F/R distribution		35.4cwt, 54.5/45.5cwt
Dimensions	Wheelbase	9ft 4.75in
	Track – front	4ft 10in
	rear	4ft 10.5in
	Length	16ft 2.75in
	Width	5ft 9.25in
	Height	4ft 6in
Suspension		As for Series II saloon
Steering and brakes		As for Series II saloon

Gearing:

Five-speed manual:

Automatic Borg Warner Model 65, 2:1 torque converter and 3.07 axle

1st – 10.99:1	Low – 18.42 to 7.68
2nd – 6.91	Int. – 11.05 to 4.61
3rd – 4.62	Top – 7.37 to 3.07
4th – 3.31	
5th – 2.76	

Tyres and wheels

Pirelli P5 205/VR or Dunlop SP Sport ER70 VR 15 covers on 6K x 15in bolt-on pressed-steel wheels (6K x 15in GKN Kent Alloy wheels optional)

Performance

Automatic transmission, 3.07 rear axle; automatic USA 'emission' model, 3.31 axle, in brackets

Standing start:

0 – 30 mph	4.2 sec	(3.7)
0 – 40	5.9	–
0 – 50	7.7	(7.4)
0 – 60	10.5	(9.6)
0 – 70	13.5	–
0 – 80	16.9	(16.3)
0 – 90	21.6	–
0 – 100	28.4	(27.8)
0 – 110	38.1	–

Standing quarter-mile: 17.6 sec (17.7)

Max. speed: 128mph (116)

Overall fuel consumption: 15.7mpg (17.5)

Max speeds in gears (at 5000rpm): 1st – 52mph

2nd – 85

(*Motor*, September 22, 1979; USA figures, *Road & Track* December 1978)

Manual transmission

Standing start:

0 – 30mph	2.8 sec
0 – 40	4.2
0 – 50	6.3
0 – 60	8.6
0 – 70	12.1
0 – 80	15.6
0 – 90	20.2
0 – 100	26.5
0 – 110	34.6
0 – 120	45.6

Standing quarter-mile: 17.2 sec

Max. speed: 131mph

Overall fuel consumption: 18.3mpg

Max. speed in gears (at 5000rpm):

1st – 35mph
2nd – 55
3rd – 83
4th – 116

Top gear: (4th in brackets)

10 – 30mph	10.3 secs (6.8)
20 – 40	9.8 (6.6)
30 – 50	9.8 (7.6)
40 – 60	9.9 (7.4)
50 – 70	10.8 (7.7)
60 – 80	12.4 (8.2)
70 – 90	14.5 (8.8)
80 – 100	15.4 (10.3)
90 – 110	21.6 (13.6)
100 – 120	– (16.6)

Jaguar XJ 3.4 Series 3 Saloon

Engine

As for XJ 3.4 Series 2 Saloon

Chassis

As for XJ 3.4 Series 2 Saloon except,
Weight (inc. full tank, air cond., and all options)
Gearing:
Five-speed manual:

34cwt 3qr

Automatic Borg Warner Model 65, 2.3:1 torque converter:

1st – 11.8:1
2nd – 7.38
3rd – 4.94
4th – 3.54 (direct)
Top – 2.95
Tyres and wheels

Low – 19.55 to 8.50
Int. – 11.9 to 5.17
Top – 8.14 to 3.54

As for XJ 4.2 Series 3

Jaguar XJ 5.3 Series 3 Saloon

Engine
As for XJ 5.3 Series 2 injection Saloon

Chassis
As for XJ 5.3 Series 2 injection Saloon except,
Weight

37cwt 3qr

Jaguar XJ6 3.6

Engine

Cubic capacity	3590cc
Bore and stroke	91 x 92mm
Valves and valve gear	Twin ohc, 0.375 in lift, four valves per cylinder; inlet valves diam. 1.39 in, exhaust valves diam. 1.17 in
Compression ratio	9.6:1 (early N. American cars 8.2:1)
Cylinder head	Aluminium alloy, pent-roof combustion chambers
Fuel injection	Lucas electronic
Max. power	221 bhp (DIN) @ 5000 rpm
Max. torque	248lb ft @ 4000rpm

Chassis

Weight and F/R distribution		33.2 cwt 53.9/46.1
Dimensions:	Wheelbase	9ft 5in
	Track – front	4ft 11.1in
	Track – rear	4ft 11in
	Length	16ft 4.4in
	Width	6ft 6.9in
	Height	4ft 6.3in
Suspension:	Front	Independent, unequal length double wishbones, coil spring, anti roll bar
	Rear	Independent, lower wishbones/upper drive shaft link, single coil spring/damper
Steering		Rack and pinion, hydraulic power-assisted
Brakes		Disc, vented 11.6 in front, outboard solid 10.9 in rear, engine driven hydraulic servo

Gearing:

Manual:		Automatic:	
1st	7.11:1	1st	8.78:1
2nd	5.59	2nd	5.24
3rd	4.93	3rd	3.54
4th	3.54	4th	2.58
5th	2.78		

Final drive 3.54 (early N. American cars 2.88:1)
Tyres and wheels

3.54 (early N. American cars 2.88:1)
Dunlop TD Sport 220 65 VR 390 on 7K x 15.3 in pressed steel wheels (alloy optional), except USA: Dunlop 215 70 VR 15 tyres on 6½K x 15 in wheels.

Performance

Standing start

0 – 30 mph	2.6 sec	
0 – 40	3.9	
0 – 50	5.5	
0 – 60	7.4	
0 – 70	9.8	
0 – 80	12.6	
0 – 90	16.3	
0 – 100	20.6	
0 – 110	26.7	
0 – 120	37.7	

	Top gear:	Fourth:
10 – 30 mph	–	8.6
20 – 40	11.5	7.4
30 – 50	11.0	7.2
40 – 60	11.2	7.6
50 – 70	12.2	7.7
60 – 80	13.4	7.5
70 – 90	14.0	7.3
80 – 100	15.9	7.5
90 – 110	17.5	8.3
100 – 120	20.4	–

Standing quarter-mile: 15.8 sec

Max. speed: 137 mph

Speeds in gears:	1st	33 mph
(at 5000 rpm)	2nd	57
	3rd	84
	4th	117

Overall fuel consumption: 20.7 mpg

Jaguar XJ6 2.9

Engine

Cubic capacity	2919cc
Bore and stroke	91 x 74.8mm
Valves and valve gear	Single ohc, 0.375 in lift, two valves per cylinder, inlet valve diam. 1.63 in, exhaust valve diam. 1.36 in.
Compression ratio	12.6:1
Cylinder head	Aluminium alloy, 'May' combustion chambers
Fuel injection	Bosch electronic
Max. power	165bhp (DIN) @ 5600rpm
Max. torque	176lb ft (DIN) @ 4000rpm

Chassis

As for XJ6 3.6 except
Weight and F/R distribution 32.7 cwt, 52/48
Brakes
Gearing:

Manual:		Automatic:	
1st	7.34:1	1st	10.29:1
2nd	5.82	2nd	5.58
3rd	5.16	3rd	3.77
4th	3.77	4th	2.75
Final drive 3.77:1		5th	3.01

Tyres and wheels

Performance

Standing start

0 – 30 mph	3.4 sec	
0 – 40	5.1	
0 – 50	7.0	
0 – 60	9.9	
0 – 70	13.2	

	Top gear:	Fourth:
10 – 30 mph	–	12.1
20 – 40	17.3	10.3
30 – 50	16.9	9.9
40 – 60	18.2	10.0
50 – 70	19.0	10.6

0 – 80	17.3		60 – 80	20.0	11.0
0 – 90	23.0		70 – 90	21.9	12.2
0 – 100	30.6		80 – 100	22.3	14.0
0 – 110	45.5		90 – 110	47.2	17.4
0 – 120			100 – 120	–	–

Standing quarter-mile: 17.5 sec
Max. speed: 117 mph
Speeds in gears: 1st   31 mph
                      2nd   54
                      3rd   80
                      4th   111
Overall fuel consumption: 19.5 mph

Jaguar XJ-S 3.6

Engine

Cubic capacity	3590cc
Bore and stroke	91 x 92mm
Valves and valve gear	Twin ohc, 0.375 in lift; four valves per cylinder, inlet valves diam. 1.39 in, exhaust valves diam. 1.17in
Compression ratio	9.6:1
Cylinder head	Aluminium alloy, pent-roof combustion chambers
Fuel injection	Lucas electronic
Max. power	221bhp (DIN) @ 5000rpm (225bhp @ 5300rpm up to mid-1986)
Max. torque	248ft lb (DIN) @ 4000rpm (240ft lb @ 4000rpm up to mid-1986)

Chassis

As for XJ-S V12 GT except:

Weight		32 cwt
Suspension:	Rear	Anti-roll bar discontinued; reinstated for 1988 models together with uprated front anti-roll bar and front and rear springs

Gearing:

Manual:		Automatic:	
		1st	8.78:1
		2nd	5.24:1
		3rd	3.54:1
		4th	2.58:1
Final drive 3.54:1		Final drive 3.54:1	

Tyres and wheels: Dunlop/Pirelli 215 70 on 6½K x 15 in alloy wheels (XJ-SC 3.6, 6K alloy wheels); 1988 models, Pirelli P600 235-60 VR 15 on 6½K wheels

Performance

Standing start:

				Top gear:	Fourth:
0 – 30 mph	2.6 sec		10 – 30 mph	12.7	8.2
0 – 40	4.1		20 – 40	11.7	7.3
0 – 50	5.6		30 – 50	10.6	6.7
0 – 60	7.4		40 – 60	10.6	6.9
0 – 70	9.9		50 – 70	11.6	7.2
0 – 80	12.4		60 – 80	12.5	7.3
0 – 90	15.3		70 – 90	13.9	7.1
0 – 100	19.7		80 – 100	15.5	7.3
0 – 110	24.6		90 – 110	16.5	8.8
0 – 120	31.8		100 – 120	19.0	11.6

Standing quarter-mile: 15.9 secs
Max. speed: 141 mph
Overall fuel consumption: 17.6 mpg

Production figures, years current and prices

The production figures have been calculated from factory listings of chassis numbers and while generally accurate to within one or two units either way, should be regarded as a guide only. The price given is that for the basic model at the time of announcement in the UK, except where otherwise indicated. The 'Produced From/To' dates indicate the period during which the model was actually manufactured at the factory; however, some cars may have been sold from stock after the latter date.

Model	Body style	Engine	Public Announcement	Produced From/To	Price on Introduction	Number Made	Chassis number Commences	Comments
S.S.I	Coupe	2054cc	Oct 9 1931	Jan 1932/ Dec 1932	£310	500	135005	No made includes 20hp.
S.S.I	Coupe	2552cc	Jan 1932	Feb 1932/ Dec 1932	£320			
S.S.II	Coupe	1052cc	Oct 9 1931	Jan 1932/ Dec 1933	£210		126268	
S.S.I 2nd Series	Coupe	2054cc	Sept 1932	Oct 1932/ Sep 1933	£325		135541	Chassis Nos in series with original S.S.I.
S.S.I 2nd Series	Coupe	2552cc	Sept 1932	Oct 1932/ Sep 1933	£335			
S.S.I 2nd Series	Coupe	2143cc	Oct 1933	Jan 1934/ Sep 1934	£335		247001	Obtainable to special order after date given.
S.S.I 2nd Series	Coupe	2663cc	Oct 1933	Jan 1934/ Sep 1934	£340		247001	
S.S.I	Tourer	2054cc	Mar 1933	Mar 1933/ Jan 1934	£325		135988	Chassis Nos of Tourer in series with closed S.S.I.
S.S.I	Tourer	2552cc	Mar 1933	Mar 1933/ Jan 1934	£335			
S.S.I	Tourer	2143cc	Oct 1933	Jan 1934/ Mar 1936	£335			
S.S.I	Tourer	2663cc	Oct 1933	Jan 1934/ Mar 1936	£340			
S.S.II 2nd Series	Coupe	1343cc	Oct 1933	Jan 1934/ Sep 1934	£260		200001	
S.S.II 2nd Series	Coupe	1608cc	Oct 1933	Jan 1934/ Sep 1934	£265			
S.S.II	Tourer	1343cc	Mar 1934	Mar 1934/ Feb 1936	£260			
S.S.II	Tourer	1608cc	Mar 1934	Mar 1934/ Feb 1936	£265			
S.S.I	Saloon	2143cc	Oct 1933	Oct 1933/ Feb 1936	£340			
S.S.I	Saloon	2663cc	Oct 1933	Oct 1933/ Feb 1936	£345			
S.S.I	Airline	2143cc	Sep 1934	Sep 1934/ Jun 1936	£360			
S.S.I	Airline	2663cc	Sep 1934	Sep 1934/ Jun 1936	£365			
S.S.I	DH Coupe	2143cc	Mar 1935	Mar 1935/ Oct 1935	£380			Last S.S.I model introduced. Obtainable to special order after date given.
S.S.I	DH Coupe	2663cc	Mar 1935	Mar 1935/ Oct 1935	£385			

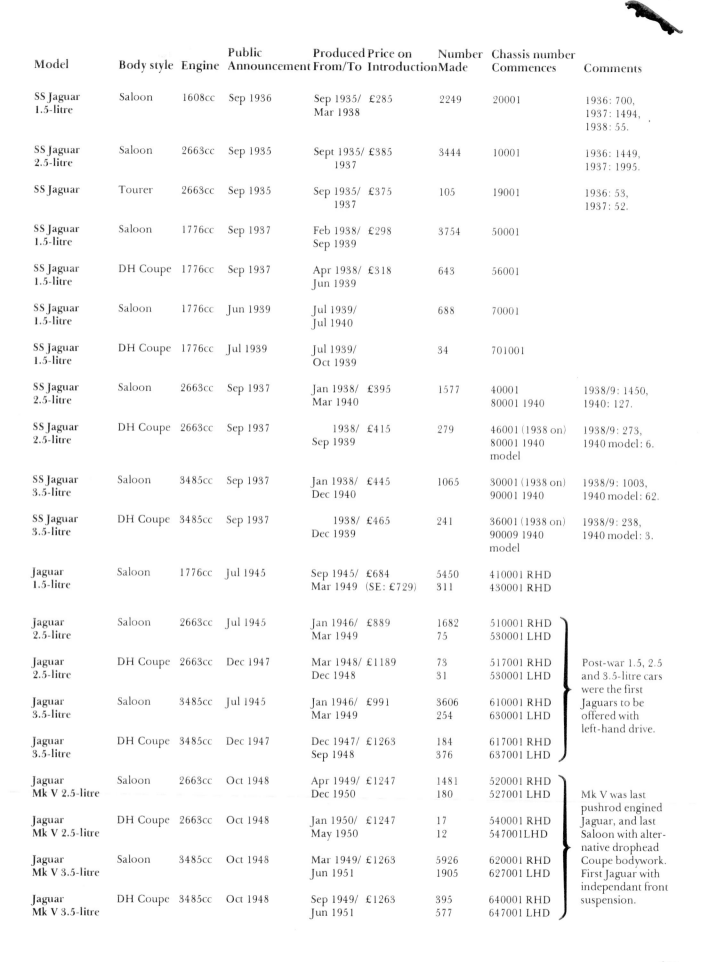

Model	Body style	Engine	Public Announcement	Produced From/To	Price on Introduction	Number Made	Chassis number Commences	Comments
SS Jaguar 1.5-litre	Saloon	1608cc	Sep 1936	Sep 1935/ Mar 1938	£285	2249	20001	1936: 700, 1937: 1494, 1938: 55.
SS Jaguar 2.5-litre	Saloon	2663cc	Sep 1935	Sept 1935/ 1937	£385	3444	10001	1936: 1449, 1937: 1995.
SS Jaguar	Tourer	2663cc	Sep 1935	Sep 1935/ 1937	£375	105	19001	1936: 53, 1937: 52.
SS Jaguar 1.5-litre	Saloon	1776cc	Sep 1937	Feb 1938/ Sep 1939	£298	3754	50001	
SS Jaguar 1.5-litre	DH Coupe	1776cc	Sep 1937	Apr 1938/ Jun 1939	£318	643	56001	
SS Jaguar 1.5-litre	Saloon	1776cc	Jun 1939	Jul 1939/ Jul 1940		688	70001	
SS Jaguar 1.5-litre	DH Coupe	1776cc	Jul 1939	Jul 1939/ Oct 1939		34	701001	
SS Jaguar 2.5-litre	Saloon	2663cc	Sep 1937	Jan 1938/ Mar 1940	£395	1577	40001 / 80001 1940	1938/9: 1450, 1940: 127.
SS Jaguar 2.5-litre	DH Coupe	2663cc	Sep 1937	1938/ Sep 1939	£415	279	46001 (1938 on) / 80001 1940 model	1938/9: 273, 1940 model: 6.
SS Jaguar 3.5-litre	Saloon	3485cc	Sep 1937	Jan 1938/ Dec 1940	£445	1065	30001 (1938 on) / 90001 1940	1938/9: 1003, 1940 model: 62.
SS Jaguar 3.5-litre	DH Coupe	3485cc	Sep 1937	1938/ Dec 1939	£465	241	36001 (1938 on) / 90009 1940 model	1938/9: 238, 1940 model: 3.
Jaguar 1.5-litre	Saloon	1776cc	Jul 1945	Sep 1945/ Mar 1949	£684 (SE: £729)	5450 / 311	410001 RHD / 430001 RHD	
Jaguar 2.5-litre	Saloon	2663cc	Jul 1945	Jan 1946/ Mar 1949	£889	1682 / 75	510001 RHD / 530001 LHD	
Jaguar 2.5-litre	DH Coupe	2663cc	Dec 1947	Mar 1948/ Dec 1948	£1189	73 / 31	517001 RHD / 530001 LHD	Post-war 1.5, 2.5 and 3.5-litre cars were the first Jaguars to be offered with left-hand drive.
Jaguar 3.5-litre	Saloon	3485cc	Jul 1945	Jan 1946/ Mar 1949	£991	3606 / 254	610001 RHD / 630001 LHD	
Jaguar 3.5-litre	DH Coupe	3485cc	Dec 1947	Dec 1947/ Sep 1948	£1263	184 / 376	617001 RHD / 637001 LHD	
Jaguar Mk V 2.5-litre	Saloon	2663cc	Oct 1948	Apr 1949/ Dec 1950	£1247	1481 / 180	520001 RHD / 527001 LHD	Mk V was last pushrod engined Jaguar, and last Saloon with alternative drophead Coupe bodywork. First Jaguar with independant front suspension.
Jaguar Mk V 2.5-litre	DH Coupe	2663cc	Oct 1948	Jan 1950/ May 1950	£1247	17 / 12	540001 RHD / 547001LHD	
Jaguar Mk V 3.5-litre	Saloon	3485cc	Oct 1948	Mar 1949/ Jun 1951	£1263	5926 / 1905	620001 RHD / 627001 LHD	
Jaguar Mk V 3.5-litre	DH Coupe	3485cc	Oct 1948	Sep 1949/ Jun 1951	£1263	395 / 577	640001 RHD / 647001 LHD	

Model	Body style	Engine	Public Announcement	Produced From/To	Price on Introduction	Number Made	Chassis number Commences	Comments
Jaguar Mk VII	Saloon	3442cc	Oct 1950	Dec 1950/ Sep 1954	£1276	12755 8184	710001 RHD 730001 LHD	Mk VII was first twin ohc engined Jaguar saloon.
Jaguar Mk VIIM	Saloon	3442cc	Oct 1954	Nov 1954/ Jul 1957	£1616	7245 2016	722755 RHD 738184 LHD	
Jaguar Mk VIII	Saloon	3442cc	Oct 1956	Sep 1956/ Dec 1959	£1830	4644 1688	760001 RHD 780001 LHD	
Jaguar Mk IX	Saloon	3781cc	Oct 1958	Oct 1958/ Sep 1961	£1994	5984 4021	770001 RHD 790001 LHD	Mk IX was first Jaguar Saloon with 3.8 engine, and last with separate chassis.
Jaguar 2.4	Saloon	2483cc	Sep 1955	Sep 1955/ Sep 1959	£1344	16250 3742	900001 RHD 940001 LHD	First unitary construction Jaguar Saloon. SE model £1375.
Jaguar 3.4	Saloon	3443cc	Mar 1957	Mar 1957/ Sep 1959	£1672	8945 8460	970001 RHD 985001 LHD	
Jaguar Mk II 2.4	Saloon	2483cc	Oct 1959	Oct 1959/ Sep 1967	£1534	21768 3405	100001 RHD 125001 LHD	
Jaguar Mk II 3.4	Saloon	3442cc	Oct 1959	Oct 1959/ Sep 1967	£1669	22095 6571	150001 RHD 175001 LHD	
Jaguar Mk II 3.8	Saloon	3781cc	Oct 1959	Oct 1959/ Sep 1967	£1779	15383 14758	200001 RHD 210001 LHD	
Jaguar Mk X	Saloon	3781cc	Oct 1961	Dec 1961 Aug 1964	£2392	9129 3848	300001 RHD 350001 LHD	
Jaguar Mk X 4.2	Saloon	4235cc	Oct 1964	Oct 1964/ Dec 1966	£2156	3720 1960	ID 50001 RHD ID 75001 LHD	
Jaguar 420G	Saloon	4235cc	Oct 1966	Oct 1966/ Jun 1970	£2237	5429 1125	GID 53720 RHD GID 76961 LHD	
Jaguar S-Type 3.4	Saloon	3442cc	Sep 1963	Sep 1963/ Aug 1968	£1669	8665 1371	IB 1001 RHD •IB 25001 LHD	
Jaguar S-Type 3.8	Saloon	3781cc	Sep 1963	Sep 1963/ Jun 1968	£1758	9717 5418	IB 50001 RHD IB 75001 LHD	
Jaguar 420	Saloon	4235cc	Oct 1966	Oct 1966/ Sep 1968	£1930	7172 2629	IF 1001 RHD IF 25001 LHD	
Jaguar 240	Saloon	2483cc	Sep 1967	Sep 1967/ Apr 1969	£1365	3716 730	IJ 1001 RHD IJ 30001 LHD	
Jaguar 340	Saloon	3442cc	Sep 1967	Sep 1967/ Sep 1968	£1442	2265 535	IJ 50001 RHD IJ 80001 LHD	
Jaguar XJ6 2.8-litre	Saloon	2792cc	Sep 1968	Sep 1968/ May 1973	£1897	13301 6125	IG 1001 IG 50001	Price given for De Luxe; Standard model catalogued at £1797
Jaguar XJ6 4.2-litre	Saloon	4235cc	Sep 1968	Sep 1968/ Jul 1973	£2253	33467 25505	IL 1001 RHD IL 50001 LHD	

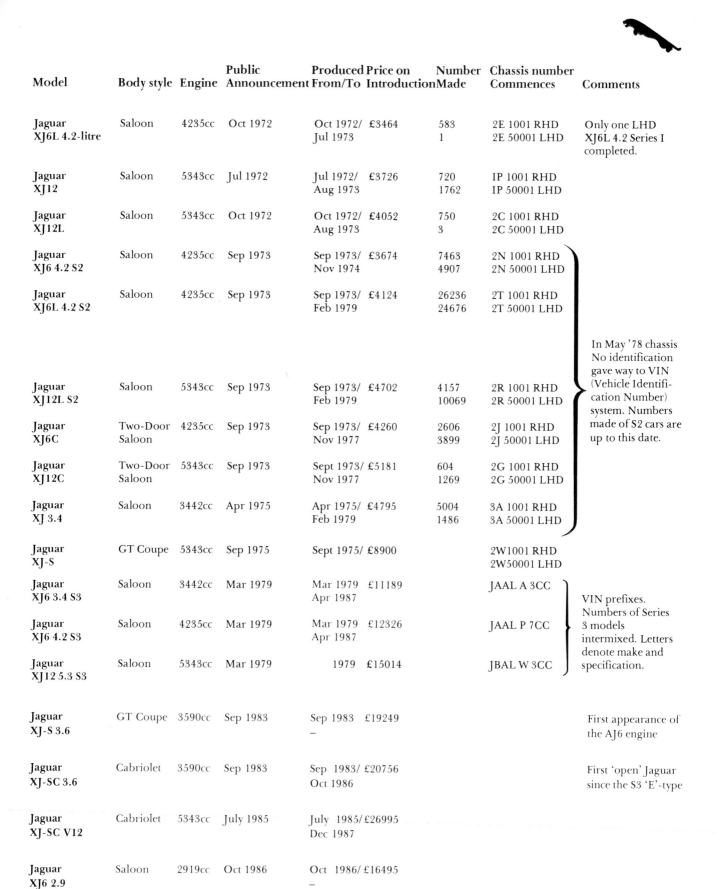

Model	Body style	Engine	Public Announcement	Produced From/To	Price on Introduction	Number Made	Chassis number Commences	Comments
Jaguar XJ6L 4.2-litre	Saloon	4235cc	Oct 1972	Oct 1972/ Jul 1973	£3464	583 1	2E 1001 RHD 2E 50001 LHD	Only one LHD XJ6L 4.2 Series I completed.
Jaguar XJ12	Saloon	5343cc	Jul 1972	Jul 1972/ Aug 1973	£3726	720 1762	IP 1001 RHD IP 50001 LHD	
Jaguar XJ12L	Saloon	5343cc	Oct 1972	Oct 1972/ Aug 1973	£4052	750 3	2C 1001 RHD 2C 50001 LHD	
Jaguar XJ6 4.2 S2	Saloon	4235cc	Sep 1973	Sep 1973/ Nov 1974	£3674	7463 4907	2N 1001 RHD 2N 50001 LHD	
Jaguar XJ6L 4.2 S2	Saloon	4235cc	Sep 1973	Sep 1973/ Feb 1979	£4124	26236 24676	2T 1001 RHD 2T 50001 LHD	In May '78 chassis No identification gave way to VIN (Vehicle Identification Number) system. Numbers made of S2 cars are up to this date.
Jaguar XJ12L S2	Saloon	5343cc	Sep 1973	Sep 1973/ Feb 1979	£4702	4157 10069	2R 1001 RHD 2R 50001 LHD	
Jaguar XJ6C	Two-Door Saloon	4235cc	Sep 1973	Sep 1973/ Nov 1977	£4260	2606 3899	2J 1001 RHD 2J 50001 LHD	
Jaguar XJ12C	Two-Door Saloon	5343cc	Sep 1973	Sept 1973/ Nov 1977	£5181	604 1269	2G 1001 RHD 2G 50001 LHD	
Jaguar XJ 3.4	Saloon	3442cc	Apr 1975	Apr 1975/ Feb 1979	£4795	5004 1486	3A 1001 RHD 3A 50001 LHD	
Jaguar XJ-S	GT Coupe	5343cc	Sep 1975	Sept 1975/	£8900		2W1001 RHD 2W50001 LHD	
Jaguar XJ6 3.4 S3	Saloon	3442cc	Mar 1979	Mar 1979 Apr 1987	£11189		JAAL A 3CC	VIN prefixes. Numbers of Series 3 models intermixed. Letters denote make and specification.
Jaguar XJ6 4.2 S3	Saloon	4235cc	Mar 1979	Mar 1979 Apr 1987	£12326		JAAL P 7CC	
Jaguar XJ12 5.3 S3	Saloon	5343cc	Mar 1979	1979	£15014		JBAL W 3CC	
Jaguar XJ-S 3.6	GT Coupe	3590cc	Sep 1983	Sep 1983 –	£19249			First appearance of the AJ6 engine
Jaguar XJ-SC 3.6	Cabriolet	3590cc	Sep 1983	Sep 1983/ Oct 1986	£20756			First 'open' Jaguar since the S3 'E'-type
Jaguar XJ-SC V12	Cabriolet	5343cc	July 1985	July 1985/ Dec 1987	£26995			
Jaguar XJ6 2.9	Saloon	2919cc	Oct 1986	Oct 1986/ –	£16495			
Jaguar XJ6 3.6	Saloon	3590cc	Oct 1986	Oct 1986/ –	£18495			

| Jaguar Sovereign 2.9 | Saloon | 2919cc | Oct 1986 | Oct 1986/ £22995 – |
| Jaguar Sovereign 3.6 | Saloon | 3590cc | Oct 1986 | Oct 1986/ £24995 – |

Part One
General Index

C

Cadillac – 367
Camaro – 386
Canada – 121, 143, 204, 230, 332, 402
Car and Driver – 310, 407
Castle Bromwich (factory) – 407
Castrol – 39
Charnock, W.H. – 44, 60
Chevrolet – 178, 310
    Corvair – 248, 255
    Impala – 344
Chrysler Imperial V8 5.4-litre – 178
    Valiant – 248
Cibié – 384, 392
Citroen, Andre – 133
Citroen – 134, 215
    "Traction Avant" – 133, 137
    7A – 133
Clayton air-conditioning unit – 118, 124
Classic Jaguar Association – 128
Clease, A.G. Douglas B.Sc – 41, 42, 56, 57
Clement Talbot – 298
Cocker Street – 20, 24, 78
Connolly – 39, 307, 334
Cooke, H.H. & Sons – 74
Car magazine – 406
Coombs of Guildford – 273, 274
Cornell Aeronautical Laboratories – 318
Corsica – 25
Cory, Bill – 223, 236, 246, 247, 254, 255
Cotral electric gearboxes – 45
Coventry – 21, 24, 77, 122, 156, 157, 162
    166, 205, 207, 220, 223, 249, 250
    282, 325, 327
Coventry-Climax – 350
Coventry Motor and Sundries Ltd – 25
Coventry Steel Caravans – 77
Cowley – 22
Craig, Peter – 110, 142, 144, 153, 166,
    189
Crisp, T. – 422
Crouch, C. – 433
Curtis, Tony – 361

D

Daimler Ltd – 113, 167, 250, 255, 256,
    257, 258, 259, 290, 353, 404, 409
Daimler
    Conquest Century – 220
    Majestic Major – 234, 250, 288,
        316, 318, 323
    SP250 – 250, 316
    2.5 V8 – 255, 256, 258, 259, 268,
        269, 288, 316
    250 – 269, 280, 290
    340 – 269

Limousine – 324, 411
Sovereign – 288, 290, 294, 347,
    348, 356, 400
    420 – 296, 321, 327, 347
    2-door – 366
    3.6 – 455
    4.2 VDP – 408
    4.5 Mk X engine – 316
    4.5V8 – 316, 318
    Double-Six – 357, 360, 365, 372,
        374, 376, 400
    Double-Six HE – 408
Dawtrey, L. – 66
Delaney Galley – 320, 334
Delco-Remy ignition – 56
Dewandre, M. – 176
Dodge Brothers – 182
Dodge – 310
    Corenet 375bhp – 286
    Hemi-Charger 425bhp – 286
Danny, Robert – 357
Duesenburg straight-eight engine – 162
Duesenburg Model J – 162
Dunlop – 36, 37, 138, 147, 199, 201,
    216, 231, 232, 234, 235, 236, 237,
    238, 248, 249, 263, 269, 273, 278,
    280, 284, 285, 289, 294, 295, 301,
    315, 318, 319, 332, 356, 377, 384,
    392, 406
Dunlopillo – 83, 93, 195
    285, 289, 294, 295, 301, 315, 318,

E

Earls Court – 144, 166
Edwardes, Sir Michael – 426
Egan, Sir John – 426, 436, 446, 458, 460
England, F.R.W. 'Lofty' – 181, 426, 433
Eustace Watkins – 25
Exchange Street – 20

F

Fairbanks, Douglas – 248
Fenton, Alice – 78
Fiat – 64
    509A – 24
    130 – 346
Ferrari – 351, 390, 407
    12 cyl. – 222
    365GT4 2-plus-2 – 381
Fletcher, J.A. – 60
Foleshill – 24, 25, 37, 43, 48, 51, 59, 63,
    64, 65, 68, 75, 78, 86, 88, 95, 108,

    114, 118, 133, 157, 158, 167, 181
Ford – 205, 271, 310, 458
    V8 saloon – 122
    8 engine – 157
    Zodiac Mk III – 286
    Zodiac Mk IV – 272
    Mustang – 286
    Cortina – 294
    Gearbox – 111
    Escort – 327
Forward Engineering – 372
Frankfurt Motor Show – 365
Fruth, Fritz – 57
Fury – 234

G

Gardner, 'Goldie', Maj. – 159
General Motors – 68, 134, 205, 328, 379
    Hydra-matic – 184
German – 104, 113, 346, 406, 407
Gibson, F. – 15
Girling – 67, 70, 80, 85, 89, 102, 103,
    104, 118, 126, 127, 132, 138, 175
    182, 216, 259, 289, 301, 328, 330,
    386
Giron, Louis – 207
Guigaro – 435
GKN Kent Alloys – 374
GKN-Sankey – 460
Gloster Aircraft Co. – 114
    Meteor – 114
Goodyear – 295
Gordon England – 25
Grant, Gregor – 230
Greville-Smith, C. – 434
Grinham, Ted – 66
Group 44 – 394
Gurney Nutting – 30

H

Hamilton, Duncan – 239, 273
Hardy – 25
Hardy Spicer – 91
Harrison, Bob – 60, 153
Harvey, D. – 417
Hassan, Walter – 93, 133, 134, 135, 136,
    157, 159, 163, 331, 350, 352
Hawthorn, Mike – 236, 237, 273
Haydens – 15
Hebb, David – 182, 183, 184
Helliwells of Walsall – 113
Henly, B. – 22
Henlys – 22, 36, 362
Hepworth Grandage Pistons – 323
Heynes, Jonathan – 345

Morgan – 151
Morgan, J. – 446
Morris Cowley Swallow – 22
Morris Motors – 22, 24, 25, 95, 96, 205
    Engines – 157
    8 – 54, 157
    Oxford – 22
    Minor – 25, 144, 173, 219
Mosquito – 110
Moss Gearbox – 125
Motor Body Builders – 20
Motor Life – 219, 220
Motor Panels (Coventry) Ltd. – 87, 113,
    165, 323, 324
Motor Show – 25, 29, 30, 51, 66, 77, 86
    95, 135, 144, 145, 164 165, 166,
    198, 358, 405
Motor Racing Magazine – 237
Motor Sport – 249, 310
Motor, The – 29, 34, 35, 39, 41, 42, 48,
    54, 56, 57, 60, 69, 80, 81, 82, 83,
    93, 99, 100, 102, 104, 113, 118,
    148, 149, 178, 179, 180, 181, 189,
    190, 201, 203, 220, 221, 222, 223,
    226, 230, 231, 234, 261, 262, 269,
    270, 281, 284, 285, 286, 292, 293,
    294, 295, 296, 313, 314, 315, 327
    338, 342, 343, 345, 357, 360, 361
    362, 364, 365, 377, 379, 381, 388,
    392, 393, 405, 406, 407, 415
Motor Trend – 220, 249
Muliner – 30
Mulliner – 114
Mundy, Harry – 352, 381, 396, 407, 418,
    419, 422
Musgrove & Green – 24

N

Nevada desert – 295
Nichols, Mel – 406
Nigerian Government – 207
Nockholds, Roy – 273
Nortons – 16
Nuneaton – 24
NSU Ro80 – 324

O

Oates, R.F. – 64, 65
Olds 98 – 220
Oldsmobile Cutlass – 335
Oliver, M. – 455
Olly, M. – 134, 328
Olympia – 25, 77
O.M. – 64
Opel Diplomat – 346

Ore, Teddy – 142
Osterreichische Touring-Zeitung – 57
Oxford Airspeed – 110

P

Panther – 113
Park Sheet Metal – 423
Patrick – 25
Pelham-Burns – 60
Perrin, S. – 446
Philco radio set – 99
Pininfarina – 434
Pirelli Cinturatos – 263
Pirelli P5 tyres – 406
Playa del Rey 'circuit' – 232
Plymouth – 310
P+M – 113
Poulton-le-Fylde – 77
Porsche – 388, 392
    2.7-litre – 381
Porsche, Ferdinand – 133
Practical Motorist – 86
Pressed Steel Co – 87, 113, 135, 165,
    166, 212, 303, 305
Pressed Steel Fisher Ltd – 323, 332, 434
Putnam, R. – 446
Pytchleys – 30, 33

Q

Queen Elizabeth – 121

R

R.A.C. Rally – 56
R.A.F. – 110
Radford (factory) – 408
Radiomobile – 118, 143
Randle, J. – 434, 436, 455
Rankin, E.W. . 68, 78, 181
Rapier Co., – 162
Renault – 162
Reutter seats – 198
Rheims circuit – 104
Riley – 60
    1.5 – 73, 96
    Pathfinder 2.6 – 234
Road Atlanta – 394
Road & Track – 178, 179, 191, 223, 229,
    231, 233, 236, 246, 247, 248, 254,
    255, 281, 282, 284, 295, 307, 311,
    312, 344, 394
Robinson, G. – 426
Roesche, G. – 298, 299

Rolls-Royce – 60, 73, 124, 184, 330,
    332, 335, 344, 357, 394
    Meteor tank engine – 167
    Silver Cloud – 320
    Silver Cloud II – 297
    Silver Shadow – 343, 362, 364,
    365, 381
    Corniche 2-door – 380
Rootes – 66, 133
Rover – 276, 457, 458
    12 – 73
    Speed 14 – 82
    SD1 3500 V8 – 239
    2000 – 271
    3500 – 327
    3500 Coupe – 335
    '77mm' 5-speed box – 381
    SD1 5-speed box – 405
Rubery Owen – 30, 113, 165
Rudge-Whitworth – 30, 67

S

Salcombe – 407
Salisbury axle – 127, 175, 190, 216
    'hypoid' bevel drive unit – 109
Salisbury Plain – 81
Salisbury Transmission Ltd – 229
Salmon, Guy – 357
Salmson – 162
Sangster, J. – 114, 256
Sankeys – 87
Sarthe Circuit – 162
Satori, Peter – 178
Sayer, Malcolm – 309, 388
Shap Fell – 42
Skan, H.V. Ltd – 369
Slumberland Group – 334
Smiths Industries – 324
Society of Motor Manufacturers &
    Traders – 51, 165
Spicer Thornton Powr-Lok – 245
Spitfire – 110, 167
Sports Car Graphic – 249
Sports Car Illustrated – 223, 224, 225, 233,
    234, 248
Standard Motor Co. – 29, 30, 32, 36, 43,
    44, 45, 46, 63, 65, 66, 90, 113,
    114, 138, 218
Standard
    Big Nine – 24
    16 – 30, 70, 73, 74
    6-cyl. engine – 30
    Little Nine – 35, 36
    Flying 12 – 82
    14 – 89
    Gearbox – 91
    Ensign – 30
Stirland, Jim – 225, 226

***

Part Two

Hahne, A. – 587
Hall, Ian – 490
Hamilton, Duncan – 524, 525, 529, 531
Hansgen, Walter – 531, 547
Harrop – 475, 511
Harveyson – 472
Hawthorn, Mike – 524, 525, 529, 534
Haynes, J.H. – 463
Healey, Donald – 519
Hébert, Jean – 493
Hedges, Andrew – 500
Hedges, John – 516
Heinz, David – 583
Hercock, Barry – 505
Heurtaux – 479
Heyer, H. – 587, 589
Hill, Graham – 474, 535, 536, 538, 540, 541
Hill, Jimmy – 513
Hinton, Graig – 528
Hoar, Graham – 513
Hobbs, David – 566, 569
Holbrook Lane – 467, 519
Hopkirk, Paddy – 500
Hotchkiss – 469, 472, 475
Howarth, G. – 473, 485
Huckvale, E. – 487
Huffaker, Joe – 581
Hughes, Barry – 509
Hulme, Denny – 538, 542, 543
Humble, G. – 473

I

Ickx, Jacques – 501, 561

J

Jabbeke Highway – 513
Jaguar Sports Cars – 472
Jane, Robert – 536, 550, 551, 553
Jennings, C. – 466
John O'Groats – 475
Johnson, Leslie – 521
Johnston, Derek – 481
Jolley, A. – 480
Jopp, P. – 473, 493, 497, 499, 541, 543

K

Kelleners, H. – 584
Kelsey, Charles – 537
Koch, G.H. – 466, 469

L

Lagerwij, N.V. – 505
Lampton, O. – 481
Lancashire Automobile Club – 490
Lancia – 470, 501
       Aurelia GT – 481, 522
Leather – 511
Leaver, Christopher – 499
Legre – 472
Lego, Claude – 497
Le Mans – 463, 467, 493, 494, 499, 510, 521, 534, 547, 556, 560
L'Equipe – 493, 560
Leschallas – 468
Lequezec, Claude – 500
Lewis, Hon Brian – 475
Leyland Cars – 563, 567, 578, 580, 583
Liddon, Henry – 500
Liege-Rome-Liege Rally – 501, 503, 508
Light, S. – 470, 472, 475
Lindner, Peter – 538, 539, 542, 543, 555, 556, 558, 559, 560, 574
Lindström – 509
Linas-Montlhery – 513
Ljungfeldt, B. – 499, 541, 543
Lister-Jaguar – 534, 547
Lotus – 535
Loughborough, Col. – 487
Lumby, Martin – 511, 513
Lumsden, Peter – 516
Lyons, Sir William – 469, 519, 547

M

MacDowel, M. – 494, 496, 497, 556
Mack, W. – 586
Makinen, Timo – 486
Mamsbridge, Joan, Mrs – 484
Mansbridge, Reg – 479, 484
Margulies, Dan – 473, 474
Marker, R. – 466
Maserati – 524
Mathieson, H. – 501
Mays, Raymond – 524
M.C.C. Round Britain Rally – 504
McCahill, Tom – 513
McCormack, J. – 584
McLaren, Bruce – 535
Merano, Italy – 465, 467
Mercedes-Benz – 473, 475, 484, 485, 491, 523, 554, 556, 561, 566, 579
Mercer – 487
Mermod, Marie-Louise – 500
M.G. – 465, 470
M.G.B. – 500
Mille Miglia – 493
Millet, Jose – 553
Mini-Cooper – 538
       'S' – 486, 500, 560

Momo, Alfred – 547
Monaco Grand Prix circuit – 480
Mongoletsi, G. – 475
Monte Carlo Rally – 463, 470, 475, 479, 481, 484, 486, 501, 504, 509, 511, 521, 524, 528
Monza, Italy – 473, 513, 516, 566, 569, 587
Morgan, F.W. – 470, 472
Morley Bros. – 492, 504, 505, 508
Morley, Donald – 505, 508
Moss, Pat – 508
Moss, Stirling – 479, 520, 521, 522, 523
Motor Show – 503
Motor, The – 465, 466, 501, 511, 513, 538, 539
Motoring News – 494
Mount Panorama – 587
Mueller, Lee – 581
Munich – 465, 467
Munto – 465

N

Needham, C. – 465, 468, 470, 472, 511
Nelson, Ed. – 493
Nice – 468, 469, 470
Nickerson ('Nicholson'), C. – 584, 587
Nilsson, Gunnar – 567, 569, 570, 575
Nocker, Peter – 538, 542, 543, 555, 556, 558, 559
Novelli – 493
Nurburgring – 555, 556, 560, 566, 567, 573, 575

O

O'Connor Rorke, H. – 473, 508
Orssich, Count – 467, 469

P

Panhard – 472
Park, Alex – 563, 569
Parkes, Mike – 535, 536
Parkes, R. – 473, 485, 491, 508
Parnell, Reg – 523, 524
Parsons, E.R. – 504
Pascoe – 475
Percy, W. – 587, 589
Perouse, Monsieur – 465
Picardie – 510
Pige – 468
Pitt, Bill – 504
Polensky, Hulmut – 501, 503
Porsche – 478, 500, 501, 505, 583
Prideaux Budge V. – 475
Procter, Peter – 500

Q

Quaker State Oil – 567
Quester, Dieter – 570, 571, 572, 574, 575, 578, 587, 588

R

Randle, J. – 584
Rankin, Ernest – 509
Rallye des Routes du Nord – 508
Renault – 475
      Dauphine – 485
Renel, Jack – 494, 500
Rheims – 463, 494, 499, 500
Rhone Valley – 518
Richard, René – 473
Riley – 466, 519, 521, 522, 529, 534
Riley Pathfinder – 504
Riley, Peter – 494, 505
Riverside, California – 547
Robinson, Geoffrey – 563
Rolland, Jean – 499
Rolt, Tony – 522, 523, 524
Rouen circuit – 493, 499
Rouse, Andy – 567, 569, 570, 571, 573, 574, 575, 578
Rowet – 490, 528
Royal Automobile Club – 469, 487, 490, 491, 492, 493, 501, 504, 521, 541
Ryder, Lord – 563

S

Saab – 486, 492, 505
Sachs, Peter – 537, 538
Sahara – 465
St. Moritz – 468, 471
Salmon, Mike – 538, 541, 542, 543
Salvadori, Roy – 524, 534, 535, 537, 540, 541, 542, 543, 574
Salzburg – 587
Sargent, Peter – 516, 537
Sawyer, John – 550
Sayer, Malcolm – 556, 560
Scott-Brown, Archie – 529, 531
Schenken, Tim – 569, 570, 573, 575, 578
Schock, Walter – 483, 491
Schluter, W. – 501, 503
Scott, D. – 490
Scottish Rally – 504, 511
Sears, Jack – 491, 492, 497, 529, 534, 535, 536, 540, 541
Sebring – 463, 547
Selsdon, Lord – 479
Senior, A. – 485
Shelsley Walsh Hillclimb – 511
Silverstone circuit – 519, 521, 524, 528, 529, 531, 534, 535, 563, 567, 569, 570, 575, 579

Simca – 485
Sims, Lyndon – 522
Skilleter, Paul – 465, 472
Small & Parkes – 473
Smith, J.C. – 490
Snetterton – 513, 534, 538
Soisbault, Annie – 500
Sopwith, T. – 490, 493, 531, 534, 535, 538, 539
Spa – 499, 529, 561, 567
Sprinzel, John – 492, 500, 509, 541, 543
'Steed, John' – 579
Stefferud, P. – 501
Stephens, Roger – 485
Stewart, Jimmy – 481, 524
Stewart, Jackie – 543, 560
Stuck, H.J. – 587
Sunbeam – 508
      Rapier – 485
      Talbot – 479
Sunday Pictorial – 513
Surtees, John – 535
Sutcliffe, Peter – 538, 542, 543
Symons, H. – 465, 467, 468, 469

T

Talbot – 472, 475
Texier, Louisette – 500
Thompson, Stephen – 567
Thomas, Parry – 466
Thomson & Taylor – 466
Tickford-bodied Healey – 519
Titterington, D. – 481, 524
Tour de France – 463, 493, 494, 499, 500, 501, 508, 556, 560
Tourist Trophy – 567, 575
TransAm Category One Championship – 581
Trautmann, R. – 485, 491
Trenowith – 584
Triumph TR2 – 493
Turin – 468
Tulip Rally – 501, 503, 504, 505, 508
Tullius, Bob – 547, 549, 581, 583
Turner, Stuart – 492

U

Unipart – 584
Uren, Jeff – 534, 540, 541

V

Vann, J.G.M. Mrs – 504
Vard, C. – 478, 480, 481, 484
Venice – 471

Verglas – 494
Vial – 472
Vienna – 466, 467
Vivian, C. – 508
Vojtech, Z. – 588

W

Walkinshaw, T. – 584, 585, 586, 587, 588, 589
Walkinshaw, Tom – 578
Waddilove, Brian – 490
Wadham – 479
Walker, Peter – 523
Walkerley, R. – 501, 511
Walton, Phillip – 485
Ward, Frank – 505
Waring, W. – 478, 479
Watkins Glen – 547
Welsh Rally – 511
Weslake-Standard engine – 519
Wharton, Ken – 478, 501, 520, 521, 522, 523, 525
Whitehead, G. – 534, 584
Whitehead, P. – 493, 494, 523
Whittaker, D. – 563
Wilkins, G. – 479
Wills 6-hour race – 551
Wisdom, A. – 508
Wisdom, T. – 472, 479 490
Wolseley 18/85 saloon – 465
Woodley, R. – 499
World Sports Car Racing Championship – 510
Word War II – 465, 466, 519
Wright – 465, 469

X

Xhenceval, Jean – 569, 578

Y

Yarborough, David – 583
Yates, Brock – 583

Z

Zandvoort circuit – 505
Zeltweg – 587
Zolder circuit – 558, 578

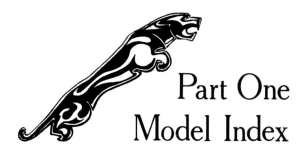

Part One
Model Index

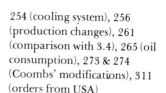

Jaguar XJ-S

General – 354, 382 (bodyshell specification), 384 (inc. manual), 385, 386, 388 (frontal area), 390-393 (manual version tested), 394 (tested in USA, and production changes), 400, 405 (manual version discontinued), 415 (manual)

HE – 415
3.6 – 418
5.3 cabriolet – 423
5.3 convertible – 425
Long wheelbase – 425

Jaguar XJ6 Series 3

General – 305, 398 (styling), 400 (specification, badging), 401-403 (equipment, interior)
4.2 manual – 405 (gearbox)
4.2 automatic – 405 & 406 (tested)
3.4 – 398, 400

Jaguar XJ12 Series 3

General – 400, 404 (engine), 409 (fuel consumption

Jaguar 'XJ40'

General – 436-440 (suspension), 440 (tyres/steering), 440-442 (bodyshell), 442-443 (styling), 443-445 (interior/instruments), 445 (heating/electrical), 447-448 (engine), 448-449 (gearbox), 449-450 (brakes), 450-454 (prototypes), 454 (1986/7 model range), 457-458 (3.6 road test), 458 (2.9 road test), 459-460 (N. American launch), 460 (1988 models)

Part Two

S.S.I & II

S.S.I. Coupe – 421, 423 (1933 Alpine), 429 (1933 Monte), 441 (1932 RAC Rally)
S.S.I. Tourer – 419, 421-423 (1933 Alpine), 424-426 (1934 Alpine), (1935 & 36 Monte), 465 (Shelsey Walsh & Brooklands)
S.S. II – 424, 426 (1934 Alpine)
Airline – 429 (1935 Monte)

SS Jaguar 2.5-litre

429 (Monte Carlo rally)

SS Jaguar 3.5-litre

429 (1939 Monte), 444 (Lancs A.C. Blackpool rally), 445, 465 (Monaco trip, 1947), 466 (with caravan)

Jaguar Mk V

432 (1951 Monte), 433 (1952 Monte), 444 (1952 RAC Rally)

Jaguar Mk VII

433 (1952 & '53 Monte), 434 & 435 (1954, 55 & 56 Monte), 444 (1952 & '53 RAC Rally), 447 (1953 Tour de France), 455-457 (Ian Appleyard's), 458 (Tulip and Round Australia rallies), 467 (at Daytona & Jabbeke), 473-475 (1952 & 1953 Silverstone), 476 (1954 Silverstone), 477 & 478 (1955 Silverstone), 479-482 (1956 Silverstone), 482 (Graig Hinton's)

Jaguar 3.4

427 (Alpine Rallies), 444 (1958 RAC), 445 (1959 RAC), 447 (1957 & '58 Tour de France), 448 (1959 Tour de France), 457 (1958 Tulip), 459 (1959 Tulip), 483-488 (in British racing), 501 (USA events, 1959 & '60), 509 (Peter Lindner's)

Jaguar 2.4

444 (1956, '57 & '58 RAC rallies), 458 (1958 Tulip & Acropolis rallies), 478-482 (1956 Silverstone), 483 (1956 Spa), 500 (in Classic Saloon racing)

Jaguar Mk II 3.8

427-428 (Alpine Rallies), 439 (1961 Monte), 440 (1966 Monte), 445 (1960 RAC), 446 (1961 RAC), 448 (1960 Tour de France), 451 (1962 Tour), 453 (1963 Tour), 454 (1964 Tour), 462-464 (European Rally Championship), 467-472 (at Monza), 489 (1960 & 61 British circuit racing), 490-492 (1962 racing), 493 (testing 1963 Six-Hour winners), 494-497 (1963 British circuit racing), 501 (1960 USA GP meeting), 504 & 505 (Bob Jane's), 506 & 607 (New Zealand & Argentinian racing), 508 (South African racing), 509 (Peter Lindner's), 510 (in 1962 & '63 Nurburgring), 512 & 513 (1963 European Touring Car Championship), 514 (1964 Championship), 515 (European events 1964-66)

Jaguar XJ6

467 (with caravan)

Jaguar XJ12

517, 533 (firetender)

Jaguar XJ12 two door

518-520 (engine development), 521 (testing), 523 (1976 Tourist Trophy), 524-528 (1977 European events), 529-532 (1977 Tourist Trophy & Zolder races), 533, 534

Jaguar XJ-S

517, 519, 521 (Group 44's), 523 (USA racing), 534-537 (Group 44's & 'Cannonball' event), 584, 587 (racing)

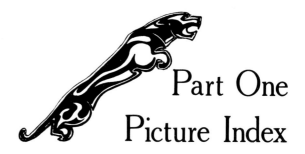

Part One
Picture Index

Mk VII

160 & 161 (prototype engines), 162–164 (engine), 165 (model of prototype), 166 (at Earls Court), 167 (at Waldorf-Astoria, New York), 168–171 (prototype), 172, 173, 174 (interior), 175 & 176 (details), 177 (chassis & engine), 178 (front suspension), 179 (in USA), 180 (under bonnet), 182 (painting), 184 (with XK 120 in USA), 185 (automatic), 186, 187 (engine), 452

MK VIIM

188, 189 (interior), 190, 191 (in church), 192, 206 (Pininfarina & Australian bodies), 207 (Ghia convertible), 208 (Queen Mother's)

Mk VIII

194, 195, 196, 197, 198, 199 (experimental), 209 (hearse)

Mk IX

200, 202, (limousine, and Radford conversion), 203 (air-cond.), 204 (last), 206 (Alroyd Lees'), 208 (for Nigeria), 209 (Beaman special)

2.4-litre

212 (engines), 213 (bodyshell), 214 (front suspension), 215 (rear suspension), 216 (prototype), 217 (standard model), 218 (interior), 219 (at Earls Court), 220 (building), 221 (at MIRA), 222, 223 (boot), 224 (for USA), 225 (cutaway drawing), 226 235 (post-1957 model), 236 (cyl. head), 240 (prototype)

3.4-litre

228, 229, 230, 232 (disc brakes), 233 (wire wheels), 234, 235, 238 (sliding roof)

Mk II

242, 243 (front suspension), 244 (interior), 245 (reclining seats), 246 (boot, & S. African-assembled), 247 (at New York show), 249, 251 (building), 252 (engines), 253 (police), 254 (air-cond.), 260 (with Colin Chapman), 261 (auxiliary tanks), 262 (3.4), 264 (2.4), 265 (2.4), 266 (1966 car), 267 (experimental interior), 274 ('County' estate), 275 (modified)

Daimler V8 – 255, 256 & 257 (engine), 258, 269

Daimler 250 – 269

240 – 268, 271, 272 (interior)

340 – 267, 272 (interior)

Mk X

3.8-litre – 298 (engine), 300 (suspension, brakes), 301 (servo), 302 (servo, steering), 303 & 304 (bodyshell), 305 (painting), 306 (dash), 307, 308, 309 (prototype), 310, 311, 312 (steering), 313 (drawing), 314 (on test), 315 (prototype), 316 (at Mira).

4.2-litre – 317 (V12 & 4.2 engines), 318 (steering), 319, 320, 321 (limousine), 326

420G – 322, 323 & 324 (Daimler DS420 limousine version), 325 (ditto Landaulette)

S-type

278, 279 (prototype), 280, 281 (export model), 282 (facia), 283, 284 (interior), 285 (3.8) 286, 287 (Bertone body), 288 (Frua body), 293 (building).

420

289, 290, 291 (Sovereign version), 292 (interior), 294 (building), 295.

XJ6 'S1'

328, 329 (front suspension), 350 (front suspension, steering), 331, 332 (tyre), 333 (bodyshell), 334 (interior), 335, 336-341 (prototypes), 342, 343, 344 (for USA), 347, 348 (Model 12 gearbox), 349 (building) 358 (6L version)

XJ12 'S1'

350 (engine), 351 (engine components), 352 & 353 (engine), 354, 355, 356 (interior), 357, 360, 361 & 362 (Daimler Sovereign version), 359 (12L version) 363 (firetender), 364, 358 & 359 (Vanden Plas version)

XJ6 S2

365, 366 & 367 (Federal), 368 (interior), 369 (engine), 397

Two-door S2 – 365, 370, 371, 378 & 379 (V12), 396 (Daimler version), 413 (convertible)

3.4 – 373, 376, 377

XJ12 S2

367, 368 (interior), 374, 375 (fuel-injection), 380, 381 (interior)

XJ-S

383, 384 (engine), 385 (interior), 386-388, 389 (inc. mid-engined prototype), 390, 391 (manual), 393 (for USA), 394 (engine), 395 (1979 model), 410 (Pininfarina Spyder)

XJ6 Special bodies – 430 (Pininfarina Spyder), 431 (Pininfarina XJ12, & Owen Sedanca), 415 (Avon Stephens Estate)

XJ6 S3

398, 399, 400 (sunshine roof), 401-404 401 (3.4), 409 (gear selector), 409 (Sovereign), 410 (Sovereign HE), 411 (Sovereign), 413 (Vanden Plas), 413, 414 (4.2 injection engines), 432

XJ12 S3
408 (May Head), 408 (engine bay), 409 (gear selector), 411 (Double Six), 412 (Sovereign)

XJS
416 (HE), 417, 418 (3.6 AJ6), 416, 420, 421 (cabriolet), 422 (roof panels), 423, 424, 425 (convertible), 425 (LBW one-off)

XJ40
436, 437, 438, 439 (rear suspension), 440 (front suspension), 441 (front dampers, body shell), 442 (dashboard), 443 (AJ6 3.6 engine), 443 (engine management system), 444 (SDVs), 445, 446, 447 (front and rear details), 448, 448 (five-speed interior), 449 (J-gate), 449 (interior), 450 (rear seats), 450, 451 (boot), 451 (2.9 engine), 452, 453, 454, 456, 457 (diagnostic system), 459, 460 (TWR)

XJ40 special bodies – 435 (Ital, Guigaro, Bertone)

Places
King Edward Avenue – 16
Bloomfield Road – 18
Woodfield Road – 18
John Street – 18
Cocker Street – 19, 23
Foleshill – 23, 47, 99, 110 & 111 (war work),117 (production engine test shop), 125 (machine shop), 152 (Mk V body line), 168
Browns Lane – 182 (paint shop), 205 (engine line), 220 (2.4 line), 227 (fire), 251 (Mk II line), 293 (S-type/Mk II line), 298 (engine test shop), 305 (painting Mk X), 307 (experimental trim shop), 311, 326, 349 (XJ6 line)
Motor Shows:
Olympia – 27 (1931)
Earls Court – 100 (1938), 166 (1950), 218 (1955)
New York – 167 (1950), 247
Geneva – 287 (1966)
Amsterdam – 328 (1968)
Brussels – 352 (1972)

Portraits
Baily, C – 159
Bertone, S – 287
Bourgeois, Mme J – 352
Egan, Sir John – 446
England, 'Lofty' – 438
Fenton, Miss A – 78
Heynes, W.M. – 66, 158
Hornburg, C – 224
Knight, R.J. – 429
Lyons, Sir W. – 235, 287, 326, 428
Lyons, Lady – 428
Moss, S – 409
Mundy, H. – 418
Rankin, E.W – 79
Robinson, G. – 429
Tarquini, Dr G – 287
Towns, W. – 343
Weslake, H. – 64
Whittaker, A. – 79

* * *

Part Two

S.S.I
466-469 (1933 Alpine), 470 & 471 (1934 Alpine), 476 (1934 Monte Carlo Rally), 477 (1935 Monte), 488 (1932 & 1934 RAC Rallies), 489 (1935 RAC), 502, 512 (1934 Scottish Rally), 548 (in Casablanca & S. Africa)

S.S.II
471, 502

SS/Jaguar
1935-1937 model – 477 (1937 Monte), 502, 520 (Brooklands), 489 (tourer, 1937 RAC)
1938-1949 model – 478 (1939 Monte), 512 (with caravan)

Mk V
479 (1951 Monte), 480 (1952 Monte), 481 (1953 Monte), 483 (1954 Monte), 490 (1951 RAC), 501 (1952 RAC), 549 (in Australia & 1950 Carrera Panamericana)

Mk VII
482 (1955 Monte), 483 & 484 (1956 Monte), 490 (1953 RAC), 491 (1958), 494 (1953 Tour de France), 503 (1953 Monte & Norwegian rallies), 504 (1954 Tulip), 520 (1952 Silverstone), 521 & 522 (1953 & 1954 Silverstone), 523 & 524 (1955 Silverstone), 525 (Tommy Rowe's & Bob Berry's), 526 & 527 ('Classic Saloon' racing)

Mk VIII
526 (course car)

2.4-litre
492 (1959), 504 (1958 Tulip), 508 (1959 Scottish)

3.4-litre
472 & 473 (1959 Alpine), 484 & 485 (1959 Monte), 495 (1959 Tour), 505 (1959 Tulip), 506 (1959 Sestriere), 507 (1959 Coronation Safari), 515 (economy runs), 530 (1957 Silverstone), 531 (1958 Silverstone GP meeting), 532 & 533 (1958 Silverstone sequence), 534 (1959 Goodwood), 544 (Albert Betts'), 549 (1959 Sebring)

Mk II 3.8
473 (1961 Alpine), 474 (1962 & 1963 Alpine), 486 (1961 Monte), 486 (1966 Monte), 492 (1961 RAC), 495 (1960 Tour), 496 (1960 & 1961 Tour), 497 (1962 Tour), 498 & 499

(1963 Tour), 500 (1964 Tour), 508 (1961 Circuit of Ireland), 509 (1963 Tulip), 516-518 (Monza), 534 (1960 Brands), 535 (1960 Silverstone), 536 (1961 Silverstone & 1962 Aintree), 537 (1962 Brands), 538 & 539 (1962 Motor 6-hours), 540 (1963 Oulton & Goodwood), 541 (Silverstone 1963), 542 (1963 Motor 6-hours), 543 (1964 Silverstone), 545 (in 1970s), 550 (Bob Jane's), 551 (in Australia), 552-554 (in New Zealand), 555-559 (Peter Lindner's), 560 (John Sparrow's), 561 (1966 Spa)

XJ6
513 (with caravan)

XJ12
Broadspeed coupe – 564 (unveiled), 565 (testing), 566 (at Browns Lane), 567 (underbonnet), 569 & 570 (1977 Monza), 571 (details), 572 (1977 Brno), 573 (testing), 574 & 575 (1977 Nurburgring), 576-578 (1977 Silverstone)

Saloon – 579 (South Africa)

XJ-S
580 (factory project), 581 & 582 (Group 44), 583 ('Cannonball' winner) 585 (Group 44), 585 (TWR), 586 (1982 Brno GP), 587 (1982 Nurburgring 6-hr), 588 (Monza, Spa and Saltzbury), 589 (Donington 1983), 589 (Monza and 1984 Spa 24-hr)

❋ ❋ ❋